Hymes

Educational Linguistics/TESOL/ICC
Graduate School of Education
University of Pennsylvania
3700 Walnut Street/Cl
Philadelphia, PA   19104

Perspectives on
American English

Contributions to the Sociology of Language

29

Editor
Joshua A. Fishman

MOUTON PUBLISHERS · THE HAGUE · PARIS · NEW YORK

Perspectives on
American English

Edited by
J. L. Dillard

MOUTON PUBLISHERS · THE HAGUE · PARIS · NEW YORK

ISBN: 90–279–3367–7

Jacket design by Jurriaan Schrofer

© 1980, Mouton Publishers, The Hague, The Netherlands

Printed in Great Britain

Contents

Contents

PART FIVE: PIDGIN ENGLISH

General Introduction

Everyone recognizes that there are differences in the way different Americans speak 'American English', just as none of those ways are identical with 'British English' or 'Australian English', etc. From isoglosses to variable rules, we have had many ways of accounting for those differences; everyone has his theory about how they came about, and as to how great they are. Two major theories, however, have always dominated the historical argument:

Language differences among heterogeneous early Americans, never completely absorbed by the 'melting pot';
Dialect differences, regionally distributed among specifically British immigrants to the continental colonies and transmitted to the speakers of other languages who came to the same colonies, some of the differences being magnified in the New World and others lost.

The second of these is by no means the older explanation; it is hardly to be found in the writings of those who made on-the-spot observations about the English of the colonies and of the new United States. It is, however, the working premise of the Linguistic Atlas of the United States and Canada, which has assumed an authority on such matters felt by some (including, apparently, the project's own members) to be unquestionable.

This approach is apparently an outgrowth of nineteenth-century historical linguistics, the triumph of which was internal reconstruction, especially of proto-Indo-European and of other proto-languages on the same model. Much of this, especially the assignment of the proto-languages and 'daughter' languages (conceived as having been formed from dialects of the original) to a 'homeland' is based on antiquated or doubtful evidence. Yet there is a tremendous academic investment in this discipline, and anyone venturing to question even some of its minor tenets may find himself ostracized.

This is apparently what Raven I. McDavid, Jr., (1975:110) means to do when he attacks,

. . . the new breed of sociolinguists, who often echo her [Glenna Ruth Pickford's]
criticism [of the Linguistic Atlas of the United States and Canada][and who] often
forget, as she did, that linguistic geography is a historical discipline in which *bench
marks* [emphasis added] are more important than numbers and in which the
bench marks provide a framework for interpretation of more extensive studies.

Bench marks, although herein undefined, seems to refer to markers
used in surveying for the purpose of marking property lines. If so, the
proprietary attitude which others have often felt to be characteristic of
the Atlas bigwigs is more pronounced than even the critics of that project
had ever realized. If these 'bench marks', once established (in a typically
authoritarian way, McDavid does not specify *how* they have been or will
be established) must always 'provide a framework for interpretation
[even] of more extensive studies,' then the history of American English is
a closed field, not a legitimate area of study.

There are, however, some who have the temerity to continue looking
upon the field as an open one. Several of those brave souls are represented in this collection. Gary Underwood, for example, in 'American
English dialectology: alternatives for the Southwest' points out how those
bench marks (although he does not actually use the term) may have been
adhered to so rigidly that more significant — or, at least, more general —
patterns have been ignored. We may not, in other words, have been lucky
enough to have placed the bench marks in the best places in the 1930s;
relocation of the basic guidelines of dialectology is a possibility, just as it is
in any live field, in which researchers are allowed to formulate their own
hypotheses and do not have to rely upon *obiter dicta*.

The most obvious data which may fall in patterns not matching the
'bench marks' of the reconstructive tradition come from bilingual studies.
Internal reconstruction, although frequently performed by linguistically
learned and even multilingual researchers, has of necessity worked with
speech communities assumed to be monolingual. In fact, some of the
early work on speech communities assumed that each was coterminous
with one language (Bloomfield 1933). More recent work (Gumperz
1962) takes into account the fact that the communities may have symbolic unity even while utilizing more than one language. Participation in a
communication network may have little to do with using one language;
several networks may exist within one language, or one network may be
made up of multilingual speakers. *Diglossia* (Ferguson 1959) is the most
familiar conceptualization of a functional relationship between languages, but many Swiss (just to take one obvious example) proclaim that
the distribution is by no means so simple as the 'H' language and 'L'
language division. In a *bi*lingual relationship, given the 'melting pot'

situation of the United States being effective to one degree or another, one language is usually assumed to give way to the other in language shift. There are, however, situations in which the community's 'original' language continues to exert some influence—what is conventionally called substratum or adstratum influence. It is almost obligatory, within reconstructive theory, to minimize the 'stratum' influence.

For some communities, however, complete language shift has obviously never taken place. These communities are frequently downplayed in studies of American English because they do not fit the prevailing theory. Partly for that reason, a large section on such communities (some of which are often sociologically characterized as 'minority' or 'disadvantaged') is included.

The more fundamental issue in the history of American English, although it has been persistently overlooked by the defenders of the bench marks, is not *bi*lingual but *multi*lingual contact. The situations are often confused. For example, Allen Walker Read's 'Bilingualism in the middle colonies, 1725–1775' (1937:95) actually describes a multi- rather than a bi-lingual situation: 'From these miniature "case histories" . . . it is apparent that the American colonies during the eighteenth century abounded in speakers of languages other than English.' Nevertheless, of works on American English perhaps only Brian Foster's *The Changing English Language* (1968) has dealt extensively with multilingualism. Foster (1968:8) points out explicitly: 'Writers on the subject of Americanisms have usually made little of the fact that in the past millions of Americans have had a foreign language as their mother-tongue . . .'

The most disadvantaged, exploited, and even ridiculed linguistic segment of the American population seems to have had a special multilingual proficiency. Read (1937:98) points out how: '. . . the implication in the next advertisement [for a runaway slave] is that the slave was exceptional in being able to "talk nothing but English." '

Groups now known as 'minority' or 'disadvantaged', like the Indians and the black West African slaves, were perhaps the most typical examples of this colonial multilingualism, but they were far from the only ones. Read points out (1937:99) that:

The cosmopolitan spirit engendered by the prevalence of many languages was an element in the pattern of colonial American culture and no doubt contributed to the breaking down of old loyalties, culminating in the American Revolution.

If bilingualism, or more precisely multilingualism, was an important factor in the development of American English, then those groups were more important in the history of the variety than has ever been acknowledged. According to Nida and Fehdereau (1970), multilingual contact may aid in the process of leveling to what may be called a *koiné*.

Evidence for such leveling is provided, almost inadvertently, by Şen (1973:121). She points out that:

I have been impressed [in her study of colonial American English] by the amount of dialect variation which existed in the early American colonies with little regional distribution or social stratification.

Within the usual dialect atlas framework, which is her *modus operandi*, Şen must mean that this great amount of variation was intrapersonal, since 'regional' and 'socially stratified' are usually taken, within that tradition, to exhaust the interpersonal possibilities. It is highly plausible that this could mean that there was social variation correlated with something other than class or caste (i.e. sex, ethnic group, professional or occupational status, age, religious affiliation, or other such factors), but Şen makes no such statement and the general tone of her article is not consonant with such an interpretation. Interpreted literally, such intrapersonal variation could well betoken the kind of individual indecisiveness often associated with the development of a standard dialect. For other developments of the same type, see Blanc (1968), Bernard (1969), and Catalán (1958). Blanc, especially, makes a noteworthy association between dialect leveling and the needs of standardization.

Whatever is concluded about the developments within the multidialectal situation, it seems unavoidable that the multilingual contact environment of the colonies is in need of the kind of consideration that it has not received since Read (this volume). The conventional formulations like interference (Weinreich 1953) can be applied to bilingual contact situations, but multilingual contact is a different case — especially where the number of languages involved exceeds four or five. It is by now commonplace that such contact is ideal for — perhaps demands — the solution of a *lingua franca*. Diverse writers (e.g. James Fenimore Cooper) about the American frontier discussed a 'lingua franca' and had their characters speaking, at least part of the time, pidgin English. And we have known since Schuchardt's time that pidgins are the ideal *lingue franche*. Gradually — almost grudgingly — some attention is beginning to be paid to American Indian Pidgin English (Goddard 1976). The section on Pidgin English in this collection, although regrettably short, represents most of what has been published on the use of that variety within the continental United States. (See, however, Dillard 1972, 1975a, 1976a.) A great deal has been published about Hawaiian Pidgin English, represented by Richard Day's article in this book.

The bilingual model (as distinct from the *lingua franca* model, although probably the two are complementary) has the limitation that it provides no 'bench marks' for the study of dialect mixing in America. No one, it is safe to assume, has ever asserted that there were only two *dialects* in contact in the colonial American situation. As a pidgin is in some sense a leveling, so the koiné that developed in the colonies (Dillard 1975a: ch. II) would be the end result of another kind of leveling.[1] As Read's article 'British recognition of American speech in the eighteenth century' (this volume) points out, the usual state of things in a multilingual contact situation is the leveling out of extreme divergences. Read also pointed out (1937:99) that

The cosmopolitan spirit engendered by the prevalence of many languages was an element in the pattern of colonial American culture and no doubt contributed to the breaking down of old loyalties, culminating in the American Revolution.

The hypothesis that regional differences in the mother country are retained and even intensified in the 'daughter' colony is not supported by such studies. In fact, it seems to have squelched any research which might otherwise have proceeded from such insights.

Early writers on American English stressed not regional British usage carried over into American dialects but the influence of the 'jargon' of the various occupations. One of those occupations — a very important one in colonial days — was sailing. Many of the forms assumed to have come from British regional dialects may actually have reflected the influence of sailors. (For a comparable hypothesis about Krio, see Hancock [1976].) Since it has not been possible to represent all occupations in this collection, the editor has chosen to emphasize the influence of the seafaring man. Others, like the mountain man and the cowboy, had almost equal importance (Dillard 1976a). But even those were not as far from maritime influence as most of us would assume. With a nod in the direction of Ramon Adams (see References), I have chosen to let the sailor carry the burden of representing occupational varieties.

Other activities, like gambling (Asbury 1936) and drinking have been important in the development of characteristically American phraseology. In recent years, spectator sports and television have had an enormous effect on our 'jargon', and most of our teenagers talk like the rock and roll lyrics' imitation of Black English at least part of the time. Someone will surely object to the leaving out of Citizens' Band radio, with its reinforcement and revivification of certain terms like *handle* 'name', presumably quiescent until picked up by the new medium. Many will say that a trend has to be significant when even Betty Ford (wife of President Ford) had her CB 'handle': First Mama. But time has not yet told whether these influences will be as longlasting (and, therefore, as 'important') as maritime and foreign influences.

Last — and not really least — there are the ethnic group affiliations of the people who make up the population of the United States. There are many of these, so many that this sampling must be virtually haphazard. There is no intention expressed, in this selection, to claim that these groups are more important than the ones left out. Frankly, mere availability of articles on a given group has been a major determining factor.[2] A few articles submitted on groups not represented (like one on the English of Polish-Americans) seemed unacceptable in quality; competent scholars who expressed an interest in preparing such articles turned out, in some cases, to be too busy to meet the deadline.

If, then, this collection has no claim to being representative, it can claim to be unusual in offering an article on the English of the American Gypsy community as well as a treatment of the speech of some Jewish Americans ('Yinglish'), the English of the Pennsylvania Germans, and the English of Puerto Ricans (whose original designation as 'Spanglish' speakers has led to a growing proliferation of terms to designate the shades of difference observable among Puerto Ricans). For the last group, there is a well-known study on their English as studied in New York City (Wolfram et al. 1971). The article by Nash concentrates on the English of the island itself because of two editorial intents: to avoid competition with Wolfram et al., and to deal, if only in a very small way, with the very important fact that American English exerts an influence far beyond the shores of the continental United States.

This collection is unblushingly, even aggressively, historical in intent. As such, it will perhaps be deemed trivial by those who expect the semantic and/or syntactic study of language (especially, as it happens, of American English) to reveal something profound about the structure of the human mind. The failure to include any such articles is not the result of a feeling that they are not important but an attempt at a modest acknowledgment of limitations. The title *Perspectives on American English* (perhaps it should have been *Historical Perspectives* . . .) does not mean to claim that *all* perspectives are treated, or that all are given equal space. The actual selection and juxtaposing of the articles was done by the editor — who, incidentally, put the articles into the sequence in which they occur according to a definite scheme. What turns out to be expressed by the book as a whole will, then, reflect something of the bias of the editor. Some (Bickerton 1977) have voiced their objections in the past to such selectivity on my part. They probably have a point, but I continue in the insistence that to ignore the matters spotlighted in this volume is also to indulge in bias.

NOTES

1. This is not really inconsistent with my view that pidgins are diffused more extensively than the prevailing theory wants to admit. The *original* leveling which formed the pidgins (at least those based on European languages, especially Portuguese, French, and English) was quite remote in time and not nearly so easy to study as transmission in more recent times.
2. Many similarities will of course be perceived between the English of Puerto Ricans and that of Chicanos.

PART ONE

Native English-Speaking Immigrants

Introduction

Speakers of American English are extremely conscious of 'accents', and jokes abound concerning how Lyndon Johnson was hailed by Texans (or, *mutatis mutandis*, some other president by some other group) as 'Finally, a president with no accent!' There is more defensiveness than real pride, however, in that attitude. Almost all Americans feel that 'good' English should somehow be neutral with respect to dialect. (It is not true, of course, that such 'accentless' speech is attributed to the American masses by Englishmen; in fact, they are usually regarded as having the very strongest of 'accents'.)

As has frequently been pointed out (McDavid 1966) there is no *geographic* locus of such accentless American English. ('Accentless' could only mean that all or most prominent, stereotypable features have been leveled out.) Some recent sociolinguists and psycholinguists (Lambert and Tucker 1969) have suggested, however, that there is a locus for such a neutral dialect in the media, especially in television broadcasting and specifically in the networks' nationwide newscasts. Thus the dominant newscasters of the 1960s and 1970s, Huntley and Brinkley and Walter Cronkhite, among others, have given us a speech pattern for imitation in which non-prevocalic (as well as prevocalic: initial and medial) /r/ is articulated but where there is no 'intrusive' /r/ (idear of it), where diphthongs like /ay/ and /aw/ have very low initial articulation points and full off-glides, and where the vowels of *Sam* and *cab* are neither lengthened as in the Southern 'drawl' nor raised as in the stereotypical New Yorker's [kɪə b]. Further than that, they have been hewed to a pattern in which subject–verb concord of the school-grammar type is held to (except when the syntax gets really complicated), double negatives are eschewed, and the impersonal *you* (as well as a personal address to members of the audience as 'you') is avoided. It would be too much to say that they have achieved the schoolteacher's ideal so perfectly as to avoid an occasional mixed metaphor, to use at all times the supposedly more forceful active voice, or to avoid occasional shifts in tense, mood, or subject. (To members of the National Council of Teachers of English, these are more important matters than the dialectologist's 'standard' and 'non-standard' usage.) But, these human failings aside, network newscasters have provided the best example of that neutral dialect that some dialectologists have regarded as 'colorless' and most linguistically naive Americans, reacting naturally, have lauded as 'good English'.

There are those who appear to think that any claim about Network Standard can be disproved by citing the many nonstandard forms that do turn up on television, some of them from speakers of high prestige like presidents and prominent ministers. What they seem to have overlooked is that such a person of high or even superordinated rank can use his non-Network forms precisely *because* he is of such high rank. If he is powerful enough, a high-ranking speaker does not have to bother to change his native dialect; he speaks on the network because the network or some other powerful organization wanted him there, and not because he impressed someone as speaking 'good' English. If, on the other hand, he had been applying for a job as an announcer with the network or an actor making a commercial, he would have had to satisfy someone's requirements as to dialect. The fact that the person in question was not a renowned dialectologist, or even a layman sophisticated about language, does not make the requirements any less real.

Network Standard, along with Black English (see Part Four), was one of the first suggested in a picture sweepingly different from that of American dialects as basically or almost exclusively geographic. Kurath (1933) made the prestigious statement that almost all followed, virtually without daring to question. Gradually, however, authors like Labov (1966), Gumperz (1958, 1962), and Blanc (1954) cast doubt on the generality of a scheme of basically geographic variation. It is noteworthy that the earlier of these studies had been performed outside the continental United States. Bernard (1969) had provided a nongeographic picture for Australian variation, and Trudgill (1974) called for an *explanatory* rather than a merely mapping model.

Examination of eighteenth-century sources, as performed by Allen Walker Read (the first article in Part One), suggests that a scheme of greatly leveled British dialects was the situation in colonial America. Şen (1973) offers some fascinating evidence of intrapersonal variation in the process of interpersonal leveling. Unfortunately, her article could not be obtained for this collection. Dillard (1975a: ch. II) went so far as to write about the American koiné among the colonists migrating from England and regrouping themselves according to something very different from their original regional distribution. Leveling in multidialectal situations is clearly established in studies like Leopold (1959). Nida and Fehdereau (1970) show that the leveling towards a koiné goes faster if other languages are in the environment of the dialects. Seaman (1972) documents the extreme leveling of dialects of Greek among immigrants to the United States.

If, however, no kind of starting point where regional differences were present to be magnified via migration can be found for American English, then some process other than the usual formulation of reconstructive linguistics (see General Introduction) must be assumed for American English. Underwood has pointed out how the old method, whereby the 'first cut' was into regional dialects and then some kind of local division into social dialects was made, may not be applicable in the United States. In his prospectus for dialect research in the Southwest — and, by implication, for other areas as well — Underwood suggests that geographic factors may not automatically be assumed to be more important than social factors, or even more important than any one social factor. Thus, place of birth or place of residence may be no greater a determinant of dialect than any *one* of such factors as age, sex, religious or political affiliation, occupation or profession, class or caste, or ethnic group. (Some of these obviously overlap, 'Jewish', for example, being a primarily ethnic designation for some and primarily religious for others. Given the striking unity of the religious practices of Blacks of the lower economic groups, not even 'Black' is a classification meaning exclusively ethnic rather than religious group.)

Herbert Pilch's 1955 article is included here as a strong statement of the attitudes and theories generally opposite to the dominant one of this book. As a member of one of the schools most concerned with linguistic system or 'structure', Pilch is bound to find a general system for 'American English', and a source for that system in British English and proto-Germanic. His comments about tracing the English of Polish-American speakers to Old English rather than Old Polish (p. 40) represent a rather strong statement of the opinion contrary to the one held by the authors of the articles in Part Three of this book. In seeing dialect variation as well as historical change as matters of subsystems within one overall system (English), Pilch articulates as explicitly as anyone I know of the considerations that have motivated the still-dominant resistance to finding adstratum influence, the looking to internal rather than external influences in change, and even to some degree the writing of panlectal grammars characteristic of recent variation theorists.

I do not know what Pilch would say about the extensive evidence for the use of pidgin English on the American frontier as it moved west. Probably, he would either reject the evidence or see the pidgin as a development internal to English. The relexification theory (Taylor 1960, 1961; Voorhoeve 1973) is certainly foreign — even anathema — to such a theoretical approach.

Nevertheless, Pilch is no practitioner of what I have called the Virginity Principle (only the first occurrence counts). See his refusal (p. 63) to treat American /æ/ as a survival of British /æ/. This focus on system is not quite the same thing as the focus on populations characteristic of sociolinguistic studies, but it can be as destructive to dogmatic conclusions if held to rigorously.

In evaluating the implications of such statements as those quoted by Read for the history of American English, it is important to realize that most of them date from about 1770 or before. Observations made by Englishmen in the nineteenth century, like the notorious ones of Charles Dickens, find quite the opposite of a 'pure' or 'classical' quality in the speech of the Americans. It is held herein, of course, that neither kind of statement can be taken at face value — that the intuitive reactions of a popular observer may be of great value but that his analysis must of necessity be almost useless. Any statements about the English of colonial Americans must, then, be considered primarily in the light of a prelude to what can be found out about succeeding decades and centuries.

ALLEN WALKER READ

British Recognition of American Speech in the Eighteenth Century*

I.

The Englishman has seldom been neutral in his attitude towards America. In the eighteenth century the political division between Whig and Tory influenced his opinion, and even in regard to language one group felt that the extension of English in America presaged a rosy future, while the other group prophesied the utter degradation of the language. How far had speech in America diverged from that in England? What were its characteristics? What was its future? What type of words had developed? Englishmen had dealt with these questions extensively even before 1800, and it is the purpose of this paper to survey a portion of their comment.

What appears to be the first proposal for a glossary of Americanisms was made in 1774 by the essayist Richard Owen Cambridge. In a light-hearted paper contributed to *The World*,[1] he wrote:

I would therefore propose, in order to render this work compleat, that a supplement be added to it, which shall be an explanation of the words, figures, and forms of speech of the country, that will most probably be the subject of conversation for the ensuing year [the American colonies]. For instance, whoever considers the destination of our present expedition, must think it high time to publish an interpretation of West India phrases, which will soon become so current among us, that no man will be fit to appear in company, who shall not be able to ornament his discourse with those jewels. For my part, I wish such a work had been published time enough to have assisted me in reading the following extract of a letter from one of our colonies. . . 'The *Chippoways* and *Orundaks* are still very troublesome. Last week they *scalped* one of our Indians: but the *six nations* continue firm; and at a meeting of Sachems it was determined *to take up the hatchet,* and *make the war-kettle boil.* The French desired *to smoak the calumet of peace*; but the *half-king* would not consent. They offered the *speech-belt,* but it was refused. Our Governour has received an account of their proceedings, together with *a string of wampum,* and *a bundle of skins to brighten the chain.'*[2]

* Reprinted, by permission, from *Dialect Notes*, Volume VI, 1933.

This nest of Indian terms shows that Cambridge had in mind the northern American colonies.[3] He was not overserious, to be sure; but nevertheless his proposal foreshadows Witherspoon, Pickering, and Bartlett. He concluded, 'A work of this kind, if well executed cannot fail to make the fortune of the undertaker. . . .'

America was far enough away for many Englishmen to have no notion of the traits of American speech. A London shopkeeper whom Boswell tells of is a case in point. When Hugh Hume, the third Earl of Marchmont, came into his shop, he observed, 'I suppose, Sir, you are an American.' 'Why so, Sir?' asked his lordship, who had a modified Scotch accent. 'Because, Sir,' answered the shopkeeper, 'you speak neither English nor Scotch, but something different from both, which I conclude is the language of America.'[4] Sometimes the Americans traveling in England yielded up information. John Wilkes, during the old quarrel about the lack of trees in Scotland, told an anecdote of an experience in the 1780s: 'I travelled through the country with an American servant, and after we had visited various places in different parts of Scotland, I enquired of him what his general opinion was of the country. "Oh, Sir!" replied the American, "it is *finely cleared*." '[5] This word evidently struck the English ear as peculiar, for in 1794 Thomas Cooper felt obliged to gloss it: 'By cleared is meant, the small trees and shrubs grubbed up, and the larger trees cut down about two feet from the ground, the stumps remaining.'[6] From Edinburgh in 1780 comes the story of a bewildered girl named Mary Muslin:

A grave looking man, who sat near me one day at dinner, said a good deal about the *fall*, and of events that should have happened before and after the *fall*. As he also spoke about *Providence,* and *Salem,* and *Ebenezer;* and as great deference was shown to everything that he said; and being, as I told you, a grave-looking man in a black coat, I was not sure that he might be some learned theologian and imagined he was speaking about Oriental antiquities, and the *fall of Adam*. But I was soon undeceived. The gentleman had lived for some time in *Virginia*; by *Providence* he meant the town of that name in Rhode-island; and by the *fall*, he meant not the *fall* of our first parents, for, concerning them he had not the least idea, but, as I suppose, the fall of the leaf; for the word is used, it seems, in the American dialect, for autumn.[7]

Even King George III was puzzled on one occasion. On July 1, 1774, Thomas Hutchinson, the Massachusetts historian, mentioned in an audience with him that the colonists 'live upon coarse bread made of rye and corn mixed'. 'What corn?' asked the king. 'Indian corn', Hutchinson was obliged to explain, 'or, as it is called in Authors, Maize'. 'Ay, I know it', commented the king.[8]

What can be expected from such a hater of America as Dr. Johnson? In introducing his *Dictionary* to public attention, Johnson announced, 'The chief intent of it is to preserve the purity and ascertain the meaning of our English idiom. . . .',[9] therefore it is a matter of surprise that he quoted the writing of an American among his authorities in the *Dictionary*. This writer, under *suppose* and *talent*[10] was the novelist Mrs. Charlotte Lennox, who lived in America to the age of fifteen and was the daughter of the lieutenant-governor of New York. Since she passed her formative years in America, she must have had an American cast to her speech. According to the *Oxford English Dictionary* Johnson himself dabbled in Americanisms to the extent of coining the word *tom-ax*, from *tomahawk + ax*,[11] but he can be exonerated from the charge because he was paraphrasing the current newspapers, where the word had already appeared.[12] In a review in *The Literary Magazine* for 1756,[13] which Boswell ascribes to Johnson, is a definite statement about speech in America. Concerning a work by the American Lewis Evans,[14] the reviewer said that 'this treatise [is] written with such elegance as the subject admits tho' not without some mixture of the *American* dialect, a tract[15] of corruption to which every language widely diffused must always be exposed.'[16] Johnson probably was offended by such of Evans' words as *portage, statehouse, creek, gap, upland, spur* (glossed as '*Spurs* we call little Ridges jetting out from the principal Chains of Mountains, and are of no long continuation'), *branch, back of, or fresh*(n.).[17]

It appears from such indications that Englishmen in the eighteenth century were well aware that the language in America had developed a character of its own. They disagreed, however, in their predictions of its future. Among those of a hopeful cast of mind was Henry Kett, who delivered lectures on English at Oxford University in the 1790s. In one of his lectures he said:

> The United States of America cannot fail to perpetuate the language of their parent country; and the spirit of literary and scientific investigation, which is rising among them, will conduce to this end; since it will encourage the study of those celebrated productions, from which the Americans have gained their knowledge of the best system of legislation, and their most correct principles of liberty.[18]

When David Ramsay's *History of the American Revolution* was republished in England in 1791, the London editor set forth his attitude toward American speech, in a tone of friendliness and understanding:

> On the whole, the western world will have possessed no language so uniform and so universal as our own is likely to be; when the British Americans shall once have peopled their new continent, which is so much more extensive than that of

Europe. Before the late American revolution, the English language had acquired its standard (as far as any living language can acquire a standard), and the British colonists had attained a remarkable perfection in it; and consequently there is no probability that any dialect can hereafter arise on either side, such as was common in barbarous ages. Englishmen then have reason to be proud of the means of communication thus offered, for benefiting, upon easy terms, so large a portion of the human race; nor will they, it is hoped, despise the opportunity of receiving benefit in return; for, it is impossible that a people descended from some of the best stocks in Europe and engaged in useful pursuits, can fail to furnish new ideas and new discoveries, like those of which the immortal Franklin has given us so many examples.[19]

Similar opinions were expressed by writers in magazines, such as one in the *English Review* in 1796, that 'the English language will, when the United States of America become populous, be spoken by a more numerous set of people than any other language in existence'.[20] Likewise a correspondent to the *Gentleman's Magazine* wrote that 'English is not the language of this island only. The whole continent of America speaks our language, and will buy an English Dictionary'.[21]

Herbert Croft, who planned an extensive dictionary to supersede Johnson's, was impressed by the desirability of recognizing American usage. He wrote of his 'Oxford English Dictionary' in 1788:

... Mr. C. does not forget over how much land the English language is spread. America, and American books, will not be neglected by Mr. C. The American ambassador has taken charge of some letters, which he advised Mr. C. to write, and which will, no doubt, produce communications from the other side of the Atlantick.[22]

By nine years later he had even decided to change the name of his project to the 'English and American Dictionary',[23] and he spoke thus highly of America:

The future history of the other three quarters of the world will, probably, be much affected by America's speaking the language of England. Its natives write the language particularly well; considering they have no dictionary yet, and how insufficient Johnson's is. Washington's speeches seldom exhibited more than a word or two, liable to the least objection; and, from the style of his publications, as much, or more accuracy, may be expected from his successor Adams. Perhaps we are, just now, not very far distant from the precise moment, for making some grand attempt, with regard to fixing the *standard* of our language (no *language* can be fixed) in America. Such an attempt would, I think, succeed in America, for the same reasons that would make it fail in England; whither, however, it would communicate its good effects. Deservedly immortal would be that patriot, on either side of the Atlantick, who should succeed in such an attempt.[24]

David Hume also looked to America hopefully. In a letter of October 24, 1767, he attempted to dissuade Gibbon from composing in French, giving as his reason: 'Our solid and increasing establishments in America, where we need less dread of the inundations of Barbarians, promise a superior stability and duration to the English language'.[25] Some years before, Hume had evidently discussed the matter with Benjamin Franklin, for on September 27, 1760, Franklin wrote him: 'But I hope with you, that we shall always in America make the best English of this Island our standard, and I believe it will be so.'[26] Hume criticized Franklin's use of the words *pejorate, colonize, and unshakable.*[27]

Some Englishmen felt, on the other hand, that the divergences in America were a menace to the language or even that a separate language would develop. Among these was the noted preacher and political controversialist Jonathan Boucher, who spent fourteen years in compiling a glossary of provincialisms. In 1801 he issued his *Proposals* for it, and as one of its objects, he stated: 'And, lastly, an Enquiry, how far the common speech of . . . the United States of North America, which, it will be readily allowed, differs materially from any spoken in this Island, is, or is not, to be regarded as dialect.'[28] In the preface to his *Glossary,*[29] he dealt bitterly with American speech:

Thus, the United States of America, too proud, as it would seem, to acknowledge themselves indebted to this country, for their existence, their power, or their language, denying and revolting against the two first, and also making all the haste they conveniently can, to rid themselves of the last. With little or no dialect, they are peculiarly addicted to innovation: but such as need not excite our envy, whether we regard their elegance, or their propriety. The progress may be slow; but if they continue to be a separate government, and a government too so eminently unpropitious to sound learning and virtuous manners, it will be sure: and it is easy to foresee that, in no very distant period, their language will become as independent of England, as they themselves are; and altogether as unlike English, as the Dutch or Flemish is unlike German, or the Norwegian unlike the Danish, or the Portuguese unlike Spanish.[30]

In reviewing the *Travels* of the Marquis de Chastellux, the *Gentleman's Magazine* selected for quotation the passage on language. The Frenchman reported that he had often heard the Americans, in contempt of the language of their 'oppressors', say to him, 'You speak very good American; American is not difficult to learn.'

They go further [continued Chastellux], and have seriously proposed to introduce a new language; and some, for the public convenience, would have the Hebrew substituted to the English, taught in the schools, and used in all public acts. You may suppose this scheme was not adopted: but you will at least conclude that the aversion of the Americans for the English could not show itself in a more striking manner.[31]

A correspondent to the magazine a few months later was appalled at this prospect, and felt that the compiler of an English dictionary need not consider America. 'If this be true', he said, 'let us leave the inventors of this motley gibberish to make a Dictionary for themselves'.[32] In 1799 an Irishman named Lucas George, resident in America, held the same opinion, in speaking of an American reviewer: 'It is not *English* that he writes, Sir; it is *American*. His periods are accompanied by a yell, that is scarcely less dismal than the warhoop of a *Mohawk*'.[33] When Lord Sheffield listed 'Books' as an article of exportation from Britain to America, he introduced the doubtful note that the language might not continue the same.[34]

II.

What characteristics of American speech struck the Englishman as being peculiar? Here was a vast laboratory for his diagnosis, because the Americans spoke copiously and fluently. Wrote Thomas Twining, concerning his tour of 1796: 'An American speaks English with the volubility of a Frenchman. On my arrival in America I was much struck with this peculiarity.'[35] Boucher also found the Americans 'eminently endowed with a knack of talking; they seem to be born orators'.[36]

Accustomed as he was to the diversity of dialect in his own island, the Englishman found a principal subject of comment in the purity and uniformity of English in America. Hugh Jones, on the basis of a residence in Virginia from 1716 to 1721, gave what may be the earliest evaluation of speech in America. He was speech-conscious enough to compose *An Accidence of the English Tongue* (London, 1724) while on American soil. He wrote, in his *Present State of Virginia:* '. . . the *Planters,* and even the *Native Negroes* generally talk good *English* without *Idiom* or *Tone*, and can discourse handsomly upon *most* common Subjects . . .'[37]

When a Scottish nobleman, Lord Adam Gordon, traveled through the colonies in 1764–1765, he gave special praise to Philadelphia: '. . . the propriety of Language here surprized me much, the English tongue being spoken by all ranks, in a degree of purity and perfection, surpassing any, but the polite part of London.'[38] Boston, moreover, he found, 'is more like an English Old Town than any in America, — the Language and manner of the people, very much resemble the old Country, and all the

Neighbouring lands and Villages, carry with them the same Idea'.[39] Johr
Bernard, who visited Boston in 1797, was similarly impressed,[40] and only
John Mair (1906) wrote disparagingly of Boston ladies in 1791: 'some oı
them are very pritty, but want the polish of language, and the easy and
eligant manner polite education gives'.[41]

The strange phenomenon of uniformity engaged the attention of
William Eddis, who wrote in a letter dated June 8, 1770:

> In England, almost every county is distinguished by a peculiar dialect; even
> different habits, and different modes of thinking, evidently discriminate inhabit-
> ants, whose local situation is not far remote: but in Maryland and throughout
> adjacent provinces, it is worthy of observation, that a striking similarity of speech
> universally prevails; and it is strictly true, that the pronunciation of the generality
> of the people has an accuracy and elegance, that cannot fail of gratifying the most
> judicious ear.
>
> The colonists are composed of adventurers, not only from every district of
> Great Britain and Ireland, but from almost every other European government,
> where the principles of liberty and commerce have operated with spirit and
> efficacy. Is it not, therefore, reasonable to suppose, that the English language
> must be greatly corrupted by such a strange intermixture of various nations? The
> reverse is, however, true. The language of the immediate descendants of such a
> promiscuous ancestry is perfectly uniform, and unadulterated; nor has it bor-
> rowed any provincial, or national accent, from its British or foreign parentage.
>
> For my part, I confess myself totally at a loss to account for the apparent
> difference, between the colonists and persons under equal circumstances of
> education and fortune, resident in the mother country. This uniformity of lan-
> guage prevails not only on the coast, where Europeans form a considerable mass
> of the people, but likewise in the interior parts, where population has made but
> slow advances; and where opportunities seldom occur to derive any great advan-
> tages from an intercourse with intelligent strangers.[42]

Nicholas Cresswell, a Derbyshire man, recorded the same in his journal
of July 19, 1777:

> Though the inhabitants of this Country are composed of different Nations
> and different languages, yet it is very remarkable that they in general speak better
> English than the English do. No County or Colonial dialect is to be distinguished
> here, except it be the New Englanders, who have a sort of whining cadence that I
> cannot describe.[43]

Boucher, who lived in Maryland or Virginia from 1759 to 1775,
testified to the same effect in a letter of December 23, 1777: 'It is still
more extraordinary that, in North America, there prevails not only, I
believe, the purest Pronunciation of the English Tongue that is anywhere
to be met with, but a perfect Uniformity.'[44] He felt that there was a

parallel between America and Italy, where various tribes, such as the Umbri, Osci, and Samnites, originally differed in dialect but upon becoming one people adopted one language.

> How exactly [pointed out Boucher] this was the case as to British America must needs be generally known. It was peopled by settlers from England, Ireland, Scotland, Germany, Holland, and Sweden, who also all differed in dialect, and many in language, from the present inhabitants of that continent. In this only the parallel fails — though in both cases the first settlers were in general of such characters as that they could not well be degraded nor debased by any future connexions, yet it does not appear that the American colonists ever mixed and incorporated, like the Romans, with the aborigines of the country.[45]

Boucher did not consider the absence of dialect an advantage, for it led to 'a corresponding scantiness of cultivation and improvement in their respective languages'.[46] When the missionary Thomas Coke visited the Methodist college near Baltimore on May 9, 1789, he found 'great propriety of pronunciation' in the young men there.[47]

The London editor of Ramsay's *History of the American Revolution* showed a liberal attitude:

> It is a curious fact, that there is perhaps no one portion of the British empire, in which two or three millions of persons are to be found, who speak their mother-tongue with greater purity, or a truer pronunciation, than the white inhabitants of the United States. This was attributed, by a penetrating observer, to the number of British subjects assembled in America from various quarters, who, in consequence of their intercourse and intermarriages, soon dropped the peculiarities of their several provincial idioms, retaining only what was fundamental and common to them all; a process, which the frequency or rather the universality of school-learning in North America, must naturally have assisted.[48] At the same time there are few natives of the United States, who are altogether free from what may be called *Americanisms*, both in their speech and their writing. In the case of words of rarer use, they have framed their own models of pronunciation, as having little access to those established among the people from whom they have derived their language; and hence they are sometimes *at variance* with us in their speech, (to say nothing of the peculiar tones of voice which prevail in some parts of the United States). But their familiarity with our best writers has in general left them ignorant of nothing which regards our phraseology; and hence their chief difference in writing consists in having *added* a few words to our language, in consequence of the influence of some local authority or of their peculiar situation.[49]

And finally, John Harriott, a military adventurer who arrived in America in 1793, testified that English 'is universally understood and better spoken by the whole mass of people, from Georgia to Quebec (an extent of country more than 1,200 miles), than by the bulk of people in the different counties of England'.[50]

This absence of dialect, so puzzling to the commentators, is now accepted as normal to any colonial speech. In the jostling of speech characteristics imported from many regions, the peculiarities are very soon worn away and a state approaching homogeneity ensues.

And yet the Englishmen may have failed to find dialectal variations partly because of a lack of intimacy with the country. After spending several years in the Southern colonies, J. F. D. Smyth, for one, found a decided change in Connecticut. 'The whole face of nature', he wrote, 'as well as the manners and dialect of the people here are widely different from that of the southern provinces, and greatly to the disadvantage of New England'.[51] Other Englishmen remarked on that intangible matter of accent. Thomas Anburey, who was a lieutenant in Burgoyne's army and crossed New England as a prisoner, recorded of the inquisitive women: 'One of them, with a twang, peculiar to the New Englanders said, "I hear you have got a Lord among you, pray now which may he be?" '[52] Even in western New York a Gael named Patrick Campbell could detect the New Englander whom he met on February 10, 1792:

> I asked him if he had come from the head of the Lake; he answered in a twang peculiar to the New Englanders, "I viow niew you may depen I's just a-comin"; "And what distance may it be from hence?" said I; "I viow niew I guess I do' no, — I guess niew I do' no — I swear niew I guess it is three miles"; he swore, vowed, and guessed alternately, and was never like to come to the point, though he had but that instant come from it.[53]

An Irishman thus described a certain Jemimah Wilkinson, living near Newport, Rhode Island, who claimed that she was Jesus Christ and had numerous followers: 'Her voice is masculine, and pronunciation the peculiar dialect of the most illiterate of the country people of New England. . . .'[54] A man named Osgood Carleton of Boston was challenged so many times because of his English-sounding accent that his business was suffering and he was constrained to insert the following advertisement in the newspaper, the *Herald of Freedom*, in 1790:

Osgood Carleton,

Having been frequently applied to for a decision of disputes, and sometimes wagers,[55] respecting the place of his nativity, and finding they sometimes operate to his disadvantage: Begs leave to give this public information — that he was born in Nottingham-west, in the State of New-Hampshire — in which state he resided until sixteen years old; after which time, he traveled by sea and land to various parts, and being (while young) mostly conversant with the English, he lost some of the country dialect, which gives rise to the above disputes.[56]

The Connecticut accent of 1744 is reflected in a record by the Scottish physician Alexander Hamilton: 'Damn me', said a horse-jockey at Norwalk, 'if you or any man shall have the jade for 100 peaunds.'[57] And John Davis could distinguish the New Jersey families that had settled in Virginia, remarking: 'The *New Jersey Man* is distinguished by his provincial dialect. . . .'[58] Smyth gives an instance from western North Carolina: the inhabitants of the region had fled to a fort during an Indian scare, and when he clamored to be given entrance, they refused it because his accent was different from theirs. They insisted that he must be a Frenchman or an enemy.[59]

A few statements have been preserved as to the character of the American accent. The Scotch philosopher James Beattie, in 1783, discussed the width of scale in speech tune and decided, contrary to the usual opinion in our own time, that a narrow range is desirable. A Londoner of his acquaintance claimed that the speech of London was the most elegant because it 'was unaccented, whereas, in every other part of the British empire, people spoke with a tone'.

And a clergyman of Virginia [reported Beattie] assured me very seriously, that the English of that province was the best in the world; and assigned the same reason in favour of the Virginian pronunciation. But every word these gentlemen spoke was to my ear a convincing proof, that they were mistaken. It is true, the North-American English accent is not so animated, as that of Middlesex, and the adjoining counties; but it is very perceptible notwithstanding.[60]

Thus, as early as 1783 the American monotone was noticeable. Boucher was even more explicit in this regard: from his observation in America before 1775 he recalled, 'One striking peculiarity in American elocution is a slow, drawling, unemphatical, and unimpassioned manner; and this, it is probable, is to be attributed, in general, to the heat of their climates, which is such as to paralyze all active exertion even in speaking.'[61] What little accent he found he explained as a survival of European origins. These he listed:

I ought perhaps to except [from the universal prevalence of dialect] the United States of America, in which dialect is hardly known; unless some scanty remains of the croaking, gutteral idioms of the Dutch, still observable near New York; the Scotch-Irish, as it used to be called, in some of the back settlers of the Middle States; and the whining, canting drawl brought by some republican, Oliverian and Puritan emigrants from the West of England, and still kept up by their undegenerated descendants of New England — may be called dialects. . . . [The English colonies] in America trace their original to a few active English cities, London, Chester, Bristol, and the like; whose phrases and accents are yet discoverable in the speech of the colonists. In Virginia, one of the oldest of the British settlements, we still hear such terms, as *holp* for *help, mought* for *might*; and several others now obsolete here, but which were in full currency at the time when that colony was first planted.[62]

Among the disagreeable characteristics of American speech was an ever-present vulgarity. Even in 1699 Ned Ward asserted concerning the New Englanders: 'Notwithstanding their *Sanctity,* they are very *Prophane* in their common *Dialect*.'[63] Shortly after reaching America in 1759 Boucher wrote to a friend in England concerning the 'forward obtrusion w'c subjects you to hear obscene Conceits and broad Expression; & from this, there are times w'n no sex, no Rank, no Conduct can exempt you'.[64] Even the language of the preachers was 'extremely vulgar and profane', according to Richard Parkinson. 'The word *damned* was a very familiar phrase', he reported, 'as much so as if we had been in a cock-pit'.[65] Others felt that the contact with negroes vitiated speech. G. L. Campbell wrote in 1746:

One Thing they are very faulty in, with regard to their Children, which is, that when young, they suffer them too much to prowl amongst the young Negros, which insensibly causes them to imbibe their Manners and broken Speech.[66]

Smyth was unable to understand his own boy attendant, and found that many of the Virginia Negroes spoke 'a mixed dialect between the Guinea and English'.[67]

III.

Less favorable were the British comments on the American vocabulary. The prevailing theory was that the words in the language were a static deposit, and any changes were bound to be for the worse. When the reviewer in *The European Magazine* found the word *belittle* in Jefferson's *Notes on Virginia,* he became eloquent:

Belittle! What an expression! It may be an elegant one in Virginia, and even perfectly intelligible; but for our part, all we can do is, to *guess* at its meaning. For shame, Mr. Jefferson! . . . O spare us, we beseech you, our *mother-tongue!*[68]

Even Noah Webster, as yet fairly obscure, received his portion of criticism. *The Gentleman's Magazine* for May 1798, spoke thus of his *Sentimental and Humorous Essays:*

In this little work, originally published in America under the title of 'The Prompter', many localities occur; which are retained, 'as it would have been uncandid to cover American ground with English leaves'. 'Some of these will appear uncouth to a reader unused to the Yankey dialect; the ideas of *rum* and *grog*, for example, which continually occur, seem unnatural to the beer-drinking Briton; and the 'dollar and quarter-dollar a corner' would sound oddly in St. James's-street; yet we approve of the phrases being continued in their original garb.'[69]

The British Critic of November 1793, assumed an attitude of paternal tolerance:

We shall at all times, with pleasure, receive from our trans-atlantic brethren real improvements of our common mother-tongue: but we shall hardly be induced to admit such phrases as that at p. 93 — 'more lengthy', for longer, or more diffuse. But perhaps, it is an established Americanism.[70]

Boucher scored the Americans because of 'their passion for innovating' and in order 'to show how very poorly they are qualified to set up for reformers of language' he collected these words from various American political pamphlets: *advocate, demoralizing,*[71] verb *progress,* the *grades* of office, verb *memorialize,* the *alone* minister, *inimical, influential,* and a *mean* for *means.*[72] It will be noticed that Boucher included *advocate* in this list, and yet in the body of his glossary he wrote of it: 'It has been said that this word is an improvement of the English language, which has been discovered by the people of the United States of North America, since their separation from Great Britain. It will, however, be seen, from the following references, that *advocate* is a very common Scotish word.' This dichotomy has run through most British writing on American speech even to the present day: on the one hand the Americans are denounced for introducing corruptions into the language and on the other hand those very expressions are eagerly claimed as of British origin to show that the British deserve the credit for them.

The British traveler found frequent occasion to comment on novel words, and his journals and reports contain many glosses.[73] The obtuse Richard Parkinson told thus of his experience:

It was natural for me now to enquire what they kept their cows and horses on during the winter. They told me — their horses on blades, and their cows on slops. I neither knew what *blades* nor *slops* were. The people seemed to laugh at me for my enquiry . . . Now to return to the slops and blades. — The latter proved to be blades and tops of Indian corn: and the slops were the same that are put into the swill-tub in England, and given to hogs; composed of broth, dish-washings, cabbage-leaves, potatoe-parings, &c.[74]

Both Wansey and Twining commented on American words:

There are many words the Americans use which we do not — *lengthy* for long, *extinguishment* for extinction, and *advocated;* the vulgar Americans pronounce the word fortune as *fortn*.[75]

Though such words as *illy, vended, to loan, to enterprise,* and a few others are to be met with in the least cultivated ranks of society, there are others which are allowable in America for their usefulness, as 'portage', applied to the *distances* goods must be carried at the locks, falls, and rapids (as the Potomac has so many *portages*), and some which are admissable both for their usefulness and greater precision, as *'boatable'* as applied to shallow rivers, instead of *navigable*, and *'immigration'*.[76]

In the Ohio country in 1775 Creswell remarked that he 'went a hunting as they call it here';[77] in Virginia, Anburey was perplexed by a road 'that has three forks (which is their manner of describing the partings in the roads)'.[78] Baily, reporting the rapid western movement of migration in 1797, explained that 'to locate, means to particularize and describe correctly the place which is intended to be reserved for the sole use and possession of the person claiming the same'.[79] Davis glossed the speech of a South Carolina man in 1799, '*Lengthy* is the *American* for *long*', and 'is frequently used by the *classical* writers of the New World'.[80] Weld at Niagara Falls found that the 'musquitoes swarm so thickly in the air, that to use a common phrase of the country, "you might cut them with a knife" ';[81] and so on — in a list that might be extended indefinitely.

The American political system was responsible for many modifications in vocabulary. In 1775 the merchants interested in the West Indies, framing a petition to Parliament, were in a quandary in speaking of the Continental Congress: if they used the American word *Congress* they would antagonize the ministry and if they used the expression 'called a Congress' they would offend the colonists. Finally they compromised on the periphrase 'a meeting held at Philadelphia'.[82] The American people were no longer 'subjects', but 'citizens'. While in America Dr. Priestley used the expression in public prayer 'in hopes of becoming *citizens* of heaven', and a British traveler who heard him considered it as 'rather trimming his sails to the wind'.[83] The *British Critic* noted that 'The Americans have coined the term *Citess*' to mean a female citizen, and the editors disapproved of it: 'But we hope not to see any jargon of the kind adopted.'[84] The first time, so far as is now known, that the word *Yankee* appeared in print (1765; with reference to a certain John Huske of

Portsmouth, New Hampshire) it was glossed by 'a North Briton' as follows: 'The epithet of Yankey, a name of derision, I have been informed, given by the Southern people on the Continent, to those of New England: what meaning there is in the word, I never could learn.'[85]

For the most part the American vocabulary was conceived to be flaccid and inaccurate. Parkinson found 'hundreds of those sorts of reptiles, flies, and bugs (all denominated bugs by the Americans)'.[86] The wild animals of America were frequently given the name of a similar animal of England, Weld found, 'because they bore some resemblance to them, though in fact they are materially different'.[87] The Frenchman Chastellux expressed the current disapproval most forcibly:

> . . . la partie de la langue créée en Amérique est extrêmement pauvre. Tout ce qui n'avait pas de nom anglois, n'en a reçu ici qu'un simplement désignatif: le geai est l'oiseau bleu, le cardinal l'oiseau rouge; tout oiseau d'eau est un canard. . . . Il en est de même des arbres, les pins, les cyprès, les sapins sont tous compris sous le nom de *pine-trees*. . . . Je pourrais citer beaucoup d'autres exemples; mais il suffit d'observer que cette pauvreté dans le langage prouve combien l'attention des hommes a été employé aux objets d'utilité. . . .[88]

The grandiloquence characteristic of America was observed also: America was believed 'to be (as they termed it) the best land in the world'.[89] When Davis was in Baltimore in 1801 a huge cheese was transported there on its way to the President of the United States from the farmers' wives and daughters of Cheshire, Massachusetts: it was called 'the greatest cheese in the world' and was known throughout the Union as 'the Mammoth Cheese'.[90] The field of religion gave scope for high-flown talk, as the Scottish physician Alexander Hamilton recorded of Connecticut on August 27, 1744:

> 'Tis strange to see how this humour [to discuss points of divinity] prevails, even among the lower class of the people here. They will talk so pointedly about justification, sanctification, adoption, regeneration, repentance, free grace, reprobation, original sin, and a thousand other such pretty chimerical knick-knacks, as if they had done nothing but studied divinity all their life-time. . . . To talk this dialect in our parts would be like Greek, Hebrew, or Arabick.[91]

More than is commonly realized, the people of the British Isles even before 1800 had an awareness of American speech. For the most part during this early period, they conceded that the general level of purity in pronunciation was high, even higher than in Great Britain; and only in the matter of vocabulary did they, on the basis of their supposition that all change in language is reprehensible, find ground for censure. Even in this field the defenders of the purity of the language were as yet engaged in reprobating Scotticisms. America was still regarded before 1800 as a land of promise, and the attitude toward speech reflected that outlook. These British commentators of the eighteenth century were finding a fulfillment of what Samuel Daniel, with a poet's clairvoyance, had predicted in 1599:

> And who, in time, knowes whither we may vent
> The treasure of our tongue, to what strange shores
> This gaine of our best glory shall be sent,
> T'inrich vnknowing Nations with our stores?
> What worlds in th' yet vnformed Occident
> May come refin'd with th' accents that are ours?[92]

NOTES

1. No. 102, Dec. 12, 1754, pp. 611–616; reprinted in *The Works of Richard Owen Cambridge, Esq.*, 438–433. London, 1803. Cambridge's train of thought may have been started by Lord Chesterfield's suggestion in the *World* essay of the previous week that Johnson compile 'a genteel neological dictionary' (p. 610).

2. Loc cit., p. 615.

3. Most of the words had entered the language in the preceding century (dates from *OED*): *scalp* (1676), *sachem* (1622), *wampum* (1636), *calumet* (1717); but *to take up the hatchet* is from G. Washington (1753), *war-kettle* has this as its first quotation, and *half-king* and *speech-belt* are not recorded. The infiltration of Indian words into England is shown in such a passage as this of 1760, supposed to be the speech of a country gentleman, Sir Politic Hearty: ' "By the bye (said the baronet), I am a great admirer of the Indian oratory; and I dare say old Hendrick the sachem would have made a good figure in the House of Commons. There is something very elegant in the Covenant-belt; but pray what a pox are those damned Strings of Wampum? I cannot find any account of them in Chambers's Dictionary." He then entered into a dissertation on the Warhoop; and turning to the apothecary, "Doctor", said he, "what do you think of scalping?" ' (*The Connoisseur*, No. 71, not in the original of July 10, 1755, but inserted into the 3rd ed., 1760, III, 41.) This ingress of words from the New World was noted at least as early as 1660, when James Howells wrote (*Lexicon Tetraglotton*, 'To the tru Philologer'); 'Touching the *English*, what a number of new words have got into her of late yeers which will be found here; as . . . perino (Carribby Islands drink) . . .'; and as early as 1621 Alexander Gill recorded (*Logonomia Anglica*, ed. Jiriczek, *QFSC*, vol. XC, 1903, p. 42): 'Yet also from the Americans we have borrowed several words [nonnulla mutuamur], as *maiz* Indian wheat, and *kanoa* a light boat from a tree trunk hollowed out by fire and flint.'

4. James Boswell, *Life of Johnson* (ed. Hill), II, 160. Oxford, 1887. It is recorded that shortly after the Revolution, the writer of ballads, Capt. Thomas Morris, wanted to compose a song against Pitt 'in the Yankee dialect', but he was well-nigh unable to find a peculiar Yankee word with which to season it. (Charles Astor Bristed, 'The English language in America', in *Cambridge Essays, 1855*, 58. London, 1855.) Speech differences were slight enough for a recent investigator to conclude, in discussing the propa-

ganda of Americans in England before the Revolution: 'One may be certain, then, that Americans often masqueraded as Englishmen. . . .' (F. J. Hinkhouse, *Preliminaries of the American Revolution as Seen in the English Press, 1763–1775,* 22. 1926).

5. [William Beloe] *The Sexagenarian; or The Recollections of a Literary Life,* II, 7–8. London, 1817.

6. *Some Information respecting America,* London, 1794, p. 87. Isaac Weld comments on the American love of cleared land: 'I have heard of Americans landing on barren parts of the north west coast of Ireland, and evincing the greatest surprise and pleasure at the beauty and improved state of the country, "so clear of trees!!" ' (*Travels through the States of North America . . . during the Years 1795, 1796 and 1797,* 24, note. London, 1799).

7. *The Mirror* (Edinburgh), No. 96, April 8, 1780, p. 383.

8. *The Diary and Letters of his Excellency Thomas Hutchinson, Esq.,* ed. Peter Orlando Hutchinson, I, 171. London, 1883. After the Revolution, in 1785, when George III received John Adams as the first emissary from the United States, the King mentioned the identity of language as one of the circumstances that should 'have their natural and full effect'. (Letter of June 2, 1785, in *The Works of John Adams*; ed. Charles Francis Adams, vol. VIII: 257. Boston, 1853; for an account of Adams' mission in England, see Robert E. Spiller (1926), *The American in England during the First Century of Independence* 103–107, New York.

9. 'Plan of a dictionary', in *Works,* ed. 1796, II, 6.

10. Edmund Malone listed these in the MS notes in his copy of the *Dictionary* now in the British Museum. The work quoted, *The Female Quixote,* appeared in 1752, five years after the *Dictionary* had been under way. For her relationship to Johnson, see J. M[itford] in *The Gent. Mag.* n.s. XX (Aug., 1843), p. 132. Under *dangler* is cited 'Ralph's Mic', but this compilation by the Philadelphian James Ralph did not contain his own writing.

11. Used in the *Idler,* No. 40, Jan. 20, 1759 (*Works,* ed. 1796, VII, 160).

12. See e.g. Benjamin Martin, *Miscellaneous Correspondence, containing a Variety of Subjects . . .,* III (Jan., 1759), p. 1: 'there is lately arrived from *America,* a *Mohawk Indian* Warrior . . . with his Face and Body painted, his Scalping-knife, and Tomax, or Battle-axe, and all other implements that are used by the Indians in Battle . . .'

13. Vol. I (Sept. 15 – Oct. 15, 1756), pp. 293–299.

14. *Geographical, historical, political, philosophical and mechanical essays: the first, containing an Analysis of a general Map of the Middle British Colonies in America; and of the Country of the Confederate Indians,* Philadelphia, 1755. All copies were printed there, but some, such as the one Johnson reviewed, had the additional line in the imprint, 'and sold by R. and J. Dodsley in Pall-Mall, London'.

15. A meaning now obsolete; = trace, trait.

16. Loc. cit., p. 294. During his tour of Scotland Johnson admitted the benefits of emigrating and recognized that the colonists 'carry with them their language' (*A Journey to the Western Islands,* in *Works,* ed. 1796, VIII, 327).

17. Op. cit. pp. iii, 1, 4, 6, 7, 8, 9, 30.

18. *Elements of General Knowledge . . .,* Oxford, 1802, I, 145. According to the *DNB* this book was compiled from his lectures at Oxford during the preceding decade. Of the five books on the English language which he recommended to his pupils (II, Appendix, p. 7), one was Noah Webster's *Dissertations* (1789; imported by Dilly in 1797). Kett's sections on language were pirated as an anonymous work, *A Dissertation on Language in General, More Particularly on the Beauties and Defects of the English Language . . .,*

(Parsons and Galignani's British Library, Prose N. 24), Paris, 1805; quoted passage, p. 56.

19. Op. cit., London, 1791, I, vi-vii.
20. 'Late Improvements on Pages and Printing', loc, cit., XXVIII (Oct., 1796), p. 388.
21. Vol. LVII, Part ii (Oct., 1787), p. 910.
22. Ibid., LVIII, Part i (Feb., 1788), p. 92.
23. *A Letter, from Germany, to the Princess Royal of England; on the English and German Languages . . .,* Hamburg, 1797, p. 3.
24. Ibid., p. 2, note 1. He wrote further (p. 8, note 1): 'During the American revolution, the idea was started of revenging themselves on England, by rejecting its language and adopting that of France. Had this taken place, the author of a dictionary of the English language could not proudly look to its being used, half a century hence, by fifteen or twenty millions of people more than exist to use it now.' In a letter of Oct. 30, 1798, Thomas Jefferson wrote to Croft that he looked forward with impatience to the publication of Croft's work. (*An Essay towards Facilitating Instruction in the Anglo-Saxon and Modern Dialects of the English Language,* N.Y., 1851, p. 3.)
25. *The Letters of David Hume* (1932), ed. by J. Y. T. Grieg, vol. II: 171. Oxford.
26. *The Writings of Benjamin Franklin* (1916), ed. by Albert Henry Smyth, vol. IV: 84. New York. Franklin continued: 'I assure you it often gives me pleasure to reflect, how greatly the *audience* (if I may so term it) of a good English writer will, in another century or two, be increased by the increase of English people in our colonies.'
27. Ibid., p. 83. Each of these had been used earlier by reputable English writers.
28. *Proposals for Printing by Subscription, in two volumes, quarto: Linguæ Anglicanæ Thesaurus; or, A Glossary of the Ancient English Language, in two parts* (n.d), 14. London. It was circulated by being stitched with an issue of the *Gentleman's Magazine* (John Nichols, *Illus. of the Lit. Hist. of the XVIIIth Cent.,* London, 1828, V, 639–640).
29. After Boucher's death in 1804, his friends published a Part I, A-aynd: *A Supplement to Dr. Johnson's Dictionary of the English Language: or, a Glossary of Obsolete and Provincial Words* (1807). London. The interest at the time did not warrant continuation; but in 1832–1833 two leading antiquaries, the Rev. Joseph Hunter and Joseph Stevenson, edited the work with the addition of their own material, printing Boucher's erudite and valuable preface of 64 pages, and proceeding as far as *blade: Boucher's Glossary of Archaic and Provincial Words, A Supplement to the Dictionaries of the English Language, particularly those of Dr. Johnson and Dr. Webster* (1832). London. In a letter of Sept. 9, 1831, E. H. Barker of Thetford. Norfolk, wrote Noah Webster that Boucher's work was complete in the provincial part from *A* to *Thirlage* and in the archaeological part from *A* to *Gib,* and that the remainder of the alphabet would have to be supplied from other sources (Webster Papers, New York Public Library).
30. Preface to his *Glossary,* op. cit., p. xxiii. The editors state that this preface was written in 1800.
31. Loc. cit., LVI, part ii (Supp., 1786), p. 1117. In the French this passage is found in *Voyages . . . dans l'Amérique Septentrionale, dans les années 1780, 1781 & 1782* (1791) (second edition), vol. II: 202–203. Paris. For a contrasting attitude by a Frenchman, note that of Roland de la Platière before the Academy at Lyons in 1789: Fernand, Baldensperger, 'Une prédiction inédite sur l'avenir de la langue des États-Unis', *Modern Philology* XV (Dec., 1917): 475–476.
32. 'D. D', in loc. cit., LVII, part ii (Nov., 1787), p. 978.
33. Quoted in John Davis (1803), *Travels of Four Years and a Half in the United States of America during 1798, 1799, 1800, 1801, and 1802,* 139. London.

34. John Baker, Holroyd, 1st earl of Sheffield (1784), *Observations on the Commerce of the American States,* 33. London.

35. *Travels in America 100 Years Ago* (1902), 117. New York. Cf. p. 167: 'I thought it not extraordinary . . . that the English language should be spoken more fluently than correctly.'

36. Under date of April 12, 1786, in his *Reminiscences of an American Loyalist 1738–1789* (1925), ed. by Jonathan Boucher, 61. Boston.

37. London, 1724, as found in Sabin's Reprints, No. 5, N.Y., 1865, p. 43. Even concerning Negro speech he wrote: those 'that are born there talk *good English,* and affect our Language, Habits, and Customs . . .' (p. 37). On the other hand, Francis Moore, visiting Savannah in February, 1735–1736, spoke of its situation on 'the bank of a River (which they in barbarous *English* call a *Bluff)*' (*A Voyage to Georgia. Begun in the Year 1735,* (1744), 23–24. London.

38. 'Journal of an Officer who Travelled in America and the West Indies in 1764 and 1765', printed in *Travels in the American Colonies* (1916), ed by Newton D. Mereness, 411. New York.

39. Ibid., p. 449.

40. 'In the genteel society of Boston I could perceive no distinctions from that of my own country. They wore the same clothes, spoke the same language, and seemed to glow with the same affable and hospitable feelings.' (*Retrospections of America 1797–1811,* (1887), 29. New York. written 1819–1827.)

41. 'Journal of John Mair, 1791', *The American Historical Review,* 12:85.

42. *Letters from America, Historical and Descriptive; comprising Occurrences from 1769 to 1777, inclusive* (1729), 59–61. London.

43. *The Journal of Nicholas Cresswell, 1774–1777* (1924), 271. New York.

44. *Maryland Historical Magazine,* 10 (March, 1915): 30. He spent his formative years in Cumberland and of English regional dialects liked that of Staffordshire best. In his *Reminiscences* (op. cit., p. 61) he corroborated: '. . . different places are there known and spoken of, not as here, by any difference of dialect (for there is no dialect in all North America) but by their being inhabited by the Fitzhughs, the Randolphs, Washingtons, Carys, Grimeses, or Thorntons.'

45. Written in 1800: *Glossary,* p. xx. He could remember only two families that claimed to have Indian blood, the Bollings and Brents, 'said to be descended from the celebrated Pocahontas, whose interesting story is related by Captain Smith in his *History of Virginia*'.

46. Ibid.

47. *Extracts of the Journals of the Rev. Dr. Coke's Five Visits to America* (1793), 111. London.

48. The 'penetrating observer' may well have been John Witherspoon, whose papers called 'The Druid' had appeared in 1781 in the *Pennsylvania Journal and the Weekly Advertiser* (as reprinted in *The Beginnings of American English* (1931), ed. by M. M. Mathews, 14ff. Chicago. This is rendered more likely because of the use of the word *Americanism* in the next sentence, a word which Witherspoon claimed to have coined (p. 17).

49. Op. cit., pp. v–vi.

50. *Struggles through Life* (1808), second edition, vol. II: 13–14. London. Cf. the comment of William Lee, who reached New York on August 21, 1786, in *The True and Interesting Travels of William Lee* (1808), 7. London.

51. *A Tour of the United States of America: containing an Account of the present Situation of that Country* (1784), vol. II: 363. London.

52. Entry of Nov. 25, 1777, in *Travels through the Interior Parts of* America, (1789), London, as reprinted in Boston, 1923, II, 32.
53. *Travels in the Interior Parts of North America, in the Years 1791 and 1792* (1793), 181. Edinburgh. Cf. the Rhode Island farmers in Harriott, op. cit., II, 43.
54. *An Historical Review and Directory of North America: containing a Geographical, Political, and Natural History of the British and other European Settlements, the United and Apocryphal States . . . By a Gentleman Immediately returned from a Tour of that Continent,* Cork, 1801, II, 36 (Preface signed Dublin, March 25, 1788). This account had appeared earlier in *The American Museum* I (February, 1787): 152.
55. Careleton's footnote: 'Several Englishmen having disputed his being born in America.'
56. August 20, 1790, as reprinted in *Quaint and Curious Advertisements* (The Olden Time Series, IV) (1886), ed. by Henry M. Brooks, 55. Boston.
57. Entry of Aug. 29, 1744, in *Hamilton's Itinerarium being a Narrative of a Journey from Annapolis, Maryland . . . from May to September, 1744* (1907), ed. by Albert Bushnell Hart, 206. St. Louis, Mo.
58. Op. cit., p. 367.
59. Op. cit., I, 278–279.
60. *Dissertations Moral and Critical* (1783), 294. London.
61. *Glossary,* p. xlviii. (Written in 1800.)
62. Ibid., p. ix.
63. *A Trip to New-England . . .,* London, 1699 (Fac. Text Soc., Ser. I, vol. VII), p. 11.
64. Letter of Aug. 7, 1759, in *Maryland Historical Magazine* 7 (March, 1912): 5. Dr. Hamilton recorded on Sept. 12, 1744, concerning his experience at a New Jersey inn: 'I was waked this morning before sunrise with a strange bawling and hollowing without doors. It was the landlord ordering his negroes, with an imperious and exalted voice. In his orders the known term or epithet of *son of a bitch* was often repeated' (*Itinerarium,* p. 229, and note the use of 'good neat bawdy', p. 217).
65. *A Tour in America in 1798, 1799; and 1800* (1805), vol. II: 460. London.
66. *The London Magazine,* 15 (July, 1746): 330. C. W. Janson (1807) (*The Stranger in America,* 383) quoted the geographer Morse to the same effect, and John Davis, in the South in 1799, wrote: 'Each child has its [Negro] *Momma,* whose gestures and accent it will necessarily copy, for children we all know are imitative beings' (op. cit., p. 86).
67. Op. cit., I, 39, 78–79, 88, 121.
68. Loc. cit., XII (Aug., 1787) p. 114, note; on the same word in a later issue (p. 273): 'A *new,* but *favourite* expression of our author.'
69. Loc. cit., LXVIII, 415.
70. In a review of *Report of the Secretary of the Treasury of the United States, on the Subject of Manufactures. Presented to the House of Representatives, Dec. 5, 1791,* in loc. cit., II, 286. It was customary to impale American words thus: '*freshets* [we are unacquainted with this word] . . .' (*Monthly Review,* 76 (Feb. 1787): 138–139, reviewing Jeremy Belknap, *Description of the White Mountains in New Hampshire.*)
71. Boucher had evidently seen the anonymous pamphlet by Noah Webster (1794), *The Revolution in France, considered in Respect to its Progress and Effects. By an American,* New York, where on p. 32 occurs the passage: 'All wars have, if I may use a new but emphatic word a *demoralizing* tendency; but the revolution in France, in addition to the *usual* influence of war, is attended with a total change in the minds of people.' Thirty-eight years later Webster annotated this passage in a copy now in the New York Public Library: 'This is the first time, this word was ever used in English. It is now common in the U. States & in England. N. W. 1832.' In 1817 he defended the term as 'so well adapted to express ideas not expressed by any other single term, that I am persuaded it

must maintain its ground' (*Letter to Pickering,* Boston, p. 15); and Charles Lyell, an Englishman who visited him in 1841, reported: 'When the lexicographer, Noah Webster, whom I saw at New Haven, was asked how many new words he had coined, he replied one only "to demoralize", and that not for his dictionary, but long before, in a pamphlet published in the last century' (*Travels in North America in the Years 1841–2* (1852), 53. New York). Webster included the word in the *Compendious* of 1806 (as also a derivative *demoralization,* before anyone is recorded as using it) and in the *American* of 1828 with quotations from the Irishman Grattan and the American Walsh.

72. *Glossary* op. cit., p. xxiii, footnote. Of these, according to the evidence of the *OED,* only *advocate* and *demoralize* are in any way American, except that *grade,* sb. 4, is recorded, with English evidence, only from 1808. Boucher's 'Absence: a Pastoral', ca. 1775, the earliest important study of American English yet pointed out, will be reprinted in the next issue.

73. These are being treated by Mr. M. M. Mathews in a valuable study now in progress.

74. Op. cit., I, 39–40. He reports the Americans as saying that they 'have once *whipped* the British', adding a bit spitefully, 'the term whipping arises from their whipping the negroes' (p. 265). In reality it was an old word that had died out in this sense in England.

75. Henry Wansey (1796), *An Excursion to the United States of North America in the Summer of 1794,* 214. Salisbury.

76. Thomas Twining, op. cit., p. 167, concerning a visit in 1796.

77. Op. cit., p. 75.

78. Letter of Feb. 12, 1779, in op. cit., II, 197.

79. Francis Baily (1856), *Journal of a Tour in Unsettled Parts of North America in 1796 & 1797,* 242. London.

80. Op. cit., p. 126.

81. Op. cit., p. 323.

82. *Lloyd's Evening Post and British Chronicle,* Jan. 6–9, 18–20, 1775, as treated in Dora Mae Clark (1930), *British Opinion and the American Revolution,* 84. New Haven.

83. John Harriott, op. cit., II, 267; and cf. II, 62: 'I used to ask some of the very staunch republicans, if they would not object to have any concern with the *King* of Heaven?' E. A. Kendall, visiting a few years later, mistook this delicate point: 'the Americans, that is, the subjects of the United States . . .' (*Travels through the Northern Parts of the United States in the Years 1807 and 1808* (1809), vol. II: 286. New York).

84. Loc. cit., VII (April 1796), p. 367, in reference to a passage of the previous month (p. 242) reviewing Peter Porcupine's *A Bone to Gnaw* (q. v., p. 13).

85. *Oppression A Poem by an American with Notes by a North Briton,* London (1765), as reprinted in *The Magazine of History with Notes and Queries,* Extra No. 71, N.Y., 1921, p. 186.

86. Op. cit., II, 364.

87. Op. cit., p. 112. John Maude, in his journal for June 23, 1800, also reported: 'I may here observe that the animals of America differ materially from those of the old Continent, yet for want of more appropriate designations, they frequently receive the names of such European animals as they most resemble; but these names are by no means settled; for instance, what are known as Partridges in one part of the Country are called Quails in another, and these birds will alight in Trees, or on Paling' (*Visit to the Falls of Niagara in 1800* (1826), 8–9. London).

88. Op. cit., I, 40. Cf. also II, 40: 'D'ailleurs en Amérique, les nomenclatures sont si peu exactes, & les observations si rares, qu'on ne peut obtenir aucune lumière en questionnant les gens du pays.'

89. Parkinson, op. cit., I. 38. On the other hand, he also found understatement (II,

453–454): 'I heard an Englishman in company very justly observe, what was termed a clever fellow in America, would be called a complete swindler in England.'

90. Op. cit., pp. 329–330.
91. Op. cit., pp. 199–200, and cf. the learned dispute in a tavern at Brandywine over the difference in meaning between *declaration* and *proclamation* (p. 17).
92. 'Musophilus', in *The Whole Workes* (ed. 1623), 100.

HERBERT PILCH

The Rise of the American English Vowel Pattern[1]

A. METHODOLOGICAL PRELIMINARIES

1. Comparability of phoneme patterns. The present paper attempts to trace in outline the history of the American English vowel pattern from the time of its geographical separation from British English. Our point of departure will be Professor Kökeritz's, reconstruction (1953) of sixteenth-century pronunciation. As a connecting link between this and the modern language we shall analyze the American English vowel pattern of 1800 as described by Noah Webster. The choice of these two rather than of other sources is for purely practical reasons. Kokeritz's work, without which the present paper could never have been attempted, is fundamental to the study of both British and American English language. Webster offers richer material on pronunciation than any other early American writer in a form consistent enough to allow of phonemic interpretation with a high degree of certainty. In order to avoid constant repetition the information supplied by other orthoepists and gathered from early rhymes and spellings by modern investigators will not be presented here in detailed synchronic arrangements, but will be referred to as the occasion arises. In the field of modern American dialects I have to rely largely on my own material[2] as the printed descriptions are with few exceptions neither phonemic nor historical, and can thus be used only for supplementary data and with great caution.

Since we conceive of vowels not as isolated units, but as the realizations of phonemes which exist as linguistic entities solely by virtue of being opposed to the other phonemes of the same pattern,[3] we propose to study the development, not of individual sounds, but of the pattern as a whole.[4] We shall thus make use of the diachronic phonemic method elaborated mainly by Professor Martinet and applied by him to a series of specific problems.

The English vowel patterns of different centuries and dialects form comparable subsystems within the total linguistic structure by virtue of their similar relationship to the latter as the sets of syllabic phonemes

Reprinted by permission of Johnson Reprint Corporation from *Word* 2:157–193 (1955).

contrasting with the nonsyllabic or consonantal phonemes of the same system.

The definition of phonemes by reference not to some extra-linguistic *tertium comparationis*, but to each other as terms of an opposition implies that different sound systems are comparable only by virtue of possessing similar oppositions, but that the individual phonemes are not comparable in isolation. For the purposes of the present paper we shall therefore call two phonemes x_1 and y_1 figuring in pattern A *the same as* the phonemes x_2 and y_2 figuring in pattern B if:

a. The distinctive feature of x_1 and y_1 are the same as those of x_2 and y_2 respectively, e.g. both in Shakespeare's and in Webster's pronunciation /i:/ and /u:/ are long high-front and long high-back monophthongs respectively.

b. All or a substantial majority of the morphemes in which x_1 and y_1 are opposed in pattern A are etymologically the same as those in which x_2 and y_2 are opposed in pattern B. For instance, the words with /i:/ and /u:/ in Shakespeare have also /i:/ and /i:/ in Webster, e. g. *feed, food*. A substantial majority of the morphemes must be held to satisfy our definition as otherwise our procedure would be intolerably cumbersome. The line will in the last resort have to be drawn arbitrarily depending on how far we wish to go into detail.

If only condition (a), but not condition (b) is fulfilled, the phonemes x_1 and y_1 will be called *substantially the same* as x_2 and y_2. For instance, the opposition of tense and lax labio-dental spirants exists both in German and Dutch, but not in a substantial number of etymologically identical morphemes, e.g. NHG, *wir* /viˑə/ ≠ *vier* /fiˑə/, Du, *vier* /viˑr/ ≠ *fier* /fiˑr/.[5]

If only condition (b), but not condition (a) is fulfilled, x_1 and y_2 will be called *distributionally the same* as x_2 and y_2. For instance, a substantial number of pairs with lax and tense labiodental spirants in German are etymologically the same as those opposing bilabial and labiodental continuants in Dutch, e.g. *wij* /ßei/ ≠ *vier* /viˑr/.

Oppositions between the same phonemes are the same. Vowel patterns which contain the same phonemes and no others are the same. Vowel patterns with distributionally the same phonemes and no others are distributionally the same, etc.

A word N will be said to be *on the same level* as some other word M, if both contain the same vowel phoneme or sequence of vowel phonemes in the same order. For instance, *off* is on the level of *taught* in Am., but on the level of *tot* in Br.[6]

It follows from our definitions that the question whether two speakers P and Q pronounce, for example, the word *whole* phonemically alike can be answered not by taking spectrograms, but only by determining its place in the sound pattern. Should it turn out that P opposes *hole* /houl/ ≠ *whole* /hol/, while for Q they are homonyms, then P and Q use different phonemes in *whole,* even if their phonetic realization agrees to a nicety.

Similarly the sound resemblance between *guard* [ga·d] in eastern New England pronunciation and *God* [ga·d] in western New England pronunciation does not entitle us to analyze them as phonemically the same, because they figure in two different patterns both of which oppose *guard* ≠ *God* along with many other pairs on the same levels, e.g. *cart* ≠ *cot, lark* ≠ *lock, sharp* ≠ *shop.* Under our definition these oppositions and consequently the phenomes entering into them are distributionally the same in the two dialects, i.e. eastern New England *guard* and *God* are distributionally the same as western New England *guard* and *God* respectively in spite of their overlapping phonetic realization.

On the morphemic level the fact that Pol. *dobić,* a perfective verb, is rendered by NHG *erschlagen* does not show the latter also to be perfective. Pol. *dobić* is perfective only by virtue of being opposed to the imperfective *dobiwać.* As this is also translated by NHG *erschlagen,* it follows that the Polish aspect correlation does not correspond to a similar correlation in German.

2. Pattern transformation. Phoneme patterns are defined by the number of their members, their distinctive features, and their distribution. A given pattern A containing $x_1 \neq y_1 \neq z_1$ as opposing terms may thus be transformed into pattern B along the following lines:

a. $x_1 \neq y_1 \neq z_1 > x_2 \neq y_2 \neq z_2$. The oppositions remain distributionally the same, but are realized with new distinctive features, e.g. the Latin opposition $\bar{e} \neq e$ appears as $e \neq \varrho$ in Proto-Romance.

b. $x_1 \neq y_1 \neq z_1 > x_2 \neq y_2$. The phonemes are reduced in number by the redistribution of the words with z_1 between x_2 and/or y_2, e.g. ORuss. *ŭ* has been shared out between *o* and *zero* in Mod. Russ.

c. $x_1 \neq y_1 < x_2 \neq y_2 \neq v_2$. The phonemes increase in number through the split of x_1 and/or y_1. A new phoneme v_2 arises, to the level of which some of the words with x_1 and/or y_1 are transferred.[7] For instance, the West Germanic opposition *ai* ≠ *io* appears as *ei* ≠ *ē* ≠ *ī* in Mod. Du., e.g. in *klein* (ei < ai), *een* (ē < ai), *veertien* (ē < io), *vier* (ī < io).

d. Changes in distribution. The opposition $x_1 \# y_1$ in pattern A remains as $x_2 \neq y_2$ in pattern B, but some words are transferred from the level of x_1 in A to the level of y_2 in B,[8] e.g. in Pol. and Czech some words with a former *o* have been lengthened and transferred to the *u*-level as in Pol. dial. *dóm,* Cz. *dům.*

If the conditions under which these changes take place can be stated and pattern A is known to be anterior in time to pattern B, it will be considered its historical antecedent. Different patterns B′, B″, B‴ will be assumed to descend from A as their common proto-pattern, if all of them are derivable from A under the methods specified.

We thus propose to examine the relationship of phonemic patterns independently of the sociological conditions under which they were actually transmitted from one speech community to another. A separate treatment of these two questions is, in my opinion, imperative in view of the fact that the history of a speech community is not necessarily the same as that of its language, however the word *same* may be defined in this context. For instance, the probable Scandinavian home of the Goths does not *per se* prove anything about a Gotho-Norse parent language,[9] nor is the Italian, Finnish, Chinese, or Essex origin of an American speaker necessarily material to determining the historical status of his dialect. By the same token popular notions of the kind that modern eastern New England speech was the 'un-American' invention of Anglo-maniacal schoolmasters will be dismissed by us not only as unrealistic, but also as irrelevant. Even assuming pattern A being transplanted through emigration into Never-never land and surviving there perfectly unchanged under the name of A′, while in the language of the nonemigrants A is transformed into B, we would not hesitate to describe A′ as the historical antecedent of B. If A = A′ and B < A, then B < A′.[10]

We thus maintain that the linguistic relationship between B and A or A′ can be investigated and determined without regard to whether the pattern was transmitted to the speakers of B by those of A or of A′ or by somebody else, and that it remains a linguistic relationship even in the extremely unlikely case of chance convergence. This principle is, in my opinion, essential. If linguistic relationship could be predicted on the basis of settlement history, the English dialects spoken as their native tongue by Americans of Polish extraction would have to be derived from OPol. rather than from OE. Conversely linguistic relationship cannot *per se* prove anything in nonlinguistic history. For instance, it does not prove the Americans mentioned to be of British rather than of Polish stock.

We are, of course, well aware that many changes of the vowel patterns studied in the present paper may be due to the influence of substrata, dialect mixture, fashionable crazes for 'the broad *a*', etc. Nonetheless they remain changes of the pattern which can be described as such, i.e. without regard to any 'causes' involved beyond the structure of the pattern itself. Denying the plausibility of this method would be tantamount to denying the linguistic relationship, for instance, of German and Russian or Tocharian as long as there is no more definite nonlinguistic evidence of the culture and migrations of the hypothetical Indo-European *Urvolk* than we now have.

In practical historical work where we have to derive a large number of modern dialects from progressively fewer known earlier dialects we always have to be content with something short of complete identity between the dialects A and A'. For instance, we usually derive PDE from OE, Low German from OS and French from Latin in spite of the fact that there were doubtless some earlier dialects closer to certain modern dialects than those from which we derive the latter in our descriptions. Similarly our results will show Webster's and Shakespeare's speech not to be the actual antecedents of all modern American dialects, but to be sufficiently close to these hypothetical antecedents to keep our procedure valid, i.e. to reduce the probability of chance convergence practically to zero. Webster and Shakespeare will thus be used by us not on the strength of any preconceived irrational conviction that they *must* be the direct historical antecedents of all modern American dialects, but as convenient terms of reference in a similar way as OBlg. or Latin are used as terms of reference in comparative work on Slavic and Romance, though they are known in some respects to differ from the protolanguages in question.

In order to fill at least some of the gaps necessarily arising from our limited knowledge of earlier American phoneme patterns, we shall also carefully investigate Webster's extensive data on dialectal and substandard pronunciation, comparing them with modern speech forms, and make further use of linguistic data not supplied by Webster. This information will prove essential to the historical interpretation of much of the linguistic diversity in PDE. For instance, the widespread Am. forms /kets̆, snets̆, git, jælou/ for *catch, snatch, get, yellow*, must be correlated with the similar forms evidenced since the fifteenth century and earlier,[11] not with Webster's and Shakespeare's pronunciation. The coalescence of the earlier sequences ōr and ār in many modern dialects is comprehensible only in terms of some earlier pattern without Webster's short /o/.[12] Though there is in this instance good contemporary evidence of such a pattern,[13] it would have to be postulated from a comparison of modern and ENE phoneme distribution if no such evidence were available. This latter procedure, i.e. reconstruction of early American phoneme patterns on the principle that if an ENE or ME opposition $x \neq y$ recurs distributionally intact in PDE, but is not evidenced by Webster or other contemporary writers, it must have survived in unknown eighteenth- and nineteenth-century dialects, will help us further to recognize in what respects the antecedent patterns of modern American speech were different from Webster's system, e.g. in the non-neutralization of *ai* and *au*.[14]

On the other hand current Southern forms like /min/ for *men* point to an earlier /men/ (as recorded by Webster) as their historical antecedent in view of the fact that the conditions under which the change occurred can be fully stated in the formula *e > i before nasals*. For the same reason the vowel lengthening and raising in items like Am. *stand* [stɛ·nd], *long* [lɔ·ŋ] must be considered an innovation over against Webster's /stænd/ and /laŋ/. Their derivation direct from the similar OE forms with lengthened vowels before *n + homorganic voiced cons*,[15] would imply that the vowels in these words remained phonemically distinct from both ME $\bar{\varrho} \neq \varrho$ and $\bar{a} \neq a$ respectively at least down to the ENE period, and is therefore not feasible in spite of the tempting phonetic similarity between the ancient and modern pronunciations.

B. NOAH WEBSTER'S VOWEL PATTERN

I. The phoneme inventory

3. Webster's approach. Noah Webster's study of the English language of his day is closely connected with the upsurge of national pride and self-consciousness which swept the thirteen American states united in the Revolutionary War. He denounces it as below the dignity of a free Republican citizen to ape 'the corruptions of a foreign court and stage', claiming linguistic as well as political independence for the United States. Against the lurid background of British decadence he paints and extols the purity of New England speech where 'any plain countryman' still preserved 'the true English' of Chaucer and Shakespeare.[16]

This approach saved Webster from merely repeating the traditional rules of British schoolmasters, but required observation of actual American speech. His express aim was to describe 'the common practice of a nation' over against peculiarities of merely local currency.[17] By comparing the two he also slips in a considerable amount of information on the dialects of his day.

At the same time he is remarkably free from the influence of mere spelling. Many of the pronunciations which he recommends are entirely at variance with the established orthography, e.g. *harsh* /hæš/ or *gape* /gæ:p/.[18] He clearly distinguishes between letters and sounds, comparing as words with organically the same vowels of different length not *hat ≠ hate,* but *let ≠ late*, etc.

These considerations rule out any *a priori* reason why Webster's data should not be accepted as they stand. For our procedure we shall assume that at least some of his contemporaries pronounced English in the way he describes,[19] and that the features which struck him as distinctive in the vowel pattern were actually so in the language of his day.

In translating Webster's analysis into the metalanguage of modern phonemics we shall refrain in particular from interpreting his speech in terms of vowel patterns known to us from other periods in the history of English. Though nobody would claim infallibility for Webster any more than for other phoneticians, this procedure is, in my opinion, likely in the long run to yield the most reliable results. Otherwise the present writer is not certain that he would always be able to resist the temptation of 'improving on Webster's description' merely for the sake of not disturbing his own pet theories on the development of English sounds and on what eighteenth-century speech *ought* to have been like.

4. Webster's phonemes. In his spelling books and dictionaries Webster recognizes 17 different vowels in English. They occur in the key words, *but, die, father, fathom, feet, fit, hall, holly, home, hone, joy, late, let, loud, pool, pull, truth.* Webster's very extensive word lists show conclusively that all of these vowels stand in opposition to each other and are therefore phonemically different. Webster's cursory references to the formation of his speech sounds remain far from yielding a full phonetic description of his pronunciation. But they indicate clearly enough the articulatory position of his vowels relative to each other, and thus invite a reconstruction of his phonemic pattern in terms of distinctive features.

4.1. The sounds of *die, joy, loud* are described as diphthongs, the remainder as 'simple sounds' (= monophthongs).[20] The latter are classified as long and short. Long vowels occur in *father, feet, hall, hone, late, pool, truth,* short vowels in *but, fathom, fit, holly, home, let, pull.* The vowels in each of the six pairs *father–fathom, feet–fit, hall–holly, hone–home, late–let, pool–pull* are organically the same, differing in duration only,[21] the vowels of *truth* and *but* are distinct both in quality and length.

4.2. The vowel of *pool* is equated with Fr. *ou* [u],[22] the vowel of *hone* with 'European' *o* [ọ] or [ǫ],[23] the vowel of *fit* with 'the short sound of the French *i*' as in *motif*.[24] The vowel of *fate* is lower than of *feet*, it is still lower in *father*. 'The largest opening of the mouth', and articulation 'deep in the throat', is required in *hall* with 'the broadest or deepest vowel'.[25] This shows that *hall* has low-back /ɑ:/ relative to raised low-front /æ:/ in *father*. The vowel of *fate* is between /æ:/ and /i:/, i.e. mid-front /e:/. As is clear from the French equivalents quoted, *feet, pool,* and *hone* have high-front i:/ (higher than *fate*, further front than *pool*), high-back /u:/, and mid-back o:/ respectively.[26] The word *truth* is pronounced with a monophthong 'between *iu* and *oo*', i.e. between high-front /i/ and high-back /u:/. This must be high-central /ɨ:/.[27]

4.3. The diphthong in *joy* is given as composed of 'broad' *a* i.e. /ɑ/, and /i/, combining as /ɑi/.[28] The diphthongs in *die* and *loud* begin 'not so deep in the throat' and with 'not . . . quite so great an aperture of the mouth' as /a/, and run into /i/ and /u/ respectively,[29] i.e. their first element is low-central /a/ (further front than /ɑ/, but not reaching /æ/). The diphthongs concerned are thus /ai/ and /au/ respectively.

The vowel of *but* is characterized merely as short and different in quality from all other sounds of the language.[30] In terms of the distinctive features so far encountered the only place left vacant for it in the pattern is mid-central /ʌ/.

4.4. Our results may be thus represented in a phonemic diagram:[31]

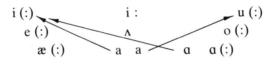

In terms of distinctive features this pattern comprises:

a. Three degrees of tongue height: high ≠ mid ≠ low.

b. Three locations of the tongue: front ≠ central ≠ back. They combine with the three degrees of height into nine distinctive tongue positions.

c. Two degrees of length: long ≠ short. They are relevant only for the monophthongal phonemes of the front and back series. In the central series the vowels are either long or short, length never figuring as the sole distinctive feature. The diphthongs are all of phonemically equal length, i.e. the length correlation is neutralized for them.

d. Stable ≠ moving tongue position. Vowels starting in a given position may either remain without perceptible movement of the tongue (= monophthongs), or move towards either high-front or high-back position (= diphthongs).[32] The latter are defined by the initial position of the tongue and the direction of its movement.[33] The digraphs /ai, au/ etc., used in our transcription refer to these two distinctive features respectively, not to a succession of two discrete stable phonemes /a + i, a + u/.[34] Of the theoretically possible 18 diphthongs (movement of the tongue from any one of its nine positions towards either high-front or high-back) only /ai, au, ɑi/, and /iu/[35] are realized.

5.1. Distributional restrictions. In stressed syllables only long vowels and diphthongs, but no short vowels occur in final position, e.g. *let, late, lay,* but no /le/. The only seeming exception *the*[36] is certainly an unstressed form 'not giving *e* its full sound', as Webster puts it elsewhere.[37]

This distribution has been characteristic of the English language throughout its known history, and remains so to the present day in the dialects which have phonemic length. It arose in prehistoric OE from the lengthening of final stressed vowels.[38] Wherever a final consonant disappeared later after a stressed vowel immediately preceding, the latter was either long or diphthongized. Cf. for example the treatment of LME *-uh, ouh, -auh* which developed either into a simple diphthong or long vowel, or into the sequence short vowel + consonant in PDE, cf. the alternation between /ɒf, ɒþ/ and /au/ in NE *trough.*[39]

5.2. /ɨ:/ occurs only between consonants as in *truth, cube,* but never after /j/. It is in complementary distribution with word-initial /ju :/ as in *union,* and with word-final /ɨu/ as in *due.*[40]

   The monophthong /ɨ:/ appears to have been a New England peculiarity used by 'any plain countryman, whose pronunciation has not been corrupted by mingling with foreigners',[41] and surviving in traces to this day.[42] Webster notes /ju:/ in *duly, new, few,* etc., as Southern, especially Virginian, and metropolitan (London and the capital towns of America).[43] He denounces /u:/ for /ɨ:/ after *r-* as in *rude* as a mannerism 'of our fashionable speakers' and a false theory of British orthoepists.[44]

5.3. Vowels are pronounced shorter before 'short consonants' as in *hat, let, meet* 'where *t* stops the sound suddenly' than before 'long' ones and in final position as in *man, tun, flee.*[45] These variations in length are nonphonemic and strictly distinguished from pairs with distinctive vowel length like *pool ≠ pull.*

5.4. /ai/ and /au/ are neutralized under a monophthongal /a/ before stops as in *fight* /fat/, *rout* /rat/.[46]

5.5. /e/ has a special allophone befo e *-r* final and preconsonantal as in *earth, birth, mercy* which is different both from the [e] of *let* and the [ʌ] of *but* 'and can be learnt only by the ear'.[47]

5.6. A glide [ə] is inserted between a long vowel or diphthong and *-r* as in *bare, mire, parent.* This 'occasions a slight change of the sound of a which can be learned only by the ear'.[48] A similar pronunciation is noted for *half* 'nearly *haef*', not giving *e* its 'full sounds'.[49] There is no indication as to possible opposition between the vowels of *half* and *staff* or *calf.*

5.7. In New England an intrusive *i* appears between *k, g, p, m, t* and /au/ as in *cow, gown, mow* 'make mouths', *power, town,* a practice 'formerly common in New England and not yet wholly extinct'. It exists to this day in New England, Va., N.C. and S.C.[50] A similar insertion of *i* only between *k* or *g* and /ai/ as in *guise, kind* is described as British.[51] /tiʌn, tšʌn/ for *tun* etc.[52] appears to be a hypothetical form invented by Webster in order to ridicule the change *ti >tš* in *nature, rapture*, etc.

II. Shakespeare's and Webster's vowel patterns

6.1. Shakespeare's vowel pattern. The vowel system of late sixteenth-century English as reconstructed by Kökeritz comprises the six front phonemes *i, ī, e, ē* (allophone *ɛ̄* before -*r*), *œ, ǣ* (allophone ā before -*r*), the mid-central phoneme ʌ (allophone ɜ̄ before -*r*, allophone *ə* as initial tongue position of the diphthongs *əi, əu*), the five back phonemes *a, ā* (dial. var. *ɒ, ɔ̄*), *ō, ū, u*, and the diphthongs *əi, əu, ai.* In a diagram:[53]

Webster's vowel phonemes are the same as Shakespeare's with the following exceptions:

6.2. Webster's new phonemes. In Shakespeare's system there is no high-central /ɨ/,[54] and the low-central [a:] occurs only as an allophone of /æ:/. Furthermore, /o:/ is the only long vowel not opposed to a short vowel of the same quality. In Webster's language this hole in the pattern has been filled, and a new series of central phonemes has been built up around /ʌ/. Historically this development involves these changes:

a. The monophthongization *jū >ɨ̄* between consonants as in *truth, duke, sure, your*,[55] and the retraction *jū > ɨ̄* in final position as in *due.*[56]

b. The lowering *əi > ai, əu > au*, while Shakespeare's [a:] has been fronted. The new diphthongs /ai/ and /au/ are monophthongized to /a/ before stops.[57]

c. The shortening *ō > o* as in *none, home* /non, hom/ ≠ *known, hone* /no:n, h o:n/, further in *bolt, boult, colt, coat, dolt, dost, doth, moult, poult, stone.*[58]

6.3. Changes in distribution. In certain sets of words Webster's vowel is organically the same as Shakespeare's, but differs in duration. Often the long and short phonemes exist side by side as alternant pronunciations. Diachronically these changes constitute lengthenings and shortenings.

a. *a* > *ā* before *-n, -ng* as in *gone, belong.* The early Spelling Books record this lengthening only in *want,*[59] *Dict.* 1828 also in *gone* 'pronounced nearly *gawn*'.[60] *Sp.* 1829 and 1837, p. 9 indicate length generally before *-ng*.

b. *ā* > *a* before *l* + *cons.* in polysyllables, and before *-ls, -lt* also in monosyllables as in *almanac, alderman, fault, false,* and under Dutch influence in *yacht.*[61]

Webster's remaining variant pronunciations are between phonemes which alternated in the same manner and under the same conditions in sixteenth-century English. The fact that the doublets concerned are not always recorded at that time in the same words as in Webster is due to the accidental character of our evidence, and, in some cases, to later borrowing and spelling pronunciation.

C. FROM WEBSTER TO MODERN AMERICAN ENGLISH

1. The transformation of the long-short oppositions

7.1. The dephonemicization of length. The most fundamental change in the vowel pattern of American English between Webster and the present has been the dephonemicization of length, the length correlation being in most instances transformed into one of stability ≠ movement (= monophthong ≠ diphthong), e.g. Webster's *e* ≠ *ē* > PDE *e* ≠ *ei*. This process is doubtless connected with the general nonphonemic lengthening of vowels in modern speech before voiced consonants, voiceless spirants, and in final position, e.g. in *led* /led/ > [le·d], and the simultaneous shortening before voiceless stops, e.g. in *late, let* (with phonetically shorter vocalic nuclei than *laid, led*).[62] The initial stages of this new distribution of quantity are already indicated by Webster, and even earlier by Elphinston in 1765 and by Cooper in 1685.[63] The new nonphonemic length differences as in [le·d] vs. [let] must have increasingly impinged on the margin of security protecting the distinctive length correlation of *laid* /le:d/ ≠ *led* /led/, *late* /le:t/ ≠ *let* /let/, and finally have led to its dephonemicization. It will be attempted in the present paper to account for some major dialect differences in contemporary American English and between American and British English in terms of different reactions of the pattern to this fundamental situation.

Though on principle we view the development as in the nature of a push-chain with nonphonemic lengthening as the cause and diphthongization as the effect, this relationship should not be conceived of as strictly mechanical. Already in Webster's time there certainly existed allophonic variants in such a way that not every realization of a given short phoneme /x/ was exactly the same in quality as every realization of the corresponding long phoneme /x:/. The new complementary distribution of vowel length depending on the following consonant must have led speakers, in cases of possible confusion, to favor those allophones of /x/ which were maximally different from certain other preferred allophones of /x:/. At the same time the very existence and growing frequency of such organically different allophones made it possible for the new nonphonetic lengthening to assume ever-increasing proportions without interfering with intelligibility. Thus there is no simple mechanical one-way relationship *cause* → *effect,* but constant interaction, either side stimulating the other.

7.2. The dephonemicization of length has operated through an intermediate stage in which, as in Br., Du. and some dialects of NHG, duration was distinctive in conjunction with quality. Webster himself already takes note of small organic differences between vowels with distinctive length in his later writings, describing, for instance, the vowel of *bat* as 'Nearly' the same as the one in *father* shortened.[64] W. Bolles[65] and J. E. Worcester[66] still regard length as the only distinctive feature in the oppositions in which it figured in Webster's description. Even O. F. Emerson[67] records the length correlation as general in the Ithaca dialect of the late nineteenth century, and emphasizes the monophthongal pronunciation of *feet, fate, boot, boat* against H. Sweet's British diphthongs. He adds, however, that 'the separation of *æ*/*ǣ* is made more difficult because of half-long *æ* before voiced consonants'.[68]

On the other hand, *Dict.* 1865, W. D. Whitney,[69] *Dict.* 1890, and E. S. Sheldon[70] combine the length correlation with one of open ≠ close,[71] lax ≠ tense,[72] and/or monophthong ≠ diphthong, the former two indicating the diphthongization[73] of $\bar{e} > ei$, $\bar{o} > ou$, the latter two also of $\bar{\imath} > ii$, $\bar{u} > uu$.[74]

Today length has totally lost its phonemic significance in those oppositions in which it was formerly distinctive.[75] It reappears, however, in some, notably in 'r-less' dialects as $a \neq \bar{a} < a \neq \bar{æ}$ with a very high functional yield.[76] Different degrees of lengthening in different environments with subsequent leveling and the coalescence of voiced and voiceless consonants have in some cases also given rise to new length distinctions which are distributionally different from those in Webster's system.[77]

8. *The high and mid phonemes of the front and back series.* If the old length distinctions were to be distributionally maintained even after the

dephonemicization of length, the latter had to be replaced by some other distinctive feature.[78] For this purpose the movement ≠ stability correlation, being realized in Webster's pattern in the low order and in high-central position only, offered a number of unused combinations such as ei, ou/ for which the long–short opposition was already neutralized.[79] In the high and mid order of the front and back series this solution, i.e. transformation of long ≠ short into moving ≠ stable, has been adopted all over the country: $\bar{\imath} \neq i > ii \neq i, \bar{e} \neq e > ei \neq e, \bar{u} \neq u > uu \neq u, \bar{o} \neq o > ou \neq o$, e.g. Webster *fit* /fit/ ≠ *feet* /fi:t/ > PDE /fit/ ≠ /fiit/, Webster *whole* /hol/ ≠ *hole* /ho:l/ > hol/ ≠ /houḷ/, etc.

9.1. The central series. In the central series length was already redundant in Webster's pattern since it did not figure as the sole distinctive feature of any two vowels. Apart from the effect on /ʌ/ of a following -r, the phonemes concerned have therefore remained unchanged.

The dialectal diversity in the pronunciation and distribution *i̵, ī̵u, jū* described by Webster survives to this day, monophthongal [ů:] or diphthongal [ʋu] being found besides diphthongs moving from high-front or high-central to high-back.[80] The coalescence of /i̵:/ and /u:/ under the latter phoneme which is noted by Webster after *r-* has in some dialects been extended to positions after *l-*[81] or even after all dentals.[82] Thus minimal pairs like *rude-rood, lute-loot, due-do* are today homonyms for some speakers, but distinct with /i̵u/ (or /iu/) ≠ /uu/ for others.

The wide-spread high-central /i̵/ in Am. *just* adv., etc.[83] which goes back to ENE shortening of /jů:/[84] presupposes a length distinction $\bar{\imath} \neq i̵$ in eighteenth-century American dialects not described by Webster. As in the case of the other high vowels this has been transformed into a monophthong ≠ diphthong correlation: $i̵ \neq \bar{\imath} > i̵ \neq iu$, e.g. *just* /džist/ ≠ *juice* /dži̵:s/ > PDE /dži̵st/ ≠ /dži̵us/.

9.2. In the mid order the retraction $e > ʌ$ before -*r* final and preconsonantal noted with disapproval by Webster has become general. Distinctions like *earn* ≠ *urn* have disappeared,[85] /er/ surviving only in a few odd forms like *weren't* /went/ (R.I.)[86] and *err* /er/ (N.Y. City,[87] New Haven, Conn.). Its place in the pattern has been occupied by the former /e:r/ being shortened to /er/ as in *bare.*[88]

Before -*r* final and preconsonantal, /ʌr/ (incl. ʌr > er) has been fronted and merged with the following consonant into the *r-* colored vowel /ə'/ through a change from successive to simultaneous articulation.[89] Thus Webster's opposition *bird* /bʌrd/ ≠ *bud* /bʌd/ turns up as PDE /bə'd/ ≠ bʌd/. Where the *r*-color has disappeared, the opposition is distributionally maintained as:

a. fronted /ə/ ≠ retracted /ʌ/ (N.Y. City,[90] eastern New England, Deep South).

b. fronted and lengthened /ə:/ (< əə)[91] ≠ retracted and unlengthened ʌ/ (Br.).

c. diphthongized /əi/ ≠ monophthongal /ʌ/ (N.Y. City). [92] In view of the general transformation of long vowels into dipthongs in Am., we propose to derive /əi/ from earlier /ə:/ lengthened as in Br. and diphthongized ə> əi with the dephonemicization of length.

Before vowels Webster's sequences *er*, ʌ*r* developed either like in final and preconsonantal position *er* > ʌ*r* > ə' or like *e*, ʌ before consonants other than -*r*. As the development has been different in different words, many speakers have today oppositions like /ə'/ in *worry, thorough, cour-age, squirrel, very, American* ≠ /ʌ/ in *hurry*,[93] *curry*, and /e/ in *merry*, etc.

9.3. Webster's low-central /a/ which occurred only before stops in com-plementary distribution with both /ai/ and /au/[94] does not to my knowl-edge survive in the U.S. The modern dialects have kept ENE /ai/ and /au/ distinct in all positions, thus presupposing a similar eighteenth-century pattern in which the opposition *ai* ≠ *au* was not as in Webster neutralized under [a] before stops and in which the only two organically different phonemes in the lower order were /æ/ and /ɑ/. The diphthong in *bay* must have been /æi/ because of its distinction from /ɑi/ in *boy*, while the nucleus of *bough* which began in the same tongue position as /æi/[95] must have been /æu/.

10. The low phonemes. Webster's length correlations *æ* ≠ *ǣ* and *a* ≠ *ā* of the lower order could not be as readily transformed into stability ≠ movement as those of the mid and high order, since diphthongs starting from low tongue position existed already in both series: *ai, æi, æu.* In terms of the distinctive features characterizing the pattern the only unused combinations offering an escape from the overcrowded low order were the hitherto unrealized /ɑu/ and the mid-back /o/ in those dialects which did not already possess it.[96] Both these holes in the pattern were adjoining the back vowel /ɑ:/. While the latter thus had 'a choice' between diphthongization and raising, the low-front /æ:/ was contained on all sides. Even if it followed up close behind /ɑ:/ after the latter's theoreti-cally probable displacement *ā* > *o* or *ā* > *au*, it would with the dephonemicization of length coalesce with the original /ɑ/. In the dialects with /o/, e. g. in New England, the functional yield of the oppositions *o* ≠ *ō* and *o* ≠ *ā* was so low that a trespass on the margin of security or merger in one direction or the other would not give rise to much homonymity beyond *whole* = *hole* or *whole* = *hall*. Thus there were three spaces in the pattern (low-front, low-back, mid-back or diphthong *au*) among which the former four phonemes *æ* ≠ *ǣ* ≠ *a* ≠ *ā* had to be redistributed. Varying solutions to this problem have been adopted in different dialects.

10.1.

This is the most common development in western New England and the Midwest. The old /ɑ:/ is raised to /ɔ/ as in *taught, law, forty, hall.* The items with /æ:/ partially follow in its wake by retraction *ǣ* > *ā*, and partially remain in low-front position. With the abolition of length as a distinctive feature they coalesce with /ɑ/ and /æ/ respectively, giving rise to the familiar homonyms *aunt = ant* /ænt/, *balm = bomb* /bɑm/, and the rhymes *father: bother* /ɑ/, *starry: sorry* /ɑ/.

On the eastern seaboard between Jersey City and Baltimore the development has been the same except for the rounding of *a* (< *ǣ*) >ɒ, e.g. /ɒ/ in *balm, father* ≠ /ɑ/ in *bomb, bother*.

Phonetically /ɔ/ as in *taught* varies between mid-back [ǫ, ǫə] in N.Y. City[97] and southwestern New England, raised low-back rounded [ɒ] in Nebr., and intermediate [ɔ] in Chicago. At the same time there is a tendency of compensatory fronting of [ɑ] > [a] as in *cot.* In New Haven, Conn., some speakers use the latter vowel in complementary distribution with phonemically the same [ɒ] before *-r* as in *cart, heart.*

The exact redistribution of /æ:/ between /ɑ/ and /æ/ has been determined by the following conditions:

a. When arising from ENE /æ/ lengthened before voiceless spirants or (in certain words) from ME *au* before *n* + *cons.*, /æ:/ alternated with /æ/ in Webster's time, except after *w-*.[98] Length not being morphemically distinctive in these instances, its dephonemicization led to no more than the coalescence of different allomorphs belonging to the same morpheme. Thus the words concerned have /æ/ today, e.g. *staff, ask, path, dance.* The items with *-ǣf* > LME *-auf* were treated on the analogy of the *staff* type, e.g. /æ/ in *calf, half, laugh.*

b. *The words with -ǣr* were retracted *ær* > *ar* in the wake of the raising *ār* >ɔr. Thus they coalesced with the original /ɑ/, e.g. *heart* /hæ:rt/ > hɑrt/ on the same level as *hot* /hɑt/. The sequences /æ:r/ and /ɑ:r/ were in complementary distribution with /ær/ and /ɑr/ respectively in Webster's pattern, the former occurring in final and preconsonantal positions, the latter between vowels.[99] The coalescence of the former /æ:/ and /ɑ/ under the conditions described thus did not produce any homonymity. However, it put a very high functional yield on the opposition *zero ≠ r* after *a* as in *cop ≠ carp, stock ≠ stark, cod ≠ card,* etc. The confusion to be expected on this count in the 'r-less' dialects has been forestalled either by the preservation of the epenthetic *-ə-* before *-r* or by relengthening of the vowel simultaneously with the loss of *-ə*,[100] e.g. pot /pɑt/ ≠ part /pɑət, pɑ:t/.[101]

c. The remaining words with /æ:/ (< ME *au* or *w* + *a*, and *father*) were under no particular compulsion either way as regards their redistribution. They were free to join either of the two developments described, some dialects generalizing /æ/ and others /ɑ/ in items like *balm, calm, palm, psalm, father, sauce, waft, haunt.* The dialects with /ɑ:/ or /ɑə/ (*<ǣr*) as in *part* /pɑ:t, pɑət/ have this nucleus rather than /ɑ/ in the words mentioned, opposing, for instance, *father* /fɑ:ðə/ ≠ *bother* /bɑðə/, *balm* /bɑ:m/ ≠ *bomb* /bɑm/. Elsewhere the homonymity *balm = bomb* has sometimes been eliminated by the reintroduction of *-l-* into *balm* /bɑlm/, *calm, psalm,* etc. This *l* is either from the spelling, or from an earlier unknown dialect where ME *-l-* remained unvocalized before *-m*, at the same time with its dark color preventing the fronting *a > æ* of the preceding vowel.

This redistribution of the former /æ:/ between /ɑ/ and /æ/ is indicated as early as in *Dict.* 1865, *Dict.* 1890 and by Worcester. They all teach a longer vowel before *-r* as in *far,* and in *father* than before voiceless spirants as in *after. Dict.* 1865[102] quotes a personal communication from Smart to the effect that his much discussed 'compromise vowel' in items like *pass* was intermediate between *part* and *pat* in quantity, not in quality. The confused descriptions of the grammarians as to its quality are reconciled by the theory of *Dict.* 1865 and *Dict.* 1890[103] that the vowel of *pass* fluctuated organically between the levels of *part* and *pat,*[104] later coalescing with the former in eastern New England,[105] with the latter elsewhere.

Summary of development in keywords:

œ < œ	*œ < ǣ*	*a < ǣ*	*a < a*	*c < ā*
have	halve	balm	bomb	talk
ant	aunt	aren't		long
rather		father	bother	trough
hat		heart	hot	haughty
			shot	short
tat		tart	tot	taught
cat		cart	cot	caught
marry		starry	sorry	forty
			collar	caller

10.2.

This pattern with the full merger in all positions except before -*r* and -*m* of the two pairs of organically the same phonemes formerly different in length is characteristic of the Far West.[106] Low-back /ɑ:/ and /ɑ/ coalesce and are raised to /ɔ/ as in *caught = cot, taught = tot, saw: law, long, log, god, dross, water, watch, orange, origin, borrow, forty*. The low-back position is taken up by the change *ǣ > a* in *father* and before -*r* and -*m* as in *large, palm*. In all other items ENE /æ:/ remains low-front, coalescing with earlier /æ/ as in *aunt = ant, halve = have*. The key-words quoted at the end of § 10.1 thus appear in the same forms as there except for the merger under /ɔ/ of those listed with *a < a* and *c < ā*.

10.3.

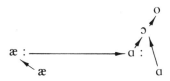

This development is common in eastern New England. As in the dialects described in § 10.1–2 Webster's /ɑ:/ is raised *ā > ɔ* as in *taught, law*, with /æ:/ following in its wake *ǣ > a* (phonetically [a] or [ɑ]) as in *father, launch, half, hard*. The coalescence of this phoneme with the old /ɑ/ which in view of the loss of final and preconsonantal -*r* in the dialects concerned would have given rise to large-scale homonymity[107] was avoided by raising *a > ɔ* in its turn. In this position it was either merged with the former /ɑ:/ which had been similarly raised before, or pushed the latter further upward, making it coalesce with the /o/ of *home*.

The former development, which occurs in R.I., Vt., Me., and most of Mass., produced the homonymous pairs *cot = caught* /kɔt/, *tot = taught* /tɔt/,[108] *shot = short* /šɔt/, *often* = orphan /ɔfn/, *wan = warn* /wɔn/, etc. A slightly raised allophone of /ɔ/ is used after *w-*, before voiced consonants, voiceless spirants, and in final position as in *water, draw, gone, broad, dog, off, cost*.

Under the second type of merger, which is found with some Boston speakers, the former /ɑ:/ coalesced with /o/, but continued to be distinct from the old /ɑ/. Thus the pairs quoted as homonyms for R. I. etc. are opposed as ɔ ≠ o (< a ≠ ā), but *hall* = *whole* /hol/ (distinct from *hole* houl/), *horse* = *hoarse*[109] /hoəs/, *law* = *lore* /loə/, *paw* = *pour* = *pore* poə/, *awe* = *or* = *oar* /oə/ etc.

Some Bostonians show a compromise between these two 'extremes', merging the former /ɑ:/ with /o/ in some words, notably in final position and before -*d*, -*z* as in *saw* /soə/ 'tool for sawing' (≠ *saw* /sɔ/ 'did see'), *laud* lod/, *clause* /kloz/, but retaining it on the level of ɔ (< a) in others as in *long, tall, talk* (ENE *ā*), thus reproducing the list of homophones given above for R.I.

The words with ENE *æ* lengthened *æ* > *ǣ* before voiceless spirants and *nasal + cons.* have often generalized their short alternants. One of my informants has *a* <*ǣ* before -*th* as in *path, bath,* but /æ/ in *last, craft, example, can't, ant* (≠ *aunt* /ant/).[110]

Summary of development in keywords (in dialects where /ɑ:/ and /ɑ/ have been merged under /ɔ/):

æ < *æ*	a < *ǣ*	c < a	ɔ <*ā*
have	halve		
	balm	bomb	talk
ant	aunt = aren't		long
rather	father	bother	trough
hat	heart	hot	haughty
		shot	short
tat	tart	tot	taught
cat	cart	cot	caught
marry	starry	sorry	forty
		collar	caller

10.4.

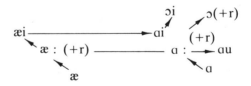

This development is characteristic of Southern Hill Speech, e.g. Tenn. The long vowels diphthongize by the same token as their mid and high counterparts: *æ* > *ǣi* as in *half* /hæif/, *ā* > *au* as in *talk, saw, brought, long,*

off. At the same time the original /æi/ is retracted *æi > ai*, the original *ai* is raised *ai > ɔi.*

Summary of development in keywords:

æi < æ	*ai < æi*	*ɔ < ai*	*æu < æu*	*au < ā*	*ou < ō*
laugh	life	loin	howl	hall	hole
half	rice	voice	mouth	moth	whole
calf	knife		owl	all	old
	buy	boy	loud	law	low
			gown	gone	tone
				taught	tote

Before *-r* final and preconsonantal, /ɑ:/ is raised *ā > ɔ* as in the other dialects, with /æ:/ following up close and coalescing with the original /ɑ/. Thus *ɔ < ā* in *forty, born, a < æ* in *barn, farther,* etc.

A similar shift has sometimes occurred in *father* with /æi/ beside /a/,[111] *brought* with /ɑu/ and /ɔ/ used in free variation by the same speaker, etc. The words *balm, calm, palm, psalm* have /ɑ/ or /æ/. Words with ENE /æ/ before voiceless spirants often generalize their short alternants, e.g. /æ/ in *staff ≠* /æi/ in *calf, grass.*

The word *want* (Webster: /wɑ:nt/) has coalesced with *won't* 'will not' under /wount/ through rounding *au > ou* under the influence of *w-.* The other words with initial *w-* have not been similarly affected, e.g. /ɑu/ (*< ā*) in *wall,* /ɑ/ (*< a*) in *was, what: hot, water: hotter.*

II. Phonemic lengthening

11. Changes in distribution. Up to the eighteenth-century the lengthening of short vowels as it occurred before *s, f, þ, r* was phonemic, i.e. it meant their transfer to the level of the corresponding long phonemes, thus modifying the distributional structure of the pattern, e. g. in *off* /af > ɑ:f/ or *far* /fær > fæ:r/. When in the nineteenth-century length ceased to be distinctive, the lengthening of short vowels as it became general at this stage before voiced consonants and voiceless spirants[112] was only of allophonic significance, i.e. it produced no phonemic changes, but merely variant pronunciations of the same phoneme as in PDE [bɪ d] vs. [bɪt]. This tendency, which was closely connected with the dephonemicization of length,[113] cannot have overtaken all dialects and all words in any one dialect at one stroke, but must have affected them one by one.[114] Thus a few early items which in some dialects increased in duration before vowel quantity had been systematically abandoned as a distinctive feature could still be transferred to the level of the respective long phonemes and share in their further development.[115]

11.1. This is regularly the case with /ɑ/ before *-n, -ng* as in *gone* /gɑn > gɑːn > gɔn/ and *long* /lɑŋ > lɑːŋ > lɔŋ/, where lengthening is noted in more and more words even by Webster in his later works,[116] and frequently also before *-g* as in *dog* /dɑg > dɑːg > dɔg/, in the word *God* /gɑd > gɑːd > gɔd/, and before *r + vowel*[117] as in *sorry* /sɑri > sɔːri > sɔri/. Today many American speakers pronounce some or all of these words with /ɔ/ on the same level as *taught, law,* opposing them to /ɑ/ in *job, cod, hot,* etc.[118]

There is much fluctuation in detail in the preference for one or the other of the two alternant forms. Before *-n, -ng,* /ɔ/ is universal in *wrong, song, gone* etc., but in the North and the Midwest it is opposed to /ɑ/ in *on.*[119] Further /ɔ/ is heard frequently in *God, dog* from speakers who use ɑ/ rather than /ɔ/ in one or several of the items *hog, frog, log, fog, cog, bog, clog, agog.* Before a medial *-r,* /ɑ/ and /ɔ/ alternate in *sorry, tomorrow, authority, foreign, borrow, orange,* etc. I have heard the same (New Haven) speaker use either form of *sorry.*

11.2. The treatment of the low-front /æ/ is exactly parallel to low-back /ɑ/. Under the same conditions as the latter it was lengthened and raised *æ > æ > ɛ̄* as in *stand* [stænd > stæ·nd > stɛ·nd], *marry* [mæri > mæ·ri > mɛ·ri],[120] so that two different vowels are heard in *stand pat* ['stɛ·nd'phæt] or *marry Jack* ['mɛ·ri'džæk]. Often [ɛ·] is replaced by, or is in free variation with, [ɛə]. In some dialects it reaches even mid-front [ẹ], so that the vowels of *stand* [stẹnd] and *stencil* [stẹnsl] differ in duration only. Unless specified otherwise we here write /ɛ/ to include all of these phonations insofar as they are phonemically different both from /e/ and /æ/ as heard in *pet* and *pat* respectively.

In normally strongly stressed monosyllables, /ɛ/ before nasals is common in the Northeast (as far west as Buffalo, N.Y.) and in parts of the South as in *can't* /kɛnt/, *man* /mɛn/, *can* 'tin' /kɛn/, but somewhat less frequent before other voiced consonants as in *bag* /bɛg/, *bad* /bɛd/. This /ɛ/ usually stands in opposition to /æ/ in more commonly weakly stressed and in polysyllabic items as in *can* /kæn/ 'am able', *had* /hæd/, *manager* /mæn-/, *badminton* /bæd-/. Before *-r* an especially high vowel is heard in Me., e.g. in *marry* [mɛri] ≠ *merry* = *Mary* /meri/. In Waterbury, Conn.,[121] I have heard [ɛə] for /æ/ used by teenagers consistently in all environments, even before voiceless consonants, e.g. in *have, map, tap, cat.* This is a complete shift *ǎ > ɛə* which has only substantial, but no distributional significance.[122]

11.3. The raising $æ > ɛ$ narrowed down the margin of security which originally separated /æ/ from /e/. This led to a compensatory shortening and raising in the environments concerned of the former /e/ and/or to its merger with either /ɛ/ ($> æ$) or /i/. Thus some New England speakers who pronounce *pan, marry* as /pɛn, mɛri/ use a shortened and/or raised allophone of /e/ in items like *pen, merry.* In parts of N.Y. State (Otsega Co., Lake Placid) the original /ær/ has become /e·r/ as in *marry = Mary* /me·ri/ on the level of *many* /me·ni/, while a vowel organically the same, but shorter, is heard in items with original /er/ as in *merry* /meri/. Complete coalescence of the former /ær/ and /er/ on the level of the latter is characteristic of most of the Midwest, Farwest, and the South, e.g. *marry = merry* /meri/, *character* /ker-/, *narrow* /ner-/. This development is strictly parallel with the raising $a > ɔ$ before $r + vowel$ and the rhyme *sorry: warry* in the back series.

Coalescence of /e/ and /i/ under /i/ with an allophone slightly lower than the [ɪ] of *bid* is found consistently before nasals in the South all the way between Texas and Ind. and as far northwest as Nebr., e.g. in *pen = pin* /pin/, *any* /ini/, *many* /mini/, *strength* /strinþ/, *length* /linþ/, *chemistry* /kim-/ etc. There is no parallel raising *on > un* in the back series as the dialects concerned did not have the late eighteenth-century /o/.

11.4. In the Southern dialects where the former /æ:/ and /ɑ:/ have been diphthongized $ǣ > æi, ā > au$, their short opposites /æ/ and /ɑ/ lengthened under the conditions specified share in their transformation: $ǣ > ǣ > æi$, $a > ā > au$, e.g. in *hand* /hæind/, *flag* /flæig/, *have = halve* /hæiv/, *gone* /gaun/, *long* /laun/, *God* /gaud/, *hog* /haug/, *fog* /faug/, *office* /aufis/.[123] In parts of the South and in N.Y. State a comparable transfer $e > ē > ei, i > ī > ii$ also occurs in the mid and high order before -g[124] as in *egg* /eig/, *leg* /leig/, *big* /biig/,[125] and on all three levels of the front series before -*š* and *ž*,[126] e.g.

/æi/ ($< ǣ < æ$) in *gnash, cash, passion, fashion, national.*

/ei/ ($<ē < e$) in *flesh,*[127] *expression, possession, measure, pleasure, treasure.*[128]

/ii/ ($<ī > i$) in *fish, admission, initiate, Patricia,*[129] *vision.*

In the central and back series similar lengthening does not to my knowledge occur before -*š, -ž*, though there is occasional diphthongization $ʌ > ʌi, u > ui, ā > ɔ > ɔi$ on the analogy of the front series, e.g. in *mush* /mʌiš/,[130] *push* /puiš/,[131] *wash* /wɔi̯s/.[132] In certain Negro dialects the transfer $e > ē > ei$ seems to have been generalized before all voiced *consonants and voiceless spirants*, e.g. /ei/ in *head, dead, bless, then, when,* while the former /æ/ has been lowered to /e/ in *hand, thank, fat, back.*[133]

12. New length distinctions. Over against the cases of phonemic lengthening discussed so far which today are recognizable as such only through historical reconstruction, e.g. *fog* /fɔg/ < fɑ:g/ (lengthened from /fɑg/) ≠ *foggy* /fɑgi/ (unlengthened), vowel length has in certain dialects been systematically reintroduced as a distinctive feature under the following conditions:

12.1. The rest of their environments being equal, vowels tend today to be longer in final position than before voiced consonants or voiceless spirants. They are also longer before simple consonants, in monosyllables, and under strong stress than before consonant clusters, in polysyllables, and under weak stress respectively. In paradigms and derivational groups where final and nonfinal, premonoconsonantal and prepolyconsonantal, and monosyllabic and polysyllabic forms alternate as in *agree–agreed, add–adds, cough–coughing*, the longer vowels have, in some dialects along the northeastern seaboard,[134] been transferred from the former to the latter forms, e.g. [əgriːd, æ·dz, khɔːfɪn] lengthened on the analogy of the infinitives [əgriː., æ·d, khɔːf]. Such forms all stand in opposition to short vowels in similar environments where no such analogical transfer took place, as in *greed* [grɪ·d], *adze* [ædz], *coffin* [khɔ·ɪn]. Similarly words frequently occurring under weak stress generalize their shorter vowel alternants in all positions, e.g. /æ/ in *had* [hæd], *has* [hæz], *can* 'am able' [khæn] stands in opposition to /æ:/ in normally more strongly stressed words like *bad* [bæ·d], *jazz* [džæ·z], *can* 'tin-can' [khæ·n].

12.2. As vowels are longer before voiced than before voiceless stops, the /æ/ in *latter* is shorter than in *ladder*. This originally merely allophonic difference has, in certain dialects, acquired phonemic significance by virtue of being maintained even when /d/ and /t/ coalesced under [ɾ] between stressed and unstressed vowels as in *latter* /lærə'/ ≠ *ladder* /læːrə'/, and similarly in *writer* ≠ *rider, pouter* ≠ powder, etc.[135]

Further a length distinction *ē* ≠ *e* has in some dialects reappeared before *-r* and *-n* as a result of a complicated series of changes, as in *stand* ste·nd/ ≠ *stencil* /stensl/, *marry* /me·ri/ ≠ *merry* /meri/. This has been discussed supra § 11.2–3.

NB. All these new length distinctions are distributionally different from those in Webster's system.

III. Phonemic shortening

13. Shortening before -k. Just as originally short vowels could be lengthened before voiced consonants early enough to be merged with the corresponding long phonemes, a few ENE long vowels transferred to the level of the originally short phonemes through early shortening before voiceless consonants. A frequent instance of this is *ē > e* before -*k* as in *take* /tek/, *naked* /nekid/, *make* /mek/, *snake* snek/.[136]

14. Shortening before -r. Before -*r* Webster's long vowels had diphthongal variants consisting of *vowel* + *ə* e.g. *beer* [biˑər].[137] The [iˑ] in this sequence must have been somewhat shorter than the phonemically same [i:] in other environments, e.g. *beer* [biˑər] vs. *bead* [bi:d].[138] In the subsequent organic differentiation of long and short vowels the somewhat shorter variants of the long phonemes before -*ər* often coalesced with and joined in the development of the earlier short rather than of the long nuclei. At the same time the sequence -*ər* was simplified by the loss of -*ə* as in *here* [hiˑər > hir], *Mary* [meˑəri > meri]).

14.1. In 'General American' as described by Kenyon the coalescence of the former long and short vowels before -*r* is nearly complete in the case of *ī, ē, ū, ō*, e.g. *spear it = spirit* /spirit/, *Mary = merry* /meri/, *during* /durin/ on the level of /u/ in *put, hoarse* /hors/.[139] It has sometimes also carried away earlier /i:ə/ of different origin as in *theatre* /þitəˈ/ *theory* /þiri/.[140] The original long vowel has been retained chiefly in derivatives from words with long phonemes not followed by -*r*, e.g. in *Jewry* /džuuri/ (with /uu/ from *Jew*) ≠ *jury* /džuri/, or in *we're* /wiir/ (with /ii/ from *we*) ≠ *weir* /wir/.

In the dialects where the eighteenth-century /o/ did not exist, its place in the pattern being later taken by *ɔ < ā*,[141] the sequence /o:r/ shortened under the conditions specified was transferred to the level of the latter as in *more* /mo:r<mɔr/, and in this way coalesced with *cr < ār* over most of the country except in eastern New England and upstate N.Y., giving rise to the homonyms *hoarse = horse, wore = war, born = borne, for = four,* etc.

In parts of the South. e.g. in Mo. and La., the late eighteenth-century sequence /ɑ:r/ was also shortened *ār > ar* as in *short* šɑ:rt > šart/, thus coalescing with *ar > ær* as in *cart* /kɑrt/ > kæ.rt/, but remaining distinct from *cr< ōr* as in *court*/kɔrt/, e.g. *cart: short* /-ɑrt ≠ *sport* /spɔrt/, *far: war* /ɑr/ ≠ *wore* /wɔr/, *barn* = /bɑrn/ ≠ *borne* /bɔrn/, etc.[142] In southern Utah I have similarly noted /ɑr/ in *fork: bark, horse:*

sparse, but /ɔr/ in other items with earlier /ɑːr/, e.g. in *or = oar, short: court.*

The retraction *œr > ar* left vacant the place of *low-front vowel + -r final or preconsonantal.* This has in parts of eastern New England and N.Y. State *been taken by ēr < œr* or *ɛr* as in *there* /ðeːr/ > ðær, ðɛə/, *care* /Reːr/ > kær, kɛə/, *secretary* /-eːri > -æri/.[143] This transfer completes the chain shift *ēr→œr→ār→ɔr.* e.g. *fair* /feːr/ > fær/, *far* /fær > fɑr/, *for* /fɑːr > fɔr/.

14.2. In parts of eastern New England only [uˑər] and [oˑər] have coalesced with organically the same short vowels, while *ī, ē, æ, ā* developed before *-r* like in other positions, yielding PDE /ii/ in *here,* [144] /ei/ in *Mary, there,* /ɑ/ in *hard,* /ɔ/ in *for.* Where /ɑː/ coalesced with /ɑ/ under ɔ/ as in *taught = tot,* there is *for* /fɔə/ < fɑːr/ ≠ *four* /foə/ < foːr/, but when /ɑː/ was merged with /o/ as in *hall = whole,* they were leveled under /o/ in *for = four* /foə/ etc.[145]

14.3. These developments provide a clue to the history of the groups *marry–merry–Mary,* and *morrow–morning–mourning* which in Webster are /mæri, meri, meːri, maro, maːrnin, moːrnin/ respectively. Modern dialects show the following types of distribution:

a. The eastern New England development discussed supra §14.2 reduces the back series to two phonemes, i.e. *morrow* on the level of *morning* /mɔ-/ ≠ *mourning* /mo-/, or *morrow* /mɔ-/ ≠ *morning = mourning* /mo-/, while the three distinctions of the front series are maintained with the former opposition *e ≠ ē* remaining distributionally intact as *e ≠ ei* or *e ≠ eə.* In N.Y. City the distribution is the same as in Boston with /ɑ/ in *morrow ≠* /ɔ/ in *morning = mourning.*[146]

b. The shortening *ēr > er, ōr > ɔr* gives rise to *Mary = merry* /meri/ ≠ *marry* /mæri, mɛri/, *mourning = morning* /mɔr-/ ≠ *morrow* /mar-/. This pattern is common in western New England, and in the front series also occurs in Me.

c. The same shortenings in conjunction with the lengthening and raising *ær > ǣr > er, ar > ār > ɔr*[147] bring about homonymity in *Mary = merry = marry* /meri/, *mourning = morning* on the level of *morrow* /mɔr-/, e.g. in large areas of the Midwest and Farwest. In Waterbury, Conn., *er* has been raised to *ɛr* after the shortening *ēr > er,* so that the coalescence *Mary = merry = marry* is under /mɛri/ on the level of *pat* /pɛt/, not of *pet* /pet/. Compensatory shortening of the original /er/ yields the distribution *marry = Mary* /meˑri/ ≠ *merry* /meri/ in upstate N.Y.[148] Owing to the difference of conditions arising from the absence or the rare occurrence of /o/ and the retraction *ǣr > ar,* the development of the front and back series is not always exactly parallel. For instance, La. has *Mary* = *merry* = *marry* /meri/, but *morrow* on the level of *morning* /mɑr-/ ≠ *mourning* /mor-/.[149]

D. CONCLUSION

British and American English vowel patterns

15. Standard British has changed much less in its vowel pattern than Am. since the late eighteenth century. The British vowel pattern described by Webster's contemporary J. Walker[150] is the same as Webster's apart from the absence of the opposition *o* ≠ *ō* as in *whole* ≠ *hole* (the words with /o/ in Webster having /o:/), the use of the diphthong /iu:/ as the distributional equivalent of Webster's /ɨ:/, and the non-neutralization of /ai/ and /au/ before stops. As in the U.S., the impetus for change came from the nonphonemic lengthening of vowels before voiced consonants. Since the Br. and Am. vowel patterns were very much alike in structure, they reacted to this stimulus in the same way by transforming the long phonemes of the high and mid order into the 'virtually present',[151] but hitherto unrealized diphthongs *ii, ei, uu, ou,* and by moving the low vowels in the direction of the hole in the pattern arising from the absence of /o/, as in Br. *ǣ → ā → ɔ̄*, and *a > a,* e.g. *far* /fæ:r > fɑ:/, *for* /fɑ:r > fɔ:/, *foreign* /fɑrin > fɔrin/.[152]

15.1. The allophonic lengthening which stimulated these transformations has, however, been less violent in Britain than in the U.S.[153] The attendant changes of the pattern having been carried proportionately less far, the vowel system of Standard British is still roughly the same as described for American English in *Dict.* 1865 with 'interdependent'[154] quantitative and qualitative differences figuring as distinctive features. In both patterns a set of long vowels and diphthongs stands in opposition to one of organically different short vowels, as in Br.[155] *ii, ei, ai, ɔi, uu, ou, au, ā, ɔ̄, ɔ̄* (< ʌr) ≠ *i,e,æ, u, ɒ, ʌ,a, ə.* Here length has not been totally dephonemicized as in American English, but has merely been linked to organic differences in conjunction with which it is still distinctive.[156]

15.2. By the same token the British vowel pattern proves rather conservative from a distributional point of view. Nearly all of Walker's oppositions between vocalic nuclei have remained distributionally intact, including those of the lower order *æ* ≠ *ǣ* ≠ *a* ≠ *ā* which in most Am. dialects have lost one of their member phonemes; cf. the tables supra § 10 with Br.:

æ < œ	*ā < œ*	*ɒ < a*	*ɔ̄ < ā*
have	halve	collar	caller
	balm	bomb	talk
ant	aunt = aren't	long	
gather	father : rather	bother	
hat	heart	hot	haughty
		shot	short
cat	cart	cot	caught
tat	tart	tot	taught
marry	starry	sorry	forty

15.3. The shift *er* > ʌr and the transformation of the eighteenth-century opposition ʌ + *r* ≠ ʌ + *zero* into ə ≠ ʌ as in *bird* /bʌrd > bə:d/ ≠ *bud* /bʌd/ has been distributionally the same in Br. and Am., but is limited in the former to preconsonantal and final positions, e.g. Br. /ə:/ in *occur*, but /ʌ/ in *occurrence, courage, thorough, worry*, /i/ in *squirrel*, /e/ in *American*.[157]

In its neutralization of the former opposition iū ≠ ū after *r* and *l* as in *rude = rood, lute = loot*, Br. is keeping a middle position between the Am. dialects with no coalescence at all or only after *r-*, and those which have extended it to all positions after stressed dentals as in *due = do, tutor = tooter, suit: root, new: shoe*.[158]

15.4. Owing to its less violent changes in vowel quantity Br. has also remained unaffected by the phonemic lengthening before voiced consonants and the phonemic shortening before voiceless ones as described for Am. supra §§ 11–13.[159] Thus Br. *long* /lɒŋ/, *gone* /gɒn/, *dog* /dɒg/, *morrow* /mɒrou/, *stand, man, bad, marry* have remained on the levels of *cot* and *cat* respectively, not being transferred to those of *caught* and *merry* or of a new raised mid-phoneme /ɛ/.

As in most types of Am. the long vowels ī, ē, ū, ō underwent phonemic shortening before *-ər* in Br. except in a few derivatives such as *doer* /duuə/ ≠ *dour* / duə/, while the shorter allophones before *-ər* or *æ̃, ā* developed like /ae:, ɑ:/ in other positions. Shortened [oˑə] was lowered to [ɔə] under similar conditions as in Am.,[160] thus reproducing the familiar homonyms *hoarse = horse, four = for*, etc. On the other hand, *-e* in Br. only after (< æ ə̇r) and [ɔə] (< ɑ ə̇r, o ə̇r), the vowels concerned being automatically restored to the length of the allophones occurring in positions other than before *-ɑ:* [ɑə > ɑ:, ɔə > ɔ:]. Thus *Mary* /meəri/ ≠ *merry* /meri/, *spear it* /spiərit/ ≠ *spirit* /spirit/ continue to be distinct in Br. as in eastern New England speech. Some speakers also preserve *-ə* after [ɔə < oˑ ər], but not after [ɔə < ɑˑər]. Thus *hoarse ≠ horse, four ≠ for* etc. are opposed with /ɔə/ ≠ /ɔ:/ in a correlation distributionally the same as /ɔə/ ≠ /oə/ in some Am. dialects. All these developments are linked to a series of further vowel shifts before -ə some of which recur in the 'r-less' dialects of Am.: eə > [ɛə] (phonemically /eə/), or eə > æə as in *Mary* (parallel to oə́>ɔə in the back series), uə→oə→ɔə→ɔ: as in *sure* /šuə. šoə, šɔə. šɔ:/ which may or may not be opposed to *shore* /šɔə. šɔ:/, aiə →aə¹⁶¹→aə, auə→aə→a:, as in *tire* /taə/ ≠ *tower* /taə/ ≠ *tar* /ta :/. Loss of -ə in the first two items may also yield an opposition /a :/ ≠ /a + :/ ≠ /ɑ :/.¹⁶²

15.5. The alternants with long and short vowels which arose from the ENE lengthening of /æ/ and /a/ before voiceless spirants have been treated differently in British and American English. Standard Southern British favors the short alternants of the back series,¹⁶³ but the long alternants of the front series, e.g. Br. *loss* /lɒs < las/ on the level of *cot*, but *pass* /pɑ:s < pæ:s/ on the level of *father*. On the other hand, Am. consistently uses the lengthened forms in the back series, while preferring the short ones in the front, as in *loss* /lɔs < la:s/ on the level of *caught*, but *pass* /pæs < pæs/ on the level of *gather*. Even those Am. dialects, esp of eastern New England, which maintain the former opposition æ ≠ ǣ in *ant* ≠ *aunt* as /ænt/ ≠ ant/ today tend to use the originally short /æ/ before -*s*, -*f*, -*p*.¹⁶⁴ This generalization of different alternants accounts for the prevalence of Am. /æ/, Br. /ɑ:/ (< ǣ in *half, graft, staff, class, last, grasp, path, rather* etc.,¹⁶⁵ and of Br. /ɒ/ (< *a*), Am. (č̃/ (< *a:*) in *off, cough, loft, cross, cost, moth, trough*.

NB. The Am. /æ/ in the former words is neither 'archaic' nor 'Elizabethan'. On the contrary, the neutralization of the former opposition æ ≠ ǣ consitutes an innovation over against the continued distinction of distributionally the same phonemes as æ ≠ *a:* in Southern British.

Many more variations between prevalent Br. and Am. speech forms, some of which have been widely publicized, are due to the generalization of different alternants, e.g. *shone*, Br. /šɒn/, Am. /šoun/; *partition*, Br. pɑ:t-/, Am. /pət-/. Their explanation will in most instances be obvious from the more general principles already proposed in the present paper.

NOTES

1. In this article I have used the following abbreviations and symbols:

Am.   Modern American English.
Br.   Modern British English.
Dict.   Noah Webster, *An American Dictionary of the English Language,*

quoted by year of edition, page, and column (a,b). References to the 1828 edition whose pages are unnumbered are by the page numbers of the 1841 edition.

Diss.   Noah Webster (1951), *Dissertations on the English Language*, ed. by H. R. Warfel. Gainesville, Florida.

LA.   *A Linguistic Atlas of New England*, ed. by H. Kurath, quoted by number of map.

LA Records   Unpublished maps for the Linguistic Atlas of the United States. (For access to these maps I am indebted to Mr. Raven McDavid of Western Reserve University.)

PDE   Present Day English.

Sp.   Noah Webster, *An American Spelling Book* (or *A Grammatical Institute of the English Language* volume one), quoted by year of edition and page.

A = B:A is homonymous with B.

A ≠ B:A stands in opposition to B.

A: B:A rhymes with B.

2. I am profoundly indebted to all of my informants in different parts of the U.S., especially to Mrs. Carol Craddock, New Haven.

3. Cf. the definition of the phoneme by Troubetzkoy, *TCLP* 7: 32–36; the terms *vowel pattern* and *vowel system* are used here to translate Troubetzkoy's *Vokalsystem,* and *opposition* for his *phonologischer Gegensatz,* cf. op. cit.: 30, 87.

4. For the diachronic phonemic method in general, on the definition of such technical terms as *push-chain, margin of security,* etc., cf. A. Martinet (1952), *Word* 8: 1–32, and, by the same author (1955), *Économie des Changements Phonetiques,* Berne, A. Francke.

5. These forms are from North German colloquial pronunciation and from the Flemish variety of *Algemeen Beschaajd Nederlands* respectively.

6. Cf. infra § 15.5.

7. Cf. the detailed description of this process by A. J. Haudricourt and A. G. Juilland (1949), *Essai pour une Histoire Structurale du Phonétisme français,* 6–8. Paris.

8. When this happens in all words with x_1, this case is the same as treated sub (b).

9. Cf. my discussion in *Word* 10: 98:103.

10. This is an axiomatic statement on the analogy of the transitive relation between real numbers in mathematics.

11. Cf. *NED*.

12. Cf. infra § 14.1.

13. Cf. infra note 96.

14. Cf. infra § 9.3.

15. Cf. Luick (1921–1940: § 268).

16. *Sp.* 1783 Preface, *Diss.* 108 fn., 135, 152, 171–179.

17. *Diss.* 168 f.

18. These forms are well evidenced in modern dialects.

19. The same reservation applies to our references to ME, Br., Am., etc. They mean that, in my opinion, a substantial number, but not necessarily all or even a majority of the speakers concerned pronounce or pronounced English in the way indicated. Similarly the statements on the geographical distribution of different phoneme patterns which are chiefly based on my observations as I happened to come across willing informants

during a short tour of the U.S. should be considered purely tentative and may contain major errors.

20. Cf. Webster's definition: 'Whenever a sound can be begun and completed with the same position of the organs, it is a simple sound. A *diphthong* is a union of two simple sounds pronounced at one breath' (*Sp.* 1798, 11).

21. 'The only difference in the sound that can be made by the *same* configuration of the parts of the mouth is to *prolong* or shorten the *same* sound. According to this principle we observe that *late* and *let* being pronounced with the same aperture of the mouth, and with the same disposition of the organs . . . must contain the same vowel. The same rule will apply to the other examples' (*Sp.* 1798, 13; similarly *Diss.* 82–84).

22. *Dict.* 1828, Liii b.

23. 'I know of no language in Europe, in which *o* has not one uniform sound, viz. the sound we give it in *rose*' (*Diss.* 119).

24. *Diss.* 104.

25. *Dict.* 1841, Lvi a, Lxxi a.

26. Webster's equation of the vowels of *fate* and *fall* with the pronunciation of Arab. *fatha* is based on erroneous information.

27. *Diss.* 151. Cf. Wallis' description approvingly quoted by Webster: 'Hunc sonum Extranei fere assequentur, si diphtongum iu conentur pronunciare; . . . (ut in Hispanorum *ciudad*, civitas). *Non tamen idem est omnino sonus, quamvis, ad illum proxime accedat;* est enim *iu* sonus compositus, at Anglorum . . . *u* sonus simplex' (*Diss.* 150 f.).

28. *Sp.* 1798, 14; *Diss.* 85.

29. *Sp.* 1798, 12, 14; *Diss.* 84, 86; *Dict* 1828, Lvi a.

30. *Diss.* 85.

31. The length mark placed in brackets (:) indicates that the vowel occurs both short and long and that length is phonemically distinctive. Vowels combining in diphthongs are connected by an arrow pointing to the second component.

32. Other types of tongue movement, e.g. the ingliding diphthongs occurring before -*r*, are nondistinctive, cf. infra § 5.6.

33. This definition has already been suggested by A. Martinet (1937), *La Phonologie du Mot en danois*, 50. Paris.

34. In view of the diachronic developments studied later, this approach which permits us to conceive of the transformation of long vowels into diphthongs as merely a change of distinctive features seems to me more convenient than the impressionistic segmentation of diphthongs into two constituent phonemes. Readers who prefer the latter solution will find no difficulty in translating our terminology into theirs.

35. On *ĭu* cf. infra § 5.2.

36. *Sp.* 1798, 54.

37. *Sp.* 1783, 23.

38. Cf. Luick (1921–1940: § 103).

39. PDE forms with /ɔ:f, ɔ:þ↔/ are due to later lengthening.

40. *Sp.* 1798, 12; *Diss.* 85. Webster's apparently contradictory descriptions of /i:/ sometimes as a monophthong and sometimes as a diphthong are not mutually exclusive, but refer to the different sounds with which it is in complementary distribution.

41. *Diss.* 152.

42. Cf. [dŭ:z] with central [u:] in Portland, Me. (*LA* 563).

43. *Sp.* 1783, 7; *Diss.* 148 ff., 159.

44. *Diss.* 153–155; *Dict.* 1828, Lxii b, Lxxii b.

45. *Sp.* 1783, 22 fn; *Dict.* 1828, Liv b fn. As Webster does not define what he means by

long and short consonants, the distribution of the allophones concerned cannot be ascertained in detail. His examples suggest a pattern similar to PDE with shorter vowels before voiceless than before voiced consonants and finally.

46. Cf. on /ai/ and /au/: 'But if it is followed by a mute consonant, the last sound is prevented and we hear barely the first sound of the diphthong which is therefore a simple sound or vowel. Thus in the word *rout, ou* appears to be as simple a sound as any in the language, but in *now* the sound is evidently diphthongal' (*Sp*. 1787, 13 fn.).

47. *Sp*. 1787, 12 fn.

48. *Dict*. 1828, Liv a, Lxxii b.

49. *Sp*. 1783, 23.

50. Cf. *LA* 191 and LA Records.

51. *Diss*. 154 f.; *Dict*. 1828, Liv a, Lvii a–b.

52. *Diss*. 156 ff.

53. This phonemic analysis differs from that of A. A. Hill (*Language* 29: 550–555) in three respects: (a) Long vowels and diphthongs are treated as unit phonemes (cf. supra, § 4.4d). (b) We draw on the dialect with [a, ā] for [ɒ, ɔ]. Thus *æ, ǣ* stand in opposition to *a, ā*, but not to [aː]. (c) We recognize vowel length as distinctive. Hill overlooks oppositions like *have* /hæv/ ≠ *halve* /hæːv/ (with loss of *l*, cf. Kökeritz 1953: 310), *ant*/ænt/ ≠ *aunt* /æːnt/ (Cf. Kökeritz 1953: 341 : '[æː] was used . . . before *n* + consonant in *romance* words', *capitals* mine; cf. also Luick 1921–1940: § 522). His case for /ei/ rather than /eː/ rests exclusively on modern speech material where the fact that some dialects have [ei] and others [eː] cannot, in my opinion, prove anything either way for Shakespeare, let alone invalidate the contemporary evidence presented by Kökeritz.

54. A. A. Hill, loc. cit. himself admits the unsatisfactoriness of his attempt to argue otherwise.

55. The last two words have /uː/ elsewhere in ENE, cf. Luicks (1921–1940: § 508 fn. 3).

56. Cf. supra § 5.2.

57. Cf. supra § 5.4.

58. *Sp*. 1783, 47 fn; 1787, 59, 64.

59. *Sp*. 1798, 49. This may go back to an ENE variant with /ɑː/, cf. Jesperson 1909: § 10.72. J. Neumann's list (1924–45) in *American pronunciation according to Noah Webster*, Columbia Diss. is misleading, as in 1783 Webster does not yet discriminate between /ɑː/ and /ɑ/ and identifies the latter with the *o* spelt in *not*.

60. But *Dict*. 1828 has /ɑ/ in *wan, swan* etc.

61. Cf. Luick (1921–1940: §§ 527, 1; 580, 1).

62. Cf. G. Trager and H. L. Smith (1951), *Outline of English Structure,* 12 ff. Norman, Okla.

63. Cf. supra § 5.3. and Luick (1921–1940: § 576 fn. 2–3). Our interpretation of this lengthening as allophonic disposes of Luick's objections against accepting Cooper's testimony.

64. *Dict*. 1828, Lxxi.

65. *An Explanatory and Phonographic Dictionary of the English Language.* New London 1847, 10 ff.

66. *A Dictionary of the English Language.* Boston 1860, XI ff. The author bases his phonetics on the authority of Walker and Smart rather than on his own observation.

67. 'The Ithaca dialect', *Dialect Notes* 1 (1896): 85–173, esp. 100–102.

68. Loc. cit. 123. We take this statement to confirm our view of a direct connection between nonphonemic vowel lengthening and the dephonemicization of length.

69. 'The Elements of English Pronunciation', in *Oriental and Linguistic Studies* 2nd ser., N.Y. 1874, 202–276.

70. 'A New Englander's English', *Dialect Notes* 1 (1896): 33–42.
71. 'In each case that which is the briefer in quantity is the more open in quality of the two' (*Dict.* 1865, 'Principles of Pron.' § 8 fn.). 'Our longs differ decidedly also in quality from our shorts' (Whitney, op. cit. 207).
72. Speaking of vowels: 'All the wide are naturally short, and the narrow naturally long, because of the fixed, braced position of the tongue in the latter case and the opposite in the former' (*Dict.* 1890, 'Guide to Pron.' § 21).
73. On scattered earlier references cf. Bronstein in *Speech Monographs* 16: 228, 230, 235.
74. I prefer to write these diphthongs in this way, the first element of the digraph indicating the initial tongue position and the second marking the direction of the movement (cf. supra § 4.4d). The symbols /ii, uu/ do not necessarily imply phonetic identity of the beginning and the end of the vowels concerned, but indicate movement within the high-front and high-back zones of articulation respectively. With the provision that the way covered by the moving tongue varies between some maximum s (= spatium) and *zero*, our symbols cover both the monophthongal and diphthongal pronunciations of items like *heat* /hɪit/ or /hi:t/. Thus we avoid having to interpret as phonemically different the vocalic nuclei of, for instance, *beat, bead,* and *bee* in dialects which use a monophthong in the first and a diphthong in the two latter words. I cannot accept a transcription based on Trager and Smith's semivowel theory (op. cit. 20–22) which not only postulates many more *h*'s, *y*'s, and *w*'s, than I can hear either in English, German or Dutch, but also contains overlapping definitions. For instance, a more central and unrounded position is, in respect of low-back /a/, also a higher and fronter position. From this follows /ay/ = /ah/ (using Trager and Smith's symbols).
75. There still are nonphonemic length differences partially reflecting the former phonemic correlation, cf. R. M. S. Heffner, 'Notes on the length of vowels', *American Speech* 12: 128–134.
76. Cf. infra § 10.1 b.
77. Cf. infra § 12.
78. Cf. 'The basic assumption of the functional approach to diachronic phonology is that the distinctive role played by a given phonemic opposition is one of the factors involved in its preservation or eventual elimination' (A. Martinet, *Word* 9: 1).
79. Cf. supra § 4.4. c–d.
80. Cf. supra § 5.2. and M. Joos, *Modern Philology,* 1934, 3–6; J. S. Kenyon (1940), *American Pronunciation,* 216–221.
81. This is the most common situation today in Br.
82. This is recorded as early as in *Dict.* 1865, 'Principles of Pron'. § 29; *Dict.* 1890, 'Guide to Pron.' §§ 131–134. The coalescence is restricted to stressed syllables, cf. /uu/ in *due* = *do*, but /juu/ in *schedule.*
83. Cf. Trager and Smith, op. cit. 14.
84. With central [u:]; cf. Kökeritz (1953: 211).
85. This distinction is still noted as rare by Whitney, op. cit. 224.
86. Cf. the phrase /we'wenttu'soe/ which may mean either 'we were not too sure' or 'we went to shore'.
87. Cf. Hubbell (1950:59).
88. Cf. infra § 14.1.
89. B. Bloch, *Language* 24, pp. 34, 40 analyses /ə'/ into /ə + r/.
90. Cf. Hubbell (1950:63).
91. Cf. Luick (1921–1940: § 566f.).
92. This /əi/ has coalesced with ME *ui* when this is kept distinct from ME *oi* as in *boil* /beil/ ≠ *joy* /dʒɔi/. I suggest this as a possible explanation of the 'ir-

regular' /əi/ ≠ /ɔi/ distribution in N.Y. City described by Hubbell (1950: 67–70).

93. *hurry* has /ʌ/ in the East and South, but /ə'/ in the Midwest and Far west, cf. the isogloss line drawn by C. K. Thomas, *American Speech* 21: 112–115.
94. Cf. supra § 5.4.
95. Cf. supra § 4.3.
96. Webster's sudden elimination of /o/ from the word lists in his spelling books from 1789 onward must be due to the fact that he recognized it as a local New England peculiarity.
97. Cf. Hubbell (1950: 82 f.).
98. After *w-* the vowel /æ:/ alternated with /ɑ:/, and developed as described sub (c).
99. The 'exceptions to this rule' in derivatives from bases with final *-r* such as *starry* /stæ:ri/ are so few as to be negligible for our purposes.
100. Cf. infra §§ 14, 15.4.
101. E.g. in S.C. and N.Y. City, cf. Hubbell (1950: 60, 80, 81, 82).
102. 'Principles of Pron.' § 6 fn.
103. 'Principles of Pron.' § 6; 'Guide to Pron.' § 59.
104. Remnants of this usage survive today in some types of Br., cf. D. Jones (1956), *An Outline of English Phonetics*, § 294. Cambridge: Heffer.
105. Cf. infra § 10.3. and Whitney, op. cit. 207, where the same vowel is given for *father* and *pass*.
106. I have noted it in Utah, Cal., Ore., and Wash. On Wash. cf. C. E. Reed, *American Speech* 27: 186–189.
107. Cf. supra § 10.1 b.
108. From *LA* 379, 666 it appears that *tot* is unknown in those areas where *taught* is recorded as [tɒt].
109. These two words are already noted as homonyms by Sheldon, *Dialect Notes* 1: 35.
110. The statistics compiled by V. R. Miller, *Speech* Monographs 20: 235–246, show that this is also the most widespread distribution in eastern Mass.
111. Evidence of /æi/ in Wentworth (1944) s.v.
112. No short vowels occurred in final position, cf. supra § 5.1.
113. Cf. supra § 7.1.
114. On this point in the theory of linguistic change cf. my article 'Der Untergang des Präverbs ge- im Englischen', to appear in *Anglia*.
115. It may be set up as a general rule that in chain shifts of the type A→B→C some items with *A* are transferred to the level of *B* so early as to coalesce with the original *B* and share in its shift to *C*. Thus the LME chains *ē*→*ī*→*əi* and *o*→*a*→*æ* comprise a few jumps *ē*→ >*əi*, *o* > *æ*, as in NE *friar* < ME *frere, strap* < *stroppe*. (Cf. Luick §§ 481, 535). Similarly the Russ, *tĭlt*→*tolt*→*tolot*, and *ĕ*→*e*→*o* (before hard consonants) produce a few forms with *tolot* < *tĭlt*, e.g. *polon* <* *pĭln*, and *o* < *ĕ,/* e.g. *vjodra* < *vĕdra*. The development in hand may be symbolized as *a*→*ā*→ɔ with the jump *a*>ɔ in words like *prong, dog*.
116. Cf. supra § 6.3 a.
117. Before final and preconsonantal *-r* this lengthening was general.
118. On the different historical interpretation of ɔ < *a* in the dialects with *cot = caught* cf. supra § 10.2–3.
119. Cf. the isogloss line by C. K. Thomas, *American Speech* 22:104–107.
120. /æ/ did not coalesce in these instances with its opposite number /æ:/ except in some dialects where the latter remained low-front in the diphthong *æi* (cf. infra § 11.4). Elsewhere there had already been retraction *ǣ* > *a*, or /æ:/ had disappeared totally under the generalization of the short allomorphs, cf. supra § 10. 1–3.

121. This city is not included in *LA*.
122. The distribution in the surrounding dialects where some words with earlier /æ/ have /æ/ and others /ɛ/ makes it highly probable that even in Waterbury not all words changed *æ* > *ɛə* at one stroke, but first a few and then more and more; cf. the discussion mentioned supra note. 114.
123. The three latter forms from *LA* Records of Southern Ohio, Southern Ill., Ky.
124. The corresponding /og, ug/ of the back series did not occur.
125. Cf. Thomas, *American Speech* 10: 293; O. Stanley, *American Speech* 11: 15; Wentworth (1944) s.v.
126. /ei/ in *measure* is also heard in the Pacific Northwest, /æi/ *ash* in Nebr.
127. Tenn. speakers use /æi/ in *fresh, flesh* = *flash* on the level of /æi/ in *fashion* which does not rhyme with /ei/ in *nation*. These forms parallel the obscure development of *thrash* < *thresh* (cf. Luick 1921–1940: § 541).
128. Although it would be tempting to derive many of these words direct from MEē treated like in *great* (cf. Kökeritz 1953: 194–197), I prefer the theory advanced here in view of the parallel forms on the *æi* and *ii* levels.
129. The two latter examples from Hubbell (1950:65).
130. Scattered *LA* Records from Ind., S.C., N.C.
131. Cf. Trager and Smith, op. cit. 27, fn. 9, 10.
132. LA Records from Ohio.
133. Cf. the texts transcribed by E. K. Kane, *Dialect Notes* 5: 355 ff.
134. For the material here presented I am indebted to Professor B. Bloch.
135. Cf. Hubbell (1950:135).
136. Nebr. (*Dialect Notes* 3: 56); Tenn.
137. Cf. supra § 5.6.
138. This is explicitly recognized by Emerson: (Before *-r*) 'where the glide and vowel have together the quantity of a long vowel' 1(*Dialect Notes* 1: 101).
139. In eastern New England, *hoarse, more*, etc. are on the same level as *home, whole* with the 'New England short *o*', i.e. /o/.
140. Recorded in Waterbury, Conn.
141. Cf. supra § 10, introduction.
142. Cf. T. S. Eliot's rhymes *wars: stars: cars* in *Burnt Norton* II, *East Coker* II.
143. *æ̃* <*ē* before *-r* as in *care* /kæ:r/ (differing from the /æ/ of *cat* in length only) is noted both in *Dict.* 1890, 'Guide to Pron.' § 49. and by an observer in Jackson's time (cf. H. L. Mencken (1921), *The American Language*, 81. New York, Knopf). Emerson, *Dialect Notes* 1: 113 records [æə] in these words. The common form /væri/ for *vary* of speakers who distinguish *marry* ≠ *merry* = *Mary* does not belong here, but goes back to an eighteenth-century variant (cf. *NED* s.v.).
144. The former /i:ə/ of *real* and /auə/ of *vowel* are treated similarly, i.e. *i:ə/·/*> *iə* > *ii, aue* > *au*, e.g. in *real* = *reel* /riil/ (R.I.), *vowel: foul* /-aul/(Utah). Cf. further examples in John S. Kenyon (1940), *American Pronunciation*, § 355, Ann Arbor, George Wahr.
145. Cf. supra § 10.3.
146. Cf. Hubbell (1950: 82, 83).
147. Cf. supra § 11.1.3.
148. Cf. supra § 11.3.
149. Cf. supra § 14.1.
150. *Pronouncing Dictionary*, Philadelphia 1803 (1st Am. ed.).
151. Term translated from L. Hjelmslev's *virtuel*, cf. *Omkring Sprogteoriens Grundlæggelse*, Copenhagen 1943, 37.
152. The proposition derived here from the surprising parallelism in the history of British

and American English that similarly structured vowel patterns may react alike to similar stimuli even in geographically nonadjacent areas also follows from the fundamental assumption of diachronic phonemics that sound laws do not work blindly, but that the internal structure of a linguistic pattern is one of the factors shaping its development (cf. A. Martinet, *Word* 8:5).

153. Especially the phonemes equivalent to eighteenth-century short vowels are, on an average, perceptibly longer in comparable environments in modern American than in modern British pronunciation.

154. Term defined by L. Hjelmslev, op. cit. 32. On *Dict.* 1865 cf. supra § 7.2.

155. Organically the same vowels of different length are opposed in Br. in a few odd pairs such as *Raleigh* /rɑli/ ≠ *Charlie* /tšɑːli/ (my own record), *particular* /pət-/ ≠ *pertain* pəːt-/.

156. Cf. D. Jones, *Outline*, § 242.

157. In Am. these words often are on the same level as *occur*, cf. supra § 9.2.

158. Cf. supra § 9.1.

159. The only possible exception is the rare variant /gɔːn < gɑːn/ for *gone*. The 'drawled forms' of *dog, God, odd* noted by Ellis show merely allophonic lengthening before voiced consonants. They are 'different from E. *awed, gawd*' with /əː/ (Ellis 1869–1889, vol. VII: 1954).

160. Cf. supra § 14.1.

161. [ae] is presupposed as an intermediate stage of the shift *æ'ə* > a.ə.

162. Cf. D. Jones, op. cit. § 431.

163. With the exception of certain Public School and Oxford University dialects which pronounce *loss* /ləːs < lɑːs/, etc.

164. Cf. supra § 10.3.

165. On the origin of ENE /æː/ in *rather* cf. Luick (1921–1940: § 494), or it may be from *rath* ræːþ/.

REFERENCES

Ellis, A. J. (1869–1889), *Early English Pronunciation*. London.
Hubbell, A. F. (1950), *The Pronunciation of English in New York City: Consonants and Vowels*. New York, King's Crown Press. (Reprinted 1971 by Octagon Books, Farrar, Straus and Giroux.)
Jespersen, O. (1909), *A Modern English Grammar*, volume one. Heidelberg.
Kökeritz, H. (1953), *Shakespeare's pronunciation*. New Haven, Yale University Press.
Luick, K. (1921–1940), *Historische Grammatik der englischen Sprache*. Leipzig.
Wentworth, H. (1944), *American Dialect Dictionary*. New York.

GARY N. UNDERWOOD

American English Dialectology:
Alternatives for the Southwest

I. Among those linguists Wolfram (1971:103) labeled 'mainstream dialectologists', highest priority is given equally to two tasks: (1) editing and publishing data already collected by linguistic atlases (e.g. the Linguistic Atlas of the Middle and South Atlantic States, the Linguistic Atlas of the Upper Midwest etc.), and (2) establishing linguistic atlases in the 'unmapped' areas of the United States. Such priorities have clear implications for the Southwest. California is 'mapped' by the California and Nevada section of the Linguistic Atlas of the Pacific Coast, begun in 1951 by David Reed (Reed and Reed, 1972:135), and plans for the Linguistic Atlas of the Gulf States (LAGS) under the direction of Lee Pederson, extend the scope of that atlas as far west as the city of Laredo and Webb County, Texas (Pederson et al. 1972:229, 233, 240). We could reasonably conclude that mainstream dialectologists would say highest priority in the Southwest should be given to an atlas of central and western Texas, New Mexico, and Arizona — in other words a Linguistic Atlas of the Southwest States (LASS). But do we want a LASS? My answer is, 'No'.

When the Linguistic Atlas of the United States and Canada was inaugurated in 1931 by Hans Kurath, it was perhaps a noble project. But since then linguistics has advanced too far for us to continue to study dialects with a methodology that has not been significantly improved in half a century. Despite Kurath's repeated assertion to the effect that 'there can be no valid objection to this procedure' (1972:26), there are indeed numerous valid objections to linguistic geography as it has been practiced by Kurath and his students for the past four decades. It may have seemed reasonable then to import a dialect theory and methodology which European scholars had thought to be adequate for studying the language of a stable peasant society and to attempt to replicate successfully this type of research in America,[1] but American innocence of the 1930s is no excuse for untenable dialectology in the

Reprinted by permission of the author and of the *International Journal of the Sociology of Language*. The article first appeared in Issue 2 (1974) of that journal.

1970s. But if we compare the first American dialect atlas, the Linguistic Atlas of New England (LANE), with the newest, the Linguistic Atlas of the Gulf States, it is clear that there is no significant change in the thinking of American linguistic geographers. With minor allowances, criticism of one atlas is applicable to any other.

Linguistic atlas methodology does not need to be modified; it needs to be abandoned and replaced by a new one if we are seriously interested in a realistic, accurate account of regional and social variation in American English. Devastating criticism of American dialectology can be found in more or less overt forms in Pickford (1956), Keyser (1963), Labov (1966), C.-J. Bailey (1968a), and Dillard (1969), to mention just the most prominent critics. But the response among mainstream dialectologists has been either to proceed as if no questions have ever been raised or to make minor adjustments as gestures of keeping up with the times. My own work until 1971 was no exception. My training was in traditional linguistic geography, and the character of my early works is unmistakably conservative. For a time I was preoccupied with modifying traditional methodology to overcome valid criticisms (e.g. Underwood 1973). I have since concluded that if we objectively examine the linguistic atlas methodology, the only reasonable conclusion is that the methodology is not salvageable.

American linguistic geography has been perceptively criticized on theoretical grounds in such words as Keyser (1963), C.-J. Bailey (1968a), Labov (1966), and Troike (1971). Furthermore, generative and lectological alternatives to traditional dialect interpretations are well documented. In addition to the works just cited, see also B. Bailey (1965), C.-J. Bailey (1968b, 1972, 1973a, 1973b), Becker (1967), King (1969), Labov (1969, 1972a, 1972b), Labov et al. (1968), Loflin (1967, 1969, 1971), O'Neil (1968), Saporta (1965), Sledd (1966), Smith (1969), Thomas (1967), Underwood (1971), and Weinreich et al. (1968). For the sake of brevity consideration of analytical procedures will be set aside in deference to those who claim that linguistic atlas data can be interpreted within the construct of any theory and to ask some fundamental questions about the data themselves. (The preceding sentence must not be interpreted to suggest that I subscribe to the invalid claim.)

Typically empiricists to the extreme, American linguistic geographers generally eschew discussions of dialect theory or hypotheses. Indeed, it is no accident that the first chapter of Kurath's *Studies in Areal Linguistics* is 'From Sampling to Publication' or that the word *theory* is not to be found in the book's exhaustive table of contents (Kurath, 1972: v–vii). A look at Kurath et al. (1939), Kurath (1949), Atwood (1953), or Kurath and McDavid (1961) reveals that nowhere do the authors offer an explication of their theoretical framework. Usually the dialect geographer begins his book by outlining dialect areas or summarizing dialect differences without bothering to explain his conceptualization of dialects or his motivation for using some linguistic features instead of others to determine dialect differentiation. Even the two articles often cited as the best state-of-the-art papers, McDavid and McDavid (1956) and Atwood (1963), ignore dialect theory while describing field methods in detail. But if we look closely at the methodological statements, we can find countless unstated assumptions and untested hypotheses, and close reading will even reveal a 'strong' dialect theory.

Support for the assertion that mainstream dialect methodology is untenable can be provided by considering four basic questions: (1) What questions do linguistic geographers ask? (2) How is information elicited? (3) What kinds of Americans are interviewed? (4) In what kinds of communities are interviews conducted?

THE QUESTIONNAIRES

Because of the linguistic geographers' concern about comparability of data, every American atlas uses a questionnaire developed from the original LANE work sheets but tailored in some ways to suit the locale.[2] Despite the dialectologists' preoccupation with comparability, which is one reason they adamantly oppose any important changes in their methodology, this concern is highly and capriciously selective. They insist that items used to mark dialects along the Atlantic coast be retained by all later studies. Thus, the LAGS interviewer in 1973 asks his informants their terms for a sheaf of wheat (Pederson et al. 1972:141), just as the LANE field worker did in 1933 even though wheat may not be grown in, say, Zapata County, Texas, or if wheat does happen to be grown somewhere in the LAGS territory, to find it tied into sheaves would surely be a rare experience. On the other hand, comparability is not a concern when fieldworkers use radically different elicitation techniques, when two sets of data are collected 40 years apart, or when responses are given in a wide variety of contextual styles.

Any dialect questionnaire must be selective, and Kurath admits that the selection presents 'problems' and 'uncertainties' (1972:3–4). Though there may be questions concerning individual items to be included, Kurath has no questions about the types of data to include, for the questionnaire must 'cover the regional and/or social differences in the lexicon, the morphology, and the phonology in a given language area . . .' (1972:3). Two assumptions in that statement are obvious: (1) Dialect differences are confined to what people utter. The possibility that dialects many differ according to the acceptance or rejection of the hypothesized grammaticality of an utterance is never considered. (2) Kurath's catalog disregards dialect differences in syntax. Actually a few syntactic matters are in atlas work sheets, but they are largely confined to choices of prepositions and the use of double negatives. Several of these features are bizarrely treated as lexical items in Kurath (1949). In addition, the LAGS work sheets include deletions of articles, auxiliaries, and prepositions (Pederson 1972:18). But linguistic atlases do not provide insights into intonation patterns (a point Sledd has stressed repeatedly, e.g. 1969:1313) or syntactic features such as embedded questions, subject-verb inversion in direct questions, relativization, complementation, or indirect object inversion. Even for all his concern for phonology, the atlas dialectologist can tell us almost nothing about contraction and deletion phenomena, *l*-lessness, word-final consonant cluster simplification, and other consonant pronunciations. Consequently, the atlas work sheets are unenlightening with regard to black–white speech differences and would be even less productive when used to elicit data on Chicano or Indian English.

The linguistic atlas work sheets have a severely limited usefulness because of their unmistakable Anglo-Saxon bias. As early as 1928, three years before LANE was underway, Kurath had already concluded:

The dialect differences in the pronunciation of educated Americans from various sections of the country have their origin largely in the British regional differences in the pronunciation of standard English (1928:394).

In view of this narrow historical account of American dialect differences, it is no surprise that the kinds of evidence which atlases use as dialect markers are rigidly restricted. This limitation is revealed by Kurath's list of sources from which atlas items were taken:

The lexical and morphological features in the work sheets are selected from an extensive collection compiled largely from the regional and local word lists in *Dialect Notes* and *American Speech*; the phonetic items are derived mostly from H. Kurath's collection and from J. S. Kenyon, *American Pronunciation* (4th ed., Ann Arbor, 1930). Most of the dialect features in G. Kempl's short list (*Dialect Notes* 1, 316–318) have been included. . . . In order to facilitate comparison with British dialects, an effort was made to include as many features as possible from A. J. Ellis' *Comparative Specimen,* his *Dialect Test* and his *Classified Word List* (*Early English Pronunciation,* part V, pp. 7*, 8*, and 25*-29*: London, 1889) (Kurath et al. 1939:148).

In other words, items were chosen because they had previously been shown to have regional variants among British or Anglo-American speakers of English. Regardless of how extensive differences may be outside the domains of the work sheets, they must be ignored. Therefore, it is easy to see why Kurath could conclude:

By and large the Southern Negro speaks the language of the white man of his locality or area and of his education. . . . As far as the speech of the uneducated Negroes is concerned, it differs little from that of the illiterate white; that is it exhibits the same regional and local variations as that of the simple white folk (1949:6).

Disregarding the fact that Kurath's conclusion can be based upon the *vocabulary* of no more than 50 Blacks in the entire Atlantic coast region,[3] we can acknowledge that Kurath has empirical evidence for his conclusion. In response to atlas questions little or no differences may be found between Southern Blacks and Whites, but that does not necessarily mean that dialect differences do not exist. It may mean only that atlas interviewers were — and still are — asking the wrong questions.

Consider, for example, the types of vocabulary items that mainstream dialectologists regard as relevant for determining dialect groupings. Topics in the atlas questionnaires include subjects such as the weather, the dwelling, the farm, farm implements and tools, domestic animals, farm crops, clothing and bedding, and foods and cooking (Kurath et al. 1939:149). Since a person's entire vocabulary inventory cannot be studied, the mainstream dialectologist needs to consider whether his selections provide an accurate representation of dialect differences. It is not enough to acknowledge that his selections present 'problems' and 'uncertainties' (Kurath 1972:4). As Dillard has pointed out:

. . . of course there is nothing wrong *per se* in investigating the domain of the home or of the farm. There are, however, other domains which should not be ignored. It is particularly unfortunate if the decision about a cultural system becomes the artifact of the questionnaire applied, as has been done in observing that the Negro brought an 'agricultural' life pattern to the inner city. It would not be surprising if it were found that Southern Negroes have the same terminology for farm implements (*whiffletree, harrow*) that Southern whites have. Southern farming developed, after all, with Negro labor but with white ownership of the land and of the implements. But it would be absurd to expect Negro musical terminology to be identical to that of the whites (1969:9).

A dialect questionnaire must not be so culturally biased that it distorts the evidence gathered from speakers whose culture differs from the norm.

But notice, too, that the vocabulary questions in linguistic atlas work sheets have decidedly rural bias even though the American population is predominantly urban. But more importantly atlas questions are not just rural; they are slanted toward a rural life style that was already disappearing when LANE was organized. Kurath acknowledged that the decision in 1930 was to record the obsolescent vocabulary of pre-mechanical agrarian America before that vocabulary completely disappeared. LANE concentrated upon this vanishing vocabulary because:

Such words reflect most clearly the regional pattern of pre-industrial New England, which must be reconstructed as well as possible if we could understand fully the present speech areas and trace the sources of New England speech back to the dialects of England (Kurath et al. 1939:1).

Indeed, as Labov's recently published study of the changes in the dialect of Martha's Vineyard demonstrates, the LANE questionnaire was oriented more to the 1890s than even to the 1930s (1972c: 87, 95–102). Despite this antiquarian bias, mainstream dialectologists insist that questions significant for the 1890s continue to be used (because of the comparability argument) in the 1970s. So Pederson's LAGS questionnaire still covers such items as calls to oxen, the parts of a wooden wagon wheel, shafts of a buggy, and razor strops (Pederson et al. 1972: Index).

There is still another problem with the atlas questionnaires. Atwood notes: 'In general, the items on the list represented everyday concepts, and sought to elicit usages that would ordinarily be transmitted orally within the family rather than in the schools' (1963:11). At first glance that statement appears innocuous enough, for dialect investigators are not interested in national usages disseminated through education. But a second glance detects a powerful assumption about the transmission of dialect features. In the 1930s researchers focused upon parentally transmitted features because it was assumed that the greatest influence on a child's speech is the speech of his parents. Today, however, we know that in language parental influence is not nearly so great as peer group influence. Any study that concentrates upon features learned from parents and systematically ignores those learned from peers runs the great danger of producing a distorted version of dialect patterns.

The family bias in atlas questionnaires is dictated by the linguistic geographer's insistence that the single most important factor in determining dialect groupings is migration patterns (Kurath 1949:1). The claim has been that as a family migrates, its dialect migrates with it, and the features of that dialect are transmitted to the next generation in the new locale. Such a theory of transmission fails to explain such well-known phenomena as isoglosses cutting across seams in migration routes (see e.g. Kurath 1949: maps 27–28, and Marckwardt 1957: maps 2–3). Kurath patched up the original hypothesis by acknowledging that some dialect variants spread independent of migration as prestige forms (1964), but such an *ad hoc* explanation does not affect the important claim that children learn the language of their parents, a claim which must seem dubious even to a mainstream dialectologist. Writing of McDavid's own children, Davis laments:

It would be fascinating if I could report that the offspring of a Minneapolis speaker [Virginia Glenn McDavid] and a South Carolinian [Raven McDavid] would show phonemic splits and mergers of a novel kind, but they speak the Standard Inland Northern of their peers (1972:xi).

So there it is: the mainstream dialectologist knows that children learn the language of their peers yet conducts research predicated upon the assumption that they learn the language of their parents. Labov, whose work in nine years has probably taught us more about dialects than that of the linguistic geographers in 39 years, once again reminds us of an obvious fact:

If children's speech reflected their parents' dialects, we would not find any of the solid isoglosses which mark the regional boundaries of American speech. Whenever a family moved to a neighboring town, we would then find that the dialect of this area was diluted with the coming of the imported child, and the overall result of this mixing process would be no regional dialects at all (1971:214, n. 22).

Since the influence of parents upon a child's dialect is less permanent than that of the peer group, to continue to emphasize in dialect investigations parental factors at the expense of ultimately more important ones does not seem to be justifiable.

THE INTERVIEW

One of the claimed virtues of atlas methodology is 'interviewing in a conversation' (Pederson 1972:8), but an atlas interview more closely resembles a test than a conversation. Conversational forms were from the beginning of American atlas surveys regarded as 'especially valuable' and 'of great importance' (Kurath et al. 1939:45) because they were believed to be more natural than answers to direct questions. Because of this goal, atlas questionnaires merely list items or notions instead of questions, and each fieldworker is encouraged to develop his own elicitation techniques, but the very nature of the items often mitigates against conversation. Consequently, the frequency of conversational forms varies from field-worker to fieldworker (Kurath et al. 1939:45–46). Since true conversation is inefficient when a fieldworker is intent upon recording an informant's usage for 700 to 800 specific items,[4] fieldwor‑ers tend to resort to a procedure of eliciting one-word or phrase responses.[5] The result is, ironically, just the type of utterance Kurath wanted to avoid.

The atlas interview in which a fieldworker uses his verbal skills to elicit a response indirectly is notoriously inefficient. It wastes valuable time, and often imprecise hints result in erroneous answers. McDavid estimates that a LAGS interview containing 800 items can be expected to be completed by an experienced interviewer in about six hours. Difficult informants or inexperienced interviewers will require even more time (1972:48). There is no need to prolong interviews to such lengths, and speed is easily attained by adopting other elicitation techniques. McDavid estimates that the maximum speed for an atlas interview is three questions a minute (1972:40). But in the ALS, in contrast, questions are used only as a last resort to elicit word or phrase utterances. Using illustrations, the ALS procedure elicits 437 pronunciation features in less than 20 minutes (Underwood 1972:216); the same technique can be used not only for vocabulary, but also for morphology and syntax (Summerlin 1972).

Consider this sample attempt to get a response by Raven McDavid, who is considered the most capable of the atlas interviewers:

A long thin-bodied insect, with a hard little beak and two pairs of shiny wings; it hovers around damp places and eats its own weight in mosquitoes, etc. (Pederson et al. 1972:161).

The desired response is *dragon fly* or a synonym, but the technique is counterproductive because McDavid, not the informant, does most of the talking. The ALS abandoned direct questioning when a study of pilot interviews using direct questions revealed that our tapes contained usually 10 words from the interviewer for each word spoken by the informant (Underwood 1972:216). But more importantly, atlas-type questioning is simply misunderstood all too often. The item McDavid is trying to deal with, for example, is one which is not at all clear when the request for information is verbal, as Smith has pointed out (1968:51–57). But as Smith also shows, erroneous answers virtually vanish if an illustration is used instead of a question. Briefly, eliciting answers with oral questioning is far more complex than atlas methodology assumes. Labov (1970b:56–59) describes some fundamental presuppositions an interviewer and a respondent must share before a question will evoke a desired response, and Schatzman and Strauss (1955) demonstrate how a question, considered simple, obvious and unambiguous to an interviewer, has a wide range of interpretations by those being interviewed. The question an atlas interviewer asks and the one his informant answers are often two distinctly different requests. When that happens the informant's answer is appropriate to the question he understands, and since it may appear to the interviewer to be a legitimate response to the question he has asked, it is recorded erroneously as a valid response.

Kurath has for at least 34 years been aware of the inadequacies of atlas interviewing techniques. He noted that 'the fieldworker's method of interviewing . . . affects the informant's responses' (Kurath et al. 1939:47). He went on to observe that *the wording of the items in the worksheets* [Kurath's emphasis] . . . to some extent determined the method of inquiry and hence also, in a measure, the response'. Since standardized questions were not used, Kurath noted a tendency among fieldworkers to use literary expressions for concepts for which the informant was expected to provide his natural synonyms. Such methods result in distortions of the evidence, as Kurath well knew, yet mainstream dialectologists continue to use the same elicitation techniques despite all the reasons for dropping them. Although there were claims for improved elicitation techniques (Pederson 1971:138), the LAGS work sheets are identical in character to all the previous atlas questionnaires, the only difference being the inclusion of illustrations of elicitation methods used by two LANE fieldworkers (Bloch and Harris), Loman, McDavid, and Pederson (Pederson et al. 1972:99–100). Kurath recognizes but plays down the inadequacies of atlas elicitation techniques by saying that the 'approach may produce variants that are not strictly synonyms', but instead of attempting to develop a better methodology he excuses the procedure by saying it has 'drawbacks of which scholars must be aware' (1972:15).

Even if those serious flaws in elicitation techniques were eliminated, the resulting data would still be unsatisfactory. The evidence would not reflect a true picture of a speaker's linguistic repertory; it would at best illustrate no more than his performance in one narrow, uncomfortable communicative context. A representation of a person's linguistic capacities that encompasses just one speech style is incomplete, and more importantly, sometimes conclusions based upon such evidence can be dangerously misleading. In their own way mainstream dialectologists are just as guilty of presenting a biased representation of a speaker's linguistic ability as are such researchers as Bereiter and Engelmann, who conclude that ghetto youngsters are nonverbal, grammatically impoverished, and cognitively deficient (Bereiter et al. 1966; Bereiter and Engelmann 1966). Unlike Bereiter and Engelmann, mainstream dialectologists do *not* misunderstand the evidence but like Bereiter and Engelmann they take evidence collected within the constraints of one situational context and regard it as indicative of a person's total linguistic capacity.

In effect, the mainstream dialectologist is assuming a hierarchy of linguistic variation. Of primary importance to him are regional variables, of secondary importance are social variables, and of no importance are stylistic variables. Yet despite his efforts to insure that data collected from an informant will be internally uniform, the mainstream dialectologist finds in his field records often so much free variation that generalizations seem impossible. However, what has been erroneously regarded as un-analysable free variation is not truly free, for if the data base is expanded to include evidence recorded in a variety of contextual styles, the variation patterns regularly conform according to stylistic stratification (Labov 1966:28–62). Stylistic variation is an important consideration to dialectology, and it was encouraging to learn that Pederson planned to incorporate procedures for isolating different styles in the LAGS work sheets (Pederson 1971:138). Unfortunately, however, the latest version of those work sheets includes no such provisions (Pederson et al. 1972:99–208). Instead McDavid instructs LAGS fieldworkers that 'the form of the interviewer should be kept as conversational as possible' (1972:45), meaning, in other words, that elicitation techniques are to be the same as those used without improvement since 1931.

COMMUNITIES AND INFORMANTS

According to Kurath the choice of communities to be studied by an atlas 'is made in reference to the sociocultural characteristics of the area under consideration' (1972:11), including such factors as chronology of settlement, the characteristics of the population at the time of settlement, the development of railroad lines, early roadways, routes of migration as settlement expanded westward, and the character of the economy in past centuries (Kurath 1972:42–51). Once the settlement patterns are known, communities representative of this history are selected as sites for interviewing.

In each community an informant is selected who is 'an elderly descendant of an old local family' (Kurath et al. 1939:41). Such old-fashioned people are important 'in order that the earlier regional pattern might be accurately delineated and the oldest living forms of speech preserved as fully as possible for the historian . . .' (Kurath et al. 1939:41). In addition, a middle-aged life-long resident, usually a high school graduate, is interviewed, and in each major city a cultured informant is also interviewed. There is nothing wrong *per se* in choosing to interview such people. It is legitimate to study only middle-aged and elderly people whose families can be traced to the earliest settlers in communities that are in turn typical of the migration patterns of the first European-Americans in the region. And this is not too far removed from what linguistic geographers do. McDavid reminds us:

Whatever the current mode of interest in dialects may be, it is none the less true that the primary purpose of a linguistic atlas is that of historical linguistics, of providing a body of stable folk evidence, from which one may work backward, comparatively, to set up affiliations of the dialect regions with those in older settled areas and in the British Isles (1972:51).

Now that is a kind of candor to be admired, and it is a shame there is not more of it from mainstream dialectologists. Instead, they tend to condescend towards the 'antiquarian bias' (McDavid 1966:12) of Europeans who have 'a predilection for historical problems [in] the hope of shedding light on processes of linguistic change by observing the linguistic behavior of the folk' (Kurath 1972:13). They claim, in contrast, that American atlases yield a different sort of evidence:

This systematic record of usage of more than 1,200 persons gives us full information on the geographic and the social dissemination of the words and the phrases selected for this study (Kurath 1949:v).

As Pickford pointed out (1956:217–218), it is not true that data from American atlases provide us with an accurate representation of the regional and social variations in American English.

II. In the preceding sections I have set forth and supported several arguments against mainstream dialectology. I have advocated that we not encourage or engage in such outmoded research in the Southwest. It does not follow, however, that no dialect research should be undertaken. On the contrary, we desperately need knowledge of language variation in both rural and urban areas, we need studies of the language characteristics of Blacks and of bilinguals (and even trilinguals in some locations), and we also need to examine correlations of linguistic variation with such social factors as a speaker's degree of urbanization, age, sex, social class, occupation, cultural isolation, and ethnic background. But such knowledge requires a different methodology from that of the mainstream dialectologists.

THE QUESTIONNAIRE

We need a questionnaire which is basically model-oriented rather than item-oriented. Priority should be given to coverage of the phonological, morphological, and syntactic systems of American English instead of to vocabulary and incidental features. We should not be content with recording only a conversational or a recitation speech style, but should instead design the research tool so that we record a person's speech in a wide range of contextual styles from the most casual to the most formal. The interview should also be broadened beyond the consideration of productive competence to include evidence of receptive competence as well, to use Troike's important distinctions (1969:63–73). This would necessitate inclusion of such matters as repetition tests like those used by Troike (1969:66–67) and Labov and Cohen (1967:12–16). Similarly, we need to develop techniques for eliciting reliable grammaticality judgments such as those used by Carden (1973). Also the interview should collect data on social evaluations as well as grammatical ones. This would mean investigation of a person's linguistic self-evaluation and his evaluation of speech different from his own. Ideally the scope of the interview should be expanded beyond linguistic competence to include his communicative competence as well. Finally, a questionnaire to be used in the Southwest would have to be designed to deal with the presence of coexistent systems and bilingualism and in some cases trilingualism, and the problem is complicated further by the fact that a variety of bilingual situations exists. In Texas, for example, the questionnaire would need to account not only for Spanish interference in English but interference from German and French as well, and possibly other European languages. In other sections of the Southwest the questionnaire would have to be adapted for Indian languages. The construction of such a questionnaire will be no easy task; it is going to require the expertise not only of a team of linguists familiar with the languages spoken in the area, but also of anthropologists, sociologists, and folklorists who are knowledgeable of the various cultures in the region. Indeed, Galvan and Troike (1969) have demonstrated the indispensable role of nonlinguists in an area of relatively uncomplicated cultural diversity such as East Texas.

INTERVIEW TECHNIQUES

Obviously the proposed character of the linguistic interview will necessitate refined interviewing techniques. Atlas methods must be abandoned in total, and new procedures for eliciting speech must be developed that exploit the very best of the work of such researchers as Sapon (1957), Labov (1966), Labov et al. (1968), Bachman (1970), Underwood (1972), and Summerlin (1972), among others. The extension of the questionnaire into new domains for the dialectologist also means that we will no doubt want to turn to methods used by other kinds of linguists and nonlinguists as well. One example of this type of borrowing is suggested by Wolfram, who proposes that help in exploring differences in grammatical systems may come from those who have been studying children's acquisition of language (1971:121). It may not be enough, however, just to train a fieldworker in new sophisticated techniques. We need to learn whether the interviewer's race, sex, or social class, for example, affects the performance of the speaker. There is reason to believe these factors are important, for Anshen's data, to use one example, suggest that the race of the interviewer affected the pronunciation of some of his Black subjects in North Carolina (1970:21). Because of the complex linguistic and cultural situations in the Southwest, the interviewer may be an important constraint upon variability. Before a survey of linguistic variation is begun, we first need to conduct experiments to learn the significance of what Wolfram has called 'interviewer variables' (1971:120).

COMMUNITIES AND INFORMANTS

If a study of linguistic variation in the Southwest is to give an accurate reflection of the English of the population, atlas methods for selecting communities and informants are not viable. A refined sampling methodology has distinct advantages over judgment sampling not because it is free of bias but because all its biases are explicit, and there are empirical tests for sampling error. In addition to the superior validity and reliability of such sampling, evidence obtained by such techniques can be subjected to a wide range of statistical calculations, whereas that from judgment samples cannot. But devising a feasible methodology poses problems which the linguist alone cannot solve.

Let us consider some of the complications present in Texas alone. First, the population in 1970 was 11,196,730, of which 79.9 percent was urban. Suppose, therefore, a sample was sought that reflected this rural–urban proportion. It may not be the best sample because there is reason to hypothesize that the dialect variation (and social stratification) in the 'Anytowns', i.e. towns ranging in population from 2,500 to 50,000 (Hodges, 1964), is different from that of metropolitan areas. Galvan and Troike (1969:31), for example, note a variation in Tyler not found in four smaller East Texas towns. In Texas there are 24 such metropolitan areas

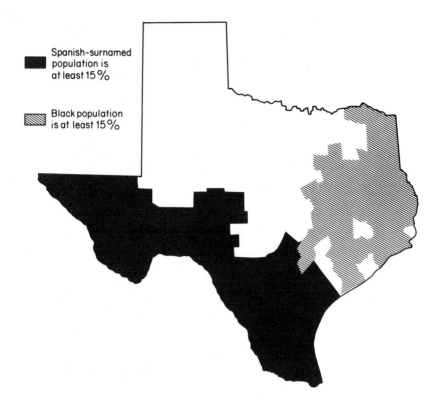

Figure 1.   *Distribution of Spanish-surnamed and Black population in Texas*

comprising 73.8 percent of the total population, leaving only 20.3 percent of the population in rural areas and a mere 5.9 percent in towns outside metropolitan areas. Furthermore, over 12 percent of the population is Black and over 16 percent is Spanish-surnamed, but these minority groups are not evenly distributed in the state (see Figure 1). If we assume a hypothesis that dialect differences correlate with cultural boundaries, we first must determine the cultural divisions of Texas. Suppose, for a purely hypothetical example, a sociological survey divides the state according to Figure 2. In areas 1, 2, and 4 the Black population ranges from 15 percent to over 50 percent in some countries, and in areas 7 and 9 the Spanish-surnamed population varies from 15 percent to over 75 percent. Note, too, the shaded areas indicating metropolitan areas. Presumably the sample would have to be extensive enough to represent adequ-

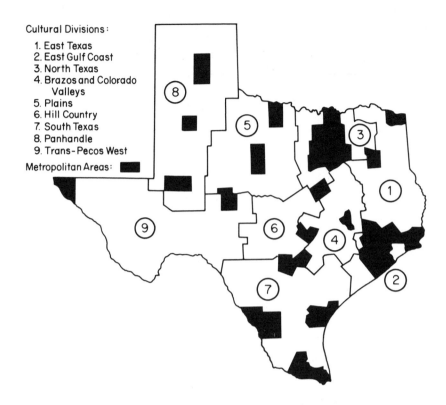

Cultural Divisions:
1. East Texas
2. East Gulf Coast
3. North Texas
4. Brazos and Colorado Valleys
5. Plains
6. Hill Country
7. South Texas
8. Panhandle
9. Trans-Pecos West

Metropolitan Areas:

Figure 2. *Cultural divisions and metropolitan areas in Texas*

ately the population character of each region, but we do not know the minimum sample that would be adequate. The sampling problems in Texas alone are so mind-boggling that one is reluctant to think about those in other Southwestern states.

III. Some people are certain to observe that what I am proposing as a replacement for traditional, mainstream dialectology is nothing more than social dialect research conducted over a large geographic area instead of in an urban area only. That is a fairly accurate observation, but there is no reason why the same methodology that works in urban areas should not work in regional studies. The dichotomy between regional dialects and social dialects is a false one anyway. Traditionally, dialectologists construct a dialect model looking something like Figure 3.

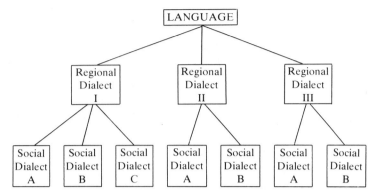

Figure 3.

But if a dialect is a variety of the language spoken by a group of speakers, differing from other varieties of the language by systematic differences in language structure, there is no requirement that those differences must be geographically distributed. Furthermore, there is no reason to assume that differences distributed geographically are inherently more significant than those with nongeographic distribution. In fact, if language variation is a social phenomenon, if it is a variation to be accounted for in terms of social factors such as age, sex, ethnic groups, social class, place of residence, cultural isolation, etc., as Dillard (1969) insists — in other words in terms of what a sociologist calls group identification and affiliation — then there is no reason to assume on an *a priori* basis that any one of these factors necessarily outranks the others. If models are desired, a more realistic one would be Figure 4.

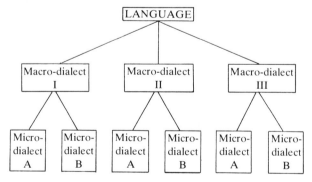

Figure 4.

Such a model makes no claims about social or regional distributions; it merely suggests that macro-dialects I, II, and III have certain fundamental differences in their systems. Micro-dialect IA shares these fundamental differences with micro-dialect IB but differs from IB in more superficial characteristics. But it must be kept in mind that such models probably have little relation to reality. They satisfy the linguist's predilection for abstractions, but their static character necessitates a ruthless segmenting of a linguistic continuum. If dialect research is to become model-oriented, our task will be to describe linguistic variables and to correlate those variables with social ones. The type of dialect research I envision for the Southwest not only calls for a combination of difficult fieldwork and theoretical models, but also for cooperation between linguists of various talents and anthropologists, folklorists, sociologists, and perhaps psychologists. Even this tentative and crude sketch of the suggested research poses such formidable problems that the likelihood that such research will even be conducted may be extremely remote. That is no justification, however, for maintaining the *status quo* of mainstream dialectology.

NOTES

1. About this point there can be little disagreement. Atwood writes: 'The methodology of the American *Atlas* has been essentially that of Gilliéron, as refined and modified for Italy by Karl Jaberg and Jakob Jud' (1963:7). Even Pederson asserts positively: 'The Linguistic Atlas of New England (LANE) Project combined the best features of its predecessors and established a standard of excellence for all of the American dialect research which has been done during the past three decades. Like Wenker and Wrede's project in Germany, Kurath's work became a model for regional research in the United States. . . . Positioned squarely in the Gilliéron tradition, the LANE Project incorporated the central tenets of dialectology instituted in ALF' (1972:8).
2. See Davis et al. (1969) for a compilation of items used in American atlas surveys.
3. The exact number is unclear. Atwood says: 'The South Atlantic materials include records of 21 more or less primitive Negro informants gathered by Loman; McDavid has added several more [from South Carolina], including some examples of educated Negro speech' (1953: 1, n.4).
4. Conversation is not just inefficient; it is practically impossible. In early pilot interviews for the Arkansas Language Survey (ALS) we attempted to elicit both vocabulary and pronunciation in conversation. Invariably we either carried on lively but unproductive conversations, or conversations deteriorated into question-and-answer sessions. The problem is simple: maintaining a conversation depends upon the interviewer's projection of genuine interest in what speakers talk about. When we let our speakers talk about topics that held interest for them, we discovered that rarely did they express interests in the semantic domains on our list. Whenever we attempted to direct the conversation to areas of our interests, speakers sometimes simply ignored our ploys. Often attempts to direct conversations resulted in tension, guarded speech, terse responses, a drop in

enthusiasm, and an increased suspicion of the fieldworker's motives. Van Riper claims to have conducted 50 interviews in Oklahoma in a conversational style (1972:177–183), but judging from the ALS experience it is highly doubtful that Van Riper was eliciting casual, spontaneous speech.

5. See Atwood (1963:11) and Pederson et al. (1972:101:208) for examples of field-worker techniques.

REFERENCES

Allen, Harold B. and Gary N. Underwood, editors (1971), *Readings in American Dialectology*. New York, Appleton-Century-Crofts.

Anshen, Frank (1970), 'A Sociolinguistic Analysis of a Sound Change', *Language Sciences* 9:20–21.

Atwood, E. Bagby (1953), *A Survey of Verb Forms in the Eastern United States*. Ann Arbor, University of Michigan Press.

— (1963), 'The Methods of American Dialectology', *ZMF* 30(1):1–29.

Bachman, James K. (1970), 'Field techniques in an urban language study', *TESOL Q* 4:256–260.

Bailey, Beryl L. (1965), 'Toward a new perspective in Negro English dialectology', *American Speech* (40):171–177.

Bailey, C.-J. N. (1968a), 'Is there a "Midland" dialect of American English?' Paper read at the summer meeting of the Linguistic Society of America (= ERIC ED 021 240).

— (1968b), 'Optimality, positivism, and pandialectal grammars', *ERIC/PEGS* 30 Washington, D.C., Center for Applied Linguistics.

— (1972), 'The integration of linguistic theory: internal reconstruction and the comparative method', in *Linguistic Change and Generative Theory,* ed. by Robert P. Stockwell and Ronald K. S. Macauley, 22–31. Bloomington, Indiana University Press.

— (1973a), 'Contributions of the study of variation to the framework of the new linguistics'. Paper read at the meeting of the International Linguistic Association, Arequipa, Perú, March, 1973.

— (1973b), *Variation and Linguistic Theory.* Arlington, Center for Applied Linguistics.

Becker, Donald A. (1967), 'Generative phonology and dialect study: an investigation of three modern German dialects'. Unpublished Ph.D. dissertation, The University of Texas at Austin.

Bereiter, Carl and Siegfried Engelmann *Teaching Disadvantaged Children in the Preschool.* Englewood Cliffs, N.J., Prentice-Hall.

Bereiter, Carl et al. (1966), 'An academically oriented pre-school for culturally deprived children', in *Pre-School Education Today*, ed. by Fred M. Hechinger 105–137. New York, Doubleday.

Carden, Guy (1973), 'Methodology and linguistic variation'. Paper read at the conference on The Expanding Domain of Linguistics, The University of Texas at Austin, Austin, Texas, March 27, 1973.

Davis, Alva L., Raven I. McDavid, Jr., and Virginia G. McDavid (compilers) (1969), *A Compilation of the Work Sheets of the Linguistic Atlas of the United States and Canada and Associated Projects.* Chicago, University of Chicago Press.

Davis, Lawrence M. editor (1972), *Studies in Linguistics in Honor of Raven I. McDavid, Jr.* University, University of Alabama Press.

Dillard, J. L. (1969), 'The DARE-ing old men on their flying isoglosses or, dialectology and dialect geography', *FFLR* 7:2, 8–10, 22.

Galvan, Mary M., and Rudolph C. Troike (1969), 'The East Texas Dialect Project: a pattern for education', *Florida FL Reporter* 7(1):29–31, 152–153.

Hodges, Harold M., Jr. (1964), *Social Stratification: Class in America.* Cambridge, Mass., Schenkman.

Keyser, Samuel J. (1963), 'Review of *The Pronunciation of English in the Atlantic States,* by Hans Kurath and Raven I. McDavid, Jr.', *Language* 39:303–316.

King, Robert D. (1969), 'Primary Change', in *Historical Linguistics and Generative Grammar,* 28–63. Englewood Cliffs. N.J. Prentice-Hall.

Kurath, Hans (1928), 'The origin of the dialectal differences in spoken American English', *MP* 25:385–395.

— (1949), *A Word Geography of the Eastern United States.* Ann Arbor, University of Michigan Press.

— (1964), 'Interrelation between regional and social dialects', in *Proceedings of the Ninth International Congress of Linguists, Cambridge, Massachusetts, August 27-31, 1962,* ed. by Horace C. Lunt, 135–143. The Hague, Mouton.

— (1972), *Studies in Areal Linguistics.* Bloomington, Indiana University Press.

Kurath, Hans, et al. (1939), *Handbook of the Linguistic Geography of New England.* Providence, R.I., Brown University Press.

Kurath, Hans and Raven I. McDavid, Jr. (1961), *The Pronunciation of English in the Atlantic States.* Ann Arbor, University of Michigan Press.

Labov, William (1966), *The Social Stratification of English in New York City.* Washington, D.C., Center for Applied Linguistics.

— (1969), 'Contraction, deletion, and inherent variability of the English copula', *Language* (45):715–762.

— (1970a), 'The place of linguistic research in American society', in *Linguistics in the 1970's* , 41–70. Washington D.C., Center for Applied Linguistics.

— (1970b), *The Study of Nonstandard English.* Champaign, Ill., National Council of Teachers of English.

— (1971), 'Variation in language', in *The Learning of Language,* ed. by Carroll E. Reed, 187–221. New York, Appleton-Century-Crofts.

— (1972a), 'The internal evolution of linguistic rules' in *Linguistic Change and Generative Theory,* ed. by Robert P. Stockwell and Ronald K. S. Macaulay, 101–171. Bloomington, Indiana University Press.

— (1972b), 'Negative attraction and negative concord in English grammar', *Language* 48:773–818.

— (1972c), 'The recent history of some dialect markers on the island of Martha's Vineyard, Massachusetts', *Studies in Linguistics in Honor of Raven I. McDavid, Jr.,* ed. by Lawrence M. Davis, 81–121. University of Alabama Press.

Labov, William and Paul Cohen (1967), 'Systematic relations of standard and non-standard rules in the grammars of Negro speakers', *Project Literary Reports* 8. Ithaca, N.Y., Cornell University (= ERIC ED 016 946).

Labov, William, Paul Cohen, Clarence Robins, and John Lewis (1968), *A Study of the Non-Standard English of Negro and Puerto Rican Speakers in New York City* (= *Cooperative Research Report* 3228). New York, Columbia University.

Loflin, Marvin D. (1967), 'A note on the deep structure of nonstandard English in Washington, D.C.', *Glossa* 1:26–32.

— (1969), 'Negro nonstandard and standard English: same or different deep structure?', *Orbis* 18:74–91.

— (1971), 'On the structure of the verb in a dialect of American Negro English', in *Readings in American Dialectology,* ed. by Harold B. Allen and Gary N. Underwood, 428–443. New York, Appleton-Century-Crofts.

McDavid, Raven I., Jr. (1966), 'Sense and nonsense about American dialects', *Publications of the Modern Language Association* 81(2):7–17.

— (1972), 'Field procedures: instructions for investigators, Linguistic Atlas of the Gulf States,' in *A Manual for Dialect Research in the Southern States,* by Lee Pederson et al., 33–60. Atlanta, Georgia State University.

McDavid, Raven I., Jr. and Virginia G. McDavid (1956), 'Regional linguistic atlases in the United States', *Orbis* 5:349–386.

Marckwardt, Albert H. (1957), 'Principal and subsidiary dialect areas in the North Central States', *PADS* 27:3–15.

O'Neil, Wayne A. (1968), 'Transformational dialectology: phonology and syntax', in *Verhandlungen des Zweiten Internationalen Dialektologenkongresses, Marburg/Lahn, 5–10 September 1965 2,* ed. by Ludwig E. Schmitt, 629–638. Wiesbaden, Steiner.

Pederson. Lee (1971), 'Southern speech and the LAGS Project, in *Dialectology: Problems and Perspectives,* ed. by Lorraine Hall Burghardt, 130–142. Knoxville, University of Tennessee.

— (1972) 'An introduction to the LAGS Project', in *A Manual for Dialect Research in the Southern States,* by Lee Pederson et al., 1–31. Atlanta, Georgia State University.

Pederson, Lee et al. (1972), *A Manual for Dialect Research in the Southern States.* Atlanta, Georgia State University.

Pickford, Glenna Ruth (1956), 'American linguistic geography: a sociological appraisal', *Word* 12:211–233.

Reed, Carroll E. and David W. Reed (1972), 'Problems of English speech mixture in California and Nevada', in *Studies in Linguistics in Honor of Raven I. McDavid, Jr.,* ed. by Lawrence M. Davis, 135–143. University, University of Alabama Press.

Sapon, Stanley (1953), 'A methodology for the study of socio-economic differentials in linguistic phenomena', *SIL* 11:57–68.

— (1957), *A Pictorial Linguistic Interview Manual.* Columbus, American Library of Recorded Dialect Studies, Ohio State University.

Saporta, Sol (1965), 'Ordered rules, dialect differences, and historical processes', *Language* 41:218–224.

Schatzman, Leonard and Anselm Strauss (1955), 'Social class and modes of communication', *American Journal of Sociology* 60:329–338.

Sledd, James H. (1966), 'Breaking umlaut, and the Southern drawl', *Language* 42:18–41.

— (1969), 'Bidialectalism: the linguistics of White supremacy', *EJ* 58:1307–1315, 1329.

Smith, Max D. (1968), 'The dragonfly: Linguistic Atlas underdifferentiation?', *American Speech* 43:51–57.

Smith, Riley B. (1969), 'Interrelatedness of certain deviant grammatical structures in Negro nonstandard dialects', *Journal of English Linguistics* 3:82–88.

Stockwell, Robert P. and Ronald K. S. Macaulay, *editors* (1972), *Linguistic Change and Generative Theory.* Bloomington, Indiana University Press.

Summerlin, NanJo C. (1972), 'The regional standard/standards: variations from it/them in the oral language of lower socio-economic Black and White students in a rural Deep South county'. Paper read at the meeting of the South Central American Dialect Society, Tulsa, Oklahoma, October 26, 1972.

Thomas, Alan R. (1967), 'Generative phonology in dialectology', *TPS* 179–203.

Troike, Rudolph C. (1969), 'Receptive competence, productive competence, and performance', in *Georgetown University Monograph Series on Languages and Linguistics* 22:63–73.

— (1971), 'Overall pattern and generative phonology', in *Readings in American Dialectology,* ed. by Harold B. Allen and Gary N. Underwood, 324–342. New York, Appleton-Century-Crofts.

Underwood, Gary N. (1971), 'Some rules for the pronunciation of English in northwest Arkansas'. Paper read at the meeting of the Midwest American Dialect Society, Detroit, Michigan, November 5, 1971 (= ERIC ED 057 652).

— (1972), 'The research methods of the Arkansas Language Survey', *American Speech* 47:211–220.

— (1973), 'Problems in the study of Arkansas dialects'. *Orbis* 22:64–71.

Van Riper, William R. (1972), 'Shortening the long conversational dialect interview', in *Studies in linguistics in Honor of Raven I. McDavid, Jr.,* ed. by Lawrence M. Davis, 177–183. University, University of Alabama Press.

Weinreich, Uriel, William Labov, and Melvin Herzog (1968), 'Empirical foundations for a theory of language change', in *Directions for Historical Linguistics,* ed. by W. P. Lehmann and Yakov Malkiel, 99–195. Austin, University of Texas Press.

Wolfram, Walt (1971), 'Social dialects from a linguistic Perspective', in *Sociolinguistics: A Cross-disciplinary Perspective,* ed. by Roger W. Shuy 86–135. Washington, Center for Applied Linguistics.

PART TWO

The Sea and the American Frontier

Introduction

Once the aboriginal Indians have been conveniently thrust aside, North American history becomes a study of peoples who first of all came across the ocean and then proceeded west through what was then a relative wilderness. Whatever 'bench marks' (see General Introduction) were laid down by plowmen and planters came later, behind the advance of scouts, trappers, and other frontiersmen. In a sense, of course, sailors had brought them all there and were therefore an important first influence. These sailors and frontiersmen were not the most conventionally moral of human beings, and they are not the ones most willingly referred to in those histories that constitute comfortable repositories of middle-class knowledge. Not only were they less respectable but also they were less homogeneous than the landowners who became the First Families of our various states. They thus appear smaller in our inventories of place names (the man who owned the land having at least some influence when it came to naming the place); and their influence on the lexical lists of farm implements, farm animals, and farm products is smaller than that of the more sedentary population that came after them.

In such matters as the generative rules of the grammar, however, it is difficult — if not impossible — to assign a greater importance to one segment of the population. And, if we look at other areas of the lexicon than the farm and the home, it may well be that the sailors who came into port, drank, and associated with the less respectable women and the cowboys who shot up the town for amusement at the end of a long, boring trail drive may have contributed as much as the farmers and sheepherders whose vices were less pronounced — or at least less public.

It may well be, as Chase suggests in the early pages of his article, that the figurative language of seafaring men was a dominating influence on the usage of the coastal towns of New England. Joanna Carver Colcord (1945) has supported that conclusion, pointing out how landsmen (including businessmen from the Middle West) use terms like *proceed under jury-rig* and *box the compass* without realizing that they have borrowed their phraseology from the sea. She also cautions, however, that landlubbers 'err' in their use of maritime terms (that is, adapt the words and phrases to their own needs and cooccurrence patterns) and that the widespread use of a phrase at sea does not prove that it *originated* there. She stresses, however, the normalizing and leveling effect of sailors' usage:

> . . . it is true that sea language is a sub-dialect of English, that it is common to both American and British seamen, and that it is subject to far less variation than exists between the various English-speaking countries, or even between different sections of the same country. An Australian sailor, for example, can go on board an American vessel and instantly comprehend all the orders given; whereas in the continental United States he would be continually puzzled to know just what was meant by what was said. Americans from both sides of the Mason and Dixon line speak the same jargon when serving in ships (1945:10–11).

Like Chase, Colcord makes a strong case for maritime uses as Americanisms. It may be the merest coincidence, but one term treated in some detail by Chase (p. 120) was condemned as an American barbarism by Dickens. In *Martin Chuzzlewit* (ch. XXVII), Martin cannot understand the American woman, significantly named Mrs. Hominy, when she asks, 'Where do you hail from?' It would seem that the maritime usage *Hail from* had by that time penetrated to some Americans but not to all Englishmen.

Among the American sea-influenced terms were, surprisingly, a couple characteristic of that U.S. invention that became international, the telephone. Bryan (1926:261–262) recounts how:

> 'Hello!' as a preliminary call-word in telephone talk, was first heard in the Menlo Park laboratory when Edison was developing a transmitter for Bell's invention, and from Menlo was carried over the world. Bell's original call-word was 'Ahoy!'

The New York *Evening Post* for August 5, 1922, deprecated the loss of 'pleasantly agitating . . . nautical associations'.[1] The term *trick* was, in the 1940s, used for 'the day's work of any one operator' (Dills 1941:133). The sea term also had a familiar application in the sense 'a prostitute's customer' or 'a stint by a prostitute', one or both of which may have been instrumental in driving the telephone expression out of use.

Neither Chase nor Colcord, nor any of the other standard writers on the English of the sea (Granville 1962; Falconer 1805; Barrere and Leland 1889; Grose 1785; Kahane et al. 1958; Layton 1955; Matthews 1935, 1937; Yule and Burnell 1903) have emphasized the maritime variety known as pidgin English as much as has — to take the extreme case — Dillard (1975a). Nearly all of these writers have, however, given examples of pidgin in nautical usage; and a very great deal more data can be gathered by consulting the writings of sailors and travelers who were not trying to place any dialectological bench marks. If these amateur observers lacked something in transcription skills, they perhaps compensated in impartiality: they had not predetermined where the bench marks were to be laid,[2] and therefore were not tempted to prejudice the data so that the markers might fall on the appropriate spots.

It would be virtually impossible to give even a representative sample of the vast amount of data available on pidgin English at sea. (See some of the comments in the introduction to the last part of this book.) Some examples are given in Dillard (1972, especially ch. III; 1975a 1976a). Many others are provided in articles by Ian F. Hancock (1969, 1972, 1976) and William A. Stewart (1967, 1968, 1970, 1972). Many more will be found in Hancock's dissertation (1971).

As it is, there is unfamiliar material enough in the writings of those who have dealt with maritime usages without dealing with pidgin English. Chase's article, although by no means the best available in terms of linguistic sophistication, is more detailed than other treatments and has not been generally known nor easily available. The articles by Berger and by Ivey-Dillard, written especially for this collection, are much more limited than Chase's treatment and more specific in their focus. Nevertheless, they do seem to complement Chase's treatment.

The article 'Sailors' and cowboys' folklore in two popular classics', by Jan Brunvand, illustrates an accident of authorship of a type that must be more frequent than is usually admitted. My Chapter IV of *All-American English* (Dillard 1975a) was based on an unconcious memory of the article, which I had read some eight years earlier. It was much less than a photographic memory that worked on that article, however, and my own intervening interests in pidgin English had a strong influence on my handling of Brunvand's comparison between the sea and the Western frontier. Instead of being outraged, Brunvand was tolerantly amused when I finally figured out what had happened — and told him. He gladly agreed to have the article reprinted. By arrangement with him, materials bearing on more specifically linguistic aspects of the sea and the frontier are included in brackets, added by me. Some of these relate, of course, to the use of pidgin English by both groups.

Signaling systems were part of the communication patterns of both the frontier and the sea, and it seems that both of them had special use for nonvocal signaling systems. Semaphore at sea is beyond the scope of this collection, and there does not seem to be a really good article on the use of sign language (taken originally from the Plains Indians) on the frontier. New circumstances, like the frontier, called for some new communication devices in addition to those, like pidgin English, that could be taken over from the sea. Many times, however, those apparently new devices, like the 'Nigger Holler', came from some unacknowledged cultural donor like the many Blacks — freed men, runaway slaves, or slaves of frontier whites — who were much more numerous on the frontier than our prejudiced historians have wanted us to know. (Fairly good correctives can be found in Katz's work [1973].) The article by Hatley and Severance, revised somewhat for this book, represents the work of folklorists, typically trained to deal with living informants and not to consult historical documents. The two authors' use of aged informants recalls the well-known survey projects, with perhaps some of the defects of those. Such an approach is otherwise absent from this collection, however, and it may even be desirable in the interests of impartiality.

I believe that the folklorist and the historian of the sea can make important contributions to the study of American English. The same may be true of the geographer, as represented by Jordan's article. I have chosen to leave unaltered even such imprecise phonetic statements as those about 'soft o' in order to preserve the original point of view from another discipline.

The absence from the literature of any really good works on the frontier has been noted before (Dillard 1975a). In fact, more can be found in the writings of Ramon Adams (1961, 1968, 1971) than in the works of any historical linguists.[3] Since Adams' quasi-dictionary approach does not lend itself to excerpting, it turns out to be virtually impossible to find anything else for inclusion here. (One popular work on the frontier's English, done by a well-known American linguist, could not be used because the author withdrew permission after reading Dillard [1975a].[4]) The frontier had many influences, with such specific varieties as what Bourke (1892) called the 'Arizona dialect'. The one certainty seems to be that there is more to be found out than is now known about the frontier language and that of the West in general.

At the risk of appearing repetitious, one must point out still another 'overlooked' facet of the history of American English. For dialect geographers interested chiefly in extending their 'bench marks' from East to West, there was no historical room for the movements from South to North, or especially for those from West to East like the spread of gambling terms (Dillard 1976a). The imposing waterway consituted by the Mississippi River could not have been anything but a major economic influence on the spreading American society, and the vast numbers of men moving along the river virtually insured that it would have some influence on the developing American variety of English. The prestigious handbooks contain, however, if possible even less about the Mississippi than about the frontier. The short list reprinted here from the Federal Writers' Project in Louisiana admittedly does little to satisfy the immense need for more information about the language of the Big River. One editor's excuse may be that, where a full meal is clearly not attainable, an appetizer may serve at least some purpose.

NOTES

1. See the comment on the frontier use of *ahoy* by Brunvand (this volume: 147).
2. Reinecke (1969:197) observes of the clause *poor boy am I* from Beecher and Harvey, *Memoirs of Henry Obookiah*, 'This exactly tallies with what I once heard an annoyed old Hawaiian woman shout: Dumb are you!' It is, of course, commonplace in post-Chomskyean linguistics that it would require even an observer as skilled as Reinecke an impossibly long time to match, from overheard utterances, even so small a corpus as that recorded for Obookiah by Beecher and Harvey. It is necessary, therefore, to utilize criteria other than those beloved of popular experts (including, occasionally, students who speak the language variety under investigation) like 'I've never heard that!' or 'I hear that all the time'. In my own recent experience, graduate students from another discipline (Education) enrolled in their first Linguistics course insist that they have 'very frequently' heard specific double-emphatic questions: 'ARE you coming or AREN'T you?' (Where all caps indicates overstress).
3. The collection of Philip Ashton Rollins' papers at Princeton seems, unfortunately, never to have been examined with this end in mind.
    It is astonishing how many such verbal comparisons can be found in casual reading about the West. In Wright (1889 /1974/:63) we find a typical example: 'In those days the "hurricane deck" of a mule was not to be despised.' Nautical-Western associations are so commonplace, in fact, that the visitor to Phoenix, Arizona, is hardly even inclined to reflect upon the name of its airport: Sky Harbor.
4. Schele de Vere (1968 [1872]) has a chapter 'The great West', which is rather good on mining terms and not bad in some other respects, although it completely omits any mention of pidgin English. Strangely, Schele de Vere calls *mountain men* 'mountaineers' (very uncharacteristic of the group he is supposedly describing) and does not utilize obvious sources like Ruxton's novels (see Dillard 1976a). Schele de Vere has a chapter entitled 'afloat', although he looked at the 'small number' of 'new words coined, or of old words used in a new meaning and form' by Americans rather than at maritime influence on American English.

GEORGE DAVIS CHASE

Sea Terms Come Ashore

It is a well-recognized fact that the figurative language of a community reflects the interests and occupations of its members. If a citizen of Sidon had written the Twenty-third Psalm, he would have said, 'The Lord is my pilot, he steereth me in safe waters.' Because the Romans were a military people, Terence could put into the mouths of his characters on stage such terms as *convasare* 'pack up the old kit bag' and *verbis protelare* 'set up a barrage of talk'. The automobile today has taught men and women to *park* their overshoes and to *skid* on the ice. A young lady was heard to say of her pet kitten, which was purring faintly, 'His battery is low.' Margaret Haley, in *With Malice Toward Some*, describes one of her hostesses as 'being gracious in all eight cylinders'.

The automobile, so much a part of twentieth-century life, borrows an appreciable part of its terminology (e.g. *fenders*) from seagoing vessels. The car influences our idiomatic usage [e.g. *back seat driver* (a person who tries to extend his authority outside his proper sphere)], but possibly no specialized idiom has ever been so well adapted to figurative use as the language of seafaring. The intricate structure and rigging of a ship and the varied operations of navigation furnish a wealth of terms and expressions. They also appeal widely to the imagination, for they are drawn from a world strange to the landsman and alluring from its mystery and adventure. They form a language of human interest and action, of experience and judgment easily transferred to human relations.

Literature has familiarized us with numerous expressions doubtless of nautical origin which have become better known ashore than at sea, such as *in deep waters* (in severe tribulation); *to pour oil on troubled waters* (to

Reprinted and abridged by permission of the University of Maine Press, Orono. The article first appeared in *The Maine Bulletin,* 44(8), February 20, 1942. Editorial abridgements, due to the great length of the original article, are frequent. Professor Chase's footnotes have often been incorporated into the text within parentheses. A few editorial additions are enclosed in brackets. Full bibliographical information for all works cited in the text can be found in the Reference section at the end of this volume.

soothe, tranquilize), referring to the practice in extremely heavy weather of heaving overboard a bag of oil to form a film on the water near by and prevent the waves from breaking so heavily; *to fish in troubled waters* (to take advantage of other's misfortune); *the sport of wind and waves* (at the mercy of chance); *tempest-tossed*, familiar in its Latin equivalent, *tempestate jactatus; wide a favoring gale* (Latin *vento secundo*); *to stem a tide* (conquer adverse circumstances from heading the bows of a ship directly against the current); and *Davy Jones's locker*, (the bottom of the ocean).

The religious exhorter can readily urge us to sail our fragile bark across the billowy ocean of life and pilot her through the rips and shallows of temptation, guided by the compass of Holy Writ, until at last we cast anchor in the safe and snug harbor of Salvation, bearing home a precious cargo. And the political spellbinder tells us that Thomas Jefferson launched the ship of state and with colors nailed to the mast defended the bulwarks of liberty and democracy.

In those early days of the American 'Ship of State', the people ashore imitated the language with which the sailor, bronzed of face and swaggering in his gait, boasted of toil and adventure and mastery at sea. The storekeeper kept his store shipshape and carried a cargo of A1 stock. The stage driver met with heavy weather and ground swells, the politicians were open and aboveboard, the wives and mothers navigated about their kitchens[1] (the men called them galleys), and everybody turned in at night and was on deck bright and early in the morning. The boys of the younger generation affected a saltier speech and reefed and tacked to their heart's content, while the young women who had found society dull in the absence of sweethearts were glad to welcome them home and hear their suggestions of splices and clove hitches. The whole community talked of sails and spars, of shoals and lee shores and breakers, of steering a straight course or of getting to windward of the other fellow.

A hundred years ago shipbuilding and seafaring were the chief occupations of the coast towns of New England. Even from settlements at some distance from the coast, men came to find employment in the shipyards or on board ship and carried their new-found sea terms back to their inland homes. Also as time went on, many families became tired of the hardships and dangers of the sea, the menfolk wearied of passing their lives apart from their families, the women dreaded an early widowhood. The country was rapidly developing westward, and families bred to the sea joined in the pioneer movement to Illinois, Michigan, and Wisconsin. Later, the War between the States struck a mortal blow to deep-water shipping, and the coast population turned to the inland cities of New England and New York. In all these ways nautical language was carried to the interior.

To be sure, as its expressions became familiar over a wider area, the exact meaning of the nautical figures was often lost or obscured. Thus Della T. Lutes, brought up in South Michigan in a family that had migrated from the East, writes, 'Lest you should think an apple dowdy all *straight sailing.'* If she had been brought up on the Atlantic Coast, she could have said 'plain sailing' (originally *plane sailing*, that is, navigating by ocean charts, as distinguished from sailing in sight of land) or 'clear sailing' but not 'straight sailing'. People heard of giving a wide berth to an unreliable person but did not always realize that *berth* referred to the position of a ship at anchor and included the space through which she might swing from wind and tide, and endanger other craft by fouling them. A vacillating, unreliable person was said to *back and fill*, a handy expression describing a recognized maneuver of square-rigged vessels in working their way down narrow passages where their chief progress was from the help of the current, adopted by people who had no notion that the figure was that of a ship now making progress with sails full and now aimlessly drifting with sails aback, i.e. filled on the wrong side. A university professor, reared in inland New Hampshire, was familiar with the expression but associated it with a tipcart backing up and filling at a gravel pit.

For a terrestrial population, maritime origin is often obscured. *Ship*, for example, is beyond question a nautical term in origin, and no one will question its transferred use when we speak of 'shipping' goods by rail. On the other hand, it requires at least some reflection for us to realize that *bill of lading* is nautical in origin and that *floating debts* and *sinking funds* suggest the sea.

Many terms originally nautical in meaning acquired their transferred meanings before the English language came to America. The earliest English use of the Norman French *voyage* applied only to the sea, although it was soon extended in meaning. Terms from Dutch, like *yacht*, *boom, deck, skipper, caboose,* and *cruise* have relatively long histories in English and relatively obvious nautical associations. The last, however, no longer means 'to scour the seas' as it once did; we can now say 'I have been cruising about town.'

The story that the first conductor on a New Jersey railway was a retired sea captain and that he was the first one to call out 'All aboard!' is potentially true, however apocryphal the details may be. The railroads, at first built near the coast, were manned largely by people of seafaring experience who transferred sea terms to trains, so that they called their roads *railways* and *shipped* goods, and conductors *ran* their trains, i.e. directed and controlled them — a causative use of *run* in the sense of manage which was definitely nautical. *Run* came to be used in a great variety of expressions at sea, such as *run afoul of, run across, run around, run down, run alongside, run athwart,* and *run astern,* all of which are now on shore. We *board* a train — as well as *ship* something on it — and are then *on board*, which originally referred to the deck of a ship. We have also borrowed *trip, passenger, fare, freight, berth,* and *cabin* on a sleeper. Tender, the fuel car attached to a locomotive, comes from *tender*, a supply or service boat accompanying a ship; and *caboose* [*camboose*, among other forms, in early attestations like James Fenimore Cooper, *sea-lions*, 1912:389], which we took from the Dutch as an alternative term for the galley or kitchen on a ship, was transferred to the car on a freight train reserved for the train crew.

I. LAUNCHING

Because the lay reader's unfamiliarity with shipping limits his understanding of how much of our vocabulary is originally nautical, I have decided upon a presentation that follows a ship's experience from launching through the process of getting out to sea. When a ship is built, first her lines are laid down, that is, architectural drawings of the hull are made; and then her keel is laid on the *ways* or *railways* — parallel timbers inclined toward the water. As the hull progresses, it is blocked and shored up and surrounded by staging. This whole structure is called the *stocks*. When the hull is completed, the blocks and shoring are knocked away and the ship is allowed to slide down the ways into the water, or is *launched*. Sometimes, if she does not slide down readily, it is necessary to *grease* the ways, as we say of the use of money, gifts, or bribes to assist in the launching of a political or business enterprise. While she is building, she is *on the stocks* or *off the ways*. A ship built for speed was a *clipper*, or *clipper-built*. Warships were heavy and solid, *frigate-built*. Whaleboats, built with overlapping strakes, were *clinker-built*. The familiar colloquial references to a woman's build are reflections of a partly obsolete nautical term.

After the ship is launched and rigged she has tout papers; that is, she is enrolled at the custom house of a port of entry by her agent, who swears to her ownership and description. She is said to *hail from* that port; derivatively, we ask 'Where does that chap hail from?' In foreign waters, she sets her national flag (colors) at her spanker peak. This was called *showing her colors*, a phrase in common use for taking a stand upon a debatable issue. The expression gains something from the fact that the action by a ship was most significant in time of war.

Upon enrollment, a vessel is *in commission*, that is, permitted to engage in commerce or to sail from port to port. If she is permanently disabled or tied up, she is *out of commission*. Of course, she may be *put out of commission* (disabled by an adversary). Every vessel is given an official rating for insurance purposes, which must be renewed periodically following inspection. The highest rating, or *first-rate*, is A1 or, as it is often called, *A Number One and a dot*.

Occasionally a vessel was put in *dry dock* for conditioning or current repairs, such as caulking, scraping, and painting the hull. She was then said to be *hauled out*, or, less often, *hove down*. These terms refer to earlier conditions, before dry docks came into use, when vessels were smaller and were actually beached and hove on their bilge for repairs. The work on the bottom had to be done at low water, which lasted only a few hours at a time. It was not the pleasantest of jobs to crawl under a vessel and work overhead on planking that was still dripping wet. The worst part of all was the plank nearest the keel, the garboard strake (or streak, as it was commonly corrupted), which was popularly called *hell*. Pitch softened by heating was often used to smear over or *pay* the seams. So the expression arose, 'There's hell to pay,' meaning 'There's tough work to be done.' In time, the expression was softened down to 'There's the devil to pay.'[2]

In the winter season, when the rivers and smaller harbors of New England were frozen up or when there was lack of business, existing vessels used to *haul up* or *be hauled up*, or *laid up;* the last is now used of a person who is physically incapacitated. It meant about the same thing to say that the ship was *tied up* to a wharf; applied to a person today, it means that he (or, usually, she) has a prior engagement. When a vessel started again in the spring, she had to be thoroughly *overhauled*. The term apparently applied first to the ropes of running rigging, to see that they were not tangled but running smoothly. In that sense it was used of any ropes or tackles that might get tangled. Next, overhaul meant to examine thoroughly and make necessary repairs on sails, standing rigging, and hull. Also, to overhaul another vessel was to overtake her, originally for the purpose of investigation in war time. Figurative uses of the term in other domains (for example, a baseball team that has been second in the pennant race overhauling the leader in the last few games) are familiar in many nonmaritime contexts.

After enrollment, the captain of a vessel, whose official title was *master* but who was always addressed as *Captain* and spoken of as *The Old Man* (a term often applied to the head of any concern) regardless of age was familiarly called *skipper* — now used for 'the boss' in many activities. The lower-ranking members of the crew *shipped* or *signed on*. At the end of a voyage they *signed off*. The crew, or common sailors, were said to *go before the mast* because they lived forward in the forecastle, while the officers lived aft in the cabin. The crew were called *hands*, and the whole crew were *all hands,* though sometimes the term was extended to include the officers, as 'all hands were lost'. The cook, addressed as *Doctor*, occupied an anomalous position, being neither an officer nor a member of the crew. Therefore, the complement on shipboard *all told* (i.e. counted) was somewhat facetiously called *all hands and the cook*. (The expression *not worth a Hannah Cook* [of no value], may derive from *a hand and a cook*.) The cook occupied a respected position, though many jokes were played on him which he was expected to take good-naturedly. The epithet *son-of-a-seacook* was offensive though meaningless.

After being fully manned, a vessel was prepared to engage in commerce. A ship went on a voyage to a foreign port. A coasting vessel made a trip to a domestic port. *Trip* is often used ashore to denote a passage one way; hence a *round trip*.[3] A person not signed up as a member of the crew was sometimes taken one way and allowed to *work his passage*. When a vessel engaged to carry a cargo she *chartered*, as one now charters a team or a bus; that is, she entered into a written contract in very precise terms.

Being loaded and have completed all her business in port she *got her clearance papers* (authority to leave port) or *cleared out*; carried ashore, the latter term is a rather scornful command to depart, roughly equivalent to 'Scram!' After all formalities had been complied with and officers and crew had *embarked*, last of all the captain went aboard and at the first opportunity the vessel put to sea, *rigged out*. The last-minute warning on passenger boats before the gang-plank is pulled, 'All ashore that's going ashore', is often used on shore more or less facetiously as a hurry-up warning.

A less fortunate vessel is often *anchored* because of conditions over which she has no control. So when a person is anchored in a town or a position, by ties of family or property, he is forced to stay there though impatient to get away. If he is forced to, or chooses to, settle down in a place he may *cast anchor* or *drop anchor* there. In the early days, cables were used to hold the anchor on a ship. The inboard end of the cable, which was attached to the bitts, was called the *bitter end*; nonnautical usage has crossed this expression with bitter, (unpleasant to the taste). When, however, the cable was let out to the bitter end, there was nothing more to be done; if worse came, the cable would carry away and the ship could drift ashore.

When a vessel at anchor *got under way*, that is, assumed controlled progress, she was *making headway*, or progress and proceeded to *make sail*. The whole procedure of departure was to *set sail*. The expressions *weigh anchor* and *get under way* from close association, are often confused, and a ship is erroneously said to *get under weigh,* which is meaningless.

The anchor was often *fouled,* by being caught on the bottom or entangled in the chain. A tangled rope was also *fouled* or *foul.* The bottom of a vessel was *foul* if it was covered with barnacles and sea vegetation. A vessel at anchor, or unmanageable, might *run afoul* or *fall afoul* of another vessel or object if she drifted against it and became entangled with it. On shore, one person may run afoul of another, a meeting that usually involves some kind of disagreement or difficulty.

In the later days of sailing vessels, the shipping was mostly confined to a few deep harbors and to large-sized vessels. These rarely sailed in and out of rivers and harbors, but depended upon tugs to tow them to and from their wharfs and anchorage. They took a tug, or were *taken in tow* when still well out to sea. We might compare the usage in which a rather large man may be taken in tow by a small but deceptively powerful girl.

In earlier times, however, vessels were smaller, many smaller harbors were still in use, and towboats were rarely available. Vessels were obliged to depend entirely upon sails. Oftentimes they made sail and *shoved off* from the wharf; today, the girl who doesn't want to take the man in tow may command him to 'Shove off!' The navigation in and out of narrow entrances, up crooked rivers, among islands, bars, rocks, and shoals, with tides, tide rips, currents, and baffling flaws of wind, required great skill and alertness until the *fairway* (a straight course, precisely as the term is used in golf) was reached. They started at *flood tide* (under favorable circumstances) when the channel was wider and deeper, and they would be sailing *with the tide* and not *against the tide;* both terms are still used for success or failure in conforming to the fashion. Constantly changing directions with frequent tacks and jibes added to the difficulties of navigation. This sort of sailing was called *close work* and was attended by many *close shaves,* an expression which I am sure has no reference to barbers, or close *calls* i.e. a nearby summons (not nautical) and was conducted in *close quarters,* a figure probably taken from the stations of men on a man-of-war.

In setting sail there was much use of ropes, usually called *lines,* whether large or small. To fasten a rope was to *make fast,* to unfasten was to *cast off.* To make fast halyards, clewlines, etc., without tying a knot was to *belay,* which was used only as a command. *Belay all* was to make everything fast. To raise sails, colors, or any weight by means of blocks or tackles was to *hoist,* which was always pronounced to rhyme with *spliced.* Many usages of the term on shore are, or once were, familiar — as in the command to a cow 'Hoist!' meaning 'Move over!'[4]

In all circumstances it is necessary to keep a *good* or *sharp lookout* at sea, and *lookout* is a thoroughly nautical term. A member of the crew, *the lookout*, was stationed at the bow of the ship day and night to *keep watch* for possible danger ahead. On approaching the shore in *thick weather* (fog, snow, or rain) or in storms, one must *look out for breakers*. 'Look out!' is also a warning call of personal danger and a general caution. In constant movement there is danger from every quarter, from ropes thrown or falling from aloft, from booms swinging and blocks slatting, from sudden lurches or seas boarding; and *look out*! is an oft repeated call, while to keep your *weather eye peeled* or *lifting,* to *keep an eye to windward* was a general precautionary rule. But no one *calls* to give an order or a warning at sea. He always *sings out* in any kind of speaking at a distance. *Call* has only one use at sea, to summon from below. You call the watch, that is, summon the watch below (the crew off duty) to *turn to,* i.e. to come on deck and go to work. When the captain *goes below* to *turn in* (go to bed) at night he tells the second mate 'Call me if it comes on to blow.' Most of these expressions have come to be widely used ashore in the same general sense. To *turn in all standing* was to go to bed without undressing.

To return to our navigating near shore. If a vessel had as many delays in getting to sea as the writer is having, she could miss the flood tide and at *low ebb* might *stick in the mud*. The first expression, metaphorically, means 'in straightened circumstances as to health, bank account, enthusiasm, or the like'; the second means a 'slowpoke' or a 'person of no energy or initiative'. Nothing is so much feared at sea as to be *befogged* (mystified, unable to see one's way clear). The danger is from *running ashore* or *aground* (figuratively, being brought to a halt by an unforeseen obstacle) in shoal water, and being left *stranded* (as, for example, being without friends or resources in a strange city) or even *high and dry* (bankrupt, utterly helpless). In a fog a sailor easily *loses his bearings* (gets out of touch with conditions) or loses sight of visible objects from which he can reckon his position and lay his course. In such a circumstance, he has to *plumb* or *sound out* (used ashore to mean 'fish for information', as in sounding out the boss as to whether he might give a raise if asked) his position by measuring the depth of the water and learning the nature of the bottom by means of a line marked off in fathoms and a lead weight (whence *plumb*) with a concave underside filled with soap to hold a sample of the bottom. When the water is too deep to *fathom* (as a boss's reason for not giving that raise might be hard to fathom) he is *off his soundings*.

Not every expression that looks wet is from seafaring. *Beyond one's depth* and *over one's head* are terms of swimming rather than of sailing. So also to keep one's *head above water*. To be *in deep water,* meaning in difficulties, refers to swimming, for deep water is the safest place for navigation. Deep-water also meant offshore, as a deep-water voyage, i.e. to foreign ports, or a deep-water sailor, i.e. one who sailed on square-rigged vessels.

Lee means shelter. The safest place to anchor is under the lee of the land, for there you are in *smooth water,* where easy progress can be made. Smooth water also makes *smooth sailing,* while *rough water* makes it more difficult to steer a steady course. The side of a vessel away from the wind is the lee side, and in the direction of that side is *to leeward.* The opposite side, on which the wind is blowing, is the *weather* or *windward side,* and *to windward* means in the direction from which the wind is blowing. A landlubber is proverbially inclined *to spit to windward,* not *to face the wind,* and to lack *sea-legs,* a lack also jocularly attributed to intoxicated persons.

If a vessel is sailing *in company* with other vessels, like a girl or boy keeping company with a member of the opposite sex, she always wishes to get to the windward of (obtain an advantage over, outwit) them. In that case she will have freedom of action on the windward side and full advantage of the wind, while she blankets the other vessels and *takes the wind out of their sails.* She is then said to have the *weather gauge* (advantage) or position, on a vessel to leeward, which may be near a lee shore but cannot *bear up* (exhibit fortitude), or haul up closer to the wind, or tack ship without incurring the danger of *running afoul* of the sail to windward. Some metaphorical usages involving *to the windward* also derive from hunting, but the difference is obvious since that position is a disadvantage to one stalking game.

II. GETTING UNDER WAY

While our vessel, all ready for sea, is waiting for her chance to *put out* (figuratively, to start in a given direction with determination) with the rest of the *fleet* (whence, obviously, *fleet of taxis, fleet of trucks,* etc.) it is well to become familiar with some of her more significant parts. The fleet or all the *sail o'vessels* in the harbor is composed of all kinds of craft — *windjammers* as they are called along the coast of Maine — from small coasting *hookers*[5] and old-fashioned clumsy *tubs* to smart, likely schooners and proud, stately ships. Some that boasted of their sailing qualities carried a broom at their masthead as an indication that they could *sweep* (move majestically, in shore talk as well) the seas. These liked to be last to set sail so that they could show off to the rest of the fleet, by sailing past them or *cutting didos* (capers) around them. Maine and Providence vessels were single-decked and had their forecastle and galley well forward to give space for deck-loads of lumber, while others were *double-deckers* (like buses, ice cream cones, or sandwiches) for cargoes entirely under hatches.

The hull of a vessel was her body, strongly *timbered* and *copper fastened*, of vital interest to her welfare and efficiency. Its widest part was under water. As it rose it sloped inward or *tumbled home*. It was a serious fault if it *hogged*, that is humped, or *sagged*, sank in the middle. If a vessel received a shot in her hull below the water, she was *hulled*. If it was at the water line, she was *hit between wind and water*, which was a dangerous injury. If after losing her spars she was abandoned at sea, she was a derelict (used in landlubber talk for an outcast, a moral wreck), a menace to navigation. If she was stripped of spars and rigging after she was no longer seaworthy, and used for storage, etc., she became a mere *hulk*, bulking and unmanageable like a hulking brute of a person.

The deck is the sphere of action, work, and discipline on a ship. To be *on deck* is to be on duty. To be *right on deck* is to be alert and prompt in action, to look alive. To be *always on deck* is to be reliable under all circumstances. Baseball borrows the term: the batter whose turn is next is *on deck*. The one after him was originally *in the hold*, a clearly nautical reference, but popular etymology or popular phonology has reduced the last word to *hole*. (Baseball teams help the process along by providing a dugout in which prospective batters wait.) 'Batter up!' is also consistent with the extended nautical metaphor.

Deck was a comparatively late term in English shipping and, like many others, was learned from the Dutch.[6] In earlier use the Saxon word *board* was used in a more comprehensive sense to designate the planking, mainly of the sides of the hull, for early ships had little or no deck planking. So *on board* and *aboard* refer to the deck, but in most other terms *board* means the side. *Inboard* and *outboard*, as all boating fans know, mean inside and outside. *Freeboard* is the portion of the side above the waterline. *Overboard* was over the side; going there was excessive, as reflected in the popular metaphor *going overboard* on a boy or girl, a new fashion, etc. To *go by the board* (to be completely ruined) comes from being lost over the side, especially of masts and rigging. To *board* a vessel is to go over the side onto the deck; ashore, it can mean to enter a conveyance like a bus or train or even to accost a person. *Above board* (frank and open, honest) comes from the nautical expression meaning 'Above the sides, not concealed from view'.

The keel, the strongest timber in the hull, was so essential to the ship's structure that it is often used metaphorically for the ship itself. It is the bottom-most part of the ship. A ship or a person *on even keel* is steady, well-balanced. A ship that capsizes or a person that faints has, however, *keeled over*.

Halfway between the ends of a vessel was *amidships* or *midships*. Her width at this part was her *beam*. If she was *broad in the beam* (a term also applied to a lady with broad hips), she was stiff; that is, she did not easily keel over. (The analogy with the lady probably does not hold.) She was apt to be slow and hard to *steer*. The rudder was controlled by the *helm*, a horizontal shaft attached to the head of the rudder after the manner of a tiller of a boat. The person steering was said to be *at the helm*, a term borrowed by business and many other activities but also notably by baseball. (In the latter, perhaps inauthentically, it was the skipper — manager — who was at the helm.) Helm was often used to include rudder, as a vessel was said to *answer* or *mind her helm* according to her readiness in responding to the movements of her rudder. The part of a vessel below decks nearest the stern was the steerage. It was used as a storeroom chiefly. In passenger ships it was fitted up for passengers, though it was the least desirable part of the vessel for such use, owing to the greater motion of the extreme end of the hull. Later it was designated the cheapest passenger quarters in any part of the ship. The afterguard in men-of-war was composed of the less efficient members of the crew stationed aft. In the merchant service to *put in the afterguard* meant, like to *bring aft*, to promote a sailor to the position of an officer, which would take him from the forecastle to the cabin. The cabin, situated aft, was the living quarters of the officers. Each officer had his private *stateroom*. The cabin and staterooms were lighted by oil lamps hung in *gimbals* which allowed them to swing freely and preserve an upright position when the vessel rolled or pitched. To put out the light was to *douse the glim*.

A few other terms for parts of the ship contributed to metaphorical usages in nonnautical English. A heavy sea which came over the stern and swept the deck fore and aft might wash all movables overboard and make a *clean sweep* — a term familiar, again, from sports where a team that wins every game in a series with a given opponent makes such a sweep. If a ship at anchor wished to leave in haste or if she was unable to heave up her anchor because of a heavy sea, she sometimes *slipped her cable*; to slip one's cable still has some currency in the sense 'leave in haste'. The smallest spar on a vessel was the *martingale* which was hung downward from the end of the bowsprit and served as a leader for forward stays. It derives its name from a town in southern France and is also the name of a part of a horse's harness that serves a similar purpose. As the word has only the latter meaning in French, it is probable that that rather than the nautical use is the original meaning.[7] In the angle of the bowspirt and stem on ships was a carved human figure sometimes suggested by the name of the ship, sometimes allegorical, as Neptune. It was called a *figure head*, known especially in politics as 'a person holding a sinecure; one whose name is used for display purposes; a puppet ruler'.

III. AT SEA

Life at sea involved hard work, and at best there was the tedium of days and weeks and months on a rolling deck with nothing in sight but sea and sky.[8] The crew was divided into watches which were on duty alternately night and day for periods of four hours (also called watches), except from four to eight p.m., the dog watch, which was split into two periods of two hours each, to make an uneven number of watches in a day and so alternate from day to day the periods of duty. The watch on duty was called *the watch on deck* and the watch off duty *the watch below*. *Below* meant living quarters, below the deck. It was also used as a hail to those below, 'Below there!' The captain stood no watches, except on smaller schooners that carried only one mate, but was *on deck* in all times of doubt or danger, and the cook had all night in. The watch below was aroused out every eight bells (four hours) and invited to *show a leg* (hurry up and get out of bed)[9] or *tumble up* and *turn in*.[10]

Among the many concerns of all the crew from the captain to the lowliest deck hand was to keep the ship from *running aground*. Figuratively, of course, that expression can mean failure in business, politics, or almost any other activity; even a love affair can run aground. A ship, like another enterprise metaphorically considered, could *spring a leak*. If it happened, literally, at sea, there was no remedy, as the bottom could be reached neither from the outside nor from within. She was sheathed inside and her cargo usually made it impossible to reach her bottom. Never a day passed at sea but the pumps were tried. If she sprang a leak it was a question of whether the water could be pumped out as fast as it ran in, and the ship kept *above water*; the same phrase means 'solvent' for even the most landlocked of businesses. The ship, or the business, needed to be kept *afloat*, in hope of *reaching port*. Either could be *swamped* and finally *sunk*. Either could *founder*. Even without leaks, the ship faced the danger of storms at sea. Sometimes in a storm the ship gave a *lurch* and the cargo shifted to one side and gave the ship a dangerous *list*. If a member of the crew was thrown overboard in a sudden lurch and could not be rescued, he was *left in the lurch*. [Americans of the 1940s, some of them never having heard the nautical term, heard the sad popular song 'Boo Hoo' with the phrase: 'You left me in the lurch; you left me waiting at the church.[11]]

Complete disaster at sea — if not in romance — was shipwreck, when a ship ran upon the reefs or shore and *went to pieces*. (As far as that is concerned, many of those left in the lurch in the sentimental songs of Tin Pan Alley claimed to have gone to pieces.) In terms of insurance she (the ship, not the jilted fiancee) became a *total loss*. The captain was said to *wreck* his ship or *cast her away*; only the second phrase applied to a girl friend. The *wreck* was *broken up, distressed*, or worse, by the action of the sea or lover, as the case may be, and floated off — the ship as *wreckage*. The crew (of the ship, obviously) became *cast-aways*, sometimes on coasts or islands from which escape was difficult. They were sometimes said to be *marooned*, though that term applies properly only to men purposely abandoned on lonely islands by pirates or mutineers.[12]

A ship *in distress* — which a maiden could also be — or peril at sea might throw overboard or *jettison* a part of her cargo. If it floated it was called by the old Norman terms of marine law *jetsam and flotsam*, and might be *salvaged* by fortunate finders. Particularly since World War II, *salvage* has been applied to the reuse of minerals even though they may never have formed part of a ship's cargo.

Sailors knew other types of distress. The chief source of sickness at sea was improper food. Canned foods were unknown and there was no refrigeration. Fresh vegetables were hard to keep — potatoes lasted longest — and on long passages the supply of food ran out. There was no fresh meat for the crew, who were fed in a separate *mess* from the officers. As an antiscorbutic, English ships served lime juice, bringing the sobriquet *limejuicers* or *limeys* to their sailors and then to the entire nation.[13] A meat stew was called *slum gullion*. Ship's bread or *hard tack,* which sometimes got wet or moldy or wormy, and potatoes, as long as they lasted, were other staples of diet. Bread made with yeast was called *soft tack*. *Bully* or *soup and bully,* a corruption of *soupe bouillie*, was served aft. It was apt to be thin, 'so thin you could see the bottom at 40 fathoms'. The recipe was expressed in the rhyme:

'Soupa de bool-yon
Three buckets of water and one onion.'[14]

Plain fare was more popular than fancy, fixed-up dishes, which were contemptuously called *kickshaws* or *manavelins*.[15]

In the wet weather which also often plagued them the sailors dressed as fishermen do, in *seaboots, oilskins,* and *sou'westers*. This was a clumsy dress, especially aloft, but a great protection in rain or snow when standing *trick*[16] at the wheel, a spell of two hours, or on lookout duty forward. In mild weather they wore *dungarees*[17] made of coarse cotton cloth of East Indian origin.

The British navy and merchant marine had been harsh in the treatment of sailors. The American service inherited much of the British practice until American admiralty law forbade laying hands on a sailor. The sailors soon learned their rights and could libel a vessel in an American port and cause her delay and expense for physical abuse at sea. But the suggestion of the old practice survived in such terms as *a taste of the rope's end* and *knock the tar out of one*, which ashore became *knock the stuffing out*, both meaning to give a sound beating. To knock *galley west*, i.e. to strike with irresistible force sometimes meant to knock a person down but more often meant the accidental striking of a person or thing by a swinging or flying object, as a boom or block. The origin of the expression is unknown. *Larrup*, to thrash, is said to stand for an obsolete *lee-rope*.[18] To *manhandle* meant to administer physical abuse, to serve 'caps'n-bar hash and belayin' pin soup'.

Ship's officers believed firmly in the old motto, 'Satan finds work for idle hands to do.' The basis of discipline at sea was to keep men employed, and the ingenuity of the mates was often taxed to find employment for the men. They began the day by *swabbing* decks and scouring brass. The sailors learned to make fancy knots and do various kinds of sea artistry, which was called *sailorizing*. A favorite occupation was to make braided mats. These were made from strands of Manila rope cut into short pieces. Their product was called *sennet, sinnet*, or *spunyarn* and the process was *spinning yarn*. Two men worked together in a sheltered place under the forward deck. It was quite, easy work and the sailors relieved the monotony by entertaining each other with long tales of experiences. The expression *spinning yarns* (telling long fanciful tales) was transferred from the labor of their hands to the entertainment of their talk and extended to story telling on other opportunities as in the dog watch on quiet afternoons, on Sundays when they did their week's washing, or in the forecastle when the *watch below* chanced to be awake. The common sailor, wonderfully well portrayed in Joseph Conrad's *The Nigger of the Narcissus*, feared doctors, whom he called *saw-bones*, and suspected clergymen, whom he called *sky-pilots*. One of his own number who was always arguing and creating dissatisfaction was a *sea-lawyer*.[19]

Much of the work on shipboard was done in rhythmic motion, as working the windlass, hauling on ropes, and rowing a boat. It was usual for one sailor to make the time by such cries as 'Yo ho', 'Yo ho ho', 'Heave ho!' etc. He was usually a man with a lusty voice whose cries were not unmusical and were encouraging and amusing.[20] The resultant short stanzas of song were called shanties, or chanties.[21] Many of them were famous and have been published. Well-known examples are 'When Paddy Worked on the Railway' and 'Derby's Ram' (mostly indecent).[22]

When a ship, after setting sail, had *worked out* or towed out of the harbor, *had cleared* the land and made the *offing* and had open water before her, she was *at sea*, headed off shore. From that point on she had *clear sailing* and it was *all plain sailing*. (Note, however, that the phrase was originally *plane sailing*. See above.) When clear of the land it was the captain's duty to begin navigating her in the strictest sense of the term, for she would soon be out of sight of land and *all at sea* (the source of the landsman's term meaning 'bewildered'), a situation quite bewildering to one who was not a navigator. The captain took his *point of departure*, a phrase well known in logical disputation, from the known position. He established his position on his chart and from that determined the exact direction in which he desired to steer, or *laid his course,* or *shaped a course*. He then *set his course* by directions to the helmsman to steer that course, and that direction was relayed to each man at the wheel until the captain changed it. A good helmsman was proud to *steer a straight course*, a term which the landsman took over to mean 'be honest and upright'.

At the same time that the captain set his course he set his taff-rail log, a form of speedometer which registered the number of nautical miles the ship *logged*, or sailed through the water. The terms *log* and *knot*, or nautical mile measured by it, refer to the earlier, more primitive device. The log attached to a reel was thrown overboard. As the vessel moved through the water, it *reeled off* the line, which was marked at regular distances. On shore, the phrase came to mean 'to relate readily at length'. The one throwing the log noted the time and read the speed of the vessel *right of the reel* (glibly, without pause).[23] The reading of the log for each hour of the day and night was recorded by the first mate of the ship in a logbook commonly called the *log*. This diary also recorded all records and important occurrences of the voyage. By reckoning from the reading of the log and from the direction steered, which was called *dead reckoning* (figuratively used for proceeding by intuition), the captain could calculate his position at any time and *steer a safe course* (behave with prudence and circumspection) provided there was no variation of the needle (of the compass) beyond that indicated on the chart, and provided there were no *cross currents* (in other domains, 'disturbing influences, running counter to the determined plan of procedure') which might carry him one side or the other *out of his reckoning* or *set him back* or *ahead*, depending on whether it was contrary or favorable, and provided his ship made no leeway. For if the wind was not dead astern but abeam, or *on the quarter*, that is, abaft the beam, or even a couple of points forward the beam, just enough to give her a *slant* (favorable chance), the ship could *hold* (to) *her course* (continue as planned), and still be carried on an indeterminate distance laterally or *make leeway*. A vessel could make the best speed with the wind on her quarter, for then all her sails would be drawing and she would still be *running free*. If it was in smooth water, the captain would set all sail and *let her fly*, elsewhere a general phrase of encouragement when things were going well.

There was no difficulty in navigating with *fair wind* and *fair weather*. Anyone could be a *fair weather sailor*. Successful navigating required a captain of coolness and judgment and a ship that could sail *by and large*. The latter phrase is widely misused, by people who have no conception of its original significance, to mean 'in general' or 'all things considered'. Large is the French nautical term *largue* 'slacked off, sheeted out', confused in pronunciation with *large*. The phrase means, then, either by, or close to, the wind, with sheets close hauled when the wind was ahead, or with sheets slacked off under a fair wind.

When the wind was ahead it was not possible to steer a course, and the order was 'By the wind'; that is, the helmsman was to steer as near to the wind as he could and keep a *good full on*; that is, keep the sails filled and drawing. The vessel pursued a zigzag course or *made a Virginia fence* in her effort to *eat to windward* or gain a more advantageous position. If the wind was dead ahead, the course was a *dead beat to windward*, or *in the eye of the wind*. On the first tack the captain would *stand off shore*, that is, away from the land, to have plenty of *sea-room*, lest he find himself suddenly *in the breakers* if he stood in too close to shore.

It was often a matter of judgment as to which tack was the more advantageous. The distance from one tack to the next was often called a leg. Two vessels sailing in company were said to sail *leg and leg* if they were evenly matched. The expression is especially used in yacht racing. After sailing a while on *one tack*, a captain might decide that he was *on the wrong tack* and *try another tack*. (The figurative used to mean 'adopt a different policy or attitude', is joined by *at every tack and turn* [constantly, annoyingly often].) He would sail *on and off* or *off and on* with regard to the land. When he was ready to *put about*, he would order 'Tack ship!' The officer on duty then ordered 'Ready about!' and ordered the watch to *stand by* ready to sheet out jibs and topsails, and the *man at the wheel* to keep her off a point or so to give her *better full*, so that she would have headway enough to *come about* on the other tack. For when she *came up in the wind* her sails would no longer draw and she would lose considerable headway, sometimes so much, especially in light weather or rough water, that when she came *up in the wind* she would *hang in the wind* and not *pay off* on the other tack. If she would not pay off she would be *in stays*, or, as it was called on square riggers, *in irons*. The last term came from putting men in handcuffs and shackles, a practice more common on shipboard than ashore.

When all was ready the order 'Hard a lee!' was given, and the wheel was put hard over or *hard up*, i.e. as far as it would go. Transferred to the shore, the last term meant 'at the end of one's resources, especially financial'. The expression goes back to the time when a ship was steered not by a wheel but by a tiller turned in the opposite direction to the rudder, i.e. to leeward. A wheel on the order 'Hard a lee!' when it is desired to bring the vessel up into the wind, is at first confusing to a landsman. In the same way the order 'Starboard your helm!' meant to turn the wheel and rudder to port and so change the direction of the vessel to the left, and 'Port your helm!' meant to steer to the right. In rough waters the waves tend to throw a ship's head off and stop her headway so that she will not come about, or if the wind is light she may not tack. In that case it is necessary to *wear ship*, that is, instead of tacking, to *keep off* (from the wind) until she describes nearly a circle, jibes, and comes up to the wind on the other tack. This operation requires plenty of sea-room and it is impossible in close work.

In sailing by the wind it is always necessary to *trim the sails* (adapt one's course to circumstances) as flat as possible, that is, as nearly in line with the keel as they can be drawn. That is done by shortening or trimming the sheet, the rope attached to the outer corner of a sail, which is done as the vessel comes about, when the sails are not filled. After she fills away on the other tack it is very difficult to trim the sheets against the wind. On square rigged ships the same result is achieved by swinging or *bracing* the yards. A yard unevenly braced or hoisted was said to be *cockbilled*. To sail close to the wind the yards must be *braced up* (figuratively used for 'stiffening one's resistance or effort'), which takes the whole strength of the watch. The inner corner of the sail, or the tack, had also to be trimmed. The order on ships was 'Aboard tacks!'

In a dead calm a vessel cannot be steered; she *drifts* and swings about *to her own head* — the first phrase being used figuratively to mean 'without purpose or direction' but the second being more nearly 'willful, stubborn'. Also in a gale of wind it is sometimes impossible to carry any sail and the vessel runs *under bare poles*. She then may be driven *off her course*. The last phrase has metaphorical application in a number of other fields.

A vessel was rigged in such a way that her masts were *stayed*, that is, held in place by her standing rigging, the loss of any part of which would weaken the whole structure. The shrouds and backstays, firmly attached to the sides of the vessel, held the masts and topmasts laterally, while the forestay from the end of the bowsprit to the foremast head held the foremast from falling backward, and the *mainstay* (not the principal one at sea, but only the stay to the mainmast; ashore it becomes 'the principal one'), in turn, running from foremast head to mainmast head held the mainmast in place. The masts were set on the keel or *stepped* with a *rake* or slant aft so that there was no danger of their falling forward. Pirate craft were low, fast, and *rakish*,[24] so that a pronounced rake suggested speed and trickery. If, then, any one of these stays parted, not only the mast which it held immediately was likely to *go by the boards* (when applied, for instance, to investments the term means 'swept away in irretrievable loss'), that is, over the side, but the others were likely to be carried with it and the vessel was *dismasted* when she was helmless. In early English she was *overwhelmed* (overcome, originally buried by heavy seas) and could only roll in the trough of the sea until a jury mast or temporary makeshift could be set up and under *jury rig* the vessel could be made manageable. When masts were carried away, the immediate danger was that they would pound holes in the vessel's hull as their shrouds and stays would hold them to her side. At the risk of life the lee lanyards that held them had to be cut away at once, a feat which the captain or one of the mates essayed. Working in the *lee scuppers* in a heavily rolling ship is comparable to nothing that the average man ashore ever experiences. The scuppers were the openings along the sides of the deck through which water could run off when the vessel *shipped a sea*. A deeply laden vessel was said to have her scuppers or decks *awash*.

When vessels met at sea, maritime law determined which one had the right of way.[25] If one was closer hauled or sailing by the wind, she held to her course, provided the other was sailing free. In that case the latter vessel must keep clear. This she often accomplished by hauling closer to the wind, or *luffing*. Vessels meeting in mid-ocean often *hailed* each other if they were *within hailing distance* and exchanged greetings and news. Captains often knew what vessels to expect and were so familiar with the sails, spars, and build of other vessels that they could recognize them by the *cut of their jib*. The polite invitation to visit was 'Come aboard!' To come nearer was to *bear towards*. The opposite was to *sheer off*. If ships were bound in the same direction they enjoyed racing, when first one then the other would crowd on sail and *forge ahead*, used by landsmen to mean 'distance competitors'.

It was always a matter of interest if another sail was *sighted,* or *hove in sight* at sea. If she was going in the same direction it was of interest to sail *in company with* her, which perhaps originally meant a race to reach port first, but later merely a trial of speed. If one out-distanced the other or changed her course they were said to *part company*.

Many expressions from naval tactics were used in the merchant service, often in a figurative sense, and in time found their way ashore. In addition to those already cited, there might be mentioned such examples as *sail in* or *into* (to attack, a person, a piece of work, or a plate of food); to *run down* (to disparage, originally to collide with). To be run down, that is, in poor physical condition, is a further extension of meaning. To *bear down upon,* from the naval manoeuver of attacking down the wind, comes to mean 'to be severe with, to persist in an argument'. To *ride* (a person) *down* comes to mean to master an unmanageable sail in furling, then to domineer over one, to break one's spirit or resistance, as 'he rode me down like the spanker'.

To *come down on*, that is, to attack from the windward, means 'to censure, to rebuke, to give one a blowing up'. A fuller expression is to 'come down upon one hot and heavy'. To *close with*, that is, to engage in battle with, to come to grips with, loses its hostile sense and means merely 'to come to terms, to strike a bargain'.

Not by a long shot is varied by *not by a long sight*, which may refer to taking a sight on a cannon, or observation of the sun. To *press into service* refers to the press-gangs in the British navy which brought on the War of 1812. It comes to mean 'to utilize as an emergency measure'. To *spike one's guns* is to forestall an adversary. *Pipe down!* is a command to shut up. *Son-of-a-gun* was originally a term of admiration, a 'thoroughbred'. It was said to derive from the days when wives were permitted to travel on their husbands' ships in the British navy, with the result that children were sometimes born at sea on long voyages. In more recent times it has become confused and used interchangeably with another term of very different origin [*son-of-a-bitch*] and connotation, which a present-day ultrarealism is allowing to appear in print.

Filibuster (to smuggle munitions of war to revolutionaries), has come directly from the navy to be used in legislative bodies to mean 'to employ tactics to prevent a bill from coming to a vote'.[26]

A *gadget* was any small, ingenious, manufactured article. In recent years it has come to be used ashore in this sense.

IV. THE RIGGING

It used to be said that a man who followed the sea must go one voyage to sea to *learn the ropes*. This in its literal sense was something of a task, for a five-masted schooner carried seventeen sails and a large ship many more, while each sail had on the average three ropes on the deck. These all had names which were, for the most part, descriptive enough though bewildering in their multiplicity. But to learn the ropes meant, in a wider sense, to learn all the parts of a ship and all the operations of seafaring, and for all this a voyage was not too long. It was this extended maritime sense which gave rise to the general meaning 'become familiar with the details of a business or occupation, understand the ins and outs of something complicated'.

A sailor had to learn to do many things that required skill and experience, and he could be sure if he was a green hand that he was observed with more or less amusement by the older men. Hoisting the lighter sails was comparatively easy. One or two men hauled directly on the halyards *hand over hand* or *hand over fist*, as fast and as easily as a lucky businessman makes money hand over fist. But some of the work was much heavier. If the last few yards hoist of the mainsail peak halyards was too much for the crew, a watch-tackle, or portable set of rope-and-block purchase, was attached to the halyards to *jig it up*, i.e. to raise with a quicker motion. The blocks were not many yards apart. If they came together, were *chock-a-block*, they could not go any further and it was said 'the *jig is up*'. [The phrase means 'nothing more can be done', but most readers will identify it with the speech of comic-strip gangsters caught in the act by the intrepid detective.] To *be jiggered* was to be treated forcibly and rapidly.

The sailing officers had to learn the signs of the weather, i.e. be *weather-wise*. The *glass*, that is, the barometer, was constantly watched. In earlier days it was the mercurial barometer which was later replaced by the more convenient aneroid barometer, which was still said to *go up* or *fall*, though the indicator moved in an arc. Most of the weather terms worked their way ashore though some had been brought from foreign waters. The *typhoon*, two Chinese words meaning 'big wind',[27] came from the China Sea. *Tornado*, Spanish and Portuguese for 'a return'[28] came from tropical waters. *Cyclone* was a book name for similar storms at sea. *Hurricane* is a word of Caribbean origin that sailors carried to all tongues of western Europe. To blow with hurricane force is to blow *great guns*, probably from the noise of a storm at sea, when a sail blown out of the ropes goes with the report of a cannon, and the general uproar is deafening. From this, the expression *Great guns!* comes to be used as an exclamation of surprise. A *dead calm*, sometimes used of an unnaturally quiet group like an unimpressed audience, was called a *white ash* breeze when a ship was *becalmed* and could make progress only by rowing. *White ash* refers to the wood of the oars. [A more customary peril is indicated by the phrase to *weather a storm*. One who did not was *under the weather*. In the figurative meaning 'indisposed, not quite well' the phrase is called 'originally U.S.' by the *Oxford English Dictionary* — which again misses the nautical point.]

Seafaring people did not always depend upon official sources for their geographical terms. *Down East*, for example, meant the State of Maine. In general, *up* and *down* as geographical terms meant 'north' and 'south', but in nautical parlance *down* is often contrasted with *out*. *Down* was a coasting term meaning along the coast line from a given starting point, while *out* meant away from the coast line. Thus *out east* meant the East Indies and *out west* was the region away from the coast when the seafaring people of New England migrated inland. In the old days of the slave trade to the west coast of Africa, ships sailed from the Atlantic ports of the United States, including New England, a course to the north of the trade winds, heading directly for the Cape Verde Islands. Returning they steered a westerly course through the Trades for the West Indies and thence northerly to the point of departure. The whole voyage described a triangle[29] of which the middle leg from Africa to the West Indies continued in later times to be called *The Middle Passage*.[30]

The officers of all vessels of U.S. registry were required by law to be American citizens. There was no such restriction for the crew, who in the larger schooners and in the deep-water craft were mainly foreigners who had never lived in the United States.[31] Many had little knowledge of the English language, but they were never allowed to use a foreign language when on duty or in the presence of an officer.[32]

Whaling and fishing were branches of seafaring and their terms were familiar aboard merchantmen and often used in a figurative sense. So either directly or indirectly they made their way ashore. In addition to the expressions already mentioned, a few of the better known may be added. Everyone knows what a *poor fish* is, and to many a *school of dog-fish* is a significant term, 'a crowd of urchins, a large family of small children'. A cargo of fish was the *fare*; a *full fare* was a full cargo. A profitable catch of seined fish was a *good haul*, figuratively 'a lucky or profitable stroke' as in 'the burglar made a good haul'. Over-greedy fish would take *hook, bait, and sinker,* like gullible persons. Some fish were fond of jumping suddenly high out of the water. If they were large like sturgeon they made a *big splurge*, figurative for 'a great display of wealth'. The sarcastic expression *a pretty kettle of fish* has in origin nothing to do with a kettle but refers rather to a kiddle or fish trap. A whale was used as a symbol of superlative size, so that *a whale of anything* was anything extremely large.

When a whale was struck, the long rope attached to the iron of the harpoon was made fast to a post in the stern of the boat called the *loggerhead*. If the whale bolted till the line was all run out, he was then *at loggerheads* with the boat; it is obvious how this expression came to mean 'in a stubborn disagreement' or 'in a controversy'.

Before vessels were required by law to carry mechanical horns for use in fog or thick weather, the straight tin horn blown by mouth was the usual means of warning at sea. This foghorn was brought ashore and metamorphosed into a fishhorn used by the fish peddler as his street cry. Applied to the nose when blown, it used to be said to a person with a cold in head, 'Blow your horn if you don't sell a fish.' [Mark Twain, in his delightful exploration of Nevada slang in 'Buck Fanshaw's Funeral', has the rough miner Scotty, trying to communicate with the Eastern minister whom he wishes to preach the funeral sermon, use the phrase 'Go in and toot your horn if you don't sell a clam.'] Clams are dug at low tide. *Happy as a clam at high water* expresses a sense of security and satisfaction. Inlanders shorten this to 'happy as a clam'. [Sexual symbolism may not be entirely irrelevant to their reinterpretation.]

V. MAKING PORT

Until the end of the Civil War coasting vessels were small and often unseaworthy. They averaged from 30 to 300 tons burthen and were engaged in miscellaneous trade, carrying lumber, ice, granite, and paving stones south, and bringing coal and pig iron north. They were looked down upon by deep-water sailors who called their crews *cow sailors*, because along the coast of Maine they farmed part of the year, or *appletreers* because they never got beyond the range of their apple trees ashore. They seldom trusted themselves to storms at sea but dodged along the coast from harbor to harbor watching their chance of fair weather to make a passage. They could anchor almost anywhere under the lee of the land in calms or storms and wait for a breeze with their lower sails still set, or *ride out a storm* in a comparative safety. The phrase for 'holding one's own during a period of stress' comes, obviously, from that nautical expression. Their navigating consisted chiefly in being weather-wise and knowing intimately every detail of the coast and where to *make for* a harbor — the source of a landsman's phrase like 'make for home'. Their motto was *any port in a storm*. They often lay in harbor *weatherbound* by headwinds or calms for days at a time. Terms like *haven* (a protected place of shelter and repose) and *harbor* (keep alive, e.g. harbor a grudge) are alive on shore, partly revived by literary usage, although the literal usages have long been out of fashion at sea.

After the tedium of a long passage the thought of reaching port was most pleasant. Fresh provisions, all night in, vegetation, new faces, were appealing. The relaxation was often disastrous to the morale of sailors and led to intemperate indulgence. A sailor after landing was soon *half seas over* (partly drunk), if not *three sheets to the wind* (drunk and rather uproarious). Even the captain was tempted on occasion to *splice the main brace* (take a drink). A *land fall* (arrival at the place aimed at or sought), was hailed with interest and satisfaction. The hardships and mishaps of the months past were accounted as *all in the course of the voyage*. It did not matter if they were *short handed* (lacking a sufficiency of help) from sickness or accident, they were in sight of land and their whole thought and attention were directed forward. Their first interest was to look for *land marks* (historic or distinguishing objects). To *see a light* (thus, figuratively, 'to comprehend') by night or a headland by day would soon help to *get their bearings* (establish a relationship, whether literally according to position and direction or figuratively with relation to people and issues). If the weather was thick they were often obliged to *take their soundings* (figuratively, to test out the views, beliefs, and attitudes of the people with whom one finds himself in contact), that is, their position with relation to the shore. As they approached nearer they could *make out* the entrance to a harbor, and *get the lay of the land* more accurately. They could *pick up* a *leading light* here or a buoy or beacon there as they *opened up*, i.e. brought into view the various features of the coast and harbour.

Even though a captain was quite capable of *piloting* his own vessel, unless fog caused him to *lose his bearings,* he was often required to employ a local pilot. Coasters learned to *steer clear* (avoid) of every danger. To *run on the rocks* was inexcusable except in thick weather, and if the tide caused a captain to *go on the rocks* he long remembered the *rock on which he split*. It was important to *get the drift* (figuratively, discover the general meaning) of the tide in entering a river or harbor. It was better to go in *on the flood*, to go with the tide, in the easiest way, rather than to try to make headway *against the tide* or on the *ebb tide*. In trying to make the entrance to the harbor, if the wind was fair but light and there was a head tide (i.e. on a *wind ebb*), he could not always *make it* or *fetch it* (gain his objective). His chances were better on a *windward flood*, when the tide was making in, even though there was an offshore breeze. In the rivers and bays of Maine vessels were often bothered by water-soaked logs floating with one end out of the water. These were called *tide-walkers*.

Every vessel entering from a foreign port was obliged to *show her colors*, that is, set the flag of her nationality at the mizzen peak. Landlubbers adopted the phrase to mean 'take a positive stand on an issue'. She must also show them on leaving port. They indicated peaceful, lawful intentions and were a claim to protection by the country indicated. A flag set upside down, that is, with the jack down, or set at half mast was a *signal of distress* equivalent to the radio SOS call. In times of war a ship showed her colors as a challenge to a hostile ship. When she *struck her colors*, i.e. hauled them down, it was a sign of surrender, the same as in the figurative language of those ashore. If she *nailed her colors to the mast*, she determined to resist to the end, never to surrender but to go down fighting. The victor came off with *flying colors*; in other endeavors, the sense is mitigated somewhat to 'with creditable success'. To *sail under false colors* was a device to deceive a hostile stranger or a trick of pirates to decoy a prospective prey, more generally 'to disguise one's real sympathy or allegiance'.

As a vessel entered harbor she began to *take in sail* and reduce her speed; in business, the phrase can mean 'to economize'. The method of taking in a sail varied according to circumstances. With triangular sails it was usual to cast off the halyards and let the sail *come down by the run*, that is without check. Its weight would take it only part way down. It was then hauled down to the spar by a *downhaul* or *brail* in the case of a jib, or *clewed up* into small compass, in the case of an upper sail or square sail, by drawing the corners together. The sails were finally *furled*, or tied up into neat parcels which were lashed to spars.

As soon as a vessel cast anchor in her port of destination, the captain hastened to go ashore or make report of his arrival to his consignees. The lashings of a boat were cast off, she was lowered into the water by her davit-tackles, and drawn along side by her painter. Perhaps she was dry after having been so long out of water and would leak. In that case she would be *bailed out*. Her rudder was hung, and she was manned by a crew of sailors who took their seats on *thwarts*, so called because they ran *athwart*, i.e. across the boat or athwart-ships. They were told to *ship oars*. They first inserted pairs of *thole pins* or wooden pegs in the gunnel (gunwale) of the boat, then laid their oars between them preparatory to rowing. The thole pins gave a *purchase* or leverage to the oars. At the order 'Give away!' they began to row. When they were near enough to the landing place, the order 'Way enough!' was given and they ceased rowing. At the command 'Unship!' they took in their oars and laid them lengthways in the boat. A ship's dory was too large to be rowed by a single person though one could *scull* her by a sort of syncopated propeller motion with one oar at the stern. To *back water* was to row backwards. At times it was necessary to abandon a ship at sea and take to the boats. All those in one boat usually shared the same fate; they were either all lost or all saved. Under such conditions it was some consolation to feel that they were *all in the same boat* (figuratively, similarly situated).

If anyone not a member of the boat's crew wished to assist in rowing he could *put in* or *shove in his oar* (figuratively, butt in). In a long pull a boat's crew could occasionally *rest on their oars* (cease effort temporarily). One who did the heaviest share of the work was said to *pull a laboring oar*. A good oarsman could *pull a strong oar*. To *burn one's boats*, like *to burn one's bridges,* meant to take a course from which there was no withdrawing for the landsman but more precisely 'cut off any chance of desertion' to the sailor. A *bum boat* was a small rowboat from which vegetables, fruit, and fish were peddled to vessels while lying in harbor.

Before anyone is permitted to land from a vessel arriving from a foreign port the captain must pass quarantine, that is, make a declaration to the health officers of the port that there is no contagious disease on board and secure *a clean bill of health* (used figuratively for any unqualified recommendation). The captain was also required to declare to the customs officers all dutiable articles on board. The temptation to *smuggle in* cigars and liquors was strong. A vessel engaged in smuggling or blockade running, attempting to enter a port unobserved by the customs authorities or the enemy must watch her chance and steal in when *the coast was clear* (when there was no danger of detection or interruption). A ship had *cubby holes*, small dark closets for odds and ends, and clever places of concealment which often escaped the careful search of suspicious customs officers.

Having obtained permission *to land* the captain put on his *shoregoing clothes* and hastened ashore to report to his consignees that he had arrived and was prepared to deliver his cargo. From that day and hour his *lay days*, that is, time within which the consignees must finish unloading, began to be reckoned. The first mate was left *in charge of the ship*, and this might be for a considerable period, for it was usual for the captain to spend most of his time in port either up town or if it was a home port, at his home, which might be a considerable distance away.

When it came a vessel's turn to dock she took a tow boat when one was available. The tow boat came *alongside* and made fast with bow and stern lines, the better to direct the movements of the vessel. It was a busy time for mates and crew with putting out leaders at every point of contact with the wharf and running lines that had to be changed constantly. With all the noise and confusion a mate had to *beller like a fog-horn* to make himself heard at a distance. Sometimes he might be guilty of a little thoughtless profanity though it took the crew of barges and lighters, or bargees, to swear properly. To *swear like a bargee* was to use profanity that would impress even sailors, and to *curse like a sailor* was proverbial among landsmen.

Before a vessel could *tie up to* the dock she had to be more or less hauled with the capstan. The order to start up the capstan was 'Heave ahead!' to stop was 'Avast heaving!' or simply 'Avast' or 'Vast!' To *heave* referred to the sailors working the windlass by their weight against the capstan bars. They were said to heave the vessel ahead or astern. If the strain on the line was too great the one *holding turn* or *holding on to the slack* was told to *surge,* that is, to slack up on the turn. If he allowed the turn to slip and some of the gain to be lost through carelessness in holding the slack he was reproved. The parting of the line called forth the exclamation 'Surge, old spunyarn!' The rise and fall of the tide was indicated on the piles of the wharf, the low point by barnacles, etc., the *high water mark* (figuratively, the top notch, the height of perfection) by the discoloration of the spikes.

In port the civil day was observed, such of the crew as *stayed by* being employed during the daytime. At suppertime they *knocked off* (were relieved from duty) and were free to go ashore during the evening. The *whole ship's company* was paid off and most of the crew were discharged in port, as their services were not needed. They went ashore with sea-chest or sea-bag of sewn canvas to spend their money and wear off the stain of tar on their hands which did not meet with the approval of their lady friends, at cheap and disreputable boarding houses. These were kept by shipping masters who would board sailors until their money was spent, and even longer. When the shipping master signed them up for a voyage he collected one month's advance wages to pay for what was owed him. This was called a *dead horse*. During the first month out a sailor was said to be *working for a dead horse*. At the end of this period it was the custom of the men in British ships to make an effigy of a horse and throw it overboard with suitable ceremonies.

The worn-out rope, metal and canvas that accumulated during a voyage was called *junk* or *old junk*. This the mate was allowed as his perquisite. In the same way the cook was allowed to sell for soap the fats and grease which he had saved up. This was called *slush*; many organizations now maintain a slush fund that may be expended for graft, lobbying, bribery, etc., without rendering an account of it on the books. The fats and grease used to be used to slush down the masts, but later prepared slush was bought. Its receptacle was called the *slush bucket* or *slush board*. The captain too had opportunities to make money on discounts from the ship's bills for the stores, etc., purchased in foreign parts. This was impossible in ports where there was a business agent for the ship, or *ship's husband* as he was called. Some ships carried a *supercargo,* or officer who had charge of the cargo — not necessarily a superfluous person as he became in shore talk. During the voyage, however, he had little to do and no duties in handling the ship.

In port a ship was infested with various kinds of undesirable people. A *wharf-rat* was a sneak-thief who had to be guarded against night and day. A *landshark* was a money-lender on usurious terms. A *beach-comber* was a derelict sailor who drifted about the water front.

The business of the home port was sometimes conducted by the captain, sometimes by a business agent or *ship's husband*. The captain usually went home and left the mates to *keep ship*. He brought home from foreign ports valuable silks and shawls and chinaware and presents of *scrimshaw work* of bone, ivory, or wood carvings and nests of boxes purchased in the East or whittled out on shipboard to while away the tedium of the voyage and destined to adorn the family whatnot.[33]

NOTES

[It should be understood from the outset that Chase did not restrict himself to 'American-isms' and that inclusion or discussion of a term does not constitute any claim that it is — in any narrow sense, at least.

1. There is more to the sea term for 'kitchen' in American English, especially in the vocabulary of the frontier. There, *caboose*, ultimately from a seagoing Dutch language variety, became first the kitchen and then the provision wagon in a wagon train and finally the last car on a freight train. See Chase's treatment of *caboose* (p. 104).
2. A long-popular etymology traces *the devil to pay* rather to the 'printer's devil' (i.e. low-ranking assistant), a very unnautical concept. Chase's accounting for that term as a 'softening down' of the sailors' term might be supposed to reflect his vested interest in sea terms. In Dr. Alexander Hamilton's 1744 *Itinerarium,* however, there is a comment upon '*the devil to pay and no pitch hot* [an] adage metaphorically derived from the manner of sailors who pay their ship's bottom with pitch' (quoted in Needler 1967:212). The Oxford English Dictionary has earlier attestations of *printer's devil,* but there seems to be no proof that '(printer's) devil to pay' occurred before 1744. Since the nautical 'hell' is near the keel, it might be expected to be a cold place to work, during most of the year, in the Atlantic. This, coupled with the frontier/sea associations discussed espe-cially by Brunvand (this volume) might explain expressions like *It's colder'n hell on them prairies* which seemed puzzling to M. W. Merryweather (1931).
3. *The Oxford English Dictionary* agrees with Chase's supposition that the nautical *trip* came first — using the term *apparently* rather than *certainly* or the like. The editor of this volume has no way of knowing how thoroughly Chase checked the sources available in his own day, and will discuss such matters again only if some really special reason for doing so becomes apparent.
4. In the form *es* (probably reflecting earlier English *heis*) the term is widely used in Krio of Sierra Leone, which has a strikingly great nautical component (see Hancock 1976).
5. Another use of *hooker,* coming more readily to the mind of the reader of the 1970s than to Chase's, also has some nautical associations. For *hooker* (prostitute), the *Dictionary of Americanisms* (Mathews 1951) accepts Bartlett's (1859) explanation: 'A resident of the Hook, i.e., a strumpet, a sailor's trull. So-called from the number of houses of ill fame frequented by sailors at the Hook (i.e., Corlear's Hook) in the city of New York.' Is it too fanciful to guess that the 'small coasting hookers' reinforced this nautical development?
6. In pidgin English, nautical words like *deck* very frequently developed uses on land with related but not identical referents. Captain W. F. W. Owen's *Voyages* (1883; II:58) contains the following example of the use of *decks* in a strictly shoreside context: . . . the two stories or "decks", as the natives called them [were referred to]: "Dat nothing; by by you come back, look um nudder deck." '
7. The OED confirms Chase in these particulars. (The resolution announced in note 3 is broken only because the nautical–horseman relationship of this term would have fitted perfectly into the scheme of Brunvand [this volume] if he had happened to think of it.)

8. Compare the descriptions of the prairie and the comparisons to the sea quoted by Brunvand (this volume).

9. There is a persistent popular explanation that, at one time or another in naval history, women were allowed to travel with the sailors but of course were not required to engage in the work of the ship. At the command 'Show a leg!' a woman could prove her sex and therefore be exempt from further commands. It is perhaps to Chase's credit that he does not even cite this belief.

10. *Turn to* and *turn out* have maritime associations which came ashore. There may very well be some connection between the sea term and *turn out* (indoctrinate a 'square' girl into prostitution). The associations seem far-fetched at first, but see material on *trick*, p. 113.

11. 'Boo-Hoo', by Edward Heyman, Carmen Lombardo, and B. J. Loeb, published in 1937.

12. Chase characteristically omits reference to *maroon* (escaped slave). See also his treatment of *middle passage* and *triangular voyage* (the latter term not really included in his list but alluded to) on p. 121.

13. The *Dictionary of Americanisms* comments that *lime-juicer* (and, presumably, by extension *limey*) is 'regarded as an Americanism . . . but the Australian used it to designate an emigrant newly arrived from England is as early as 1859.' What is documented here is the ultimate irrelevance, especially in maritime expressions, of terms like 'Americanism' or 'Australianism'.

14. Since this couplet is obviously in the context of foreigners' speech, it is possible that *soupa* contains the enclitic vowel so characteristic of contact languages. It is somewhat more likely, as a matter of fact, than some explanation like foreign accent, since French is the foreign language nearest to this context.

15. *Kickshaw* is obviously related to French *quelque chose*, but the earliest *OED* citation (1958) refers to its borrowing by Italians. *Manavelins* is called only 'of obscure origin', but many of the early citations are maritime.

16. See the discussion of this term in Dillard (1975a:32). Dana uses the term 'my trick at the helm' [p. 32, italicized, probably to indicate the technical nature of the usage] and 'neither Stimson nor I gave up our tricks, all the time that we were off the cape'.

17. This word is strangely missing from the standard historical dictionaries.

18. See the article by Margie Ivey-Dillard (this volume).

19. The *Dictionary of Americanisms* lists this term, but the first citation is 1940!

20. See the discussion by Courlander (1963:23–24) of the qualities desired for a song leader of a Black prison work gang, and the comments on singers of 'sea shanties' in Joanna Carver Colcord (1938).

21. See Colcord (1938).

22. It is a commonplace of jazz history that 'The Derby Ram' is the source of 'Didn't He Ramble?' The last line of the latter, famed for its use in New Orleans funerals, varies in different performances from *He rambled till the butcher* [i.e. death] *cut him down* and *He rambled till the women cut him down*. Elaboration of the latter is surely what Chase meant by 'mostly indecent'.

23. In the form *right off* [*sic*] *the reel* this is a well-known colloquialism. The Chase form looks like a misprint.

24. Chase's note asserts that this *rakish* has nothing to do with *rake* as in Hogarth's 'Rake's Progress'. The *OED* considers this point more doubtful.

25. The *OED* gives, but with a quite late date, the phrase in the sense of privilege of passing through another's property. The maritime sense, although very probably related, may well have existed earlier. In America today, the phrase would of course be understood to refer to automobile traffic.

26. Virtually every work on American English has traced *filibuster* from the Dutch *vrijbuiter* by way of 'Spanish'. For objections on the grounds of, especially, the initial consonant cluster development (*vr-* to *fil-*) see Dillard (1976a:38–39).
27. There is, as often, more of an international character to the history of this word than Chase knew. See the *OED* entry.
28. Chase's etymology for *tornado* is, of course, extremely naïve. In either Spanish or Portuguese, the sememe for 'twist' is more likely than that for 'turn' as a source. There is, however, as in many cases with maritime words, little certainty about the exact development. See the *OED* entry. Linguists will recognize many failings of this sort in Chase's article, and it has not been the editorial intention to point out all of them. Some of the more extreme examples have, however, been excluded in the abridging process.
29. The 'triangular voyage' of the slave trade, like many other expressions peculiar to and stemming from the consequences of that trade (see Dillard 1977) does not appear to be mentioned in the historical dictionaries.
30. Chase, like almost all other writers, glosses over the slaving implications of this term.
31. The heterogeneous and polyglot nature of ships' crews has been frequently pointed out. Hancock (1976) cites B. Traven's *The Death Ship;* others cite *Moby Dick,* Chapter 27, where it is asserted that 'at the present day not one in two of the many thousand men before the mast employed in the American whale-fishery, are American born, though pretty nearly all the officers are.' See note 32.
32. The requirement that English be used, plus the fact that few crew members knew it as a native language, of course promoted the use of a contact variety (i.e. pidgin English). While superficially the large number of native languages involved makes for extreme diversity, there is a deeper sense in which a kind of homogeneity is encouraged: a solution to the language problem, once found, spreads with great rapidity. See, as a perhaps extreme example, the discussion of *waddy* in Dillard (1975a:130) and the comparison of maritime terminology to cowboys' language (Brunvand, this volume).
33. A work by a scholar who collaborated to some extent on Chase's article, Joanna Carver Colcord (1945), utilizes much of this material in a rather different format. She also comes to conclusions differing from those of Chase. In a few cases, such as her confusing *caboose* with *calaboose*, her derivations from Chase seem unfortunate. In compensation, she offers some materials not found in Chase. Especially interesting are some forms that she traces to pidgin English:
Changee for changee 'Let's exchange'
Three-piecee bamboo 'a three-masted vessel'
So-fashion 'thus'
Joss-pidgin 'church forms and ceremonies' (the first word from the Portuguese for 'god', widely used in Chinese Pidgin English)
    In addition, she comments on *vamoose* as a contact language form brought by sailors see Dillard 1975a:127) and makes no decision between Portuguese *abasta* 'enough' and Dutch *houd vast* for *vast/avast*. Kahane et al. (1958:100) indulge in the same kind of hesitation, although the Dutch derivation seems to have little to recommend it.
    In view of Brunvand's demonstration (this volume) that Western plainsmen adopted maritime terms like *prairie schooner* and *prairie ship* for their wagons, it is interesting that Colcord reports '*Wagon.* A sailor's cant name for a ship.'

MARGIE IVEY-DILLARD

Larrupin': From Nautical Word to Multiregionalism

According to Chase (this volume) and such dictionaries as have treated the matter, *larrupin'* is a word of maritime origin, originally *lee rope*. (Colcord [1945] was skeptical.) The *Dictionary of Americanisms* omits the term entirely, and the *Oxford English Dictionary* dismisses it rather lightly. Partridge's (1970) *Dictionary of Slang and Unconventional English* records *'larrup* . . . "to beat, thrash": colloquial and dialectal; from ca. 1820.' Farmer and Henley (1890), *A Dictionary of Slang and Unconventional English*, provide essentially the same information. As an Americanism, the word hardly exists in the sense that Partridge attributes to it, although the American meaning 'extremely good' probably developed subsequently to 'to beat, thrash'.

B. H. Lehman (1921): called it 'of Southern origin, widely current in California.' J. L. B. Taylor (1923), 'Snake County [Missouri] talk' called it 'exceedingly pleasant to taste. See *lickum*.' He also points out that the noun form means 'a severe whipping' and the verb form 'to whip'. Ramon Adams (1968) has *'larrup*. "A cowboy name for molasses. To strike, to thrash" and *"larrupin"* truck. A cowboy's term for anything he considers great stuff.' With widespread sea–frontier relationships (see Brunvand, this volume), the term may have come to the cowboy separately.

A perhaps out-of-date baseball usage meant 'hitting hard line drives', especially as applied to New York Yankee first baseman 'Larrupin' Lou' Gehrig (Thorne 1974:109). This usage is probably metaphorical, refer-ring to the 'whiplike' character of his drives. The batting expertise of Lou Gehrig and Babe Ruth have often been compared. Ruth tended to hit the ball perhaps further but higher than Gehrig and, the latter's admirers insisted, without as much force.

In the United States, the term *larrupin'* is widely distributed, although one gets from informants the erroneous reaction in almost all cases that it is a quaint localism. No one interviewed so far has failed to comment in some way on the homey implications of the term — a strange develop-ment for an originally nautical term, especially in northwestern Louisiana and East Texas. Moreover, such local usage is never nautical and in no observed sense does it refer, in any literal sense, to a rope or a whip. Counting Gehrig's case, however, we have a semantic range from 'whip-like' to 'extremely good'.

Since 'whip' and 'rope' have an association in the maritime domain — the semantic shift is by no means an exceptional one — the meaning 'extremely good' seems to be the problematic one. It is also the meaning given by those informants who think of the term as homey and belonging strictly to casual or intimate speech. Lou Gehrig was an extremely good first baseman, but it would be hard to associate homey and local qualities with him. It remains to be determined how 'whiplike' can be associated with 'excellent' by some natural process, unless it is to be assumed that the two senses are unrelated.

A possible explanation was provided in a casual and almost chance interview with an elderly informant.* Familiar with *larrupin' good* and with the homey associations, the informant volunteered the information that the phrase seemed to apply most naturally to syrup. The informant came from the county of Van Zandt, Texas, an area where ribbon cane was grown and where syrup-making was extensively practiced until the 1930s. Questioned further about his subjective feelings, the informant volunteered (without use in any other grammatical form being suggested to him) that the term *larrups* was applied to the thin streaks of syrup that streamed down the container into which the newly made syrup was poured. The best syrup, he explained, rose to the top. Clearly beginning to have an insight into the matter, he went on to point out that such streaks (*larrups*) were 'larrupin' good' (the best). Questioned about cooccurrence with other forms (*larrupin' good ham*), he felt that they were marginally acceptable but that syrup was the natural domain of distribution.

Syrup-making certainly provides a rationale for the homey associations of the term. Probably no one associates syrup with formal and public activities. (In fact, so far a search for a description of the folk art of syrup-making has turned up no studies; the only available information comes almost incidentally from accounts of sugar-making.) Cane syrup is consumed in all parts of the United States, but made only in the states with a relatively warm climate. In fact, there is no report of the term in the sense 'extremely good' in the Northern states, and it may well not be known there in that sense. East Texas was the locale specified by my primary informants — but only because they came from East Texas. The

*Marvin L. Dillard, 77 years old, resident of East Texas for 62 years and now of Dallas, Texas. Mr. Dillard attended East Texas State Teachers College for two years, but has hardly traveled outside the state of Texas. This interview has since been corroborated with other informants.

apparent paradox of a nautical term becoming a localism seems to have been resolved, although it is not yet known in how many places the word is subjectively perceived as homey and local.

Gehrig played for the Yankees at a time when the American League (in fact, both major leagues) was concentrated in East Coast cities. *Larrupin'* in the sense 'whiplike', as in the case of Gehrig's line drives, must have come directly from *larrup* (to whip), a basically nautical usage. Southern cane country got *larrup* and *larrupin'* not from the East but from the sea — probably most specifically from the Gulf of Mexico. Louisiana, East Texas, and the cane-growing South used the metaphor of *larrups* for the ropelike substance overflowing the buckets of syrup and the sense of 'extremely good' developed at that point. Subjectively for the informants, such usages are localisms.

REFERENCES

Adams, Ramon (1968), *Western Words, A Dictionary of the American West*. Norman, University of Oklahoma Press.
Colcord, Joanna Carver (1945), *Sea Language Comes Ashore*. New York, W. W. Norton.
Farmer, J. S. and W. E. Henley (1890), *A Dictionary of Slang and Unconventional English*. London, A. P. Watt.
Lehman, B. H. (1921), 'A word list from California', *Dialect Notes* 5:109–14.
Mathews, Mitford M. (1951), *Dictionary of Americanisms*. Chicago, University of Chicago Press.
Partridge, E. (1970), *Dictionary of Slang and Unconventional English*. New York, Macmillan.
Taylor, Jay L. B. (1923), 'Snake county talk', *Dialect Notes* 5:197–225.
Thorne, John (1974), *A Century of Baseball Lore*. New York.

MARSHALL D. BERGER

New York City and the Antebellum South: The Maritime Connection

Writers on the 'peculiarities' of regional speech are caught in a curious semantic bind. That which is observed to be *peculiar* in the sense of merely unusual often comes to be regarded as *peculiar* in its pejorative sense, i.e. weird or ridiculous. Such is the case with the traditional pronunciation of *first, girl* and *work* in the New York metropolitan area. Journalists and other writers delight in such spellings as *foist, goil* and *woik*, but the actual sounds range from [ɜɪ] through [ʌɪ] to a relatively rare [ɵɪ]. Trained linguists, of course, are obliged to refrain from injecting aesthetic judgments into their observation and analysis of linguistic phenomena; journalists and folklorists are under no such compulsion (Mencken 1949:367–368; 1956:187–192; Needler 1968; Krapp 1925, vol. II: 185–186). Nevertheless, it is a fact that these diphthongs, having engaged the interests of both types of observers over the years, have thus far resisted all attempts to crack the mystery of their origins. It is perhaps time to take a fresh look at the problem, putting it into historical, social, and geographic perspective, while making use of structural principles of phonological analysis.

Historical perspective requires that we begin our discussion long before the present era, in fact as far back as the latter half of the seventeenth century. In that period we begin to see documentary evidence of dramatic changes in the behavior of certain vowels before *r*. For example, for words like *first, serve* and *burst*, which were originally sounded with the vowels (from an earlier [v]), [ɪ], [ɛ], and [ʌ], we find such variant forms as *ferst, furst* (first); *gairle* (girl); *parson, person* (person); and *retern* (return). This vacillation and fluctuation in usage went on for some time till shortly after the turn of the nineteenth century when most of the words in question came to be sounded alike with a central vowel of the [ɜ] type: [fɜrst], [sɜrv], [bɜrst] etc.[1] During the same period, especially toward the end of the eighteenth century, postvocalic *r* began to weaken and finally disappear in certain areas. The trend apparently started in London and spread from there to much of England and to various points along the Atlantic seaboard of the former North American colonies (Krapp 1925:217–231; Needler 1968:467). In those areas where *far, for, fear, fair, fewer,* and *fire* have lost their final *r*'s and *farm, form, fierce,* and *fairly,* their pre-consonantal *r*'s, by far the most widespread pronunciation of *first, serve, burst,* and *work* is [fɜːst], [sɜːv], [bɜːst] and [wɜːk] (Kurath and McDavid 1961:107–108; Kurath 1964:120). In the New York City area and in a substantial part of the Southeastern and Gulf State area there are large numbers of speakers whose normal vowel in these words is a diphthong of the [ɜɪ] type.[2]

Commentators on the speechways of New York City say nothing of [ɜɪ] in the early part of the nineteenth century. In fact, H. L. Mencken observes (1956:188) that the diphthong 'attracted little attention until after the Civil War'. William Cullen Bryant makes no mention of it in his *Dictionary of the New York Dialect of the English Tongue* dated about 1820 (Bryant 1941). John Russell Bartlett (1859), a Rhode Islander by birth and upbringing, asserts that '. . . residents of the city of New York are, perhaps, less marked in their pronunciation and use of words than the residents of any other city and state, the reasons for which are obvious. The population is so fluctuating, so many people from every part of the country, as well as from England, Scotland, Ireland, are congregated here, who are in daily contact with each other, that there is less chance for any idiom or peculiarity to grow up.' Such comments or lack of comment may be taken as strong indications that the diphthong had not yet made its appearance. In the case of Bartlett, particularly, if one assumes that the post-vocalic *r* had already disappeared from Rhode Island speech and that the earlier [ɜr] had become [ɜː], then his remarks suggest that a similar stage of development had been reached in New York City, or in other words, that New York City pronunciation was little different from that of eastern, especially southeastern New England in 1848.

As for Southern *r*-less speech, little work has been done in the historical phonology of that regional pattern. A thoroughgoing structural analysis may well give us new insight into the alignment of the diphthongal nucleus [ɜɪ] with the many other diphthongs of the vocalic system, but so far the task has gone begging.[3] On the other hand, a glance at a map of the Atlantic seaboard brings the geographic picture into sharp focus: the New York metropolitan area is of small compass and entirely surrounded by *r*-retaining speech penetrating deep into New York's relatively small hinterland. It is separated from the nearest *r*-less area, eastern New England, by many miles; in this area the prevailing vowel is [ɜː], often with considerable fronting. By contrast, the *r*-less South is a large, sprawling area extending from southern Maryland to eastern Texas. Moreover, it contains a number of coastal cities of historic importance: Charleston,

Savannah, Mobile and New Orleans. The last-named is the second largest port in the country, second only to the port complex of upper New York Bay.

Harking back to the early part of the nineteenth century, it was during this period when the vocalic system of New York City was in a state of flux that the maritime trade with the South picked up speed and intensity. In the antebellum period, roughly between 1820 and 1860, financial, commercial and social relations between the city and the South were at fever pitch: New York banks underwrote the plantation economy, cotton was shipped routinely from New Orleans, Charleston, Savannah and Mobile to be trans-shipped to England, and Southern planters regularly combined business with pleasure in the Big Apple of the 1800s. One historian goes so far as to say that '. . . down to the outbreak of the Civil War, New York dominated every single phase of the cotton trade from plantations to market' (Foner 1941:6). Yet another echoes this: '. . . much of the shipping that is employed in the southern ports to convey their cotton and other produce to foreign markets is owned by New York merchants' (Still 1956:150). Furthermore, many New York firms had branch houses in Southern cities, and New York entrepreneurs were deeply involved in the ownership and operation of Southern mines (Foner 1941:2, 3). Chroniclers of the time such as Joseph A. Scoville tell of business partnerships flowering between New Yorkers and Southerners, leading to warm friendships as well as, in some cases, to marriages between the sons and daughters of businessmen from both regions (Scoville 1885, vol. I:171; vol. II:290; vol. III:157–158; vol. IV:155). Even in the absence of documentation there is little reason to doubt that the same warm feelings existed between New Yorkers and Southerners on other social levels: sailors, longshoremen, store clerks, and many others involved in the maritime economy of the two regions. New Yorkers were strongly affected by the political struggles of the antebellum period. Many of the leading lights of the New York business community labored mightily to prevent the 'extremists', i.e. the abolitionists, from polarizing the country, thereby threatening the uneasy truce between the North and the South over the slavery question. But then in 1861 came the Civil War.[4]

Interestingly enough, the earlist known reference to the diphthong [ɜɪ], according to Needler (1968:466), to whom I am greatly indebted for this find, occurs in Oliver Wendell Holmes' *The Professor at the Breakfast-Table* published in 1859. Holmes describes it as:

. . . that extraordinary monosyllable which no single-tongued phonographer can make legible, prevailing on the banks of the Hudson and at its embouchure, and elsewhere, — what they say when they think they say *first,* (fe-eest, — *fe* as in the French *le*) . . . (1859:142).

It is startling to note that this is only eleven years after Bartlett's comments on the unsingular nature of the speech of New York City. It would appear that the [ɜ:] of the forties had ripened into the [ɜɪ] of the late fifties. Such a shift is hardly new in the evolution of phonological systems. In fact, Thomas (1958:95–96) finds an analogue in the diphthongizing of long, tense English vowels, citing the change of [i:] to [ɪi] and [e:] to [eɪ]. Pilch, approaching the problem structurally suggests that the shift from monophthong to diphthong took place as part of the general phenomenon of de-phonemicization of length in the vocalic systems of the nineteenth century.[5]

Over the next thirty years or so, the New York City vowel pattern developed a whole array of internal arrangements which were intimately bound up with the social and ethnic stratification of the metropolis: [ɜɪ] came to be used in *coil* as well as *curl* on the lower social levels; *r* coloring was introduced into *boil* [bɜɪ] and *point* [pɜɪnt]; all of these sounds being heard in monomorphemic forms like *goiter* and *loiter* and in inflected forms like *employed* and *enjoyed*, although not in the speech of the most privileged classes. Furthermore, the phonetic quality of the diphthongs varied greatly, ranging from a somewhat centralized [eɪ] and [aɪ] to the more usual [ɜɪ, ʌɪ] and [ɵɪ] (Hubbell 1940, 1950:67–70). Normative and aesthetic bias on the part of many popular writers have made it difficult to deal with these problems, but studies in 'phonological space' of the past few decades have sharpened our structural tools in accomplishing the task of grouping disparate sounds into discrete phonological units (Martinet 1952, 1955; Moulton 1962; Berger 1968; Heller and Macris 1967). By 1896 when E. H. Babbitt published the first scientific study of New York City pronunciation, all the features which made up the predominant structural schema of the New York metropolitan speech community were in place.[6] Since then, especially since World War I, further changes have taken place, among them the gradual displacement of the ancestral diphthong by the more general North American [ɜr] (de Camp 1941; Labov 1966: 340–341; Bronstein 1962). Thus, at least in this respect, we have come full circle.

It will perhaps be useful to recapitulate the main features of the linguistic and historical hypothesis which has been presented here:

1. By the end of the first quarter of the nineteenth century, most words like *first, serve, burst* and *work,* originally sounded with the vowels suggested by their spellings, viz. [ɪ], [ɛ] and [ʌ] come to be sounded alike with a central vowel of [ɜ] type: [fɜrst], [sɜrv], [bɜrst], and [wɜrk].

2. Within approximately the same time period, postvocalic *r* weakens and finally disappears, leaving [ɜ:] as the prevailing nucleus in *first, serve,* etc. as well as in *her, fir* and *fur.*

3. In the antebellum period, roughly between 1820 and 1860, extremely close financial, commercial and social ties develop between New York City and the South.

4. At a time when the vocalic system of the area is in a state of flux and Southern speech models enjoy high prestige among the more privileged classes, [ɜ:] before consonants undergoes diphthongization to [ɜɪ]. New Yorkers of other social levels are not immune, either: sailors, longshoremen, and even store clerks who are in contact with their Southern opposite numbers in the shipping trade.

5. Later social and linguistic developments result in a highly intricate set of internal arrangements within the vowel system, bringing the speech patterns of the community into the condition described by E. H. Babbitt in 1896.

NOTES

1. Krapp, (1925:166–184). Merger did not take place in Scotland, much of Ireland and parts of northern England. Furthermore, in some cases [ɛr] passed to [ær] and thnce to [ɑr]: *sergeant, parson* (doublet of *person*), *varsity* (clipped from *university*), *clerk* (British pronunciation), etc. At one time the centralizing process bid fair to spread to vowel + r + vowel sequences, but the scale tipped in the direction of preservation of vowel distinctions in such word types. But note the establishment of *squirrel* and *stirrup* as [skwɜrəl] ~ [skwʌrəl] and [stɜrəp] ~ [stʌrəp] in the U.S.A. Other examples could be adduced from regional and/or folk speech. See also John Kenyon (1940:192–194).
2. Kurath and McDavid (1961:15, 22); see also McDavid (1946). J. L. Dillard (1976:45) reports the use of a similar diphthong in several other widely dispersed locations, all of them either coastal or insular (Liberia, Watling Island in the Bahamas, and Charlotte Amalie, St. Thomas in the U.S. Virgin Islands).
3. Nor have scholars been able to assess the impact of the black population upon the white, and of the Huguenots of Charleston and the Creoles of New Orleans and elsewhere upon the rest of the South. These all remain open questions.
4. During the years immediately preceding the war, right up to the eve of the war, there were proposals on the part of some merchants and political leaders for the establishment of New York as a free city that would maintain commercial ties with the South (see Foner 1941:14, 285–296; Still 1956:168).
5. Herbert Pilch (p. 50). Even if one were to posit a shift directly from [ɜr] to [ɜɪ], this should hardly be surprising. Linguistic literature is replete with examples from all manner of languages and dialects, where vowel + consonant sequences, especially where the consonant is a liquid, nasal, or glide, change to diphthongs or nasalized vowels. More than fifty years ago, Krapp stated (1925:185–186): 'The difference between the very general Eastern American and British pronunciation of *first* as [fʌːst] and the New York pronunciation of the same word as [fʌɪst] is not so great as to necessitate a special explanation for the latter pronunciation. Both pronunciations are due to the absorption of the r into the preceding vowel, a process not dissimilar to that which changed [ɑ] to [ɔ] through the loss of *l* in words like *talk, chalk*, etc.'

6. The popular speech of the time was frequently referred to as *Boweryese*; the term *Brooklynese* is of much more recent date. Neither term should be taken literally.

REFERENCES

Babbitt, E. H. (1896), 'The English of the lower classes in New York City and vicinity', *Dialect Notes* 1:457–464.
Bartlett, John Russell (1859), *Dictionary of Americanisms*. New York, Bartlett and Welford.
Berger, Marshall D. (1968), 'The internal dynamics of a Metropolitan New York vocalic paradigm', *American Speech* 43:35–39.
Bronstein, Arthur J. (1962), 'Let's take another look at New York City', *American Speech* 37:13–26.
Bryant, Cullen (1941), *Dictionary of the New York Dialect of the English Tongue*, c. 1820, *American Speech* 16:157–158.
de Camp, L. Sprague (1941), 'New York City American', *Le Maître Phonétique* (April–June): 22–23.
Dillard, J. L. (1976), *American Talk: Where Our Words Came From*. New York, Random House.
Foner, Philip S. (1941), *Business and Slavery: The New York Merchants and the Irrepressible Conflict*. Chapel Hill, University of North Carolina Press.
Heller, Louis G. and James Macris (1967), *Parametric Linguistics*. The Hague, Mouton.
Holmes, Oliver Wendell (1859), *The Professor at the Breakfast-Table*. Boston, Houghton Mifflin.
Hubbell, Allan F. (1940), '"Curl and coil" in New York City', *American Speech* 15:372–376.
— (1950), *The Pronunciation of English in New York City: Consonants and Vowels*. New York, King's Crown Press. (Reprinted 1972 by Octagon Books, Farrar, Straus and Giroux.)
Kenyon, John S. (1940), *American Pronunciation*, eighth edition. Ann Arbor, George Wahr.
Krapp, George P. (1925), *The English Language in America*, volume two. New York, The Century Company.
Kurath, Hans (1964), *A Phonology and Prosody of Modern English*. Ann Arbor, University of Michigan Press.
Kurath, Hans and Raven I. McDavid, Jr. (1961), *The Pronunciation of English in the Atlantic States*. Ann Arbor, University of Michigan Press.
Labov, William (1966), *The Social Stratification of English in New York City*. Washington, D.C., Center for Applied Linguistics.
McDavid, Raven I., Jr. (1946), 'Dialect geography and social science problems', *Social Forces* (December): 170.
Martinet, André (1952), 'Function, structure and sound change', *Word* 8:1–32.
— (1955), *Économie des Changements Phonétiques*. Berne, A. Francke.
Mencken, H. L. (1949), *The American Language*, fourth edition. New York, Knopf.
— (1956), *The American Language: Supplement II*. New York Knopf.
Moulton, William G. (1962), 'Dialect geography and the concept of phonological space', *Word* 18:23–32.

Needler, Geoffrey (1968), 'On the origin of New York City's pathognomic (sic) diphthong: a new hypothesis', *Speech Monographs* 35:462–469.

Pilch, Herbert (1955), 'The rise of the American English vowel pattern', *Word* 11:57–93.

Scoville, Joseph A. (1885), *The Old Merchants of New York City by Walter Barrett, Clerk*, five volumes. New York.

Still, Bayrd (1956), *Mirror for Gotham*. New York, New York University Press.

Thomas, Charles K. (1958), *An Introduction to the Phonetics of American English*. New York, Ronald Press.

Slang and Words with their Origin on the River*

Editor's Note. The evidence is that this collection was made by Cecil A. Wright, interviewer and first-draft writer with the WPA Louisiana writers' project directed by Lyle Saxon et al., *Gumbo Ya-Ya* (1945), a popular product of the WPA project. Some of the phrases in this list were used in that book, but the complete list has never been published. Wright was no philologist, and his list perhaps represents no more than a popular impression when it asserts that the terms are 'Negro', especially if there is any speculation about the origin. There is, however, a reasonably good argument for asserting that *tote* is an Africanism (Turner 1949) in spite of rejections like this one from Schele de Vere as far back as 1872:

The strangest of all explanations is probably that given by the learned Noah Webster [NB!] in his admirable Dictionary. He says of the word, 'said to be African in origin.' This suggestion has nothing in its favor except for the simple fact, that the negroes never use any other word for carrying (Schele de Vere 1968 [1872]:643).

Schele de Vere and Wright thus agree, at least to that extent.

These materials are utilized by permission of the Archives Division of Northwestern State University, John M. Price director. They come from the Melrose Plantation collection of the WPA project referred to above, ably organized by Donald Hatley of Northwestern State University.

1. *Drift* — a man who drifts from one place to another along the various river fronts, either working or begging.
2. *Come, come get hot; money is to be made* — a phrase chanted by Negro workers in the coffee warehouse when a large shipment of coffee has been received and the Negroes have not had work for some time.
3. *Floater* — same as drift, sometimes only applies to a fisherman.

* Northwestern (Louisiana) State University Archives, WPA Writers' Project (Melrose Collection).

4. *Under the skids* — freight that is carried by means of a conveyor.

5. *Hopped up* — preferably applied to a drunk, but can mean a dope fiend.

6. *On the ways* — a term used on the oyster wharf when a Negro or any other worker stays on shore for some time due to a lull in business.

7. *Gimme a head* — term used on the coffee wharf when a Negro wants someone to help him to put a sack on his head.

8. *Gimme a bumper* — term used on the coffee wharf when a Negro wants someone to help him lift a sack on a wagon.

9. *Tote* — to carry; a Negro never uses the word 'carry'.

10. *Teering* — a term used on the coffee wharf meaning to stack coffee in piles.

11. *Totin' out* — term applied on the coffee wharf when the Negroes are carrying a load to the wagon.

12. *Git in th' hole* — term yelled by Negroes to the drivers of coffee wagons when they wish them to back the wagon.

13. *You're out* — term applied when a Negro is finished loading.

14. *Falled out* — exhausted.

15. *Spell* — a rest period during work.

16. *Bat th' hatches down* — to close the hatches.

17. *Stage plank* — old slang term for a flat ginger cake.

18. *Niggers lunch* — a stage plank and a dipper of Mississippi water (unfiltered).

19. *Barrel house* — a restaurant or a saloon.

20. *Peeler* — a police officer.

21. *Straw boss* — any Negro who has any influence with the white boss.

22. *At organheads together* — when two fellows are angry with one another.

23. *Shanty man* — the singer of a gang.

24. *Top bale* — lifting a bale of cotton over one's head.

25. *Wag* — a sailor.

26. *Marchand* — a person who prepares lunches and sandwiches.

27. *Cooper* — in today's usage a fellow who reconditions cargo.

28. *Cargodore* — in the old sailing vessel days the crew of the boat would help load her, as well as the stevedores. These men were known as cargodores.

29. *Rabbit* — a fellow who will not pay his bill.

30. *Dead head* — a fellow who will not work in order that he does not have to pay his bills.

31. *Bay mass* — ginger cakes.

32. *Elephant ears* — large jelly doughnuts.

33. *Heavy devil* —bread pudding.

34. *Shackle* — clevis.
35. *Poop* — stern.
36. *Beachcomer* — any seaman who quits his boat, loafs around, and panhandles from his mates.
37. *Possum belly* — the boiler in the engine room.
38. *The Texas* — superstructure under the wheel house.
39. *Winehead* — a fellow who drinks wine in order to get drunk — more or less applies to the wharf rats.
40. *Gunnel* — chassis.
41. *Skidding* — rolling molasses or sugar from the bank to the boat.
42. *Parbuckle* — term applied to method of loading heavy sugar rollers.
43. *Go-devil* — term applied to method of loading boilers and other heavy machinery.
44. *Nigger drivers* — term Negroes give to the first and second mate of a boat.
45. *Bullneck* — meat.
46. *Whippin' up cotton* — picking up cotton with a boom.
47. *Wharf boat* — a barge with a house built on it.
48. *Black oil* — dirty used oil from the engine room.
49. *Stage* — stage plank.
50. *Bull pen* — place where mules and other animals were kept on the steamboat.
51. *He-fog* — a fog from the gulf which is very heavy and lasts for a long time.
52. *Mud clerk* — a man who was part of the crew of the steamboat and sailed with the boat, but who went on the wharf when the boat docked to check the cotton, seed, and lumber. There were usually two on a boat.
53. *Bosom bread* — stage plank. This was the term used by the old roustabouts on the steamboats. It is the same thing that the longshoremen know as stage plank.
54. *Dress up* — term used by river gamblers when they succeed or intended to succeed in taking money from passengers on the boat by means of cards, dice, etc.
55. *Horses* — the large ropes that are used to tie a vessel to the wharf.
56. *Friendly boat* — a term used by steamboat people in referring to another boat not in competition with them. Old steamboat men considered a friendly boat in the same light as a next-door neighbor is considered today.
57. *Guard* — that portion of the steamboat deck which was used by the passengers to enjoy the river breezes. It is tantamount to the promenade deck of a modern vessel.
58. *Cabin* — term used on the steamboat to signify a large hall. It was

usually on the second deck and was divided into two portions, *ladies'
cabin* and *gentlemen's cabin*. The ladies' cabin was more or less a lounge
room and also had the captain's dining table in it, whereas the gentlemen's cabin was synonomous with the main dining room.

REFERENCES

Saxon, Lyle, Edward Dreyer and Robert Tallant (1945), *Gumbo Ya-Ya*. Boston, Houghton
    Mifflin.
Schele de Vere, Maximilian (1968), *Americanisms; the English of the New World*. New
    York, Johnson Reprint Corporation. (Originally published 1872.)
Turner, Lorenzo Dow (1949), *Africanisms in the Gullah Dialect*. Chicago, University of
    Chicago Press.

JAN HAROLD BRUNVAND

Sailors' and Cowboys' Folklore in Two Popular Classics

Walter Prescott Webb asserts (Webb 1931:487) that early travelers in
the American West, 'with one accord . . . compared the Plains to the sea.'
A few typical instances demonstrate that tendency. Josiah Gregg, for
example, describing the Santa Fe Trail in the 1830s characterized one
stretch in these terms: 'This tract of country may truly be styled the grand
"prairie ocean"; for not a single landmark is to be seen for more than
forty miles — scarcely a visible eminence by which to direct one's course.
All is as level as the sea' (Gregg 1962:32). Similarly, Francis Parkman
(1961:34, 255) again and again compared the prairies to the sea, writing
now of 'green undulations, like motionless swells of the ocean', and
now of buffalo bellowing 'like the ocean beating up the distant
coast'.

The vocabulary of early plains travel also reflected a seagoing image.
When one of Parkman's inexperienced fellow travelers wished to hail a
darkened camp, it seemed to him quite natural to shout 'Camp ahoy'.
Prairie schooner is first reported from 1841 as a term for the wagons that
were variously also called *prairie ships* (from 1851) or *prairie clippers*
(from 1851). When his caravan encamped, Gregg generally spoke of
having *made a port*, and the expression *prairie port* is recorded from 1848.
One traveler wrote of being 'becalmed on the prairie-ocean and not a sail
in sight'. Gregg was echoed by others when he said that he could see no
reason 'why the captain of a prairie caravan should not have as much
power to call his men to account for disobedience or mutiny, as the
captain of a ship upon the high seas' (1962:39). Apparently it was
inevitable for poetic minds to compare the prairies to the sea. Having
been to sea, but never in the great plains, Cooper himself pictured them
both in the same terms: 'The earth was not unlike the ocean, when its
restless waters are heaving heavily, after the agitation and fury of the

Reprinted by permission of the author and of the *Southern Folklore Quarterly*. By special
arrangement with the author, the editor has inserted examples of maritime and frontier
language in brackets. Full bibliographic information for citations within these brackets can
be found in the reference section at the end of this volume.

tempest have begun to lessen. There was the same waving and regular surface, the same absence of foreign objects, and the same boundless extent to the view' (Cooper 1950:6). The passage continues, somewhat less accurately, to suggest that on the prairie, at intervals, 'a tall tree rose . . . like some solitary vessel'.

As if to corroborate Cooper's vision, William Cullen Bryant, upon first seeing the rolling grasslands of Illinois, rhapsodized:

> Lo! they stretch
> In airy undulations, far away
> As if the Ocean, in his gentlest swell,
> Stood still, with all his rounded billows fixed,
> And motionless forever . . .
> ('The Prairies', 11. 6–10)

Washington Irving repeatedly compared the Western prairies either to the sea or to desert wastes in his first Western book *A Tour on the Prairies* (1835); in *Astoria* he wrote that John Jacob Astor's agents had to cross 'a region almost as vast and trackless as the ocean' (1961, vol. I:181).

Mark Twain (1953:7) wrote true to this established mode (although deprecating stereotyped Western travel books elsewhere) when he recalled his initial impression of the great plains: 'Just here the land was rolling — a grand sweep or regular elevations and depressions as far as the eye could reach — like the stately heave and swell of the ocean's bosom after a storm.' A later fictional greenhorn, Owen Wister's narrator in *The Virginian*, responded in the standard idiom, declaring that the first Wyoming road he traveled 'lay like a ship's wake across the huge ground swell of the earth' (1960:37). [In a letter of August 16, 1887 (Wister 1958:55), Wister quoted the Indian guide Tigie in credible pidgin English: 'Quick . . . He come them — so-so.'][2]

A generation after this, on the opening page of yet another memorable work in the literature of the West — O. E. Rølvaag's *Giants in the Earth* (1927) — a caravan of pioneer wagons is described pushing its way through the tall grass, and 'the track that it left behind was like the wake of a boat — except that instead of widening out astern it closed in again'.

Historians of the West have found a basic truth in the familiar comparison. For instance, in Ernest Staples Osgood's *The Day of the Cattleman*, the aspect of the land before the time of 'The Texas invasion' is pictured in these terms:

When the emigrant bound for Oregon or California turned his back on the

Missouri settlements and struck out along the westward trail, his condition was not unlike that of the traveler sailing out of an eastern seaport on a trans-atlantic journey. Beyond the narrow wagon track a vast waste stretched away on every side to the far horizon, its swells and hollows as lacking in identity as the crests and troughs of the Atlantic rollers. Herds of buffalo and great bands of antelope, seemingly as multitudinous as the fish of the sea, moved over the face of these great solitudes (Osgood 1929:7).

If the early traders and emigrants were the first transoceanic tourists of the prairies, it was the cowboys who were to become the professional mariners of the territory (and to inherit and extend the linguistic practices to their forerunners). These able seamen of the prairie-ocean endured occupational conditions of changing weather, great distances, and long isolation which were very much like those prevailing on ocean-sailing ships. It is not without significance that one of the favorite cowboy songs was a parody of a poem that began 'O, bury me not in the deep, deep sea' [substituting *lone prairie*] (Laws 1964: 79–82).

A comparison of two great classic books of the American sailing ship and the open range reveals how similar the lives of sailors and cowboys were (and how many parallels there were in the language situation).[1] Curiously, both books resulted from a phase of the Western cattle industry — R. H. Dana's *Two Years Before the Mast* from the early hide and tallow trade along the California coast, and Andy Adams' *The Log of a Cowboy* from the height of the Texas longhorn boom. Each book is thoroughly typical of its subject: Dana documented an adventurous trip around the Horn and back from 1834 to 1836,while Adams compressed his experiences of fifteen years on the trail into a novel, set in 1882, which covered the full sweep of a long drive from Mexico to Montana. The narrator of each book is a young man, bound for an exotic region and a new life, who is acutely aware of the sometime romance, sometimes tedium of his surroundings.

The basic impression of nature on both authors was comparable. A few days out of Boston, while still seasick, Dana reflected, 'There is something in the first grey streaks stretching along the eastern horizon and throwing an indistinct light upon the face of the deep, which combines with the boundlessness and unknown depths of the sea around, and gives one a feeling of loneliness, of dread, and of melancholy foreboding, which nothing else in nature can' (*Two* :5–6). Andy Adams' narrator, Thomas Moore Quirk, might have provided the young Boston Brahman with an equivalent in nature for the monotonous seascape, as well as a theory based upon it:

Once the freshness of the spring had passed, the plain took on her natural sunburnt color, and day after day, as far as the eye could reach, the monotony was unbroken, save by the variations of the mirages on every hand . . . if the monotony of the sea can be charged with dulling men's sensibilities until they become pirates, surely this desolate, arid plain might be equally charged with the wrong-doing of not a few of our craft (*Log*: 145).

When a boy went west to become a cowboy in the late nineteenth century he found himself in a job very much like that of sailing on the high seas in earlier days. The all-male crew [called *hands* whether cowpunchers or members of a ship's crew; see Chase (this volume 106)] lived by a code of pride in outfit, strict assignment of tasks, and long hours of hard work. The men all wore distinctive garb, and they learned to speak a common technical lingo [partly described in Dillard 1975a: Ch. I for the sea, Ch. IV for the frontier. See also works by Granville (1962) and Ramon Adams (1961, 1968, 1971).] Around-the-clock watches were needed in the open, and all hands had to sleep on-call for emergencies; sudden changes in weather generally brought on trouble and an order for the entire crew to turn out, including the cook or the carpenter, who were usually old able-bodied hands themselves. The high life that could be enjoyed in ports provided a release from the weary months of voyaging, and the crews became famous for their energetic celebrations. One old cowboy summed it up nicely in a statement in his little book of personal reminiscences:

They were a rough and ready class of men; always ready for a fight or a frolic. Like sailors on the sea, these men received no money until the drive was ended. (There is a similarity in the life of a cowpuncher to the life of a sailor.) When the cattle were sold all were paid off. There were always men and allurements at the end of these trails to get the boys' money. They had just finished a weary, long and lonesome season, and they were hungry for entertainment. It was furnished them, and again was enacted the drama of 'spending money like drunken sailors' (Rush 1930:28).

[Brushes with the law were, of course, the natural consequence of these celebrations. Particularly among the cowboys (see Dick 1954:152–153), the use of firearms, sometimes innocent but sometimes tragic, was a major feature. Like the sailor in the Pacific or even in West Africa, the cowboy could wind up in what was called the *calaboose*. For the origin and maritime spread of this word, see Dillard (1975a:129).]

Judging from these two books, cowboys, in two important respects, seem to have been somewhat more comfortable than sailors of Dana's generation were. [Dick (1954:191–192) provides a rational explanation:

'Many parents of noble blood [sent] their sons to the West' and some of the better-off American families did the same. It must have been boys like this who invented and spread the phrase *like getting money from home*, attested to by Owen Wister in 1893 (Wister 1958) as a 'Westernism' — incredibly, until one realizes how many cowboys must not have been entirely dependent upon their trail wages.] The food was better in the cow camps, and the bosses were less severe. Although both writers describe what seem like tiresome menus — weak tea, tough salt beef, and hard biscuits at sea; and beef, biscuits and coffee on the prairies — there was a great difference ashore where the bread was freshly baked, the meat often newly killed, and the coffee always strong and hot. The shipboard meat barrels were picked over for the officers' meals first, so that what reached the crew was bad enough to inspire a chant that began 'Old horse! old horse! what brought you here (*Two*:230n). The tea — thin and sweetened with molasses — was dubbed 'water bewitched' and 'tea begrudged'; and *scouse* was what Dana called 'one rare treat'; it was a stew made of 'biscuits pounded fine, salt beef cut into small pieces, and a few potatoes boiled up together and seasoned with pepper' (*Two*: 24, 245). Once or twice a week Dana and his shipmates received a pudding-like *duff* made of flour, water, and molasses with plum added for Christmas; while on the range, the cowboys' usual treats were canned tomatoes, pie made from dried fruit, and sometimes jam for their biscuits. Andy Adams also wrote of eating wild turkey eggs on the trail and of having doughnuts on a ranch. When bacon was to be had, it sometimes went by the name of *fried chicken* among the Texans (*Log*:80).

Dana's description of the discipline of sailors is notorious for an account of a brutal flogging, but even the day-to-day authoritative rule of some captains was bad enough. On the voyage out from Boston, the captain of the *Pilgrim* bragged up his power like any frontier boaster: 'I'm Frank Thompson, all the way from "down east". I've been through the mill, ground, and bolted, and come out a regular-built down-east *johnny-cake*, when it's hot, d—d good; but when it's cold, d—d sour and indigestible' (*Two*:40). [Dana, like Colcord, claims nautical origin for *haze* (to punish a sailor by hard work). Colcord (1945: 97) points out that 'college hazing got its name from the shipboard term.']

The ship's work was carried on continuously, according to what Dana said sailors called 'The Philadelphia Catechism':

Six days shalt thou labour and do all thou art able;
And on the seventh, holystone the decks and scrape the cable
(*Two*:12).

At least in Tom Quirk's outfit, there was no corresponding despotic ruler. The owner himself occasionally visited the herd during the five-month drive to check on the care of both livestock and men. The foreman, though tough and able, was a paternal sort who would advise his men: 'Don't sit up all night telling fool stories', when he left for town, and who might bring back to them a box of cigars and some Old Crow.

A spirit of fellowship prevailed among members of both crews; this is indicated by the familiar nicknames they adopted among themselves. In *The Log of a Cowboy* Tom Quirk's bunkmate was 'The Rebel', and others in the group were called 'Rod' Wheat, 'Bull' Durham, 'Moss' Strayhorn, and 'Quince' Forest. Andy Adams also gave a list of Dodge City peace officers' nicknames, as well as those of numerous prominent cowmen. Dana's first ship captain was called 'The Down-East Johnny-Cake' behind his back, while other functionaries were 'The Mate' (first mate), 'Sailors' Waitor' (second mate), 'Doctor' (the cook), 'Chips' (the carpenter), and 'Sails' (the sailmaker). A boy from Hingham, Massachusetts, was nicknamed 'Bucket-maker', and another, for reasons not clear, was 'the Reefer'; a studious passenger was christened 'Old Curious', and all the Hawaiians (Kanakas) they met became known by such whimsical names as 'Fore-top', 'Rope-yarn', 'Ban-Yan', and 'California Bill'.

[Loftis (1973:101) offers evidence that other Californians, not eager to give their real names because of the possibility of being discovered to be fugitives from justice, coined names like 'Kanaka Joe', 'French Pete', 'Boston', 'Kentuck', and other aliases. There are many other bits of evidence that Adams' cowboys and Dana's Kanakas were not so widely separated as many would assume. It is not always realized by readers of Dana that his ship operated just off San Diego for most of the voyage he describes. Dana points out that the Kanakas manned, for the most part, the vessels traveling between the 'Sandwich Islands' and California, and that many of them left the ships to accept jobs curing hides in San Diego.]

[Dana is also one of the earliest extensive sources of Hawaiian Pidgin English. The author does for the sea approximately what Rollins (1936) did for the range: 'They [the Hawaiians, called Sandwich Islanders] spoke a little English, and by a sort of compromise, a mixed language was used on the beach, which could be understood by all' (Dana 1959:180).]

[Dana quotes the 'compromise' language fairly extensively. John Reinecke (personal communication) has questioned Dana's competence in rendering the contact language, but I find it rather impressive:

'Me no eatee Cap'nee Cook! Me pickaninny — small — so high — no more! My fader see Cap'nee Cook! Me no! . . . New Zealand Kanada eatee white man; Sandwich Island Kanaka — no. Sandwich Island Kanaka ua like pua na haole — all 'e same a' you' (Dana 1959:181).

If, as Reinecke suggests, Dana's memory for the speech of the Hawaiians is unreliable, it still remains to be explained how he acquired the genuine forms *pickaninny* and *all 'e same a'*. If he heard them elsewhere and mistakenly attributed them to Hawaiians, the case for the widespread nature of pidgin English is, I submit, strengthened rather than weakened. Some of the same forms that Dana attributes to the Hawaiians also figured in the Alaskan whaler's jargon which Stafánsson (1909) asserted, or speculated, was influenced by Hawaiians.]

[The whole tenor of comments by all the writers referred to suggested that the resemblance between sailors' and cowboys' terms reflected something more than a lexical similarity — and a human rather than a geographic pattern of distribution. Cowboys, who dealt with Spanish- and French-speaking populations and were endlessly bewildered by the multitudinous variety of the languages of the American Indians, borrowed the solution of the English-speaking sailor: pidgin English. Adams (1960:373–374) represents the cowboys trying to communicate with Blackfeet: 'But our Spanish, which Quarternight and I tried on them, was as unintelligible to them as their gutteral gibberish was to us.' Communication is accidentally established when one of the cowboys chances to call a Blackfoot brave by the word *squaw* (Algonquian in origin, although transmitted through pidgin English) and draws the rejoinder: '. . . in fair English . . . "Me buck."' (Adams 1960:375). At least one Indian in the Red River Valley mixed French and pidgin English to produce 'He voisin', if we can trust the report of Harry and Elizabeth Eskew (1954:134).]

[Rollins (1936:78) made the Western and cowboy use of pidgin English as an auxiliary language, along with Spanish, explicit:

Pidgin-English contributed its quota of words and phrases. Its 'long time no see 'em' conveniently set forth the status of a searcher for some lost object, while its 'no can do' definitely expressed personal impotence.

In the extreme Northwest a few words were borrowed from the Chinook jargon of the coastal trappers and traders . . .

Although Rollins had this very early insight into the use of trade language or frontier *lingua franca* by the cowboys, not even Ramon Adams (1961, 1968, 1971) followed up that very important lead.]

On either a long cattle drive or sailing voyage the steady routine of the work fostered a mood of creeping boredom; the common response of sailors and cowboys was to fall back on a stock of traditional devices to kill time, and their similar conditions of life were mirrored in a matching folklore. Since talk was cheap and easy, storytelling was the most general recreation among the crews.

The best time of day for telling stories, as in the old-time logging camps, was between supper and bedtime. Loggers, who also lived much like sailors or cowboys, have been described as spending the evening until the nine o'clock lights-out, 'tending to small chores, whittling, smoking, talking ... [and sometimes] singing, step dancing, and storytelling'. Dana's description of the ship's watches from four to six and six to eight o'clock is remarkably similar:

As the dog watches come during twilight, after the day's work is done, and before the night watch is set, they are the watches in which everybody is on deck. . . . The crew are setting on the windlass or lying on the forecastle, smoking, singing, or telling long yarns. At eight o'clock eight bells are struck, the log is hove, the watch set, the wheel relieved, the galley shut up, and the watch off duty goes below.

Several times Dana returned to descriptions of this peaceful, social time; one regular event of the dog watches when the ship was anchored was for men who had been ashore to recount their day's activities.

Substitute the terms first, second and third *guards* beginning at eight o'clock, and you have the cowboys' equivalent gathering — the campfire circle. Andy Adams wrote:

We had a splendid camp-fire that night, of dry live-oak logs, and after supper was over and the first guard had taken the herd, smoking and storytelling were the order of the evening. . . . After the labors of the day are over, the men gather around the fire, and the social hour of the day is spent in yarning (*Log*:25).

Time and time again Adams described these fireside evenings when 'jokes and songs helped to while away the weary hours of the night.'

Both Dana and Adams commented on the broad range of stories told by their companions. Dana referred to 'the usual strain of conversation, inquires, stories, and jokes, which one must always hear in a ship's forecastle', and he observed that they were 'after all, no worse, though more gross and coarse, than those one may chance to hear from some well-dressed gentlemen around their tables.' According to Andy Adams, the cowboys' repertoire was equally comprehensive: 'The stories told may run from the sublime to the ridiculous, from a true incident to a base fabrication, or from a touching bit of pathos to the most vulgar vulgarity.'

Certain topics of conversation were popular whether they led to traditional tales or not. Tom Quirk's fellows spent nights discussing 'revisiting the old states', while Dana and his shipmates considered 'home, and what we should do when we got there.' Other subjects that the Texans talked about were Mexicans, Indians, horses, dogs, and their old sweethearts, about in that order; while the New England crew, on the other hand, told whaling yarns, 'queer Negro stories', and legends about condemned meat served to sailors and brutal captains set over them. Both groups had tall tale specialists among them — a sailmaker who was 'remarkable for drawing a long bow' with Dana, and a cowboy who was 'inclined to overcolor his statements' with Tom Quirk. The former raconteur was considered very amusing, but the latter, according to Andy Adams, drew only 'respectful attention . . . as a cheerful, harmless, liar'. Another folktale expert was Tom Quirk's bunkmate, who sometimes annoyed his partner by telling war stories and jokes late into the night as they lay in their bedrolls. The brig *Pilgrim* also had a chief mate who considered himself '*ex officio* the wit of the crew' and told 'coarse jokes' at which Dana and the crew felt obliged to laugh.

Both cowboys and sailors welcomed a chance to meet other parties who had new tales. Andy Adams characterized one camp visitor as 'a good conversationalist, meaty with stories not eligible to the retired list'; another one was full of 'news and scarey stories'. The young cowboy also spent several hours listening to storytelling by old-timers in Dodge City, and when some Montana prospectors visited the camp, the whole outfit outdid itself telling old tales in hopes of drawing out fresh ones. Dana's captain hailed passing ships for news, and on occasion held up for longer talks; a certain visiting captain, Dana claimed, once stayed on board for four hours telling a single continuous yarn and then he left only because a good breeze had come up. We also learn from Dana what readers of *Moby Dick* found out a decade later — that on whalers this visiting between ships was called *gamming*.

An accident now and then reminded sailors and cowboys of some of the real dangers inherent to their calling; it also prompted more stories. After coming upon the fresh grave of a cowboy who had been killed by a chance shot, the men told nothing but gloomy tales at the evening campfire; the general feeling was that '[an] accident might happen to any of us', although one man maintained: 'You can't avoid it when it comes, and every now and then you miss it by a hair.' The sailors were equally casual about their risks:

Whatever your feelings may be, you must make a joke of everything at sea; and if you were to fall from aloft, and be caught in the belly of a sail, and thus saved from instant death, it would not do to look at all disturbed, or to treat it as a serious matter (*Two*:24).

Bad luck *was* a serious matter, however, and when a ship's crewman accidentally drowned, there was talk about possible forewarnings. Some men reported that the unfortunate sailor had recently spoken of his fear of drowning; others thought he was jinxed from the start because he had been unwilling to go on the voyage; a third man saw an evil omen in the victim's talking about his family the night before. The Negro cook's imagination was fired by the tragedy so that he not only gave Dana further accounts of death warnings, but also went on to tell legends of the Flying Dutchman and to describe his experience with the power of Finns to call up a wind. Other maritime superstitions that Dana reported are that the actions of St. Elmo's fire on the mast predicts weather, that certain ships have prevailing good or bad luck, that the third attempt to round the horn never fails, and that, on a northern passage in the Atlantic: 'If the Bermudas let you pass

You must beware of Hatteras'.

The cowboys of Andy Adams' experience seemed to have been considerably more hard-headed than this. The only general superstitions that he included had to do with card playing and choosing good horses by their color. One man provided an especially convincing demonstration of 'gambler's luck' in Ogallala, Nebraska, and also confessed the reason behind his personal superstition against wearing spurs.

Although Andy Adams alluded to cowboys singing around the campfire, and other sources corroborate the practice, all of the folksongs described in *The Log of a Cowboy* are sung by the night guards to soothe the cattle. As Adams explained it, this was a communal effort: 'Every once in a while a song would be started, and as it surged up and down the line, every voice, good, bad, and indifferent, joined in.' He wrote that 'the guards usually sing or whistle continuously, so that the sleeping herd may know that a friend and not an enemy is keeping vigil over their dreams.'

Parts of several night guards' songs were threaded into the narrative. At the fireside one night a guard was overheard singing 'Little Black bull come down the hillside long time ago', and the foreman remarked: 'Whenever my men sing that song on guard, it tells me everything is amply serene.' On another occasion, as the narrator rode out for a shift, the previous guard was just finishing a verse of 'Shortnin' Bread' [probably Black in origin and not so innocent in content as sometimes thought, since bakery symbolism is usually sexual symbolism among American Blacks. See Guy B. Johnson (1927), and Dillard (1977:Ch. II).] Yet a third singer preferred this ditty:

Sure it's one cent for coffee and two cents for bread
Three for a steak and five for a bed.

Sea breeze from the gutter wafts a salt water smell
To the festive cowboy in the Southwestern hotel.

Adams wrote that this verse 'had been composed, with little regard for
music or sense, about a hotel where they had stopped the year before', but
closely parallel lines are found in old New York state canallers' songs
collected from Irish-American singers. (Thompson 1939:228–229).

Andy Adams also referred to what he called an 'old rear song: . . . go
'long little doggie, you'll make a beef-steer by-and-by.' He wrote about
'the farewell songs generally used in parting with a river', and he gave
'One More River to Cross' and 'Roll, Powder, Roll' as songs saved for the
last stretch of their drive — through the Powder River country of Wyoming and Montana. Apparently night herd singing soothed men as
well as cattle, for Adams reported nostalgically: 'We spent our last
night with the herd singing songs, until the first guard called the relief,
when realizing the lateness of the hour, we burrowed into our blankets'
(*Log*:231).

The sailors' work songs — sea shanties — had a purpose quite different
from cowboys' singing; Dana explained it in detail:

> The sailors' songs for capstan and falls are of a peculiar kind, having a chorus at
> the end of each line. The burden is usually sung by one alone, and at the chorus all
> hands join in — usually the louder the noise the better. With us, the chorus
> seemed almost to raise the decks of the ship, and might be heard at a great
> distance ashore. A song is as necessary to sailors as the drum and fife to a soldier.
> They must pull together as soldiers must step in time, and they can't pull in time,
> or pull with a will without it (*Two*:209).

Among sailors as among cowboys every man had to sing as best he
could, but a sailor who could sing really well was regarded as a great
benefit to the rest of the crew. Dana described one instance during the
hide-loading stage of the work when some new hands on the job provided
a set of fresh songs, and he admitted: 'I have no doubt that this timely
re-enforcement of songs hastened our work several days.' Dana listed the
titles of eleven shanties: 'Heave to the Girls!' 'Nancy O!' 'Jack Crosstree',
'Cheerily Men', 'Heave Round Hearty!' 'Captain Gone Ashore!' 'Dandy
Ship and a Dandy Crew', 'Time for us to Go!' 'Round the Corner', 'Tally
High Ho!' and 'Hurrah! Hurrah! My Hearty Bullies'. Some of these were
special favorites sung again and again; 'Cheerily Men' in particular was
one which the crew liked, but stubbornly refused to join in just after a
flogging, and later raised again loudly, even in bad waters, when they
were sailing home. At this the captain commented: 'That sounds like a
lively crew. They'll have their song so long as there's enough left for the

chorus!' The Americans did not sing, however, while rowing to shore, as foreign crews often did, a fact which Dana lamented. Instead his countrymen 'pulled the long distances to and from the shore, with our loaded boats without a word spoken, and with discontented looks.'

Sometimes the sailors sang purely for entertainment rather than to accompany work. One night when a multitude of foreign ships was in a California harbor, the crews on shore, and two vessels prepared to sail next day, the men gathered for a sort of farewell hootenanny at one of the hide storing houses. 'We had songs', Dana wrote, 'of every nation and tongue . . . and we three Yankees made an attempt at the "Star-Spangled Banner"' Later when Dana's ship *The Alert* was loading, a ship just in from Boston brought some musical sailors who could sing 'the latest sailor songs . . . battle-songs, drinking songs, boat-songs, love-songs, and everything else'. Dana named, ' "All in the Downs", "Poor Tom Bowline", "The Bay of Biscay", "List, Ye Landsmen", and other classical songs of the sea'.

He also mentioned one night of fiddling and dancing on the ship deck — a 'regular sailors' shuffle' — when a boy from Cape Cod performed, who 'could dance the true fisherman's jig, barefooted, knocking with his heels and slapping the decks with his bare feet, in time with the music.' In general, however, it appeared to the author that Americans danced poorly, compared to the performance he saw of a fandango at a Spanish wedding ashore.

Andy Adams described no comparable cowboy songfest, but he did include details of a fiddling match in town. A Negro cook from a Texas outfit was matched against a local player, more as a practical joke on both than as a bona fide match. The contestants were instructed to play a waltz, a jig, and a sacred piece, but by the third number the musicians had caught on to the joke, and the darky played 'The Arkansaw Traveler', while his opponent performed 'The Irish Washerwoman'; the cowboy judges declared the match a draw, and everybody rushed away to see a shooting in another part of town.

When the sailors had heard every crewman's stock of stories, sung all the songs they knew, and exhausted the topics of conversation, they fell back in desperation on any device that might relieve the boredom of a long pull. Dana felt it to be 'a windfall' when the ship's carpenter, a Finn, was put in his watch to replace an injured man; he wrote, '[he gave me long accounts of his country — the customs, the trade, the towns . . . [and] his marriage and courtship.' When even companions failed him, Dana used his own 'deliberate system of time-killing' repeating to himself a long string of memorized mathematical, historical, biblical, and literary matters in several languages. [It is ironic that, while these accounts are of little value, his later memories of pidgin English — which he would hardly have granted the status of a language — may constitute his real contribution to language history.]

Books — or any printed matter — were treasured on the ships to be read and reread and then traded for new ones when chances were offered. Dana read several volumes during his voyage, including William Cowper's letters and poems, Godwin's *Mandeville*, 'a romance in five volumes', and even a jest book. On the day the ship's hold was fumigated before loading hides he spent his whole time of deck reading aloud to a circle of crewmen from Scott's *Woodstock*, omitting, he said, only 'many of the reflections and political parts'.

J. Frank Dobie (Introduction to Siringo 1950: xx–xxvii) has written knowledgeably of cowboys' insatiable appetites for reading matter on the trail, but Andy Adams had no readers among the boys of the outfit. The closest they came to print was toying with a jam can and speculating about the people pictured on the label. The favorite general recreations he described were card playing, horse racing, and pranks. There was 'seven-up', 'freeze-out', 'monte', and 'faro', as well as some varieties of poker. [The influence of the last two games on frontier terminology, and afterwards on the phraseology of the entire United States, moving from west to east, is described in detail in Asbury (1936), partly summarized in Dillard (1976a). It further fits into Brunvand's pattern that poker was an international game, transmitted by sea, and entering the United States through the port of New Orleans. Rollins (1936:80) also stresses the popularity of keno, '. . . of which the Sacramento Chinaman said, "Fline glame. Velly simple. Dlealer slay 'Kleno' and ellybolly ellse slay 'O hlell' ' ". The absurd phonological device of having a Chinese intrude /l/ almost haphazardly, instead of simply indicating a lack of contrast between /l/ or /r/, does not mark Rollins as an infallible linguistic observer; but he is too good elsewhere to be dismissed out of hand for such a failing.]

Another diversion mentioned by Adams was a rigged horse race by means of which the cowboys were neatly relieved of most of their ready money and a good part of their personal equipment. Some of their pranks were hazing the acting foremen, hiding a fancy hanky and garter in the cook's pocket, and having a man impersonate a Kentuckian before a real one. [Rollins describes the cowboys' jocular use of Indian terms like *making medicine* (preparing for a journey) and the use of what Indian sign language they knew 'in order to dress up light-hearted conversation'.]

Two Years Before the Mast and *The Log of a Cowboy* are rich in authentic details of nineteenth-century ocean sailing and Western trail riding. We have seen how the books illustrate the likenesses of these callings, and we have found good examples in them of the similar folklore of sailors and cowboys. Both of these works, however, are much more than simple, realistic documents of bygone romantic trades. They have been widely read and glowingly praised, by literary scholars and lay readers alike, as great, evocative treatments of their subjects. The *Literary History of the United States* (Spiller et al. 1953), for instance, declares that *Two Years Before the Mast* 'was and is a classic' and that Andy Adams 'the best of the cowboy novelists' produced in *The Log of a Cowboy* 'the best of his work'. The reputation of Dana's book, of course, is secure; Andy Adams has recently moved well out of the shadows of relative obscurity with the paperback printings of some of his works and the publication last year of a biographical and critical study which concludes: 'There can be no doubt about the artistic excellence of *The Log of a Cowboy*, the only acknowledged masterpiece in the literature of the cattle country' (Hudson 1964:226). These two books are, in short, the popular literary classics of two early American trades; taking for granted the appeal of their subject matter, we might briefly inquire now what part folklore plays in their shaping.

It is immediately apparent that the style and viewpoint of the books are essentially the same, although one was written by a Harvard undergraduate and the other by an ex-Texas cowboy with very little schooling, and one was presented as travel memoirs, the other as fiction. The important facts are that each writer began with direct personal experience, each tried to tell the truth, and each wrote with earnest, youthful, vigor. Both books are *first* books that deal with voyages of discovery, and both put a perceptive first-person narrator in the framework of a long, adventurous journal. The language of each telling is concrete, direct, and proverbial, while the structuring of chapters is simply chronological or anecdotal.

Surely the appraisal that Mark Van Doren made of one of these storytellers applies equally well to the other:

He is not mystical, or mythical, or metaphysical. His ideas are of the simplest sort, intelligible at any time. And his language has nothing [in it] of splendor. . . . There is something in [the] narrative that cannot die. It is something as familiar in life as it is rare in art. It is the simple truth. Or so we say as we read these pages in which there is so little ostentation of art that we may think there is no art at all (Introduction to Dana 1959: viii–ix).

This passage refers to Dana's book, but one of the most typical characterizations of Andy Adams' style is very similar. It was written by Walter Prescott Webb (Hudson 1964:202) in a letter to Eugene Manlove

Rhodes: '[he] has produced a peculiar kind of fiction, which is fiction and so much like fact as to be disconcerting.'

It seems to me that such qualities as we find in these books are among those that distinguish the best of verbal artists in folk tradition. These are the characteristics of the master narrator of pithy anecdotes, the skilled raconteur of supernatural belief stories, the reciter of social protest jokes, the teller of dialect stories, and even the singer of traditional ballads. To some extent the appeal of *Two Years Before the Mast* is like that of 'Sir Patrick Spens', and the effect of *The Log of a Cowboy* is like that of 'The Old Chisholm Trail'.

Not only did Dana and Adams succeed in representing a natural oral style, but also each of them used authentic folklore skillfully and unobtrusively, weaving together strands of invented, reported, and traditional material into scenes of pleasing variety and balance. The chapters that describe setting out on the two trips illustrate this. In Chapter III of *The Log of a Cowboy*, titled 'The Start', the foreman gives his final instructions, and a typical day of slow, steady travel ends by the campfire with storytelling, or on night guard with singing. There is some friendly banter at the fireside as men ride in and out to change guards, and finally a prank is sprung on one wisecracker in order to 'cure him of sucking eggs and acting smart'; at this the campfire circle breaks up and men roll in their blankets to sleep. In Chapter II of *Two Years Before the Mast*, titled 'First Impressions', Dana describes his captain's initial orders and the first days at sea. The men were 'singing out' as they worked and telling tales when they rested, and one of them prescribed a home cure for the new hand's seasickness so that he could 'begin on a new tack', and settle 'into that routine of sea life which is only broken by a storm, a sail, or the sight of land'.

Both of these books reward the folklorist [and the historian of American English] with rich accounts of similar occupational traditions; they preserve for the literary critic's attention examples of a style that intrigues by managing to be very effective and yet to seem artless. The books have given ordinary readers a sense of authentic, thrilling experience related quite simply. There are no pirates, no rustlers, no pretty schoolmarms, and no detectives in either book, and there is neither any straining for effect nor any apology for bluntness. In sum, these books have become the classics of two historic American callings largely because they are true to the life, the spirit, and to the folklore of their subjects.

NOTES

1. *Two Years Before the Mast,* published in 1840 (New York: Bantam Books, 1959), hereafter cited as *Two*. *The Log of a Cowboy,* published in 1903 (Garden City, N.Y., Doubleday Dolphin edn., 1960), hereafter cited as *Log*. I have selected modern paperback editions to cite, considering them fitting sources for investigating popular literature. (Unhappily, the Dolphin edition was allowed to go out of print in March, 1964. A new paperback edition has been published by University of Nebraska Press.)
2. References in bracketed comments are in References to Introduction.

REFERENCES

Cooper, James Fenimore (1950), *The Prairie.* New York, Rinehart Editions.
Gregg, Josiah (1962), *Commerce of the Prairies: The 1844 Edition, Unabridged.* Philadelphia, Lippincott.
Hudson, Wilson M. (1964), *Andy Adams: His Life and Writings.* Dallas.
Irving, Washington (1961), *Astoria: The 1836 Edition, Unabridged.* Philadelphia, Lippincott.
Laws, Malcolm (1964), *Native American Balladry,* revised edition. Philadelphia, The American Folklore Society.
Osgood, Ernest Staples (1929), *The Day of the Cattleman.* Chicago, Phoenix Books.
Parkman, Francis (1961), *The Oregon Trail.* New York, Signet Classics.
Rølvaag, O. E. (1927), *Giants in the Earth.* New York.
Rush, Oscar (1930), *The Open Range and Bunk House Philosophy.* Caldwell, Idaho.
Siringo, Charles A. (1950), *A Texas Cowboy.* New York.
Spiller, Robert E. et al., editors (1953), *Literary History of the United States,* one volume, revised edition. New York.
Thompson, Harold W. (1939), *Body, Boots and Britches.* Philadelphia.
Twain, Mark (1953), *Roughing It.* New York, Rinehart.
Webb, Walter Prescott (1931), *The Great Plains.* New York, Grosset and Dunlap.
Wister, Owen (1960), *The Virginian.* New York, Popular Library.

TERRY G. JORDAN

The Origin of *Mott* in Anglo-Texan Vegetational Terminology

It was perhaps inevitable that the vital and influential Anglo-Texan subculture would leave its mark on American English. The most important contributions have been to vocabulary, both through the introduction of Spanish loanwords into English and the coinage of new words such as *maverick* and *gobbledegook*. The subject of the present essay is the Anglo-Texan word *mott*, pronounced mŏt and frequently encountered in its alternate spelling *motte*. In Texan vegetational terminology, *mott* means 'a copse or small stand of trees on a prairie', 'a clump of trees in a prairie', a small thicket of bushes or trees, or a grove of trees. *Mott* occurs in Texas both in the vernacular and as a generic place name suffix. As will be discussed below, linguists have traditionally considered it to be a modified Spanish loanword, in the same category as *lariat, ranch, bronc* and many others. The Spanish word *mata* has been proposed as the parent of Anglo-Texan *mott*. It is my thesis that there are a number of other plausible origins for the word and that *mott* may not be derived from Spanish at all.

An important clue to the origin of *mott* may be revealed by its spatial distribution in Texas. As a generic place name suffix, it occurs mainly in the coastal prairie adjacent to the Gulf of Mexico, particularly in the 'coastal bend' country from the lower Colorado River southwestward to Baffin Bay (Figure 1).[1] The eastern boundary of toponymic *mott* is rather sharply drawn, for only one example has been found east of the lower Colorado. *Mott* place names are only occasionally found in the interior prairies of Texas.[2] In several instances, rural communities in Texas have been named for a nearby *mott*, as in Long Mott, a Calhoun County hamlet, and Elm Mott, a growing suburb of Waco in central Texas. The term is much more widespread in the vernacular than as a place name suffix. E. B. Atwood has mapped its usage in folk speech, concluding that *mott* is concentrated as a vernacular term 'mostly in the Corpus Christi

This article is a revision of 'The Origin of "Motte" and "Island" in Texan Vegetation Terminology', published originally in the *Southern Folklore Quarterly* 36 (1972):121–135.

area', though it 'has spread to a considerable portion of South Central and Southwest Texas.[3] (See also Figure 1.)

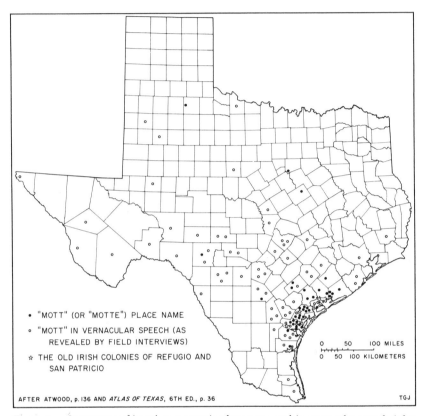

Figure 1.   *Occurrence of 'mott' as a generic place name and in vernacular speech (after Atwood [1962:136] and* Atlas of Texas *[fifth edition], 36)*

Additional assistance in determining the origin of *mott* can be gained by ascertaining, as nearly as possible, the place and date of its first usage in the vernacular. The earliest known written reference to *mott* dates from 1841. George Wilkins Kendall, a native of New Hampshire and resident of New Orleans who was newly arrived in Texas, wrote that the word 'mot' was used by Texans to describe small clumps of woods in a prairie.[4] Kendall first encountered the term in the south-central part of the state, near or within the present zone of major *mott* usage, and it was obviously new to him. The famous Texas adventurer 'Big Foot' Wallace, describing his experiences of the mid-1830s, spoke of 'mots of wild cherry and plum trees',[5] but his account was not written until the 1870s and it is impossible to know when *mott* became a part of his vocabulary. In 1846, the traveler William A. McClintock, a native and resident of Kentucky, saw 'here and there a "motte" of thorns and brambles' near the Aransas River near the Gulf Coast, within the area where *mott* usage is most common today.[6] McClintock's account is the first known written reference in which one of the two correct spellings of the word is employed. Still later, in 1857, William H. Emory, a native of Maryland who was taking part in the United States–Mexican border survey, referred to 'clumps of post-oak called *mots*' in Texas.[7] He apparently first encountered the term in the coastal prairie near Matagorda Bay, and it was obviously not previously known to him. The written evidence suggests, then, that *mott* probably entered the Anglo-Texan vernàcular during the 1830s and that a current spelling was employed at least by the mid-1840s, if not earlier.

In addition to the commonly assumed Spanish origin, there are a number of possible explanations for Texan *mott*. Similar words are found in French, English, and Erse. In modern French, *motte* means 'clod', 'ball of earth', 'mound', or 'a slight elevation, either natural or artificial', none of which are close enough to the Texan meaning to excite further interest.[8] The Louisiana French use of *île* to mean 'grove' further damages any claim for direct French origin of Texan *mott*, as does the absence of French colonization in the zone of *mott* concentration. It is true that the French explorer La Salle visited that part of the coastal prairie of Texas in the late 1600s, but no place names of any sort were left behind by his ill-fated expedition.

The French word *motte* was introduced into English speech through the Norman invasion, surviving the transplanting with spelling and meaning intact. The first meanings listed for *motte* in any English dictionary are 'clod', 'clump', 'hillock', and 'a type of palisaded mound common in prehistoric Europe', all of which virtually duplicate the definitions of the French parent word. It is true, however, that the preferred English version is *mote*, pronounced with a hard 'o' and meaning 'height', 'eminence', or 'hill'. The use of *motte/mott* to mean 'a clump of trees in a prairie' follows only as a secondary definition, accompanied by the remark that this latter usage is found only regionally in the United States.[9] It is conceivable that the Texan *mott* was derived from the English noun *mottle*, which means 'a colored spot' or 'an appearance like that of having colored spots, blotches, or cloudings'.[10] Related words include 'mottled' and 'motley'. To describe groves of trees in a prairie as *mottles* would be quite in keeping with the meaning of the word. There are, however, some serious difficulties involved in accepting an English or Anglo-American origin of Texan *mott* by way of *mottle*, not the least of which are the

altered spelling and pronunciation. It is not common for the 'l' sound to
be lost through contraction in English. Furthermore, it is difficult to
explain why Anglo-Americans would have developed this word only in
parts of Texas, for they encountered groves of trees in the prairies along
the entire perimeter of the American frontier, from Minnesota to Texas.
In short, it seems unlikely that the Texan *mott* was derived directly from
English *motte* or *mottle*. This supposition is further strengthened by the
absence of *mott* as a place name or vernacular term in Louisiana, the
former home state of many of the Anglos who settled the Texas coastal
prairie.[11]

As was suggested above, the generally accepted theory for the origin of
the Texas *mott* is that it is derived from the Spanish *mata*. In Castilian
Spanish, this word can mean 'a piece of ground covered with trees of the
same species', 'copse', 'orchard', 'a young live oak tree', and cane-
brake.[12] Even more promising are the Mexican-Spanish meanings for
mata, which include 'a group of trees in the middle of a prairie' and 'a hill
or a forest . . . that is small or of limited extent'.[13] So convincing is this
evidence that it has been accepted by the Texas linguistic expert E. B.
Atwood[14] and the editor of *The American Heritage Dictionary of the
English Language*,[15] among others. The borrowing would fit Dillard's
'second stage' of language contact between Spanish and English, a time
when many loanwords, some modified almost beyond recognition,
entered English speech.[16] Particularly numerous were loanwords relating
to horsemanship and the management of cattle from horseback.

It is here proposed that the Texan *mott* is perhaps not derived from
Mexican-Spanish *mata*, both because there are certain difficulties
involved in accepting the Spanish origin theory and because plausible
alternative explanations exist. First, the most convincing meaning of
Mexican-Spanish *mata*, 'a group of trees in the middle of a prairie', is
found in *southern* Mexico, the part of that country farthest removed from
Texas.[17] In Texas, *mata* normally refers to canebrakes, as in Matagorda,
'big cane'. Second, many Spanish words ending in 'a' were absorbed into
the Anglo-Texan vernacular, including *reata, acequia, resaca, remuda,*
and *hacienda*, but only rarely with the loss of pronunciation of the final
'a', such as would have occurred had *mata* been the basis for *mott*.
Moreover, Anglo-Texans typically flattened the sound of the Spanish *a* in
loanwords, as in 'ranch', 'dally rope', 'savvy', 'cavvieyard', and 'wrangler', a modification which did not occur if *mott* was derived from *mata*.
Also worth noting is the fact that *mata* is invariably a prefix when used in
Spanish place names, while in Texas *mott* is always a suffix. Almost none
of the Texan *motts* have a Spanish-Mexican prefix.[18] Even around the city
of Victoria, founded by the Mexicans on the coastal prairie in the mid-

1820s, they bear names such as Sutton Mott, Kentucky Mott,[19] and Blue Mott, suggesting non-Mexican origin. The only exception detected so far is Alazan Mott in Kleberg County, but its Arabic-Spanish prefix was derived from nearby Alazan Bay by Anglo-Texans. In short, the transition from *mata* to *mott* does not parallel changes or lack of changes in spelling and pronunciation observed in other words borrowed from Mexican Spanish by Anglo-Texans. *Mott* may be one of the words traditionally attributed to borrowing from Spanish which 'turn out not to be explainable in terms of English phonological interference on Spanish'.[20]

Still, the temptation to accept the Spanish *mata* origin might remain compelling if no attractive alternative existed. However, there are such alternatives. The coastal prairie in the zone of *mott* concentration is today peopled not only by the descendants of Anglo-Americans and Mexicans, but also by persons of Irish, German, Czech, Danish, Swedish, and Polish ancestry.[21] Of these diverse European minority groups, only the Irish were present as early as the 1830s, when *mott* presumably entered Texas English. The Irish colonists came to Texas in the late 1820s and early 1830s at the encouragement of the government of Mexico, which sought to impose a human barrier of Catholic Europeans in the path of the westward expansion of potentially disloyal Protestant Anglo-Americans.[22] The major Irish settlements founded were San Patricio, named for the patron saint of the colonists and located on the Nueces River upstream from present-day Corpus Christi; and Refugio, at the site of an old abandoned Spanish mission some forty miles northeast of San Patricio. It is significant that both of these colonies lay in the zone of present *mott* concentration (Figure 1). The Irish quickly spread out from these villages, scattering through much of present-day Refugio, Aransas, and San Patricio counties. As late as 1850, persons of Irish birth or parentage constituted the largest single ethnic group in these counties, accounting for almost fifty percent of the population.[23] By contrast, Spanish-surnamed individuals were only one-sixth as numerous as the immigrant Irish in the two counties combined in 1850.

Since the Irish settled in a largely unpopulated region between the clusters of Anglo and Hispano population, it stands to reason that they were the people responsible for naming many of the environmental features of the area. Only some of the streams, bays, and other prominent features had been named previously by the Spaniards. The adoption of cattle ranching by many of the Irish settlers in the 1830s caused them to spread out and become familiar with the vegetational features of the surrounding areas. The cattle often found refuge from the heat of summer in the shade of *motts*.

The leading European source area of the Irish immigrants was County

Wexford, situated in the east of Ireland, in the coastal region south of Dublin.²⁴ Perhaps some of the colonists had at least a partial knowledge of Erse Gaelic, the ancestral Celtic tongue of the Irish, but for all of them English was the mother tongue. The eastern location of County Wexford meant that Anglo-Norman influence from England had been strong over the centuries, though the population there had clung tenaciously to Roman Catholicism.

Significantly, there are many *mottes*, or *motes*, in County Wexford and other parts of Ireland (Figure 2). To be sure, these are *mottes* in the traditional British-English sense, defined as man-made mounds dating from antiquity. In the words of the geographer A. R. Orme, an expert on Ireland, 'the motte or mote was a twenty to forty-feet-high, steep sided, artificial mound of earth, topped by a thirty to one hundred-feet-wide summit flat defended by a timber palisade and blockhouse. . . .'²⁵ Most of these *mottes* were established as fortifications in the late twelfth and early thirteenth centuries, at a time when Anglo-Norman efforts to conquer Ireland reached a peak.²⁶ The use of the word *mote* or *motte* in Ireland can be attributed to the French spoken by these Norman invaders, and it has survived in the vernacular English of the Irish. The word, modified as *móta*, also entered the vocabulary of Celtic Erse.

Once accepted into the Irish vernacular, the term *motte* or *mote* subsequently came to mean any artificial mound, including some which predated the Norman invasion. Graves of chieftains and other hallowed places came to bear the name, and perhaps by such association numerous Norman *mottes* came to be venerated. In addition, various Irish saints sometimes ascended such mounds to speak to the gathered peasantry, lending the *mottes* a special religious significance. For these reasons, the *mottes* were generally not tilled or grazed, with the result that in time the artificial slopes and summits became covered with trees. In later times, particularly in the 1600s, some landlords deliberately had trees planted on *mottes*. Significantly, the forested *mottes* were among the few timber-covered places anywhere in Ireland, for the countryside became almost completely deforested. The *mottes* stood as islands of timber, rising impressively from the surrounding fields, pastures, and meadows, visible for many miles. To be sure, some of the *mottes* remained devoid of trees, covered simply by grass, but there is no doubt that a significant number of them were tree-covered in the early 1800s, when the Wexford emigrants left for Texas. The numerous *mottes* found in Wexford, especially in the south, along the Slaney and Barrow valleys, surely made a lasting impression on the superstitious peasants of the province (Figure 2).

The evidence reveals, then, that *motte* was used in parts of nineteenth-century Ireland, including Wexford, to describe mounds that were often,

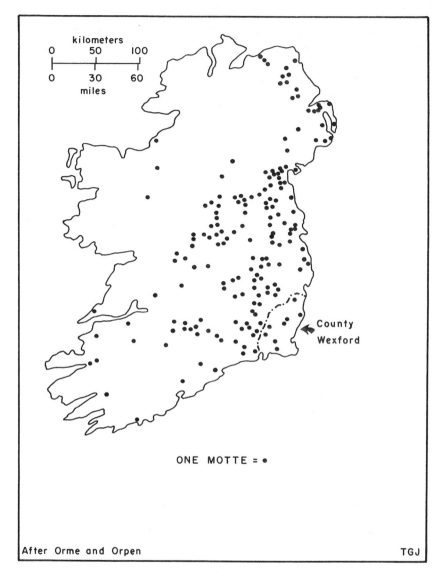

Figure 2. *Distribution of mottes in rural Ireland (after Orme and Orpen)*

if not usually, tree-covered. Confronted with oak groves which rose impressively from the table-flat coastal prairie of Texas, the Wexford emigrants could quite understandably have employed *mott* to describe them. Indeed, the similarity becomes almost compelling when one considers that some of the Texan *motts* occupy slightly raised ground, small natural mounds and salt domes which abound on the otherwise level coastal plain. An example is Lund Motte, which occupies a low height overlooking Tres Palacios Bay in the Coastal Prairie of western Matagorda County, Texas.[27] Still further evidence supporting Irish origin of the Texan *motts* can be detected in certain of the place name prefixes, as in the case of O'Leary Motte in Refugio County.[28] In addition, it is perhaps significant that an accepted spelling of the Texan *mott* duplicates one of those of the proposed Norman-English-Irish parent word.

The principal difficulty with this Irish origin theory, and a major one, lies in pronunciation, for in Ireland *mote*, pronounced 'moat', is the preferred form.[29] Still, it is possible that the Wexford Irish were familiar with a soft-'o' pronunciation of *motte*. The word has apparently disappeared from the Wexford vocabulary, and was unknown to some rural Irish folk living in the vicinity of *mottes* in the early years of the twentieth century.[30]

Another possible Irish origin is offered by the Erse word *mothar*, which means a clump of brush, a thicket, or an area of thick brushwood.[31] Wexford was one of the most Anglicized parts of Ireland, and the Celtic language had probably passed out of use there even by the 1820s, when the Texas migration occurred. Also, the *th* sound in Celtic and English speech tends to be persistent and is rarely hardened to a *t* by native speakers of these languages, as would have been necessary if *mothar* 'mothered' *mott*. Still, it is a possibility which should not be overlooked. At the very least, we can say that the Irish were preconditioned by their own vocabulary to accept the Spanish word.

Those who are disinclined to accept an Irish origin of *mott* should consider Spanish words other than *mata* as the possible parent. Of particular interest is the Spanish word *mota*, equivalent to French *motte*, meaning 'mound', 'hummock', or 'an eminence of low altitude which rises above a plain'.[32] Unlike *mata* in its 'grove' meaning, *mota* was widely used in Texas as a generic place name, especially in Kenedy and Brooks counties on the southern fringe of the *mott* usage core area. There one finds numerous such hillocks, such as Mota Verde, Mota Casa, Mota del Tacon, and Mota Negra. A variety of other names, such as La Mota Ranch and San Pedro de las Motas appear in the same general area. Some of these *motas* are tree-covered and surrounded by prairie or brush country. *Mota* is probably the explanation of the intriguing toponym Paderones Mot which appears on a 1794 Spanish map of the southernmost part of Texas, located north of modern Edinburg.[33] Another Spanish word, *moto*, means 'landmark' or 'guidepost', and it is conceivable that a grove of trees in a prairie might have served such a function.[34]

The diffusion of *mott* from its core area-cradle of usage in the coastal prairie to certain other parts of Texas is fairly easy to explain. The coastal prairie corridor served as a funnel through which Anglo-Texan cattlemen passed westward.[35] The grasslands of Refugio and San Patricio counties were home to hundreds of cattle ranchers in the 1840s and 1850s who later moved into portions of southern, southwestern, and western Texas. These ranchers were in all probability the agents of *mott* diffusion within the state, and they may well have carried the term as far as adjacent eastern New Mexico. This would help explain why *mott* spread so far to the west of the coastal prairie core area but failed to make any substantial headway eastward from the old core area.

I hope I have sufficiently clouded the waters that a closer scrutiny of 'obvious' Spanish loanwords and generic place names such as *mott* will be made. Texas was and is an ethnically diverse state, not simply a contact zone between Anglo and Hispano. Individual elements of the Texan subculture are often rather more complicated to explain than has previously been recognized, involving numerous ethnic groups other than Anglo-Americans and Mexican-Americans.[36]

NOTES

1. Data on the generic place name *mott* were collected from United States Geological Survey topographic maps, county highway maps, county and local histories, ranch histories, and field observation. See the map by Terry G. Jordan (1976), 'Selected generic place-names describing vegetational features', in *Atlas of Texas*, fifth edition, ed. by Stanley A. Arbingast et al., 36. Austin, The University of Texas Bureau of Business Research; and Margaret Gidley Clover (1952), 'The place names of Atascosa County, Texas'. Unpublished Master of Arts thesis, University of Texas, Austin. The *motts* in this core area for which specific prefixes have been found are: Alazan Mott (Kleberg Co.), Black Mott(e) (Refugio Co.), Black Mott (San Patricio Co.), Blue Mott (Victoria Co.), Crop Mott (Refugio Co.), Eagle Mott (Refugio Co.), Grape Mott (Jackson Co.), Kentucky Mott (Victoria Co.), Larry Mott (Refugio Co.), Long Mott (Calhoun Co.), Lower String Mott (San Patricio Co.), Lund Motte (Matagorda Co.), Money Mott (Refugio Co.), Mustang Mott (DeWitt Co.), Mustang Mott (Refugio Co.), Mustang Motts (San Patricio Co.), Nine Mile Mott (San Patricio Co.), Oak Mott (San Patricio Co.), O'Leary Motte (Refugio Co.), Peach Mott(e) (Refugio Co.), Peelers Mott (Atascosa Co.), Rattlesnake Mott (San Patricio Co.), Round Mott (Wharton Co.), Shepherds Mott (Matagorda Co.), Sutton Mott (Victoria Co.), The Motts (Nueces Co.), Turtle Mott (Matagorda Co.), Twin Mott (Refugio Co.), Umbrella Motte (Jackson Co.), Upper String Mott (San Patricio Co.), Well Mott (Refugio Co.), and Wildcat Mott (Matagorda Co.). There are undoubtedly more.
2. The toponymic *motts* found outside the core area are Cedar Mott (Edwards Co.), Cottonwood Mott (Motley Co.), Elm Mott (Johnson Co.), and Elm Mott (McLennan Co.).
3. Elmer Bagby Atwood (1962), *The Regional Vocabulary of Texas,* 91, 136. Austin, University of Texas Press.

4. George Wilkins Kendall (1844), *Narrative of the Texan Santa Fé Expedition*, vol. I:39–40. London, Wiley and Putnam.

5. John C. Duval (and William A. A. Wallace) (1966), *The Adventures of Big Foot Wallace*, 15–16. Lincoln, University of Nebraska Press.

6. William A. McClintock (1930–1931), 'Journal of a trip through Texas and northern Mexico in 1846–1847', *Southwestern Historical Quarterly* 34:154, 237–238.

7. William H. Emory (1857), *United States and Mexican Boundary Survey, Report of William H. Emory, Major First Cavalry and U. S. Commissioner*, vol. I, part I: 56. House of Representatives, 34th Congress, 1st Session, Ex. Doc. No. 135. Washington, D.C., Cornelius Wendell, Printer.

8. Paul Robert (1966), *Dictionnaire alphabétique et analogique de la langue française*. Paris, Société du Nouveau Littré, Le Robert. Denis Girard et al. (1962), *The New Cassell's French Dictionary of the English Language*. New York, Funk and Wagnalls.

9. William A. Neilson et al., editors (1955), *Webster's New International Dictionary of the English Language*, second edition, unabridged. Springfield, Mass., Merriam.

10. *Webster's New International Dictionary*, (1955).

11. Personal correspondence, Randall A. Detro to T. G. Jordan, April 7, 1970. See also R. A. Detro (1970), 'Generic terms in Louisiana place names: an index to the cultural landscape'. Unpublished Ph.D. dissertation, Louisiana State University, Baton Rouge.

12. *Diccionario de la Lengua Española* (1970). Madrid, Real Academia Española; Edgar A. Peers et al., editors (1960), *Cassell's Spanish Dictionary*. New York, Funk and Wagnalls.

13. Francisco J. Santamaria (1942), *Diccionario General de Americanismos*. Mexico City, Pedro Robredo, and, by the same author (1959), *Diccionario de Mejicanismos*. Mexico City, Porrua.

14. Elmer Bagby Atwood (1962), *Regional Vocabulary of Texas*, 109. Austin, University of Texas Press.

15. William Morris, editor (1969), *The American Heritage Dictionary of the English Language*. Boston, Houghton Mifflin and the American Heritage Publishing Co.

16. J. L. Dillard (1975), *All-American English: A History of American English*, 131. New York, Random House.

17. See the two works cited in Note 13.

18. Refer to the list of *mott* place names in Notes 1 and 2.

19. Rendered as 'Kentucky Mutt' on the United States Geological Survey topographic map quadrangle, no doubt by a puzzled non-Texan draftsman!

20. J. L. Dillard (1975), *All-American English: A History of American English*, 127–128. New York, Random House.

21. See Terry G. Jordan (1970), 'Population origin groups in rural Texas', Map Supplement No. 13, *Annals, Association of American Geographers* 60: 404–405; large color map in pocket at end of June issue of the *Annals*; and Stanley Arbingast et al., editors, *Atlas of Texas*, (fifth edition), 29. Austin, the University of Texas Bureau of Business Research.

22. The best source on the Texas Irish colonies is William H. Oberste (1953), *Texas Irish Empresarios and Their Colonies*. Austin, Texas, Von Boeckmann-Jones. See also Hobart Huson (1953), *Refugio: Comprehensive History of Refugio County*. Woodsboro, Texas, Rooke Foundation.

23. Terry G. Jordan (1969), 'Population origins in Texas, 1850', *Geographical Review* 59: 87, 98, 99; hand-count of Manuscript U.S. Census population schedules, Refugio and San Patricio counties, 1850.

24. Walter Prescott Webb and H. Bailey Carroll, editors (1952), *The Handbook of Texas*, vol. II:456. Austin. Texas, Texas State Historical Association.

25. Antony R. Orme (1970), *Ireland*, 107. Chicago, Aldine. See also pages 104, 106, 111, 198, 267. For additional information on Irish *mottes*, see vol. I: 339–343, vol. II: 343–344, and map following p. 344 of Goddard H. Orpen (1911), *Ireland Under the Normans, 1169–1216*. Oxford, Clarendon Press; M. A. O'Brien (1957), 'Place names', in *A View of Ireland* , ed. by James F. Meenan and David A. Webb. Dublin, British Association for the Advancement of Science; Goddard H. Orpen (1906), 'Mote and Bretesche building in Ireland', *English Historical Review* 21:435–444; and Goddard H. Orpen (1907), 'Motes and Norman castles in Ireland', *English Historical Review* 22:228–254, 440–467.

26. Most of the information in the remainder of this paragraph and all of the following paragraph was derived from personal correspondence, Antony R. Orme to T. G. Jordan, May 22, 1971.

27. United States Geological Survey, topographic map, 'Turtle Bay, Texas', quadrangle, scale 1:24,000, published 1952.

28. United States Geological Survey, topographic map, 'Tivoli SW Texas', quadrangle, scale 1:24,000, published 1952.

29. See, for example, Michael Traynor (1953), *The English Dialect of Donegal: A Glossary*, 187. Dublin, Royal Irish Academy. Orpen uses *mote* throughout his various works, though Orme apparently prefers *motte*. In English dictionaries, preference is normally given to hard- 'o' *mote*, while *motte*, in the meaning of hillock, is often completely omitted.

30. Goddard H. Orpen (1906), 'Mote and bretesche building in Ireland', *English Historical Review* 21:437.

31. *Mothar* was brought to my attention by Richard G. Underwood and D. W. Meinig of Syracuse University.

32. *Diccionario de la Lengua Española* (1970). Madrid, Real Academia Española; Edgar A. Peers et al., editors (1960), *Cassell's Spanish Dictionary*. New York, Funk and Wagnalls.

33. Florence J. Scott (1969), *Royal Land Grants North of the Rio Grande, 1777–1821*, 81. Rio Grande City, Texas, La Retama Press.

34. Edgar A. Peers et al., editors (1960), *Cassell's Spanish Dictionary*. New York, Funk and Wagnalls.

35. See Terry G. Jordan (1969), 'The origin of Anglo-American cattle ranching in Texas: a documentation of diffusion from the lower South', *Economic Geography* 45:63–87.

36. In this context, the recent discovery of a significant Irish impact on vernacular architecture in south Texas is enlightening. See Ada L. K. Newton (1973), 'The Anglo-Irish house of the Rio Grande', *Pioneer America* 5(1):33–38.

DONALD HATLEY and KATHLEEN THOMAS SEVERANCE

Communication in a Frontier Society

When the early white, Anglo-Saxon settlers of Red River Parish moved into North Louisiana, they brought with them problems in communication which have still been only partly solved. Some of these involved actual language differences, as with Indian groups, or ethnic class/caste exclusions which made some communication minimal and even undesirable, except under prescribed conditions, to that group of settlers. In maintaining the communication network with friends and relatives left behind, as well as with those who lived close by, illiteracy was perhaps the greatest problem.

People who could not read and write had to rely on those who could or go on having messages delivered by word of mouth. On the frontier it was common for travelers to repay their hosts by reciting, at random, long lists of names and places and messages they had collected on the chance that some of the information would be pertinent. This method of 'passin' the news', as it was called, often caused messages to find their destinations in surprising ways with suprising results. One Red River Parish resident tells of the time her family, after listening patiently to a long list of names, heard a familiar name with good news attached, and the whole family 'come up ashoutin''. She chuckled and added, 'Hit like to of scairt that poor man to death.'

Those who could write, or got someone to write for them, 'mailed' letters; however, misspelling frequently proved a problem. Names were usually spelled according to a rough idea of letter–sound correspondence, and the shortening of names was a common practice. For example, Melissa frequently became Lissie or Lis; then, with the substitution of z for s, Liz or Lizzie.

After getting the name right, the letter writer had to contend with the address. Just how could a writer address a letter to someone who might be anywhere west of the Mississippi? As one of the informants explained:

A preliminary version of this paper was published in 1976 in *Louisiana Folklife Newsletter* 1 (2), October. The article is reprinted with the permission of that periodical.

'When most folks set out, they didn't know where they was goin' or what they'd find when they got there. Might start out for Texas and wind up in California. Folks just started off alookin' for a good stoppin' place, and if things didn't work out there — why there was plenty other places to go to. Just pick up and light out again, that 'uz all a body had to do. Seems like the whole world was amovin' back then.'

One common form of address was 'John Doe, Louisianer Terr'. Another was 'John Doe, somewheres on the Red River'. Common or frequently used names sometimes required further identification. Thus, for example, a John Doe might be described as 'Jack Doe's boy, out of Butler County, Alabama, married to Jane Smith from there, somewhere near Texas'.

If the letter writer was lucky enough to have the name of the town where the relative or friend lived, that was a help but no guarantee that the letter would be delivered, because while the letter was being carried, either the relative or the town 'could of dried up and just blowed away, or picked up and moved on'.

Even though 'things were might chancy back then', letters still had to be mailed, and mailing usually consisted of finding someone headed in the right direction and asking him to carry the letter as far as possible and then pass it on. To help insure delivery, a writer frequently sent, by different people, as many as fifteen copies of the same letter. At times, carriers were paid, but usually letters were carried without charge because travelers realized that they would require similar favors in the future.

Letters passed from hand to hand were sometimes 'in the mail' for years. There are stories about letters being carried across the continent, to California and back, and then delivered to the right person not fifty miles from the point of origin. This happened in Fate Ivy's case. He roamed the West for seventeen years and was actually returning home when a letter caught up with him. Fate, who could not read, stuck the letter in his pocket, knowing that his mother would read it for him when he got home. When he finally reached home, the first thing he did was present the letter to his mother. 'Why, Fate Ivy', she exclaimed, 'this here letter is the one I wrote you seventeen years ago! If I'd knowed you was comin' back so soon, I wouldn't a writ.'

There were times however, when the 'news' couldn't wait seventeen years for delivery. When a letter had to be delivered quickly, as in the event of death and legal complications, a rider was employed. Generally, hired riders were paid only after they proved that they had delivered the mail. Writers frequently took stringent precautions to insure delivery, especially when sending money, because of the infamous Spanish Trail riders and other less-organized brigands who made a practice of robbing travelers. One such precaution was to tear bills in half, across the serial number, and to send only one half to the addressee. When proof of receipt was delivered, the other half was sent. If the first half was lost or stolen, the sender could use half of the bills and his list of serial numbers to have it replaced.

'Passing the news' over long distances presented many problems, but early settlers also had to solve problems in communication within the newly established frontier settlements. One of the most interesting of the methods they used was that known as the 'nigger holler'.[1] Its origins were not known to the informants, and its primitive name gives no indication of the true sophistication of the form. At one time, the 'nigger holler' served as a language in itself. By using this cross between a yodel and a yell or scream, practiced hollerers could convey even complicated messages over surprisingly long distances.

By the 1930s, the holler had degenerated into a kind of 'all's well' signal. This method of communication was most often used in the evening to let other people know that everything was all right. One man would start the holler, and others would take it up. They would continue hollering until the 'message' had gone completely around the settlement. A man needing help had only to remain silent, and the neighbors would converge on his house to render assistance.

Settlers also used the holler for private family purposes. One man who made the day-long trip by wagon from his farm to Coushatta, seat of Red River Parish, and back, hollered at successive points on the way home to let his wife know that it was time to prepare the evening meal. At each holler, she would put something else on the fire. The husband's last holler coincided with the wife's call to supper.

Most of the intercommunity communications were of a simple signal variety. As one informant said: 'When folks worked a good distance from the house, as they did back then, a body had to save some way of callin' 'em in to dinner.' Some beat a spoon against a pan; some rang the dinner bell, though bells were not common in a poor area like Red River Parish. Many people used a cow horn, locally called a 'dog horn', blowing one long blast and one short blast close together.[2]

Three short, quick blasts on a 'dog horn', repeated at regular intervals, was an urgent call for help and brought people from miles around. Later, after people started using breechloaders, three quick shots served the same purpose. Jangling a bell at any time other than at meals was another emergency signal, and there are still places around the parish where a child who 'fools around with the big bell' can get quick punishment.

Then, as now, in North Louisiana where hunting is extremely popular, continuous blowing on a 'dog horn' meant someone was lost. If the blowing continued for too long, the neighbors would quickly gather to help. Three spaced blasts on a horn or gun told people that the lost was found.

Other sounds indicated that a neighbor was in distress. As one resident of Red River Parish said: 'Folks paid attention to things, and if a man had reason to believe a neighbor was in trouble, he didn't wait to be asked. He saddled up and went, on shank's mare [walking], if necessary.'

One of these sounds was that of a horse running past a house. As a matter of courtesy and plain common sense, 'You just didn't run a horse past a man's house unless there was bad trouble'. One man tells a story of himself and his brother and the time they got the whipping of their lives for running a horse. It all happened because of an argument over a pretty girl. Both wanted the first dance with her at a party which was to take place that night. They decided that a horse race would settle the argument, and it did. But to this day, neither of them remembers who won. What they do remember is the whipping they received when they returned home to find the neighbors waiting to see that the proper punishment was meted out for giving a false danger signal.

People also developed a system of trail signs. For example, the first group of a large party of hunters or loggers who went up a certain trail cut a pine top (the top portion of a pine tree) and put it along the trail with the butt pointing out the direction taken. 'Chunking', placing a chunk of wood alongside the trail, served the same purpose, but was not quite as obvious. The chunk said as plainly as words, 'Look for a turnoff', and indicated the direction. Individuals or groups had their own special signs, sometimes blazing, painting, or otherwise marking trees, rocks, or even fence posts to denote passage or settlement. These special markings on or around a homeplace have been known to aid in the delivery of a straying letter. 'John Doe, his mark' was more than an 'X' during the early days on the North Louisiana frontier.

Sticks were used beside trails in the same way, and some people developed elaborate codes, using notched sticks, different-sized or broken sticks, or rocks and sticks together to 'write' detailed, exact messages.

Of course, it was the attitude of the people in a community that made these and other forms of communication work. The settlers paid attention to what was going on around them, and sometimes, as a result of noticing some small thing missing, added, or out of place, they answered a call for help before it was officially given. Smoke from a farmhouse at the wrong time of day, or no smoke at the right time, the sudden brief urgency of an axe sounding or the absence of such a sound — any least thing out of the órdinary — alerted these early Louisianians to possible danger, and in a time when the individual's life and safety directly depended on the life and safety of the whole community, a hint was enough to bring immediate response.

When there was good news to communicate, the neighbors were more than happy to help. Gossiping old women today are merely, in many cases, attempting to fulfill the function demanded of them in the early days. It was the responsibility of every citizen to disseminate both vital as well as unimportant information. People were, by the very nature of their society, required to 'spread the word'.

News was also 'published at the church'. This meant anything from having the preacher or one of the deacons make an announcement, doing it oneself, or putting up a notice or hand-written, decorated invitation, to simply 'talking it up before or after the meeting'.

At best, communicating in the early days in Louisiana was a difficult matter, and at worst, impossible. But, as one Red River Parish resident said; 'We didn't have too bad a time here even before we got the telephone. I mean, nowadays, it's a lot easier — but it used to be a lot more fun.'[3]

NOTES

1. For an overall treatment of the holler, see Peter T. Bartis (1971) 'An examination of the holler in North Carolina White tradition', *Southern Folklore Quarterly* 39:209–217.
2. The term *dog horn* does not appear to be recorded in any of the historical dictionaries, and we have no theory as to where or how the term originated.
3. The informants cited in this paper are all natives of Red River Parish. They range in age from twenty-four to ninety-one years and include: Miss Lonie Breedlove, W. R. Hawthorne, Robert McCart, Travis Price, Lavinia Robinson, Elria Thomas, Estella Page Thomas, Zara Zimmerman Thomas, Celeste Walker, Felix Walker, and Josie Walker. The time period covered in the anecdotes is from the 1700s through the 1940s, after which telephone service was made available to a majority of the parish residents. According to C. R. Smoth, South Central Bell Telephone Company representative, prior to 1950, only 30–35 percent of the parish householders had telephones; in 1976, the percentage had risen to 73 percent. Use of signaling devices is still common in the rural areas of the parish; even those residents who now have telephones often prefer to use a dog horn, a gun, or a bell.

PART THREE

Immigration and Migration

Introduction

In 1919, H. L. Mencken broke ground in the study of American English with his *The American Language*. In that volume, which in many ways presented a more consistent picture than his later productions on the same subject, Mencken considered what is now being called the obvious about Americans and their language: We are basically a nation of immigrants, and not by any means of immigrants only from the British Isles. Mencken's thesis, that a new language called 'American' had been formed as a close relative of 'English', was almost unanimously rejected by linguists, but this data were utilized by a number (see Pyles 1952) who laid claim to a higher degree of professional sophistication than Mencken possessed. With that kind of dismissal — and with the gradual absorption of Mencken into the tradition in his three later editions and two supplements — the original thesis was effectively dead and almost forgotten. By the time the abridged fourth edition (1963), edited by McDavid and Maurer, came out, incorporating many of the findings of the Linguistic Atlas of the United States and Canada, Mencken had been effectively absorbed into the tradition. Mencken was praised as an originator and a catalyst, and no sane linguist ever dared compete with him as a prose stylist, but his linguistic accomplishment was regarded as little or nothing.

There is, however, some evidence that Mencken, instead of originating the tradition that attributed 'American' to the influence of immigrants, rather continued such a tradition as it had developed outside linguistics. Stephen Graham's *With Poor Immigrants to America* (1914) had already used the phrase 'The American Language' as a chapter title. Graham was even less a formal linguist than Mencken, but he shared the latter's ear for accents and also his willingness to generalize. What's more, Graham (1914:244) even had a little to say about maritime influences on the immigrants' English:

Suddenly a bell was rung on the steamer, and a little man came forward and announced in broken English: "Somebody wan' to come on the boat; the time is supp."

Inhibited partly by the reconstructive tradition (see General Introduction), formal dialectologists have long been unwilling to hear ethnically correlated 'accents' or dialects; McDavid (1973a) cautions us to 'go slow' on ethnic attributions in a conventional if thoroughly unimaginative way. It is noteworthy, however, that Graham, like Feinsilver (this volume: pp. 223, 241) recognized the particularly Jewish use of *should* and gave an example as indicative of the kind of change going on in American English.

Some have intimated that Feinsilver's work falls halfway between Leo Rosten's popular nonlinguistic book (consisting more of Jewish jokes than of language materials) *The Joys of Yiddish* (1968) and 'The Linguistic and Cultural Atlas of Yiddish'. McDavid (1973b) predictably condescended to Feinsilver's *A Taste of Yiddish* (excerpted in this volume) as a 'worthy competitor' for Rosten's book and a preparation for 'understanding the significance of the scholarly endeavors of the Weinreichs and their associates'. McDavid also, more professionally, pointed out the omission of David Maurer's studies (1939) of 'the role of Yiddish in the argots of criminal subcultures'. I feel that McDavid has here, as he did in his early study of Negro dialect and Gullah (McDavid and McDavid 1951), come right up to the brink of a significant point without quite recognizing it. Feinsilver has dealt not with the arcane use of Yiddish by special, underground, or even underworld populations but with its function in and influence on everyday American English. It may take no special field techniques to recognize that influence, but it does take a certain amount of broad-mindedness to acknowledge it.

Sometimes it seems, as Mencken insisted, that linguists need to go out and use their eyes and ears during the time they spend reading the literature and administering questionnaires. In the *New York Times* for March 31, 1975, for example, food critic Craig Claiborne stood corrected on his Yiddish by a reader who wrote: 'From cooking you know; from Yiddish you don't, but that's all right. Nobody is perfect.' A few weeks before that I had heard an impressive paper on whether anyone spoke 'Yinglish'; the linguist who gave the paper rather preferred to think that nobody did. But when I asked an Introduction to Linguistics class at Ferkauf Graduate School the same question, the brightest in the class answered immediately, 'What else?'

Among other things, Feinsilver points out (as is also, possibly, obvious to everyone except research linguists) how much Yiddish has influenced our popular culture. The unflattering Yiddish terms *schmaltz* and *boraxy* could be applied to American radio broadcasting (especially to its music), television, and movies. But it helps a little bit, in retrospect, to know that not everybody involved in those mass medias was operating exclusively on the mental level of twelve years old. It could even make middle-aged academic Americans feel better about their youth to realize that, when they laughed at the verbal slapstick of Jack Benny and Bob Hope, someone at least was deriving a verbal double meaning from words like *schnook*. Some of us perceived a little of that complexity — maybe more than was actually there. Naively, we assumed that *schlemiel*, like *schmuck*, had a sexual second meaning; and we snickered with ignorant pseudosophistication. When one of Jack Benny's stooges repeated the formula line 'Today I yam a man', we (not knowing of Bar Mitzvah) thought the laughter of the studio audience (New Yorkers all) must be for the palatal glide before the initial vowel of the verb. But at least we had a slight bit of exposure to something more than Middle America, data ready to be reinterpreted if we ever made it to the big city and got some inkling of the real function of those Jewish expressions. (Middle America was just as naïve, of course, about other foreign languages. As late as the 1960s, an Italian restaurant in Waco, Texas, found it necessary to change its sign from *Pizzeria* to *Pizza-ria* because many passers-by thought the former was related to *pissoir*.)

American advertising, also, probably merits our horrified feeling that it is the world's worst. Jingles designed to sell soap are all too deeply imbedded in our childhood memories, but it helps, again, to realize that there was some cultural influence from Jewish immigrants and not just monolingualism combined with the profit motive. When Mrs. Feinsilver (1970:291) tells us how, . . . an ad of El Al airlines asking 'Why is this airline different from all other airlines?' actually provided four answers in the style of the Haggadah, each beginning 'On all other airlines . . . ', we somehow feel a little better about making the world's airlines and airports over in our own image; there have been some other influences admitted, however unconsciously, and American material culture has not destroyed everything else in its path.

Pennsylvania German, when it came to general attention, was even less well recognized than Yiddish influence. The Broadway play *Papa Is All* probably impressed most Americans in the hinterlands, if they even read about it, as having a sentimental title equivalent to *Papa Is the Whole Show* or something like that. Those who attended the show, and a few studious types who read about it later, probably got the information that the Pennsylvania German-English *all* meant more nearly 'exhausted, finished, done for'.

The Pennsylvania Germans, unlike the Jews and the Blacks in their differing ways, have never needed to have the attention of Americans in general. They have rich farm lands to support them, and do not have to make their way in the ghetto or even in the city. They can afford to issue publications poking mild fun at their own language variety as *Verhoodled English*, and they can afford to perpetuate 'stereotyped' expressions like,

The pants are too tight; I'll have to leave out the seat.
Throw your father down the stairs his hat.

When we find the learned Professor Otto Springer repeating some of these, we feel as though we had read an article giving the formulae to generate the Black English Vernacular sentence:

Who dat say who dat say who dat?

But a people as comfortable as the Pennsylvania Germans perhaps do not need to be afraid of caricature or of stereotyping.

Gypsies, with their past history of hundreds of years of slavery, could hardly be so comfortable, in America or anywhere else. Americans, who use a phrase like *to gyp* without any thought of ethnic slur, confuse the Romani with Irish horse traders — in fact, that should probably be the meaning assigned to *Gypsy* in the American lexicon; some appropriate form of *Rom* would better designate the group that migrated ultimately from India. Ian F. Hancock is certainly as well qualified as anyone alive to describe their English. A militant and outspoken former secretary of the Romani Literary Society, Hancock once silenced the television talk show emcee who introduced him as 'the king of the Gypsies' with the sharp retort, 'There's no such damned thing as the king of the Gypsies'. Besides writing on the creoles (including most of what has been done with Papia Kristang and with the Gullah of Bracketville, Texas) he has produced most of the serious study of the 'ethnolectal' English spoken by his own people.

Alone, perhaps, of the groups represented herein, the 'Gypsies' may be identified primarily by linguistic means. Hancock, who has published studies of their folklore and who is intensely interested in their history, uses a primarily linguistic criterion for membership in the group: A Rom learns at least some of the traditional language (in one or another of its various forms) and is identified with the group in an ultimately minimal way in that they will refuse to call him *gažo*.

The various Latin-American, Spanish-American, Mexican, or Chicano groups in the United States have the same problem of group nomenclature and the same principle of group identification through the use of Spanish. Often, however, groups that have been in the United States for more than one generation have a minimal use of Spanish and the Spanish surname, along perhaps with Roman Catholic religion, is the strongest identifying factor.

Puerto Ricans are only one of those groups, but they stand out, in a way, in having allegiance to their island home so that 'immigration' to the continental United States seldom involves any final separation from their childhood home. Many Newyorricans (Puerto Ricans who grew up in New York) who go back to the island speak English, their peer group language, better than Spanish. Often, that English is tinged with Black English Vernacular forms (Wolfram et al. 1972; Silverman 1975). In some cases, such as absence or 'deletion' of the concord marker for the third person singular, non-past, clearcut transmission or influence of the native language corresponds to what would automatically be termed the result of 'language universals' elsewhere.

American English is an important factor in the speech repertory of the island itself, so much so that some Hispanic purists have warned against 'loss' or 'corruption' of Spanish and a genuine language shift seemed to be in progress until there was a wholesale alteration of language policies in the 1950s. Newyorricans returning to the island find even their own compatriots extremely willing to talk to them in English, so that the hypothetical case of a Puerto Rican by 'blood' living on the island for a long time without mastering Spanish is at least possible. Puerto Ricans typically regard English as the language to be used with outsiders, and even some Spaniards and South Americans complain about Puerto Rican insistence upon using English (Dillard 1969).

Any danger of a complete shift to English seems to be obviated by the very nature of the English Puerto Rican islanders speak, however. It is strongly reminiscent of Spanish in accent, structure, and semantics. False cognates are institutionalized to the degree of being present in names of companies and in permanent, elaborate, neon-lit signs. Like Irishmen, whose variety of English can serve the function of group identification even if they do not speak any Celtic language, Puerto Ricans would be able to preserve their affinities through the variety of English that they speak.

Pedagogical considerations have been very strong for those who have been concerned with Puerto Rico. English as a Second Language teachers, armed with the perhaps not entirely undebatable slogan 'They Need English', have been very much in evidence. The ESL movement on the island gathered strength during the period when Fries and Trager–Smith dominated linguistics and were very influential on applied linguistics, so that the ultimately impossible (for a large group) aim of native speaker pronunciation occupied a disproportionate amount of time and effort. In such a context, characteristic Puerto Rican varieties of English have been regarded as 'errors' and taxonomies of those 'mistakes' have been compiled in hope of improving English teaching.

Rose Nash is one of the few who have not fallen into this error nor into the political fallacy which colors the writing of so many native Puerto Ricans on the language of their native land. Besides her training in linguistics, she brings a background of childhood multilingualism and an experience of some ten years — a long time in the highly mobile academic community of the island — along with considerable experience in language contact situations (she is the compiler of a quadrilingual dictionary of linguistic terminology) to the study of the Puerto Rican situation. We conducted the correspondence concerning my use of her article for this collection entirely in Spanglish ('You have reason. I no onnerestood.'), which should do something to prove that it is a genuine language variety.[1]

Something should probably be said, somewhere in this collection, about caricatures. Overly straight-laced linguists (some of them with inflated reputations) tend to relegate any variety that has been widely caricatured to the status of nonexistent variety, ignoring the obvious fact that a caricature in any other area is a distortion of *something*. (We do not conclude that President Carter has no teeth, simply because caricaturists represent them as impossibly large.) The late Eddie Lopez was the champion of Spanglish caricaturists. His Candid Flowers bears an impossible name in English, even though Candido Flores is a perfectly good Spanish name if we are so gringo-influenced as to omit the matronymic. Candid's famous line, 'You are the brassiere of your family', is too extreme a case of 'false cognates' ever to occur in actuality, although *el sostén* does translate as either 'the brassiere' or 'the support'. But when we see, in San Juan, a huge and expensive neon sign advertising LOPEZ AND GONZALES [not actual names] FABRICATORS, we are happy that we know about the possibilities. We permit ourselves, with no fear of being considered prejudiced, to rejoice in the knowledge that these partners might be considered by outsiders to have called themselves 'liars', but are known by insiders to have claimed only to be 'manufacturers'.[2]

Very many United States citizens are bilingual in English and Spanish, but so are many others in English and some other language. Since Mencken (and Graham) there has developed the fashion, however, of looking to other factors — primarily British regional dialects — to explain variation in American English. In fact, numbers of the collections purporting to inform educators about variety in American English (e.g. Bailey and Robinson 1973) hardly touch on the subject of bilingualism at all. (They certainly do not deal with multilingualism.) In the context of the fashions of the last few decades, Professor Magner's suggestion (p. 284) that local variants in American English may derive from languages originally competing with English is outright daring. To many, however, it seems that such factors have been too long overlooked.

NOTES

1. I overlook, here, Nash's distinction between 'Spanglish' and 'Englañol'.
2. These materials bear out fairly well William Nemser's statement (1971:123) that 'the contact situation should . . . be described not only by reference to the native and target languages of the learner . . . but by reference to the learner system as well.' One can agree with Nemser here and still wish that he had not made such a misstatement as the following (1971:120): '*hypercorrection* [occurs when] Spanish-English speakers often substitute [ŋ], which does not have phonemic status in Spanish, for /n/: English /sʌn/→Spanish-English /saŋ/.' It is, of course, absurd to refer to this process as 'hypercorrection'. [ŋ] is the allophone of the Spanish /n/ (or of Spanish /N/) which regularly occurs in final position. No reference to 'hypercorrection' is necessary; in fact, this articulation is definitely not an instance of that process. A somewhat closer approximation, orthographically, comes in the use of SOUL TRAIM [sic] as the name for a small Santurce bar. The attempt to achieve the English distinction between nasals, rather than the Spanish neutralization, in final position leads to the misspelling with -*m*.

STEPHEN GRAHAM

The American Language

Even Americans of the highest cultures and of Boston families speak
English differently from any people in the old country. The difference
may not be obvious to all, but it is there, and it is a thing to rejoice in, not
to be sorry for. The American nation is different from the British, has a
different history and a different hope; it has a different soul, therefore its
expression should be different. The American face as a type is different; it
would be folly to correct the words of the mouth by Oxford, or Eton, or
Granville Barker's theater, or the cultured Aberdonian, or any other
criterion. The use of American expressions of quite moderate tone
amounts to a breach of good taste in many British drawing-rooms; and if
you tell a story in which American conversation is repeated with the
accent imitated, you can feel the temperature going down as you proceed;
that is, if you are not merely making fun of the Americans. Making fun of
any foreign people is always tolerable to the British; a truly national and
insular trait. The literary world and the working men and women of
Britain can enter into the American spirit, and even imitate it upon
occasion; but that is only the misfortune of our populace, who ought to be
finding national expression in journalism and music-hall songs and dancing, and who are merely going off the lines by imitating a foreign country.
It is loss to Britain that the Americans speak a comprehensible dialect of
our tongue, and that the journalist of Fleet Street, when he is hard-up for
wit, should take scissors and paste and snip out stories from American
papers; or that commercial *entrepreneurs* should bring to the British
public things thought to be sure of success because they have succeeded in
America — 'Within the Law', 'I Should Worry', 'Hullo Ragtime!' and the
rest. The people who are surest in instinct, though they are sympathetic to
a brother-people, hate the importation of foreign ugliness, and the substitution of foreign for local talent.

The American language is chiefly distinguished from the British by its

This article previously appeared as Chapter XV of the author's book *With Poor Immigrants
to America* (1914), and is reprinted here by permission of the Macmillan Company.

emphatic expressive character. Britain, as I have said, lives in a tradition; America in a passion. We are laconic, accidental, inarticulate; our duty is plain, and we do it without words. But the American is affirmative, emphatic, striving; he has to find out what he's going to do next, and he has got to use strong words. Britain also is the place of an acknowledged caste system; but America is the place of equal citizens, and many American expressions are watchdogs of freedom and instruments of mockery, which reduce to a common dimension any people who may give themselves airs.

The subtler difference is that of rhythm. American blood flows in a different *tempo*, and her hopes keep different measure.

Americans commonly tell us that theirs is the language of Shakespeare and Shakespearian England, and that they have in America the 'well of English undefiled'. But if they have any purely European English in that country it must be a curiosity. Shakespeare was a lingual junction, but we've both gone on a long way since then, and in our triangle the line subtending the Shakespearian angle gets longer and longer. O. Henry makes a character in one of his stories write a telegram in American phraseology, so that it shall be quite unintelligible to people who only know English:

His nibs skedaddled yesterday per jack-rabbit line with all the coin in the kitty and the bundle of muslin he's spoony about. The boodle is six figures short. Our crowd in good shape, but we need the spondulicks. You collar it. The main guy and the dry goods are headed for the briny. You know what to do. — Bob.

This is not Shakespearian English, but of course it is not Shakespearian American. The worst of the contemporary language of America is that it is in the act of changing its skin. It is difficult to say what is permanent and what is merely eruptive and dropping. Such expressions as those italicized in the following examples are hardly permanent:

'One, two, three, *cut it out* and work for Socialism.'
'*I should worry* and get thin as a lamp-post so that tramps should come and lean against me.'
'*Him with the polished dome.*'
'She hadn't been here two days before I saw her kissing the boss. Well, said I, *that's going some.*'
'This is Number Nine of the Ibsen, *highbrow* series.'
'*Do you get me?*'
'I'll *put you wise.*'
'And how is your *yoke-mate?*'

'He thinks too much of himself: *too much breathed on by girls.*'
'A low lot of *wops and hunkies: white trash.*'
'Poor negroes; *coloured trash.*'
'She is *one good-looker.*'
'She is *one sweetie.*'
'My! You have *a flossy hat.*'
But I suppose 'He is a white man' is permanent, and 'Buy a postcard, it'll *only set you back a nickel.*'
'She began to lay down the law: *thus and so.*'
'Now *beat it!*'
'Roosevelt went ranching, that's how he got so *husky.*'
'Is it far? It is only *a little ways.*'
'Did they *feed that to you?*'
'When he started he was in a poor way, and carried in his hay in his arms, but now he is quite *healed.*'

But the difference in speech is too widespread and too subtle to be truly indicated by this collection of examples, and the real vital growth of the language is independent of the flaming reds and yellows of falling leaves. In the course of conversation with Americans you hear plenty of turns of expression that are unfamiliar, and that are not merely the originality of the person talking. Thus in: 'How do they get on now they are married?' 'Oh, she has him feeding out of her hand', though the answer is clear it owes its form to the American atmosphere.

Or, again in: 'I suppose she's sad now he's gone?' 'Oh! He wasn't a pile of beans to her, believe me', you feel the manner of speech belongs to the new American language. The following parody of President Wilson's way of speaking is also an example of the atmosphere of the American language:

So far as the prognosticationary and symptomatic problemaciousness of your inquiry is concerned it appears to me that while the trusts should be regulated with the most unrelentful and absquatulatory rigorosity, yet on the other hand their feelings should not be lacerated by rambunktions and obfusticationary harshness. Do you bite that off?

Punch would have no stomach for such Rabelaisian vigour.

But wherever you go, not only in the cities, but in the little towns, you hear things never heard in Britain. I go into a country bakery, and whilst I ask for bread at one counter I hear behind me at the other:

'Kendy, ma-ma, kendy!'
'Cut it out, Kenneth.'
'Kendy, kendy, kendy!'
'Oh, Kenneth, cut it out!'

Or, as I sit on a bank, a girl of twelve and her little baby sister come toddling up the road. The little one loses her slipper, and the elder cries out: 'Slipper off again! Ethel, perish!'

America must necessarily develop away from us at an ever-increasing rate. Influenced as she is by Jews, Negroes, Germans, Slavs, more and more foreign constructions will creep into the language — such things as 'I should worry', derived from Russian-Jewish girl strikers. 'She ast me for a nickel', said a Jew-girl to me of a passing beggar. *'I should give her a nickel*, let her work for it same as other people!' The *I shoulds* of the Jew can pass into the language of the Americans, and be understood from New York to San Francisco; but such expressions make no progress in Great Britain, though brought over there, just because we have not the big Jewish factor that the Americans have.

Today the influence that has come to most fruition is that of the Negro. The Negro's way of speaking has become the way of most ordinary Americans, but that influence is passing, and in ten or twenty years the Americans will be speaking very differently from what they are now. The foreigner will have modified much of the language and many of the rhythms of speech. America will have less self-consciousness then. She will not be exploiting the immigrant, but will be subject to a very powerful influence from the immigrants. No one will then be so cheap as the poor immigrant is today. Much mean nomenclature will have disappeared from the language, many cheap expressions, much mockery; on the other hand, there will be a great gain in dignity, in richness, in tenderness.

OTTO SPRINGER

The Study of the English of the Pennsylvania Germans

The effects of the *mutual impact of English and Pennsylvania German*, which cannot be ignored even by the casual students of this dialect, present such an exemplary illustration of what happens when two languages meet, that a more systematic investigation of the problem English vs. Pennsylvania German in itself should be urged, for the benefit of the hundred similar cases all over the world which may be more remote from us in space and time, cases which have left us solely with the final results of a conflict whose physical, social, and cultural constellation, therefore, can only *a posteriori* be reconstructed in faint relief.

In the struggle of Pennsylvania German and English, which has continued with varying intensity for more than two hundred years and which is still continuing under our very eyes, in this gradual linguistic Americanization of the Pennsylvania German settlers, we can observe, often step by step (as Hans Kurath once put it) 'the linguistic adaptation to a new physical, social, and cultural environment; we can follow up the gradual transition of minority groups from the imported language to the national language, and ascertain the survival of features of the submerged language in the dominant language.'

The influence of English on Pennsylvania German, while leaving its phonology and morphology untouched, may be felt in certain syntactical features, but strongest of all in the vocabulary of the Pennsylvania Germans, a statement which merely goes to confirm the old truth that sounds and grammatical forms are the stronger, syntax and words the weaker part in linguistic structure.

Learned (1889: *passim*) and Buffington (1937:284) have pointed out many examples of Pennsylvania German constructions formed on English

Reprinted, by permission of the author and the editors, from the *Journal of English and Germanic Philology* 33 (1943): 18–27. The excerpting of these pages is done with the approval of the author. The original article was much longer and dealt primarily with Pennsylvania German as such. According to Professor Springer (personal communication), this article has been revised and updated in his *Arbeiten zur germanischen Philologie und Zur Literatur des Mittelalters* (1975), 35–74.

patterns, although most of their illustrations might rather be classified as literally translated idioms, such as: [wiːɪç dsuːkumə bɪn] 'when I came to', NHG *wie ich zu mir gekommen bin*; or, [sɛlɪs uf dsuː diər] 'that's up to you', NHG *es kommt auf dich an*, etc. Most systematically has the English influence on Pennsylvania German syntax been studied by J. W. Frey (1941b:184–243), but even he finds only a few cases which might be counted here with certainty: [sɛlɪs mɪç] 'that's me', NHG *das bin ich*; or, with the adverb at the end: [ɪç wɔːərɪm ʃtɛdəl gwɛst gɛʃtroːwət] 'I was in town last evening', NHG *ich war gestern abend in der Stadt;* or, using the possessive pronoun with parts of the body: [sɪ hɔtɪːərə beː gəbrɔχə] 'she broke her legs', NHG *sie hat sich die Beine gebrochen.*[1]

It is, of course, in the vocabulary that the influence of English is most easily recognized. For almost a century, scholars and laymen have taken particular delight in exposing these intruders, especially the words whose adaptation to the phonemic patterns of Pennsylvania German happened to result in amusingly sounding forms. As a matter of fact, ever since A. J. Ellis, because of the English element in Pennsylvania German, likened the dialect to Chaucer's mixture of Anglo-Saxon and Norman-French (1871:652), it has been this admixture of English words which in the eyes of many outsiders seemed to constitute Pennsylvania German. However, as Buffington (1941) has pointed out very convincingly, the number of English loan words in Pennsylvania German has been greatly exaggerated, partly, perhaps, because the English words will impress themselves on the English-speaking listener in a way completely out of proportion to their actual number, and, partly, because a great many words, such as [fɪʃ], [æpəl] pl., [fleːʃ] are likely to be taken for English loan words by people who know little of the true linguistic relationship of English and German (cf. Buffington 1941:67).

Thus E. H. Rauch claimed 18–20 percent of all Pennsylvania German words to be of English origin (1879:iii ff.), while Horne (1875, 1896, 1905, 1910) among his 5,522 entries listed only 176 English words, i.e. only three percent. There were soon many who eloquently protested an overrating of the English element in Pennsylvania German, such as E. D. Leisenring in 1882: "'S net wohr, dass der Pennsylvanier 'n Vertel so viel Englisch in seiner Sproch schwätzt wie ihr schreibt' (1882:71), and similarly, a generation later, E. W. Hocker (1910) and C. C. Ziegler (1908).

The first to investigate this question on a scientific level was again M. D. Learned, in a special chapter of his book (1889:87–114) entitled 'English Mixture'; he even ventured to discuss, besides the proportion and the character of the English admixture, the causes and the 'laws' of the borrowing from English. The tabulation of the material, which he took largely from printed sources and divided into a southwestern and north-eastern section, yielded proportions from 'nil to 12 or 15 percent,' divergences which were largely due to the fact that some of the passages happened to be so brief that the presence or absence of English loan words was largely a matter of chance.

Much more reliable are the figures quoted in a recent article by A. F. Buffington (1941), who again follows up Learned's stimulating sugges-tions of more than fifty years ago and develops them in a more systematic way. To be sure, Buffington's proportions of English loan words, like Learned's, are based on printed and literary material, namely on three samples of 10,000 words each, taken from the prose writings of Pumpernickle Bill, Solly Hulsbuck, and Boonastiel. However, after com-paring them with his own native dialect of Pillow, Dauphin County, Buffington claims that the prose selections from these three Pennsylvania German writers 'are fairly representative of the spoken dialect' (1941:67). While in the spoken language, according to Buffington, the proportion of English loan words is five to six percent among the older, and seven to eight percent among the younger generation, the three literary samples rank as follows: Pumpernickle Bill (William Troxell — Lehigh Valley) two and one-half percent, Solly Hulsbuck (Harvey Miller — Dauphin County) less than four percent, and Boonastiel (Thomas Harter — Center County) five percent.

Thus Buffington's tabulation, while reducing the popular figures for the proportion of English loan words to a minimum ranging from two and one-half to five percent for literary material and from five to eight percent from the spoken dialect, confirms what Learned suggested (1889:68 ff.) and B. Bausman as early as 1870 surmised (1870:112), namely that the percentage of English admixture varies in different sections of the Pennsylvania-German-speaking area, depending upon the varying degree of influence from the surrounding or infiltrating English speech. A more accurate determining from township to township will have to wait for the progress of the geographical survey in connection with the Linguistic Atlas.

The problem of the adaptation of English loan words to the phonemic patterns of Pennsylvania German has been discussed, very ably, by A. F. Buffington in his dissertation as well as in several articles (1937, 1938, 1939, 1941, 1942) and by J. W. Frey in a special chapter of his disserta-tion (1941b:54–64), which with some minor changes has recently been published in the April number of *American speech*. According to Frey 'the following general phonemic principles operate in adapting English loan words to Pennsylvania German: (1) English consonants are unvoiced, especially in final position; (2) The stops and spirants of loan words follow the phonemic correlations of those patterns characteristic of native words; (3) Substitutions are made when the English phoneme does not exist in Pennsylvania Dutch, e.g. [i:dər] *either.* In fact, Pennsylvania German has fewer phonemes than English, hence the necessity for substitutions; (4) Vowels of loan words, when not identical with their values in modern American English, can usually be traced to some earlier pronunciation' (1941b:101 ff.).

Moreover, just as E. Haugen from older Norwegian speakers has heard pronunciations and words which are now extinct or obsolescent in the American English of that region (1942:45), Frey notes that certain words borrowed by the Pennsylvania Germans at an early date reflect an older American pronunciation. Thus [blɛndɪ] is the 'Dutch' word for 'a lot of', while English *plenty* is pronounced [plɛnɪ] in Pennsylvania today (Frey 1942:94). And H. Penzl (1938) explained the pronunciation of certain English loan words in Pennsylvania German with Middle English (short) *a* before *r*, such as [ʃmæərt] *smart*, [kæ:ərpət] or [kærəpət] *carpet*, [pæ:ərdɪ] *party*, etc., as reflecting an earlier dialect pronunciation of these words in American English. On the other hand, as J. W. Frey suggests, since the same words 'are also pronounced (as in English) with the *a*-sound in certain sections, it is highly possible that these loan words followed the regular twofold development according to which Middle High German high or mid vowel+*r* becomes *a* or *æ* in Pennsylvania German' (1941b:xxi). That is to say, since MHG *Kirche* is represented in Pennsylvania German by [karɪç] or [kærɪç], it may have been in analogy to this pattern of differentiation that English *smart* was pronounced [ʃma:rt] and [ʃmæ:ərt] in Pennsylvania German.

Yet the most intriguing problem in connection with these loan words has always been the question as to which gender would be assigned in Pennsylvania German to the 'genderless' nouns of English. Starting from A. W. Aron's stimulating paper on 'The gender of English loan-words in colloquial American German' (1930), according to which the gender is determined by the gender of the German word (*der arm-chair*), by meaning (*der actor*), by grammatical or by rhyme analogy (*der dash, die balcony*), by the 'feminine tendency' (*die aisle*, in spite of *der Gang*), or by gender differentiation to express differentiation of meaning (*die joint* 'Gelenk', *der joint* 'disreputable place'), C. E. Reed recently divided the material gathered through his and L. W. J. Seifert's field work into the following four classes: (1) nouns that have taken over the gender of the German nouns which they displace; (2) nouns having a type of suffix that normally characterizes a particular gender in German; (3) nouns whose gender is determined by the sex of a living being, specifically a human being; (4) nouns that have been given the feminine gender, because the

English definite article [ði:/ðə] resembles phonetically the dialectal German definite article [di:/də].

The chief merit of Reed's study is his endeavor, often successful, to identify the actual German dialect word which was replaced by an English loan word and therefore bestowed its gender on its English-born successor. Thus in the case of Pennsylvania German [dər kamfərt] from English *comfort* 'bed cover', Reed explains the masculine gender as due to its Pennsylvania German equivalent [dər dɛpɪç], while the standard German equivalent *die (Bett) Decke* would suggest the feminine; similarly Pennsylvania German [dər barlı] from English *barley* is masculine in accordance with the gender of the Pennsylvania German dialect word [dər/garʃt], while in standard German it is feminine: *die Gerste.*

From a study of the lists compiled by Learned (1889:94–114) Buffington (1941:69–80), and Reed (1942:26–28), it seems to me that the great majority of English loan words in Pennsylvania German owe their gender to the gender of the Pennsylvania German native word which they replace (Class 1 according to Reed). In a way, even the loan words whose gender seems to be determined by sex (Class 3 according to Reed) might be considered a subdivision of Class 1 since their gender naturally is the same as that of their Pennsylvania German native equivalents: if [dər dɔ:dɪ] *daddy* is masculine and [di:mæm] *mamma* is feminine, the gender agrees with the German equivalents.[2] Moreover, the number of English loan words whose gender is explained as due to the association of the English ending with a similar one in German (Class 2 according to Reed) may have to be reduced considerably. Several nouns with endings such as ['ɪŋ] *-ing* fem., [-ɪ] *-y* fem., [-ər] *-er, -or* masc., whose gender is attributed to the similarity of their endings to German [-uŋ] *-ung* fem., [-ɪ:] *-ie* fem., [ər] masc., may rather owe their gender to the German words which they replace: PaG [di: si:lɪŋ] from English *ceiling* — German *die Decke*; PaG [di: pæ:ərdɪ] from English *party* — German *die Gesellschaft, die Partei;* PaG [di: ʃtɔ:ərɪ] from English *story* — German *die Geschichte*; PaG [dər kaundər] from English *counter* — German *der Ladentisch*; etc. In many cases which cannot be decided clearly in favor of the one or the other explanation we shall have to content ourselves with a statement of the several explanations that compete.

The similarity of the English definite article [ði:/ðə] to the German feminine article, which, as far as I know, was first suggested by K. Knortz (1873–1874) as an explanation of the feminine gender of certain English loan words in Pennsylvania German, should be reserved and recognized as a last resort. Reed (1942:28) lists ten loan words whose feminine gender in Pennsylvania German he is inclined to attribute to this factor. But the question remains: Why did this factor have this effect only and just in these ten cases? Why not in the several hundred other loan words which in English were likewise preceded by a definite article [ði:/ðə]? Why was English [ði:/ðə flɔ:r] not taken over as [di: flɔ:ər], but as [dər flɔ:ər] in accordance with the gender of the native Pennsylvania German word *der (Fuss) Boden* [dər bɔdən], whereas English [ði:/ðə fɛns] *fence* was adopted by the Pennsylvania Germans as [di: fɛns], in spite of the masculine gender of the native word *der Zaun?* Moreover, since the form of the English definite article which happens to resemble German *die*, namely [ði:], is used before nouns with initial vowel, should we not expect that above all those loan words which begin with a vowel would have been adopted with the feminine article [di:] in Pennsylvania German? As a matter of fact, not one of the words listed by Reed in Class 4 begins with a vowel; only English [ði: ʌmbrɛlə] *umbrella*, taken over as [di: ambərɛl] would be a case in point, but even this word is used, besides, as a masculine, probably in accordance with the gender of German *der (Regen) Schirm.* The gender of PaG [di: grɪk], from English *creek*, finds a much more natural explanation in the gender of the German word *Bach* which in the dialect of large areas of Germany, including the Palatinate, is known to be feminine; similarly PaG [di: blaus], from English *blouse*, is likely to derive its gender from the association with German *die Bluse*, which in the sense of '*Frauenbluse*', '*Arbeitsbluse*', occurs in all the dialects of the region near the middle Rhine;[3] or, PaG [di: flu:], from colloquial English *flu* 'influenza', is feminine probably according to German *die Influenza*, which is used quite generally in German dialects (beside *Erkältung*, etc.).[4] In many cases, to be sure, the question of gender remains obscure. Perhaps the compilation of the Pennsylvania German vocabulary according to topics may suggest additional associations which were responsible for the assignment of a certain gender in some puzzling cases; others may forever defy any plausible explanation.

The reasons why these English loan words were adopted in Pennsylvania German speech have been discussed by Haldeman (1872:28 ff.) and more thoroughly by Learned (1889:111–114) and Buffington (1941:80–82).[5] Learned, who is followed by Buffington, lists as the most prominent causes the following: (1) The unintelligibility of German to the English speaker; (2) the insufficiency of the colloquial German vocabulary for the emergencies of the new environment; (3) the recognition of English as the only official speech; (4) the loss of puristic speech-consciousness by the decline of the German pulpit and schools; and (5) the inclination to despise the Pennsylvania German vernacular. Yet the problem will have to be carefully reconsidered as soon as a more complete compilation of English loan words in Pennsylvania German and a survey of their geographical distribution have been carried out.

However, not only the influence of English on Pennsylvania German, but also that of *Pennsylvania German on the English spoken by the Pennsylvania Germans* has been the subject of scholarly research, casual comments, and often of ridicule, from the traditional 'make the door shut' to our latest contemporary 'Papa is all. . . . ' The pronunciation of English as modified according to the phonemic patterns of Pennsylvania German has been often discussed, especially by R. W. Tucker (1934), G. G. Struble (1935), E. R. Page (1937), and in two articles by J. W. Frey (1940, 1941a). Naturally, the same phonemic principles which we observed in connection with English loan words adopted in Pennsylvania German will be functioning again (see above): voiced stops and fricatives, especially in final position, are unvoiced, [brɛt] *bread*, [ʃeːf] *shave*, [d] will be substituted for English [ð], and [s] for English [θ], as in PaG [badərə] *to bother*, and [fɪlsɪ] *filthy*. Less attention has been paid to such intangible matters as intonation, sentence rhythm, etc., although in these particular domains the effects of bilingualism have been felt most generally and most instinctively.

As we would expect, accidence and word formation of the English speaking Pennsylvania German reveal little German influence, whereas syntax, vocabulary, and phraseology are full of it; cf. the rich collections of examples by G. G. Struble (1935, pp. 167 ff.) and J. W. Frey (1940, 1941a). Struble has also touched upon the important problem of a German influence on the meaning of words in English which is due to the fact that words of cognate forms extend their sphere to include what the corresponding German terms include. Thus we may hear in the English of the Pennsylvania Germans 'a load of ground' (= soil, in accordance with German *Grund*), 'a soft-cooked egg' (= soft boiled, German *weich-gekocht*), or sentences like the following: 'Though she never used force, she was a very *strong* teacher' (= strict, German *streng*); perhaps it was through Pennsylvania German influence that the word *dumb* in American English (and differing from British English) has come to mean, almost exclusively, 'stupid', 'ignorant' (*Dictionary of American English* [Chicago, 1940].[6] Struble also discusses the confusions arising from the fact that German happens to have only one word to express a thing or an idea which in English is split up and therefore covered by two or more terms (and *vice versa*). Thus the Pennsylvania Germans may use the English word 'to loan' for both 'to lend' and 'to borrow' because German *leihen* may be used for either, or, having only the one verb *lassen* in their German vernacular, they may confuse English 'to leave' and 'to let', a confusion which Struble so beautifully illustrates by the shocking experience of a customer who, while trying on a ready-made suit in a Lebanon clothing store, is told by the Pennsylvania German salesman: 'Since

you are rather large in the hips, I shall have to leave out the seat. . . . .'
Only if in our future gathering of Pennsylvania German material for
the proposed atlas and dictionary we no longer limit ourselves to the
vernacular, but include liberally all English features which more or less
habitually slip into Pennsylvania German, as well as all traces of Pennsylvania German in the English spoken by the Pennsylvania Germans, will
we be able to deal systematically and satisfactorily with the mutual impact
of English and Pennsylvania German, for the benefit of the study of
Pennsylvania German in particular and of the problems of bilingualism as
a whole.

NOTES

1. However, as to the last two cases, Standard German and certain German dialects with no
   English influence present may occasionally show the same constructions; if so, the
   English influence in PaG would have merely encouraged a tendency which was prevalent
   anyway. Even the use of the accusative instead of the nominative in constructions such as
   Das ist mich is found in various dialect areas of Germany.
2. If the natural gender or sex were the decisive factor, English *girl*, if borrowed, should be
   feminine; yet, according to my *Sprachgefühl*, and to both *Der Grosse Duden*, p. 195, and
   Der Sprach-Brockhaus, p. 227, the word is neuter in Pennsylvania German, das girl, in
   accordance with the gender of *das Mädchen*.
3. Cf. J. Müller, editor (1933), *Rheinisches Wörterbuch* volume one (Bonn und Leipzig),
   806: [di: blu:s] Arbeitsbluse'. More frequently: 'Frauenbluse', = NHG.
4. Cf. *Rheinisches Wörterbuch*, (Berlin, 1935), 1089.
5. Cf. also, for American German in general, Aron (1930:14 ff.).
6. Cf. G. Struble (1935:170). Even if there should be no dialectal *weichgekocht*, the
   expression 'soft-cooked' would find its explanation in the fact that PaG uses 'to cook' for
   both 'to cook' and 'to boil' under the influence of dialectal [kɔχə].

REFERENCES

Aron, A. W. (1930), 'The gender of English loan-words in colloquial American German', in
   Curme Volume of Linguistic Studies, 11–28. Language Monographs 7, Baltimore.
Bausman, B. (1870), 'Introduction to the word list', in *Harfe; Gedichte in Pennsylvanisch-
   Deutscher Mundart* by B. Harbaugh, 111–112. Philadelphia.
Buffington, A. F. (1937), 'Pennsylvania German; a grammatical and linguistic study of the
   dialect', Unpublished Ph.D. thesis, Harvard University.
— (1938), 'Characteristic features of Pennsylvania German; an attempt to correct some
   erroneous impressions concerning the dialect', *'s Pennsylfawnisch Deitsch Eck*, December
   10 and 17.
— (1939), Pennsylvania German; its relation to other German dialects', *American Speech*
   14:276–286.
— (1941), 'English loan words in Pennsylvania German', in *Studies in Honor of John
   Albrecht Walz*, 65–85. Lancaster, Pa.

Buffington, A. F. (1942), 'The Pennsylvania-German dialect', in *The Pennsylvania Germans*, ed. by R. Wood, 259–281 Princeton, Princeton University Press.

Ellis, A. J. (1871), Pennsylvania German the analogue of Chaucer's English', in *On Early Pronunciation with Especial Reference to Shakespeare and Chaucer*, part 3, 652–663. London.

Frey, J. W. (1940), 'The English of the Pennsylvania Germans in eastern York County', *'s Pennsylfawnisch Deitsch Eck* May 18.

— (1941a), 'Some observations on bilingualisms in eastern York County', *'s Pennsylfawnisch Deitsch Eck* February 15.

— (1941b), 'The German dialect of eastern York County, Pa. Unpublished Ph.D. thesis, University of Illinois.

— (1942), 'The phonemics of English loan words in eastern York County Pennsylvania Dutch', *American Speech* 17:94–101.

Haldeman, S. S. (1872), *Pennsylvania Dutch: a Dialect of South German with an Infusion of English*. London and Philadelphia.

Haugen, E. (1942), 'Problems of linguistic research among Scandinavian immigrants in America', in *Conference on Non-English Speech in the United States* 35–57 American Council of Learned Societies, Bulletin 34. Washington, D.C.

Hocker, E. W. (1910) 'A defiant dialect: Pennsylvania German in fiction', *The Pennsylvania German* 11:598–602.

Horne, A. R. (1875, 1896, 1905, 1910), *Pennsylvania German Manual*. Kutztown (first edition); Allentown (second – fourth editions).

Knortz, K. (1873–1874), 'Deutsch-Pennsylvanisch', *Der deutsche Pionier* 5:66–70.

Learned, M. D. (1889), *Pennsylvania German Dialect*, part one. Baltimore, also published (1888, 1889) in *American Journal of Philology*, 9:64–83, 178–197, 326–339, 425–456; 10:288–315.

Leisenring, E. D. (1882), 'Pennsylvanisch-Deutsch', *Der deutsche Pionier* 14:70–71.

Page, E. R. (1937), 'English in the Pennsylvania German area', *American Speech* 12:203–206.

Penzl, H. (1938), 'Lehnwörter mit mittelenglisch *a* vor *r* im pennsylvanisch-deutschen Dialekt'. *JEGP* 37:396–402.

Rauch, E. H. (1879), *Rauch's Pennsylvania Dutch Hand-Book/Rauch's Pennsylvania Deitsh Hond-Booch*. Mauch Chunk.

Reed, C. E. (1942), 'The gender of English loan words in Pennsylvania German', *American Speech* 17:25–29.

Struble, G. G. (1935), 'The English of the Pennsylvania Germans.' *American Speech* 10:163–172.

Tucker, R. W. (1934), 'Linguistic substrata in Pennsylvania and elsewhere', *Language* 10:1–5.

Ziegler, C. C. (1908), 'Is Pennsylvania German a dialect?' *The Pennsylvania German* 9:66–68.

LILIAN MERMIN FEINSILVER

The Yiddish is Showing

In 1945, on entering a New York publishing office in a new dress, I was greeted by a co-worker with, 'Mm-m-m . . . zaftig'. An out-of-towner, I was surprised to hear this Yiddish word rolled so authentically on an Irish-American tongue. But of course this was New York, home of half the Jews in America, where Yiddish had for years been adding *tam* to the American language. Here, I reminded myself, many Gentiles understood and even used a variety of Yiddish expressions, like *mazel tov, shikse, shlemiel*, etc.

What was true in New York in 1945 is becoming more and more so across the country. The process, to be sure, is uneven. Many a Gentile reader has to come running to Jewish friends for explanations of the Yiddish terms strewn around the pages of recent novels, and many a young Jewish reader comes to older relatives for the same purpose. Others without such handy interpreters are apt to feel frustrated and annoyed, wondering why the terms are not translated, or why the book has no glossary. It is a rare publisher today who bothers to provide such explanations [as those provided immediately below].

a for instance (or *a forinstance*); *give me a forinstance*

Two popular Yiddish expressions are involved here: *gib mir a moshel* 'Give me an example', and *l'moshel* 'for example'. In translating the former into English, the first generation was influenced by the frequency of 'for instance' in English and also by its Yiddish counterpart, *l'moshel*. (The latter derives from Hebrew *l'mashal*, which is quite common in rabbinic literature.)

The second generation quoted 'a forinstance' in good-natured jest. Now it's being adopted generally. Notice a sample from a syndicated book review by John Barkham: 'A forinstance is the case of a Ring

Reprinted, by permission of the author and of A. S. Barnes and Company, Inc., from *The Taste of Yiddish*, New York, 1970.

Lardner story he included in an anthology of humorous talks'; and from a news conference by former Secretary of State Dean Rusk: 'Will you specify and give me a forinstance.' It's even been put in the plural, as in a Pennsylvania radio commercial: 'We'll give you a couple of forinstances here' and in a TV line introducing gift ideas: 'Here are a few forinstances.'

The process is reminiscent of the spread of the form 'irregardless'. Starting as an error (presumably influenced by the word 'irrespective'), this was humorously quoted by those who knew better. It began to appear in print, with the irony not always understood, and found its way into the latest edition of *Webster's New International Dictionary* (as a 'nonstandard' form).

again with the . . . !

This annoyance at a person who has repeated some irritating statement or behavior has a Yiddish flavor. It can be followed by almost any part of speech, repeating whatever the annoyance has been. Ex.: the novel *The Conversion of Chaplain Cohen* by Herbert Tarr had a line in which the objection is to the use of the adjective 'brave': 'Again with the brave, David groaned.'

For the next stage of exasperation, see Ch. II, Ann. and Arg., *noch a mul . . . un vidder a mul . . .* *

a little nothing for 'almost nothing'

From *a kleyn gurnit*, this is common in American Jewish speech, in such a sentence as 'He picked it up for a little nothing.'

The phrase presumably inspired the naming of the 'little nothing' black dress which was featured in the early 1960s and which was followed by the ' "little nothing" bras' of Saks Fifth Avenue and the ' "Petit Rien" bikini panty girdle'. Even hosiery got on the bandwagon, with the TV ad: 'The Cantrice stocking in the black box is the little nothing by Cameo. . . .'

. . . already for ' . . . now'

The use of 'already' at the end of a sentence is a direct translation of the Yiddish *shoyn*, as in *Kum, shoyn*! 'Come, already!' or *Genug shoyn*! 'Enough, already!'. English would normally use the mild 'now' as in 'Come, now' or the stronger 'Come on, now!' But 'Enough, already!' and 'Let's go, already!' have been widely used on TV and seem to be making inroads into general speech.

* All internal references to chapters etc. in this article refer to Lilian Mermin Feinsilver (1970), *The Taste of Yiddish*. New York, A. S. Barnes.

Pennsylvania German also has a final 'already', but it is somewhat different: 'He has lost his respect for her long already.'

. . . and finished! for ' . . . and zoom!'

This translation of *un fartik!* (Ch. II, Exclam.) may take the place of 'to make a long story short' or 'before I knew it', as in the account a mother gave me of the time she was settling into a new home and left her young son alone for a few minutes: ' . . . and finished! The kid had everything in a mess.'

I've heard the expression in the English speech of both Jewish and Gentile Germans, and assume it must occur in German as well as Yiddish.

And how! See Ch. II, Exclam., *Noch vi.*

Answering a Question With a Question

This common feature of Jewish speech is associated with intonation and probably grew out of Talmudic discussion. As noted in Ch. II, Greetings, the question *V' azoy geyt es?* 'How is it going?', may be replied to with the shrugging irony: *V'azoy zol es geyn?* 'How should it go? Or notice the joke about the three U.S. Army chaplains who were playing cards while sitting in a tent and idly discussing the question of honesty. Both the priest and minister express the idea that lying is sometimes necessary; the rabbi holds that under any circumstances lying is sinful. Suddenly the commanding officer comes into the tent and asks, 'Father Murphy, have you been playing cards? You know my rules on the subject.' The priest says, 'No, sir, I haven't.' The CO asks the minister, and he too says, 'No, sir.' The CO then asks the rabbi whether *he* had been playing cards, and he replies: 'With whom, sir?'

On hearing this story, my daughter asked, 'What would have happened if the Jewish chaplain had been asked first? Oh! I know! He would have answered: "Who, *me*, sir?" '

According to an old quip, a Jew was asked why he always answered a question with another question, and he replied, 'Why not?' We must agree this is in tune with tradition, considering that many centuries earlier Cain answered an inquiry about Abel with: 'Am I my brother's keeper?' (As one writer has pointed out, Cain wasn't Jewish, but the chronicler was!) Answering a question with a question is a favorite habit of psychiatrists and social workers. Perhaps this was an unconscious contribution of Freud's Jewish background! Interestingly enough, a newspaper financial column by William Doyle recently attributed this tendency to the Irish. I would venture to guess that if it *is* a characteristic of the Irish, they must have picked it up from the Jews — in Ireland and the United States.[1] An old Yiddish conundrum pokes fun at the whole process by asking why a kugel tin is wide on the top and narrow on the bottom. The answer: 'Why isn't it narrow on the bottom and wide on the top?' (The double incongruity here is that only the order of the question has been reversed, not its facts.)

bagel

American English spelling of *beygel* (Ch. II, Food and Drink).

In TV production lingo, a bagel is a show with a hole in it, lacking something.

The word has also been used as a synonym for 'Jew' or 'Jewish'. In Brooklyn's Crown Heights, the Jewish anti-crime patrol has been dubbed 'The Bagel Lancers', and this phrase has appeared in the title of a book on Jewish humor. In the summer of 1966, columnist Earl Wilson noted that the ordinary New Yorker's escape from the heat was a delicatessen at 'Bagel Beach, 54th St. and 7th Ave'. A generation ago, this might have been a slur. I remember the term as an in-group deprecation for a certain Connecticut beach frequented by lower-class Jews. And I recall in my early childhood being taunted by Gentile children with the epithet 'Jew-bagel'. Perhaps symbolic of the changing times is the fact that several years ago, when a Gentile track star named Begel (pronounced like the food) on Yale's team started off, the good wishes called out to him were: 'Lox of luck, Begel'. Too, Jack Altshul of *Newsday* has reported a rock 'n roll group called 'The Bagels'. He explains: 'You've heard of hard rock; they claim they're hard roll.' But Lender's Bagel Bakery hastens to advertise on the radio: 'Contrary to popular opinion, the frozen bagel is not a new rock band. You will find Lender's frozen bagels in freezers in supermarkets across the country.'

In London, reportedly, the term has been heard pronounced 'bygel' and even 'bageel'!

As noted in Ch. II, in Yiddish the plural is the same form as the singular. I have seen a similar usage in English on the labels of a bread supplier to the A & P: 'Jewish Rye; Pumpernickle (sic); Bagel.'

See *It can't hurt* and IIIB, *bialys*.

Better . . . should for '. . . might better' or '. . . would have done better to'

This seems to derive from Yiddish *Besser zol ich* . . . 'Better I should . . .', but may also reflect German, and Pennsylvania German, influence.

I've heard it in radio announcer's lingo ('Better we should stop the clock') and seen it in Inez Robb's syndicated newspaper column ('Better the boys should save their breath to cool their porridge') as well as in Howard Nemerov's poetry (' "There's nothing in this for me", he said aloud; "Better the snow should be my lonely shroud." ')

See also *should* and *shouldn't* for 'may' and 'may not. . . .'

Be well; Stay well; Go well (and come back well)

These translations of *Zay gezunt* and *Gey gezunt* (*un kum gezunt*) occasionally appear in unexpected places. I recall the Kurt Weill musical *Lost in the Stars* (lyricist Maxwell Anderson), in which a departing father's line to his daughter is 'Stay well, my child' and her reply is, 'Go well, my father.' Recently I heard Mimi Benzel signing off her WNBC radio program with the line: 'Mother, stay well'. And Joe Franklin on WOR likes to say: 'Stay well and stay tuned.' Such references to health on parting are common among Jews but often puzzling to Gentiles. Apparently, though, they're spreading out.

See also *Wear it in good health.*

bit for 'routine' or 'stuff' See *shtik.*

borax

In furniture, architectural, and decorating lingo, this means cheap furniture of poor taste — the kind so often bought by poor immigrants on the installment plan. It's believed to derive from Yiddish and German *borgen* 'to borrow'. My guess is that it was a rendition of the colloquial noun *borgs* 'something on loan'.

The term is sometimes used as an adjective for anything gaudy and even as an exclamation. 'Borax-house' is a firm selling such merchandise. (Cf. *shofel.*)

boss

Though derived from the Dutch word *baas* 'master', this English term may also have been reinforced to some extent by the Yiddish *balebos* 'proprietor', from Hebrew *baal ha-bayis* 'master of the house'.

Cf. IIIB, 'What are you *balesbostev*in' about?'

bubele See Ch. II, Endearment.

by for 'at'

In Yiddish, the similar-sounding *bay* is the equivalent of French *chez* 'at the home of'. It is natural, then, that the first generation would say 'He's by Alfred' instead of 'He's at Alfred's'. A similar sentence appears in a book by Nelson Algren: 'I'll buy you a drink by Antek'. But the usage hasn't spread too far as yet.

by for 'to'

The Yiddish *bay*, mentioned above, can also mean 'to'. *Ex.: Bay mir bistu sheyn* 'To Me You Are Beautiful'. This was the title of a song which became very popular in bilingual form in the late 1930s. The words *bay mir bistu sheyn* were not translated literally in this popular version, which noted that the expression 'means that you're grand'.

In August 1969, a financial newscaster on WNEW radio noted that stocks were off a little but had rallied, and the regular announcer commented ironically: 'That's by you a rally — it's off .44!' (Cf. *by* for 'with'.)

by for 'with'

Again, the influence of the versatile Yiddish *bay*, as in *bay mir peylstu* (Ch. II, Exclam.). It shows up in 'It's O.K. by me' or 'It's all right by me' and in ' . . . fine by . . . ' as in chatty prose like the following in the *New York Times:* 'He is regarded as a youngish-type people's critic, rather than middle-aged people's or dodderers', and this is fine by Mr. Fiedler.'

The popular Jewish American greeting 'How's by you?' and its good-natured reply 'By me is fine' have this same origin and have been picked up to some extent by other Americans. The inverted order is reminiscent of the Pennsylvania German 'Throw me from the train a kiss', which graced the popular-song list some years ago. (See: Inverted Sentence Order.)

called up (to the Torah)

This refers to the honor of being called from a worshiping congregation to participate at the pulpit. (See Ch. II, Rel. and Cul., *alieh.*) One may hear, 'He was called up at temple last night, and was he thrilled!'

chutzpa, chutzpah, chutspa, chutspeh, chuzpa, hutzpa, etc.

This Yiddish term for nerviness (Ch. II, Char. and Des.) has been heard on TV and seen in much current journalistic writing. It is listed in several dictionaries, including the Funk and Wagnalls' *Standard College Dictionary*, which in 1967 and 1968 advertised itself in the *New York Times* as 'the only college dictionary with "chutzpah".' According to the *Jewish Post and Opinion*, a new real estate holding company in Philadelphia is 'Chutzpa, Inc.'!

See Ch. II, Food and Drink, end of *beygel*.

The adjective *chutzpadik* is common among Jews and sometimes crops up in odd places. The late American rabbi Stephen S. Wise was once in conversation with the late Dr. Edouard Beneš, president of Czecho-slovakia, when a student barged in to remind Dr. Wise that he was late for his (the student's) wedding, at which he had promised to officiate. Beneš is reported to have asked whether the intruder was a student, and Wise to have replied, 'A *chutzpadik* student.'

cluck, kluck

This term for an oaf, often in the redundant 'dumb cluck,' was popular a generation ago and seems to have come from Yiddish *kluhtz*.[2] In recent years the authentic 'klutz' and 'clutz' have been appearing (I have heard 'dumb klutz' on TV), with the companion adjective 'klutzy'. *Time* has even made a verb of it: 'Choreographer Kenneth MacMillan has attempted a compromise between dancing and acting that too often leaves Nureyev and Ballerina Margot Fonteyn with nothing to do but klutz around the stage like actors who have forgotten their lines.'

cobber

Reportedly an Australian term for 'pal', 'chum', this is believed to come from Yiddish (and Hebrew) chaver (Ch. II, Greetings).

compote

This French word for stewed fruit, which appears in both Yiddish and English, has been given an impetus in English through its use by American Jews. As noted in Ch. II, Food and Drink, the dish is a traditional holiday dessert. It is interesting that while most packers of mixed dried fruit call their products just that, a major brand-name stocked by independent grocers (including the average Jewish neighborhood store) calls it 'compote'.

dairy for 'dairy products'

Ex.: 'We're having dairy for supper.' Refers to milchiks 'milk type of food', as differentiated from fleyshiks 'meat type of food'. (See Rel. and Cul., *kashres*.)

This is so common a usage that French's mustard ran an ad in a Jewish monthly in 1963 advocating that its product be used for 'any meat sandwich', adding: 'Great with dairy, too!' A 1966 full-page ad in *Commentary* heralded a new Mazola margarine that is '100% dairy-free'. This is a way of saying that the margarine is now *parev* (Ch. II, Food and Drink).

The abbreviation is similar to that in 'Danish' for 'Danish pastry' below.

Danish for 'Danish pastry'

This short-form is common among lunch-counter personnel and at least partly reflects the American tendency to abbreviate terms, also seen in 'coffee an' ' or 'He's collecting unemployment' for ' . . . unemployment insurance' or 'Have a happy' for 'Have a happy day'. Yet in Jewish speech there are similar short-cuts like 'the Joint' for 'the Joint Distribution Committee' or 'enjoy' for 'enjoy yourself' (see 'enjoy' as an intransitive verb) and 'entitled' for 'entitled to' (see 'entitled' without the 'to it'). A sentence like 'They have wonderful Danish' — which I seem to have heard only in the speech of American Jews — has to my ear a Yiddish ring. It seems pertinent that the term appears in ads in American Jewish weeklies, like the one of Dugan's bakers which headlines 'Great Danish in the morning'.[3]

Declarative Form in Questions

Yiddish is of course not the only force at work here, but the use of this type of question in popular journalism often strikingly reflects Yiddish intonation. Witness: 'This is moral decadence?' (reader in Billy Graham's syndicated column questioning Graham's appraisal of American morality); 'TV's Topmost — *This* is America?' (critical evaluation of TV programming in the *New York Times*): 'It took somebody all this time to figure *that* out? Sheer brilliance . . . ' (Xerox Corp. ad in *Time*); 'This is Art?' (*Reader's Digest* heading for an item on a Londoner's technique of throwing tubes of paint on a large canvas on the floor and then driving a sports car over it); etc.

Such sentences sometimes begin with 'So', as in an editorial head in my local newspaper: 'So We Have a Permanent Acting Postmaster?' (See 'so' at beginning of sentence.)

See also end of Inverted Sentence Order and . . . *no*?

Do me something.

This blithe defiance, which is a translation of *Tu mir eppes* (Ch. II, Ann. and Arg.), is being picked up generally. Psychiatrist Eric Berne, in *Games People Play*, uses it to designate a 'second-degree hard form' of the game 'Why Don't You — Yes But.' ('The patient refuses to do the housework, for example. . . .')

The expression is of course a companion to 'Sue me!' — which has had a wider impact, chiefly through entertainers. The related 'do me' for 'do to me' is sometimes heard in 'What can he do me?'

See IIIB, 'Call me *pisher.*'

Don't ask!

This translation of *Freg nisht!* (Ch. II, Exclam.) has been showing up lately in newspaper and TV advertising copy. Notice the Ezra Brooks whiskey ad: 'Have we got troubles? Don't ask! There we were, minding our business and . . . SUDDENLY THE ROOF FALLS IN! Overnight, everybody discovers our rare old Sippin' Whiskey. We're a hit! We're also way behind in our orders.' Or witness the Chesterfield TV commercial which starts with a woman talking incessantly about why she likes Chesterfield King cigarettes and follows with: 'Why does everybody like the taste of Chesterfield King? Don't ask!'

Double Negative

Although frowned upon by English teachers, the double negative has a natural drive in many languages, including English and Yiddish. The Yiddish occasionally bolsters the tendency in English, as in *He don't know from nothin'*.

drek, dreck (taboo)

In the blunt shop talk of garment manufacturing, this means shoddy merchandise, junk. But it's not a word for polite company. It's a Yiddish equivalent of the four-letter word for excrement. Interestingly enough, it appeared in the term *drek-apotek*, assigned to the class of medieval medical remedies involving animal excrement. (Jewish opinion was critical of such practice.) The word comes from German but in that language means merely 'dirt'.
Cf. IIIB, 'A.K.'

Drop dead!

My guess is that this originated in Jewish circles. It reflects the spirit of Yiddish imprecation and is very close to several Yiddish forms, for which it is a common translation: *di ptire zolstu ayn-nemen* and *Zolstu krign dem toyt* 'May you catch — or get — death', as well as the double-barreled *Shtarb a teyte* 'Die a dead one'.

The expression was widely used in the 1940s — I even remember it in a form of pun and super-climax: D.D.T. (Drop Dead Twice) — and is still heard and seen occasionally. A striking instance was the AP dispatch on Dec. 18, 1968, headed ' "Dear Santa, Drop Dead!" Says Methodist Minister'.

dynaschmo

Variety coined this term, which is a combination of 'dynamo' and 'shmo' (see *shmo*). It was offered as a description of an operator who 'makes like a whirling dervish, acts as though he knows everything, but in the final showdown always comes up blank'.

enjoy as an intransitive verb

Though previously a rare form, this has become fairly common in recent years — largely encouraged, I believe, by the usage of American Jews.

'Enjoy yourself' was abbreviated to the simple 'Enjoy' by the solicitous Jewish mother. Harry Golden, editor of the *Carolina Israelite*, made it popular around 1960 with his collection of reminiscences entitled *Enjoy, Enjoy!* In July 1964 the magazine *Prevention* carried an ad of *Quinto Lingo* urging: 'Just read, enjoy, absorb!' and some months later a bank advertising on my local Pennsylvania radio station advised: 'Save now, enjoy later.'

In June 1966, over New York's radio station WQXR, Murray Shumach reported an interview with famed violinist Mischa Elman, quoting the musician's denial of being bitter: 'I get a great kick out of life. I know how to enjoy.' And several months later my local paper quoted Harry Balmer, a New Jersey sculptor, as saying: 'Some people live to enjoy. I enjoy to live.'

entitled without the 'to it'

Harry Golden called attention to this ethnic English with his volume *You're Entitle'!* It has since been picked up in sundry quarters, such as the Congress of Racial Equality (CORE), which in 1964 offered a 'Freedom Hat' in a circular which declaimed, 'Yes, we changed it a little.[4] We're entitled, it's our idea.' Or witness the women's-store ad for Mother's Day in my community in 1965: 'She Baked Your Birthday Cakes . . . She Held Your Hand in the Dark . . . She Jollied Away Unhappiness . . . She's Your MOM . . . SHE'S ENTITLED!'

eppis

This term was reported in 1966 from carnival lingo on the West Coast as meaning 'nothing' and being spoken with a shrug to indicate poor business. It may be an ironic use of Yiddish *eppes* (Ch. II, Exclam.), perhaps influenced too by the somewhat similar Pennsylvania German *ebbes*.

fall in for 'drop in'

From Yiddish *araynfaln*, this is heard in both the present tense ('Straighten up the living room in case company falls in') and the past tense, as in a description of a family who chose the wrong time to stop by: 'They fell in on us — just at suppertime!'

finif, finnif, fin

These slang terms for a five-dollar bill are from the Yiddish number five, *finif* (from German *fünf*).

fire for 'firebrand' or 'hothead'

'She's a fire' is a common second-generation description of a teenage daughter. It's from *Zi'z a bren.*

first for 'just' or 'just begin to'

This is common in the speech of American Jews, reflecting the impact of Yiddish *ersht* Witness: 'Here it was eight o'clock, and she first began to get dressed' (account of a daughter who does everything at the last minute); 'They work till ten o'clock, and then they first go out for a good time till three in the morning' (a woman telling me of her son's experience in a camp job). Molly Picon in her autobiography quoted her grandmother as saying, 'If a person can't have that feeling to joke any more, then it is first really serious.' Even in literary usage, notice this line: 'After the novel was published, I first realized that the main character, Yankel, must have come from a great hidden affection for my father. . . .' (Jerome Charyn, quoted in a review of his novel, *Once Upon a Droshky*).

from for 'of'

The often-heard 'What do you want from me?' is a direct translation of the exasperated *Vos vilstu fun mir (hobn)?* (Ch. II, Ann. and Arg.). The more normal English would of course be, 'What do you want of me?' Yiddish *fun* means either 'of' or 'from', as does German *von*, and it is likely that German has had some influence too.

The slang 'from hunger' is probably from Yiddish *Er shtarbt fun hunger* 'He's starving from hunger'; hence, 'is in need, inadequate', where the 'from' again takes the place of 'of'. Other phrases from the entertainment world, like 'strictly from borsht', referring to the style associated with the borsht circuit (IIIB), may be related.

See also *know from* for 'know'.

from hunger See *from* for 'of'.

ganef

This Yiddish word for 'crook' or 'sharpie' (Ch. II, Char. and Des.) turns up in a variety of spellings in England and the U.S.: 'gonnif', 'gonoph', 'gunnif', 'gunef', etc. There is also the short-form 'gun', presumably from the latter pronunciation and unrelated to the firearm. In South Africa there's an old cant term 'goniv' for a buyer of stolen diamonds, as well as 'goniva' for such a diamond — presumably from Yiddish *ganeyve* 'theft'.

'Ganef' derives from Hebrew *ganov* 'thief' — not, as was suggested over a hundred years ago, from English 'gone off'! In English cant it has usually meant a pickpocket. In the United States it is a more general synonym for 'crook' or 'robber', though it has also been applied of late to a male homosexual. In the 1940s it was reported in use by carnival men for 'fool'.

England also has a somewhat similar term for simpleton, 'gnof' or 'gnoffe', which goes back to Chaucer's time. It too is credited to Hebrew *ganov* (having spread at a time when the Jews themselves were officially banned). The two terms appear to have reinforced each other. (See middle of III.)

'Ganef' has been used as a verb here and in England, but in Yiddish the verb has different forms from the noun.

The Yiddish plural, *ganeyvim*, has cropped up in science fiction as the name of the police (spelled 'Ganavim') on a corrupt trans-galactic planet.

gelt

This underworld term for money has a long history in international thieves' slang. It was originally German, meaning tribute, payment. Its currency in the United States — sometimes as 'geld' (Dutch) — has been at least partially bolstered by the Yiddish form. (See incident in beginning of III.)

According to Sholem Aleichem, *gelt* is something that everyone wants and nobody has.

Get lost.

From the Yiddish *Ver farloren* (Ch. II, Ann. and Arg.), this has been used for years in the comics and on radio and TV. In 1964 I noticed a sign in front of Alitalia Airlines on Fifth Avenue in New York urging, 'Get lost! Get lost!' In November 1968 a foldout page in *Life* contained just two words: 'Get lost'. The inside page elaborated: 'Get lost where you've always wanted to get lost. Anywhere in the Americas. Cut out the Del Monte items in grocers' ads, and get a free family vacation.'

See also *Verlier*.

Give a look.

Equivalent to the normal English 'Take a look', this comes from the

Yiddish *Gib a kuk*. It's been picked up in popular journalism and dialogue, and has led to the popular 'Give a listen' on radio and TV. Recent variations are 'Give it a listen' — which I saw in *Dig*, a teenage magazine in 1964. ('That record is so full of warmth and feeling, I can't believe it. Give it a listen.' — and 'Give a little listen' — which Altec Lansing used for promoting its hi-fi equipment in a 1967 *Harper's* ad.)

'Give a listen' seems quite parallel to the long-established 'give an ear'. When I heard the Englishman David Frost say on his New York TV show in August 1969, 'Take a listen . . . ', I thought it sounded odd, even though it derives from the normal idiom 'Take a look'.

The catchiness of *gib a kuk* has also invaded modern Hebrew, which now has the equivalent *naton mabat*.

In first-generation speech, 'Give a . . . ' takes still other forms, like 'Give a run over' for 'run over'. This is often 'Give a run over by' for 'Run over to'. (See 'by' for 'to' above.)

Give me a call.

This appears to have developed from 'Give me a ring', the Yiddishism of an earlier generation. The announcers on several Pennsylvania radio stations invite comment with 'Give us a call' and one of them often acknowledges listeners' responses with the awkward 'Thank you for giving us a call'. A local florist advertises 'Just give Merwarth's a call; they'll do it all.'

give toco; give toks See *tokus.*

Go as an ironic substitute for 'Try and', 'You just can't', etc.

This is from Yiddish *gey* and has been used for years on TV in such expressions as:

'Go be nice to people!' (See what it gets you!)

'Go know.' (*gey veys* — Ch. II, Resig.)

'Go fight City Hall.' (A lot of good it'll do!) The more normal English is 'You can't fight City Hall.' The expression has been played on in picture squibs of an American Jewish weekly, the *American Examiner*: 'Go Fete City Hall' (a presentation to New York City's Mayor) and 'Go Light City Hall' (a Chanuka menorah being lighted at City Hall). These of course change the irony of the Yiddish and are more in the class of the normal English 'go' seen in the heading of an ad for a marble-frying kit in *Mechanix Illustrated*: 'Go Fry a Marble!' That in turn has elements of humor, from its similarity to the negative 'Go fly a kite!' (See IIIB, *'gey fight. . . .')*

'Go figure it out!' (I'll be darned; can you match that?) This is a frequent heading for oddities presented in the *Jewish Digest*. It has appeared in other places, sometimes cut to 'Go figure', as in the conclusion of a recent *New York Times* article on culture in Indianapolis: 'It might be added that the new Clowes Hall is . . . one of the best sounding halls in the United States. Its acoustic properties, with clouds and everything, were designed by the same Bolt, Beranek & Newman who were responsible for Philharmonic Hall. Go figure.'[5] (As music lovers know, the acoustics of Philharmonic Hall were for some time less than ideal.)

See Ch. II, *chazen, aleh Yidden kenen zayn chazonim . . .* re, *Gey zay a shammes.'*

goniv; goniva See *ganef.*

gonnif, gonoph See *ganef.*

Good goods!

This smiling judgment of a fellow Jew's new wearing apparel — accompanied by a fingering of the material — is apparently derived from *Guttes' choyre* (Ch. II, Char. and Des.), and is heard in both the United States and Canada.

In England, 'good goods' and 'best goods' have been informal characterizations, as in 'He was rather good goods'.

gun; gunef, gunnif See *ganef.*

gunsel, gunzel, guntzel, etc.

This underworld and hobo term for an inexperienced young boy is probably from German *Gänsel* 'gosling', reinforced by the same Yiddish form. The term may also mean a sneak or crook, and it is possible that it was also influenced by 'ganef' (see *ganef*).

Among carnival men, 'guntzel' has reportedly been used for 'fool'.

In England, the low 'go the guntz' — which means 'go all the way' — may have borrowed from this term as well as from Yiddish *gants* 'whole'.

Cf. Ch. II, Food and Drink, *ganz.*

guy

This slightly derogatory U.S. slang for 'fellow' may have been influenced by Yiddish *goy* (Ch. II, Tribalism), as suggested a generation ago. In England there are a number of other uses of the word, though a nineteenth-century cant one meaning a Christian ruffian, as against a Jewish one, may also have been related to Yiddish.

hame

In jazzmen's lingo, this is the place where a musician is working. It would seem to be from the Yiddish word for home: *heym*.

He don't know from nothin'.

This is the form in which *Er veyst nisht fun gornisht* made its entry a generation or more ago. It has since been showing up in more sedate forms like 'He doesn't know from nothing'; 'He knows from nothing'; 'He doesn't know from anything'. (But note, all use the extra 'from'. See *know from* for 'know, . . . ')

As is common in Yiddish, the idiom has also been appearing with the pronoun 'I'. Witness the recent widely quoted statement by Attorney Dean Andrews, convicted of perjury in connection with his conflicting testimony regarding President Kennedy's assassination: 'I don't know from nothing. What I got is a vivid imagination'. Indeed, a character in the comic strip *Dr. Kildare* by Ken Bald[6] combined this kind of usage with that noted under 'know from' for 'know, . . .': 'Don't pull the "too proud to fight" bit on me, Kildare. I don't know from all this noblesse oblige.'

hole in the head

One of the most common of recent Yiddish borrowings, this comes from *Ich darf es (azoy) vi a loch in kop*, which is often fully translated, 'I need it like a hole in the head' or 'I need that the way I need a hole in the head'. It appeared in Saul Bellow's *Herzog*: ' "I need this outing like a hole in the head", he thought as he turned the key.' In a Connecticut hospital in 1967, I heard a Gentile nurse comment on hearing an ambulance siren: 'More business — like we need a hole in the head!' On the other hand, a Gentile Pennsylvanian soon to undergo the special skull-drilling operation for Parkinson's disease smilingly informed his friends that he *needed* a hole in the head!

See also *I need it like I need. . . .*

The term was used as the title of a Broadway show and a movie (*A Hole in the Head; Hole in the Head*) and also showed up in lyrics for a television marionette show: 'Wise men in fact/Are just a little cracked,/So be glad there's a hole in your head.' Even cigar companies have made use of it. The Roi-Tan firm, which pioneered in the punctured 'head', originally used the slogan 'The Cigar with the Hole in the Head'; but as other cigar makers picked up the idea and emphasized it with such text as 'Notice the Hole in the Head', Roi-Tan changed the wording on its boxes to: 'No biting off ends. The Hole in the Head Draws Easily.'

J. D. Salinger's *Catcher in the Rye* used the variation 'as much use as a hole in the head' in the irreverent sentence: '. . . the Disciples . . . were about as much use to Him as a hole in the head.' A recent book on language puts the expression in the plural: ' . . . if any of these people were here in this room, and instead of writing I were to start creating, with my tongue and my teeth and the holes in my head the intermittent sounds which we call speech, they would know immediately what I am thinking.

In the comics, it has come through in the plural and in a question: 'Ya think I got holes in my head?' (*Kerry Drake* by Alfred Andriola); as well as in a strange Russian-Cockney: 'Before he hexpired, Ian Flemm *Tried* to tell me . . . 'is publisher's haddress in Hamerica — But 'e couldn't remember the ZIP CODE — due, I Hassume, to th' 'ORRIBLE 'OLE IN 'IS 'EAD!' (*Li'l Abner* by Al Capp).

Finally, the phrase has become an adjective, in such copy as that offered by a Chevrolet dealer on Philadelphia TV: 'How about those hole-in-the-head prices?'

hoo-ha

In Yiddish an exclamation (Ch. II), this has become an English noun meaning 'to-do', 'issue', 'argument', as in this London dispatch to the *Nation* regarding current English and American satire: 'The great hoo-ha has been the American scene.'

The term has been bandied about in other ways. *Time* has made it a verb in ' "He's got to be joking!" hoo-ha'd Elizabeth Taylor, 34.' My local radio station made it into an adjective, closer to the Yiddish meaning of 'Oh boy!' when it featured week-end comedians on the 'Hoo-ha Theater' and musical selections from the 'Hoo-ha Library'. One less-than-decorous use occurred on the TV 'Tonight' show, when Phil Ford and Mimi Hines described the laying of a square egg by a 'Hoo-Ha Bird': When the egg was part-way down, the bird said 'Hoo', and after the egg was out, the bird said 'Ha'. The scriptwriters may have been aware that in England the term can also mean an artillery demonstration or even a water closet. (Eric Partridge, in his *Dictionary of Slang and Unconventional English*, lists the additional spellings of 'hoohah' and 'huhhah'.)

T. S. Eliot used the term as a plural noun to refer to the difficulties of middle age: 'You've had a cream of a nightmare/dream and you've got the hoo-ha's coming to you.'

How sweet it is!

This famous line of TV's Jackie Gleason is reminiscent of *Oy, iz dos zis!* (Ch. II, Endearment), which may have been in the mind of a Jewish scriptwriter. The Yiddish itself may have been inspired by the Biblical

'Behold, how good and how sweet it is for brethren to dwell together in unity' (Psalm 133).

The line appeared in a *New York Times* headline several years ago, above an article reporting untoward friendliness in certain political circles: 'Suffolk Politics: How Sweet It Is!' A pictorial history of television by A. Shulman and R. Youman is entitled *How Sweet It Was*.

ich! See *ickle*.

ickie, icky, ikky

This old adjective of distaste — which became a noun in jazz lingo for someone who didn't like or understand swing music, and which has since been an occasional synonym for 'cornball' or 'square' — may have been influenced by Yiddish *ikkel* nausea, and perhaps by English 'sticky', the old description of sentimental music.

See also *ickle*.

ickle, ikkle

This verb 'to upset' or 'to gripe' seems to have come from Yiddish *ikkelen* 'to make nauseous'. Rabbi Samuel Silver, who digests the Yiddish press for the *Jewish Post and Opinion*, tells me he once heard a girl in Texas say 'That ikkles me', quite oblivious, he was sure, of the Yiddish origin of the term.

Some American Jews remember the pronunciation of *ekkelen* rather than *ikkelen*; others may have heard *ichelen*. This last form, I would guess, is related to the old playful expression of distaste, *Ichel-pichel* (Ch. II, Exclam.). This same *ichel* may partly account for the slang 'ich!' — variation of 'ugh!'

In England, 'ickle' is baby-talk for 'little' and is probably unrelated.

if not higher

This is a translation of the title and last line of a famous story by I. L. Peretz about the Rabbi of Nemirov, who used to vanish Friday morning at the time of the Penitential Prayers (Ch. II, Rel. and Cul., *sliches*) and who, his disciples said, ascended into heaven. A skeptic decides to get the facts and hides himself in the rabbi's quarters. He discovers that the rabbi, disguising himself as a peasant selling wood, visits the cottage of a sick Jewish woman and not only offers her the wood on credit but puts the wood upon her fire, reciting the Penitential Prayers as he does so. Thereafter, when the rabbi's disciples boast of his annual ascension to heaven, the skeptic no longer scoffs but quietly adds, 'if not higher'.

Jews familiar with the story may quote the line in reference to well-deserved praise.

If you'll excuse the expression See *You should excuse me.*

I need it like I need . . . ; *I need this the way I need.* . . .

These ironic responses to an unwelcome situation are related to 'I need it like a hole in the head' and have been picked up by many non-Jews. The Dannon Yogurt Co. has used the first form in New York radio advertising: A haughty millionaire states, 'I need yogurt like I need a rich relative'; or a slim girl comments, 'I need Dannon Yogurt like I need a parking ticket. Why do I eat it? I *like* it!'

See also *I need it very badly* and *That's all I need.*

I need it very badly.

This translation of the ironic *Ich darf es zeyer hobn*[7] has been used on TV and elsewhere but seems, as yet, less widely adopted than 'I need it like I need. . . .'

Inverted Sentence Order

The usual order of words in an English sentence puts the subject first and then the predicate. In oldest English, the opposite was often true. There are still many types of sentences in which the old inverted order is naturally used, as in questions 'Where did they go?', quotations (' "Not at all", replied our visitor'), etc. However, in recent years the inverted order seen in popular advertising and journalism seems strongly related to Yiddish with its characteristic intonation and irony. Notice the banana ad in *McCall's*: 'Mistakes we make. But we don't label them "Chiquita".' Or the Beaunit Fibers ad in the *New York Times*: 'Maybe a great drummer he's not, but he looks so gorgeous in his Mr. Wrangler, Jr.'s, who cares?' Or the small-college ad in *Time*: 'Viterbo College: Berkeley we ain't.'

Witness further *Time*'s comment on Julie Andrews: 'A Liz Taylor she's not.' Or Douglas E. Kneeland's discussion of pigs in the *New York Times*: 'But for all the things hogs are, he conceded, returning to his wife's adamant contention, humorous they are not.'

A striking use of this order appeared in Earl Wilson's Broadway column, when he discussed the divorce plans of David Susskind, quoting Susskind's wife of twenty-five years as saying: 'Pneumonia I will give him . . . divorce, NEVER!'[8]

Most popular, perhaps, is the smiling irony: 'On you it looks good.' This even appeared as the title of a novel in 1963.

My husband tells the story of a newspaper ad asking for a physicist who is unmarried and free to travel. A little Jewish man answers the ad and is asked, 'Are you a physicist?' 'No. I'm a tailor.' The interviewer proceeds, 'Are you single?' 'No. I have a wife and seven children.' 'Are you free to travel?' 'Of course not. How could I be, with a wife and family?' 'Then what', the interviewer explodes, 'are you doing here?' 'I just came to tell you', the applicant replies, 'on me you couldn't count.'

In Jewish speech, the word 'maybe' also often appears in an abnormal position, sometimes in a declarative question,[9] and such usage has already turned up in magazine ads ('You were expecting maybe another get-tough-with-Avis ad?' — Hertz Rent-a-Car) and in the comics: 'You were expecting maybe a BRASS BAND?' (*Batman*, by Bob Kane).

Ish Kabibble

Several theories have been offered about the derivation of this old slang term, which was a nonchalant rejoinder meaning 'I should worry'. The most likely is that it came from Yiddish *Iz nisht gefidelt*. (See Ch. II, Resig., *Nu, iz nisht gefidelt* under *Nu, iz nisht*.) Polish pronunciation tends to slur *nisht* to *nish*, from which *ish* is just a step.

'Abe (*or* Abie) Kabibble' was presumably a derivative. I've seen this as an adjective: 'Abe Kabiblish'.

I shoulda (should have, should've, should of) stood in bed.

This clowning expression of self-disgust at 'one of those days' comes from the immigrant generation's confusion of 'stood' and 'stayed' — due to the fact that Yiddish *shtey* means both 'stay' and 'stand'. Boxing promoter Joe Jacobs is supposed to have been responsible for spreading it around the country a generation ago. In recent years, it's been heard a good deal on TV, as in Art Carney's comment on seeing the Sorcerer's Apprentice: 'I should have stood in bed', followed by a song which poked fun at the expression itself: 'I'd Still Be Standing In Bed.'

On radio, I heard a Pennsylvania announcer berate his slips of the tongue with, 'Better I should have stood in bed'. This combines the expression with another Yiddishism (see *Better . . . should*).

In 1962 *Time* used the expression with 'could' instead of 'should' and without the usual implied element of failure. Noting that Arkansas Governor Orval Faubus had gone sleepless on election night, it observed: 'As it turned out, Faubus could have stood in bed: he pulled in about 52 percent of the votes, more than the combined total won by . . . also rans.'

Associated with 'stand' are Yiddish *shtey*'s further meanings of 'say' or 'state', as in *Es shteyt geshribn* (lit., 'It stands written, it says in writing')[10] or *Vu shteyt es geshribn?* 'Where is it written?' (Ch. II, Ann. and Arg.). Swedish-American speech has a similar use of 'stand'.

Is it good for . . . ? See Ch. II, Tribalism, *'Siz gut far di Yidden?*

It can't hurt.

This is from *Shatn, ken es nit* (lit., 'Hurt, it can't'). It's common in the speech of American Jews, who also use a number of variations like 'It wouldn't hurt', 'Would it hurt?' etc. All are showing up in advertising. Witness the sign on a New York automat: 'Have a bagel. It can't hurt' or the subway poster: 'Bagel lovers — Would it hurt to try Lender's for a change?'

The approach isn't limited to bagel barkers. Nestle's Chocolate uses 'It couldn't hurt' on TV: 'Well, it's no substitute for a mother's love or a big bankroll, but it couldn't hurt . . . Nestle's Crunch! Have one! It couldn't hurt!' And the firm of A. B. Dick, in *Time*, uses '. . . won't hurt', substituting two words for the 'it' ('Knowing this won't hurt') in an ad which begins with the English idiom, 'What you don't know about copying and duplicating won't hurt you' and ends with the Yiddish-inspired usage: '. . . you only need to know one thing: in copying and duplicating we have more answers than anyone else. . . . Knowing this won't hurt.'

It could always be worse; could be worse.

Whether this came directly from Yiddish, which has the equivalent *S'ken alts zayn erger*, is hard to say, but it must have been bolstered by the latter, for the philosophical acceptance of fate that is mirrored here is thoroughly Jewish. A classic story tells of the Jew who is relating his family troubles to an old friend: his wife has had a lengthy illness and is going into the hospital for a risky operation and he doesn't know whether she'll live or die. 'Could be worse', the friend comments. 'But you haven't heard anything yet', the man continues, 'Last month my daughter ran off with a traveling salesman and I don't even know where she is.' 'Could be worse', the friend repeats. 'It's *takeh* worse', the man declares. 'With all my worrying about my wife and daughter, the doctor tells me I've developed an ulcer. Just what I need!' 'It could be worse', his friend assures him. *'oy'*, the man goes on, 'I'm not through. On top of everything, business is terrible. I owe so much I'm afraid my creditors are going to foreclose on me any day.' The friend clucks sympathetically but insists, 'It could still be worse'. 'What do you mean?' the man complains, 'how *could* it be worse?' 'Easy', the friend replies, 'it could have happened to me!'[11]

A cartoon by Jim Berry in 1966 showed two bums sitting on a step, one looking worried and the other saying: 'Things could be worse — if you were a pensioner, you'd be the REAL victim of inflation!'

It shouldn't happen to a dog.

This popular denunciation of fate is of course directly from *Tsu a hunt zol es nit trefn.*[12] It began infiltrating American slang at least a quarter-century ago and has become quite common in recent years, in newspaper headlines and on TV. A late-summer brochure from a department store recently utilized it: 'August — the Indians called this season of the year "Dog Days" — but what happened to us — "Shouldn't happen to a Dog". We looked thru our books and find that this month — YOU DON'T OWE US A CENT!'

The expression was used in the affirmative, *It Should Happen to a Dog*, as the title of a wry little play by the English writer Wolf Mankowitz. See *should* and *shouldn't*.

It's just to . . . for 'It's enough to make you . . .'

This Yiddishism cropped up in a song which Sophie Tucker sang on the Ed Sullivan TV show in 1964: 'There's so much to do in so little time . . . There's so much to do, that it's just to cry. . . .'
Cf. *What's to. . . .*

It's their America.

A translation of *'Siz zeyer Amerike*, this is still heard in comment on the success of the younger generation. It mirrors the same immigrant view of the United States as that in *Amerike ganef*! (Ch. II, Exclam.).

Joe Smoe See *shmo*.

Joosh for 'Jewish'

This is a good-natured in-group pronunciation, poking fun at the first generation's Yiddish-tinged English speech. Several years ago at a Bar Mitzvah celebration a woman who was greatly enjoying the refreshments grinned at me as she picked up a tiny *knish* and asked, 'Aren't you glad you're Joosh?'[13]

But note, when used by outsiders, as in 'Joosh pipple', the term is resented. (Cf. Ch. II, introduction to Tribalism.)

keek

A manufacturer's look-out man, especially in the garment industry, who spots what competitors are doing — presumably from German *kieken* 'to peek or peep', reinforced by the Yiddish verb to look, *Kuken* or *kiken* and the noun *kuk* or *kik*. (Cf. *Give a look.*)

The term also appears in English, Scotch and Irish dialect for 'look' or 'see'. A 'keeker' in Scotch coal mines is the man who checks on the quality of coal sent up the shaft.

kibitzer

This expressive term for someone who is looking on at other's activity and occasionally putting in his two cents' worth — often at cards — is generally credited to Yiddish, which probably drew on both German and Hebrew. In German, *Kiebitz* or *Kibitz* 'pee-wit, lapwing, or plover', has reportedly long been applied to an onlooker at cards, especially one who offers advice. In Hebrew, there is the verb *kibeytz* 'to gather'.

A movie of the 1930s, *The Kibitzer*, featuring an innocent Jewish meddler, did much to diffuse the term.

Bilingual verbal forms like 'kibitzing' and 'kibitzes' are common. In 1955, when Margaret Truman substituted for Edward R. Murrow in covering the presidential family on his *Person to Person* TV show, her mother was at one point walking from one room to another murmuring to herself. Margaret admonished her with: 'No kibitzing, Mother, no kibitzing. No kibitzing.' *Time*'s account carried a picture of the Trumans with the caption: 'No kibitzing allowed.' In 1942 the title of an article in *Word Study* by Julius G. Rothenberg was 'A Devoted Reader Kibitzes the Lexicographers.' That made the verb transitive. A similar use appeared in a recent issue of the *Las Vegas Israelite*, in the caption for a picture of comedian Jackie Mason looking over the shoulder of card-playing *Sun* columnist Ralph Pearl: 'Mason Kibitzes Pearl.'

The root of the word is sometimes used to mean 'chew the rag' or 'shmoose' (which was the original Yiddish meaning), as in the old popular song 'My Baby Just cares for Me': 'She don't like a voice like Lawrence Tibbett's,/She'd rather have me around to kibitz.' In this sense it's sometimes heard as a noun, as in 'a good kibitz'. But note, this is different from Hebrew *kibbutz*, a cooperative settlement, which is accented on the last syllable. Someone once wrote me she was sorry I was away; she was 'in the mood for a good kibbutz'!

kike

This pejorative word for a Jew is supposed to have originated among German Jews in the United States who used it to refer to the lower-class Jewish immigrants from Eastern Europe.

One explanation, suggested by Prof. Gotthard Deutsch over a generation ago, is that it came from the Yiddish term for 'circle', *kaykel*, which an immigrant peddler he knew used in various ways to mark his account books. A refinement of this theory, attributed to Philip Cowen, an old United States immigration inspector, is that the circle was first used by

Jewish immigrants on Ellis Island, when they signed their names with this mark in lieu of an 'X', which had Christological associations for them, the inspectors thenceforward speaking of such signers as *kaykel, kaykele* or *kayki* and finally *kayk* or 'kike'.

Though at least one writer has objected that *kaykel* is not the Yiddish word for 'circle' (which is more properly *rod* or *krayz*), the term appears in the Harkavy dictionary (1910). Peter Tamony has suggested two additional influences: the German *kieken*, to peep (see 'keek' above) and the diminutives of Isaac, 'Ike' and 'Ikey' — the latter pejoratives, according to his account, having been common among German and Austrian Jews who were displaced in U.S. clothing manufacturing by the newer immigrants. (The terms have a history in English cant, where they have presumably been limited to the 'out-group'.)

Leo Rosten reports that the peddler was also known among Gentiles as the 'kike man'. In structure, at least, this is reminiscent of the term 'Jew peddler', reported from Nevada speech over a generation ago, as well as of the common slur 'Jew boy', which may well have begun as simple description.

Cf. Ch. II, Tribalism, *yeke*.

klutz See *cluck*.

know from for 'know', 'know of', 'know about'

This influence from Yiddish is seen in various ways. First, there is the extra 'from' where English would normally use only 'know', as in the popular 'He don't know from nothin' ' and its derivatives discussed above. Among Jews, a similar usage shows up in the variations of 'not to know from *borsht*' (IIIB).

As a substitute for 'know of' or 'know about', it is common in Jewish speech, as in the exclamation of a character in Jerome Charyn's fiction, recalling a poor childhood: 'Who knew from school!' A line like this came through on TV in the *Beverly Hillbillies* in 1964, deprecating someone's acquaintanceship with English actors: 'What does he know from English actors?' (Here the usual English meaning would be quite different.)

Also common among Jews are expressions like 'You shouldn't know from such things' (see end of *should* and *shouldn't*).

kosher; not so kosher

These figurative uses of the dietary term, to mean respectively, 'on the up and up' and 'unreliable', have become fairly common in detective fiction and journalism and in the speech of many Gentiles. Among the last-named a generation ago, 'kosher' was sometimes used slurringly as a synonym for 'Jewish', as in 'a kosher cutie' for an attractive Jewish girl. (Cf. 'motsal'.) Today, it's generally more respectable. The late Senator Everett Dirksen, interviewed about his union membership after he made a bestselling phonograph record, remarked in 1967: 'This I can tell you. Everything seems to be kosher.' In 1964 on TV's *McHale's Navy*, McHale stated: 'There's something about all this that just doesn't smell kosher to me.'

In the dietary sense, 'kosher' is also being used as a noun meaning 'kosher products' or kashruth, the system of kosher observance. Witness the booklet issued by the public-relations firm Joseph Jacobs Organization, 'What You Should Know about Kosher', which states: 'In line with the general Spiritual Revival, more Jewish people are paying more attention to their religion — and this means more attention to "kosher".' In accordance with such advice, Dugan's bakers advertise that they are 'Finest for Kosher'.

Jews also speak of 'keeping kosher' and 'eating kosher', and kosher butchers advertise the advice to 'buy kosher'.

See early part of III; Ch. II, Rel. and Cul., *kashres*.

lox See Ch. II, Food and Drink, *laks*.

make with for 'give out with'

This translation of *mach mit* has been heard on the radio ('These famous voices make with "What's the Use?" ') and in popular journalism, where it has led to 'making with' as in a book review by John Barkham: 'Having uttered his gripe, Smith moves into pleasanter pastures and begins making with the gags.'[14]

matzo, matzoh

This unleavened bread of Passover is being used at times by some Christian clergymen as a communion wafer[15] and by many other Americans as a low-calorie cracker (being so advertised on the radio). Even the Air Force, if it didn't before, now has a pretty good idea of what a matzo is, for a New Jersey woman reported an Unidentified Flying Object as looking like a big matzo, with tiny holes around the edge!

The word has shown up in a number of quips. *Time* has referred to Sam Levenson as a 'matzo-barrel philosopher' and 'matzo-barrel humorist'. Velvel, ventriloquist Ricky Lane's dummy, has commented on TV, 'That's the way the matzo crumbles'. And poet Louis Untermeyer has described his wife, a singer, as a 'matzo soprano'.

Cf. *motsa*.

maven

This spelling of the Yiddish term for connoisseur or expert, *mayven*, has been used in a number of special ads by Vita Herring concerning the 'Herring Maven', which elicited a surprising response from readers of the *New York Times*. Thousands of these proved willing to pay for Herring Maven forks or to copy a detailed drawing for the prize of a fork and an 'I Am a Herring Maven' button. Canada Dry has been touting its product as 'Maven's Choice', in American Jewish weeklies, where Switzerland Emmentaler cheese announces itself with: 'Calling all Mayvinim!'

See Ch. II, Ann. and Arg., *oych (mir) a . . ., oych mir a meyven*; Passing Judgment, *Zingn ken ich nit, ober a meyven bin ich*!

mazel tov

This Hebrew and Yiddish expression of congratulations and good wishes is being more and more widely used and understood. Ten years ago I heard a female radio m.c. say, 'Well congratulations and mazel tov'. About the same time it appeared in the movie *Please Don't Eat the Daisies*, where the characters were of course not Jewish. Since then, a Philadelphia radio station has been carrying a musical program for young people entitled *Mazel Tov* ('the Show with Young Ideas'), and a pop group has been organized in England (new in 1966) calling itself 'Mozzle Toff'. (According to the *London Jewish Chronicle*, only the drummer was Jewish.) When former Secretary of State Dean Rusk's daughter married a Negro in 1967 the comment for publication by Negro leader Bayard Rustin was: 'Mazel tov'. And in January 1968 a Pennsylvania radio announcer reported on the temperature: 'We got to 23 — mazel tof'.

A silver bracelet charm on sale at jewelers' in recent years has a four-leaf clover on one side and engraved good wishes in many languages on the other, including *'mazel tov'*.

As a private joke, in Raeburn Van Buren's comic strip *Abbie an' Slats,* a wealthy dowager bent on marrying off her daughter was named 'Ma Zeltov'. To celebrate said daughter's decision to marry 'a man of character instead of cash', she 'planned her specialty — fresh fish à la Ma Zeltov!' It took a certain corn-oil producer to advertise: 'MAZOLA-TOV; Congratulations, you've found our 10¢ off Coupon . . . !' Appropriately enough, a dating bureau for Jewish singles, advertising in the *Nation* in 1969, is 'Operation *mazel tov*'.

mazuma, mezuma, mazoomy, etc.

This old slang term for money or cash comes from Yiddish *mezume*, which derives from Aramaic *m'zumon*. It has sometimes been shortened to 'mazoo' or lengthened to 'mazoola' (combining with another slang term for money, 'moola').

metsieh, metziah, mitsia, etc.

Reported a generation ago to mean, in jewelry auctioneers' lingo, a flashy but defective diamond, this is from the ironic Yiddish *a gantse metsieh* (Ch. II, Char. and Des.).

Jewish residents of Great Neck, New York, have been smiling at the name of the new automobile dealer in their area selling Toyota, the Japanese car: 'Mitsia Motors'.

mish mash, mish-mash, mishmash; mish mosh, mish-mosh, mishmosh

Another example of a foreign word adopted by English and later given impetus from the Yiddish which had also borrowed it. German *mischmasch* came into English about five hundred years ago as 'mishmash', with a short 'a'. In recent years it has become common in the entertainment world, pronounced with a broad 'a' as in Yiddish and accordingly sometimes spelled with an 'o'.

In 1964 when Governor Scranton of Pennsylvania used the term on TV, pronouncing it with the short 'a', he received a letter from comic actor Groucho Marx, advising him that if he planned any campaigning in Jewish neighborhoods, he had better change his pronunciation to rhyme with 'slosh'. The Associated Press quoted Scranton as saying, 'Ever since then, I've been trying to do that for Groucho'. This incident was capitalized on immediately in TV's Dick Van Dyke show. Two writers were discussing a script in process. 'What have we got? A mish mosh', said one. 'So we've got a mish mash', replied the other. And the first one exclaimed, 'Mish mash? It's mish *mosh*. Can't you speak English?'

Composer Leonard Bernstein, writing in *Vogue* a decade ago, made a verb of it: 'There was Gothic melodrama with dancing girls in tights, and comedy songs, and long speeches by Stalacta, Queen of the Golden Realm; there were gnomes and demons and Zamiel the Archfiend, and Swiss peasant maids — all mishmashed together.'

See Ch. II, Rel. and Cul., *medresh*.

mishugge; mishuggene

These Yiddish terms for — respectively — 'crazy' and 'crazy one' have been picked up in the entertainment world and have been heard on Broadway, in movies, and over radio and TV. An old lively radio musical group was called 'The Mishuggenes' (The Nuts). A recent book by comedian Henny Youngman was described in a *New York Times* ad as

'Mishugah!' — the spelling being based on the Hebrew from which the term derives.

In Yiddish, *mishugge* is a predicate adjective and knows no gender (*er iz mishugge* 'he's crazy'; *zi iz mishugge*, 'She's batty'), while *mishuggene* is the feminine form of the adjective when it precedes a noun (*a mishuggene meydel* 'a dizzy girl') and also the feminine form of the noun (*ot kumt di mishuggene* 'here comes the nut'). The masculine form of the latter term is *mishuggener* (*a mishuggener mentsh* 'a wacky person'; *er iz a mishuggener* 'he's a nut'). However, as usually heard in American slang, *mishuggene* applies to either sex.

See Ch. II, Char. and Des., *mishugge* and *mishuggener*.

mitsia See *metsieh*.

mix in for 'butt in' or 'get mixed up in'

'Don't mix in' is common in the speech of the second generation and sometimes shows up in the patter of Jewish comedians. It seems to derive from *mish zich nit (arayn)* — Ch. II, Advice.

mockie

My hunch is that this old slurring term for a Jew came from Yiddish *makeh* (Ch. II, Imprec., *A makeh im!*). I would also guess that the parallel slur 'Makalairy', which Maurice Samuel reports from the England of his childhood, is a combination of Yiddish *makeh* and *chalerye* (Ch. I, Imprec., *zol dir chapn a chalerye!*). The term 'moggy', in English dialect, means cow, calf, or ass, and this may conceivably have been involved too.

Cf. *sheeny*.

Money is round.

This homespun observation that money is undependable and can roll away is common among second-generation American Jews, often as an equivalent of 'Money isn't everything', particularly with regard to a prospective suitor. It comes from the Yiddish *Gelt iz kalechdik — a mol iz es do, a mol iz es dorten* 'Money is round — sometimes it's here, sometimes it's there'.

See also Ch. II, Advice, *Mit gelt ken men nit shtoltsiren.* . . .

motsa, motser, motzer

Although I have never heard it myself, 'motzer' is listed in Berry and Van den Bark's *The American Thesaurus of Slang* as a slurring term for a Jew. I would guess it comes from *matzo* (Ch. II, Food and Drink), as did presumably the old, relatively rare, derogation 'motsy'.

'Motsa' and 'motser' have been reported as Australian slang for a large sum of money, as in 'He made a motsa'.

mouchey

Another relatively rare derogatory term for a Jew, this is believed to derive from the Yiddish name *moyshe* 'Moses'. German has a somewhat similar verb, *mauscheln*, to speak with a Jewish accent or intonation or to speak in Yiddish.

nash, nasch See *nosh.*

nebbish

This term for a poor fool, from *nebbechel* (Ch. II, Char. and Des.) has shown up on TV ('He's a nebbish'), in newspaper columns ('Kovacs, who played a noble nebbish, turned the piece into a personal gambado'), in the comics (Fearless Fosdick's 'Shhh!! — This is direct from the Nebbish Desert' in Al Capp's *Li'l Abner*), etc. It was popularized in the retail trade in the 1950s with the 'nebbish' gift items 'for the man who has nothing'. (The line even included a 'nebbish bank' for children, advertised on TV, from which the money came right out at the bottom.)

Note that some of these uses make the word an adjective. It's been used this way to describe a humble approach in advertising copy. Witness the statement by Norman B. Norman quoted in *Harper's* regarding the approach of Doyle Dane Bernbach, who directed the Avis Rent-a-Car campaign: 'It's always *nebbish*, always apologetic.'

As a noun the term is often shortened to 'neb': 'He's such a neb!'

The verb 'to neb', meaning to be inquisitive, was reported a generation ago for southwestern Pennsylvania and West Virginia, but this may be from German and unrelated.

nik See IIIB, 'nogoodnik'.

Nisht Amool

This is the name of a horse that was reportedly running in 1968 races. It is Yiddish for 'Not Sometime' (but Now!).

. . . no?

Asking a question by tacking 'no?' onto a statement is common in the speech of first- and second-generation American Jews. The practice presumably came from German, which influenced both English (the usage appears in Shakespeare) and Yiddish, with Yiddish helping to intensify it in the United States.

Note that this 'no' is different from Yiddish *nu* (Ch. II, Exclam.). The editorial writer in my local paper once confused the two: 'Esoteric, Shmesoteric — It's interesting, nu?'

nosh

This form of Yiddish *nash* 'snack' (Ch. II, Food and Drink) has appeared in various places: in a cracker named 'Nosh-o'-Rye' (a pun on *nasheray*) — with its rhymed advertising slogan 'By gosh, what a nosh!' — and in the title of a cookbook *A Rage to Nosh.* In Florida a hotel snack bar is 'Ye Noshery' (which I've heard pronounced like the cracker), and in the nation's capital a fancy Chinese restaurant was named 'Chinese noshery'.[16]

An establishment specializing in *knishes* has been dubbed 'Nish Nosh'. Isaac Gellis packages a 'Salami Nosh' (chunks of salami for snacks). Stuff to nibble on has been called 'noshables' in a food column; and Earl Wilson has quoted Burl Ives in a restaurant asking for 'just a little something to nosh on', the column being headed 'Burl Ives Takes Off Weight, but Noshing Puts It Back On'.

On TV, the term has been used in various forms for over a decade now — from the line of Richard Willis the beauty expert to a stocky woman, 'I'll bet you nosh all the time'; to the fancy chef on a Steve Allen show named 'Neville Nosher'; to Danny Thomas's comment on a $70 bill for luncheon at the Plaza, 'Somebody must have been doing some noshing'.

On the radio, a food product has been recommended as 'a posh nosh'. And a recent ad for frozen *blintzes* in the *New York Times* read: 'Noshniks of the world, unite! Join the Golden Blintz Revolution!' As mentioned previously in III, paper napkins are available with the invitation 'Have a Nash'. I have also seen 'nasch time', in publicity for a holiday celebration of a synagogue sisterhood.

A distinction between 'nosh' and 'nibble' was made in an ad in the *Hadassah Magazine* for Dromedary Date-Nut Roll, in which two slices were shown, one with a large bite in it, the other with a smaller one, the text reading: 'NOSH or NIBBLE it . . . Stack it HIGH . . . keep it handy to serve when guests drop by!'

nudj, nudje See Ch. II, Char. and Des., *er nudjet.*

nudnik

This popular Yiddish term for a bore or pest (Ch. II, Char. and Des.) has been turning up in various places — from an author's pseudonym, to the *Li'l Abner* character 'Liddle Noodnik', to the punning 'nudenik' in a Broadway column for a photographer persistently urging undraped posing. It has even been misused in a series of animated cartoons about a pathetic little character for whom everything seems to go wrong. The poor fellow is really a *shlimazel* (see Ch. II, Char. and Des., *shlemiel*).

of beloved memory

The *Ellery Queen Mystery Magazine* has been wont to attach this phrase to the name of any person departed or thing defunct. This is of course common usage among Jews, who get it from *zecher livrocho* and *olev 'a sholem* (Ch. II, Death).

only for 'just'

English sometimes uses 'only' for 'just', as in 'If I could only. . . .' The impetus from Yiddish *nor*, which also has both meanings, is most colorfully seen in such a statement as 'He should only break a leg!' (Cf. *should* and *shouldn't.*)

On you it looks good. See Inverted Sentence Order.

oonshick

This term for 'a person of low intelligence' is reported from Newfoundland usage by Eric Partridge, who wonders whether it may be of Amerindian origin. I suggest it is a snappy short-form of Yiddish *unshikenish* 'a dire happening'. The exclamation *an unshikenish!* (Ch. II, Ann. and Arg.) gives vent to annoyance at the person who is a calamitous pest, and this might often be a boring nincompoop or 'imbecile'.

out of this world

Yiddish has the counterpart of this expression — Ch. II, Char. and Des., *An oys nem (fun der velt)*! It may have had something to do with the American slang expression.

shamus, shammes, shammus, shommus

This term is well known to readers of detective fiction as a synonym for a cop, a flatfoot, or more frequently a house detective. Though some observers have related it to the Irish surname 'Seumas', noting that there are many Irishmen connected with police work, it seems much more likely to have come from Yiddish *shammes* 'the synagogue beadle', (Ch. II, Rel. and Cul.) who was the keeper of the premises and object of a certain deprecation. (Hebrew *shamosh* means keeper, guardian or servant.)

The short form 'sham' is believed to be a derivative, though some argue that this is short for 'shamrock', symbol of the Irish. It's also been suggested that this is the standard word 'sham', implying a lack of police integrity. It could also conceivably be a short form for the old Indian word for medicine man, *shaman*, which had disparaging connotations.

Leo Rosten has decried the absence of the term in the latest edition of Mencken's *American Language*, but it does appear there, as it did in that work's Supplement II of 1948.

sheeny

An old derogatory term for a Jew, this probably came — as A. A. Roback suggested back in 1938 — from the Yiddish imprecation *a mise meshinne* (Ch. II), and as I believe other anti-Semitic slurs came from different commonly heard Yiddish imprecations (see *mockie*).

shemozzel, shemozzle, shimozzle, schlemozzle, etc.

In British and Canadian slang, this means a misfortune, difficulty, or 'row', hence an affair of any kind. It's also used as a verb, to mean 'make tracks', 'get moving'. In the United States, it's occasionally seen as 'schlemozzle' for 'uproar'. The origin would seem to be Yiddish *shlimazel* (Ch. II, Char. and Des.)

shice See *shyster*.

shick See IIIB, 'shikkered'.

shickser, shikster, shakester, etc.

Yiddish *shikse* 'Gentile girl', (Ch. II, Tribalism) is believed to be the source of these low terms used in England to mean, at various periods, a lady or a not-too-respectable female.

shlag, shlak See *shlock*.

shlemiel

In retail jargon, this may mean a sucker. In general slang, its use is increasing, reflecting its Yiddish meaning of poor fish, dope (see Ch. II, Char. and Des.).

Contrary to Leo Rosten's assertion, the term is included in the 1963 edition of Mencken's *American Language*. It also appeared in Supplement I in 1945.

shlep, schlep

This root of the verb *shleppen* 'to drag', is common in American Jewish speech ('Why should you shlep all those packages if you can have them sent out?') and has been spreading. The term was reported two decades ago among retail furniture salesmen, for the act of moving furniture around on the floor. I recall an S. J. Perelman play on TV in 1959, in which a Jewish psychiatrist remarked: 'If I want an orange, I don't have to go shlep myself to some supermarket.' A New York department store recently used the term as both verb and noun, advertising a new shopping bag in three sizes: 'Schlep!', 'Son of Schlep', and 'Super-Schlep'.

I've also heard 'shlep' as an abbreviation of *shlepper* (Ch. II, Char. and Des.), as in the statement actor Walter Mathau made to radio interviewer Arlene Francis: 'I like to go around looking like a shlep.' Asked to explain, he said a 'shlep' was a guy who went around wearing an old lumber jacket.

Also common are a number of bilingual forms, like 'shlepped', 'shlepping', 'shlep along', 'shlep around' and 'shlepping around'. A much-quoted pun about a weekend when former President Lyndon Johnson went to the Catskills was: 'LBJ shlepped here.' An old Mickey Katz musical parody was 'Schleppin' My Baby Back Home'. In 1957 the New York *Post* reported: 'Queen Elizabeth will schlep along 95 pieces of baggage on her trip here.' A year before, it reported that a truck driver had found a purse in the road, noting that there was '$11 in it and the usual trifles that a woman — in this case Mrs. John B. Kelly, Grace's mother — might schlep around'. In 1962 Earl Wilson's syndicated column used the verb intransitively: 'While schlepping around Waikiki in my swim trunks, I met Debbie Reynolds. . . .' — the item being headed in a Pennsylvania paper: 'Schlepping at Waikiki Becoming a Popular Sport'! Similarly, in 1967 society columnist Suzy (Aileen Mehle) noted in the New York *Daily News* that 'Charlotte Ford Niarchos has been schlepping around the Greek islands with her ex-husband, Tanker King Stavros Niarchos. . . .' Apparently neither Earl Wilson nor Suzy was aware that in Jewish usage, 'shlepping around' usually connotes a point-less courtship (see Ch. II, Family, *arumshleppen*).

The program for the 1967 musical burlesque 'P.D.Q. Bach' in New York featured a 'Schleptet'.

In England, a 'shlepper-in' is a barker, i.e. a person who drags in the customers.

In underworld cant, 'make the shleps' means 'get the bundle'.

shlimazel See Ch. II, Char. and Des., *shlemiel.*

shlock, schlock, shlak, shlag, schlag, shlog

This current slang term, seen and heard mostly in 'shlock-shop', for a store with third-rate merchandise and without fixed pricing, seems to have been influenced by several Yiddish words: *shlak*, 'a stroke' (See Ch. II, Imprec., *A shlak zol im trefen*!); *shlacht* 'slaughter', as in *shlacht-hoyz* 'slaughterhouse; and *shlogen* 'to hit'. Back in the 1920s it was reported in the retail shoe business, as 'schlach-joint'. 'Shlock' has also been used to mean an overcharge or a junky bit of merchandise or, as in theater box-office lingo reported over a generation ago, a brutal situation, a very poor ticket sale. Among circus people the term appears (along with 'slum', 'junk', 'garbage') for the cheap wares sold by concessionaires. In underworld cant it's also used as a synonym for 'junk', but there 'junk' means narcotics.

In TV lingo, a 'shlock-meister' is a hander-out of junk or shlock: i.e., a fellow who arranges for indirect commercial 'plugs' to be used in TV scripts and who passes out gifts from the companies whose products are so mentioned. In the radio trade, a 'shlock-minister' is a preacher who exhorts his listeners to send in contributions.

The word has also appeared as an adjective, e.g. in 'shlock job' for a fill-in or pot-boiling assignment in the theater, and as a verb, meaning to overcharge.

In Australia and Britain, to 'shlog (or slog) it on' means to up the price.

shlub (shluhb)

This recent synonym for slang 'jerk' is being used by many a Gentile. It has appeared on TV and in popular journalism, as in the following line in the New York *Daily News* over a decade ago: 'Telvi had a contract for $500 . . . to punch some shlub around.' It is apparently from Yiddish *zhlob* 'a yokel, a big dope, a lumbering idiot'.

shlump, schlump

Probably from Yiddish *shlumper* 'slut, slattern', this usually means 'slob'. But it has been used in the comics for 'jerk' ('So you admit you were a shlump?') and has appeared in a *Time* movie review as a verb indicating something like 'laze' or 'slink' ('Spirited performers also lend *Sylvia* a sorely needed touch of class, and Actress Baker shlumps through the role at a wry deadpan pace, obviously enjoying her buildup as Hollywood's sex queen pro tem.').

shm- See IIIB, 'fancy-shmancy, etc.'

shmaltz, schmaltz, schmalz, etc.

This musicians' term for sentimental music is of course the Yiddish word for poultry fat, so commonly used in the Old Country recipes. It has appeared in reference to greasy hair dressing and also as an adjective, as in *Time*'s reference to 'Schmalz Pianist Liberace'. Usually, though, one sees the bilingual adjective 'schmaltzy', as in the 1968 Barton's candy ad: 'This Valentine's Day, women are longing, waiting to be wooed the schmaltzy way.'

To 'schmaltz it up' in music or writing means to make it more sentimental. Maurice Samuel has spoken of the Broadway hit *Fiddler on the Roof* as 'a shmaltzification of Jewish life'.

shmaychel, shmeikle

This verb to con or fast-talk is from the Yiddish verb shmeychlen or shmaychlen 'to smile'. As with the English 'gladhand', the ideas of pleasure and deception are combined.

Cf. IIIB, '*shmay* around'.

shmear, schmear, schmeer

In 1930, this term was reported as being used by furniture salesmen to mean to flatter a customer. It's believed to come from the Yiddish shmiren (from German *schmieren*) 'to smear or grease' hence 'butter up' and thence to 'tip' or even 'bribe'.[17]

The term may also denote to win dramatically against, as an intensified form of 'smear', particularly with respect to football: i.e. when you shmear a player from the opposite team, you knock him over, hence 'wipe the ground with him' or 'smear' him.

The word also appears as a noun ('It was a real shmear'). An interesting extension is seen in the statement which a New York chemist told me he had heard from a Gentile salesman: 'I've got the whole shmear'. Apparently this means. 'I've got the complete line; it'll outclass any competitor's'. This usage has become more generalized, so that in February 1969 WOR's John Wingate employed it in the sense of 'shebang' when he said of the play *The Wrong Way Light Bulb:* 'Everything that's happening in New York is in that play . . . the whole shmear. . . .'

shmecken, schmecken

Dope addicts mean by this 'narcotics'. It's the Yiddish word to smell, from the German word to taste. Dope may of course be either sniffed or tasted, and both languages are probably involved.

Among Chicago addicts as reported a generation ago, 'smecker' meant one of their kind.[18]

shmegegge See Ch. II, Char. and Des.

shmeikle See *shmaychel.*

shmo

From the widespread use of this slang term, you might never guess that it comes from a taboo Yiddish word (*shmok* — from German *Schmuck* 'ornament' — denoting the male organ and, figuratively, 'fool'). Indeed, the popular 'Don't be a shmo' seems to be a direct rendering of *Zay nit keyn shmok* 'Don't be a fool'. With the dropping of the last letter, the word was cleaned up a bit, but it's always been unsettling for me to see it in children's TV films (a potentate, 'The Shmo of Shmoland'; 'The Schmohawk Indians') or to hear it in the spot announcement on racial intolerance: 'Don't be a shmoe, Joe,/Be in the know, Joe' — to say nothing of the jingle appearing on the box of a family type of puzzle, 'What's Your Hi-Q?':

'If you take a week,
You're an average Joe.
If you give it up,
You're just a schmoe.'

The height — or depth — of this trend was reached with Remco's 'Shmo' game, about which TV ad copy proclaimed, 'It's fun to play Shmo, to watch a shmo, to *be* a shmo!', but whose box carried a more accurate message: 'I'm a shmo, and that ain't good!'

Vulgar terms of course frequently travel up the scale of acceptability. Slang like 'snafu', 'all bollixed up' can similarly trouble those who are sensitive to the terms' origins.

In World War II 'Joe Shmoe' was common American Army slang, producing an alternate form, 'Joe Smoe'. This same dropping of the 'h' I think explains the vulgar term 'smock', which in England is used in many phrases of a licentious nature and is doubtless related to the Yiddish and German terms (as is the low English 'schmock', a fool). Similarly, I assume that the English slurring term for a Jew, 'shmog', with the same derivation, was the source of two epithets reported by Maurice Samuel from his childhood in England: 'smoggy' and 'smoggy Van Jew'. The process was obviously known to the writer of advertising for Smucker's jams, which had a man with a knowing look saying: 'With a name like this, it *has* to be good!'

The pronunciation 'shmuck', as noted in Ch. I, Vulgarity, has been heard in a recent Broadway play. I have since heard it in the 1969 movie *Good-bye, Columbus* and recall it earlier in the Broadway musical *West Side Story*. It has appeared in several recent novels, spelled 'schmuck', even being quoted in an advance review by the Kirkus Service: ' "Everything is itch and scratch, skin, surface, and advertising copy", declares the narrator, a "Jewish schmuck", who memorializes the world of drugs. . . .'

In modern fiction from England, I've seen the spelling 'shmook' (see *shnook*).

The outright term may well be supplanting 'shmo'. I have even heard the bilingual adjective 'shmucky' in teen talk, voiced without any awareness of the taboo nature of the word.

Cf. *shmoo* and IIIB, 'fancy-shmancy, etc', and Ch. II, Char. and Des., *shmegegge*.

shmoo

This imaginary animal created by cartoonist Al Capp which lays eggs, gives milk, provides meat, and in its author's words 'represents the earth in all its richness' has been the subject of speculation by several linguists. Capp himself once indicated the term came to him on a cross-country trip as a symbol of the lushness of our countryside, but two pertinent observations have been made: *Shmu* was used by German Jewish businessmen a generation or two ago to mean somewhat illicit profit, and *shmue* is taboo Yiddish for the female organ. The satirical Mr. Capp, who has gone on suggestive capers before, even without the protective screen of Yiddish (and been taken to task for them by the New York Board of Regents), has had his own big joke — topping it with a 1963 sequence about the Shmos of Outer Shmongolia in which he gaily pointed out the difference between a 'shmoo' and a 'shmo'.

Franklin D. Roosevelt, Jr., was quoted in 1966 as using the phrase 'the old schmoo' to describe turning on the charm.

shmoose, shmooze

This slang term for 'chat' or 'chew the rag' can be a verb or noun and comes from Yiddish *shmus* (from Heb. *sh'muoth* 'news or tales'). It's often heard in the bilingual 'shmoosing'.

Several South African colloquial terms have a similar origin: 'smouse', 'smouch', and 'smouser' for a peddler; and 'smousing', peddling. (A peddler is an itinerant, who would bring news of other places.)

In England, opprobrious terms for a Jew in the eighteenth century were 'smous(e)' and 'smou(t)ch'.

shnook

This recently popular synonym for 'sucker' or 'fool' *could*, as Thomas Pyles has suggested, be a minced form of taboo 'shmuck' — perhaps through its occasional form 'shmook' (see *shmo*); but I wonder whether the Yiddish *shnuk* for 'snout' or 'trunk' may have been involved, in a further association with the sexual organ.

Over a generation ago, both *shnuk* and *shnukel* reportedly meant an easy mark to retail salesmen, and H. L. Mencken thought they might be related to German *schnucke* 'small sheep'. I always heard the word as *shnukel* in first-generation speech and have assumed that 'shnook' was an American shortening of the term. But if the more licentious origin is truer, the suffix was of course added.

I have a gift apron, purchased at Lord & Taylor, New York, which proclaims: 'Any shnook can cook!' (I think it would be more appealing if it said 'I'm no shnook; I can cook!') The comic-strip *Mary Worth*, by Kevin Ernest and A. Saunders, over a decade ago had the line: 'If I weren't a blind, rockheaded jingle-brained charter member of the "Schnook-of-the-month club", I'd be married to September Smith.' In 1962 a pre-Christmas AP Newsfeature for children was titled 'Mr. Shnoo's Zoo', and I wondered whether the name was from 'shnook' or 'shmoo' (see *shmoo*) or both. It may even have involved a variation of shm- play on the children's character 'Mr. Magoo' — I recall a TV line, 'Magoo, Mashmoo, I'll kill the miserable wretch!' (See IIIB, 'fancy-shmancy, etc.')

shnorrer See Ch. II, Char. and Des.

shofel, shofle, shoful

A cant term for counterfeit money, this came into English from German *schofel* 'worthless', which in turn is supposed to have come from the Yiddish form of Hebrew *shaphal* 'low, base'.

In 1929 it was reported as an adjective in the speech of borax-house salesmen: 'If business is bad, it's shofle.'

shon, shonk, shonky, shoncker, shonnicker

These opprobrious terms for a Jew in England are supposed to have come from Yiddish *shoniker* 'petty trader or peddler'.

should — ironic

This Yiddish influence is seen in popular ironies like 'I should worry' or 'I should tell him he can't do it!' — the implication being 'Why should I?' Sources are the ironic *Hob ich a dayge* 'I've got a worry', and *mayn dayge* (Ch. II, Resig., *'Siz mayn dayge*). An old popular song, 'I Should Care', built on the expression: 'I should care,/I should let it upset me. . . .'

The irony of this 'should' was coupled with another Yiddish-derived 'should', that of wishing, in the defiant children's rhyme of my generation: 'I should worry, I should care,/I should marry a millionaire.' (See *should* and *shouldn't.*)

should and *shouldn't* for 'may' and 'may not'

This translation of the Yiddish particle *zol* shows up in a number of expressions popular among Jews and fast infiltrating general speech: 'I should live so long' (Ch. II, Life and Health, *Ich zol azoy lang lebn!*); 'So it shouldn't be a total loss'; 'We should be so lucky'; 'That should be your biggest worry' (Ch. II, Advice, *Zol dos zayn dayn ergste dayge*); 'You should only be well'; etc.

An aquarium sticker being sold and used by pet shops declaims: 'It Should Knock in Your Head like You Knock on the Glass.' On WQXR, Murray Shumach in 1966 quoted a violinist's comment about his fellow artist Mischa Elman: 'God should keep him a long time.' (Elman was seventy-five at the time.) Going a step further, a Miami Beach hotel has advertised: 'You should live to 120.' This is of course a good-natured rendition of *Biz a hundert un tsvantsik yor* (Ch. I, Superstition). The added statement was: 'If you know how to live, you'll live longer. If you don't know, you'll learn at the Sans Souci.' A caption in *Time* under a picture of Joseph M. Katz, leading gift-paper manufacturer, was: 'Santa? He should live forever'.[19]

On a recent *Tonight* show on TV, a young singer presented a song about the trials of film stars, ending with the line: 'It ain't easy — it should happen to me!' This is a direct translation of *af mir gezugtgevoren* (Ch. II, Destiny). Several years ago, when I was in a restaurant with husband and children, we all knew just what we wanted, and the waitress exclaimed: 'All my orders should be given this easily!' Chiquita Brand bananas, advertising in a recent issue of the *Reader's Digest*, detailed its care in packing the product, 'otherwise known as the Special Delivery Banana', and added: 'The U.S. Mail should have it so good'.

I've also heard 'You shouldn't know (from) such things' and 'You shouldn't know it' in the speech of a young Jewish woman who grew up with Gentile friends and married a Gentile. These are of course from *Zolst nit visn fun azelche zachen* (Ch. II, Destiny). Closely related is the title of a book prepared by a volunteer group in New York listing sources of help for various citizens' problems: *The Book You Shouldn't Need.*

See *You should excuse me.* . . .

shtarker

'Strong one' in Yiddish, this term has been used in Vita Herring ads for a large hero sandwich including a number of other fillers in addition to herring.

shtik, shtick

Yiddish for 'routine' or 'bit' (Ch. II, Char. and Des.), this has been

picked up in show business. Note entertainer Sammy Davis's comment in
1966, quoted in the *New York Times*, about his projected TV show: 'The
show won't be for hippies only. That inside *shtick* is not for me'. Some
months later, Harry Belafonte on the Joey Bishop show explained how
hard it was to substitute for m.c. Johnny Carson: 'They see right through
your shtik'.

The popular use of 'bit' in this sense — as in the comic strip *Mark Trail*
by Edd Dodd: 'You mean you're going to do the scout bit? . . . Birds and
bees *and* leaf collecting?' — may be a derivative.

shtunk, shtoonk

This word for 'stinker', often heard in 'He's a shtunk', comes from
Yiddish *farshtunkener* 'a stinky one'. Al Capp has used it in *Li'l Abner*
as the name of an animal, the 'Slobbovian Shtoonk', which 'is not
only sneaky, smelly, and surly, but — yak! yak! — just try to EAT
one!!'

shyster

In both the United States and England, this adjective or noun usually
refers to an unethical lawyer, but may mean any worthless person. Its
source appears to be the taboo German term for a defecator *(Scheisser)*,
with at least some help from the related Yiddish *shays*, which is supposed
to have been responsible for the vulgar eighteenth-century adjective
'shice'. Another possible Yiddish influence may have been *shayker*
'falsehood, liar'.

slog it on See *shlock.*

smecker See *shmecken.*

smouse, smouser See *shmoose.*

snide and shine

In England, this used to connote a Jew, particularly a Jew of East
London. One theory has connected 'shine' with slick looking hair and
another with *shayn*, a variant of *sheyn* 'pretty, beautiful', as in a merchant's statement, *Dos klayd iz shayn* 'The garment is beautiful'. My own
hunch is that the phrase came from the exclamation *Shnayd un shoyn (or
shayn)!* 'Cut and done already!' which a Jewish tailor might voice regarding the length of time it would take to make something, the equivalent of,
'Before you can say Jack Robinson'.

so at the beginning of a sentence

This characteristic of first-generation American Jewish speech probably was influenced by Yiddish *tsi*, which in formal Yiddish is often used at the beginning of a question. In recent years it has been showing up in popular journalism, often before a declarative question (*see* "Declarative Form in Questions").
      See also *So what else is new?*

So it shouldn't be a total loss. See *should* and *shouldn't.*

So what?

This has been credited to the shrugging Yiddish *iz vos* 'So is what?' It's been used in popular journalism and advertising in England as well as the United States. Indeed, it appeared as the title of a book by Charles Landery published in London in the 1930s.

So what else is new?

Among American Jews, this is an ironic way of changing the subject after unpleasant matters have been discussed, a kind of Americanized form of *Lo'mir redn fun freylicher zachen* (Ch. II, Exclam.).
      The expression is so common, it has appeared on a comic paperweight made in Israel, a little bronze figure of a man with a humorously pathetic look, a sort of nebbish made in Israel. It's been appearing in general use, too, from TV commercials to newspaper ads,[20] to Hy Gardner's joke book with that title, to a recent novel by James Stevenson in which a television show is named SWEIN, short for 'So What Else Is New?' My local electric company used it in a mail brochure, but stuck in an unnecessary comma: 'So, what else is new?' (This is just the opposite of the situation with the ironic 'yet', where Yiddish seems to need the comma (see *yet* as Ironic Intensive).)
      The variant 'What Else Is News?' appeared in a recent ad in the *New York Times Magazine*: 'What Else Is News at Nat Sherman's? (the 'what else' being 'Pink cigarettes for weddings — Blue for Bar Mitzvahs').

Sue me. See *Do me something.*

Talk to the wall!

This ironic expression of exasperation means 'I might just as well be talking to the wall' and comes from Yiddish *Red tsum vant!* (Ch. II, Ann, and Arg., under *Red tsum lomp!*).
      A rather sedate version was quoted from an anonymous European

diplomat, in comment on General Charles de Gaulle's intemperate statements in Canada in the summer of 1967: 'You might as well speak to a wall. The man is getting old — he is nearly seventy-seven.' Other forms, like 'We're tired of wasting our time talking to the wall', have appeared in advertising[21] and on TV. A guest on WNBC radio's Long John Nebel Show criticized Columbia University's attitude during the student protests of 1968: 'The University has no means for student redress. The students can talk to the walls.' (This use of the plural 'walls' appeared also in the Israeli cartoon mentioned under *Red tsum vant*! referred to above.)

That's all I need.

From the ironic *Nor dos feylt mir*, this is fast invading popular speech, along with the other ironic complaints about fate that Yiddish is replete with (see *I need it like I need . . . ; I need it very badly; Who needs it?*). John Wingate exclaimed on WOR radio in February 1969, 'Another snowstorm? That's all we need!'

The apple doesn't fall far from the tree.

This common observation among Jews, noting that children are usually not too different from their parents (either good or bad), comes from the Yiddish *Der epl falt nit vayt fun beym*. The same thought also appears in German and Dutch proverbs.

The end was for 'The result was'

From *Der sof iz geven*, this is common in first-generation American Jewish speech, and the second generation often quotes it smilingly.

to for 'against'

'What do you have to him?' in first-generation speech comes from *Vos hostu tsu im?* — in which the Yiddish *tsu*, which sounds so much like 'to', means 'against'. One even hears it in the bilingual 'I have a *tayne* to you,' from *Ich hob tsu dir a tayne* (Ch. II, Ann. and Arg.).

Cf. IIIB, '*Tsu* whom . . . ?'

tocker

This underworld term for a murderer may be related to Yiddish *toches*. See the concluding discussion under *tokus*.

tokus, dokus, tokis, tukis, tookis, tuckus, tochas

These are all variations of Yiddish *toches* 'rump' (Ch. II, Char. and Des.), which have been heard in one form or another in various parts of the country for over seventy-five years. Among Gentile Germans in the

West over a half-century ago, the spelling was 'tookis' and 'tukis' and the meaning was reportedly 'anus'. One modern slang dictionary lists a current taboo meaning of 'rectum'. About fifteen years ago, a young Jewish New Yorker teaching in a southern private school heard the headmaster tell a group of boys that they had better buckle down to work or they would get it in the 'tokus'. Playing dumb, he asked the headmaster about the word and was told it was just a localism!

Several children's diminutives have developed in the United States. One is 'tush' (which was used a number of times in Noah Gordon's best-selling novel *The Rabbi* as well as in mystery parodist Sol Weinstein's series on the war between Israel and TUSH — Terrorist Union for Suppressing Hebrews!). On Art Linkletter's TV program, a young boy who was asked what he wanted to be when he grew up replied: 'A doctor'. When Linkletter asked 'Why?' the boy replied: 'So I can give people shots in the tush'. Unaware, Linkletter asked: 'What's a tush?' and the boy spread his arms and shrugged saying: 'It's a tush'. Still unknowing Linkletter asked: 'Do I have one?' and the audience howled. Understandably, the name of British actress Rita Tushingham has been cause for snickering among American Jewish children!

Another diminutive is 'tushie'. This spawned 'tushie slide', which a Gentile social worker in the Midwest told me over a decade ago meant to her Jewish charges 'a slide down a slope on your bottom'.

Pre-teens and teenagers have in recent years been using the comment 'tough tukis' to mean 'tough luck', 'too bad'. And Jewish adults have been using a playful word-and-motion to express 'How stupid of us': a repeated jabbing of the index finger at the temple, with the spoken word *toches*, which is short for 'It *toches* (took us) a long time to figure it out!' (In conversation with me at a Connecticut Hospital in 1967, a Gentile nurse used this same finger motion at her temple and commented about herself: 'No kidneys'. Cf. IIIB, 'No *kop* and no *toches*'.)

Apparently England's Eric Partridge did not recognize the term when spelled 'tochas'. Note his theorizing in his *Dictionary of the Underworld* (1950):

Tochas. Testicles (?): 1938, James Curtis, *They Drive by Night*: 'I could do three months on me tochas. How'd you like to be hung?' extant. Origin? If we can alternatively spell it *tockers*, we obtain the following: Tockers suggests tick-tockers, reminiscent of a clock pendulum, which swings; therefore compare slang danglers (testicles).

Indeed, his 'tick-tockers' might seem more pertinent to the underworld term 'tocker', a murderer, for the latter truly 'does time'. But it would seem more likely that 'tocker' — which Partridge indicates is American in origin — relates directly to *toches*, because a murderer is a 'lifer', or someone who sits on his *toches* or tocker. Unwittingly, however, Partridge has come close to a meaning for *toches* which is sometimes implied in Yiddish, as in the phrase *a kalter toches* 'a cold fish'.

I suspect that Yiddish *toches* may also help explain the expressions used in England, to 'give toco' or to 'give toks', denoting a thrashing.

See also IIIB, introduction, 'tochi'; 'T.L.'; T.O.T.'

tough tukis See *tokus*.

tsuris

A common alternate for *tsores* (see Ch. II, Char. and Des., *tsore*), this was given wide circulation by a full-page *New York Times* ad in July 1969 which presented El Al airline's 'Cure for Terminal Tsuris' — a new waiting room at the Kennedy Airport.

Harrison D. Horblit, well-known book collector, likes to use the bilingual adjective 'tsuritic' for 'troubling' or 'worrisome'. This is a joking pronunciation of Yiddish *tsuridik* and is similar to the humorous pronunciation of *rebbitzen* mentioned in the note to that item (Ch. II, Rel. and Cul.).

tumeler, tumuler

This Yiddish designation for a real fun-guy is now part of American slang — chiefly through its application to the staff member of Jewish resort hotels assigned to livening things up among the guests. (See Ch. II, Char. and Des., *tumel.*) Danny Kaye and other entertainers got their starts as tumelers in the Catskills. Among the second and third generations, one may hear, 'Boy, is he a tumeler!' Cutting up or clowning is 'tumeling around'.

In underworld cant the word has been reported to mean a rough criminal.

tush, tushy, tushie See *tokus*.

Use it in good health See Wear it in good health.

Verlier

A generation ago, this term was reported as common among furniture salesmen when they had a customer on the hook and wanted another hovering salesman to go away and leave them quiet waters. The meaning is 'Lose' — short for 'Lose yourself' — and suggests both German *Verlier dich* and the related Yiddish *Farlir zich*, the latter being the active form of *Ver farloren* (see 'Get lost').

'Lose yourself' has of course been heard in general slang for some time.

Wear it in good health; Wear it well.

Reported in 1943 as common among second-generation Jews, these two translations of *Trog es gezunterheyd* (Ch. I, Concerns about Life and Health)[22] have been making steady inroads in American usage. From Ann Sothern on TV to Elizabeth Taylor in films, to Gentile merchants who have picked it up from former Jewish employers, a bevy of sources have been transmitting the sentiment to American ears. At a testimonial dinner for Pennsylvania's State Senator Jeanette F. Reibman in 1967, I heard a Gentile officer of the State Democratic Committee present pearl and diamond earrings to the senator with the words: 'Wear them in good health'.

The eyes too are being exposed. A New York maker of pulpit robes and academic gown prints on the little envelope containing spare buttons: 'All of us here at Bentley & Simon who made your robe wish you to enjoy Your Robe and wear it well'; and a well-known maker of raincoats attaches a label to its products saying: 'Misty Harbor wishes you health to wear this. . . .' To top it all, a 1966 series of ads of the Chiquita banana company showed young people with the paper seal of the banana pasted onto their foreheads, in line with the advice: 'Look for the seal on the peel and wear it in good health'. (This stimulated a fad.) But my favorite was the installment of the comic strip *Miss Peach* by Mell Lazarus in which Ira, having broken his arm, was showing off his new sling with wooden splint and plaster cast, and his friend answered: 'Wear it in good health'.

Related is 'Use it in good health' — said to someone who has acquired new furniture and sometimes put in the hybrid 'Use it *gezuntherheyd*'.

The variation 'Eat it in good health' appeared in a recent editorial in my local paper which commented on the raise in Congressional salaries from $30,000 to $42,500 a year after Senator Everett Dirksen reported picking up a luncheon tab for $160: 'that's $1,500 to cover the 5 percent) cost-of-living increase and $11,000 for lunch. Eat it in good health, boys'.

What . . . need with for 'What . . . need for'

Molly Picon, in *So Laugh a Little*, quotes her grandmother as saying, 'What do I need with a mirror?' The same idiom has been creeping into the speech of TV performers, as in a recent line of Jackie Gleason's: 'What they need with that I'll never know'.

What's to . . . ? for 'What is there to . . . ?'

This showed up a few years ago in a lengthy ad for Heinz ketchup on the back cover of the *National Jewish Monthly*: 'What's not to like about calf's liver?' and in a recent one for ZBT baby powder in *My Baby*: 'How can there be this much to know about Baby Powder? . . . What's to know? Just this. . . .'

I also heard it in a sentence where normal English would, in addition, use a participle after the 'to': two professional women were discussing their summer plans, and one with a projected graduate study, noted that her younger daughter could keep house; the other responded, 'Keep house? What's to keep house? The other kids are away, and you'll be home half the day!'

What's with . . . ?

In *Hamlet*, the question is put, 'What's the news with you, Laertes?' In Yiddish, the same question is reduced to, 'What's with you?' (*Vos iz mit dir?*), and this elliptical form has been appearing in various places. Note the 1962 cartoon *Carnival* by Dick Turner showing a man who has just come out of the shower and grabbed the phone, answering: 'Oh, just catching a little pneumonia. What's with you?' Or witness the advertising flyer: 'What's with fashion? A wardrobe of Garay belts!'

Even the sense of 'What's the matter with', which is common in Yiddish, has been showing up in general use. A 1958 AP dispatch about the Burlington Liars Club quoted the club's president: ' "What's with Alaska?" Hulett demanded. "They're bigger than Texas, but we didn't receive a lie from them in '58." ' A 1962 editor's note in the nationwide insurance magazine *Minutes* asked: 'Whatever became of rest? What's *with* people, anyway? Always on the go. . . .'

'What's with . . . ?' is combined with 'What's this?' in a cartoon mail-insert distributed by the Bell Telephone Company of Pennsylvania, in which a woman asks her husband, 'Harry, what's this with the telephone directory?' Indeed, some of the recent popular uses of 'What's with . . . ?' seem to be a breezier form of 'What's this with . . . ?' A 1963 instalment of Ken Bald's comic strip *Dr. Kildare* had a waitress say to a nervous young man: 'Something's wrong with you, mister. What's with the shakes?'

Who needs it?

Especially popular in recent years has been this cheerfully defiant Yiddish question (*Ver darfes?*) — strikingly used in the title of an April 1969 cover article in the *New Republic*: 'The ABM: Who Needs It?'[23] It is closely related to 'Who asked for . . . ?' (*Ver hot gebetn . . . ?*), which as suggested earlier, reflects the Old World Jew's difficult situation and his daily round of blessings and prayers. Constantly asking God for help, he naturally assumed, when he came up against something that did not suit him, that someone else had asked for it. That is, 'Who would have asked for this? Who *needs* it?'

Other words or phrases have been substituted for the 'it' as in the book title *Who Needs a Road?* or the radio ad 'Who needs a can-opener now that Carling Black Label Beer comes in the tab-opener can?' The expression is sometimes preceded by 'so' and even by an entire sentence as in this real estate ad in the *New York Post*: 'So tell me. Who needs Miami with a view like this?'[24]

Many other variations are dressing up current advertising and journalism. Notice these uses of introductory clause or phrase: 'If this is Acrilan, who needs wool?'; 'With Dylan Thomas and Richard Burton, Who Needs Stereo?' As it often does in Yiddish, the expression has also been appearing as an exclamation. A Union Oil Company ad asked 'Profit? Who needs it!' Mutual of New York advertised 'I could hit it big with beavers. Who needs life insurance!' Another MONY ad retained the question in the first part but put the exclamation in negative form: 'Health insurance? *There's* an expense I don't need!' (Cf. *That's all I need.*) The whole expression was used as a noun in the TV line: 'I've been thinking about what you said about school being a waste of time and who needs it. Well, I'm going to drop out too'.

A related question common among Jews is, 'With a friend like him, who needs enemies?' It's sometimes a statement: 'With a friend like him, you don't need any enemies.' These have also been appearing in the comic strips and on TV in such forms as 'With such friends (*or* 'With neighbors like this), who needs enemies?'[25]

Seemingly stimulated by 'Who needs . . . ?' is the growing use of a similar 'Who wants . . . ?' Witness the *Harper's* filler presenting statistics on the overwhelming number of psychiatrists in the District of Columbia: 'Who Wants an Explanation?' or the Lear Jet stereo ad in *Time*: 'At times like this who wants to hear football scores.'

See Ch. II, Advice, '*Siz nit neytik.*

Who's counting?

This humorous question is popular among American Jews and comes from an old joke about the woman who is being offered a tray of tidbits and tells her hostess, 'I've already had three, but they're so delicious I'm going to have another' — to which the hostess replies, 'You've had five, but who's counting?'

The idea was used on TV's *Ozzie and Harriet* show, when a visitor remarked, 'This is about the third time I've happened to be in the neighborhood around suppertime' and the reply was, 'Well, it's the fourth time, but who's counting?'

The joke may be subtly related to the superstitious avoidance of counting discussed in Ch. I.

Who sent for him?

The translation of *Ver hot far im geshikt?* is common in American Jewish speech, as an equivalent for, 'Who asked for him?' (See *Who needs it?*)

Who's minding the store?

This is the punch line of an old Yiddish joke about the storekeeper on his deathbed who asks for his wife, then for each of his children. When the last one responds, 'Yes, Pop, I'm here', the old man exclaims, 'Then who's minding the store?'

The ironic line has been widely used in recent years — from the title of a movie with Jerry Lewis, to newspaper and radio political commentary. In 1960, Washington columnist George Dixon complained: 'While Ike is away on his amiability amble who's minding the store?' Several years earlier, a WQXR announcer had asked: 'Who's minding the store at the White House?'

The verb was slightly changed in 'Who Minds the Store?' — a heading for a 1962 column by Howard Taubman in the *New York Times* which noted that long theater runs go stale without supervision. It was further changed in a *Times* article squib in 1968: 'ORGANIZATION–ANTI-ORGANIZATION MAN — To attract today's college students into business and industry, all signs indicate that the campus recruiter is going to have to get with it. Otherwise, who's gonna mind the proverbial store?' A recent movie with Milton Berle and Joey Bishop changed the last word: 'Who's Minding the Mint?'

Substitute verbs have shown up too. A 1959 column by Victor Riesel, deploring a Supreme Court decision against the employee-screening of the Industrial Personnel Security Program, ended: 'Okay, they won. Now who watches the store?' And a *Life* editorial in 1964, discussing what might be happening in the Communist Party while Khrushchev was in Cairo, was headed: 'Who's Running the Red Store?'

The comment has also appeared as a statement in various forms. Presidential aspirant Adlai Stevenson, in a famous Madison Square Garden speech, declared: 'Someone has to mind the store.' TV's 'Chief Half-Town' on the Popeye Theater explained to his young viewers in 1962: 'Sally Star has a vacation for the entire month of January. I'm here trying to mind the store for her.' In the society page of the Philadelphia *Sunday Bulletin* in 1963, a picture of a couple who were keeping an eye on a horse-racing stable in Palm Beach for the absent owner was headed

'Minding the Store'. Here too the verb has sometimes been changed, as in the statement in the 1961 novel *The Scar* by Eric Rhodin: 'Such was the way for a saloon-keeper; you always had to have somebody taking care of the store — life, death or high wind.'

with for 'of'

This influence of Yiddish idiom is seen in the common exclamation, 'Enough with the nonsense!' in place of "Enough of your . . . !' or 'Enough of that!'
Cf. *again with the . . . !*

Would it hurt to . . . ? See *It can't hurt.*

yet as Ironic Intensive

One of the most popular Yiddish borrowings in recent years, this has shown up on TV and in a variety of newspapers and magazines. A translation of *noch* (Ch. II, Exclam.), it is often equivalent to the ironic '. . . no less', as in the article heading in *Consumer Reports*: 'another vegetable peeler (electrically powered, yet).' It has even appeared in a comic 'superclimax' on containers of the confection halvah: 'With NUTS YET' and 'Without NUTS YET'.[26]

The usage is also common in the speech of Pennsylvania Germans, but Yiddish appears to be the dominant carrier. Notice that sometimes the 'yet' is preceded by a comma, other times not. For me, the comma helps convey the Yiddish intonation.

yock, yok, yog

In England, 'yock' is an alternate form for 'yog', which is East London back-slang for *goy* 'a Gentile or a fool'. (See discussion in introduction to Tribalism, Ch. II.)

In the United States, 'yock' is an old vaudeville term for 'a loud laugh' — sometimes pronounced 'yak' or 'yuck' — and apparently unrelated to Yiddish.

You should excuse me; You should excuse the expression; If you'll excuse (or pardon) the expression; etc.

The first of these is a direct translation of the Yiddish *Zolst mir antshuldiken!* (Ch. II, Exclam.) It was a popular bilingual joke a generation ago to ask at a party, 'Would you like — you should excuse me — a cocktail?' This punned on the Yiddish *kak* (see IIIB, 'A.K.').

The locution has fanned out beyond American Jewish speech, appearing in a variety of lighthearted forms. Notice the simple extension to 'You should excuse the expression', which Zero Mostel used in a monologue years ago: 'I walked down to Delancey Street for — you should excuse the expression — a breath of fresh air' and which appeared in a recent Stanley and Janice Berenstain cartoon in *Look*: 'This — you should excuse the expression — is my room'.

That form has also joined with more idiomatic English to popularize 'if you'll excuse the expression', as in the 1956 radio broadcast by a pet expert listing meats for dogs: ' . . . and, if you'll excuse the expression, pork'. The latter form — which was given wide circulation around 1930 by the old radio comic Ursul Twing — later became ' . . . an expression . . .' in one of the lyrics for Broadway's *South Pacific*: 'If you'll excuse an expression I use, I'm in love. . . .' A 1964 AP dispatch helped widen the possibilities of who or what might do the excusing: 'The American Institute of Hypnosis, in a burst of Thanksgiving spirit, has some advice that should make turkeys grateful until they die — if turkeys will excuse the expression.'

The 'if' version (probably influenced by the idiom 'if you will pardon my saying so') also became 'if . . . pardon the expression', in more than one way. First there was the simple 'if you'll pardon the expression', as in the George Clark cartoon of a wife who has opened up a pile of cans and announced to her husband, 'Dinner, if you'll pardon the expression, is ready'. Then greater variety was given to the person or thing doing the pardoning. A 1967 *Commentary* review by Walter Goodman noted: 'The "careful analytic neutrality" to which the doctor lays claim turns out to be pure benevolence toward Hiss and a hatred of Chambers so relentless that, if everybody will pardon the expression, it seems unconscious'. A 1959 *Harper's* article by William S. White went further, using the whole expression as a substitute for 'with apologies to': 'This experience produced (if the *Reader's Digest* will pardon the expression) some of the Most Unforgettable Characters I ever met. . . .' And another *Harper's* article, by Russel Lynes, in 1965 used the form with 'they' and 'forgive': 'The new volume introduces two chroniclers of the suburbs who have emerged in the last decade, Charles Saxon and James Stevenson, both sociologists at heart (if they will forgive the expression), both extremely able. . . .' In addition, 'expression' has been replaced, as in the song sung in the 1968 Miss Pennsylvania Pageant on TV: 'Sometimes, if you'll pardon the word, I sweat.'

In further variety, the 'pardon' version has sometimes dropped the 'if', as in Pulitzer Prize winner Relman Morin's AP feature: 'Are we all heading straight toward (you'll pardon the expression) togetherness?' It has also taken on 'me' as in the *Time* letter writer's 'Thank God (and I hope the people of Venice will pardon me the expression). . .'. It took

Harry Golden to combine 'pardon me' with the original 'should' in: 'Most of the folks in the South, reflecting the attitudes of the dominant society, would like to have a rabbi (you should pardon me) who does not look "too Jewish". . . .'. Intriguingly enough, a 1963 installment of the cartoon *Brother Juniper* by Fr. Mac uses the 'should' with 'pardon': The good Brother is coaching a children's baseball game and yells: ' "STEAL!" '. . . you should pardon the expression'.

Finally, we've been hearing the brief 'excuse the expression', as in the TV disc jockey's 'That sounds like garbage — excuse the expression,' and the similarly brief 'pardon the expression', as in the 1963 UPI feature quoting a woman about to embark on a weight-losing fast: 'I see no reason why my upcoming fast can't be, pardon the expression, a huge success'. And I'm sure we ain't (you should pardon the slang) heard nothin' yet.

NOTES

1. In the fall of 1966, attending the Helen Hays Theater in New York, I discovered I had no program and asked a female usher if I could have one. Her response — 'Why not?' — was especially striking because of its intonation, which was equivalent to the notes La, Sol. Most Americans, I think, would use the opposite intonation, more closely approximating Fa, Sol. Though I did not inquire into the lady's background, she looked as though she might be Irish, and that might support the statement of Mr. Doyle; but it is also possible that an Irish person in New York would have picked it up from Jewish speech, in which intonation is often La, Re, Fa (Why no-ot?).

   Perhaps Pennsylvania German was at work. That dialect tends to start questions on a high note and to end them on a lower one; but whether the questioning reply itself could also be Pennsylvania German I am not certain. (Susan Sontag has reported 'Why not?' to be a common response in Sweden.)

2. See Ch. II, Char. and Des., *a por kluhtzim*.
3. Cf. Ch. IV, note *re.* 'I'm an Orthodox. . . .'
4. This was presumably changed from the *yarmulke* which the freedom riders had previously used. See Ch. II, Rel. and Cul., *yarmulke*.
5. I am indebted for the clipping to Dr. Marshall D. Berger.
6. Whether this name is a pseudonym I don't know, but the two words in Yiddish mean 'Can Soon' or 'Know Soon.'
7. See Ch. I, Famil. with God.
8. This is reminiscent of the cussing in Ch. II, Imprec., *a makeh im*! as well as of the story under Family, *get*.
9. See 'Declarative Form in Questions.'
10. See Ch. I, Punning, *re.* pun on *alles shteyt in talmud*.
11. This line is related to some extent to the concern about destiny, as in 'It should happen to me!' See 'should' and 'shouldn't'. . . .
12. See Ch. I, Famil. with God.
13. This sentiment has shown up in advertising, as in the picture of a gloved and monocled Englishman exclaiming, 'By Jove, it's great to be Jewish and enjoy Rokeach Gefilte

Fish.' Lest the Gentile feel left out, the makers of Levy's Rye Bread have for some time been pointing out: 'You don't have to be Jewish to enjoy Levy's rye. . . .' (The poster noting this with a picture of an Indian has been reproduced and sold in the recent craze-market for posters!) Indeed, the opinion advanced of late by the communications industry, through both Jewish and Gentile performers, is that 'When you're in love, the whole world is Jewish.'

14. See also IIIB, end of 'a whole *megille.*'
15. The wafer is of course based on the unleavened bread of the Last Supper. (See Ch. II, Rel. and Cul., *seyder.*)
16. For other examples of such cultural syncretism, see Ch. II, Advice, note to *az me ken nit aribergeyn*. . . .
17. See Ch. II, Passing Judgment, *az me shmirt di reder*. . . .
18. Re. the dropping of the 'h', see discussion under 'shmo'.
19. Note the different wish for Santa under 'Drop dead!' above.
20. Particularly intriguing was the 1966 ad in the *New York Times*: 'So what else is new for Christmas? The Hamilton Beach Oral Hygiene Center, that's what.'
21. This appeared in a recent ad of Weyenberg Massagic Shoes in the *New York Times*, along with 'knocking our heads against the wall' ('For months now, we've been knocking our heads against the wall trying to convince you that Weyenberg Shoes are better than Portage shoes'). See Ch. II, Ann. and Arg. *klap kop in vant!*
22. Page 31.
23. I am indebted for the clipping to Professor James Macris.
24. The clipping was kindly provided by Dr. Marshall D. Berger.
25. As may be seen in Ch. II, Destiny, a number of Yiddish expostulations at fate call up a relationship to friend or enemy, and these are often heard in translation. See also Char. and Des., last par. under *finster.*
26. These halvah designations were reported to me from California by Dr. Irving Babow.

IAN F. HANCOCK

The Ethnolectal English of American Gypsies

Existing practically unnoticed, but everywhere to be found amidst the greater population, the Rom are one of America's smaller ethnic minorities. Popularly known as 'Gypsies', the Rom are ultimately of Indian origin, and among themselves speak dialects of a language which descends from Sanskrit.

There are a great many such dialects, but they are by no means all mutually intelligible despite their close linguistic relationship. It is usually on the basis of differences of speech that the Rom most readily distinguish the different ethnic subgroupings within the overall race; these have been discussed by Lee (1967–1969). The present treatment will deal with just two of these, the Romnichals and the Rom, who together constitute the great majority of Gypsies in North America.

The history of the Gypsies may be found in more detail elsewhere (e.g. Hancock 1975a, 1979); briefly, the ancestors of the modern populations entered Europe perhaps 700 years ago from India, via Persia and the Byzantine Empire. This journey from India to Europe probably took another seven centuries before that. The entry into Europe, and the subsequent treatment of Rom there was directly the result of the increasing hostility between Muslim and Christian; since the wars against the Seljuks had seriously depleted Balkan manpower, the Rom, forced across the Dardanelles by the advancing Turkish hordes, were by 1370[1] forced into slavery, a condition which lasted until 1855. This is of some importance linguistically, since the abolition of slavery bears directly upon the presence of Rom in the USA and to some extent upon their linguistic behavior *vis à vis* the rest of the American population.

Not all of the Rom who entered Europe were made captive in the Balkans; others pushed on into western and northern Europe, the ancestors of the group now known as the Romnichals entering Britain by 1505.[2]

The Romnichals, like the Gitanos in Spain, the Kale in Finland and the Roteparattor in Norway and Sweden, all ethnically Gypsies, spread across Europe during the years between ca. 1250 and 1550, though the descendants of the Balkan Rom, today equally widespread, only began leaving southeastern Europe in large numbers in the 1860s. This two-stage diaspora has had an interesting effect; speakers whose ancestors arrived in Europe during the earlier period have in the main adopted the respective host languages as their mother-tongues, a process called *cainoglossia*; nevertheless the ancestral tongue, in greatly modified form, *is* maintained within the group, though it may not be learnt until the speaker is nine or ten years old.

The language of the Romnichals is referred to here as Angloromani, since as in Spain and elsewhere it developed as a contact language between speakers of Romani and the local people — in this case speakers of English. This hypothesis claims that the contact took place in Britain as early as the first half of the sixteenth century, and that for a time Angloromani and the older, inflected Romani were coexistent. This latter is now practically extinct in England, and survives with vigor only in northern Wales (see Hancock 1979). An alternative hypothesis suggests that Angloromani dates from the nineteenth century, and is the result of gradual language loss and a simultaneous replacement with English, Romani-derived vocabulary being retained in an English grammatical matrix (Kenrick 1971).

In contrast, the Rom retain Romani as the first language, though everywhere being able to speak one or more other languages with varying degrees of proficiency. Monolingualism in Romani is rare, and where it occurs it is restricted to very small children.

Romnichals have been reported in America since 1665, though they were not the first Gypsies to arrive here. As early as 1580 the Spanish had also begun transporting unknown numbers to the Americas, and were followed by the French by 1600. But it was the English who, in an effort to rid their country of its unwanted elements (e.g. nomads, vagrants, Irish and Scottish prisoners of war, etc), sent many Gypsies to the colonies. The Rom on the other hand only began arriving on a large scale after about 1865; although all ultimately descend from the Balkan slave popu-lation, few families came to North America directly from there. Some had spent a number of years in Russia, Serbia, and even South America before eventually making a home in the United States. According to Trigg (1973:224), ' . . . in the latter half of the nineteenth century many more Gypsies, mostly from Slavic countries, were to arrive in the United States. By 1885, however, Gyspies were excluded by immigration policy and returned to Europe'. But this policy was not entirely effective, since Rom were able to enter illegally across the Canadian and Mexican borders, and in any case it is not always possible to identify a Gypsy by appearance alone, and since there is no indication of ethnic origin on a passport, government ruling was only successful when immigrants arrived in large, easily identifiable groups.

Traditionally, Gypsy culture forbids extensive socializing with non-Gypsies (called *gajé* in Romani), while at the same time the various means of livelihood depend upon working within the greater population; thus it is important to know that population's language. It appears to have been acquired for just this purpose, after initial arrival in this country, and having once been learnt, developed separately within the Romani community, with only minimal direct reinforcement from the outside world.

Inflected Romani has a complex morphology, and a phonology which differs considerably from that of English, and while English and Romani are usually learnt simultaneously, the English is an ethnolectal variety used within the home, rather than that of non-Gypsy Americans. It is still widely felt that attendance at school is contrary to the traditional Gypsy way of life (*romaníya*), since it means physical and cultural exposure to the *gajé*; nevertheless an increasing number of children are attending public school for shorter or longer periods of time, and as a result are being exposed to general American English from an earlier age than their parents.

The ethnolectal English of the Rom is distinguished by extensive intrusion from Romani. Romani also exhibits considerable interference from English as might be expected (see Hancock 1975b). An increasing number of people also command a more acrolectal variety, and using this is called 'speaking like an American'. Linguistic behavior is a very powerful factor in one's identity as a Rom, and Romani English, rather than general American English, is used within the community whenever Romani is not being spoken. To talk a standardized variety would be considered affected, and would not be tolerated for long, even though the ability to do so when making out-group contact is praised as being a useful skill.

In particular, Romani-English is distinguished phonologically by a lack of contrast between /w/ and /v/, /t/ and /θ/, /d/ and /ð/, and aspirated and nonaspirated stops. Thus pronunciations such as ['wɔlwo] 'Volvo' (a brand of car), ['tɛləwɪʒn] 'television', [dɛt] 'that', [tɪŋk] 'think', etc., are common. Less common are hyperurbanized forms such as [θri] 'tree' or ['θaɪpraɪdə] 'typewriter'.

In being adopted into Romani, English words are made to conform to Romani phonology, in many cases taking a final vowel and, if a noun, being assigned to a particular gender class. In Romani there are two distinct verbal paradigms into which all loanverbs fit (Hancock 1975a:101). Sometimes an English word which has been adopted into Romani will be used in Romani-English in its assimilated form: 'don't

gimme that [bi'yɛso]' (don't give me that BS); 'they live over in [si'adla]'
(they live over in Seattle); 'it was a letter from the [gɑvə'mɑnto]' (it was a
letter from the government). Perhaps the most noticeable feature lexically is the abundance of malapropisms, some of which have been listed
elsewhere (Hancock 1975a), resulting from English words being heard
but not verified in print: 'volumes' (Valiums — a brand of tranquilizer),
'world's fair check' (welfare check), and so on. Words may be otherwise
confused, thus ['fo:ni] in Romani-English, and as an adoption into
Romani, means 'funny', but appears to be based on the English word
'phoney' (in Romani, 'funny' is *p^hirása*, and 'phoney' is *t^hodiné*). Similarly
one hears 'electrical currency', 'car exhaustion', 'Al Capulco' (for the
Mexican town of Acapulco), 'knowlogy', and so on. While these are
usually restricted to families or single individuals, some have very wide
currency.

Because of the insulation from the rest of the population, and the fact
that English was acquired first in the late nineteenth century from (usually) nonstandard speakers, forms which are either obsolescent or regional in American English survive; 'gramophone' or 'victrola' (phonograph), 'subpeeny' (subpœna), 'extry' (extra), and so on. Grammatically,
a shibboleth is the use of 'because' for 'that' as complementizer, both
words being translated by *ke* in Romani: 'did you hear because he's sick?'

Among the Romnichal population, the situation is rather different, for,
whatever its history, their ethnic speech has become a variety of English,
and the original inflected variety is not known except to a very few
individuals, and there is little interaction with the inflected-Romani-
speaking Rom here. The English of the Romnichals is therefore not
subject to other-language interference the way the English of the Rom is.
Illiteracy is almost as common as it is among Rom, and examples of otosis,
or ear-error, are similarly common: 'delations' (relations), 'device'
(advice), 'mopheridyke' (lesbian — 'hermaphrodite'), 'tippoty' (anti-
pathy), and in particular modified forms such as 'composement' (compos-
ition), blends such as 'muddly' for 'muddy', and overcorrected pronunciations like ['θərməsk], [wʌnst] and [naɪst] for 'thermos', 'once', 'nice'. An
example of a very widespread reinterpretation of a standard English word
is 'gorgeous', which being understood as containing the root ['gɔ:dʒə]
'non-Gypsy' has come to mean 'pertaining to the *gajé*'. Another word
with a special interpretation in the English of American Romnichals is
'glamorize', which is used in the sense of 'charm' or 'bewitch'. Comment-
ing on the similarly idiosyncratic character of the English of the Romnichal population in Britain, Dr. Thomas Acton, a specialist in Gypsy
politics and education, questions whether items like the above should be
' . . . considered as mistakes in English usage, which would hinder the

educational development of the child, and were a symptom of verbal inadequacy, or whether they were to be considered as valid coinage within an ongoing tradition, of whose relation to standard English older Gypsies, at least, were aware' (1971:18).

Currently, no examination is being made in this country of the educational situation of the Romnichal population here; as with the Rom, few Romnichal children attend school for long, and since they remain within an all-Gypsy environment outside of working hours, the question of the rightness or wrongness of their speech does not arise, and it would only be labeled a 'problem' once the *gajé* became involved.

Romnichal speech fluctuates along a continuum, with English at one extreme and Angloromani at the other. Unlike the situation with the Rom, who are able to say at any given time what language they are speaking, despite cross-interference from the other system, there is no clear-cut division between Angloromani and Romnichal English, although the greater the incidence of non-English lexicon an utterance has, the 'deeper' it is said to be. Generally speaking, the language is 'deeper' in the United States and Canada than it is in Britain, though such statements mean little since the line between natural and conscious speech is hard to define. Certain Romani-derived words occur constantly in Romnichal English quite spontaneously, while an attempt to speak at length on a topic using an absolute minimum of English words would be extremely difficult for many people. There are a number of individuals who can do this, and who have earned reputations for themselves for this ability.

An example of mesolectal Romnichal language approaching the English end of the scale is found in a book of essays by Romnichal children, again in Britain since nothing similar is found here,[3] produced by the National Gypsy Education Council:

> . . . at night when they come out of the kitchema, they get in their cart and go back to the vardos. They sit around the old yog, and they get a piece of board and they tap dance on it. They gilly around the yog. The little chavvies are in the vardos asleep. When the little chavvies gets up, they take the grais down to the pani and they wash the grais down, and then they ride the grais up and down the drom. Then we all go to the kitchema and we all have bread and kel and a piece of stinger (Zilla Roberts, National Gypsy Education Council [1976:6]).

The author of the above piece has attended school since she was eleven — a total of three years — and nonstandard features in her speech are negligible ('the little chavvies gets up', in the above selection); but even though this excerpt is from a school essay, it is quite representative of how she would speak English in her home environment. Half of all the nouns she uses are Angloromani[4] ('stinger' for 'onion' is of Cant rather than Romani derivation), but such a proportion is not unusual in Romnichal English, and would increase sharply as a speaker shifted into Angloromani. Angloromani itself, with examples of the language from the United States, Canada and Britain, has been dealt with in detail elsewhere (Hancock 1979).

Mention may be made of a similar, though ethnically unrelated situation in this country, that of the Irish Travelers who live in Georgia and a number of other southern states, and who ' . . . speak and use in their daily lives an argot derived from Irish Gaelic which they call "the Cant" ' (Harper 1969:iv). Thus they too speak a 'secret' language, and, as with the Romnichals, though to a lesser extent, it influences their everyday variety of English.

Most of the Irish Traveler population in the United States traces its history here from the time of the potato famine of 1845–1852, which drove over half of the population of Ireland overseas. Jared Harper, who is the only person so far to have worked on Cant in this country, collected about 150 different words from Travelers over a five-month period, which he estimated fairly represents the total extent of the vocabulary.

Cant derives from an earlier speech called Shelta, which also survives in North America as well as in Britain (Hancock 1974a) but the Travelers, who despite their name are settled for much of the time, are not familiar with it. Even Cant is becoming lost in the settled communities; it ' . . . is a road language used only between Travelers wandering the highways and byways of the land, and it is only they who know it well . . . some road traders simply forget Cant when they retire from the road . . . ' (Harper 1969:80). Shelta itself is a contact language between Irish and English, and differs from Cant in extent of Irish-derived lexical content (between one and two thousand items) and Irish-derived idiom.

Although some Cant words are common in Traveler English, e.g. [ni'dʒeʃ] 'no', it does not intrude into that language to anything like the extent Angloromani does into the English of American Romnichals. When it is spoken, Cant serves as a conscious barrier between Travelers and the rest of the population, and would be used to discuss the price or the merits of a horse, for example, in front of a customer. Samples taken from Harper of Cant items occurring spontaneously in an all-Traveler social environment include 'he's kind of [θərki]' he's kind of quarrelsome); 'they laid the [grɔmp] out there' (they laid the tent out there); 'she's [lirki]' (she's crazy); and 'rub his [dʒiːl]' (rub his self, i.e. rub him). The samples of Traveler English found elsewhere in Harper indicate features commonly associated with Irish or other nonstandard kinds of

English, 'them's strange people'; 'there's still somes [*sic*] that uses it, but they ain't got no sense'.

There are a number of idioms similar to the above surviving in America; among others, the Polari of sections of the male homosexual community (Hancock 1973; Collier 1976) and the Boontling of northern California (Adams 1971). How far professional or cryptic vocabulary may influence the colloquial English of these speakers, and to what extent we are justified in treating other-language interference (as in Romani-English) and 'cryptic register interference', for lack of a more suitable term (as in Romnichal English or Irish Traveler Cant) as extensions of the same phenomenon, however, has yet to be explored.

NOTES

1. Vaux de Foletier (1970:24) says: 'The first Gypsies mentioned in the Rumanian archives, toward the middle of the fourteenth century, were already slaves. In 1386, Mircea I, the Lord of Wallachia, confirmed a gift made about 1370 by his uncle Vladislas to the Monastery of St. Anthony, near Voditza, of forty Gypsy families.'
2. There are in fact suggestions that they may have already entered the British Isles as much as a century before that.
3. It ought to be stressed that apart from the educational aspects, the linguistic situation in the USA closely parallels the British one. With the exception of the discussion of Irish Traveler Cant, below, observations in the present paper are all based on the writer's personal involvement with various Gypsy communities in this country.
4. These are *chavvi* 'child' (cf. Romani *čavo* 'boy', Sanskrit *śāva*, Hindi *chokarā*); *drom* 'road' (cf. R. *drom* < Greek δρόμος); *gilly* 'sing' (cf. R. *gili*, S. *gīti*, H. *gīt*); *grai* 'horse' (cf. R. *grai*, S. *ghoṭa* H. *ghoṛā*); *kel* 'butter' (cf. R. *k il*, S. *ghṛta*, H. *ghī*,); *kitchema* 'tavern' (cf. R. *kirčuma* < Old Slavic кръчьма); *pani* 'water' (cf. R. *pani*, S. *pānīya*, H. *pāṇī*); *vardo* 'wagon' (cf. R. *verdo, vurdon* < Ossetic ـبردون [u:rdɔn]); and *yog* 'fire' (cf. R. *yag*, S. *agni*, H. *āg*). The Cant mentioned here does not refer to the Shelta-derived speech of the same name mentioned below.

REFERENCES

Acton, Thomas A. (1971), *Current Changes Amongst British Gypsies and Their Place in International Patterns of Development*, Oxford.
Adams, Charles C. (1971), *Boontling, an American Lingo*, Austin and London, University of Texas Press.
Collier, Barbara (1976), 'On the origins of Lingua Franca', *Journal of Creole Studies*, 1(2):281–298.
Hancock, Ian F. (1973), 'Remnants of the Lingua Franca in Britain', *The USF Language Quarterly* 11:35–36.
— (1974a), 'Shelta, a problem of classification', in *Pidgins and Creoles: Current Trends and Prospects*, ed. by David DeCamp and Ian F. Hancock, 130–137. Washington, D.C., Georgetown University Press.

— (1974b), 'Identity, equality and standard language', *The Florida FL Reporter*, 12:49–52, 101–104.
— (1975a), *Problems in the Creation of a Standard Dialect of Romanés.* Social Science Research Council Working Paper in Sociolinguistics, XXV, May.
— (1975b) 'Patterns of lexical adoption in an American dialect of Romanés', *Orbis*, 25(1):83–104.
— (1979), 'Pidginization and the development of Anglo-Romani', *Journal of the Gypsy Lore Society* 4th series, 1(3).
Harper, Jared V. (1969), 'Irish Traveler Cant: an historical, structural, and socio-linguistic study of an argot. Unpublished M.A. thesis, University of Georgia, Athens.
— (1971), ' "Gypsy" research in the South', in *The Not So Solid South*, ed. by J. Morland, 16–24. Southern Anthropological Society Proceedings No. 4, Athens.
Harper, Jared V. and Charles Hudson (1971), 'Irish Traveler Cant', *Journal of English Linguistics* 5:78–86.
— (1973), 'Irish Traveler Cant in its social setting', *Southern Folklore Quarterly*, 37(2):1;1–104.
Kenrick, Donald (1971), 'Anglo-Romani today', in *Current Changes Amongst British Gypsies and Their Place in International Patterns of Development*, ed. by Thomas A. Acton, 5–14. Oxford.
Lee, Ronald (1967–1969), 'The Gypsies in Canada', *Journal of the Gypsy Lore Society* 46:38–51; 47:12–28; 48:92–107.
National Gypsy Education Council (1976), *The Travelling Man and Other Stories: An Anthology of Writing by Gypsy and Traveller Children.* Sheffield, National Gypsy Education Council.
Trigg, Elwood B, (1973), *Gypsy Demons and Divinities.* Secaucus.
Vaux de Foletier, F. de (1970), 'L'esclavage des Tsiganes dans les principautés roumaines', *Etudes Tsiganes* 16(2/3):24–29.

ROSE NASH

Spanglish: Language Contact in Puerto Rico

Although the influence of American English is present, to some extent, in all parts of Spanish-speaking America, Puerto Rico is unique in having both English and Spanish as official languages.[1] In accordance with the government policy of bilingualism, English is taught as a required subject in all schools from the first grade through the university level.[2] The close contact of Puerto Rican Spanish and American English since the turn of the century has greatly intensified in recent years, largely because of the ever-increasing number of Newyorricans (New York Puerto Ricans) who have returned to the island to live, bringing with them the language and culture of Spanish Harlem.[3] In the metropolitan areas of Puerto Rico, where Newyorricans play an influential role in the economic life of the island, there has arisen a hybrid variety of language, often given the slightly derogatory label of Spanglish, which coexists with less mixed forms of Standard English and Standard Spanish and has at least one of the characteristics of an autonomous language: a substantial number of native speakers.[4] The emerging language retains the phonological, morphological, and syntactic structure of Puerto Rican Spanish. However, much of its vocabulary is English-derived. That it is an autonomous language has been recognized not only by some Puerto Rican intellectuals, most of whom strongly disapprove of it for reasons that will appear later, but also by the New York School of Social Research, which has offered a course in Spanglish for doctors, nurses, and social workers (see Varo 1971). The other well-known language mixtures, such as Franglais, Yinglish, Japlish, or Honglais, have not, I believe, achieved such distinction.

This paper will briefly describe some typical examples of Spanglish used in Puerto Rico; they were collected over a period of five years from a variety of sources: newspapers, radio, television, public signs, and conversations heard on buses, at parties and meetings, and in classrooms,

This article first appeared in *American Speech* (1970):223–233. It is reprinted by permission of the author and of *American Speech*.

post offices, stores, banks, and hospitals — in short, everywhere that language is used in daily affairs. First, however, the term *Spanglish* must be defined because it has been applied to more than one cross-language phenomenon.[5] Although the division between what is and is not Spanglish is not always clear-cut, utterances of the following type can be excluded:

No speak very good the English [no espik beri gud di inglis]. 'I do not speak English very well.' = *No hablo muy bien el inglés.*

Utterances of this kind, in which English words are put in Spanish order and pronounced in a Spanish manner, are common enough on the streets of San Juan, and journalists have used the technique of word-for-word translation consciously for fun and profit.[6] To accept such an obviously ungrammatical English sentence as Spanglish, however, would leave no reason to reject an equally ungrammatical sentence that might be produced by an English monoglot:

Yo hago no hablar español muy bueno [you hagow now hablar espanyol muwiy bweynow]. 'I do not speak Spanish very well.'

Also excluded from consideration as Spanglish is switching from one language into the other for a special effect, unless the switching takes place within an utterance in a natural way. Examples of such deliberate switching that will not be considered Spanglish can be seen in two-language advertisements, such as:

Buy your home in Levittown Lakes, *donde la buena vida comienza* (radio advertisement).
Yo y mi Winston — *porque* Winstons taste good like a cigarette should (advertisement, sung in a movie house).

To put it differently, Spanglish as defined here is neither language containing grammatical errors due to interference nor intentionally mixed language.

Examples of Spanglish can be conveniently, although somewhat arbitrarily, divided into three main types, each with subtypes. Type 1 is characterized by the extensive use of English lexical items occurring in their original form in otherwise Spanish utterances. These items fall into several groups. First, there are international terms in science and technology, which also appear in many other languages and are therefore not uniquely characteristic of Spanglish.

Second, there are simple substitutions of high-frequency English words that have Spanish equivalents:

Juan estaba en el army, pero se pasó al navy. 'John was in the army (ejército), but he transferred to the navy (a la marina).'
El bos dijo que había que trabajar overtime este weekend. 'The boss (jefe) said that we had to work overtime (extra) this weekend (fin de semana).'
Hágalo anyway. 'Do it anyway (de todas maneras).'
La gente de mi building vive del welfare. 'The people living in my building (edificio) are on welfare (bienestar público).'
Cógelo easy. 'Take it easy (con calma).'
¿Qué size es? 'What size (tamaño) is it?'
Voy al shopping center. 'I'm going to the shopping center (centro comercial).'
Ella tiene ojos braun. 'She has brown (carmelita) eyes.'
Mi prima es bien nice. 'My cousin is very nice (muy agradable).'
Se me perdió el lipstick. 'I lost my lipstick (lápiz labial).'

As such common English words gradually replace their Spanish equivalents, the Spanish words tend to become obsolete through disuse, or change their status from colloquial to formal. In Puerto Rico today it is rare to hear a *freezer* referred to as a *congelador*, or a *truck* called a *camión*.

Third, there are cultural borrowings, many of them slangy expressions. Some, like *hotpants*, are untranslatable English idioms. Others could be rendered in Spanish only by awkward and often unrecognizable paraphrases. Examples of this category are the following:

El baby está bonito con su T-shirt. 'The baby is pretty in his T-shirt.'
El beisbol es mi hobby favorito. 'Baseball is my favorite hobby.'
Deme dos hamburgers plain sin lechuga y tomate. 'Give me two hamburgers plain without lettuce and tomato.'
Esto es un rush job. 'It's a rush job.'
¡Qué down! 'What a letdown!'
¡Qué groovy! 'That's great!'
Lo mío es love. 'My thing is love.'
Todos los substitute clerk carriers están off mañana. 'All the substitute clerk carriers (postal workers) are off tomorrow.'
Cartas airmail para stateside con menos de 11¢ son surfaces. 'Airmail letters going out stateside with less than 11¢ are surface mail.'
Vas al coffee break ahora. 'Take your coffee break now.'
Amplio parking gratis. 'Plenty of free parking.'

Finally, the vocabulary of American merchandising, the names of business establishments, and the slogans and mixed-up messages of advertising are a rich source of type 1 Spanglish, as in the following examples:

Sears de Puerto Rico: Use nuestro plan de compra Lay-Away. Use el plan Easy Payment de Sears. Use el plan Revolving Charge de Sears (signs in a store).

Este album contiene el hit de gran combo (on a record jacket).
Recurt's Office Supplies: folders, máquinas de escribir, account books, papeleria, sillas, desks (sign on a store window).
Design Mens Salon, toupées a la medida, hair weaving y pelucas stretch para caballeros (advertisement in the yellow pages of the telephone book).
Marco Discount House: Cabecera con frame, 2 mesas de noche, 1 triple dresser con 2 espejos. Fibra lavable, 2 corner bed y ottomon en azul. Elegante sofacama (newspaper advertisement).

The last example presents an interesting case of lexico-semantic fusion. *Bed* and *cama*, which are identical in meaning, are used as synonyms in the same advertisement, in which English and Spanish have converged. In effect, the words *bed* and *cama* have become, for this advertiser, part of the same language. Many Puerto Ricans who classify themselves as monolingual speakers of Spanish are quite unaware that some of the words they use naturally and unselfconsciously are English in origin.[7] One of my colleagues at the University of Puerto Rico relates an anecdote about a visitor from Spain who was to give a lecture on the campus. When he asked a campus guard for directions to the *paraninfo*, the guard replied that he was sorry but he did not understand English. After the visitor clarified what he meant, the guard informed him that the Spanish word for that was *asemblijol* (assembly hall).

In type 2 Spanglish, English words lose their non-Spanish identity. Their pronunciation changes more noticeably to conform to Spanish phonology, and they frequently appear in written form spelled according to Spanish orthography. Nouns and verbs assume the morphological characteristics and inflections of Spanish words. Thus the feminine articles *la* and *las* and the masculine articles *el* and *los* agree in number and gender with their nouns, though I have as yet been unable to determine the exact rules for assigning gender to borrowed nouns. Many, but not all, nouns take the grammatical gender of the Spanish words they replace, for example *el rufo* 'roof' replacing *el techo*.[8] Some nouns appear in both masculine and feminine forms, following the pattern of gender marking in such pairs as *la hermana* 'sister' and *el hermano* 'brother', for instance *la bosa* and *el bos* 'boss'.

Among the most frequent types of phonological and orthographic adaptation are the following (the Spanglish spelling is cited when it is attested; the pronunciation is cited when a spelling is not available or the pronunciation does not follow Spanish orthoëpy):
Addition of a final vowel: *bosa* 'boss', *rufo* 'roof', *caucho* 'couch', *norsa* 'nurse', *ganga* 'gang'.
Addition of a final vowel and shift of stress to the penultimate syllable:

marqueta [malkéta] 'market', *furnitura* [fulnitúra] 'furniture', *factoria* 'factory', *grocería* 'grocery', *carpeta* [kalpéta] 'carpet'.

Addition of an initial vowel before [s] plus a consonant and change of the [s] to [h] (in accordance with the allophonic rules of Puerto Rican Spanish): [ehtrí] 'street', swich [ehwíc] 'switch', [ehtínyi] 'stingy', [ehtófa] 'stuff', [ehlíp] 'slip'.

Change of /r/ to [l] in syllable final position: *norsa* [nólsa] 'nurse', *frizer* [frísel] 'freezer', [álmi] 'army', [fólman] 'foreman', [míhtel] 'mister'.

Change of [m] to [ŋ] in final position: [obeltáyŋ] 'overtime', [ruŋ] 'room', *suera* 'sweater',[9] [líhti] 'lipstick', *saibo* [sáybol] 'sideboard', [depármen ehtól] 'department store'.

Ephenthesis: *gauchiman* 'watchman'.

Interpretation of *ge* as [he]: *tinager* [tinahél] 'teenager'.

Verbs in Spanglish are created by taking on the productive infinitive suffixes *-ar*, *-ear*, and *-iar*. They are then conjugated for person, number, and tense according to the regular Spanish paradigms, producing such forms as the following: /flunkár/ 'to flunk (an examination)', /flúnko, flúnkas, flúnka/ 'I, you, he flunk(s)', /flunké, flunkaré, he flunkádo/ 'I flunked, will flunk, have flunked'.

New verbal formations reflect the activities of everyday life, which is the primary source of Spanglish vocabulary, and may, if used in written form, have variant spellings, depending on the user's familiarity with the English form or the frequency with which the adaptation occurs. Some common words, such as *parquear* 'to park', have well-established orthographic forms, and their use cuts across all social classes. Others are in a state of flux with regard to spelling, but not pronunciation. In the home, for example, one hears *bakear, mopear, heatear, freezear, vacuunear*; in the office, *taipear, chequear, clipear*; and in sports, *pitchear, batear, catchear, hitear, trainear, rollear, slipear, flipear, bowlear*. One also hears *lonchear, flirtear, foolear*, and new creations appear every day with no loss of intelligibility.

Some words of type 2 exhibit a range of meaning more restricted than that of the English words from which they were derived. Thus the Spanglish word *estofa*, from English *stuff*, refers only to narcotics. There are also semantic expansions: the Spanish word *ganga* 'sale' converges in Spanglish with *ganga* from English *gang* and can be used in either sense depending on context. A similar case is Spanglish *yarda* from English *yard*, which in pre-Spanglish usage referred only to cloth measurement, but now is also used in the sense 'patio'.

There are also lexical innovations of several kinds. *Zafacon* 'garbage can', a uniquely Puerto Rican word of unknown origin, has been connected by folk etymology with a supposed English source, *safety can* or *save-a-can.* Other creations are *chinero* 'china closet' and *clipiadora* 'stapler'.

Some examples of sentences using type 2 Spanglish are the following:

No jangues por aqui. 'Don't hang around here.' (*janguear* 'hang')
Yo no estoy fuleando. 'I'm not fooling.' (*fuliar* 'fool')
El rufo liquea. 'The roof leaks.' (*liquiar* 'leak')
Limpia la yarda. 'Clean up the yard.'
¿Cuál es tu job en la factoría? 'What's your job in the factory?'
Jumpió la batería. 'He jumped the battery.' (*jumpiar* 'jump')
Deme la clipiadora. 'Give me the stapler.'
¿Sabes taipiar? 'Do you know how to type?'
Me friso. 'I freeze up.' (*frizar* 'freeze')

Type 3 Spanglish includes such things as calques, syntactic idioms, and some original expressions that can be recognized as a distinctive new form of Spanish evolving under the influence of English, much as English itself was influenced by Norman French. Syntactic influence directly from English is not always easy to pin down because some of the manifestations attributed to it, for example excessive use of the redundant nonemphatic subject pronoun, as in *yo no sé* 'I don't know', have been shown to be widespread in other Spanish-speaking areas not in close contact with English or can be traced to literary usage. The examples here are therefore limited to well attested instances of calques cited in a recently completed dissertation by Páulino Pérez-Sala (1971) the conventional Spanish equivalent is in parentheses):

El es un drogadicto. 'He's a drug addict.' (*Es un adicto a las drogas.*)
Lo mataron por ninguna razón. 'They killed him for no reason.' (*Lo mataron sin razón alguna.*)
Mi salario compara con el de E.U. 'My salary compares with that of the U.S.' (*Mi salario es similar al que se paga en los E.U.*)
El está supuesto a venir. 'He is supposed to come.' (*Se supone que el venga.*)
Ahora sí esto hace sentido. 'Now it makes sense.' (*Ahora esto sí tiene sentido.*)
Eso hace una diferencia en mis planes. 'That makes a difference in my plans.' (*Eso cambia mis planes.*)
Nos unimos en simpatía con usted. 'We join you in sympathy.' (*Le acompaño en el sentimiento.*)
Le daré pensamiento a eso. 'I'll give it some thought.' (*Hay que estudiar el problema.*)
Alberto es 20 años viejo. 'Albert is 20 years old.' (*Alberto tiene 20 años.*)
El pasado año 'last year' (*el año pasado*).
El plan parecía uno demasiado costoso. 'The plan seemed to be a very expensive one.' (*El plan parecía demasiado costoso.*)

¿Cómo le gusta Puerto Rico? 'How do you like Puerto Rico?' (*¿Le gusta Puerto Rico?*)
El sabe como hablar inglés. 'He knows how to speak English.' (*Sabe hablar inglés.*)
Llámame para átras (= *pa'atras*). 'Call me back.' (*Vuélveme a llamar.*)
Tráigalo para átras. 'Bring it back.' (*Devuélvalo.*)

Loan translations of the more obvious kind, such as *perro caliente* for *hot dog*, *Caballo Blanco* for *White Horse (Whiskey)*, and *Siete Arriba* for *Seven-Up* are relatively rare, which perhaps makes their use particularly effective, as in the following:

¡Está en la bola! 'He's on the ball!'
Felicidad es comprar en Pueblo. 'Happiness is shopping at Pueblo (Supermarket).'

Other expressions in common use (with the conventional Spanish in parentheses) are the following:

demasiado mucho 'too much' (*excesivo*)
salvar tiempo 'to save time' (*ahorrar tiempo*)
el alto costo de la vida 'the high cost of living' (*la carestida de la vida*).

The last group of examples, which most nearly represent a merger of Spanish and English into a new dialect, contains elements of all three types and something more. English and Spanish are not only mixed, but fused into expressions with a special Puerto Rican flavor that goes beyond linguistic analysis because it reflects the life of the speakers:

Estás en algo. 'You're in!'
Estás hecho. 'You have it made.'
Estaba tripiando anoche. 'Last night he turned on with pot.'
Todavía está en el tinegeo. 'He still acts like a teenager.'
Quiero un jamón sandwich. 'I want a ham sandwich.'
Tengo dos cheeseburgers trabajando. 'I've got two cheeseburgers working.'
María esta en la high. 'Maria is in high school.'
Está ahora en el grin. 'The traffic light just turned green.'
La estofa está caliente. 'The stuff is hot (illegal).'
¡Qué fallo! 'What a let-down!'

In summary, Spanglish may be characterized as a gradual relexification of Puerto Rican Spanish through borrowings, adaptations, and innovations of the kind observable in every living language. The vocabulary of Spanglish is the vocabulary of practical everyday living and working in a two-language world, in which not everyone commands those two languages fluently. A person must, therefore, select from each source the linguistic materials he needs in order to communicate freely, economically, and intelligibly with other members of his speech community. In a great majority of cases, the English lexical item meets these requirements better than its Spanish counterpart, though the reasons for substitutions are various. A Puerto Rican buys a *freezer* rather than a *congelador* because that is the word he sees in the advertisements; he speaks of *la high* rather than *la escuela superior* because it is shorter; he can express a keener sense of disappointment with ¡ *Qué fallo*! than with the bookish ¡*Qué desengaño*! And in every case, he knows that he will be immediately understood by his peers without need of clarification, because this is their common language.

The chief purpose of this paper has been to present a brief description of some types of Spanglish chosen from a continuum of use that is too complex both linguistically and sociolinguistically for thorough treatment here. It would not be proper, however, to conclude without mentioning the attitudes towards the use of Spanglish expressed by Puerto Rican educators, intellectuals, and political leaders and the effect of those attitudes upon that group in society with which I am most familiar — people of college age. For although from the linguist's point of view such creative activity may be considered normal, healthy, and even inevitable, given the existing language contact situation, there are bitter disagreements about its cultural significance. Puerto Ricans today are a people living in two worlds simultaneously — the world of Spanish colonial traditions and the world of modern American industrial society. They do not want to give up the former, and they cannot escape the latter. The Spanish language holds a cherished place in their search for a national identity, and any indication that Spanish is being replaced is seen as a symptom of cultural breakdown. The fear of losing their language is in fact one of the strongest arguments in the movement for political independence. Regardless of political persuasion, everyone agrees that Spanish must remain the dominant language.[10] There is, however, considerable disagreement concerning what Spanish is and what to do about the 'dangerous' influence of English.

The most optimistic opinion is held by Ruben del Rosario, professor of philology at the University of Puerto Rico, who has written extensively on language change in Spanish America: *La lengua es lo que se dice* 'language is that which is spoken', and there is no cause for alarm. Puerto Rican Spanish, he says, has been enriched by vocabulary from many different languages, and the changes that have occurred are no different in kind from those in other Spanish-speaking countries. Syntactic interference from English, he feels, is minimal, and he sees little possibility that Spanish will be replaced, whether or not English is present as a second language.

Sharply opposed to this view is the opinion of Salvador Tío, a journalist and literary figure. He sees language mixture as a degradation and impoverishment of the glorious tongue of Cervantes and castigates those who speak Spanglish. The true culprit, he believes, is the official policy of bilingualism, and he would do away with the required teaching of English altogether, so that its presence could not encourage language mixture.[11]

Supporters of the bilingual policy feel that the solution to the problem of language mixture lies in raising the standards of education. By improving the teaching of both Spanish and English, they feel, it will be possible to keep the languages functionally separate. Luis Muñoz Marin, the island's first elected governor, who instituted the present school policy in 1950, had the vision of a truly bilingual society, in which the two great world-languages would flourish. Yet he warned his fellow countrymen not to mix English and Spanish, lest they become 'semilingual in two languages'.[12]

The official disapproval of Spanglish is hardest psychologically on the college student, who feels he is being unpatriotic when he uses English words instead of the 'perfectly good Spanish words' that he does not know or cannot remember. This feeling frequently carries over into an aversion for learning English itself. There is an anecdote about one student asking another, 'How come your English is so bad? Is it because you're patriotic, or are you just stupid?'

This is the linguistic dilemma of Puerto Rico today: a generation of students who feel inadequate about their Spanish, uncomfortable with their English, and guilty about their culturally unacceptable Spanglish.

NOTES

1. The only exception, to my knowledge, is the state of New Mexico, where Spanish has a legal status equal to English.
2. Until 1950, English was the medium of instruction in the public schools. It is still maintained in many private schools. For a discussion of this highly controversial issue, see Epstein (1970).
3. For an in-depth study of Newyorricans, see Fishman (1968).
4. In addition to the presence of Newyorricans, several other factors may be mentioned that encourage language mixture. First, there is a large English-speaking population, including military personnel, non-Puerto Rican permanent residents from various parts of the United States, and transient tourists. Second, virtually all of the products sold in Puerto Rico are manufactured in the United States and are referred to by their English

names. Third, Puerto Rico is geographically isolated from other Spanish-speaking areas, so that borrowings from English quickly become institutionalized.

5. I reserve the term *Spanglish* for English-influenced Spanish as a first language, distinguishing it from Spanish-influenced English spoken as a second language, which I call *Englañol*. The latter will be treated in a subsequent paper.

6. The late journalist Eddie Lopez was a master of this literary genre. He created a character called Candido Flores, whose letters, written in hilariously mangled English, appeared periodically in the *San Juan Star*, Puerto Rico's English-language newspaper.

7. In general, the level of awareness is proportionate to the level of education, but this has little effect on the frequency of usage. Ease of communication is the chief motivation for employing English words, although the prestige factor, for some speakers, cannot be ignored.

8. Exceptions are *la marqueta*, also *la marketa*, replacing *el mercado*, and *el window*, replacing *la ventana*. Use of the inappropriate article, such as **la window*, is considered ungrammatical.

9. The attested spellings *cuara* and *suera* derive from articulatory similarities between Spanish /r/, which is a single-tap voiced alveolar, and the English voiced variant of /t/ in intervocalic position, which is voiced alveolar stop. English speakers with voiced /t/ may make no distinction between *latter* and *ladder*. In such words, the Spanish speaker 'hears' /r/, and therefore uses the *r* grapheme. The Spanish phoneme /d/ is realized in intervocalic position as the fricative [ð]: *todo* 'all' [tóðo], *toro* 'bull' [tóro].

10. During the Governors' Conference held in San Juan in 1971, one of the American governors from a southern state said publicly that English would have to become the dominant language if Puerto Rico were to continue its association with the United States. The mayor of San Juan, who was with him, immediately left the stage in protest and refused to speak to him again. The mayor belongs to the Statehood party.

11. Tío claims credit for inventing the term Spanglish in a bitterly satirical article written in 1952. Pronouncements against the menace of English are made with great frequency by highly placed cultural, professional, and educational leaders, but have little noticeable effect on speech habits. Some examples of vituperative remarks, translated from the Spanish-language newspaper *El Mundo*, are the following: 'For Puerto Rico, bilingualism is the dissolution of its national personality through the loss of its language' (a prominent attorney); 'The only bilingualism which exists in Puerto Rico is the struggle between English, which attempts to impose itself, and Spanish, which wishes to save itself' (director of the Institute of Puerto Rican Culture); 'Puerto Ricans should not permit a foreign language in one's mouth or in one's soul' (independentista professor). Members of the intellectual elite strongly identify with Puerto Rico's Hispanic cultural heritage and minimize the contribution of Africa, as well as other European countries and the United States.

12. In a speech before the Teachers Association of Puerto Rico in 1953.

REFERENCES

Alvarez Navario, M. (1956), *La Naturaleza del Español Que se Habla en Puerto Rico*. San Juan.

Dillard, J. L. (1975), *All-American English, A History of the English Language in America*, chapter VI. New York, Random House.

De Granda, German (1968), *Transculturación e Interferencia Lingüística en el Puerto Rico Contemporaneo (1898–1968)*. Bogotá.

Epstein, Edwin H., editor (1970), *Politics and Education in Puerto Rico: A Documentary Survey of the Language Issue.* Metuchen, N.J.

Gil Gaya, Samuel (1965), *Nuestra Lengua Materna.* San Juan.

Fishman, Joshua, editor (1968), *Bilingualism in the Barrio*, two volumes. Washington, D.C.

Navarro Tomas, T. (1948), *El Español en Puerto Rico.* Río Piedras.

Pérez Sala, Páulino (1971), 'Interferencia del Inglés en la Syntaxis del Español hablado ne la zona metropolitano de San Juan'. Unpublished Ph.D. dissertation, University of Puerto Rico.

Porras Cruz, J. L., et al. (1968), *Recomendaciones para el Uso del Idioma Español en Puerto Rico.* San Juan

Rosario, Ruben del (1971), *La Lengua de Puerto Rico*, seventh edition. Río Piedras.

Tio, Salvador (1954), *Teoria del Espanglish, A Fuego Lento, Cien Columnas de Humor y una Cornisa.* Río Piedras.

Varo, Carlos (1971), *Consideraciones Antropológicas y Políticas en Torno a la Enseñanza del 'Spanglish' en Nueva York.* Río Piedras.

THOMAS F. MAGNER

The Melting Pot and Language Maintenance in South Slavic Immigrant Groups

The metaphor of the 'melting pot' has not been in good repute in recent years. The term seems to have been coined by Israel Zangwill who used it as the title of one of his plays, *The Melting Pot*, produced on Broadway in 1908. Like other inventors of apt phrases, Zangwill himself has retreated into obscurity while his term has lived on in popular usage to characterize the American policy and practice of assimilation; the term is much alive today but in many quarters it has come to signify the destruction of cultures, both immigrant and indigenous, by the dominant group of Americans of Anglo-Saxon background. The metaphor implied the 'melting away' of distinctive national characteristics and the acquisition of new, broadly shared 'American' cultural characteristics. In its time this process of homogenization was seen as eminently desirable by the older settlers in this country and even by immigrants themselves though in truth they had no voice in the matter. One should, however, be cautious about imposing today's attitudes on a historical process such as the accultura-tion of immigrant groups in America; doing so might be emotionally satisfying to those who feel that their forebears were unjustly forced into the American mold, but it does not alter the history and attitudes of earlier eras.

Negative attitudes toward immigrants who spoke a language other than English have prevailed from the very beginnings of this country. In 1753 that eminent American, Benjamin Franklin, was complaining (in a letter to a friend) about the German colonists in Pennsylvania who insisted on maintaining their German culture and language.

Few of their Children in the Country learn English. They import many Books from Germany; and of the six Printing-Houses in the Province, two are entirely German, two half German half English, and but two entirely English. They have one German Newspaper, and one half-German. . . . The Signs in our Streets have Inscriptions in both Languages, and in some places only German. They begin of

This is a revised version of an article which appeared in *General Linguistics* 16(1976):59–67.

late to make all their Bonds and other legal Instruments in their own Language, which (though I think it ought not to be) are allowed good in our courts, where the German Business so increases, that there is continual need of Interpreters; and I suppose in a few Years they will also be necessary in the Assembly, to tell one half of our Legislators what the other half say (Smyth 1905:140).[1]

Franklin's prescription for remedying the situation was an early version of the 'melting pot' as he proposed 'to distribute them more equally, mix them with the English, [and] establish English Schools, where they are now too thick settled'.

Proponents of the 'melting pot' could in the past point with pride to an immigrant such as Michael Idvorsky Pupin who came to New York City at the age of fifteen in 1874. Pupin, a Serbian lad from the tiny village of Idvor in the Banat, then part of Austria-Hungary, welcomed Americanization and his autobiography, *From Immigrant to Inventor*, eloquently portrays his love for his adopted land. Even his marriage reflects his commitment to America and that of his Serbian mother back in Idvor who had told him: 'You must marry an American girl if you wish to remain an American, which I know you do' (Pupin 1930:276). And yet this famous scientist and inventor never abandoned his Serbian people and in fact was instrumental in mobilizing war relief for his fellow Serbs during World War I. An objection here might be that Pupin was unique, as great men always are, and that the real tragedy was that of the hordes of immigrants from countries around the world who paid for the benefits of American life by sacrificing their ancestral cultures and languages.

To understand the importance attached to Americanization or the workings of the 'melting pot', it is instructive to read the words of President Woodrow Wilson (a friend and admirer of Pupin), words which he addressed to several thousand immigrants on the occasion in May 1915 of their naturalization as American citizens,

... While you bring all countries with you, you come with a purpose of leaving all other countries behind you — bringing what is best of their spirit, but not looking over your shoulders and seeking to perpetuate what you intended to leave behind in them. I certainly would not be one even to suggest that a man cease to love the home of his birth and the nation of his origin — these things are very sacred and ought not to be put out of our hearts — but it is one thing to love the place where you were born and it is another thing to dedicate yourself to the place to which you go. You cannot dedicate yourself to America unless you become in every respect and with every purpose of your will thorough Americans. *You cannot become thorough Americans if you think of yourselves in groups. America does not consist of groups. A man who thinks of himself as belonging to a particular national group in America has not yet become an American, and the man who goes among you to trade upon your nationality is no worthy son to live under the Stars and Stripes* [my italics — T.F.M.] (Wilson 1917:115–116).

President Wilson was not the first or the last to offer new immigrants such a rationale for the 'melting pot'. The effect of such injunctions on immigrants was quite powerful, inducing them to shed their 'non-American' customs and traits. Writing in 1921, Constantine M. Panunzio, an immigrant from Sicily, interpreted typical American attitudes this way,

. . . how unkind, how cruel are the methods sometimes used in connection with our so-called Americanization program. Think of our saying to these foreign peoples, some of whom have been in this country for perhaps a brief period: Forget your native land, forget your mother tongue, do away in a day with your inherited customs, put from you as a cloak all that inheritance and early environment made you and become in a day an American *par excellence*. This was precisely the talk I used to hear when I first came to this country. There was then as now, I regret to say, a spirit of compulsion in the air (Panunzio 1921:194).

The 'melting pot' did work effectively for certain nationalities, for example the Irish and the Germans, but less well for others such as Italians and Slavs. Latter-day opponents of the 'melting pot' concept take pride in the continued existence of such 'unmelted' groups or subcultures and see them as a source of strength for America. One spokesman for the new ethnicity puts it this way:

The new ethnic politics is a direct challenge to the WASP conception of America. It asserts that *groups* can structure the rules and goals and procedures of American life. It asserts that individuals, if they do not wish to, do not have to 'melt'. They do not have to submit themselves to atomization. 'Subcultures' are refusing to concede the legitimacy of one (modernized WASP) 'Superculture' (Novak 1971:270).

Language is a criterion for the identification of a people though it is not an essential one: the Austrians, for example, speak German but consider themselves to be distinct from the German people, and one would hardly confuse the Irish and the English even though they both speak English. But most of the immigrant groups arrived in America not only with distinctive sets of characteristics and customs but with distinctive languages. Some immigrants could function in specific settings without ever learning English but obviously the next generation had to master the language of the new country. The transition from monolingualism (i.e. the imported language) to bilingualism (i.e. the imported language and English), however imperfect, back to monolingualism (i.e. English) has been and still is a phenomenon characteristic of the first few generations of immigrant groups. Certain groups have managed to maintain their bilingualism but most of the groups of hyphenated Americans no longer control the ancestral language. Mexican-Americans are conspicuous by their success in language maintenance but they are a contiguous culture group in the sense that they are physically close to Mexico, the mainspring of their culture and language. Another group which has succeeded in maintaining both language and culture is the Old Order Amish, who exist in about fifty communities in North America. The Amish, who along with other groups of German descent are popularly known as 'Pennsylvania Dutch', came to this country over two centuries ago from the Rhineland, bringing with them a German dialect which still functions for them at home and work. The Amish have been able to maintain their German speech alongside English only because they have chosen to avoid the seductions of American culture and technology; they literally live in a horse-and-buggy culture.

In his outstanding study of the Norwegian language in this country, Einar Haugen describes the American attitude toward bilingualism as follows:

Americans have tended to take it for granted that 'foreigners' should acquire English, and that a failure to do so was evidence by implication of a kind of disloyalty to the basic principles of American life. . . . It has seldom been recognized that the bilingual might have problems of adjustment which called on the best efforts of students and scholars for their solution. Even linguists have rarely exploited the possibilities of immigrant bilingualism for its bearing on linguistic theory. Bilingualism has been treated as a necessary evil, a rash on the body politic, which time might be expected to cure without the need of calling in the doctors (Haugen 1969:2).

Disdain and suspicion of bilingualism do indeed characterize American attitudes. While bilingualism is accepted as natural and even admirable in many countries of the world, it is regarded in America as a kind of defect. This attitude toward other languages and bilingualism often shows up in college courses of 'English for Foreigners' where the mastery of another language is somehow regarded as a type of retardation to be corrected by kindly instruction in basic English. Once in giving a general lecture about the makeup of Yugoslavia to an audience of college-educated people, I had occasion to detail the ethnic and linguistic diversity characteristic of that country. At the end of the talk one member of the audience arose and exclaimed: 'You said these peoples have all those languages: Slovenian, Serbo-Croatian, Macedonian, Albanian, Hungarian and others. Why in the world do they want that many languages? Why don't they just settle on one and forget the rest?' How does one explain to a person who has such a monolingual view of the world, who really feels that all these peoples with the strange names would be better off speaking English, that most peoples, perhaps all peoples, regard their particular language as an essential part of their very identity.

It is beyond the scope of this paper to determine why American culture is so intolerant of languages other than English. But the effect of this intolerance on bilinguals is quite clear, as Haugen points out:

As for the bilinguals themselves, some have accepted their lot with enthusiasm, others with resignation, but many more have sought to evade it by becoming anglicized as soon as possible. However prominent bilingualism may be as a trait of American life, it is eclipsed by the continual flight of the bilinguals themselves from bilingualism (Haugen 1969:2).

There is, however, another side to any consideration of immigrant bilingualism. In discussions about language maintenance in ethnic groups it is usually assumed that bilingualism is a worthy goal. This assumption is fortified by the widely held belief that knowledge of a foreign language is the sign of an educated person. Actually, the two situations are vastly different: in the ethnic group an individual may use one language at home and another one, the common language of the country, in school and public life; in the academic situation a person usually controls the national language, English in this country, and tries to acquire a command of one of the more prestigious languages in the world, say French, Spanish, German, or Russian. In these two situations social pressures differ greatly: an immigrant or his descendant is judged, sometimes harshly, on his control (or lack of it) of the national language, while the person exercising a foreign language learned in school will suffer only personal and temporary disappointment if his efforts to communicate while in the foreign country are not successful. Bilingualism, the coping with two different language systems, can be a source of learning difficulty and can result in limited social movement for the person who is reared in a subculture where a non-English language is still dominant. Daniel J. Boorstin, the distinguished American historian, has a particularly relevant quote on a negative aspect of bilingualism.

Only recently the Governor [of Puerto Rico] expressed his fear that the pressure to learn two languages had made islanders not bilingual but 'semilingual in two languages' (Boorstin 1960:156).

The value of ethnic bilingualism is even more questionable in the case of many of our South Slavic communities, particularly where the representatives of the first generation speak one of the many, and often very different, dialects of Serbo-Croatian or Slovenian. Even today in Yugoslavia there is controversy about the nature of the standard Serbo-Croatian language with some scholars claiming that there is as yet no such standard language. Many of the Yugoslav Americans in San Pedro, California, speak a version of a dialect from Vis, an island off the Dalmatian coast; this dialect would be incomprehensible in many parts of the Serbo-Croatian speech territory in Yugoslavia. Similarly, in Steelton, Pa. Yugoslav Americans speak a dialect strongly influenced by the village *kajkavian* of their ancestors. It is doubtful that a Yugoslav American from San Pedro could communicate with a Yugoslav American from Steelton in their respective dialects. The ancestral dialect serves as a cultural link between the first generation (the immigrants) and the second generation (born in America) but the value of such a linguistic bond rapidly decreases in present-day America. If an ethnic group remains in a specific occupation, e.g. agriculture or fishing, and a specific territory, the ancestral language can be maintained, as in the case of the Amish mentioned above, and a true and effective bilingualism can flourish, a situation characteristic of the Amish or the Portuguese-American fishermen of New England. But active participation and integration in the larger monolingual American culture deprive the earlier bilingualism of its utility.

In considering the fate of South Slavic immigrants in America, one can do no better than to start with the observations of that most perceptive immigrant from Slovenia, Louis Adamic.

Of all the Bohunks[2] — which includes the Poles, Slovaks, Czechs, and other Eastern and Southeastern Europeans whose lot it is, along with that of the Italians, Mexicans and Negroes, to perform most of the dirty work of the United States — the Yugo- or South-Slavs are perhaps the largest ingredient in the Melting Pot. They are to be found in large numbers — running to a total of nearly two millions, though a good half of them are still carried in official American statistics as Austrians — in the great mining regions of Pennsylvania, Ohio, Illinois, West Virginia, Colorado, New Mexico, and Arizona, on farming lands in the Middle West and the West, in New York City, Chicago, Cleveland, Pittsburgh, Cincinnati, and other industrial centers, in the woods of Maine and the Northwest, on fishing smacks along the coast of Southern California, and on countless construction jobs all over the country (Adamic 1927:319).

In an article a year later (1928) Adamic explains why and how Slovenes, Croats and Serbs tended to disappear within the American context.

In the case of the Slavic immigrants from Southeastern Europe fifteen or twenty years ago, at which time they came over in a steady stream, the first, although to them not the most important, difficulty arose in making the people here — native-born Americans and aliens of other nationalities — understand who they were and whence they hailed. The difficulty lay basically in the fact that many of them were not clear on the point themselves. If, say, a Slovene was asked what his nationality was, very likely he replied that he was a Kranjec or Carniolan, from Kranjsko (German: Krain; English: Carniola). Only a few Czechs, Styrian Germans and Italians from Trieste and Gorizia knew what it meant. It was as if a citizen of some such obscure State as Nevada, arriving in Belgrade or Warsaw, should announce that his nationality was Nevadan. If he really knew what he was, he declared himself a Slovene, but that, to the average American, Irishman or Scandinavian, meant no more than Carniolan.

Croats, Serbs and Montenegrins fared no better, Adamic continues, most of them receiving the designation 'Austrian' while their language became just another variety of the 'Austrian' tongue (Adamic 1928:319–320).

In his 1927 article, 'The Yugoslav speech in America', Adamic considered what he calls 'a third language' resulting from the infiltration of English terms into the South Slavic languages.

Considering that this Yugoslav population in America is relatively meagre and, besides, is spread out all over the country, it is small wonder that its vulgate, within the last thirty years, should have undergone considerable changes. The Yugoslav immigrant, as a rule, learns the American language as well as his new environment permits him — in some cases very well indeed — but at the same time he keeps up with his native Slovene or Serbo-Croat, insisting, for purely sentimental and selfish reasons, that his children learn it, and resenting, on occasion, any attempt to corrupt it. Simultaneously, however, he goes on building and using, perhaps unknowingly, a third language, fashioned from the materials of the first according to the genius of the second (Adamic 1927:320).

Some of his examples are: *kična* 'kitchen'; *štof* 'stove'; *kara* 'car'; *šuhi* 'shoes'; *lonč-boket* 'lunch-bucket'; *vurkati* 'to work'; *lajka* 'he/she likes'. Surnames are sometimes changed either on the basis of sound similarity, e.g. Oblak to O'Black; Bizjak to Busyjack; Stritar to Streeter; or by simple translation, e.g. Belič [Belić] to White; Podlesnik to Underwood (Adamic 1927:320–321).

One of the oldest South Slav colonies in the United States is that of the Takos who started to settle in the marshlands of southeastern Louisiana in the first decades of the nineteenth century.[3] Coming from Dalmatia, these Croats became specialized as oyster fishermen and established a close community, undisturbed by the outside world until recent times. But now, as in other ethnic 'islands', the outside world has intruded through compulsory schooling, urbanization and greater mobility, and the Takos are caught up in the seemingly inexorable assimilation of the 'melting pot'. The ancestral language is one of the first distinctive traits of such a subculture to be affected by the dominant non-Croatian culture.

In some of the Croatian homes, the Croatian language is still used exclusively, and occasionally the children do not speak or understand English when they enter school. The fact that this situation is rapidly changing is a cause of real concern among many of the parents. They resent the fact that there is a growing reluctance on the part of the younger generation to learn how to speak, to read, and to write Croatian. Personal observation reveals that the younger people are more proficient in the use of the English language than their parents. Many times the Croatian language is used only when the child feels it would be inappropriate or disrespectful to do otherwise (Lovrich 1966–1967:103).

In similar fashion the ancestral language (Serbo-Croatian or Slovenian) endures and then wanes in other South Slavic communities in this country.[4] Sometimes the language acquires renewed life through latter-day immigration as in the Serbian settlement in Milwaukee but most often it loses its vitality and usefulness as the immigrant generation itself moves from the living present into American history.

The story of the importation of South Slavic languages into the United States, their gradual retreat and ultimate demise in our English-dominant culture is not unique; the same pattern obtains for scores of other immigrant languages. But there is one aspect about this process of linguistic disintegration which deserves the attention of the linguist. Do these imported languages disappear completely or do they leave their mark on American English? The answer to both parts of this question could be yes: certain languages sink into immigrant history without a significant trace, while others contribute distinctive elements to the English of their region.

Little if any research has been done on the influence of the South Slavic languages on American English. To illustrate the possibilities, however, I would like to quote from Buffington's study of the influence of Pennsylvania German on Pennsylvania English. Buffington (1968:33–40) found a carryover of phonetic features (e.g. nonoccurrence of voiced stops in word-final position; thus, *bet* and *bed* pronounced alike), special intonational patterns, many lexical items (e.g. 'The meat has too much speck on it' [Pennsylvania German *Schpeck* 'fat']; *hair* as a plural e.g. 'I see you have a haircut. When did you get them cut?'), particular syntactic usages (e.g. 'It wonders me' [Pennsylvania German *es wunnert mich*]; extensive use of the verb 'make' e.g. 'Make the door open'), etc. Buffington (1968:40) concludes:

The influence of the Pennsylvania German dialect on the English spoken today in the northern part of Dauphin County, the southern half of Northumberland County, Snyder County, and the western part of Schuylkill County can be observed in the pronunciation of certain sounds, in the intonational melodies or patterns, in the vocabulary, and in the syntax. Furthermore, there seems to be no indication that the English as spoken on various levels among the people living in these sections will change very rapidly toward standard English, even though the Pennsylvania German dialect seems to be yielding increasingly to English. Certain phonemic patterns and peculiar usages are so well established in the English spoken in the Pennsylvania German area that they will probably survive long after the Pennsylvania German dialect itself has died out.

Just as immigrants from particular countries have made distinctive genetic contributions to the physical structure and appearance of Americans, so also their languages have had the possibility of contributing unique elements to the resources of American English. Many regional features of English may well be echoes from other languages which competed with English for a time and then ostensibly disappeared.

NOTES

1. I am indebted to my colleague, Professor Hugo A. Meier, for this reference.
2. 'Bohunk' was a pejorative term formed from the words 'Bohemian' (i.e. Czech) and 'Hungarian'. Another such term was 'Hunky' from 'Hungarian', though it was applied to Slavs as well. The latter term suggested 'Honky' which was used in recent years by certain Blacks as a derisory term for white Americans. (T.F.M.)
3. 'The term "tako" means "so, so" in Croatian. When the Anglo-Americans would meet a Croatian they would ask him how things were. He would answer them *tako, tako*; hence the nickname "Takos." ' (Lovrich 1966–1967:38).
4. A special issue of *General Linguistics* (Volume 16, Nos. 2–3, Summer/Fall 1976) contains valuable articles on four other South Slavic communities: Alexander Albin, 'A Yugoslav community in San Pedro, California' (78–94); Joseph Paternost, 'Slovenian language on Minnesota's Iron Range: some sociolinguistic aspects of language maintenance and language shift' (95–150); Charles A. Ward, 'The Serbian and Croatian communities in Milwaukee' (151–165); and Dunja Jutronić, 'Language maintenance and language shift of the Serbo-Croatian language in Steelton, Pennsylvania' (166–186).

REFERENCES

Adamic, Louis (1927), 'The Yugoslav speech in America', *The American Mercury* 12(47):319–321.
— (1928), 'The Bohunks', *The American Mercury* 14(55):318–324.
Buffington, Albert F. (1968), 'The influence of the Pennsylvania German dialect on the

English spoken in the Pennsylvania German area', in *Helen Adolf Festschrift*, ed. by S. Z.
  Buehne, J. L. Hodge, and L. B. Pinto. New York, Frederick Ungar.
Boorstin, Daniel J. (1960), *America and the Image of Europe*. New York, Meridian Books.
Haugen, Einar (1969), *The Norwegian Language in America*, second edition. Bloomington,
  Indiana University Press.
Lovrich, Frank M. (1966–1967), 'Croatian in Louisiana', *Journal of Croatian Studies*
  7–8:31–163.
Novak, Michael (1971), *The Rise of the Unmeltable Ethnics*. New York, Macmillan.
Panunzio, Constantine M. (1921), *The Soul of an Immigrant*. New York, Macmillan.
Pupin, Michael (1930), *From Immigrant to Inventor*, fifteenth printing. New York,
  Shribner's.
Smyth, Albert H., editor (1905), *The Writings of Benjamin Franklin*, volume three. New
  York, Macmillan.
Wilson, Woodrow (1917), *The Messages and Papers of Woodrow Wilson*, volume one. New
  York, Doran.

PART FOUR

Black English

Introduction

Historically, there can hardly be any doubt that the variety now known as Black English is the most complex of American dialects. Long held to be the result of direct and exact transmission of older Southern White English, retaining archaic features while the language of the whites changed, Black English has recently been shown to be closely related to the varieties spoken in the West Indies (e.g. Jamaican) and Surinam (Sranan Tongo) and even to West African forms like Cameroonian and Nigerian Pidgin English and Krio of Sierra Leone. The very existence of Gullah, an obvious Creole language, should have suggested that possibility; but Gullah was conveniently shunted aside as something 'isolated'. If, however, the equating of Black English Vernacular grammatical forms with Gullah, in some historical sense, necessitated a complex theory (decreolization, according to Stewart [1967, 1968]) there were turns of phrase like *love come down* (Dillard 1977) and a wide range of rootwork conjure terminology so blanketing the Black communities in the United States as to preclude any possibility of transmission by a few migrating Gullahs and offering excellent evidence of the ultimate unity of Black dialects. Of the works on those collocations or 'idioms', perhaps none have been better done than the demonstration regarding *cut-eye* and *suck-teeth* by Rickford and Rickford (this volume).

In the early 1960s, when linguists and dialectologists knew Afro-American varieties (unless they happened to be familiar with Herskovits and Herskovits, *Suriname Folk-Lore*) only through the studies of Jamaican Creole by DeCamp and LePage (1960), Cassidy (1961), and Cassidy and LePage (1968), it was easy to imagine Jamaican and Gullah as exotic but rather insignificant varieties separated by a lot of water and not matched by anything spoken elsewhere. With the new emphasis on the development of the Afro-American varieties from an originally maritime pidgin (Hancock 1976, Dillard 1972; in that general spirit are also Taylor [1961] and Voorhoeve [1961, 1973]), there came an interest in studying other populations of African provenience in other places. An interesting outgrowth of this new emphasis is Holm's article on Miskito

Coast Creole. In addition to a lot of expected borrowing from Spanish, Miskito shows a great deal of what is intermediate between 'deep' creole and decreolized Black English Vernacular.

Holm points out how many creole structures resemble those of African languages like Yoruba, thus already providing a more complex history for a variety of New World English than had been dreamed of by the Linguistic Atlas projects. There is, however, even more complexity than that. As Creolists have long recognized, and as John Birmingham points out in his article in this volume, many of the English varieties have striking similarities to dialects and to languages that could not possibly have come from English — British or otherwise. Somewhere, in the historical background wherein speakers of hundreds of West African languages learned to communicate in languages at least lexically European, was the tradition of the maritime Lingua Franca, academically known since the days of Schuchardt (1909) but hardly given the attention it has deserved. The Lingua Franca was the language of seafaring men. If, as Birmingham has asserted, Papiamentu is the 'Long-lost Lingua Franca' (Birmingham 1976) and if, as he asserts (this volume), Black English has roots near Papiamentu, then the historical affinities of the Black English Vernacular are complex indeed. And such complexities should surely not be hidden under 'bench marks'.

If, in fact, we discard the conventional homey British origin for Black English, a great many other things in American dialect history may also have to be changed. If Southern Whites did not somehow pass on their dialects in exact form to the African slaves, who by some strange process retained an 'archaic' form of white speech after the Whites had changed, then there may be other explanations of how the white Southern dialects themselves arose. The folk explanation, given serious consideration in Dillard (1972:ch. V), has always been that southern White English was 'corrupted' by contact with the slaves and their distinctive language. Factoring out any pejorative connotation of popular terms like 'corruption', we can see the likelihood of just such influence on 'southern dialect'. In fact, Wolfram (1974:525) expresses something of the same viewpoint in terms of a non-Creolist dialectology:

It seems only reasonable to conclude that Southern whites speak more like Blacks than Northern whites (although of course not identically), not only because of the settlement patterns of British dialects but because some of the distinct Black speech, if you will, rubbed off.

The attacks of the American Creolists (Bailey, Stewart, Dillard) on standard Anglocentric historical theory have caused adherents to the latter theory to begin looking at a source of American dialect forms almost never considered before — Anglo-Irish. In particular, the striking public demonstrations which Stewart began making around 1964 of the Black use of 'time-extending' *be* (*he all the time be doing that*) contrasting with another structure of less marked time extent (*he doing that right now*) tended to be explained away as originating from Anglo-Irish 'consuetudinal' *be*. This explanation was more agreeable to the Anglicists — in fact, it seemed almost like a miraculous rescue to some of them. It overlooked, unfortunately, the paucity of other material (even vocabulary) traceable to the Irish. And it overlooked — which would seem to be unforgiveable in the traditions of linguistics — inconvenient syntactic relationships like the negation pattern:

He be doing that   He don't be doing that
He doing that   He ain't doing that

and many others (see Loflin 1967, 1970; Fickett 1970, 1975).

Nevertheless, the entry of the Irishman broadens the historical picture for American English, and that is a desirable result. My own initial reaction to the Irish source for South Texas *mott* in Jordan's article (this volume) was ambivalent and even unfavorable: there are contact language explanations for the failure of Texans to articulate the final vowel of *mata* even though they do pronounce the final one in *enchilada*, *mañana* — if not with a perfect 'Spanish accent'. Nevertheless, the evidence that Jordan provides should not be overlooked, nor should the Irish English origin of some Black English features be rejected without a hearing, no matter how absurd it seems to risk the label Black Irishmen.

What is much more objectionable than Anglocentrism and far-fetched Irish sources is the appeal to 'sound symbolism', 'pig Latin', and the like for the vast amount of still-unexplained terminology associated with the big city ghettoes of the United States. (Many of the same usages are, of course, current among Blacks in the rural South, and usages like *zoot* and *cool* have analogues as far away as Liberia). An excellent example of a terrible etymology (Major 1970) is the derivation of *ofay/fay* 'white man' (with pejorative connotations) from *foe*. This facile derivation takes advantage of a chance resemblance to pig Latin practices. However, Frederick G. Cassidy, himself best known as an Anglicist, has established the strong possibility that the source is rather *ofé*, from Yoruba or (more likely) from a complex of closely related West African languages. Cassidy concludes (1975:89): 'That this word could have been brought to the United States by slaves is altogether possible.'[1]

As Dalby (1972) seems already to have established, this is only the beginning. *Ofay/fay* is still confined almost exclusively — with the exception of borrowing by a few teenagers devoted to rock and roll music — to Blacks. *O.K.* is another matter entirely. Dalby's daring suggestion that this 'most representative Americanism' may actually have begun as an Africanism brought on a furious storm of protest, but Dalby's arguments seem more persuasive than those of his opponents — which are, frankly, little above the 'pig Latin' stage of etymological sophistication. The familiar Southern explanation of borrowing from Blacks, that aristocratic Whites had Black 'mammies' and learned a lot of language from them, modified by the sociolinguist's realization that 'mammy's' children, who constituted a temporary peer group, were much more plausible agents of transmission, has even received some acceptance from more orthodox students of dialect. (See the quotation from Wolfram, above.)

It cannot, of course, possibly be maintained that the totality of Black English grammatical structure derives from Anglo-Irish. Neither can the baby talk or language deficit explanations be considered to have any surviving adherents in the respectable academic tradition. The remaining barrier to acceptance of the Creolist formulation is the appeal to language universals. This is a highly respectable and significant part of modern linguistics, and no one really wants to argue against the position that language universals do exist. It could still be asked, however, that the appeal to universals be applied impartially: if it is to affect one's interpretation of a list provided by Joan Baratz (1969, 1970, 1971), it should also be applied to the materials of Cleanth Brooks (1935).

Some changes have been made in recent years, and rightly so, in our notions of language acquisition. Carol Chomsky (1971) has given us an excellent argument that acquisition of a grammar goes on longer than linguists had assumed in the days when they glibly called the child aged five or six (sometimes four!) a 'linguistic adult'. Nevertheless, C. Chomsky's demonstrations with regard to differentiating *promise John to go* and *tell John to go* surely do not cancel out what had been learned earlier about the acquisition of suffix morphemes. In the case of markers like the *-s* of the possessive, such studies as exist (*pace* Wolfram 1974:525) do seem to indicate that children of five or so are 'beyond the age of language acquisition' *for that particular form*. And elicitation from ghetto children six to ten years old, that shows unmarked possessives (*Mary hat, he book*) may still be taken as evidence for the Creolist hypothesis.

Multiple negation in Black English has regularly been claimed as an Anglicist characteristic, since the veriest sophomore can quote a line from the Prologue to Chaucer's Canterbury Tales containing three negative markers. Significantly, multiple negation is never referred to 'linguistic universals', probably because orthodox linguists have been able to reach the desired conclusion without utilizing the new weapon. As Labov (1972) shows, however, Black English does not have merely double negatives or multiple negation but *negative concord*. Birmingham's article (this volume) compares, however tentatively, BEV multiple concord to the negation patterns of Papiamentu. No study of Papiamentu negation comes even close to the scope of the Labov article, but it is clear that Papiamentu adds negative markers where Spanish, notorious for its 'double negative', would not. The evidence does seem to suggest that Papiamentu has a concord-like negation rule; something of the same type has developed in the Black English Vernacular since about 1830 (Dillard 1972).

Unpidgin-like as negative concord seems, the beginnings of Black English in West African Pidgin English nevertheless seem to provide the best solution for the development of the negative concord rule. The process involves not only creolization but partial decreolization, clearly stated by Stewart (1967, 1968) but rather carelessly disregarded by many critics. Neither have the Creolists ever asserted that the whole process reflects 'African influence' or the like, without any relationship to other nonstandard American English dialects. (In fact, such influence is precisely what is subsumed in 'decreolization'.) Starting from a pidgin/creole negation base of,

NP no VP

Black English has expanded the all-purpose negator *no* to *didn't, ain't, don't* (and, in some cases, *not*) to match the underlying verbal categories of the variety (Fickett 1975). The careful analysis of the negation pattern made by Labov (1972) together with the data about the nature of pidgin languages give us an important insight into the history of Black English.

A new crop of young linguists, not tied by training to the Anglocentric theory, is beginning to provide historical insight into the relationship between Black English and other Afro-American varieties. Birmingham's work has been mentioned above. John and Angela Rickford provide valuable comparisons to West Indian language forms, especially those of Guyana (formerly British Guiana). John Holm adds much to the little that is known about the Creole English of the Caribbean shore of Central America. Along the way, he adds evidence (see, also, Dillard 1971) that the 'zero copula' could hardly have been produced by 'contraction and deletion' of the English present-tense forms of *be*, since it occurs freely with past-time adverbs. (See also Loflin et al. 1973.) There seems to be a further valid objection to Labov's (1969) contraction–deletion rules in that they are not independently motivated in the BE phonology but brought in ad hoc to explain away what otherwise would be syntactic rules.[2]

Ian F. Hancock's work (1969, 1972, 1976) on English Creole and related varieties, especially Krio, is already well known. In Part Four his article on Texan Gullah gives one of the first accounts of a relatively isolated population of speakers of something very like the dialect of the Low Country ('Sea Islands') first given academic currency in Turner (1949). By the standards of Stewart (1967, 1968) and Dillard (1972) it is not necessary to assume that such a creole-like variety of Black English is 'Gullah', since their thesis is that Gullah itself is merely a localized survivor of a generalized plantation creole. Hancock does, however, draw some convincing specific parallels to the Sea Island variety; and his contention that the South Carolina–Georgia coastal dialect probably extended down to Florida, whence the Seminoles migrated to Texas and beyond, is well taken.

Robert Berdan and Riley Smith are more immediately concerned with what the academic and linguistic world now knows as 'Black English'. They provide further documentation of the thesis, advanced as early as 1965 in an article by Beryl Bailey, about grammatical differences between the Black English Vernacular and ordinary English. At the time of the Bailey article, syntax was automatically considered to be synonymous with 'deep structure', with no reference to semantics needed, and the argument for a deep structure difference was an earth-shaking argument indeed. Since that time, linguistic theories about deep structure have gained much sophistication. It is not, then, surprising that Berdan and Smith do not stress the 'deep structure' aspects quite so much as Bailey (or as Loflin, for that matter). Still, they represent serious research work on the language variety called Black English, and they find differences that are more significant than a mere percentage of 'deletions' of the /-z/ of the third person singular, non-past verb.

Barth's article may be said to have opened, in its quiet manner, the way into exploring lexical and semantic independence for Black English. (Thus, even if 'deep structure' is no longer defined in the terms in which B. Bailey defined it, her perception of deep structure differences may still be valid within the changing framework.) Barth's researches not only found Black–White semantic differences and displayed them in a valid research framework with interpretations perfectly in line with the best traditions of relativism; he also predicted the reactions of some who did not have that sophistication and would see 'deficient' language.[3]

It is not enough, however, to mouth the conventional pieties about Black English being 'not deficient'. Any linguist, for about one hundred years, would have agreed with that statement. A little more commitment is necessary if any kind of significance is to be achieved. Grammatical differences have been claimed by Stewart (1967, 1968, 1970, 1972), Loflin (1967, 1970), and Fickett (1970, 1975), among others. In many cases, it is claimed that such statements are 'outdated', that 'newer developments' in linguistics show the triviality of those merely syntactic insights.

If that be the case, then the semantic implications of materials like those of Rickford and Rickford on lexical collocations (see also Dillard 1977) become of increasing importance. Their materials, and those of Dalby (1972) do not happen to be presented in the currently fashionable format of the pluses and minuses of semantic features, but the presentation could easily be translated into that form. And the significance of differing collocations of lexical material — either the combinations would not be made in other dialects of English, or they would not have the same meaning — has surely not been bypassed by linguistic fashion.[4]

NOTES

1. Ian F. Hancock (personal communication) points out that *zydeco*, a term for a type of Black folk music in Louisiana, may have a more respectable etymology than *les haricots*, the dominant folk etymology for the word. Yula, a Gur language of French West Africa, has *zade-ko* 'dance', where *ko* appears to be a copula. See Dillard (1977:39) for some commentary on the origin of *rock* (*and roll*), where I am also indebted to Hancock.

It must be emphasized that we are not doing 'etymologies' in the conventional sense that we think we have identified the African language picture, for the slave population was far too complex for that. But a bald claim that Yula is 'the source' for *zydeco* would be no more naïve than the derivation of e.g. *ofay* from 'pig Latin'. Even though exact tracing may never prove to be possible, at least we feel that we can disprove some of the absurd notions that have been in vogue, especially such ideas as that Black English has some special relationship to children's language games.

Nevertheless, the probability of African vocabulary survivals in special vocabularies — like 'infantile' *yum yum* (see Dillard 1975a) — is strengthened almost every time we probe deeper into special language varieties. Goldin et al. (1950) list, for example, *yam yam* '(Negro term: rare among whites). An opium-gum pill, especially for chewing or dissolving in the mouth'. For other special applications of Afro-Creole *nyam nyam* see Major (1970) and Dillard (1977).

2. I owe this observation to Mervyn Alleyne, in a talk before the Linguistic Institute in 1976, not, insofar as I know, otherwise published or scheduled for publication.

Obviously, the form *you Ø* (from *you are*) is independently motivated by a phonological rule of Black English, almost all varieties of which are 'r-less' in nonprevocalic position.

The occurrence of forms like, 'I'm Adj, You Adj, He Adj', leads almost paradigmatically to the assumption of contraction and deletion. The assumption that contraction has taken place in the first is, however, considerably complicated by the widely observed occurrence of both *I'm is* and *I'm am*. Careless application of the 'deletion' rule can produce horrors like the following, from Ronald Wardhaugh's *Topics in Applied Linguis-*

tics (1974:190–191): 'Likewise, the use, or non-use of *be* is different, as in *He be here soon* and *He here soon*'. Any kind of care in reading the sources that Wardhaugh cites should have made him aware that, '*He here soon' is completely ungrammatical in the Black English Vernacular. It is doubly unfortunate that this book is on applied linguistics, for teachers who may deal with Black students. There are many respects in which Black English forms seem like deletions and may be perceived to be grammatical matters only through historical comparison or observation of hypercorrection in acropetal (i.e. toward more Standard English) shifting. A sentence like: 'You suppose to say "I doesn't"?' can be very misleading, since virtually everyone can be assumed to have been exposed to the superficial phonological information that the 'd' of *supposed to* is never articulated (except in hyperformal styles, like perhaps that of the word caller at a spelling bee) by a native speaker of English. But the question form, in an acrolect-oriented style which is not, like basilect, without *do*-support, yields further information: 'Do you suppose to say "I doesn't"?' See Berdan's article (this volume) for an excellent illustration of how rules that are phonological by superficial observation, turn out, on fuller examination, to be syntactic.

3. For a survey of deficit theory, see Baratz and Baratz (1969).

4. Bickerton (1977) apparently misses this point. Otherwise, he might not have objected so strenuously to my inclusion, in *Perspectives on Black English*, of J. A. Harrison's 'Negro English', which contains interesting cases of such collocations even if it is worthless otherwise.

ERNEST A. T. BARTH

The Language Behavior of Negroes and Whites

In developing the principle of linguistic relativity Benjamin Whorf has contended that language shapes man's view of the world so thoroughly that 'users of markedly different grammars are pointed by their grammars toward different types of observations and different evaluations of externally similar sets of observations, and hence are not equivalent as observers but must arrive at somewhat different views of the world'.[1] While this position emphasizes the functions of language for the individual it underplays the significance of the social role of language.

Roger Brown has suggested a distinction between *language*, which is a formal system composed of a phonology, a morphology, and a grammar; and *thought* which he defines as a set of cognitive categories manifest in the discriminating use of names.[2] With respect to meaning (equated in some ways with 'thought') Floyd Allport rejects the doctrine of linguistic relativism, asserting that 'meanings . . . cannot be originally given by signs of objects. They are not "mediated", but are derived directly from dealing with the objects themselves.'[3] Allport is obviously stressing the development of the relationship between meanings and signs which occurs in the process of socialization. He goes on to observe that 'much confusion has arisen because of the tendency to identify meaning in toto with language and to think that when we have covered the semantic aspect we have solved the problem'.[4] The process of learning to associate meaning with symbols takes place in a social setting. Given changes in the character of this setting there will be changes in the meanings attributed to symbols.

Applying this line of reasoning to the specific context of social relations it may be concluded that there is a direct relationship between the forms of social organization experienced by a child and the meaning which that child comes to attach to symbols used in communication concerning these relationships. In an article entitled 'Language, logic and culture', Mills presents a similar view. Emphasizing language as a process, he asserts

Reprinted from *Pacific Sociological Review* 4(2): 69–72 (Fall 1961) by permission of the publisher, Sage Publications, Inc.

that 'newly sanctioned social habits force new meanings and changes in old meanings'.[5] He further contends that 'language, socially built and maintained, embodies implicit exhortations and social evaluations. . . . A vocabulary is not merely a string of words; immanent within it are societal textures — institutional and political coordinates. Back of a vocabulary lie sets of collective action.'[6]

A test of the relationships between meaning, patterns of social organization, and the formal organization of a symbol system is very difficult when the subjects studied do not share a common language. It is a simpler task when a common symbol system exists as is the case with American Negroes and American Whites. Under these circumstances if one could show that different patterns of social organization are systematically associated with different meanings for mutually used terms, or if one could show that converging patterns of social organization are associated with convergences in the meanings of terms, a substantial step would have been taken in the development of a theory of language.

This paper reviews a pilot study undertaken to explore one approach to the identification of linguistic differences between Negroes and Whites. The following rationale underlies our expectation of differences in the language behavior of Negroes and Whites.

American communities are characterized by a high degree of residential and institutional segregation of the Negro population. Thus, the rates of interaction *within* racial groups are much higher than they are *between* racial groups. As a result of their position as a minority racial group, the vast majority of Negroes experience common status problems. These are manifest in their conceptions of self, in their relations with other Negroes, and in their relations with Whites. The high rates of interaction among Negroes, combined with the status problems they experience produce certain norms common to Negroes within the Negro community. In addition to these normative differentials numerous studies have documented the existence of differences in the forms of family, political, economic, and religious organization as compared to the white community. In such a setting it is to be expected that the social experiences through which words take on meanings for these Negroes will be differentiated from those experienced by Whites. Words associated with these settings will have systematically different meanings for members of the two racial categories.

What is the nature of these differences in meanings? The following suggestions are based upon the analysis of a series of recorded interviews with Negro family members from a project designed for another purpose. The language behavior of these Negroes appeared to differ in three ways from that of Whites of a comparable status level. First, words seemed to have a more *personalized meaning* for the Negroes. They were used to refer to self and self experiences. Second, they appeared to be used in an *evaluative, emotive fashion* rather than in a denotative fashion. Finally, the subjects tended to use words in a *less abstract*, categorical manner than do Whites.

A word of caution might be added at this point. It is not contended that there will be no differences in the linguistic patterns within the Negro population. Differences would be expected to arise as a result of variations in class and regional background.[7] In addition, some Negroes will not have been raised within the setting of the Negro community and would therefore not be expected to follow the linguistic patterns of that community.

THE STUDY

General Approach: There are several possible approaches to the study of racial linguistic patterns. For example, Roher and Edmonson examined differences in dialect among Negroes in New Orleans.[8] In another study Johnson found that Negro respondents were particularly sensitive to certain words and phrases often used by Whites.[9] The emotional reactions to these resulted in communicative barriers between Negroes and Whites.

In this study the approach was slightly different. It consisted of an analysis of differences in the use of words which are common to the vocabulary of both Negroes and Whites. It seems likely that if Negroes and Whites use the same words in communicating with one another and yet attach different meanings to these, effective communications across racial lines would be difficult and interaction strained, even in situations characterized by approval of interracial contacts.

Study Design: Fifteen white and fifteen male Negro respondents were interviewed. They were all students at the University of Washington and their ages ranged from 18 to 21 years. In all cases but one their fathers had completed at least some college and on this basis they were roughly classified as 'middle class'.

Data Collection: The data were collected by means of a questionnaire administered in a personal interview by a student interviewer. A list of ten words was presented with sufficient space following each word for the respondent to write a short paragraph defining that word. The following instructions were given:

On this and the next page we have listed several words. Following each word space is provided for a short paragraph. We would like you to define each word in your own way, telling us what it means to you. Work as rapidly as possible and try to indicate how you would use the word in your normal conversation.

At the end of the questionnaire, additional information was secured on the subject's age, residential history, father's occupation, and father's educational attainment. The ten words selected for use are listed in Table 1.

Table 1. *Number of respondents making self references in their definitions of ten words — by race of respondent*

	Race of respondents	
	Negro	White
Word defined	(N = 15)	(N = 15)
Home	9	9
Color	6	1
Minority	6	0
Father	7	1
Neighborhood	4	0
Scholarship	0	0
Job	8	1
Slum	0	0
Sex	1	0
Policeman	0	0

Data Analysis. Three categories of analysis were used in classifying the data. They included (1) self reference–no self reference in the definition of the term; (2) the level of generality characteristic of each definition; and (3) the degree of emotionality reflected in each definition.

If in his definition, the respondent made use of any personal pronouns such a I, my, or our, the definition was classified as 'self reference'. If, in any fashion, he indicated that the phenomenon being discussed was one of a class, his definition was classified as 'high generality'. Finally, if any emotion-denoting terms were used in the definition, it was classified as 'high emotionality'.

The selection of these categories was based in part on direct experience in communication with Negro family members. They are, however, closely related to three of four categories used by Schatzman and Strauss in their analysis of modes of communication reflected in interview protocols from working and middle class respondents. One of their categories, 'perspective or centering', which they define as the standpoint from which a description is made is similar to the one we have labeled 'self reference'. Our 'level of generality' category closely resembles their 'classification and classificatory relations'. Finally, our 'emotionality' category fits into their conception of 'organizing frameworks and stylistic devices'. The definition for each of the ten terms was coded dichotomously on each of these three dimensions. Word by word tabulations were then made.

THE FINDINGS

In general, the findings appear to bear out the hypothesis that differences in word usage between Negroes and Whites do exist and that they may be identified in the fashion noted above. Table 1 presents the findings concerning the use of self reference in the definition of these words. It may be noted that in general, the Negro respondents made references to self far more extensively than did the Whites. This was particularly true of the words *father, minority, color, neighborhood*, and *job*. A majority of the respondents in both groups made reference to self in defining the word *home*.

Table 2 presents the findings on the use of emotion-denoting adjectives. Again, the words *color, minority, father, neighborhood*, and *job*, evoked different responses from Negroes than from Whites with the Negroes reflecting a higher level of emotionality. The word *home* evoked more frequent emotionality from the white respondents, as did the word *sex*, although the differences here are small.

The patterns of response analysed on the basis of level of generality are presented in Table 3. Here, except in the case of the words *color* and *minority*, the data do not bear out the hypothesis. In fact, the words *father, scholarship*, and *sex*, appear to evoke more general definitions from the Negro respondents.

INTERPRETATION

On the basis of what we know in general about the socialization of Negro children, a process which usually leaves them acutely conscious of their racial status, we would expect that any symbols related to minority status would be associated with significant personal emotional experiences. Our findings with respect to the patterns of meaning associated with two such words (i.e. *color* and *minority*) support this expectation. Additional sup-

port comes from the findings that words such as *father, neighborhood*, and
job, all more or less specifically expressive of specific aspects of the Negro
minority status, evoked more personalized and emotional connotations
from our Negro respondents.

Table 2. *Number of respondents using emotion-denoting adjectives
in their definitions of ten words—by race of respondent*

Word defined	Race of respondents	
	Negro ($N = 15$)	White ($N = 15$)
Home	8	11
Color	6	0
Minority	6	3
Father	7	3
Neighborhood	6	3
Scholarship	0	0
Job	4	2
Slum	2	1
Sex	1	3
Policeman	0	1

Table 3. *Number of respondents reflecting a low level of generality
in their definitions of ten words—by race of respondent*

Word defined	Race of respondents	
	Negro ($N = 15$)	White ($N = 15$)
Home	7	8
Color	11	5
Minority	11	5
Father	4	7
Neighborhood	7	7
Scholarship	2	7
Job	6	5
Slum	6	6
Sex	3	5
Policeman	5	5

The failure of words such as *scholarship, slum*, and *policeman* to evoke differential patterns of response from Negroes and Whites is probably a consequence of our selection of middle-class respondents. For the most part these students have been raised in an integrated school system. There have been no excessive slum areas in Seattle even in the Negro areas of the city and repeated investigations have failed to uncover any systematic police brutality toward minority people. Obviously, with such scanty evidence as we have here, any speculation about the relationship between position in the social organization and the meanings of verbal symbols is tenuous. However, further study of this relationship seems warranted on the basis of the findings which have been presented.

IMPLICATIONS

There are two immediate implications deriving from this line of research. One of these involves the diagnosis of some educational problems facing Negro children in integrated school settings. It would appear that the Negro child coming from a segregated community comes to school equipped with a basically different pattern of linguistic orientation from that of his white teachers and his fellow students. Academic failure among such students has frequently been attributed to 'poor motivation' and to 'poor home training'. To the extent that academic performance is also a product of linguistic differences, if there is failure to understand the teacher because of these linguistic barriers to communication, then the provision of 'equal educational opportunities for minority children' would seem to be a far more difficult task than it has thus far been considered. It will involve far more than a simple equating of physical facilities and a mechanical social integration in the class room. Far more attention will have to be directed to the problem of facilitating effective interpersonal communication.

There is a second implication in this approach to the study of Negro–White relations. It may be helpful in advancing our understanding of *cliquing behavior* in certain types of situations. Repeated notice has been made of the fact that Negroes and Whites tend to form racially segregated cliques in settings relatively free of the more obvious forms of racial prejudice and where participants in the situations are actively interested in promoting more friendly relations. Examples of such behavior have been observed in integrated housing developments, churches, and among the student bodies of integrated schools. It seems likely that the type of linguistic barriers to effective communication here discussed could produce feelings of uneasiness and frustration for both Negroes and Whites when they interact. Because they appear to share a common language, members of both groups tend to explain that the social strains they experience in interaction as a result of racial differences — 'they're just different from us'. This leads to a withdrawal into racial cliques.

One final interpretive comment: if extensive and systematic linguistic differences are established in future research, these differences could be used as a basis for establishing the boundaries of the minority Negro community, and would facilitate the study of the minority community as a subsystem within the setting of the larger dominant community. It is apparent that the visibility criterion is inadequate for this purpose in view of the rather complete dissociation from the minority community of some Negroes who live and work in the larger community.

NOTES

1. Harry Hoijer (1954), *Language in Culture*, p. 132. Chicago, University of Chicago Press.
2. Roger Brown (1958), *Words and Things*, p. 260. Glencoe, The Free Press.
3. Floyd Allport (1955), *Theories of Perception and the Concept of Structure*, p. 573. New York, John Wiley and Sons.
4. Ibid., p. 573.
5. C. Wright Mills, (1939), 'Language, logic, and culture', *American Sociological Review* 4 (October):676.
6. Ibid., p. 677.
7. Leonard Schatzman and Anselm Strauss (1955), 'Social class and modes of communication', *American Journal of Sociology* 64 (January):329–338.
8. J. H. Roher and M. Edmonson (1960), *The Eighth Generation*. New York, Harper and Brothers.
9. R. Johnson (1957), 'Negro reactions to minority group status', in *American Minorities*, ed. by Milton Barron. New York, Alfred A. Knopf.

IAN F. HANCOCK

Texan Gullah: The Creole English of the Brackettville Afro-Seminoles

INTRODUCTION

The Afro-Seminole population dealt with in this article is linguistically related to the Gullah speakers of the Georgia and South Carolina coast and the Sea Islands, speaking a closely related dialect within the community in certain social situations. The historical and linguistic links between the Texas/Mexico and the Atlantic coast dialects is briefly dealt with in this study, which is in two parts. These were circulated separately as Occasional Paper No. 3 (April 1975) and Occasional Paper No. 7 (March 1977) of the Society for Caribbean Linguistics. The first presents conclusions based upon analysis of a tape-recording of a dialogue in English with an inhabitant of the town of Brackettville, before a field trip to that community had been made. The second was written two years later, after a preliminary survey of the linguistic situation in Brackettville had been undertaken. In large part it confirms the suggestions presented in the earlier study.

More recent investigation indicates that the same language also survives in Hughes, Seminole, Okfuskee and Okmulgee counties in Oklahoma, and possibly in Florida and the Bahamas as well.

I. CREOLE FEATURES IN THE AFRO-SEMINOLE SPEECH OF BRACKETTVILLE, TEXAS

1.0.0. The present transcription is from a tape-recording made by Mr. Walter Wakefield of Austin, Texas, in Brackettville, on August 1st 1970. Credit and thanks are due to him for making it available for study.
1.0.1. The following is a brief historical account[1] of a community inhabiting several towns in the Texas–Mexico border area, but centered mainly in Brackettville, Texas. Apart from its involved and turbulent history, the community is notable for its dialect of English, which appears to have preserved many Afro-American creole features acquired in Georgia and Florida during the eighteenth and nineteenth centuries.

1.1.0. *Historical background*

1.1.1. During the early decades of settlement in the North American southeast, Indian slavery was almost as widespread as the slavery of Africans. In South Carolina in 1708, for example, there were 1,400 Indian slaves, and slightly more than twice that number of African slaves. At that time, Florida was dominated politically by Spain, and runaway slaves, both Indian and African, were able to find refuge and protection there according to Spanish law. The area which is now the state of Georgia did not become a Royal province until 1755, and was inhabited largely by the Creek nation. Florida did not join the United States until 1819.

1.1.2. Many different Indian peoples settled in the Florida hinterland,[2] although the Creeks were by far the most numerous. These came to be known as the *Seminoles*, a Creek word meaning 'fugitive' or 'maroon'. The term does not refer to a specific ethnic group. The Seminoles in Florida were entitled to settle on whatever unoccupied land they could find, and were accorded the same rights and privileges as the rest of the population. They soon established many semi-independent settlements throughout northwestern Florida, where escaped African slaves were made welcome.

1.1.3. The Seminoles, like the Whites, still maintained a master–slave relationship with the Blacks, but here the similarity ended. Africans in Seminole communities were able to own homes, farms, and cattle, and were given considerable freedom in comparison with their earlier situation. They were required to give a portion of their income to their owners, but as Foster (1935:28) notes, their influence within the communities was so great that they 'in fact . . . governed' the Seminoles themselves.

1.2.0. At the close of the War of Independence in 1783, the authorities of the new State of Georgia reportedly drew up a treaty with the Creek Indians, who occupied 100 towns through the region, providing for the return of all Blacks who were living at that time under the protection of the Creeks. The Creeks subsequently denied the existence of such a treaty, and failed to comply with its terms. A troubled period followed, with outbreaks of hostilities between the Georgian Whites and the Georgian Creeks, until in 1789 government intervention established calm between them.

1.2.1. At this time, the Georgian Creeks took it upon themselves to speak on behalf of the Florida Seminoles over the border to the south. This was unjustified since the Seminoles (also known as the 'Lower Creeks') regarded themselves as Spanish rather than American citizens.

1.2.2. The trouble between Georgia and Florida continued, with Georgia sending contingents into Florida in (usually unsuccessful) attempts to bring back the renegade slaves. The situation was not improved for the Georgians with the renewal of British–American hostilities in 1812; in 1814, Lord Cochrane arrived in Maryland and proclaimed that all who were still loyal to the Crown would be settled as free persons in the British West Indies. Even though the British were unsuccessful, slaveowners in Georgia found it difficult to maintain the support of their slaves, who were anxious to leave for the Caribbean and liberty.

1.2.3. While this was going on in the southeast, British attacks in New Orleans during the same year (1814) were being successfully repulsed by the American troops. American concern about the free Seminole settlements in Florida continued, especially since it was felt that such settlements were a disruptive influence upon the U.S. slave states bordering them.

1.2.4. In 1816, the U.S. Army set out once and for all to destroy the Seminole forts. The army, with 500 Georgian Creeks (who were still hostile to the Seminoles because of the 1789 incident, see 1.2.1. above), attacked Fort Nichols, the 'Negro Fort', which was a major Seminole stockade on the Appalachicola River. This was entirely successful, and none of the Seminoles escaped unhurt.

1.2.5. After this initial victory, the U.S. troops moved on to other settlements, but the inhabitants here were better prepared, and after two years of fighting with a 50 percent loss of men on both sides, the U.S. withdrew defeated.

1.3.0. Despite their victory, the Seminoles and their African slaves had suffered such a loss that they had become easy prey to continuous independent raids from the north, and as a result were steadily losing slaves. The subagent for the Florida Indians formally claimed that the situation had reached a point where any further American aggressions would inevitably result in more unnecessary loss of life, and suggested that a wholesale relocation of the population further west was in the Seminoles' best interests.

1.3.1. This ran counter to the aims of the U.S. government who wanted to see the Seminoles reunited with the Creeks and their slaves also returned to the United States. Nevertheless the agent was proven right, and in 1833 the U.S. government arranged for eight Seminole chiefs to tour the central states in order to find suitable territory for relocation.

1.3.2. Although this was just an exploratory trip, when the chiefs returned to Florida they found that their lands had been sold in their absence, and that relocation was inevitable.

1.3.3. The Seminoles and Blacks realized that they were being taken advantage of by the Americans, and decided that war was the only solution. Two hundred and fifty Blacks and 1,660 Indians prepared to fight rather than to continue to lose their land and fellow men, or be relocated against their will.

1.3.4. In December 1836, fighting began. During the months which followed the Seminoles and renegade Blacks had several minor victories, but suffered overall, and by mid-1837 reluctantly agreed to migrate west.[3] At this time some of the Seminoles accepted an invitation from the Cherokees to settle with them on their land, while several hundred others were able to remain in Florida. The majority however left for Arkansas, Oklahoma and elsewhere. The entire conflict had cost the U.S. government forty million dollars.

1.4.0. Eastern Arkansas was not very far from Creek-occupied country, and it was not difficult for the Creeks, who were still antagonistic toward the Seminoles, to organize vendettas against them. They were so successful in stealing the Seminole Blacks and selling them as slaves in Arkansas — a slave state — that the Seminoles felt once again compelled to move on. Thus in 1849 ca. 300 Indians and Blacks left for Mexico.

1.4.1. Journeying southwestwards through Texas, they encountered the Kickapoo who had been relocated earlier, and together they crossed into Mexico at Eagle Pass. Exclusive of the Kickapoo, the number of Blacks and Indians who settled in Musquiz (then Santa Rosa) in Coahuila State, was about 300. Soon after the community moved once more, to an allotment of land in Colonia Nacimiento comprising some eight square miles, about ten miles from Musquiz. Life here was comparatively peaceful except for occasional slave-seeking raids from Texas during the 1850s, usually to the disadvantage of the Texans.

1.5.0. During the late 1860s, west Texan Indian groups such as the Kickapoo and Kiowa were causing considerable trouble by preventing white overlanders from settling in the area. The Afro-Seminoles in El Nacimiento had a reputation as good fighters, and the U.S. government met with the government of Mexico in 1870 to negotiate for the resettlement of some of the Seminole Blacks in Texas to help quell the Indian fighting there.

1.5.1. In August 1870, an estimated 75 to 125 Afro-Seminoles settled in Fort Duncan at Eagle Pass, and in Fort Clark (now Brackettville), to act as scouts for the U.S. army against the Indians.

1.5.2. Here they established their own Amerindian way of life, quite distinct from the Afro-Americans around them. Even today, the Brackettville Afro-Seminoles refer to other Americans, both black and white, as 'American race' or 'state race' people. Although almost wholly African racially, culturally the scouts were Indian, and resisted formal education for fear of losing their Indian ways as a consequence (Foster 1935:48).

1.5.3. In 1914 the need for military scouts came to an end, and Fort Clark was dismantled. The Afro-Seminoles dispersed to other localities: Del Rio, Ozona, Kerrville, San Antonio, and others, but the majority settled in Brackettville itself. Foster (1935:49) counted 67 Afro-Seminole families in Brackettville in 1935; today that number appears to have diminished somewhat.

1.5.4. Because of earlier miscegenation laws, it has been the practice of the El Nacimiento and Brackettville communities, separated from each other by some 200 miles of road, to find mates within their own and each other's communities. This intercommunity relationship continues, although there is an increasing occurrence of outmarriage with Afro-Americans. Despite an overwhelmingly African genetic ancestry, the present-day Afro-Seminoles call themselves Seminoles, or even more specifically 'Mikasuki' or 'Kickapoo', and regard themselves as being quite distinct from the surrounding population.

2.0.0. *Linguistic background*

2.0.1. It is apparent from the present data that the African maroons who took refuge with the Florida Seminoles spoke and retained a creolized variety of English. Whether it was specifically Gullah or not is another matter; nevertheless it had many features in common with Gullah and the other Atlantic creoles. There is some evidence that this same Gullah-like speech has been transmitted to the Seminoles still living in Florida (Moore-Wilson 1928:*passim*) and may also be found in the Oklahoma Seminole communities (Foster 1935:52).

2.1.0. According to Chafe (1962:166), the Kickapoo language is still spoken in the northern Mexico community by approximately 500 people, an equal number speaking the language in the Oklahoma and Kansas reservations. The Creek language however does not seem to have survived among the Texas/Mexico Afro-Seminoles, although Foster (1935:50) notes that their English and Spanish are 'poor and mixed with various Indian words'.

2.1.1. Foster was not a linguist, and may be forgiven for stating that 'there is not enough difference in their language to require a great deal of attention' (1935:53). He notes (1935:53) that

Their English shows a few particularly noticeable characteristics. The use of 'him' for 'her' and 'he' for 'she' is very common. 'It' may be used for man or woman. This use is found among the Seminole Negroes of Oklahoma, showing similar backgrounds.
Other peculiarities exist which show that these Seminoles had Southern contact

years ago, but a few of them are peculiar to the Seminole Negroes. The misuse of the pronouns above is one of them. Most of the older persons cannot express the future perfect in any manner so that it can be understood by a stranger. Their usage of English words varies enough from ordinary English to merit this question: Can you understand Creek? This question will frequently be asked a stranger. Many of them think that the term Creek really expresses the name of the language they speak.

2.1.2. Foster gives examples of Afro-Seminole English:

De Mexicans did not know dat we wus dere eder. John Horse he told dem when we wus ready to tell de Mexicans dat we wus dare. Later Wild Cat took sick with de pox and he die. We all wus crying fur we done lost him. He was so good. John Horse, or Juan Cavallas, our next head man, but de Injuns most of dem been gone back to de territory (1935:43).

She was a good man. She was an Injun-fighter. She was tuff; she didn't care how a big a bunch dey wus; she wint into 'em every time; she look after his men; his men was on equality too; she didn't stand back and dey go jonder, she would say 'come on boys, let's go get 'em' (1935:47–48).

2.1.3. The above representations differ somewhat from the text that follows, which exhibits less interference from standard (and eye dialect!). It is transcribed from a tape-recorded interview with one Brackettville resident, Mr. Alfred Gordon, who was born in 1889 to Isaac Gordon, a Seminole scout, and who has lived and worked in various parts of the South and Southwest.
2.2.0. While a more detailed and accurate linguistic analysis remains to be undertaken,[4] some of the more obvious points of grammatical similarity with the Atlantic creoles may be demonstrated. These are discussed following the transcription. This consists of excerpts from a much longer tape-recording, and is given in sequence, though not contiguously. The orthography is broadly phonemic and employs IPA notation. Intonation contours are not shown, though these share some similarity with Caribbean English Creole rather than Gullah, in places. Pause is indicated by / and //.
2.2.1. Mr. Wakefield who made the recording had the impression that the informant was making efforts to standardize his speech for the interview, and normally spoke a more basilectal variety.

3.0.0. *Transcription*

1. bʌd aʸ hæd ə liːdl̩ aʸ hæ⊢d ə fiːəl// maʸ daːdiʸ had əfiːəl n̩ aːftə hiʸ daʸ wɛl

2. aʸ plan dæⱡt təl afdɜ now wɔ:də dɛn aʸ kwɪtʔn̩ *(indistinct)* bəd dat *(indistinct)*

3. wəz wiʸ own // bəd aʸ wəz dɪ ownliʸ / yʌŋgɛs maⱶn dat bɪnz *(?)* ə bɔɪ dat bɪn lɛf //

4. a: yɛs // a:tə də twɛlß mɪ əz dɪ oʷnlɪ wʌn lɛf // aʸ pla:ntɛn / had ə lɪdl̩ go:t n̩

5. hɔ:sɛz / n̩ kaʷtɪl də bɔ:də // aftə ɪ gɪt so draʸ aʸ saʸd tə kwɪt n̩ kʌm oʷn bæk oʷ ɛə //

6. ðeʸ da:diy / aʸ dɪdn̩ gɛt tu noʷ ðɛm da:diy / kəz a wəz / aʸ gɛs aʸ wəz tuw smɔ:l //

7. bəd ɒ:l dɪ bɪlɒksiʸ dɛm / ɒ:l dʌ ʸd ʌp / bət wʌn ə dɛ: sʌn / bət dat ɪz ɪn sanandžɛloʷ //

8. sʌm lɪß iʸn nasəmyɛntə tuʷə də faktə dɛm / ən / sʌm ə ðə wɪlsən/bʌt ðe kɒ:l əm

9. baskəs / yu siʸ dɛm *(indistinct)* bɛ mɛskən neʸm /bʌt ðeʸ fɑ:ðə wəz wɪlsən //

10. roʷzə θeʸ / hiʸ dʌ ʸd / sʌm ə hɪz da:tə / wɛl naʷdə se:m wʌn aʸm təlɪn y əbaʷt

11. ə: džɛɪ danyəl / hiʸ marɪd tə wʌn ə roʷzə fe: da:tə / hiʸ li:v daʷntaʷn ɔn dɪs haʸwe /

12. das we: ɒn də lɪdl laʸt yuʷsə klaʸm ʌp ɒn də hɪl raʸd ɒn də raʸd ha:n saʸd fo yu klaʸm

13. də lɪdl hɪl raʸt we: šiʸ lɪb / džɛɪ danyəl //

14. džɒn gɔt ə sʌn bʌt dat ɪz ʌp ɪn oʷzoʷnə / neʸm ə fraŋk džɛfəsɪn kɜʸliʸ də ʌdə sɔ:n

15. bəd hiʸz wɜʸkɪn aʷd ɒn ə ræntš|/'das liʸrɔʸ džɛfəsən //dɛm tuʷ bredəz//dɛm hæv sɔ:n /

16. džɒn n̩ kɜʸliʸ // dɔliʸ'džuwlaʸ / ə / deʸ gad ə da:tə luʷsiʸ / huʷlɪv ʌp ɒn də hi:l /

17. hiʸ hʌzbən ɪz džoʷ wɪlsən / hɪ wɔz ə soʷldžə / n̩ džɒn džuʷlaʸ hiʸ lɪb raʸd in taʷn

18. ɒn də nɛks striʸt //

19. džuʷlyə pe:n / hiʸ wəz mʌ:ʸ mɔrɪnlɔ: / hiʸ / ɔ:l hɪz sɔn n̩ da:tə dɛm dʌ ʸd ʌp / ɔ:l

20. dʌ ʸd ʌp //

21. ɛlsə šiʸ dʌ ʸ tuʷ / hiʸ / hiʸ / hiʸz niʸs dɛm ɪz in mɛsɪko //

22. siyzə / hiʸ wəz wʌn ə dɛm danyəl / wɛl a noʷ yʌŋ siʸzə / dat wəz kən džɔniʸ sɔn /

23. hi wɜᵏkɪn ʌp dɛ :rɒn ə ræntš // bəd aʸ gɛs me:biʸ yuʷ də miʸn dɪ o:l siʸzə iz ɔŋkʊl //

24. las mʌnt wɛn / wɛn dɪs wʌn yʌ ɪm kʌm / a a:ks əm ṇ šiʸ tɛl miʸ de dɪdṇ gɛd ɪt aʷt

25. yɛt / ṇ a tɛl əm wɛl doʷn troʷ dɛm pɪktšəz weʸ / a wɔʷn dɛm pɪkšə //

26. dɛm nɛvə gɛt tə siʸ dɛm mʌðə / wɛn dɪs wʌn yiə / dɪs o:ldɪs wʌn / ɛn dɪs nɛks gɜl /

27. wən dɪs wəz sɪks ye: ṇ dɪs wʐ faɪ / wɛl dɛn dɛm mʌdə daʸ // niʸdə wʌn nɛbə gɪt tə noʷ

28. dəm mʌdə // ɪf de mʌdə wəz lɪbən de kʊdə kʌm o:ə iyə ṇ nɛbə niʸd no pe:pə / bʌt yʊ

29. siʸ deʸ fa:də ɪz ə mɛsəkən sɪtɪzṇ / ɛn de to: miʸ dat de kya:n biʸ ə / ma grantšɪrən

30. dɛm kʊdṇ biʸ əmɛrɪkŋ sɪdɪzṇ //

31. de hæftə gɪd aʷd ə pəmɪt //

32. ɪm a:ks mɪ m̩ sɛ yuʷ ɪz əmɛrɪkŋ sɪdɪz ṇ ? // a tɛl ʌm a:m əmɛrɪkŋ sɪdɪzṇ ṇ ma waʸf ɪz

33. əmɛrɪkən sɪ / sɪdɪzṇ / boʷf əv əs bɒ:n in br / ɪn ə nyuʷnaʸdɪd ste:t ɪn brakɪt //

34. dɛn yɒ:l toʷl miʸ ðat *(indistinct)* mʌs bɪn brɪŋ dɪ / dɪ mʌnɪ ṇ yɒ:l kʊd ə fɪks ɪt ʌp //

35. yuʷ kya:n fɪks noʷ kaʸn ə pe:pə fə yə grantšɪlən //

36. šiʸ stʌdɪyɪn fə nɜʸs / wɛl šɪ sɛ šiʸ stʌdɪyɪn fə dat bɪkʊ ɪ maʸd marɪd ṇ ɛn ɪ maʸd

37. nɔt / ṇ ɛf ɪ gɛt tə o:ʷl leʸdɪ i av sʌmtɪŋ tə duʷ / ə lɪdḷ i:ziʸ džɒb //

38. ṇ aʸ had ə pɪkšə bət aʸ do:n no:ʷ // ɒ:lwe:z wɛn a pak əm i:n ma bɪlfo:l bʌt a

39. gɛs a dʌn te: əm ʌp //

4.0.0.

'But I had a little — I had a field — my daddy had a field and after he die I plant that till after no water, then I quitting (. . .) but that (. . .) was we own. But I was the only — youngest man that beens (?) a boy that been left. Ah yes. After də twelve me 'uz the only one left. I planting, had a little goat and horses, and cow, till the border. After he got so dry I decide to quit and come out back over here.

They daddy, I didn't get to know them daddy, because I was — I guess I was too small.

But all the Biloxi them, all died up but one of their son, but that is in San Angelo.

Some live in Nacimiento, two of the Factor them, and, some of they Wilson, but they call them Vascos (?) you see them (. . .) bear Mexican name, but their father was Wilson.

Rosa Thay (?), he died — some of his daughter — well now, the same one I'm telling you about ə Jerry Daniels, he married to one of Rosa Thay daughter; he live down town on this highway. That's way on the little light, used to climb up on the hill, right on the right hand side before you climb the little hill right where she live. Jerry Daniels.

John got a son, but that is up in Ozona; name of Frank Jefferson. Curly the other son, but he's working out on a ranch. That's LeRoy Jefferson. Them two brothers them have son, John and Curly. Dolly July, ə they got a daughter Lucy who live up on the hill; he husband is Joe Wilson — he was a soldier. And John July, he live right in town on the next street.

Julia Payne, he was my mother-in-law. He — all his son and daughter them died up; all died up.

Elsa, she died too. He — he — his niece them is in Mexico.

Cæsar — he was one of them Daniel — well I know young Cæsar, that was Cou'n Johnny son — he working up there on a ranch. But I guess maybe you də mean the old Cæsar, his uncle.

Last month when — when this one here him come, I ask him and she tell me they didn't get it out yet, and I tell him, "well don't throw them pictures away, I want them picture. . .".

Them never get to see them mother. When this one here, this oldest one, and this next girl, when this was six year and this was five, well, then them mother die. Neither one never get to know them mother. If they mother was living, they could have come over here and never need no papers, but you see they father is a Mexican citizen, and they told me that they can't be a — my grandchildren them couldn't be American citizen.

They have to get out a permit.

Him ask me him say, 'you is American citizen?'. I tell him I'm American citizen and my wife is American ci- citizen, both of us born in Br- in ə Nyunited State in Brackett.

Then y'all told me that (. . .) must been bring the — the money, and y'all could have fix it up.

You can't fix no kind of paper for your grandchildren.

She studying for nurse; well, she say she studying for that because he might married and then he might not, and if he get to old lady, he have something to do, a little easy job.

And I had a picture, but I don't know — always when I pack əm in my billfold, but I guess I done tear əm up.'

5.0.0. *Principal characteristics of Alfred Gordon's speech*

5.0.1. Phonologically the informant's speech shares several characteristics with Gullah and other creoles. The examples listed here are followed by line reference to the transcription (pp. 310–312). Comparisons are made with other creoles and are also referenced.
5.0.2. Forms such as the following are especially reminiscent of the creoles: [nyuʷnaˑtɪd] (33), cf. Gullah [ɲuˈnɒɪtɪd] (Turner 1949:243), also Jamaica and elsewhere; [marɪd] (36) 'marry', also Krio, Gullah (Gonzales 1922:312), Jamaican (Cassidy and Le Page 1967:294); [da:tə] (10, 19) 'daughter', widespread Caribbean; [brɛdə(z)] (15) 'brother(s)', also Gullah (Gonzales 1922:290), Jamaican (Cassidy and Le Page 1967:68), and widespread Caribbean.
5.0.3. Most of the nonstandard features of Alfred Gordon's speech, however, while occurring in the Caribbean creoles, and in Gullah especially, are also widely found in decreolized dialects of Afro-American. These include: [kya:n] (29, 35) 'can't'; [dɛm] (*passim*) 'them'; [sʌmtɪŋ] (37) 'something'; [kən] (22) 'cousin'; [(gran) tšɪrən] (29), [(gran) tšɪlən] (35) 'grandchildren'; [mɔrɪnlɔ:] (19) 'mother-in-law'; [boʷf] (33) 'both'; [nɜˑs] (36) 'nurse'; [kɜˑliˑ] (14, 16) 'Curly'; [wɜˑkɪn] (15) 'working'; [lɪb] (17) 'live'; [lɪbən] (28) 'living'; [nɛbə] (28) 'never'; [te:] (39) 'tear'.

5.1.0. *Unmarked grammatical relationships*

5.1.1. *Ø-preterite*: 'after he die' (1–2), 'them never get to see them mother' (26), 'I tell him I'm American citizen' (32), 'then them mother die' (27).
Cf. Gullah 'I finish pay for this' (Cunningham 1971:55), 'I call [əm] to cut my hair' (Cunningham 1971:47); Jamaican *aata im dai, di fuors taim mi sii im, mi kaal im fi kot mi iir*; Krio *afta i dai, di fɔs tɛm we a si am, a kɔl am fɔ bab mi ia.*

5.1.2. *Ø-auxiliary*: 'she studying' (36), 'John got a son' (14), 'I planting' (4), 'he married to one of Rosa Thay daughter' (11).
Cf. Gullah 'I still looking' (Cunningham 1971:66); Jamaican *im stodiin, Jan gat a son a plaantin, im marid a wan a Ruoza Tie daata*; Krio *Jɔn gɛt bɔi-pikin.*
5.1.3. *Ø-plural*: 'one of Rosa Thay daughter' (11), 'goat, and horses, and cow' (4–5), 'one of their son' (7), 'some of they Wilson' (8), 'some of his daughter' (10), 'them have son' (15).
Cf. Gullah 'these teacher good', 'I done get them check' (Cunningham 1971:31); Jamaican *wan a Ruoza Tie daata, guot, haas an kou, wan dem son, som dem Wilsan, som a im daata, dem gat son*; Krio *wan Roza Te gyal-pikin, got, ɔs ɛn kau, wan dɛm bɔi-pikin, sɔn dɛm Wilsin, dɛm gɛt bɔi-pikin.*
5.1.4. *Ø-future*: 'if he get to old lady, he have something to do' (37).
Cf. Gullah 'I be too glad to see y'all' (Cunningham 1971:79). In Jamaican and Krio future is generally marked by *wi* and *go* respectively; in both however the aspect marker JC *a*; Kr *de*, can include the future (see Bailey 1966:46): Jamaican *mi naa tel im di truut* 'I am/will not tell/telling him the truth'; Krio *a nɔ de go tɔŋ* 'I am not going/will not go to town'.
5.1.5. *Ø-genitive*: 'cou'n Johnny son' (22), 'Rosa Thay daughter' (11).
Cf. Gullah 'we been see that man thief that man car' (Cunningham 1971:65); Jamaican *ko Jani son, Ruoza Tie daata, da man kyaa*; Krio *kɔz Jɔni bɔi-pikin, Roza Te gyal-pikin, da man ka.*
5.1.6. *Ø-3rd person sg. agreement*: 'he live down town' (11), 'where she live' (13).
Cf. Gullah 'she shake my hand' (Cunningham 1971:77), 'he stay a preacher' (Cunningham 1971:50); Jamaican *im lib dong tong, we im lib, im shiek mi an*, Krio *i tap dɔŋ tɔŋ, we i tap, i shɛk mi an.*
5.1.7. *Ø-copula*: 'Curly the other son' (14).
Cf. Gullah 'how your boy?' (Cunningham 1971:148), 'I not no singer' (Cunningham 1971:83). Not discussed for Jamaican (which regularly has *a*: '*Kuorli a di oda son*'); very rare in Krio (which regularly has *na*: *Kuli na di ɔda pikin*), but cf. Krio *tide us de? tide mi bafde* 'what day is today? today is my birthday'.
5.1.8. *Ø-gender distinction*: 'he husband is Joe Wilson' (17), 'he was my mother-in-law' (19), 'his niece them is in Mexico' (21), 'because he might married' (36).
Cf. Gullah 'he ask me to clean the house' (Cunningham 1970:47); Jamaican *im ozban a Juo Wilsan, im waz mi madanlaa, im niis dem de a Meksikuo, kyaang im maita marid*, Krio *i man na Jo Wilsin, i na bin mi mɔdɛnlɔ, i nis dɛm de Mɛksiko, bikɔs sɔntɛm i bin fɔ mared.*

5.2.0. *Other features primarily considered creole*

5.2.1. /bɪn/ *as past-marker*: 'a boy that been left' (3), 'must been bring the money' (34).
Cf. Gullah 'we been see that man', 'you feel like you been feel' (Cunningham 1971:65); Jamaican *wan bwai we (b)en~bin lef, mos (b)en bin~bring di moni*; Krio *wan bɔbc we bin lɛf, mɔs bin briŋ di kɔpɔ kam*.

5.2.2. /də/~/ə/ *as copula:* 'after də twelve' (4) (?), 'the same one I'm telling you about ə Jerry Daniels' (10–11), 'ə they got a daughter Lucy' (16) (?).
Cunningham (1971:40) lists only *is* as the equative verb, although earlier texts show /də/. Cf. *dish'yuh duh de oxin* (Gonzales 1922:75). Jamaican has *da~a: aata a twelv, di siem wan mi a tel yu bout a Jeri Danyelz, a dem gat a daata Luusi*. Krio has only *na: di sem wan we a de tɛl yu bɔt na Jɛri Danyɛls, na dɛm gɛt wan gyal-pikin we nɛm Lusi*.

5.2.3. /də/ *as aspect marker*: 'you də mean the old Cæsar' (23).
Cf. Gullah 'he də try for sing a song' (Cunningham 1971:54), 'I still də look' (Cunningham 1971:67); Jamaican *im a trai fi sing sang, mi stil a luk*; Krio *i de trai fɔ siŋ wan siŋ*.

5.2.4. *Demonstrative for personal pronouns*: 'John got a son, but that is up in Ozona' (14), '. . . one of their son, but that is in San Angelo' (7), 'when this was six year and this was five' (27).
Not recorded in Cunningham or Bailey for Gullah or Jamaican. Cf., however, its parallel in Krio: *Jɔn gɛt pikin, bɔt da de Ozona, we dis bin ol siks yia ɛn dis bin ol faiv yia, na dat gi mi di sup*.

5.2.5. /-dem/ *plural*: 'all the Biloxi them' (7), 'two of the Factor them' (8), 'them two brothers them' (15), 'all his son and daughter them' (19), 'his niece them' (21).
In Gullah this survives only as an 'and Co.' indicator. Cf. 'Richard-them is my mother brother', 'they don't allow no man in there around the sister-them', (Cunningham 1971:29). Both functions (i.e. and Co. and plural) occur in Jamaican and Krio: Jamaican *Ruupat dem* 'Rupert and his group', *di tuu breda dem, aal im son an daata dem, im niis dem*, Krio *Rupat dɛm, di tu brɔda dɛm, ɔl ĩ pikin dɛm*.

5.2.6. /əm/~/ʌm/ *as 3rd person object pronoun*: 'I guess I done tear əm up' (38–39), 'I tell ʌm I'm American' (32), 'always when I pack əm in my billfold' (38).
Cf. Gullah 'I couldn't be see əm' (Cunningham 1971:72), 'I call əm happy' (Cunningham 1971:106); Jamaican *mi kudn sii am, di wie di taim tan, mi kyaan uon am* (Cassidy and Le Page 1967:8); Krio *a nɔ bin ebul fɔ si am, a kɔl am api, luk am*.

5.2.7. /say/ *as complementizer*: (?) 'Him ask me əm say, "You is American citizen?" ' (32).
Cf. Gullah 'I tell my wife say, "well, I must got cramp" ', 'you ain't hear say a snake bite Sarah's child?' (Cunningham 1971:48); Jamaican *mi tel mi waif se mi mosa gat kramp, yu no yier se sniek bait Siera pikni*?, Krio *a tɛl mi wɛf se a mɔs dɔn gɛt kramp, yu nɔ yɛri se snɛk bin bɛt Sera ī pikin?*.

5.3.0. *Nonstandard features less specifically creole*

5.3.1. *Variable pronominal case*: 'me 'uz the only one left' (4), 'they daddy' (6), 'he husband' (17), 'we own' (3), 'them daddy' (6), 'them bear Mexican name' (9), 'him come' (24).
Cf. Gullah 'them give əm little bit' (Cunningham 1971:24), 'I married she' (Cunningham 1971:43), 'she name is Bertha' (Cunningham 1971:92, 21), 'me gwine gie you six day mo' (Jones 1888:70), 'hongry biggin fuh ketch we' (Gonzales 1922:231); Jamaican, *dem gi im likl bit, mi marid shi, honggri bigin fi kech wi*; Krio *dɛm gi am lili bit, aŋgri bigin fɔ kech wi, mi nɔ no we im brɔda de*.
5.3.2. *Use of pronoun after noun*: 'Elsa, she died too' (21), 'Rosa Thay, he died' (10), 'Jerry Daniels, he married' (11), 'John July, he live right in town' (17), 'Julia Payne, he was my mother-in-law' (19), 'Cæsar, he was one of them Daniel' (22), 'when this one here him come' (24). Cf. also 5.2.5. above.
Cf. Gullah 'Buh Rabbit him say "Hey titter, enty you guine tan one side?" ' (Jones 1888:8); Jamaican *den a we Mieri him de?* (Bailey 1962:40); Krio *mi a nɔ wā go*; Cameroon Pidgin *mi sef a de go, i sef i de čɔp am* (Dwyer and Smith n.d.:380).
5.3.3. *Use of 'is' for 'are'*: 'his niece them is in Mexico' (21), 'You is American citizen?' (32).
Cf. Gullah 'them is the king of the rattlesnake' (Cunningham 1971:41), and for 'am', 'I is a citizen of Edisto' (Cunningham 1971:92); Jamaican *dem iz som a mi fren, yu iz a fuul, sa*. This does not occur in Krio.
5.3.4. */for/ as infinitive marker*: 'she studying for nurse' (36) (?).
Cf. Gullah 'he də try for sing a song' (Cunningham 1971:177); Jamaican *im a trai fi sing sang, im a stodi fi nuors*; Krio *i de trai fɔ siŋ wan siŋ, i de stɔdi fɔ nɔs ~i de stɔdi fɔ bi nɔs*.
5.3.5. *Double negatives*: 'never need no paper' (28), 'neither one never get to know . . .' (27), 'you can't fix no kind of paper' (35).
Cf. Gullah 'he ain't got no kin folks' (Cunningham 1971: 82), 'You can don't plant none, you ain't go get none' (Cunningham 1971:84); Jamaican *non a di pikni dem neba si notn, no waata no de a hous*; Krio *i nɔ gɛt nɔn fambul, n'ɔn di pikin dɛm nɔ si natin*.

5.3.6. /done/ as completive aspect marker: 'I guess I done tear əm up'
(38–39).
Cf. Gullah 'that chicken be already done stew' (Cunningham 1971:124),
'you see, you done do it' (Cunningham 1971:69); Jamaican *mi don tel
unu trii taim se unu aal fi guo, im don wiekop aaredi*; Krio *a dɔn tɛl una tri
tɛm se una fɔ go, i dɔn wek, di rɛs dɔn kuk*.
5.3.7. *Nominal absolute with 'own'*: 'that . . . was we own' (2–3).
Cf. Gullah 'that house is Bee own' (Cunningham 1971:41), 'wear hənə
own' (Cunningham 1971:22); Jamaican *fi yu hous biga dan mi pupa uon,
dat a wi uon*; Krio *dat na bin wi yon, da os na Bi yon, yu os big pas mi dadi
yon*. Note that while absolute forms with *own* occur both in West African
Creole and in Guyana and Trinidad where West African Creole influence
is extensive, it is not recorded for Barbados, which uses *mi wan, hi wan*,
etc., or Sranan, which uses *fu mi, fu en*, etc.

II. FURTHER OBSERVATIONS ON AFRO-SEMINOLE CREOLE

'The sable slave, from Georgia's utmost bounds,
Escapes for life into the Great Wahoo.
Here he has left afar the savage hounds
And human hunters that did late pursue;
There in the hommock darkly hid from view,
His wretched limbs are stretched awhile to rest,
Till some kind Seminole shall guide him thro',
To where by hound nor hunter more distrest,
He in a flow'ry home shall be the
red man's guest'
Albery Whitman, *Twasinta's Seminoles*

6.0.0. Since I wrote the earlier part of this article, further investigation
has provided answers to several of the points raised therein.
6.0.1. It was suggested that Mr. Alfred Gordon[5], upon a recording of
whose speech the first part of the article was based, was employing an
acrolectal variety and otherwise spoke something more creolized. This
has proved to be the case. The question of whether or not the source of
Brackettville Afro-Seminole Creole was in fact Gullah was also addressed, but left unanswered; it is now possible to confirm that with very few
differing characteristics, the language as spoken in Brackettville and El
Nacimiento today represents an offshoot of Georgia Gullah,[6] and is in
some respects more conservative or archaic than the modern Atlantic
Coast dialects of that language.

6.2.0. The history of the Brackettville Seminoles was outlined in my earlier discussion; a few additional observations are included here.

6.2.1. Sturtevant (1971:103) places the beginning of the Seminoles as a distinct group at around 1770, when their first settlements in Florida were being formed. The earliest documented use of the term *Seminole* is found in an English report dated 1765.[7]

6.2.2. It seems that there has been in fact less intermarriage between African and Indian Seminoles than previously supposed; Sturtevant (1971:109) remarks on 'evidence of social separateness in the fact that blood group frequencies prove that the modern Florida Seminoles have almost no Negro ancestry'. Nevertheless Indian characteristics, cultural and physiognomical, are evident in the Brackettville population; family names such as *Warrior* ['wɔɪə] and *Bowlegs* ['boleɪg(z)] occur, and certain of their songs are clearly of Indian origin. In addition, some individuals were able to produce words and phrases in an (unidentified) Indian language: [kwa] and [kwa'hi], 'greetings', ['tonoko'ke:tɛʔkætoʔ] (meaning unknown), [kewa:n' ɪkɪnoʔke:pɑko:kɔʔ], 'What have you done today?', ['kɔka'yɛna], 'I worked today' and so on.[8] A popular local dish in Brackettville called ['sʌfki], prepared with ground corn, is known among the Florida Seminoles, and its name is of Muskogean origin (Musk. *sá·fki*) according to Sturtevant (1971:113).

6.2.3. It is possible that the Indian genetic element may in part be traceable to intermarriage with the Kickapoo (in ASC ['kɪkipu]), who although historically unrelated to the Seminoles live very near the community at El Nacimiento in Coahuila State, Mexico, from which the Brackettville families descend. Although current reports from various individuals give the impression that there is now no socializing between the Seminoles and the Kickapoos at El Nacimiento, others writing earlier speak of the first Seminole (Blacks) who 'made friends with the Kickapoos and other neighboring Indians and intermarried with them' (Foster 1935:46).

6.2.4. The Indian element is further weakened by the fact that most of the Indian Seminoles remained in Oklahoma, from where the Mexican group had come in 1849. Wright (1957:237) notes that of the over 2,000 Seminoles now resident in Oklahoma, 'approximately 50 per cent . . . are fullblood Indian . . . Some admixture with Negro is found, but has not been socially recognized, these people mostly living among the freedmen, descendants of former Negro slaves in the Seminole Nation'.

6.2.5. It was also the case that the Indians among the group settling in Mexico soon returned to Oklahoma, leaving just two families among the Afro-Seminole remainder (Sturtevant 1971:109; Foster 1935:46) and in addition, it appears that around 1866, a journey was made from El

Nacimiento to the Oklahoma-Arkansas settlements and a further ca. 37 Seminole Blacks were brought back to Mexico.[9]

6.2.6. Dickerson (1952:592) puts the number of El Nacimiento Seminoles who came to Texas in 1872 at about 500 (cf. Foster's figure of about 300). They were asked to come and man Fort Clark, now a tourist resort in Brackettville, in order to help the federal troops drive the Plains Indians out of West Texas in the 1874–1875 campaign;[10] this they were able to accomplish successfully under the command of General Bullis. These scouts and their descendants are buried in the Seminole Scout Cemetery some four miles southwest of Brackettville, and a Seminole Scout Cemetery Association has been established in recent years to ensure its upkeep.

6.3.0. After Fort Clark was dismantled in 1914 the Seminoles were treated rather ungratefully by the U.S. government, whose reply to a letter dated July 22, 1914, from Henry Breckenridge, Assistant Secretary of War, suggesting that the Seminoles were entitled to a 'portion of some Indian reservation where they could be made self-sustaining', bears reproducing as a prime example of bureaucratic double-talk:

If any rights as Indians still existed in these people, it would come by virtue of their Seminole blood. By Section 2 of the Act of April 26, 1906 (34 Statute L. 137), the rolls of the Seminole tribe were closed as of March 4, 1907, since which date the Secretary of the Interior has no power to add any names thereto. Having no other Indian blood in their veins they would not be entitled under existing laws, to either land or money with any of the other Indian tribes of the United States. It is not seen, therefore, how this Department is in a position to extend any relief to the persons referred to in your communications (Woodhull 1937:127).

6.3.1. Another communication from the Secretary of the Interior answering a similar enquiry noted the same year that, 'No allotments can be made to them as Seminoles and, of course, there is no provision of law for making allotments to them as Negroes' (Woodhull 1937:127).

6.3.2. Today the community in Brackettville has no land of its own except the cemetery, and lives among the 1,400 or so other inhabitants of the town itself, working mainly on the surrounding ranches and sheep farms.

7.0.0. *Linguistic discussion*

7.0.1. Those who provided conversation and discussion in and about their language included among the men, WW (about 47 years), CD (63 years) and CB (42 years), and among the women EB (57 years), EW (about 53 years), HD (74 years), AF (about 60 years), MP (69 years) and VJ (about 70 years).

7.1.0. Afro-Seminole Creole is still spoken by nearly all members of the community older than about 50, though one of the best speakers was a man in his mid-40s. People younger than this usually cannot speak the Creole, though most of them understand it. The language seems to be disappearing, though as a result of nonuse by succeeding generations rather than by gradual decreolization, as is the case with Gullah.

7.1.1. Speakers are quite aware that ASC, usually called by them ['sɪmɪnol], is something different from English, and despite a certain amount of variation (cross-interference) in each system, are able at any time to say what language they are speaking. Only one woman, interestingly by repute the best speaker in the whole community, called the Creole 'Flat English', and used the name *Seminole* to refer to the Indian language, presumably Creek (cf. 1.2.2.).

7.1.2. While knowledge of ASC is widespread, it seems seldom to be used in everyday conversation, Spanish or English being used instead. It may indeed be that the widespread knowledge and use of Spanish has slowed down the decreolization process. Afro-Seminoles have possibly been bilingual in Spanish and ASC since the beginning, acquiring the Spanish language in Florida and only later learning English after arrival in Texas; evidence of Spanish among the Oklahoma or Bahamian groups would support this hypothesis. Although Foster comments to the contrary (1935:52), Mexican-Americans in Brackettville have remarked on the 'good quality' of the Spanish of the Afro-Seminoles, and one suggested that it didn't sound like any of the local varieties.[11]

7.1.3. The English of some of the very old people in particular is clearly influenced by ASC (but cf. 2.2.2.); one lady who claimed that she couldn't speak the Creole said she [nʌ no haʊ fə tɔ:k əm] 'didn't know how to speak it', and it was said of another, who was particularly proud of her speech, that she wouldn't [laɪt̩n ʌp ɪ tʌŋ fə nobadi], 'lighten up her tongue (i.e. speak English) for anyone'.

7.1.4. The term ['bækrə] ~ ['bʌkro] has acquired an extended meaning in ASC; while in Gullah it means only a White, in Brackettville it has come to mean 'outsider', 'non-Seminole', also referred to as 'state raise' or 'American raise' people, black or white. One woman whose husband was an Afro-American was said to have married a ['bʌkro].

7.1.5. It is generally believed that an even more basilectal variety of Creole is spoken in El Nacimiento, where the only languages are ASC and Spanish, English being unknown. It is also said that despite a knowledge of ASC in that settlement, the everyday language there is Spanish.

7.1.6. Two people in Brackettville said that they had encountered West

Indians, and one had met some Pidgin-English-speaking students from Nigeria; all three commented on the similarities shared by the speech of those people and ASC.[12]

7.1.7. Despite an awareness of the distinctive character of ASC and of the fact that it is different enough from English to be unintelligible, a fairly widespread feeling is evident that it is an inferior mode of speech. It may be because of this and its resulting suppression outside the group that many local Whites were unaware of its existence when questioned,[13] despite the fact that interracial social contacts are surprisingly relaxed for that part of the South. No segregation was apparent in bars, neighborhoods or churches among Seminoles, Mexican-Americans or Whites. Representatives of each group were pleased to draw attention to this fact.

7.2.0. The first characteristic in a comparison between ASC and Gullah is the apparent absence of extensive African-derived lexicon in the former. Only a few of those items listed in Turner (1949:190–208) were recognized, viz. [tot] 'carry', ['kutə] 'tortoise', from KiKóongo and Manding respectively, though both also widely used outside Gullah territory, and ['bʌkrə], discussed above at 2.1.4. from Efik, found in Gullah, Jamaican, and Sranan, but not Krio.

7.2.1. Since of Turner's ca. 450 Gullah words of African origin a great proportion are of Mende (Sierra Leone) origin (Hair 1965:81–82; Hancock 1979) this is to be expected, since the Mende did not reach Freetown or the Sierra Leonean coast until the early nineteenth century (Fyfe 1962:6; Hancock 1971:447), and were not transported into Gullah-speaking North America until long after the Afro-Seminoles had made their separation. While it is possible to determine early influence from Krio upon Gullah, influences from Sierra Leonean Mende, Fula, and Vai are probably post-1820.[14]

7.2.2. The problem of establishing the *immediate* source of Gullah still remains; by 1720 African slaves already outnumbered West Indian slaves in Gullah territory, yet the acoustic impression of ASC is markedly Caribbean; this is all the clearer since when using English the speakers employ an intonation much closer to that associated with Black English. This is apparent in the following recorded example of code-switching:

[ɪf yu wɒnt tə seɪ yə fɑːðə yə seɪ yu daːdɪ]
'If you want to say 'your father' you say [yu daːdɪ]'

7.2.3. Other 'West Indian' intonational patterns are especially noticeable in such words as *bròthêr, sìstêr, bàbŷ, màmmŷ, sòmebŏdŷ* and so on. Similarly, the durative marker [də] ~ [ə] and forms of the verb with {-ɪn} are also Gullah and Caribbean, but not West African outside of Liberia. Expressions which have parallels in West Indian, such as [yu dɛ pɑ:n fu:l] 'you're being foolish' and [a tɛl əm fə gɪd ɪ rɑ:s aʊd ə he] 'I told him to get his ass out of here' also occur in Krio.

7.2.4. It appears to be the case that the earliest form of Gullah was a West Indian creole, and that influence from Krio (discussed in Hancock 1978) came later, and increased while West Indian influences gradually decreased. It is also possible that the intonation preserves the characteristics of earlier forms of English-derived Atlantic Creole, and that it has since become modified in Krio due to intense re-Africanization between 1820–1850, though the fact that Sranan does not share it either might argue against this.

8.0.0. *Grammatical characteristics*

8.0.1. Afro-Seminole Creole exhibits most of the features found in earlier transcriptions of Gullah, the differences being mainly phonological (the palatals [c] and [ɟ] recorded by Turner do not seem to occur, for example) and lexical (cf. 2.2.0.); note also that the customary action marker *blan*, rare even in Gullah and probably a late introduction from Krio, is unknown in ASC, and no use was recorded of the complementizer *se*, common in related creoles (cf. Cunningham 1970:167–168), including some varieties of Black English; [dæt], which is also the relativizer, is used instead: [a bɪn yɛdɪ dæt ɪ stan so] (EW) 'I heard that it was like that', [tɪŋz dɛm dæt ɪ ni:d] (EB) '(the) things that he needs'. Intonational patterns also differ from Gullah; recordings of contemporary basilectal South Carolina Gullah[15] played to a group of ASC speakers were readily understood, but it was remarked that the speakers were 'trying to speak Seminole', and not entirely convincingly.

8.1.0. Unmarked verbs usually have past reference:
[mɛk ɪm nə k3m]? (WW) 'Why didn't he come?'
[ʌ wek ʌp we: yandə fo de brʌk su:n də mɔ:nɪn] (CD) 'I woke up well before daybreak, early in the morning'.
[mi no du ɪt] (WW) 'I didn't do it'.
[ɑ:tə dɛm gʊ ho:m] (WW) 'Afterwards, they went home'.
There is one instance recorded of an unmarked verb with future reference: [yʊ bɛdə mɛk mɑ:nʌs, a gi yʊ wʌnbaha:n lɪk yʊ nɛvə fəgɪt] (CD) 'You'd better make your manners, or I'll give you a back-hand lick you'll never forget'.

8.1.1. As with all northwestern creoles,[16] the aspectual and copula markers (Krio and Sranan _de_ and _na_ respectively) have fallen together in ASC as [də]~[ə] (in Jamaican, _da/a_):

Aspect

[a:s dɪ bʌkrɛ wɔ ɪ də duɪn yʌ] (WW) 'Ask the outsider what he's doing here'.

[də we yʊ də gwaɪn]? (CD) 'Where is it you're going?'.

[haʊ hənə də du]? (WW) 'How are you (pl.) doing?'.

[yʊ də kɔ:l yʊ sɪstə, mɑ:n, yʊ wɔ̃:n ə fə kʌm ŋ si wɔ yʊ wɔ̃:, kʌm yʌ tɪtʌ] (CD) 'You're calling your sister, man, you want her to come and see what you want: come here [tɪtʌ]!'.

[yʊ də traɪ lɔv sʌmbɑdɪ dɛn] (CD) 'You're trying to love somebody, then'.

[wɛn dɪ pi:pɪl də gɛdə təgɛdə fə pre] (EB) 'When the people are gathering together to pray'.

[hudæ də de de də kraɪ]? (WW) 'Who's there crying?'.

[yʊ də laʃ əm, yʊ də wel əm] (CD) 'You lash him, you whale him'.

[wɔ yɔ:l dɛ se, yɔ:l də tɔ:k ɪndyɪn]? (EB) 'What are you (pl.) saying; are you speaking Indian?'.

Copula

[də hɪm de dɪ wɜn] (AF) 'He's the one'.

[bʌbə, dæ də yʊ brʌdə] (CD) '[bʌbə], that's your brother'.

[a nə də yɔ: ɔŋkl̩] (CD) 'I'm not your uncle'.

[nʌdə wʌd fə kutə də gofə] (WW) 'Another word for "cooter" is "gopher" '.

[hɪm də mi ɑ:ntɪ ɛn dɛm də sʌm ə wi kʌzn̩] (WW) 'She's my aunt, and those are some of our cousins'.

Aspectual [də] has the form [ə] after anterior marker [bɪn]:

[dɪs yeɪz bɪn ə hʌt mi ba:d dɪs pa:s tu tri de] (EB) 'This ear has been hurting me badly these past two or three days'.

[ɔ:l mɪ pi:pl̩ bɪn ə tɔ:k əm, haʊ a nɛbə gwaɪn tɔ:k əm]? (CD) 'All my people spoke it; how wouldn't I (also) speak it?'.

8.1.2. There is high consistency of occurrence of prephrasal [də], now rare in Gullah:

[də wɪsɛ yʊ bɪn yɛdɪ əm]? (EW) 'Where did you hear it?'.

[də we yʊ də gwaɪn] (EW) 'Where are you going?'.

[də dat mɛk ɪ dõ: wʌk] (CD) 'That's why it doesn't work'.

[də hɪm də dɪ wɜn] (AF) 'He's the one'.

[də dat ɪ ɲus fə du] (MP) 'That's what she used to do'.

8.1.3. The locative verb is [de]:

[nʌfə piːpɪl bɪn de] (CD) 'Plenty of people were there' (or perhaps better, 'there were a lot of people').

[nʌfə piːpl̩ de de, plɛnti ə de de] (CD) 'Plenty of people were there, plenty were there'.

[wɪtʃwe ɪ de]? (CD) 'Where is it?'.

[hudæ də de de də kraɪ]? (WW) 'Who's there crying?'.

[lɛf da wɔrə de rat naʊ] (CD) 'Leave that water be right now' or 'leave that water there right now'.

8.1.4. Future is indicated most commonly with [gwaɪn]~[gwʌ̃], etc.:

[ɪ nʌ gwã laɪtn̩ ʌp ɪ tʌŋ] (EB) 'She's not going to "lighten up her tongue" '.

[yu gwaɪn dɛd wʌn ə diːz deɪz] (WW) 'You're going to be dead one of these days'.

[yu gon daɪ tu] (WW) 'You're going to die too'.

The same speaker (WW) has the form [enə] (reduced from [gwaɪn] + [ə]):

[i na enə halə] 'He won't shout out'.

[i no ena se nʌtn̩] 'He won't say anything'.

[yu enə ded tu] 'You're going to be dead too'.

8.1.5. The past (anterior) marker is [bɪn]:

[a bɪn ʃʌm] (EW) 'I saw it'.

[də wɪsɛ yʊ bɪn yɛdɪ ʌm] (EW) 'Where did you hear it?'.

[dɛm bɪn ɲus fə tɔːk sɪmɪnol mo] (CD) 'They used to speak Seminole more'.

[de bɪn pʊt mi in dʒeːl] (WW) 'They put me in jail'.

[dɛm ɔːl bɪn krɔs ʌp] (CD) 'They were all crossed up' (i.e. of mixed ancestry).

There is one recorded instance of [bɪn] used verbally:

[hɪm bɪn ə laɪə] (WW) 'He was a lawyer'.

8.1.6. The completive aspect marker is [dʌn]:

[a dʌn brʌk əm naʊ] (EB) 'I've broken it now'.

8.1.7. [fə] 'should' and [bɪn fə] 'should have' occur in the following:

[yʊ fə lɛf da wɔrə] (CD) 'You should leave that water'.

[ɪ bɪn fə deːd] (WW) 'He should have died'.

[fə] might be functioning prepositionally (cf. West African Pidgin English) in:

[hi gɑt fə gɪt bæk fə skul] (EB) 'He has to get back to school'.

One instance of the use of [kʊdə] 'could have' was recorded:

[a kʊdə tɛl yʊ dat iːzɪ] (CD) 'I could have told you that easily'.

8.1.8. The usual negator is preverbal [nə] (~[nʌ]~[na]~[no]). This does not seem to have given way to forms deriving from *ain't* or *don't* except in one recorded example ([də dat mɛk ɪ dõː wʌk] (CD) 'That's why it doesn't work'), which is one of the first replacements to be made in the decreolization process. The ASC forms have probably survived because of the similar syntactic function and phonological form of Spanish *no*:

[tɪkyæ yʊ nʌ lɔs əm] (EB) 'Take care that you don't lose it'.

[nə lɑ:f] (WW) 'Don't laugh'.

[mi nə no] (VJ) 'I don't know'.

[a nʌ ʃʌm] (EW) 'I didn't see her'.

[mɛk ɪm nə kʌm] (WW) 'Why didn't he come'.

[a nə də yɔ: ɔŋkl̩] (CD) 'I'm not your uncle'.

[nʌ wes da glɑ:s ə ti] (HD) 'Don't spill that glass of tea'.

[a nʌ no] (WW) 'I don't know'.

[mi no du ɪt] (WW) 'I didn't do it'.

[na tri:t mi lak dat] (WW) 'Don't treat me like that'.

[ɛf yʊ no bɪliv mɪ] (WW) 'If you don't believe me'.

[yʊ na gɑt tɑɪm fə tɔ:k] (CD) 'You don't have time to talk'.

[i na enə halə] (WW) 'He's not going to shout out'.

[ɪ na dɛ pɑ:n fu:l] (CD) 'He's not being foolish'.

A number of examples were found with [nɛvə] as a marker of simple negation, parallelling the Eastern Nigerian Pidgin English use of the same word:

[a nɛvə mɛmbə] (EB) 'I don't remember'.

[haʊ a nɛbə gwaɪn tɔ:k əm]? (CD) 'How wouldn't I speak it (too)?'.

In one sentence [nɛvə] has the meaning 'never':

[wʌn bahɑ:n lɪk yu nɛvə fəgɪt] (CD) 'A back-hand lick you'll never forget'.

8.1.9. The pluralizing morpheme [dɛm] may occur after any noun phrase; in Gullah this has become restricted in use to plus-human noun phrases:

[fə rid ɪ bʊk dɛm ɛn raɪt tɪŋz dɛm dæt ɪ ni:d] (EB) 'To read his books and write (the) things he needs'.

8.2.0. Variation in the pronominal system is illustrated in the following sentences:

8.2.1.

[a nʌ no kʌ:, mɛkso mɪ no du it] (WW) 'I don't know, Cou(sin), why I didn't do it.

[yʊ kā: kɔ mi ɔŋkl̩ kouz a nə də yɔ: ɔŋkl̩] (CD) 'You can't call me "uncle" because I'm not your uncle'.

[a dɛs sə tæŋkfl̩ tʊ mɪ gɔ:d dæt a lɪb fə si: dɛm dʒɛnəre:ʃn̩] (EB) 'I'm just so thankful to my God that I've lived to see the generations (of grandchildren)'.

[a də gwaɪn ho:m fə si ma ʊmən n̩ fə i:t sʌmʔm fo a go də tʃʌtʃ (WW) 'I'm going home to see my wife and to eat something before I go to church'.

[dæs maɪ frẽːn saɪlɪs hɔːl] (WW) 'That's my friend Silas Hall'.
8.2.2.
[tɪkyæ yʊ nʌ lɔs əm] (EB) 'Take care that you don't lose it'.
[a nə də yɔː ɔŋkl̩] (CD) 'I'm not your uncle'.
[dæ də yə brʌdə] (CD) 'That's your brother'.
[yu oːn bɪgə] (EB) 'Yours is bigger'.
[iːt yʊ bɪtl̩ miːn iːt yʊ fuːd] 'Eat your victuals means eat your food'.
8.2.3.
[wɔ ɪ də duɪn yʌ] (WW) 'What is he doing here?'.
[ɪ dõː wʌk] (CD) 'It doesn't work'.
[də dat ɪ ɲus fə du] (MP) 'That's what she used to do'.
[ɪ tɛk yʊ maːmɪ ɔ yʊ daːdɪ fə du ɪt] (CD) 'It takes your mother or your father to do it'.
[haʊ ɪ stan] (CD) 'What's it like?'.
[hi gɑt fə gɪtbæk fə skul naʊ bɪkʌz nilɪ skul sun aʊt tu mɔnt] (EB) 'He has to get back to school now because school will soon be out in two months'.
[hɪm tɛk lɪl tes ə dɪ maʃ] (WW) 'He took a little sip of the whisky'.
[hɪm hɪt tʃu] (WW) 'He hit you'.
[hɪm də mɪ ɑːntɪ] (WW) 'She's my aunt'.
[wʌ də hɪm] (CD) 'What is it?'.
[oːbə tə hɪm ræntʃ] (EB) 'Over at his ranch'.
8.2.4. No examples of [wi] in subject position recorded:
[lɛ wi go ŋ gi əm tə rəm rad əwe] (EB) 'Let's go and give it to her right away'.
[fə kip seːdənt fəm wi do] (CD) 'To keep Satan from our door'.
8.2.5.
[mɛkso hənə nə staːt wɪdaʊt mi] (WW) 'Why didn't you (pl.) start without me?'.
[haʊ hənə də du] (WW) 'How are you (pl.) doing?'.
[sʌmʌtʃ ə tɪŋ fə tɛl hənə] (CD) 'So many things to tell you (pl.)'.
[dɛm də hənə frɛn, ɛntɪ] (WW) 'They are your (pl.) friends, aren't they?'.
[wɔ yɔːl dɛ se, yɔːl də tɔːk ɪndyɪn] (EB) 'What are you (pl.) saying; you're speaking Indian'.
8.2.6.
[de bɪn pʊt mi in dʒeːl] (WW) 'They put me in jail'.
[dɛm bɪn ɲus fə tɔːk sɪmɪnol mo] (CD) 'They used to speak Seminole more'.
[dɛm də sʌm ə wi kʌzn̩] (WW) 'They are some of our cousins'.
[ɑːtə dəm gʊ hoːm fə mɛk beːbɪ] (WW) 'Afterwards, they went home to make love'.

[a no dɛm gwã̄ fəgɪt dɛm ɪnstəmənt] (CB) 'I know they're going to forget their instruments'.

8.3.0. *Notes on individual items*

[bɪtl] 'food' (< victuals); Gullah and Caribbean, but not West African.

[brʌk] 'break'; derived from English preterite form *broke*. Common creole; cf. ASC [lɛf], [lɔs].

[bʌbə] 'brother'; also Gullah but not Caribbean; cf. Krio [bɔ̀bɔ́] 'small boy'.

[dɛ pɑːn fuːl] 'be acting foolishly'; this appears to be a frozen expression, use of Krio and Caribbean [de pan] as a habitual action marker being otherwise nonproductive in ASC.

[dɪʃʌ] 'this', also Gullah.

[duɪt] 'do it' may not be a decreolization of [du ʌm] since the two forms cooccur in Jamaican Creole as well.

[ʔɛʔɛ] Common exclamation of surprise in all Atlantic creoles.

[ɛntɪ] 'Questioning or reaffirming tag', Gullah and Krio: ASC [ɛntɪ dɪ maːnbɪn tɛl əm]? (WW) 'Certainly the man told him, didn't he?'.

[he] 'here' (more commonly [yʌ] or [hyʌ]). Same form in Guyanese; cf. [de] 'there'.

[hənə] 'you' (plural). Common Gullah form. Cf. Krio, Caribbean [una], [unu].

[kãː] 'can't'. The verb *can* has this negative in all Atlantic creoles outside of Surinam. Palatalization ([kyãː]) was noted but is rare in ASC where it would be expected in the light of its occurrence in Gullah and even some Texan varieties of Black English.

[laɪə] 'lawyer'; cf. [paɪzn̩].

[lɔs] 'lose'; ASC form derived from English preterite *loss*, probably originally present in the speech of the British sailors which the Africans first heard, since the Southwestern dialects (e.g. Dorset, Devon) have *loss* 'lose', *broke* 'break', *leff* 'leave' and so on.

[mɛk(so)] 'why'; Also Gullah. Probably reduced from an earlier phrase *[wɔ mɛk so]; cf. Krio [wetin mɛk], Jamaican [wa mek], 'why'.

[nʌfə] 'a lot of', also Gullah. Krio and Caribbean have [nɔf] (< *enough*), 'plenty'.

[ɲayam]~[ɲaŋam] 'eat'; apparently only for use with children, and not known to all speakers: [ɛf yʊ wɔ̃ː ʃo tʃɪlən haʊ fə iːt yʊ se ɲayam] (CD) 'If you want to show children how to eat, you say [ɲayam]'. Common creole.

[ɔ:l tu] 'both'. Gullah, Krio, etc.

[o:n] 'own', a common creole formation of possessive absolute construction: [yu o:n bɪgə dən hɪm o:n, ɛntɪ] (EB) 'Yours is bigger than his, isn't it?'.

[pi:pɪl] 'people'. In AF's speech the unstressed vowel in this word and others was [ɪ]. Noted also in [trɔbɪl] 'trouble' and [saɪlɪs] 'Silas' from other speakers.

[paɪzn̩] 'poison'. Retention of earlier [aɪ], modern [ɔɪ]. Also Gullah, Caribbean, but not Krio. Cf. [laɪə], 'lawyer'.

[rɑ:s] 'arse'; Krio and Caribbean; probably also Gullah but not recorded for that language.

[rəm] Form of the third person singular object pronoun after preceding word-final high back vowels: [gi əm tə rəm] (EB), 'Give it to her', noted as a feature in the same speaker's English as well. Also Krio and Gullah.

[sʌmʌtʃ] 'so much'; Gullah.

[swɪndʒ] 'Singe (feathers)': [swɪndʒ əm gʊd] (CD), 'Singe it well'. Also Gullah, Caribbean, and Krio.

[sɛdaʊn] 'sit'; also Gullah. Cf. Krio [sidɔm], Sranan [sidon], etc.

[sta:n] 'be like'; [aʊ ɪ sta:n]? 'what's it like?'.

[ʃʌm] 'see/saw him/her/it'; Also Gullah.

[tə] 'to; at'. Possibly related to Gullah prepositional[də], cf. ASC[dɛm pipɪl obə tə nasəmyɛntə] (EB), 'Those people over in Nacimiento', but *to* is also found with this function in southern U.S. dialects.

[tɪkyæ] 'take care'; Gullah, Krio, etc.

[tɪtʌ] 'sister'; Gullah. Cf. Jamaican [tita], Krio [tìtí], 'young girl'.

[traɪ] 'try', though in the sense recorded could have been interpreted as 'succeed' or 'try successfully', in which case parallelled by Krio and WAPE [trai].

[tʌmʌtʃ] 'too much', also 'very much': [a laɪk əm tʌmʌtʃ, yu də traɪ lɔv sʌmbadi dɛn] (CD), ' "I like her very much"; you're trying to love somebody, then'.

[tʃi:ʌ] 'chair'; Gullah, Krio, Caribbean.

[wɔɾə] 'water'; Gullah.

[wɪsɛ] 'where' (< *which side*), with the variants [wɛsə], [wɪsə] and [wɪtʃwe], cf. Krio and (older) Sranan [usai], Gullah [ßɪsaɪ].

[yaɪ] 'eye', common creole.

[yɛdɪ] 'hear', Gullah, cf. Krio [yèrí] (also archaic Jamaican).

[yeɪz] 'ear', Gullah, cf. Krio [yes], Jamaican [iez].

8.4.0. *Connected passages*

8.4.1.

[gʊt iːvnɪn, gʊt iːvnɪn, haʊ hənə, haʊ hənə də du, a hop hənə də du
faɪn, aɪ də du owraɪt, naʊ a dʌs kɜm yɜ təs iːvnɪn tə si: haʊ yɔːl dʊɪn n̩ tə
pe mi rɪspɛks tə də deːd, dæs mʌɪ frɛːn saɪlɪs hɔːl n̩ hi də deːd, yʌ i də
deːd, yə no i bin fə deːd, naʊ nə lɑːf, nə lɑːf, yu gon daɪ tu, yu gwaɪn dɛd
wʌn ə diːz deɪz, si də mɑn raɪt dɛə, i də ded, ɛf yʊ no bəliːv mi go ovə
dɛə n̩ pɪntʃ ɪm, i na enə halə, i no ena se nʌtn̩, yu enə ded tu] (WW)

'Good evening, good evening, how are you, how are you doing, I hope
you're doing fine, I'm doing all right, now I've just come here this
evening to see how you are doing, and to pay my respects to the dead;
yes, he's dead; you know he should have (= was going to?) died, now
don't laugh, don't laugh, you're going to die too, you're going to die one
of these days. See the man right there? He's dead; if you don't believe
me go over there and pinch him, he's not going to holler, he's not going
to say anything; you're going to die too'.

8.4.2.

[sɪstə fɪlɪs, də wʌn tɪŋ a də no, də we yu gɪt də oːl diːp beɪd aʊt dɛː frɑm,
d ol beɪd so dip i dyɛ lʌɪk ə mɑn fə lɛdaʊn iːn ɪz greib, i hæfə stɑːn ɔp fə
tɜːn oːvə in ɪt] (WW)

'Sister Phyllis, there's one thing I (want to) know, and it's where did
you get the old deep bed out there from? The old bed's so deep it's just
like a man would be lying in his grave; he has to stand up to turn over in
it!'.

NOTES

1. Based especially upon the works of Brevard (1924–1925), Foster (1935), McReynolds
   (1957), and Porter (1950).
2. Including the Fox, Timukwa, Mikasuki, Sauk, &c.
3. Mass debating among the followers of the Seminole chiefs Taskogee and Hallec Hajo
   and those of General Jessup, who was acting as mediator for the U.S. government,
   climaxed on February 8th with the Seminole Omission of 1838, a proposal that the
   Seminoles and their slaves not be admitted to the western territories, but instead remain
   in southern Florida. This was rejected by the U.S. Secretary of War, however, and plans
   to migrate were put into effect (see Brevard, vol. I:150–151).
4. The most recent discussions of the Seminole communities are to be found in Dillard
   (1972:150–155; 1975:47, 137, 182).
5. Mr. Gordon passed away in January of this year.

6. Or perhaps Florida Gullah, since there are indications that it was at one time spoken further south than it is now.

7. The word is originally the Spanish *cimarrón* (French *marron*, English *maroon*), adopted into Muskogee as *simaló ni* and *simanó li*, and was first applied to plants and animals in the sense of 'wild' or 'runaway' (Sturtevant 1971:105).

8. The most likely Indian languages to have been acquired or partly acquired by the Afro-Seminoles are Muskogee (Creek) and Hičiti (Mikasuki), both spoken in the Florida settlements, Biloxi, probably encountered in the Arkansas-Oklahoma settlements, and Kickapoo, which has some 500 speakers living near the Seminole community in El Nacimiento, Mexico.

9. While the Florida and Oklahoma Seminole groups are predominantly Indian, the El Nacimiento and Brackettville communities are without question almost wholly of African ancestry; there is one other Afro-Seminole community, on Andros Island in the Bahamas, established there several decades before the later groups left for the West (Porter 1945; Goggin 1946).

10. An information officer at Fort Clark maintained that the true story was that the first Afro-Seminoles arrived destitute and uninvited at the fort, and asked to be cared for. There is no evidence whatsoever to support this, while evidence to the contrary, in the form of documents and citations from the federal army to the scouts, are abundant, and are readily produced by the various families who own them.

11. Another observer said, however, that it was indistinguishable from ordinary Brackettville Spanish.

12. Lilith Haynes (1976:par. 2.2.2.) also mentions someone who had encountered 'Geechee' in his travels with the U.S. Army, and who thought ASC might be related to that. 'Geechee' here probably means Gullah, although as elsewhere in Texas, the word was thought to have to do with Louisiana in some way.

13. Though several people knew of Whites in Brackettville who were able to speak ASC.

14. Especially in view of the lateness of the arrival of Africans into the area. Bancroft (1931:359–360) mentions a cargo of some 420 Africans being put off near Augusta in December 1858. Curtin (1969:158) notes that '. . . Georgian slave imports from Africa after 1766 show a heavy but nonquantifiable bias toward Senegambia and Sierra Leone — thus approximating the South Carolinian pattern'.

15. Kindly provided by Prof. William A. Stewart.

16. I use the term *northwestern creoles* here to refer to all the English-derived creoles in the western hemisphere outside of Surinam; the Sranan-Djuka group are *southwestern*, while the Guinea Coast group are *eastern*. This division is based on linguistic as well as geographical criteria.

REFERENCES

Bailey, B. L. (1962), *A Language Guide to Jamaica*. New York.
— (1966) *Jamaican Creole Syntax: A Transformational Approach*. Cambridge, The University Press.
Bancroft, Frederic (1931), *Slave Trading in the Old South*. Baltimore, Furst.
Brevard, Carolina M. (1924–1925), *A History of Florida from the Treaty of 1763 to Our Own Times*, two volumes, New York.

Cassidy, F. G. and R. B. Le Page (1967), *Dictionary of Jamaican English*. Cambridge, Cambridge University Press.

Chafe, Wallace L. (1962), 'Estimates regarding the present speakers of North American Indian languages', *International Journal of American Linguistics* 28:162–171.

Cunningham, Irma A. E. (1970), 'A syntactic analysis of Sea Island Creole ("Gullah")'. Unpublished Ph.D. dissertation, University of Michigan.

Curtin, Philip D. (1969), *The Atlantic Slave Trade*. Madison, Wisconsin University Press.

Dickerson, W. E. S. (1952), 'Seminole Indians', in *The Handbook of Texas*, ed. by W. P. Webb et al., 592. Austin, The Texas State Historical Association.

Dillard, J. L. (1972), *Black English: its History and Usage in the United States*. New York, Random House.

— (1975), *All-American English: A History of the English Language in America*. New York, Random House.

Dwyer, D. and D. Smith (n.d.), *An Introduction to West African Pidgin English*. East Lansing, Michigan State University Press.

Foster, Laurence (1935), *Negro-Indian Relationships in the Southeast*. Philadelphia, University of Pennsylvania Press.

Fyfe, Christopher (1962), *A History of Sierra Leone*. London, Oxford University Press.

Goggin, John (1946), 'The Seminole Negroes of Andros Island, Bahamas', *The Florida Historical Quarterly* 24(3):201–206.

Gonzales, A. E. (1922), *The Black Border: Gullah Stories of the Carolina Coast*. Columbia, S.C.

Hair, Paul E. H. (1965), 'Sierra Leone items in the Gullah dialect of American English', *African Language Review* 4:79–84.

Hancock, Ian F. (1971), 'A study of the sources and development of the lexicon of Sierra Leone Krio'. Unpublished Ph.D. dissertation, S.O.A.S., London.

— (1979), 'Gullah and Barbadian: origins and relationships', *American Speech*, 54(3): 33–48.

Haynes, Lilith M. (1976), 'Candid Chimæra: Texas Seminole'. Paper presented at the Fifth Annual Southwest Areal Linguistics Workshop, San Antonio, April, 1976, and to appear in the published proceedings.

Jones, Charles C. (1888), *Negro Myths from the Georgia Coast, Told in the Vernacular*. Boston and New York.

McLoughlin, Wm. (1974), 'Red Indians, black slavery and white racism: America's slaveholding Indians', *American Quarterly* 26(4):367–385.

McReynolds, Edwin C. (1957), *The Seminoles*. Norman, Oklahoma.

Moore-Willson, M. (1928), *The Seminoles of Florida*.

Porter, Kenneth (1945), 'Notes on the Seminole Negroes in the Bahamas', *The Florida Historical Quarterly* 24(1):56–60.

— (1950), 'Negro guides and interpreters in the early stages of the Seminole War', *Journal of Negro History* 35(2).

— (1952), 'The Seminole Negro-Indian scouts', *Quarterly of the Texas State Historical Association* January.

Sturtevant, Wm. C. (1971), 'Creek into Seminole', in *North American Indians in Historical Perspective*, ed. by Eleanor Leacock and Nancy Lurie, 92–128. New York, Random House.

Turner, Lorenzo D. (1949), *Africanisms in the Gullah Dialect*. Chicago, Chicago University Press.

Whitman, Albery A. (1880), *Twasinta's Seminoles.*

Woodhull, F. (1937), 'The Seminole Indian Scouts on the border', *Frontier Times* 15(3):118–127.

Wright, Muriel H. (1957), *Guide to the Indian Tribes of Oklahoma.* Norman, Oklahoma University Press.

JOHN C. BIRMINGHAM, JR.

Black English near its Roots:
The Transplanted West African Creoles

Much has been said and written over the years about the characteristics
and the grammar of American Black English, but until relatively recently
not much had been revealed about how Black English acquired those
characteristics and that grammar. There has been a good deal of guessing
— intelligent and otherwise — by linguists and nonlinguists alike, and the
result of this guessing has been an attempt to explain the peculiarities of
Black English on the basis of certain British dialects of English. It apparently has not occurred to these investigators to question the logic of their
explanation: how could one who has never lived in the British Isles pick
up all these traits of speech, even if one lived among people who had?

What is beginning to seem fairly obvious, thanks to the work of J. L.
Dillard (1975, especially the bibliography), William A. Stewart (1975),
and others, is that Black English, or whatever else we choose to call it, is
the product of a relexification of an earlier creole, with a postcreole shift
toward Standard English. This creole was itself probably based on an
even earlier pidgin which in its turn may well have been merely a relexification of the now-extinct Lingua Franca,[1] and it more than likely
developed, perhaps as early as the sixteenth century, in Portuguese slave
camps (or *factorias*, as the Portuguese called them) along the west coast of
Africa. Since slaves were drawn from differing tribes and could not
necessarily understand one another's language, they naturally had to find
a common language to serve their communication needs in the slave
camps, where they were held until there were enough slaves to constitute
a shipload. This common language seems to have been a Portuguese
pidgin imposed by the Portuguese slavetraders, and some form of it may
have been the language the slaves took with them to the New World and
elsewhere.

The purpose of this present study will be to compare Black English
(especially Early Black English, or Plantation Creole, as Dillard
[1972:72] calls it) with a few creoles still spoken in the New World, most
particularly with Papiamentu, an Afro-Iberian (probably Afro-
Portuguese) creole of the Caribbean, spoken by some 200,000 people,

mostly the descendants of African slaves, on the three Netherlands Antilles islands of Aruba, Bonaire, and Curaçao,[2] sometimes known as the ABC islands. Papiamentu in its present state may be seen as a partially relexified version of the Portuguese pidgin of West Africa, brought to the New World beginning about the middle of the seventeenth century by the slaves who were imported by the Dutch, for whom the island of Curaçao, under almost continuous Dutch control since 1634, quickly became a booming slave depot for the distribution of slaves to all parts of the hemisphere. Despite efforts by the Dutch to eradicate Papiamentu, it continues to thrive in its tropical environment. But like the Taki-Taki (or Sranan Tongo) and the Saramaccan of Surinam, the Creole English of Jamaica, the extinct or nearly extinct Negerhollands or Black Dutch of the Virgin Islands, the Palenquero of the coast of Colombia, and other such creoles of the Caribbean and elsewhere, Papiamentu has been going through a constant process of relexification and decreolization.[3] These transplanted and relexified Afro-European creoles, however, will prove to have many features in common with Early Black English and even with Modern Black English. I shall therefore seek to show that Black English as we know it is very probably a relexification of the West African Portuguese Pidgin, keeping in mind the very obvious possibility that some similarities in the various speech forms may well be due to the workings of certain linguistic universals, particularly as regards pidgins and creoles.[4] I have chosen to deal almost exclusively with Papiamentu because, of the New World creoles, it is probably the most representative of creoles in general and of the Afro-Portuguese-based creoles in particular, and because it, unlike the other New World creoles, seems to have remained relatively unchanged from the original Afro-Portuguese model in syntax and morphology, although in its lexicon it has been strongly influenced by Spanish, Dutch, and English.[5] I shall not go into detail about the native African substrata because such is not within the scope of my study.

It would be difficult — and perhaps ill-advised as well — to pick out one single feature of Black English that stands out above all its other features; but certainly one of the most noticeable and (by Whites) most criticized features of Black English is the nonredundant or zero plural, the process of marking nouns for plural by prefixing a number or some other adjective of quantity: *two boy, a basket of peach*, etc. Papiamentu utilizes the same process. But of course Black English and Papiamentu are not alone in using the nonredundant plural, for some of the present-day West African Portuguese creoles, for instance, do the same (see, for example, De Oliveira Almada [1961:91, par. 126]). What most Whites do not understand, however, is that Black English uses the English plural morpheme -*s* where it is necessary for clarification. According to Dillard (1972:62) Black English has used the -*s* plural since at least the early 1700s. In any event, Papiamentu, like Black English, observes the non-redundant plural and also has a plural morpheme which it uses for clarification. This plural morpheme is [nãŋ], which is also a third-person pronoun meaning 'they, them, their'. Thus, ['hɔmbərnãŋ] 'men', but [dos 'hɔmbər] 'two men'. From a syntactic and morphological point of view, this Papiamentu [nãŋ] finds its exact counterpart in the Jamaican Creole English plural morpheme *dem* (Bailey 1966:26), from Standard English 'them', serving also as a personal pronoun. For example, Jamaican Creole speaks of *di manggo* 'the mango (a specific one)' and *di manggo-dem* 'the mangoes' (Bailey 1966:27). However, to talk about mangoes in general, Jamaican Creole would say simply *manggo* (Bailey 1966:27), which shows no inflection for plural, nor does it need to. Papiamentu does precisely the same thing: [mi gu:sta 'mãŋgo] means 'I like mangoes (in general)', while [mi gu:sta ɛ 'mãŋgonãŋ] means 'I like the (specific) mangoes'. The IPA transcriptions show the tonality of the typical dissyllabic Papiamentu verb, the colon here representing vowel lengthening and the subscript numbers 2 and 1 showing falling pitch and rising pitch, respectively. This tonality, however, is not universal and follows a rather complicated pattern, as does the use versus the omission of the Papiamentu pluralizing morpheme. Leaving aside the aspect of tonality — undoubtedly a vestige of African morphology in Papiamentu and perhaps also in Black English, if it exists in the latter — it is certainly the complicated nature of the situation which leads traditional-minded linguists to the only partially correct conclusion that Black English has no plural morpheme.

The double negative is another feature of Black English which comes readily to mind in any discussion of the dialect, be it Early Black English (Plantation Creole) or Modern Black English. While Nonstandard White English also exhibits the double negative, the phenomenon is more often associated (whether rightly or wrongly) with Black English. This use of the double negative — perhaps more accurately the multiple negative — is also an outstanding feature of Papiamentu, a feature which is present in Papiamentu not only in those instances in which the parent Iberian language would demand at least a double negative, but also in situations where even Spanish and Portuguese would shun the use of more than two negatives. Spanish, for example, to express the idea 'I have never said anything', would say (among other possibilities) *Nunca he dicho nada*, employing only the two negatives *nunca* and *nada*. Papiamentu, on the other hand, would say (again, among other possibilities) ['nũŋka mi no a bi:sa 'nada] or, more idiomatically, ['nũŋka mi na bi:sa 'nada] (the element [na] representing the contraction of [no] and [a]), in either case using three negatives. The fondness for multiple negation which characterizes Black English could well come from the Portuguese pidgin base, merely relexified into English, like so many of its other characteristics. Labov, who sees ' . . . a Creole origin . . . ' for Black English, gives examples of what he calls *negative concord.*[6] One such example is, 'None of 'em can't fight', which translates very nicely into Papiamentu as [nĩŋ'gũŋ di nãŋ no por brĩ:ŋga]. The Hispanic languages would not admit the second negative (here [no]) in this type of construction.

The above Papiamentu examples open up a whole series of similarities between the two speech forms. Such things as the use of *me* for the subject pronoun *I* (cf. Papiamentu [mi] above), and others to follow, are so well documented in Plantation Creole (and in other varieties of Negro English, in West Africa and the Caribbean, for example) that we can safely assume that they are among the features of Black English that have been lost as the dialect has moved closer to Standard English. Dillard (1972:90), for instance, has the following short dialogue between a Lord Kidnapper and a Virginia slave named Cudjo:

Lord Kidnapper — Can you shoot some of them rebels ashore, Major Cudjo?
Cudjo — *Eas, massa, me try.*
Lord Kidnapper — Would you shoot your old master, the Colonel, if you could see him?
Cudjo — *Eas, massa, you terra* [i.e., tell] *me, me shoot him dead.*

Negation with *no* for Standard English *do not, am not,* etc., is likewise well attested in Early Black English and has an exact parallel in Papiamentu and, indeed, in many another creole, particularly and most obviously in the Iberian-based or Iberian-influenced creoles. Dillard (1972:94) quotes a source from the year 1807, which has the Plantation Creole phrases: *I no likee this massa Fopling* . . . and . . . *he no half so good as Jemmy Seamore.* . . . It is curious here, by the way, to note Standard English *I* as the first-person subject pronoun in *I no likee*, where we would probably expect *me*, as in *me try* and *me shoot*, above. As late as the time of the American Revolution we still see the subject pronoun *me* in American Black English, as well as negation with *no*; and Dillard (1972:87) quotes a paragraph from J. F. D. Smyth's *A Tour of the United States of America*, published in London in 1784, in which the author records the speech of a North Carolina slave as follows:

Kay, massa, (says he), you just leave me, me sit here, great fish jump into de canoe, here he be, massa, fine fish, massa; me den very grad; den me sit very still, until another great fish jump into de canoe; but me fall asleep, massa, and no wake till you come; now, massa, me know me deserve flogging, cause if great fish did jump into de canoe, he see me asleep, den he jump out again, and I no catch him; so, massa, me willing now take good flogging.

This *me* and this negation with *no* can doubtless be traced to the Portuguese Pidgin and perhaps even farther back than that, back perhaps to the Lingua Franca (see my note 1), in which the form *mi* apparently serves all grammatical first-person functions ('I, me, my, mine, myself'), as [mi] definitely does in Papiamentu. And there is in Papiamentu, for example, the phrase [mi no sa:bị] or, as it would be colloquially, [min'sa] 'I do not know', which is echoed in the Jamaican Creole English *mi no sabi* 'I do not know', now largely replaced by *mi no nuo* (see Cassidy 1971:208), showing the substitution, by relexification, of English *know* for Portuguese Pidgin *sabi*. These points are all very neatly tied together in a sentence which Dillard (1972:174) quotes from Charles William Day's *Five Years Residence in the West Indies* (1852, London), giving a sample of the Negro English of the Caribbean island of St. Kitts at about the middle of the nineteenth century: *Me no sabby why dat officer make noise wid dat ting.* It would therefore seem, if these transcriptions are to be trusted, that the slaves of the New World used *me* as a subject pronoun, apparently the same [mi] which we observe in Papiamentu and other creoles. The *I no catch him* of Smyth's passage above, however, seems to show that *me* at least occasionally varied with *I*, again, that is, if the transcription is accurate.

Perhaps of more linguistic import than the above similarities (*me, no,* and *sabi*) is the fact that the Papiamentu verb is invariable from one person to the next, like the Plantation Creole verb, with the result that a subject noun or pronoun must nearly always be expressed. There are in Papiamentu perhaps no more than three verbal constructions which omit the subject noun or pronoun, one of these being the so-called impersonal construction, as in [ta jọ:bɛ] 'It rains, is raining', in which [ta] serves as an aspect marker to express present or habitual time. This [ta] also functions as an independent verb carrying the meanings of the copula verb 'to be', and as such it may never be omitted. However, when it functions as an aspect marker, its use or omission depends on two very distinct factors. First, it is normally used only with verbs of physical motion (there are exceptions), but even with those verbs it is omitted in cases of doubt, hypothesis, or other subjunctive-like constructions. Let us compare:

['ora ɛ ta baj kas|ɛ ta sosɛ'ga]
'When he (she) goes home, he (she) rests.'
['ora ɛ baj kas | loɛ sosɛ'ga]
'When he (she) goes home, he (she) will rest.'

The second Papiamentu sample above shows the future marker [lo], most likely deriving from Portuguese *logo* 'soon'. It also shows the omission of [ta] in the first clause to indicate an action still pending: he or she has not gone home yet. Secondly, this [ta] is almost always omitted before verbs of mental attitude (knowing, wanting, etc.), although there are, again, some exceptions.

In other words, the concept of the copula is a highly developed one in Papiamentu, while Black English tends toward the zero copula. The common Papiamentu verb [baj] 'to go', forms of which we saw above, is conjugated in the present aspect as follows:

[mi ta baj]   [nos ta baj]
'I go, am going'   'we go, are going'

[bo ta baj]   ['boso ta baj]
'you go, are going'   'you go, are going'

[ɛ ta baj]   [nãŋ ta baj]
'he (she, it) goes,   'they go, are going'
is going'

It is very clear from the above paradigm that there is no change in the verb form from one grammatical person to another. This fact is significant because this invariability is still a very strong tendency in Modern Black English (*I is, you is, he is,* etc.). And besides Papiamentu's inability to distinguish among *he, she*, and *it* in several of the above samples, a Black English tendency which we shall discuss shortly, it is also of interest to note that both the Papiamentu and the Black English invariable verb form many times seems to be based on the third person singular of the European verb: [ta], perhaps from Portuguese *está* 'he, she, it is', [baj], most likely from Portuguese *vai* 'he, she, it goes', and the universal *is* of Black English, which is unquestionably the third person singular.[7]

The other tenses or time aspects in Papiamentu are likewise expressed by invariable aspect markers or verbal particles, such as the past marker [a], as seen in the above phrase ['nũŋka mi no a bi :sa nada] and its variant, which gets across not only the idea of a present perfect ('I have not said anything') but also the idea of a simple past ('I did not say anything'), as in the French *passé composé*. This past marker [a] may or may not be the same as the particle *a* in Dillard's example (1972:97) of the English of the West Indies of the early nineteenth century: *Matty a l'arn matty* 'Friend taught friend'.

But one thing is sure: Papiamentu, like Black English, does not make gender distinctions, most pronouns taking the etymologically masculine forms, as in the Black English phrase, *He a nice girl*. (Note also the Black English zero copula.) Papiamentu not only does not, but cannot, make gender distinctions in pronouns; in the above illustrative phrase [ɛ tabaj], the pronoun [ɛ] serves for 'he' and 'she', and also, incidentally, for 'it' in a specific (that is, not impersonal) situation such as 'It (the box, the merchandise, etc.) is here'. This invariable and nondistinguishing pronoun [ɛ] is better thought of as [ɛ1] ~ [ɛ], since before a vowel it is [ɛ1] and in any other environment it is [ɛ]. In the matter of adjectives, too, Papiamentu rarely observes grammatical gender; and, although this type of agreement would be of little concern to a speaker of English, it is significant that Spanish and Portuguese, for example, maintain a strict masculine–feminine agreement between nouns and adjectives, with typical masculine nouns and adjectives ending in *-o* (Papiamentu, like Portuguese, tends to close final [o] to [u]) and typical feminine nouns and adjectives ending in *-a*. In Papiamentu, most adjectives display the etymologically masculine form, with any apparent agreement being merely accidental: [ūŋ 'hɔmbər 'prɛtu] 'a black man', but likewise [ūŋ mu'hɛ 'prɛtu] 'a black woman', in which the Iberian tongues would demand a feminine adjective (and a feminine article), most likely ending in *-a*, such as *[*'prɛta], which does not exist in Papiamentu. (Neither does it exist in Spanish; a similar form is *prieta*, but *preta* is pure Portuguese.)

Interestingly enough, Papiamentu rarely makes gender distinctions in nouns either, although it can do so, unlike the situation in the case of pronouns. Besides the fairly obvious distinctions, such as the above ['hɔmbər] 'man' versus [mu'hɛ] 'woman', Papiamentu generally prefers all-inclusive forms, such as [mu:ča][8] 'boy/girl; child' and [ru'măŋ] 'brother/sister; sibling'. If the language is forced to make a gender distinction in cases such as these, it merely adds ['hɔmbər] or [mu'hɛ]: [ru'măŋ 'hɔmbər] is 'brother' (literally 'sibling-man'), and [ru'măŋ mu'hɛ] is 'sister' ('sibling-woman'). This device is reminiscent of Caribbean Negro English expressions like 'boy-child' for 'son', and a similar expression in Papiamentu is [ju 'hɔmbər] 'male offspring, son'. A [ju mu'hɛ], of course, is a daughter, the simple word for offspring of either gender being [ju].

Bringing our comparison closer to home, we see another tendency which Papiamentu shares with Black English, and that is the tendency to maintain statement word order in a question, distinguishing between statement and question only by intonation. This feature of Papiamentu can be illustrated like this:

[ri'kardo por ju'dami]	'Richard can help me'
[ri'kardo por ju'dami?]	'Can Richard help me?'

Perhaps an even better illustration, certainly in relation to Black English, is this one: [na 'ŭnda bo ta¿]⁹ 'Where are you?', literally '(In) where you be?' or '(In) where you is?' The significance of these comparisons is that the Iberian tongues, like Standard English, normally require inverted word order for a question, while Black English and Papiamentu prefer a static word order. This preference may be due to the native African substrata, or it may stem directly from the Portuguese Pidgin (perhaps going back to the Lingua Franca?); but in either event the above comparisons may help to explain such typical Black English constructions as *What time it is?*

In the early days, in the days of Plantation Creole, there was a tendency on the part of the slaves to drop prefixes (such as *vorce* for *divorce*) and to reduce consonant clusters (such as *dress* for *dressed*). And the same tendency is still seen in Modern Black English with its *have* ([hev]) for *behave* and its *tes* for *test* and *tole* for *told*. This tendency is also characteristic of Papiamentu, which favors forms that are apocopated versions of the equivalent etymological Iberian forms. For example, [kos] 'thing' derives from Iberian *cosa, cousa,* or *coisa* 'thing', without the final -*a*, and is reduced even further in certain combinations, such as the interrogative [pa'kiko¿] 'why?' (literally 'for what thing?'). It is in the etymological past participles forms that we can see the process of apocopation perhaps more graphically than anywhere else, as in [sa'bi] 'known', from Iberian *sabido*; [ma'ta] 'killed', from Iberian *matado*; [ro'ba] 'stolen', from Iberian *robado, roubado*; and so forth. Papiamentu normally reduces consonant clusters by epenthesis, or the addition of a support vowel which, by assimilation, is usually the same as the vowel in the preceding syllable. Thus we see forms like [kolo'ga] 'to hang', from Iberian *colgar*, and [dɛlɛ'ga] 'thin', from Iberian *delgado*. The consonant cluster [gw] is typically reduced by dropping the [g], as in ['awa] 'water', from Iberian *agua, água*. This process would seem to be in line with the Black English penchant for dissolving consonant clusters.

There were, at least in Plantation Creole, numbers of 'fancified' Black English noun forms ending in -*ment*, such as *divorcement, separament, scatterment, worryment*, and *dividement*, forms which do not exist in Standard English. Here we see a very striking and perhaps revealing similarity in Papiamentu. Let us start with the very name *Papiamentu* itself: the word derives from the Portuguese (or perhaps Old Spanish¹⁰) verb *papear* 'to babble, to chatter', plus the typical Portuguese noun-deriving suffix -*mento*, with closing of final [o] to [u], as in Portuguese. The resultant form *Papiamentu* thus means something like 'babblement' or 'babbling', but nowadays it has none of the negative connotation of the Portuguese Pidgin original; it means merely 'talk' or 'talking': [tīŋ 'hopi papja'mɛntu] 'There is much talk.' (This phrase shows not only the form [papja'mɛntu] in the sense of 'talk', but also the Dutch-derived[11] ['hopi], literally 'heap' or perhaps 'little heap', to mean 'much, many'. The resemblance of this ['hopi] to Pidgin English 'heap' as a qualifier is interesting [see Dillard 1972:175–176].) Likewise, the Papiamentu verb [pa̩:pja] 'to speak, to talk' derives from the same Iberian verb *papear* but does not carry any of the negative force of the original.[12]

But let us see some of the many other common Papiamentu nouns ending in ['mɛntu] formed by the creole itself, that is, nouns which do not exist in the Iberian tongues but which were created by the creole from its native stock and according to the same specific creole pattern which produced the form *Papiamentu*. The following can serve to illustrate:

[duna'mɛntu]	'giving'
[kibra'mɛntu]	'breaking, breakage'
[muri'mɛntu]	'death, dying' (also ['mɔrtu])
[komɛ 'mɛntu]	'eating, meal'
[ponɛ'mɛntu]	'putting, setting, laying (of eggs)'
[jama'mɛntu]	'calling'
[purba'mɛntu]	'proving, proof'
[risibi'mɛntu]	'receiving, reception'
[skirbi'mɛntu]	'writing, spelling'
[kuminda'mɛntu]	'greeting'
[brĩŋga'mɛntu]	'fighting, quarreling'
[hĩŋka'mɛntu]	'sinking, thrusting, sticking'
[lɛsa'mɛntu]	'reading, lecture'

This process holds a further point of interest for students of Black English: as J. A. Harrison (1975:173) points out, Black English has or at least had a tendency to stress the last syllable of words like *wonderment* (that is, *wondermént*) and *judgment* (*jedgmént*) (his transcriptions). While Harrison (1975:173) attempts to trace this feature to Elizabethan English or to nineteenth-century Huguenot or creole influence, it is just as probable — in fact, more so — that Black English, much earlier than the nineteenth century, only partially relexified these words ending in *-ment* (given the common Latin base of the noun-deriving suffix) and kept, at least for a while, the original Iberian stress pattern.

Among the less conspicuous pecularities of Black English is its tendency to repeat the antecedent of a relative pronoun by means of a so-called personal pronoun placed at the end of the phrase (Dillard calls this process the 'redundant relative'), as in 'This is something that I want to talk about it', in which *it* repeats the antecedent *something*.

Papiamentu does exactly the same. For example, whereas Standard English would say 'This is the man with whom your daughter is in love' or, less formally. 'This is the man your daughter is in love with', Papiamentu would say [ɛsa:ki ta ɛ 'hɔmbər ku bo ju mu'hɛ ta namo'ra di jɛ], literally, 'This is the man whom your daughter is in love with him'. This construction is unknown in the Iberian languages.

There are other and more isolated points of morphological and syntactic similarity between Black English and Papiamentu, such as the rejection of simple words for 'both', using instead a circumlocution like 'all two' or the redundant 'all bofe', as in Dillard (1972:93–94) and Stewart (1969).[13] Nonliterary Papiamentu regularly uses the expression [tur'dos], literally 'all two', for 'both', although the Iberian *ambos* 'both' nowadays seems to be replacing [tur'dos] in newspaper usage, an area in which there is and traditionally has been a strong decreolizing influence from Spanish.[14] The nautical nature of the slave trade gave rise in Papiamentu to a number of sea-related items which may also have their counterparts in Black English, as the use of the word ['bjaha] 'trip' (Iberian *viaje, viagem*) for 'time' in the sense of 'instance': [ūŋ 'bjaha] 'one time, a time'. This is certainly reminiscent of the slang expression 'not *this* trip!' for 'not *this* time!' Other instances of nautical influence are reflected in the Papiamentu forms ['banda] (Iberian 'side of a ship') for 'side' in any sense, and [bi:ra] 'to become, turn, go (crazy, etc.)', from Iberian *virar* 'to turn, tack, veer': [ɛl a bi:ra 'ʃɛgu] 'He (she) went blind'. And I have not even touched on the phonological similarities between the two speech forms, such as the short, simple [u] sound for the Standard English diphthongized offglide [uw], as in Black English [du] for Standard English [duw] 'do'. This and other phonological features of Black English may well derive from the same Portuguese and/or Spanish sources — or, perhaps, from more generalized Romance sources like the Lingua Franca — which also carried over into Papiamentu, with some almost certain phonological influence from native African languages, particularly as regards intonation and pitch. But in closing, suffice it to say that the similarities are there if one will but look for them and that these similarities will be of invaluable help to us in our search for Black English near its roots.

NOTES

1. My own theory can be seen in my article on Papiamentu (1976c).
2. For an in-depth treatment of Papiamentu, see my unpublished Ph.D. dissertation (1970).
3. For specific examples, see my paper on Papiamentu (1976a).

4. A good treatment of such linguistic universals can be found in Douglas Taylor (1971).
5. See Note 3.
6. William Labov (1972). Labov's reference to a creole origin for Black English can be seen on p. 774, note 4, and his example 'None of 'em can't fight' appears on p. 786.
7. The same tendency, that of basing the entire conjugation on the third person singular, is also to be seen in Afrikaans, the Dutch-based creole of South Africa. For example, the present tense of the verb *wees* 'to be' uses *is* (from the Dutch third person singular *is*) all the way through. For a fuller treatment of this type of conjugation, see my article on Papiamentu and Afrikaans (1977). The Black influence on Afrikaans is very clearly set out by Marius F. Valkhoff (1975).
8. Tonality in Papiamentu is not limited to verbs; other parts of speech as well show this feature, the only stipulation apparently being that the form must be dissyllabic.
9. The inverted question mark indicates an 'information' question, while the normal question mark indicates a 'yes-or-no' question, as suggested by Leonard Bloomfield (1933:114–115).
10. It is interesting to note that the verb *papear* is still used in modern colloquial Brazilian Portuguese, but it also existed in Old Spanish: *Fervos he sin los ojos, si mucho papeades*. . . . (Free translation: 'I shall pluck out your eyes, if you *talk* too much.') The quotation is from the early Spanish poet Gonzalo de Berceo's *Vida de Santo Domingo de Silos*, and can be seen, for example, in Chandler and Schwartz (1967, vol. I:14).
11. The Dutch word is *hoop* (phonetically [hop]), but the Papiamentu ['hopi] seems to derive from the Dutch diminutive *hoopje* or the dialectal Dutch *hopie*, in the same way that Papiamentu ['buki] 'book' derives from the Dutch diminutive *boekje* or *boekie*, literally 'little book'.
12. This same verb *papear* gives rise to similar forms for 'to speak, to talk' in other Afro-Portuguese creoles, such as the creole of the Cabo Verde islands, off Africa's west coast. Maria Dulce de Oliveira Almada (1961:157) gives the following example from Cabo Verde Creole: *ę tą pąpią mų̧tu čę̧u* (*ele fala muito*) 'he talks much'. Compare Papiamentu [ɛ ta pa:pja̧ 'hopi], same meaning. See Note 11 for ['hopi]. See also my article on this subject (1976b).
13. The same 'all two' for 'both' appears in Gullah, as I point out in my article on Papiamentu (1976c).
14. See Note 3.

REFERENCES

Bailey, Beryl Loftman (1966), *Jamaican Creole Syntax: A Transformational Approach*. Cambridge, The University Press.
Birmingham, John C., Jr. (1970), 'The Papiamentu language of Curaçao'. Unpublished Ph.D. dissertation, University of Virginia.
— (1976a), 'Papiamentu: new trends in decreolization'. Paper presented at the Conference of the Society for Caribbean Linguistics in Guyana, August 1976. (Revised title: 'Lexical decreolization in Papiamentu'.)
— (1976b), 'Papiamentu's West African cousins', in *1975 Colloquim on Hispanic Linguistics*, ed. by Frances M. Aid et al., 19–25. Washington, D.C., Georgetown University Press.
— (1976c), 'Papiamentu: the long-lost Lingua Franca?'. *The American Hispanist* 2 (13).

— (1977), 'Papiamentu and Afrikaans: two Black-influenced creole languages', *Kristòf* (Curaçao) 3 (5):193–203.

Bloomfield, Leonard (1933), *Language*. New York, Holt.

Cassidy, Frederick G. (1971), 'Tracing the pidgin element in Jamaican Creole', in *Pidginization and Creolization of Languages*, ed. by Dell Hymes, 203–222. London, Cambridge University Press.

Chandler, Richard E. and Kessel Schwartz (1967), *A New Anthology of Spanish Literature*. Baton Rouge, Louisiana State University Press.

De Oliveira Almada, Maria Dulce (1961), *Cabo Verde: Contribução para o Estudo do Dialecto falado no seu Arquipélago*. Lisbon, Junta de Investigações Científicas do Ultramar.

Dillard, J. L. (1972), *Black English: Its History and Usage in the United States*. New York, Random House.

— (1975), *All-American English*. New York, Random House

Harrison, J. A. (1975), 'Negro English', in *Perspectives on Black English*, ed. by J. L. Dillard, 143–195. The Hague, Mouton.

Labov, William (1972), 'Negative attraction and negative concord in English grammar', *Language* 48 (4):773–818.

Stewart, William A. (1969), 'Negro dialect in the teaching of reading', in *Teaching Black Children to Read*, ed. by Joan C. Baratz and Roger W. Shuy, 197–198. Arlington, Va., Center for Applied Linguistics.

— (1975), 'Sociological factors in the history of American Negro dialects', in *Perspectives on Black English*, ed. by J. L. Dillard, 222–232. The Hague, Mouton.

Taylor, Douglas (1971), 'Grammatical and lexical affinities of creoles', in *Pidginization and Creolization of Languages*, ed. by Dell Hymes, 293–296. London, Cambridge University Press.

Valkhoff, Marius F. (1975), 'África do Sul e Portugal: algumas reflexões sobre os dialectos crioulos', in *Miscelânea luso-africana*, ed. by M. F. Valkhoff. Lisbon, Junta de Investigações Científicas do Ultramar.

JOHN R. RICKFORD and ANGELA E. RICKFORD

Cut-Eye and Suck-Teeth:
African Words and Gestures in New World Guise

In the New World, things African are usually associated with the unusual and the exotic. Thus, *cumfa*, with its frenzied drumming, would seem a natural candidate for inclusion in any list of African 'survivals'. So also would a folktale or folksong which included several lines of obscure incantation. Or a word which made use of very un-English phonotactics, like *kpoli*, or was matched against a more standard equivalent (*nyam* versus *eat*).

Our suspicions would be particularly aroused if the cultural or linguistic item were rarely used, if, for instance, we 'got' it for the first and only time from the ageing grandchild of some erstwhile slave, now living an isolated life far from the masses of people. For academics and laymen alike, it is of such stuff that true New World Africanisms are made.

In keeping with this pattern of intuition and reasoning, we never attached any historical significance to *cut-eye* and *suck-teeth*. The gestures to which these refer are performed daily in our native Guyana by all kinds of people, in urban center and rural area alike. And the compounds we use to describe them could hardly be more ordinary, composed as they are of simple English words — *cut, eye, suck,* and *teeth.* With such unpromising clues to go by, it is hardly surprising that we used them every day without giving any thought to their source.

However, while doing graduate work in Philadelphia in 1971, we happened to notice a curious division between American Whites and Blacks with respect to these very gestures. While the Blacks would 'cut their eyes' and 'suck their teeth' in much the same manner that people did in our native community, Whites apparently never did, and were often ignorant of the meanings of these gestures when they were directed at them.

On the basis of this chance observation, we began to consider the possibility that both the gestures and the words we used to describe them might represent African 'survivals', and we began to study more sys-

Reprinted by permission of the authors and the American Folklore Society from the *Journal of American Folklore* 89(353), 1976.

tematically the extent to which they were used and recognized across three broad areas: the Caribbean, the United States, and Africa. This paper reports on the results of this investigation.

We shall first briefly describe the methods we used to obtain data on these areas and then summarize the findings for *cut-eye* and *suck-teeth* under separate headings. In the conclusion, we discuss some of the larger implications and research directions which grew out of our research.

METHOD

Data on the use of *cut-eye* and *suck-teeth* in the Caribbean area were obtained from several sources. For the detailed physical and ethnographic descriptions of the gestures in Guyana we drew mainly on our own observations and experience, supported by comments and criticisms from fellow Guyanese. For other areas in the West Indies, we first consulted available dictionaries and glossaries,[1] then carried out our own interviews with several West Indians, representing Antigua, Barbados, Haiti, Jamaica, Trinidad, and St. Kitts.

Data from the United States are based on original fieldwork conducted by the authors. Within the framework of a questionnaire designed to explore linguistic and cultural differences between black and white Americans, we asked the following question:

Now we want to consider some things that people say and use a lot. Do you know what the following things mean (in terms of the actions and 'social significance'):
(1) To 'cut your eyes' on someone
(2) To 'suck your teeth'[2]

In each case, the informant was asked to give a physical demonstration and to discuss the meaning freely. A corpus of seventy American informants was interviewed, in Philadelphia, Boston, and New York. Thirty-five of these were black, and thirty-five were white. Within each group, there were eighteen males and seventeen females. Informants represented a diverse range of native geographical backgrounds, including Pennsylvania, New York, California, Alabama, Georgia, Illinois, and Massachusetts.

Our African data were limited by the small number of accessible informants, and by the fact that so few dictionaries of African languages had entries classified in terms of English. Nevertheless, among students at the University of Pennsylvania and in Guyana, we managed to locate speakers of the following languages: Twi, Temne, Mende, Igbo, Yoruba,

Swahili, Luo, Banyang, Krio, and Cameroon Pidgin. They were first asked if they were familiar with the gestures, and then asked to provide data on their use and equivalent terms from their native languages if any existed.

CUT-EYE

In Guyana, *cut-eye* is a visual gesture which communicates hostility, displeasure, disapproval, or a general rejection of the person at whom it is directed. The very existence of a well-known term for this particular gesture indicates its centrality in the wide range of gestures in the culture, not all of which have comparable verbal labels.

The base *cut-eye* gesture is initiated by directing a hostile look or glare in the other person's direction. This may be delivered with the person directly facing, or slightly to one side. In the latter position, the person is seen out of the corners of the eyes, and some people deliberately turn their bodies sideways to achieve this effect. After the initial glare, the eyeballs are moved in a highly coordinated and controlled movement down or diagonally across the line of the person's body. This 'cut' with the eyes is the heart of the gesture, and may involve the single downward movement described above, or several sharp up-and-down movements. Both are generally completed by a final glare, and then the entire head may be turned away contemptuously from the person, to the accompaniment of a loud *suck-teeth*. See Figure 1 for the main stages of this sequence.

Part of the effectiveness of a *cut-eye* as a visual 'put-down' lies in its violation of what Erving Goffman has called the 'information preserve' of the individual, one of his important 'territories of the self'.[3] The information preserve is 'the set of facts about himself to which an individual expects to control access while in the presence of others', including 'what can be directly perceived about an individual, his body's sheath and his current behaviour, the issue here being his right *not to be stared at or examined* (emphasis ours)'.[4] As Goffman goes on to point out, since staring constitutes an invasion of informational preserve, it can then be used as 'a warranted negative sanction against somebody who has misbehaved'.[5]

A *cut-eye* provides even more of a 'negative sanction', since one not only invades, but with the eyes, rummages up, down, and about in another's preserve. It is as if the recipient has no power to prevent this visual assault, the very fact that someone else's eyes can run right over him like this proclaiming his worthlessness. The 'cut' is made even deeper

when the eyes are finally turned away — the implication here being that
the victim is not even worth further attention.

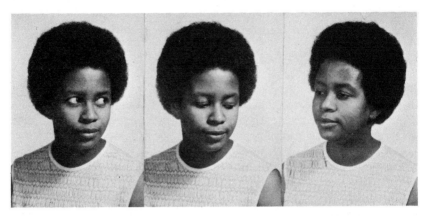

Figure 1. Sequence of movements in a cut-eye. *Note accompanying
suck-teeth (in this case, closure is made with the tongue against the alveolar
ridge)*

This kind of visual 'put-down' or 'cut-down' comes to the fore in
'buseings' or fierce arguments between two or more protagonists, especially between women. The argument is waged as much with words as
with eyes, each protagonist 'cutting up the eyes' on the other in a
threatening and belligerent fashion. But there may not be any verbal
argument at all. In any situation where one wishes to censure, or challenge someone else, or convey to him that he is not admired or respected,
a *cut-eye* may be conveniently employed.

Thus an old woman rebuking an eight-year-old for hitting her younger
brother on the street might receive a *cut-eye* from the child (challenging
her authority to intervene) in response. Similarly, a male who whistles at a
female may be met with a cold *cut-eye* suggesting that she does not
appreciate this form of greeting, and that he fails to win her interest or
favor. In both these cases, the recipient is guilty of some infringement of
what the sender considers his 'rights', and the provocation for the *cut-eye*
is clear (whether others consider it justified or appropriate is another
matter).

Sometimes however, the 'misbehavior' which earns someone a *cut-eye*
is not as obvious on the surface. The recipient need not have said or done
anything to the person who directs the gesture to him. But there is
something in the way he dresses, looks, or behaves, which, while not

necessarily intended, rubs someone else the 'wrong way'. This is particularly true if others around interpret the situation as one in which the recipient is trying to 'show off'. If, for instance, someone drives up in a big new car or arrives at a party in expensive clothes on the arm of a well-known figure, others around might cut their eyes on that person as a way of suggesting that they are not really impressed. The *cut-eye* is a way of saying 'you're no big thing at all, not to my mind at least'.

In fact, however, it frequently is the case that the recipient *is* someone in a situation which many people, including the sender, respect and envy. Thus, while the gesture might express genuine resentment and dislike, it is sometimes an attempt to nullify the appeal of another's attributes or circumstances when these are precisely what the sender would like to have. This is clearer when the sense in which people also talk of cutting their eyes on *something* is considered. A woman who sees a prohibitively expensive dress in a store window might report to her friends that she had to 'cut her eyes' on it and walk away. The phrase is used here to symbolize a rejection of something one would really like to have, but cannot or should not, because of personal circumstance.

The gesture of *cut-eye* is performed most frequently (and most skillfully!) by women. Men do not use this gesture as often and may experience real difficulty in trying to imitate the darting, highly coordinated movement which women can control. The gesture is often used when the other party in an encounter, conversation, or dispute, is enjoying his 'turn' to talk, and may prompt the latter to interrupt his turn to give a more powerful *cut-eye* or some form of verbal retort in return. One common verbal retort is *Look*, cut-eye *na a kill daag* 'Cut-eye doesn't kill dogs'. This acknowledges that an invasion or affront has been made but attempts to vindicate the recipient by claiming that it can do him or her no bodily harm.[6]

Another pattern can be seen in a turn-of-the-century description of a classic type of court dispute.[7] In the course of giving his testimony, the complainant notices that the defendant has 'cut his eye' on him. He interrupts his testimony to ask, *A who you a cut you yiye pon*? 'Who are you cutting your eyes on?', to which the defendant simply replies, *you see um* (which is roughly equivalent to 'If the shoe fits, wear it!'). In this particular incident, the exchange was followed by further verbal provocation and retort which is often called 'shotting' or 'rhyming' in Guyana, 'talking broad' or 'rhyming' in other Caribbean territories.[8]

The physical and ethnographic account of *cut-eye* given above still does not tell the whole story, but we have attempted to make it reasonably detailed, partly because of the limited data available on patterns of nonverbal communication generally, and also because we hope it might be more easily recognizable elsewhere by other researchers. As we ourselves discovered since beginning this study, it is certainly known and used in other parts of the Caribbean. The term is listed in the *Dictionary of Jamaican English* for what is clearly the same gesture with the same meaning:

> *Cut-Eye*: to catch (someone or something) with the eyes, then quickly close them and turn or toss the eyes aside. The purpose of the action may be to avoid temptation . . . but it is usually directed against another person . . . and is usually insulting.[9]

The editors also add that the action may combine insult and temptation into provocation, and they cite the following definitions from Miss Joyce Nation:

> To cut one's eyes is to toss one's head away from a man's glance in a contemptuous but sexually provoking fashion: Little girl to a little boy, 'You come a me yard' (cutting her eyes) 'come if you name man.'[10]

While this 'provocative' use of *cut-eye* is also found in Guyana, it is usually distinguished from the more hostile use of the gesture in very subtle ways, involving different privileges of cooccurrence with other paralinguistic features or 'kinesic markers'.[11] The difference may reside in nothing more than whether the *cut-eye* is accompanied by a slight smile, or by a *suck-teeth*, and sometimes males misread the meaning of a female's *cut-eye*, to their own embarrassment.

The term, the gesture, and its meaning, as discussed above were all instantly recognized by the various West Indians whom we interviewed. From Karl Reisman (personal communication), we also learned that it can be frequently observed in Antigua. A Haitian informant provided a dramatic demonstration of the gesture as soon as it was mentioned and explained that it was known in Haiti as *couper yeux* — literally 'to cut (or cutting) the eyes'. We find it very striking that the Haitian expression for this gesture should consist of morphemes which literally refer to *cut* and *eye*. The same phenomenon may be observed in Saramaccan (example provided by Ian Hancock): *a ta koti woyo* 'she's cutting eye'. These examples seem to suggest different New World relexifications of an expression which existed either in one or more African languages or in a proto-Pidgin, and which included morphemes for *cut* and *eye*. We will return to this point briefly when considering the data from African languages.

The results of our questionnaire investigation of familiarity with *cut-eye* in the United States were more dramatic than we expected. As Table

1 indicates, almost all the black informants were familiar with the term. Among the 'meanings' volunteered were 'a look of disgust'; 'expression of hositility'; 'to threaten'; 'act of defiance or disapproval'; 'bad feelings'; 'when you're mad at someone'; 'to show you don't like somebody'. All the black women understood the term and were able to perform the gesture easily and expertly.

Table 1. *Number of American informants familiar with* cut-eye *according to race and sex.*

Sex		Blacks		Whites
Males	(N=18)	16	(N=18)	2
Females	(N=17)	17	(N=17)	2
Total	(N=35)	33	(N=35)	4

Two of the black men were not familiar with the term. The other sixteen, although clearly aware of the meaning of the gesture, could not execute it as skillfully as their female counterparts, and they kept excusing themselves by saying, 'Mostly women do that.' As we have noted above, this situation is parallelled in the Caribbean. Some of the men felt it would be a 'cop-out' for a man to keep using this gesture to express his feelings — physical or verbal expression ('sounding') would be the more masculine thing to do. Barring this, one should simply 'keep one's cool' — remain silent, apparently unperturbed.

As Table 1 also indicates, *cut-eye* as a lexical item and as a cultural form of behavior is almost totally unknown to white Americans. Only four of the thirty-five white informants displayed familiarity with the term. Of these, three said 'to stare at someone', and one suggested 'to look at someone out of the corner of the eye'. These are good descriptions of the initial stage of the gesture, but not of the complete sequence. And in none of the cases could a white informant execute the full gesture.

Sixteen Whites plainly admitted that they had never heard the term before and had no idea of its meaning. The other fifteen in the sample provided idiosyncratic and highly varied responses: 'expression of religious ecstasy'; 'to go to sleep on someone'; 'to stop looking at someone'; 'expression of horror'; 'to look at someone attractively for a long time'. This sharp divergence between the responses of Blacks and Whites is all the more revealing because many of the black informants were middle-class individuals completing their college education and might otherwise be considered highly acculturated to the mainstream American culture.

Some of the black informants mentioned that 'rolling the eyes' is sometimes used instead of 'cutting the eyes' in black American communities to refer to the very same gesture. This is confirmed in Kenneth Johnson's description of 'rolling the eyes' among American Blacks which accords with our description of *cut-eye* in Guyana on several points.[12] Unless it omits certain details, however, the following description from another researcher would suggest that the physical movements involved in 'rolling the eyes' might be slightly different:

If a girl in a lounge does not want to be bothered when a cat comes up to rap, she might lift up one shoulder slightly, rolling her eyes upward in her head as though saying, 'what a drag!'[13]

Whether or not this is the case, note that the meaning and usage of the gesture will register dislike, disapproval, or hostility. The fact that the general public usually associates 'rolling the eyes' with ingratiation and 'Uncle Tom' behavior (an image partly propagated by television and the cinema) suggests that Blacks might have endowed the gesture with a systematic ambiguity which they exploited to permit safe and subtle expression of their more genuine feelings. As we shall see later, *suck-teeth* can be similarly used with a strategic ambiguity.

Before presenting the results of our research on *cut-eye* with African informants, we feel a few remarks are in order. Several scholars have attempted to pinpoint the African languages which, for various historical reasons, may be assumed to have had the greatest influence on the New World pidgins and creoles. The lists are somewhat different from one scholar to another, and the relative importance of particular languages (like Wolof) is a matter of some dispute.[14]

The absence of universal agreement in this area is sometimes problematic. When considering possible etymologies for New World forms, it can be difficult to determine which languages must be examined and what weight must be assigned to the evidence of one language as against another. However, this problem is not always as critical as it might seem, because as many observers have noted, many New World Africanisms go back to generalized features of West Africa, even of sub-Saharan Africa as a whole.[15] Given the multiplicity of areas from which slaves were taken, it is easy to see why this might have been so. 'Survivals' were more likely to survive if they were supported by the common experience of Africans from several areas and tribal affiliations, rather than restricted to a single group.

We cannot claim to have exhausted all the 'key' languages in the lists referred to above. However, the picture which emerges from the languages for which we do have data is that the concept of a *cut-eye* or *suck-teeth* gesture is familiar in several areas of both West and East Africa, and it is described by a verbal label in many of the languages spoken there.

The Mende, Banyang, and Luo examples make use of morphemes with the literal meaning of 'cutting the eyes' or 'sucking the teeth', and thus provide the kind of models we would need to classify our New World compounds as straight cases of loan-translation. However, we are in no position to claim that any one of these provided a particular immediate source. Neither Banyang (a 'minor' language spoken in Cameroon) nor Luo (an east coast language) are normally rated as 'key' languages where the business of seeking etymologies for New World forms is concerned. Mende certainly is a 'key' language in this sense, but several others for which we do not have data may provide equally plausible prototypes for loan-translation. The whole point of our discussion is that all this is not crucial. We shall probably never know which language or languages provided the immediate source; wherever the particular description of 'cutting the eyes' may have come from, it received support from the fact that what it referred to was familiar everywhere.

All of the African informants with whom we talked, for instance, recognized the *cut-eye* gesture immediately. They provided the following equivalent expressions:

> Twi: *obu ma ni kyi* 'He breaks the backs of the eye on me'.[16]
> Yoruba: *mólójú* 'making expressions with your eyes to show disapproval'.[17] R. Abraham also lists *mónlójú* cross-referenced to *món* (D.2) under which the following items are listed: (I) *ó mónjú* 'He looked away contemptuously', (II) *ó món ni lójú* 'He looked at me in scorn', (III) *àwòmon jú* 'a scornful look'.[18]
> Cameroon Pidgin: *no kɔt yɔ ai fɔmi* 'Don't cut your eye on me'.
> Banyang: *a kpot a mek ne me* 'She cut her eyes on me'.
> Luo: *kik ilokna wangi* 'He is cutting his eyes'.
> Swahili: *usinioloka macho* 'to roll one's eyes'.

The last two languages provide an interesting comparison. They are both spoken in Kenya, Swahili as the more widespread and better known East African lingua franca. The terms in Luo and Swahili correspond to the two American variants: to 'cut' and to 'roll' the eyes respectively. Data from other languages may provide other possible sources for the alternation between these terms.

SUCK-TEETH

Suck-Teeth refers to the gesture of drawing air through the teeth and into the mouth to produce a loud sucking sound. In the basic *suck-teeth* gesture, the back of the tongue is raised toward the soft palate and a vacuum created behind a closure formed in the front part of the mouth. This closure may be made with the lower lip against the upper teeth (as in Figure 2), or with the tip or blade of the tongue just behind the upper teeth, on the alveolar ridge (as in Figure 1, although not clearly seen). When the closure is suddenly relaxed, air outside the mouth rushes in audibly.

Figure 2. A suck-teeth *made with the inner surface of the lower lip pressed against the upper teeth.*

The gesture is accomplished by the same velaric ingressive mechanism used to produce the 'clicks' of Khoisan and Southern Bantu languages.[19] The differences lie mainly in the fact that the closure for 'clicks' may be formed at several other points in the mouth, and that while 'clicks' are stops — produced by one sharp release of the closure, a *suck-teeth* is more like a prolonged fricative — after the closure is relaxed, air continues to rush in turbulently through the narrow opening.

There are all kinds of minor variations in the way the gesture is produced. It can be made with the lips tensely pouted, or with them spread out, or pulled to one side. There are variations in the duration and intensity of the sound produced depending on the tightness of the closure and the pressure of the inrushing air. These variations depend to some extent on personal habit, but are governed also by the situation — how angry one is, whether one is in a place (like a church) or in company (a circle of parents' friends) in which a loud *suck-teeth* might be frowned on. In general, however, the longer and louder the *suck-teeth*, the more forceful and expressive its 'meaning'.

Suck-teeth, also known in Guyana and the Caribbean as *stchoops* (*-teeth*) or *chups* (*-teeth*), is an expression of anger, impatience, exasperation, or annoyance. It shares some of the semantics of *cut-eye* and, as mentioned before, is often used in combination with the latter. It can be more open and powerful, however, and it is considered ill-mannered in certain situations. For instance, while people of all ages do it when something annoys them or someone makes them angry, its use by children in the presence of their parents or other adults is considered rude and insubordinate. As J. Cruickshank noted in 1916: 'A sulking child is told sharply, "Wha you suck teeth fo?" . . . With eyes lowered and lip pouting, it pictures disgust, discontent — rebellion with the lid on.'[20]

The prohibitions against the use of this gesture are sometimes justified by the claim that it means 'kiss my ass' or 'kiss my private parts'. This meaning may have become attached to it because of the close resemblance between the sound made in producing a *suck-teeth* and the sound sometimes made for 'calling off' a girl on the street. This latter sound is made with pouted lips (the teeth not involved as articulators), and is supposed to represent a forceful kiss (among other things). It has much cruder sexual connotations than other ways of attracting a girl's attention (like whistling, or saying *psssssss*), and these seem to be attached also to the *suck-teeth* sound.

To avoid actually sucking the teeth in situations where it might be considered vulgar or ill-mannered, people sometimes say the words *stchoops* or *chups* without making the sound itself. Other interjections like *cha*, *cho*, or *shoots* may also be used, and children in particular will purse or put their lips as if preparing to make a *suck-teeth*, but again, without making any audible sound. The advantage of this latter strategy is that it can be carried out behind the back of a reproachful adult without fear of discovery or reprimand.

Interviews with informants from Jamaica, Trinidad, Barbados, Antigua, and even Haiti (where, we understand, it is sometimes referred to as *tuiper* or *cuiper*) confirmed familiarity with this oral gesture, its meaning, and the social prohibitions against its use as outlined above. In Antigua, according to Karl Reisman (personal communication), *stchoops* to describe the action of sucking one's teeth is convergent with the word for 'stupid', and the ambiguity is well exploited (*Wuh yuh stchoopsin yuh teeth fuh? Yuh stchoops or wuh?*). This reinforces the negative social connotations of the gesture.

The West Indian dictionaries and glossaries all contain some reference to *suck-teeth* or the alt rnate terms *stchoops* and *chups*. The *Dictionary of Jamaican English* defines *suck-teeth* as 'a sound of annoyance, displeasure, ill nature or disrespect (made) by sucking air audibly through the teeth and over the tongue.'[21] Hyman Rodman refers to it as an 'expression of disdain or mild disgust', and gives as an example of its usage: 'When I suggested that she visit them, she said *stchoops*.'[22]

Frank Collymore, writing on Barbados, describes it as indicative of distrust or sulking, but attempts also a more detailed classification of the different kinds of *chupses* or *suck-teeth* which is worth reprinting:

(i) the *chupse* of "amused tolerance", used in retort to some absurd remark or statement, a sort of oral shrugging of the shoulders; (ii) the *chupse* "self-admonitory" when the chupser has done something of which he has no occasion to be proud; (iii) the *chupse* "disdainful", accompanied by a raising of the eyebrow; (iv) the *chupse* "disgusted", in the performance of which the eyebrows are almost closed; (v) the *chupse* "sorrowful", in reality a series of quickly emitted chupses, the head being shaken slowly from side to side; (vi) the *chupse* "offensive and abusive"; (vii) the *chupse* "provocative", a combination of (iii), (iv) and (vi) which often leads to blows.[23]

This description certainly seems to justify the statement attributed by Collymore to the lead-writer of the *Barbados Advocate*, 'the *chupse* is not a word, it is a whole language . . . the passport to confidence from Jamaica to British South America.'[24]

The immediately preceding statement appears, however, to have set too closely the northern limits of the area in which *chupse* or *suck-teeth* is known. This is clear from Table 2, which reveals that many Black Americans are also familiar with it.

Table 2. *Race and sex.*

Sex		Blacks		Whites
Males	(N=18)	10	(N=18)	0
Females	(N=17)	14	(N=17)	1
Total	(N=35)	24	(N=35)	1

If we compare Table 2 with Table 1, it is clear that black Americans are slightly less familiar with *suck-teeth* than with *cut-eye* (nine persons who recognized the latter failed to recognize the former). But the recognition rate is still quite high (68.5 percent), with the black females again slightly in the lead.[25] Among the 'meanings' given by black informants were: 'when disgusted'; 'act of defiance, disapproval'; 'sign of frustration'; 'impatience'; 'to show disappointment'.

What is particularly striking about Table 2, however, is that only *one* white American, a woman, was familiar with *suck-teeth*. Twenty-six of the white informants did not even attempt to suggest possible meanings, and the eight who did were far off the intended track: 'to shut up'; 'to stammer'; 'to express that you like food'; 'after eating to clean teeth'. This last 'meaning' was suggested by four informants, and in fact is the only one given for 'sucking the teeth' in the *Oxford English Dictionary*. Under entry 10b for the verb *suck* is listed: 'to apply one's tongue and inner sides of the lips to (one's teeth) so as to extract particles of food.'

Now while West Indians rarely speak of 'sucking the teeth' in this 'Standard English' sense, they sometimes use it as a cover or excuse for the everyday *suck-teeth* of annoyance or insubordination. For example, a student who responds to the teacher's instructions to write an essay in class with an inadvertent *suck-teeth*, might claim as she approaches him with an icy stare, that he was just 'trying to clear out his teeth'. Given the demonstrated divergences between what black and white Americans most commonly understand by this gesture, it is not at all difficult to imagine that many a slave might have been able to use it on his masters with equally feigned innocence, to express feelings of exasperation and rage for which there was no other outlet.

As early as 1951, Richard Allsopp had observed that 'words exist in West and East African languages which contain a sound produced by sucking air between the teeth. What connection this may have with sulking or defiance, however, as it does in our (Guyana) dialect, I do not know.'[26] It is not clear from this whether Allsopp is referring to the famous "clicks" of certain African languages (which so far as we know have no connection with rudeness or defiance). However our interviews with African informants some two decades later confirmed that they were in fact familiar with the gesture, and that many of their languages had verbal labels referring to it. Some of the African informants pointed out spontaneously that 'sucking your teeth' in front of your parents was very rude, likely to earn you a slap or a whipping. This is, as we pointed out before, also true of Guyana and the rest of the Caribbean.

The African equivalents for *suck-teeth* which we collected were the following:

Mende: *i ngi yongoi γofoin lc nya ma* 'He sucked his teeth on me' (literally, 'He his teeth sucked me on').[27]
Temne: *tós nė* 'to suck to self'.
Igbo: *íma osò* 'to make a sucking noise with the mouth'.
Yoruba: *kpòše* '(vb.) 'to make a sucking noise with the mouth'.
òše '(n.) 'sucking noise made with the mouth'.[28]
Luo: *ichiya* (vb.) 'to make suck-teeth noise'.
chiyo (n.) 'suck-teeth noise'.
Krio: *no sck yu tit pan mi* 'Don't suck your teeth on me'.
no sɔk tit mi 'Don't suck-teeth me'.
Cameroon Pidgin: *no sɔk yɔ tif fɔ mi* 'Don't suck your teeth on me'.

There is the possibility too that *chups* and *stchoops* also have their roots in an African expression for the gesture involving the word 'suck'. We had always assumed that these were merely onomatopoeic creations for the sound made in sucking one's teeth. But as Hancock points out (personal communication), the Papiamentu and Sranan expressions for the gesture include a morpheme *tšupa*, which is very similar, of course, to *chups* or *stchoops*. It may derive from the Portuguese *chupar*, which, not surprisingly, means 'to suck'. But it is also significant that in Gambian Krio ('Aku'), the term for *suck-teeth* is *tšipú*, adopted from Wolof. As Hancock himself was the first to suggest, the Caribbean forms *chups* and *stchoops* may possibly represent a convergence of the Portuguese and Wolof forms.

If *chups* and *stchoops* turn out to be more than mere onomatopoeic New World creations, so also do the other equivalents or substitutes mentioned above: *cho, chu*, and *tcha*. There is first the possibility that these are merely abbreviated forms of *chups*. But there are other possibilities. The *Dictionary of Jamaican English* describes *cho* (with variants /*cho, cha, chut, chu*/) as 'an exclamation expressing scorn, disagreement, expostulation, etc.', and provides two possible West African sources: 'Ewe *tsóò* — interjection of astonishment, anger, impatience, disappointment', and 'Twi *twéaa* — interjection of uttermost contempt'.[29] The editors add that 'English *tcha* can hardly be the source', because the earliest citations for *tcha* in the *Oxford English Dictionary* are later (1844, 1887) than the Jamaican attestations (1827, 1835).[30] In fact, far from being the source, English *tcha* may well be a later reflex of the Ewe or Twi interjections, perhaps via the Caribbean forms *cho* and *cha*.

This expanding network of possible African derivations which grew out of our original research into *suck-teeth* does not end here. After reading an earlier version of this paper, Ian Hancock mentioned that the Yoruba have a term (*šumú, šùtì*) for the gesture we discussed above of pursing the lips for a *suck-teeth* without actually making the sound. We wrote back, without taking it too seriously, that people sometimes refer to this in Guyana as *faul biti maut* 'mouth shaped like a fowl's behind'. When Hancock replied excitedly that speakers of Krio in Sierra Leone also use this very metaphor — *luk we yu de mek yu mɔt leke fol yon* 'look how you make your mouth like a fowl's behind', we felt the similarity could hardly be due to coincidence. Once again we were struck by the pervasiveness of the African influence which lurks behind so many of the symbols, patterns, and institutions we manipulate in the New World from day to day.

CONCLUSION

Cut-eye and *suck-teeth* provide clear evidence that 'Africanisms' in the New World may reside not only in the exotic, but also (and perhaps more frequently) in the commonplace. In general, the identity of such items will not be obvious, either to 'natives' or 'outsiders'. However, it may be revealed by careful attention to disparities in usage between Whites and Blacks, and to the recurrence of the same patterns in different communities which have sizable African-derived populations.

To discover other nonverbal patterns, we need to be interested not just in rare and elaborate rites, but also in the more 'ordinary' rituals involved in everyday behavior: how people walk and stand; how they greet and take their leave of each other; what they do with their faces and hands when conversing, narrating, or arguing, and so on. Karl Reisman has come across some examples of just this type in Antigua quite recently,[31] and of course Herskovits had suggested several others over three decades ago which still warrant further investigation.[32]

In terms of linguistic survivals, we can translate the need to look for the commonplace into an increased alertness for loan-translations and cases of convergence between English (or other European) and African forms. Like *cut-eye* and *suck-teeth*, these will look like ordinary English words; sometimes it is only the subtlest 'non-English' shades of meaning and usage which will help to give them away.[33] In fact, where a particular form and meaning have become generalized in almost every part of the English-speaking world,[34] we will not have even this clue. Difficulties of this sort (and others) can make the search for loan-translations and convergences more harrowing than the search for direct loans of the *nyam* and *goober* type.

On the other hand, the very English facade which makes them difficult to recognize today has undoubtedly helped them to survive in larger numbers. Like *cut-eye* and *suck-teeth* they may be actively used even among those people who are striving most consciously toward the prestigious 'standard' language and culture, and in whose speech direct African loans like *nyam* are unlikely to be found.

There is an additional significance to the study of loan-translations and convergences. As Dalby has suggested, they must have been invaluable in the creation and maintenance of a subtle code by means of which slaves could communicate with each other without fear of detection or punishment by Whites.[35] From our suggestions above, too, of the ways in which the gestures discussed in this paper might have been passed off with more acceptable 'meanings' (*cut-eye* as ingratiation, *suck-teeth* as the effort to remove food from the teeth), it is clear that the code was not restricted to linguistic material. Both verbal and nonverbal resources were utilized for its creation. *Cut-eye* and *suck-teeth*, Africanisms both as words and as gestures, are themselves evidence of this.

Other examples abound. Reisman notes the existence of a side-up turn of the head in Antigua which seems to be of African origin; it is used today as a greeting, but it also resembles a Euro-American head-gesture which might have been used as a command ('Come over here!') in the plantation environment.[36] Investing the latter gesture with the 'African' interpretation of a salutation would have provided a measure of personal satisfaction, 'a way to redress the harshness of the slavery situation'.[37] Similar to this is the story told to us by Richmond Wiley, a native of the South Carolina Sea-Islands, of a slave who used to answer his master's queries and commands with the words 'You-ass, sir!' The insult, so obvious to his fellow slaves, was passed off on the master as the slave's slurred pronunciation of 'Yes, sir!'

More urgently and directly communicative was the way slaves would raise the spiritual refrain 'Wait in the Water' from one plantation to the next to warn a runaway that bloodhounds were on his trail — a signal interpreted by the masters as their expression of religious zeal. In all these cases, the existence of public and more 'acceptable' interpretations is exploited by Blacks for the communication of more private or 'unacceptable' meanings.[38] The value of Africanisms in this more general strategy is that they provided one of the sources (though not the only one) of its fuel.

As we hope this paper has itself been able to demonstrate, there is more to be done with 'Africanisms' than presenting them in a list with possible sources. Viewed from the standpoint of different cultures and social groupings in both the present and the past, they have much to tell us about how peoples of African descent adapted to the experience of the New

World, and how much they were understood by their social and political superiors. Finally, as we should like to stress again, the most telling Africanisms from this point of view might involve the most ordinary items of everyday behavior — how that person is looking at you across a room, or what that woman is yelling down the street.[39]

NOTES

1. These include Frederick G. Cassidy and Robert B. LePage, editors (1967), *Dictionary of Jamaican English*. London, Cambridge University Press. Frank Collymore (1970), *Notes for a Glossary of Words and Phrases of Barbadian Dialect*. Bridgetown, Advocate. J. Graham Cruickshank (1916), *Black Talk, being Notes on Negro Dialect in British Guiana*. Georgetown, Demerara, Argosy. Carlton R. Ottley (1971), *Creole Talk of Trinidad and Tobago*. Port of Spain, Ottley; and the glossary in Hyman Rodman (1971), *Lower-Class Families in the Culture of Poverty in Negro Trinidad*. New York, Oxford University Press.

2. Discussion of some of the other items which appeared in this questionnaire and provided evidence of sharp discontinuities in the linguistic competence of Blacks and Whites is contained in J. Rickford (1975), 'Carrying the new wave into syntax — the case of B. E. BIN' in *Proceedings of the Second Annual Colloquium on New Ways of Analysing Variation*, ed. by Roger Shuy. Washington D.C.

3. Erving Goffman (1972), *Relations in Public*, 28–61. New York, Basic Books.

4. Ibid., p. 39.

5. Ibid., p. 61.

6. Compare one of the standard rejoinders to *verbal* insult or mockery:
   'Sticks and stones can break my bones,
   But words can never hurt me.'

7. Michael 'Quow' McTurk (1899), *Essays and Fables in the Vernacular*. Georgetown, Demerara, Argosy.

8. Roger Abrahams (1972), 'The training of the mans of words in talking broad,' in *Rappin' and Stylin' Out*, ed. by Thomas Kochman, 215–240. Urbana, University of Illinois Press.

9. Cassidy and LePage, p. 139. Compare also the brief descriptions in Collymore, p. 38, and Cruickshank, p. 31.

10. Miss Nation's contributions to the *Dictionary* were made on the basis of her analysis of the spontaneous conversation of Jamaican children.

11. This is one of the useful terms for the basic units of contrast in body-motion communication derived from Ray L. Birdwhistell (1970), *Kinesics and Context*. Philadelphia, University of Pennsylvania Press.

12. Kenneth Johnson (1971), 'Black kinesics — some non-verbal communication patterns in the Black culture', *Florida Foreign Language Reporter* (Spring/Fall):17–20.

13. Benjamin Cooke, 'Non-verbal communication among Afro-Americans — an initial classification', in *Rappin' and Stylin' Out: Communication in Urban Black America*, ed. by Thomas Kochman, 32–64. Urbana, Ill., University of Illinois Press.

14. Compare the list of 'key' languages in Lorenzo Dow Turner (1949), *Africanisms in the Gullah Dialect*, Chicago, University of Chicago Press, with the list in David Dalby, 'The African element in American English', in *Rappin' and Stylin' Out*, 170–186.

15. On this point, see Mervyn C. Alleyne, 'Acculturation and the cultural matrix of creolization', in *Pidginization and Creolization of Languages*, ed. by Dell Hymes, 175–176. Cambridge. England, Cambridge University Press, and Ian F. Hancock (1971), *A Study of the Sources and Development in the Lexicon of Sierra Leone Krio*, 652. Ph.D. Thesis, University of London.

16. This metaphorical reference to 'breaking the back of the eye' is evocative of the straining of the eye muscles which one actually feels when delivering a good *cut-eye*.

17. For all Yoruba examples cited in this paper, v́ = high tone, v = mid tone, v̀ = low tone, and v⁼ mid-high rising tone.

18. R. C. Abraham (1958), *Dictionary of Modern Yoruba*, 423, 427. London, University of London Press.

19. Peter Ladefoged (1967), *Linguistic Phonetics*. Los Angeles, UCLA Press; D. Westerman and Ida C. Ward (1933), *Practical Phonetics for Students of African Languages*. London.

20. Cruickshank, p. 50.

21. Cassidy and LePage, p. 428.

22. Rodman, p. 235.

23. Collymore, pp. 30–31.

24. Ibid.

25. Some of the black females pointed out that 'titting your teeth' is sometimes used instead of 'sucking your teeth' for the same gesture.

26. Richard Allsopp (1950), 'The language we speak', *Kyk-Over-Al* 3 (11):25.

27. We wish to thank Richard Allsopp for contributing this example.

28. R. C. Abraham, p. 490, describes *òse* (1a) as 'a sign denoting unhappiness'. I. O. Delano (1969), *A Dictionary of Yoruba Monosyllabic Verbs*, 2, Ile-Ife, Nigeria, Institute of African Studies, University of Ife, p. 91, glosses *pòšé* thus: 'to express impatience or dissatisfaction by saying "pshaw".'

29. Cassidy and LePage, p. 441.

30. Ibid.

31. Karl Reisman (1970), 'Cultural and linguistic ambiguity in a West Indian village', in *Afro-American Anthropology*, ed. by Norman E. Whitten Jr. and John F. Szwed, 132–133. New York, Free Press.

32. Melville J. Herskovits (1941), *The Myth of the Negro Past*. New York, Harper.

33. On this point, see Frederic G. Cassidy (1961), 'Multiple etymologies in Jamaican Creole'. *American Speech*, 4:211–214, and Jay G. Edwards (1974), 'African influences on the English of San Andres Island, Colombia,' in *Pidgins and Creoles: Current Trends and Prospects*, ed. David DeCamp and Ian F. Hancock, 1–26. Washington, D.C., Georgetown University Press.

34. Like 'O.K.,' the informal signal of assent or agreement, which is discussed in David Dalby.

35. Ibid., p. 174.

36. Reisman, pp. 132–133.

37. Ibid., p. 133.

38. Reisman, ibid., provides the most detailed discussion of the different ways in which all kinds of linguistic and cultural symbols in Antigua have been subject to a process of remodeling and reinterpretation which allows them to 'mediate at least two sets of cultural identities and meanings'.

39. This article represents a revised version of a paper entitled 'Cut-Eye and Suck-Teeth' originally prepared in June 1973, and circulated in mimeo. We wish to thank Karl Reisman and Ian Hancock, who helped with data collection and provided both encour-

agement and criticism. We should also like to thank the many Americans who partici-
pated in our questionnaire, and the various West Indian and African informants, too
numerous to mention by name.

JOHN HOLM

The Creole 'Copula' that Highlighted the World

There is evidence for the genetic relationship between various creole and West African languages in the existence of the highlighting copula, the topic of this paper. Although this grammatical element is found both in the Atlantic creoles and in languages native to West Africa, it is not present in the creoles' European parent languages. Evidence will be presented to link this highlighter to the introducing *i's* of U.S. Black English, in which the 'copula' simply does not delete according to Labov's general rule; it will be argued that this is in fact a single morpheme descended from the creole and African ancestors of Black English.

The creoles, unlike their European lexical-source languages, have a variety of 'copulas' (as the term is used in Labov [1969]), the uses of which are determined by certain syntactic and semantic restrictions (Holm 1976). Specific West African languages whose influence on the formation of these creoles is historically probable, such as Yoruba, were found to have a similar variety of copulas with parallel distributional restrictions, and seem likely sources for this phenomenon in creoles.

Subsequent fieldwork[1] has shown that copulas are found in a similar range, unknown in Standard English, in the creole English spoken on Nicaragua's Caribbean shore, Miskito Coast Creole (MCC):

1. *iz* equating two *noun phrases*:

/rigl *iz* jos a shaat ting/ 'A riddle is just a short thing.'[2]

2. *o* before *adjectives* (a subclass of verbs):

/nansi — frii/ 'Anancy was free.'[3]

3. *de* indicating *location*:

/i no kom we a *de*/ 'He doesn't come where I am.'

4. The preverbal *progressive* aspect marker, properly not a copula at all although indicated in Standard English by *be*, was found in the basilect (or variety of creole least influenced by Standard English) to be *de*:

/a *de* trai/ 'I'm trying.'

Few violations of these rules are to be found among basilect speakers.

The highlighter, the topic of the present discussion, constitutes a fifth syntactic category for 'copula' in MCC. In the basilect, this highlighter takes the form *a* and can, among other functions, focus attention on a question word by introducing it:

5. /bot *a* wa tu duu/ 'But what to do?'

The nearest English equivalent seems in this case unidiomatic: 'But what *is it that* I can do?' Another possible English gloss, *the hell*, as in 'What the hell can I do?' is a syntactically similar questionword emphasizer, although its semantic and sociolinguistic restrictions are clearly distinct.

A structure not traceable to any Standard English syntactic pattern results in the mesolect when basilect *a* relexifies to *iz* and highlights an embedded question:

6. /yuu no nuo *iz* huu/ 'You don't know who it is.'

In Jamaican Creole (JC), closely related to MCC historically, a similar question-word highlighter is found:

7. /*a*-wa Anti sen fi mi/ 'What has Auntie sent for me?' (Bailey 1966:88).

'If any of the constituents *nominal, manner, locative*, and *time*, as well as the nominal modifiers *determiner* and *specifier*, is to be the focus of the question, the sentence is inverted, with the focus moved to the front position and ... preceded by *a*' (Bailey 1966:88). Accordingly, *a* can also highlight the question words /huu, hou, we, wen, homoch, wich/. In fact, Bailey (1966:90) prefers to treat the occurrence of these items alone as instances of 'deletion of introductory "*a*" '.

A distinct function of JC *a* is to equate two noun phrases in the basilect:

8. /dis *a* di liida/ 'This is the leader.' (Bailey 1966:87).

Under pressure from the standard, equative JC *a* can be replaced by *iz* (Bailey 1966:139), yielding /dis *iz* di liida/, identical to MCC equative *iz* in (1) above.

A third function of JC *a*, in which its uses as a highlighter and equator merge, is as an introducer of noun phrases:

9. /*a* Mieri/ 'It's Mary' (Bailey 1966:87).

Again, JC *a* can relexify to *iz*, the usual MCC form in this structure:

10. /*iz* truut/ 'It's the truth.'

Although the phonological proximity of mesolect *iz* to standard *it's* allows *iz* to 'pass' and be easily understood by Standard English speakers (whose contracted pronoun and copula is clearly the etymological source of *a*'s relexified form), it would be difficult to justify the analysis of MCC *iz* as anything except a single morpheme; indeed, there are no synchronic phonological rules in the creole mesolect that could yield a contraction of /it iz/. Perhaps a more helpful analogy (for which I am indebted to Richard Hudson) is that of the French presentative *voilà*, which functions synchronically as a single morpheme, or Russian *bot*, which also introduces a noun phrase in a pattern requiring no verb.

In American Black English Vernacular (BEV), Labov (1972:116) found that the copula did not contract and delete in the usual manner after *it*. While one might well find a zero copula in a BEV sentence like *Pat good*, one does not find **It good* despite the parallel phonological environment for deletion of the copula, but rather *I's good*. Labov provides phonological rules to reduce *it ## iz* to *is* (vowel reduction, contraction, assibilation, and deletion), but offers no explanation as to why these rules do not apply to nonpronouns as in his own counterexample, *Pat good*. In light of MCC /iz truut/, it would seem that the first element in BEV /is di truuf/ is derived from a *single* syntactic unit in an earlier creole which functioned like the JC and MCC introducer *iz*. BEV *is* is restricted to this syntactic function, *iz* occurring elsewhere (among other forms). In noninterrogative sentences JC and MCC introducing *iz* can be replaced by *das*, which may have a slightly stronger deictic force:

11. /*das* wai yuu kom/ 'That's why you came.'

12. /*das* di smuok/ 'That's the smoke.'

Although the lexical source of *das* clearly lies in the contraction of two English morphemes, the creole word functions syntactically as a single unit; cf.:

13. Das *would be de bes' place* 'That would be . . .' (Cassidy and LePage 1967:197).

A possible parallel to a historical transitional form might be found in Texan Afro-Seminole Creole:

14. /*dʒ* hɪm *dʒ* dɪ wɜn/ 'He's the one' (Hancock 1977:9).

Although the two underlined copulas are likely to correspond to introductory and equative *a* (or *iz*), a Standard English speaker might 'interpret' them along the lines of the roughly equivalent: 'That's him, that's the one'. Interestingly enough, the first word in Afro-Seminole:

15. /*dæs* mai frē:n/ 'That's my friend' (Hancock 1977:13).

corresponds in function and t-loss to JC and MCC *das*, strongly suggesting a common historical source. In fact, the introducer *tha's* occurs in BEV, paralleling *i's* in function (Labov 1972:116). The fact that these items are not normally used by white Americans lends credence to the hypothesis that they are of creole origin. While Labov's phonological rules for t-loss are certainly of diachronic importance, it is less certain whether they are synchronically functional, although *wha's* and *lo's* (Labov 1972:116) could be interpreted as evidence that the rules are still productive.

In seeking the source of JC *a*, it will be helpful to look at one more of its functions; in order to distinguish this use from those discussed above (equating and introducing), it will be referred to as highlighting:

16. /a Mieri waan di buk/ 'It's *Mary* who wants the book' (i.e. not Jane)

17. /a di buk Mieri waan/ 'It's the *book* Mary wants' (i.e. not the pencil) (Bailey 1966:86).

Given *a*'s mesolectal form *iz*, one might be tempted to analyze such sentences as nothing more exotic than front-shifting with deletion of a subject relative pronoun, quite possible in nonstandard British and American dialects:

18. It's Mary wants the book.

19. BEV: It's a bush grow up like that (Smith 1973:93).

However, this analogy will not account for MCC highlighting of verb phrases:

20. /so i sista driim somting, bot *iz* driim somting bad/ 'So his sister dreamt of something, but it was something bad she dreamt of.'

Finally, we are clearly dealing with a structure unknown among the Indo-European languages when verbs (and adjectives, a subclass of verbs) frontshift to a position following an introductory highlighter, but maintain their position in the original sentence structure by means of reduplication:

21. /a tiif Jan tiif di manggo/ 'John *stole* the mango' (he didn't pay . . .).

22. /a sik Samwel sik/ 'Samuel is *sick*' (not tired)' (Bailey 1966:86).

This structure, rather ambiguously called 'predicate-clefting' by Bynoe-Andriolo and Yillah (1975:234), is found in a variety of creole and West African languages. It will be useful to examine several of these to see whether the particle introducing this easily identifiable verbal structure can also fill any of the other functions of JC and MCC *a* / *iz*; if this is found to be the case, it is evidence that the highlighters — and, indeed, the languages themselves — are related.

The Yoruba particle *ni* does not precede but follows[4] the word it highlights. It is used with the predicate-clefting construction discussed above:

23. /nínà *ni* ng ó nà á/ lit. 'Beating *it is* I will beat him' or 'I'll give him a good beating.' (Rowlands 1969:158).

24. /pípá *ni* nwón pá á/ lit. 'Killing *it is* they killed him' or 'They actually killed him' (Rowlands 1969:189).

Yoruba has a variety of 'copulas', the uses of which are determined by syntactic and semantic restrictions parallel to those of the MCC copulas outlined on page 368: (1) Yoruba *se* and *jé* (the latter for innate characteristics) equate noun phrases like MCC *iz*; (2) Ø is used before adjectives in both languages; (3) Yoruba *wà* indicates location (cf. MCC *de*); (4) *ń* is the Yoruba preverbal progressive aspect marker (cf. MCC *de*, Ø). With such a wide range to choose from, it is striking that Yoruba uses *ni*,[5] the highlighter for a predicate-clefting parallel to JC *a*, in precisely the same way JC uses *a* to fill other functions, viz. with question words and noun phrases:

25. /ta *ni*/ 'who?'; /ki *ni*/ 'what?' (Rowlands 1969:26).

26. /èmi *ni* mo fó o/ lit. 'me *it was* I broke it' (Rowlands 1969:27).

Regarding (25), it is interesting to note that the Yoruba question words and highlighters are virtually inseparable. That Bailey (1966:90) treated JC question words in terms of the deletion rather than the addition of *a* (noting that this deletion occurred under pressure from Standard English) is testimony to the accuracy of her native-speaker's intuition, however counterintuitive the procedure might strike a native speaker of Standard English.

Cameroon Pidgin English, probably the descendant of an earlier pidgin linking West African languages with Caribbean varieties of English, has a parallel range of copulas: roughly, (1) *bi* equates NP's; (2) *zero* for the progressive (Todd 1973). Yet it is the highlighter *na* that introduces:

27. Predicate clefting: /na dans a bin dans/ 'I *danced*' (Todd 1973:11).

28. Noun phrases: /na Pita bin ron kwik go si-am/ 'It's Peter who ran fast to go see him' (Todd 1973:12).

29. Question words: /na usaı ı ae?/ 'Where is he?' (Todd, personal communication).

/a no sabi *na* usai i de/ 'I don't know where . . . ' (Todd, personal communication).

There seems to have been a syntactic category 'highlighter' in the mother tongues of many of the first West Africans who reanalyzed Portuguese, English, and French into the pidgins that became the Atlantic creoles. In the same way that the 'need' of English and French speakers for an expressed subject will lead them, in speaking Spanish, to keep on using personal pronouns as subjects for verbs whose conjugational inflections render the subject quite clear and its expression in the form of a pronoun completely unnecessary and ultimately wrong, there seems to have been a 'need' for a highlighter among Africans that was so great that words were found to fill this slot despite the lack of any such syntactic category in the European languages in question. One Portuguese creole spoken in Guinée seems to have lighted on what had been a relative pronoun:

30. /baka *ki* si pápe/ *Le boeuf, c'est lui qui est son supérieur* (Chatagnier 1963:46).

The West African languages spoken in the same area have a similar highlighter between subject and verb: Mandingo *le* and Wolof *a* (Chatagnier 1963:46). The creole French of Haiti has:

31. /sé soulié *ki* kônê si chosèt gê trou/ 'It is shoes that know if the socks have holes' (McConnel and Swan 1960:102).

This construction seems quite French until the use of *sé* above is compared to that in the more African predicate-clefting structure:

32. /sé travay 1 (i) ap travay/ 'He's working (Bynoe-Andriolo and Yillah 1975:234).

This suggests that Haitian *sé* is not simply French *c'est*, but rather what was the handiest European word available to Africans in Haiti to fill a syntactic need, just as *a* and *iz* were the handiest words for their brothers and cousins in Jamaica. That other lexical solutions were possible is illustrated by parallel structures in the creole French of Mauritius:

33. /mo-*mem* pu fer sa/ 'I (highlighter) will do that' (Baker 1972:87).

34. /zape *mem*, to pa kon zape/ lit. 'Bark (highlighter), you not know bark' or 'Don't you even know how to bark?' (Baker 1972:195).

Before concluding, it should be pointed out that there were certain European dialect structures that were less mismatched to the African syntax than those in the standard language. In fact, a case could be made for the positive reinforcement of *iz* in the English creoles by structures in the English of Irishmen. Rickford (1974:107) points out that by the middle of the seventeenth century the Irish had become the biggest sector of the white population in the British West Indies, and equally important, that Irish bond-servants seem to have been the only white group which had close social contact with the slaves. In Hiberno-English we find a single sentence pattern with both an introductory and equative 'copula' (in the widest sense):

35. *It's* himself*s* the boy-o! 'He's quite a playboy' (Todd personal communication).

This can be seen as influenced by an underlying Irish structure with a single copula:

36. *S'é sin an buachaill o!* lit. 'Be him that the boy oh!' (Todd, personal communication).

The introductory copula *s* is a reduced form of *is*; this Irish copula could well have influenced the earliest Irish speakers of English to articulate the middle phoneme in *it's* lightly (if at all), and it is conceivable that this pronunciation was passed on to the Africans with whom the Irish came into contact in the West Indies, leading eventually to JC and MCC *iz* or BEV *is*. Regarding its use in JC predicate clefting,

37. /iz wok im a wok/ 'He's *working*' (Bynoe Andriolo and Yillah 1975:234)

it is interesting to note Hiberno-English,

38. It's breaking my heart you are! (Todd, personal communication)

which clearly has no Standard English parallel.

To conclude, the highlighter we have examined was born of an African syntactic concept fulfilled by a variety of mismatched European words. Its only identity being syntactic, this highlighter is an amazing chameleon that has blended almost imperceptibly into the surrounding lexicon of creole languages stretching halfway round the world, from the Indian Ocean to the Caribbean (and possibly the Pacific).

This discovery of the basic unity of the functions of all these highlighters — in all probability a single concept springing from a single general area — would scarcely have been possible, had this, like so many other African constructions, had close European parallels. Yet its existence, once discerned, should serve to point up again the relatedness of the creole languages not only to one another but also to their African as well as European parent languages; it should also point to the need for a

workable theoretical model in terms of which this interrelatedness can be
more precisely defined and more systematically explored.

NOTES

1. I am indebted to the University of London's Central Research Fund, which financed my
   fieldwork in Nicaragua. I am also grateful to the National Endowment for the Humanities
   in Washington, D.C. for providing the initial grant that allowed me to begin my study of
   Black English.
2. All sample sentences not otherwise identified are transcriptions of my tape recordings of
   Miskito Coast Creole.
3. The glossing of Ø as 'was' rather than 'is' is not arbitrary; it refers to the time-setting of the
   story from which this sentence was taken. In another context, e.g. /mista borti sik/ 'Mr.
   Bertie is sick', the Standard English gloss could well refer to the present tense. Although
   it is possible in MCC to mark adjectives and other verbs for tense (e.g. /a did tayad/ 'I was/
   had been tired'), this is normally only done at the beginning of a narration to set the scene
   chronologically, or in the middle of a narration to signal a shift in the period of time under
   discussion. Although it is usually impossible *not* to mark a European verb for tense, the
   MCC system of tense marking is found in many creoles (cf. Baker 1972:106) and
   languages native to West Africa (Rowlands 1969:76 ff.). This system is also relevant in
   working out a coherent description of Black English tense marking. The absence of a
   copula before adjectives in creoles, which require an equating copula before noun
   phrases, is of course highly relevant to Labov's finding (1969) that Black English is much
   more likely to delete copulas before adjectives than before noun phrases. The Yoruba
   data suggests that the origin of this phenomenon is to be found in Africa (copula deletion,
   unlike zero third person singular present tense marking, having no parallels in British
   dialects). Miller (1972) to the contrary, Africa is the most likely source of copula deletion
   even in the speech of Southern Whites (cf. Wolfram 1974). Although the psycho-
   sociolinguistic explanation of this phenomenon is beyond the scope of this paper, it may
   be noted that the speech of Whites in the Caribbean has long been influenced by the
   creoles (Cassidy 1961:22).
4. The Mauritian French highlighter occurs in this position also (see below), as does the one
   in Rama Cay Creole (RCC). The latter is spoken by Amerindians who have some contact
   with MCC, although RCC seems to be a distinct linguistic system influenced by the
   group's original language, now practically extinct. The RCC highlighter comes after the
   word emphasized: /i no nuo wa-*da* hu duu/ 'He doesn't know what to do'; /huu-*da* hu
   bliem/ 'Who's to blame?' The latter could well be related etymologically to the /huu-da/
   or *who-dat* personal question word form so widespread in the creole English of the
   Caribbean and West Africa, and once associated with U.S. Southern Blacks. (I am
   grateful to Barbara Assadi of the University of Missouri for the RCC tape transcript from
   which the above sentences were taken.)
5. *ni*, with a similar function; occurs in Swahili and other Bantu languages of East Africa; *na*,
   again with the same function and identical in form to the Cameroon Pidgin highlighter
   (see below) occurs in Twi. For this information I am indebted (respectively) to Derek
   Nurse and Philip Baker, both of the University of London's School of Oriental and
   African Studies.

REFERENCES

Bailey, Beryl Loftman (1966), *Jamaican Creole Syntax: a Transformational Approach.* London, Cambridge University Press.

Baker, Philip (1972), *Kreol: A Description of Mauritian Creole,* London.

Bynoe-Andriolo, Elsa and M. Sorie Yillah (1975), 'Predicate clefting in Afro-European creoles', in *Proceedings of the Sixth Conference on African Linguistics,* 234–239.

Cassidy, F. G. (1961), *Jamaica Talk: Three Hundred Years of the English Language in Jamaica,* London.

Cassidy, F. G. and R. B. LePage (1967), *Dictionary of Jamaican English.* London, Cambridge University Press.

Hancock, Ian F. (1977), 'Further Observations on Afro-Seminole Creole'. Society for Caribbean Linguistics Occasional Paper. Mona, Jamaica.

Holm, John (1976), 'Copula variability on the Afro-American continuum'. Paper presented at the Conference of the Society for Caribbean Linguistics *New Directions in Creole Studies* (Turkeyen, Guyana).

Labov, William (1969), 'Contraction, deletion, and inherent variability of the English copula', *Language* 45 (4):715–762.

— (1972), *Language in the Inner City: Studies in the Black English Vernacular.* Philadelphia, U. of Pennsylvania Press.

Miller, Joy L. (1972), 'Be. Finite and absence: features of speech — Black and White?', *Orbis* 21:22–27.

McConnel, H. and E. Swan (1960), *You Can Learn Creole.* Petit-Goâve, Haïti.

Rickford, John R. (1974), 'The insights of the mesolect', in *Pidgins and Creoles: Current Trends and Prospects,* ed. by David DeCamp and Ian F. Hancock. Washington, D.C., Georgetown University Press.

Rowlands, E. C. (1969), *Teach Yourself Yoruba.* London, The English Universities Press.

Smith, Riley B. (1973), 'The interrelatedness of certain deviant grammatical structures in Negro non-standard dialect', in *Black Language Reader,* ed. by R. H. Bentley and S. D. Crawford, 90–95. Glennview, Illinois, and Brighton, England.

Todd, Loreto (1973), 'To be or not to be — What would Hamlet have said in Cameroon Pidgin?', *Archivum Linguisticum*:1–15.

Wolfram, Walt (1974), 'The relationship of White Southern speech to Vernacular Black English', *Language* 50:498–527.

ROBERT BERDAN

Have/Got in the Speech of Anglo and Black Children

For the past century *have/got*, as used in (1), has been the subject of considerable contention:

1. He*'s got* long hair.

Writers of grammar handbooks and teachers alike have damned the collocation *have got* with such epithets as 'redundant', 'pleonastic', and 'nonsensical' (Crowell 1955:2). Many would agree with Richard White, who in 1870 condemned it as 'not only wrong, but if right, superfluous' (Rice 1932:284). These prescriptivists would allow only:

2. He *has* long hair.

A. C. Bartlett (1949:280) described this proscription as coming from the 'New Rich English speakers and writers, those who have learned enough about their language to be self-conscious but not enough to be certain of anything'. Actually the use of possessive *have got* dates back to at least 1516; it was used by Samuel Johnson in his dictionary. The list of authors who have used it in their writings reads like a bibliography for an English literature course.

Not surprisingly, such arguments have little to do with what people, children in particular, actually say. Among children, at least, (1) and (2) are only two of a larger set of alternatives used for the possessive verb. All of the forms in (3) may also occur:

3. a. He *have* long hair.
    b. He *haves* long hair.
    c. He *got* long hair.
    d. He *gots* long hair.

Data for this paper are from studies done at SWRL Educational Research and Development with Anglo and Black children ranging in age

This article was presented as a paper to the Annual Meeting of the Linguistic Society of America, December 27, 1972, Atlanta, Georgia.

from kindergarten to sixth grade, low- to middle-income neighborhoods in Los Angeles.

Several elicitation procedures were employed to obtain *have got* data. The first was adapted from the Baldwin and Garvey's (1970) convergent communication studies in Baltimore. In this procedure two children are seated at opposite sides of a table. An opaque screen is placed between them so that they cannot see each other, but can communicate freely. In a typical desk, one child is given a set of pictures, and the other child is given one picture from the set. To perform the task successfully the children must determine which picture in the set is identical to the single picture.

Tasks of this type have been found to generate constructions of the kind in (1–3) at relatively high frequency; much higher than in casual conversation. They occur in affirmative statements, in questions, and with negation. Analysis of these protocols showed that certain kinds of descriptive statements tended to be formed with the copula while others were formed with some realization of *have*. For example, when the child described attributes of the whole subject, e.g. its size or color, the typical statement employed some form of the copula:

4.   He'*s* big and green.

But when the description involved some part of the object, it typically employed some realization of *have*:

5.   He *has* a pointy hat and big feet.

Using this information in subsequent interviews, sets of tasks were constructed with pictures of pairs of objects, with members of a pair differing in some one property (Berdan and Pfaff 1972). The children were asked to describe the difference between the two objects. It was possible to develop a fair degree of control over the syntactic constructions employed in the children's responses, without biasing the response by giving them any model to repeat. For example, when two objects differed by the presence or absence of some part, if the object with the part was shown before the object without the part, the answer took the form:

6.   a.   This one *has* a hat and this one *doesn't.*
      b.   This one *have* a hat and this one *don't.*

If the order of the objects was reversed so that the object with the part was shown last, the response took the form of (7) with a negated verb and reduced form of the affirmative:

7.   a.   This one *doesn't have* a hat and this one *does.*
      b.   This one *don't have* a hat and this one *do.*

Zwicky (1970) uses two criteria — susceptibility to contraction and tag question formation — to establish three classes of *have*. The first class may be called auxiliary *have*. It allows contraction (8a) and forms tag questions with *have* (8b) rather than *do* (8c):

8. a. John's eaten his sandwich.
    b. John's eaten his sandwich, *hasn't* he?
    c. *John's eaten his sandwich, *doesn't* he?

The second class of *have* includes the main verb *have* 'in its central senses of possession, location, availability, and the like' (Zwicky 1970:329). Main verb *have* does not normally allow contraction (9a) and forms tag questions with either *have* (9b) or *do* (9c). The terms 'auxiliary' and 'main verb' are used here in a traditional sense:

9. a. *John's a salami sandwich.
    b. John *has* a salami sandwich, *hasn't* he?
    c. John *has* a salami sandwich, *doesn't* he?

Zwicky's (1970:329) third class includes the main verb *have* 'in various restricted, idiomatic, or derived usages'. These do not allow contraction (10a) and form tag questions only with *do* (10c), not with *have* (10b):

10. a. *John's a drink every night.
     b. *John *has* a drink every night, *hasn't* he?
     c. John *has* a drink every night, *doesn't* he?

Of these three classes, only main verb *have* meaning *possess* may be substituted by *have got* without change of meaning. The sentences of (11) paraphrase (9), but (12) is ungrammatical, and (13), if grammatical, does not mean the same as (10):

11. a. John's *got* a salami sandwich.
     b. John's *got* a salami sandwich, *hasn't* he?
     c. John's *got* a salami sandwich, *doesn't* he?

12. *John's *got* eaten his sandwich.

13. John's *got* a drink every night.

Have, got, and *have got* all occur in a variety of constructions where the meaning is not that of sentences (1–3). In (14) *got* has the meaning *obtain* or *receive*, rather than *possess*. Some American speakers, like the British, also use got, rather than gotten, as the past participle of *get* (15b):

14. a. Mary *gets* a lot of mail.
     b. Mary *got* a letter yesterday.
15. a. Mary *has gotten* a lot of mail this week.
     b. Mary *has got* a lot of mail this week.

Besides in the possessive sentences in (11) and in the possible perfective sense of *obtain* in (15b) *have got* is used as a quasi-modal of obligation (16):

16. He's *got* to finish before midnight.

This paper, however, will consider in detail only the possessive uses of *have, got*, and *have got*, as in sentences (1–3).

Main verb *have* retains the meaning *possess* with any sequence of tense auxiliaries in (17):

17. a. John *has* his billfold in his back pocket.
     b. John *had* his billfold in his back pocket.
     c. John *has had* his billfold in his back pocket.
     d. John *had had* his billfold in his back pocket.
     e. John *will have* his billfold in his back pocket.
     f. John *will have had* his billfold in his back pocket.

This is not true with *got. Got* has the meaning *possess*, rather than *obtain* only in the sequence *have got* (18a). Neither the past auxiliary *had* (18b), or any other tense auxiliary may be used and retain the meaning *possess*:

18. a. John *has got* his billfold in his back pocket.
     b. *John *had got* his billfold in his back pocket.
     c. *John *will get* his billfold in his back pocket.
     d. *John *will have got* his billfold in his back pocket.

There are other syntactic and semantic restrictions on *have got* that do not apply to main verb *have*. Rosenbaum (1967) argued that verbs may be categorized according to which complementizers they may dominate. The restrictions on *have got* appear to be rather the complementizers *by which* it may be dominated. Main verb *have* may occur in any of the complement constructions of (19). However, *have got* may only be dominated by the *that* complementizer (20a):

19. a. Richard pretends *that* he *has an idea*.
     b. Richard pretends *to have* an idea.
     c. Richard discourages *having* ideas.
20. a. Richard pretends *that* he *has got* an idea.
     b. *Richard pretends *to have got* an idea.
     c. *Richard discourages *having got* ideas.

The restriction on the use of *have got* with the complementizers in (20b) and (20c) is not a general restriction on a sequence of auxiliary and main verb, even with auxiliary *have* and main verb *get* in the sense of *obtain* as shown in (21):

21. a. Richard pretends *to have gotten* the idea.
     b. Richard dislikes *having gotten* secret information.

A similar pattern occurs with modals and quasi-modals. Either auxiliary *have* (22b) or main verb *have* (22a) may follow modals, but *have got* (22c) may not:

22. a. I expected that John *would* still *have* his old car.
     b. I expected that John *would have gotten* his old car back.
     c. *I expected that John *would* still *have got* his old car.

Each of these syntactic facts about the differences between the distribution of main verb *have* and *have got* may be accounted for by one generalization: *have got* may not occur in any context in which *have* is not subject to person–number agreements. This precludes any tense except simple present tense (17–18); the *poss–ing* complementizer of (20c) which requires the participle; the *for–to* complementizer of (20b) which requires the uninflected infinitive; and the modals and quasi-modals, which also require the infinitive.

There are also semantic restrictions on *have got* that do not apply to *have*. The restrictions more or less parallel Zwicky's distinction between main verb *have* and other peripheral meanings of *have*; i.e. the sentences which do not allow *have* tag questions cannot have *have got*:

23. a. Henry always *has* a good time, *doesn't* he?
     b. *Henry always *has* a good time, *hasn't* he?
     c. *Henry always *has got* a good time.

24. a. Henry's wife has a baby every twelve months, *doesn't* she?
     b. *Henry's wife *has* a baby every twelve months, *hasn't* she?
     c. *Henry's wife has *got* a baby every twelve months.

25. a. Henry always *has* a drink before he goes home, *doesn't* he?
     b. *Henry always *has* a drink before he goes home *hasn't* he?
     c. *Henry always *has got* a drink before he goes home.

At least part of the distinction noted by Zwicky appears to be the difference between the stative and nonstative use of *have*. Sentences which do not allow *have* tag questions and do not allow *have got*, generally can occur in the constructions claimed to be diagnostic of stative verbs (Lakoff 1966):

26. a. (Pseudocleft) What Henry did was *have* a good time.
    b. (Complement of *persuade*) I persuaded Henry to *have* a good time.
    c. (Do–so) Henry *had* a good time and Richard did so too.
    d. (Progressive) Henry is *having* a good time.
    e. (Imperative) *Have* a good time, Henry.

On the other hand, sentences which do allow *have* tag questions and *have got* (27) do not occur in these environments (28):

27. a. John *has* a ruptured appendix, *hasn't* he?
    b. John's *got* a ruptured appendix.

28. a. *What John did *was have* a ruptured appendix.
    b. *I persuaded John *to have* a ruptured appendix.
    c. *John *had* a ruptured appendix and Mary did so too.
    d. *John *is having* a ruptured appendix.
    e. **Have* a ruptured appendix, John.

There are other syntactic restrictions on main verb *have* and *have got*. They do not occur in the passive except in certain idioms (29, 30).

29. a. *The books were *had* by John.
    b. *The books *have been got* by John.

30. I've *been had*.

Neither main verb *have* nor *have got* allows indirect object inversion, although inversion can occur with *get* in the sense *obtain* (Bates 1970):

31. a. I *have* a bear for Bill.
    b. *I *have* Bill a bear.

32. a. I've *got* a bear for Bill.
    b. *I've *got* Bill a bear.

33. a. I've *gotten* a bear for Bill.
    b. I've *gotten* Bill a bear.

It appears that *got* adds no lexical information to the stative main verb *have*, and occurs only in constructions in which *have* would in fact have the meaning *possess* in some stative sense. Further, *have got* is restricted to surface syntactic constructions in which Standard English marks *have* for person agreement.

BLACK ENGLISH HAVE/GOT

As already stated, the actual speech of the children, as expected, departed in some respects from this idealized standard. Sentences with *have got* comparable to the taboo sentence (1) were not used by the Black children, though not for any of the reasons which would be countenanced by the prescriptive grammarians. All of the rest of the forms in (2) and (3) were used by Black children.

The difference between (2) and (3a) is obviously the presence or absence of person/number agreement. Dillard (1972) and others claim that in Black English there is no marking for number agreement. For some Black children this appears to be true, though definitely not for all, particularly the children of the Black middle class.

The agreement markers for *have* and *do* in Standard English are irregular; *has* and *does* rather than *haves* and *do's* as one might expect from the general rules applying to other verbs. It was found that children who used uninflected *have* also used uninflected *do*. Sentence (34b) is the question equivalent of (34a), and (34c) is its negation:

34. a. This one *have* a window.
    b. D⌣ this one *have* a window.
    c. This one *don't have* a window and this one *do*.

Some of the children showed variation between the use of uninflected forms (34) and the inflected forms in (35). However, most consistently either did or did not use inflected forms of *have* and *do*:

35. a. This one *has* a window.
    b. This one *doesn't have* a window and this one *does*.

The use of inflection with other main verbs was also examined and it was found that children who do not inflect other main verbs do not inflect the irregular *have* and *do*. But there are some children who do inflect regular verbs and do not inflect *have* or *do*.

The situation with *haves* as in (3b) is not quite so clear. It was used only by Black children and only by children in the lower grades, primarily from the school in the middle-income neighborhood. Children who used *haves* also inflected *do* and the regular verbs. Some of these children also used *has*. For these children who alternated between *haves* and *has*, it was very tempting to say that they showed variation between regular and irregular use of agreement. However, it may have been the case that, for these children at least, *has* represented not the Standard English *has* but the application of consonant cluster simplification to the final consonants of

third singular *haves*. The surface results are the same, of course. None of
the children who showed this alternation between *has* and *haves* also used
do's. The children's treatment of other final sequences of sibilants has not
yet been examined and until that has been done, the status of *has* for these
children will remain unclear.

The use of *got* in Black English is quite different from its use in
Standard English. None of the sentences in (36) occurred:

36. a. This one's *got* a window.
     b. *Has* this one *got* a window?
     c. This one *hasn't got* a window.

Instead *got*, like any other main verb, formed questions and negation with
do (37):

37. a. This one *got* a window.
     b. *Do* this one *got* a window?
     c. This one *don't got* a window.
     d. This one *don't got* no window and this one *do*.

This leads to the interesting, but potentially confusing situation, in which
Black English possessive *got* in (37a) can only mean *obtained* in Standard
English, while the sequence *have got*, which is only possessive in Standard
English, can mean either *possess* or *have obtained* in Black English.

Some children who used agreement with other main verbs also
used agreement with *do*, giving the sentences of (38) rather than those
of (37):

38. a. *Does* this one *got* a window?
     b. This one *doesn't got* a window.

A few of these children who used agreement also inflected *got* in the
affirmative statement (39):

39. This one *gots* a window.

Clearly, for these children *got* is a regular main verb which inflects for
agreement and requires Do–Support.

However, there were some other children who used *gots* in sentences
like (39) who also used it in (40). For these children *gots*, rather than *got*,
appears to be the underlying form.

40. a. *Do* this one *gots* a window?
     b. This one *don't gots* a window.

Most of the children consistently used forms with *got* or forms with *have*;
few used both.

The Anglo children interviewed never used uninflected *have* in third singular contexts; none used the inflected form *haves*. However, this is not to say that all Anglo children use only Standard English forms. No kindergarten or first-grade children used the sequence *have got*; older Anglo children did. When younger Anglo children used *got* it was used as a main verb, as by Black children, but always with agreement, as in (38) and (39). The exception to this was the use of *don't got*. *Don't* is the negation of both *do* and *does* for some Anglo children, and some who used affirmative *has got* and *have got* used only *don't got* in the negative.

In environments where contraction is possible, affirmative statements, the *have* of *have got* was always contracted; none of the children used the full forms *have* or *has* in these environments. In the environments which allow contracted *have*, some children used *got* with no auxiliary; this happened only with *have* for Anglo children; never where agreement required *has*.

THE GRAMMARS OF HAVE/GOT

Standard English

These facts have several implications for the construction of grammars. First the grammar for Standard English.

There is no semantic motivation for identifying main verb *have* with auxiliary *have*. There is no notion of the perfect in possession; nor is any sense of possession inherent in the temporal notion of perfect. This becomes even more apparent when one looks at languages other than English. Few show any lexical similarity between perfective auxiliary and possessive verb, if in fact such a verb exists in the language. Arguments for deriving main verb *have* and auxiliary *have* from a common source are presented in Bach (1967). That paper does not consider any of the syntactic arguments presented here, nor does it deal with *have got*.

There also seems to be no syntactic motivation for identifying the main verb with the auxiliary. Many of the parallels that obtain between the copula *be* and the tense auxiliary *be* do not hold for the auxiliary *have* and the main verb *have*. Consider the paradigms (41) through (47). In each of these auxiliary *be*, copula *be*, and auxiliary *have* exhibit one type of behavior while possessive *have* exhibits another behavior identical to other main verbs.

I. *Questions* *Be* is preposed in questions whether it is used as a copula

(41a) or as an auxiliary (41b). Auxiliary *have* (41d) may be preposed, but not main verb *have* (41c). *Have* may be preposed in *have got* (41e):

41. a. *Is*   John the new vice-president?
     b. *Is*   John running for vice-president?
     c. **Has* John his instructions?
     d. *Has* John received his instructions?
     e. *Has* John *got* his instructions?

Like other main verbs, *have* forms questions with Do–Support in American Anglo English.

42. a. *Does* John *like* his instructions?
     b. *Does* John *have* his instructions?

II. *Contracted Negation*   The same pattern is apparent with Neg. contraction: *be* may be attached to the contracted Neg. either as auxiliary or as copula. Main verb *have* (43c) requires Do–Support (44):

43. a. John *isn't* the new vice-president.
     b. John *isn't* running for vice-president.
     c. *John *hasn't* his instructions.
     d. John *hasn't* received his instructions.
     e. John *hasn't got* his instructions.

44. a. John *doesn't like* the new vice-president.
     b. John *doesn't have* his instructions.

III. *Auxiliary Contraction*   Likewise with auxiliary contraction. *Be* may contract either as verb or auxiliary; *have* may contract only as auxiliary (45):

45. a. John*'s* the new vice-president.
     b. John*'s* running for vice-president.
     c. *John*'s* his instructions.
     d. John*'s* received his instructions.
     e. John*'s got* his instructions.

IV. *Auxiliary Shift*   This rule is used by Baker (1971) to transpose the auxiliary and certain preverbs if the auxiliary is not stressed:

46. a. John *is already* angry.
     b. John *is already* running for vice-president.
     c. *John *has already* his instructions.
     d. John *has already* received his instructions.
     e. John *has already got* his instructions.

V. *Auxiliary Attraction*   Certain negative preverbs allow the auxiliary to be preposed (Fillmore 1966):

47. a.   Only rarely *is* the bus on time.
     b.   Only rarely *is* anyone actually working.
     c.   *Only rarely *has* John his instructions.
     d.   Only rarely *has* John received all the instructions he needed.
     e.   Only rarely *has* John *got* all the instructions he needs.

In each of these five constructions possessive *have* is unlike auxiliaries, but like other main verbs. *Have got* appears to be a sequence of auxiliary and main verb. In the two following constructions *have* has properties both of an auxiliary and of a main verb.

VI.   *Tag Question*

48.   a.   John *has* a new car, *hasn't* he?
     b.   John *has* a new car, *doesn't* he.

49.   a.   John *has got* a new car, *hasn't* he?
     b.   John *has got* a new car, *doesn't* he?

Sentences (48a, 49a) follow the pattern of an auxiliary; (48b, 49b) follow the pattern of a main verb. However, if the main sentence is negated, only the auxiliary to which the negative is attached may occur in the tag question (50):

50.   a.   * John *doesn't have* a new car, *has* he?
     b.   John *doesn't have* a new car, *does* he?

51.   a.   John *hasn't got* a new car, has he?
     b.   * John *hasn't got* a new car, *does* he?

VII.   *Conjunction Reduction*   Reduced conjoined sentences show a pattern similar to tag questions except that negative *hasn't got* may be replaced either by *has* (55a) or *does* (55b):

52.   a.   John *has* a new car and so *has* Mary.
     b.   John *has* a new car and so *does* Mary.

53.   a.   John *has got* a new car and so *has* Mary.
     b.   John *has got* a new car and so *does* Mary.

54.   a.   * John *doesn't have* a new car and neither *has* Mary.
     b.   John *doesn't have* a new car and neither *does* Mary.

55.   a.   John *hasn't got* a new car and neither *has* Mary.
     b.   John *hasn't got* a new car and neither *does* Mary.

In clearly possessive contexts the verb *have* exhibits the characteristics of a main verb, not of an auxiliary. These facts warrant positing at least one main verb *have* in the grammar of Standard English. And given the acceptability of sentences like (56) but the strangeness of (57) one might want to claim there is more than one such verb:

56.   Every night John *has* a scotch and soda, Bill a Manhattan, and Martha a Tom Collins.

57.   *Every summer John *has* a new car, his wife a baby, their son a drink, and their daughter a cold.

The status of *have got* may be considered next. First, in each of these constructions *got* is semantically void; it adds nothing to the meaning of the sentence. Second, although *have* does not take on the meaning of the perfective in *have got*, it does function syntactically as an auxiliary. Third, there are restrictions on the occurrence of *have got* that are not normally nor easily stated in the lexicon. For example, one must account for the fact that (58a) is possessive but (58b), if grammatical, is not:

58.   a.   It seems that John*'s got* some more money.
      b.   John seems to *have got* some more money.

All of this suggests that *got* may best be inserted by transformational rule. These arguments are similar in form to the arguments which have been advanced for There-Insertion and Do-Support.

The Got-Insertion rule must perform two operations. It moves *have* to the auxiliary and inserts *got* in its place, converting (59a) to (59b):

59.   a.   John [present]$_{aux}$ [*have*]$_{verb}$ big hands
      b.   John [present *have*]$_{aux}$ [*got*]$_{verb}$ big hands

As desired, this allows *have* to function as an auxiliary but assigns it no notion of the perfect. There are some restrictions in the structural index on the application of the rule. It must occur in the environment of present tense. This precludes the ungrammatical sentences of (18). And if the rule is made last cyclic, it precludes (58b) as well as (20b, 20c) where the complement process deletes tense.

Anglo-English

This Standard English grammar accounts for most facts observed in speech of the Anglo children without modifications. However, for the kindergarten and first-grade children who inflect *got* in the third singular to *gots* and form questions with *does got*, there seems no reason to posit any rule of Got-Insertion. These children seem to have two possessive verbs: *have* and *got.* Each of them functions for the child like any other main verb.

The other fact which needs explanation for Anglo children is the use of *have got* in questions, but *don't got* in negation. For these children the use of *got* reflects some of the characteristics of the Standard English grammar and some of the characteristics of the development grammar of the younger children.

Black English

In the speech of the Black children there appear to be two independent verbs of possession: *got* and *have.* There is no motivation for any kind of transformation between them.

Loflin (1970) described Black English as having no auxiliary *have.* His data were drawn largely from the speech of one fourteen-year-old boy. Based on the assumption that there is no *have* auxiliary, Loflin developed a tense system for Black English different from the Standard English tense system.

If the *have* of *have got* is in fact identical to auxiliary *have* with other verbs, and if Loflin is correct that Black English has no auxiliary *have*, it is possible to account for the Black English *got* rather than *have got* from the general absence of *have* auxiliary, assuming of course that Black English has no Got-Insertion rule as has been suggested for Standard English.

However, another study by Labov et al. (1968) has shown that *have* auxiliary does in fact exist in Black English. In this study the same children who never used *have got* did use auxiliary *have* with other main verbs. But as Labov has also shown, the *have* auxiliary was frequently deleted.

One could argue that Black English is just like Standard English with respect to *have got*, except that the independently motivated rules of auxiliary contraction and deletion delete *have* from *have got*. However, the auxiliary contraction and deletion rules do not operate in all environments. For example, when the auxiliary is preposed in question or when it occurs with contracted negation the contraction and deletion rules block, giving (60):

60. *Have* you ever eaten pork?

It is exactly these environments, question and negation, in which *got* occurs only with *do* auxiliary, not *have*. The contraction and deletion rules cannot be used to explain Black English *got*.

CONCLUSIONS

The facts of *have/got* are somewhat confounded by the multitude of nonpossessive uses, both of *have* and of *got*; and by the dialectical differences in their use. Within the speech of children, at least, many variations occur. Some of these appear to result from different lexical representations, such as the use of *gots* in all instances, rather than *got*. Some differences result from differences in rules: The difference between Anglo-English *have got* and Black English *got*. For some forms, such as the use of *haves*, it is difficult to determine whether there is a difference in the morphology or a difference in underlying forms. *The facts of Standard English seem best described by positing a rule of Got-Insertion. There is no evidence for such a rule in Black English.*

Acquisition of this construction does not seem to be complete for all children at the kindergarten and first-grade level. There are forms used by these children which do not occur elsewhere, notably *haves*, and a lack among young Anglo children of *have got*.

There are also social differences in use associated with income level. Particularly, children from Black schools in lower-income neighborhoods used person–number agreement much less frequently than did Black children in middle-income areas.

REFERENCES

Bach, E. (1967), '*Have* and *Be* in English syntax', *Language* (43):462–485.
Baker, C. L. (1971), 'Stress level and auxiliary behavior in English', *Linguistic Inquiry* (2):167–181.
Baldwin, T. and Garvey, C. (1970), 'Studies in convergent communication: II. A measure of communication accuracy'. Report No. 91, Johns Hopkins University, Center for the Study of Social Organization of Schools.
Bartlett, A. C. (1949), '*Get, have got*, and *have got to*', *College English* (10):280–282.
Bates, R. R. (1970), 'A study in the acquisition of language'. Unpublished doctoral dissertation, University of Texas, Austin.
Berdan, R. and Pfaff, C. (1972), 'Sociolinguistic variation in the speech of young children: an experimental study'. Professional Paper 21. Los Alamitos, California, SWRL Educational Research and Development.
Crowell, T. L., Jr. (1955), 'A study of the verb *get*'. Unpublished doctoral dissertation, Columbia University, New York.
Dillard, J. L. (1972), *Black English*. New York, Random House.

Fillmore, C. J. (1966), 'On the syntax of preverbs'. Unpublished paper, Ohio State University.

Labov, W., P. Cohen, C. Robins, and J. Lewis, (1968), 'A study of the non-standard English of Negro and Puerto Rican speakers in New York City'. Final Report, Cooperative Research Project 3288. Washington, D.C., Office of Education.

Lakoff, G. (1966), 'Stative adjectives and verbs in English', in Report No. NSF-17, ed. by A. G. Oettinger. Cambridge, Mass. Harvard University Computation Laboratory.

Loflin, M. C. (1970), 'On the structure of the verb in a dialect of American Negro English', *Linguistics* (59):14–28.

Rice, W. (1932), '*Get* and *Got*', *American Speech* (April):280–296.

Rosenbaum, P. S. (1967), *The grammar of English predicate complement constructions*. Cambridge, Mass., M.I.T. Press.

Zwicky, A. M. (1970), 'Auxiliary reduction in English', *Linguistic Inquiry* (1):323–336.

RILEY B. SMITH

Interrelatedness of Certain Deviant Grammatical Structures in Negro Nonstandard Dialects

Research in highly divergent dialects of American English, especially in what has been termed Negro Nonstandard English (NNE), has lately been thriving, and quite a number of hitherto unnoticed divergences have been disclosed and published.[1] The findings themselves have for the most part been categorized in terms of the standard language, and though there is at present a theoretical controversy over descriptive methods,[2] some highly creative work has been done toward explaining certain features of NNE within both models. The data in any case are always valuable, and the explanations themselves are often highly insightful. But there may be relationships between divergent features of a dialect which would tell us more about that dialect, and the researcher should not shrink from speculating about his findings in the dialect's own terms, i.e. of the divergences' relations with each other within the dialect.

Generative-transformational linguists have quite properly used the phenomenon of intracode ambiguity (constructional homonymy within their own dialects, as in 'the shooting of the hunters') as a discovery tool and as a rhetorical device. That such intracode ambiguity is a phenomenon in all dialects of all languages should require no defense. But that certain divergent dialects of American English have terminal formatives which grammatically 'ambiguate' underlying phrase-markers different from those of standard English (SE), or indeed 'ambiguate' phrase-markers not at all ambiguable in SE, should be considered a possibility offering dialectologists a powerful tool.

Notice has admittedly been given to this phenomenon of ambiguity peculiar to a dialect, but it has generally been restricted to dialect homophony, as in *stock–stalk* (western Pennsylvania), *pin–pen* (South Midland and western South),[3] and *right–rat* (NNE), this last still the subject of controversy.[4] And though the locative-existential transformation *it* + *be*, as in *It's a lot of wires down here,* was pointed out as early as

Reprinted by permission of the author and editors, from the *Journal of English Linguistics* 3(1969): 88–88.

1953 with reference to the speech of West Virginia and the Chesapeake Bay area,[5] has since been randomly noticed as a feature of certain South Midland dialects (especially in Oklahoma and Texas), and has subsequently been checklisted as a feature of NNE,[6] the potential intracode ambiguity of this structure with the extrapositional *it* + *be*, as in *It was six of the boys what saw a lizard*, has not been pursued. Thus, *It was a man under the bed* is ambiguous in NNE and in some other American English dialects in a way that it is not in SE, reflecting the SE translations *There was a man under the bed* and *It was a man under the bed* (*who* + *VP*).

The unavailability of the dialect-informant qua dialectologist is, of course, the principal and rather overwhelming reason why this technique of dialect analysis has been hitherto ignored. But it is also true that speakers of dialects of SE, under certain conditions at least, are quite deaf to grammatical divergences of nonstandard dialects. Aretha Franklin's hit song of last spring is labeled *Ain't No Way*, but it is almost always referred to by white disc-jockeys as *There Ain't No Way*, seldom as *It Ain't No Way (for me to love you if you won't let me* — the lyric actually repeated in the 'refrain'), except by those whose dialects generate this structure. But researchers who have worked intensively with a particular dialect are able to recognize structural ambiguation within the dialect, and the analytical tools this recognition offers them are invaluable.

Few linguists have dealt at all with the phenomenon of cross-code ambiguity, a phenomenon doubtless peculiar to the domain of dialectology. It has usually been treated as a curiosity of fortuitous phonological skewing, resulting in the near homophony of lexical items across dialect boundaries, such as in *hard* (eastern New England)–*hide* (certain South Midland dialects).[7] But the phenomenon exists also at the syntactic level, as in *It was a man under the bed*, and such types of ambiguations perhaps result in serious barriers to communication and learning, especially in those areas where there has been recent ethnic resettlement. The inability of the disc-jockey to hear Aretha Franklin's locative-existential transformation, *It Ain't No Way*, can be attributed, I think, not so much to the divergence itself, but to the cross-code ambiguation it would cause with a structure in his own SE dialect.

The persistence of some 'ungrammatical' forms of NNE has been accounted for by citing causes of ethnic identity, self-conceptualization within the subculture, and language loyalty. Though these are certainly important factors, the English teacher's frustrations perhaps attest that they are not completely satisfactory explanations.[8] The phenomenon of cross-code ambiguation is offered in this paper as a collateral explanation of the persistence of certain 'ungrammatical' forms of NNE.

The two deviant grammatical structures of a dialect of NNE to be discussed in this paper are (1) the pleonastic subject pronoun, and (2) the deletion of the subject relative pronoun. A relationship between the two structures within the dialect will be shown, and some conjecture about interference phenomena attributable to the relationship will be made. And it is hoped that this discussion will have more general ramifications for future research and analysis in dialectology.

Among Negro informants of East Texas,[9] the frequency of the pleonastic subject pronoun is extremely high among speakers of all age-groups, and its occurrence is quite widespread.[10]

So the older peoples *they* got herbs and stuff and help made medicine theirself (67, Atlanta, #122).[11]
My mother *she* used to wash and iron and cook (46, Marshall, #101).
And then my daughter *she* is a secretary for a store manager (46, Marshall, #101).
My brother from Lubbock *he* visit to get his wife and baby (17, Tyler, #085).
Some of them *they* put the needle in the fire (9, Tyler, #041).
Teenager(s) *they* don't much like his rock (14, Nacogdoches, #065).

Among this same group of informants, the frequency of the deletion of the subject relative pronoun (usually *what* in this dialect of NNE), not optionally deletable in SE as it is in this dialect, is extremely high and its occurrence is widespread.

He look like a little man have on a hat with a round circle on it (8 Marshall, #021).
This here is one family eat anything (53, Nacogdoches, #121).
I have a brother work at Ralston Purina here in town (13, Nacogdoches, #061).
She be the kind like to go (17, Tyler, #085).
It's a bush grow up like that, and it's good for fever (67, Atlanta, #122).

Further, in strings where both of these structures occur in this dialect, the pleonasm is highly stable even where the relative pronoun is present.

The one stay here in Clarksville *she* don't do anything at all (44, Clarksville, #101).
    The one who lives here in Clarksville doesn't do anything at all (SE translation).
The man *what* own(ed) the land *he* come over (18, Clarksville, #084).
    The man who owned the land came over (SE translation).
The boy won *he* did a three (15, Tyler, #069).
    The boy who won did a three (SE translation).
My other sister *she* fourteen go to Dogan (10, Tyler, #047).
    My other sister is fourteen who goes to Dogan (SE translation).
    Not: My other sister who is fourteen goes to Dogan.

These strings, which consist of *one* sentence, not two, suggest that there is an interrelatedness between the two structures such that the high frequency of the deletion of the relative pronoun exerts an influence in some way on the stability of the pleonastic subject pronoun, or that the pleonasm is in some sense itself a disambiguating formative.[12]

The string *I saw the man did it* is ambiguous in NNE in a way that it cannot be in SE. In the shorthand derivations below, the second sentences of both A and B are embedded, but in A they are relativized, in B they are nominalized. (The dotted line indicates a possible but infrequent deletion transformation.)

Negro Nonstandard English

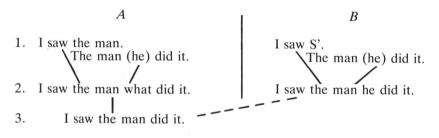

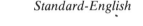

Standard-English

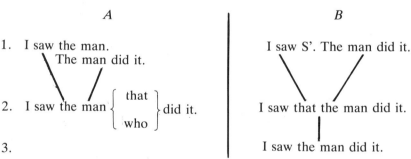

It will be noted that though the *what* in NNE above (A2) could be retained — i.e. the deletion transformation could be blocked — to disambiguate, the relative *what* is a rare formative in any terminal string, and the pleonasm usually takes over this function, i.e. its deletion is usually blocked. The relatives *who* and *that* in SE (A2 above) are not deletable and therefore the string never ambiguates with B3. It will be further noted that there is cross-code ambiguity between the terminals (3) of NNE and SE, such that the speakers of the two dialects may decode different underlying phrase-markers for the terminal string *I saw the man did it.*

To the speaker of NNE, the SE string *My sister plays the piano* may reflect not a sentence, but a noun-phrase with an embedded relative clause: i.e. *My sister who plays the piano.* The pleonastic pronoun is usually present in NNE, as in *My sister she play the piano*, to disambiguate the two structures. Thus both intracode and cross-code ambiguation militate against the NNE speaker's learning to leave out the subject pronoun pleonasm, which seems to have more a grammatical than a strictly stylistic function in his dialect.

There is at present no clear way to describe what appear to be synchronic influences of transformational rules upon each other, rules apparently unrelated except that they have the potential of generating ambiguous terminal strings within a dialect.[13] Optionally deletable markers occasionally, though rarely, perform such a disambiguating function in Standard English. *I see the men do it* is ambiguous in SE, reflecting phrase-markers which are clearly different when we pronominalize *the men*: (1) *I see they do it*, and (2) *I see them do it.* But the SE speaker normally disambiguates with the clause marker *that* when he wants to reflect the structure of (1): *I see that the men do it.*

Analogously, the NNE string *The man did it* is ambiguous; *The man he did it* disambiguates with the pleonasm. Whatever the generative provenience of the pleonastic subject pronoun (it appears to be neither a clause-marker nor a relative pronoun in the SE sense), it is a marker in the sense that it marks nonrevitalization of the following verb-phrase, a function stabilized by the regular deletion of the relative pronoun in this dialect of NNE.

Acrolect pressure on the basilect compounds the communication and pedagogical problems further. The failure of the NNE speaker to recognize the complexity of certain ambiguations between divergent dialects is certainly no more serious than this same failure on the part of the SE speaker. The dialectologist should look for relationships within a dialect which may be indispensable to a proper description of it. And the English teacher, in her struggle against 'ungrammatical' forms, should begin to recognize that some of her students' failures may be identical to her own, resulting from a blockage of understanding of the grammatical structures of the unfamiliar dialect because of ambiguity across dialect boundaries.

NOTES

1. An earlier version of this article was presented as a paper at the annual meeting of the American Dialect Society, December 28, 1968, in New York.

2. The bases of this controversy are clearly shown in William Labov and Paul Cohen (1967), 'Systematic relations of Standard and Non-Standard rules in the grammar of Negro speakers', ERIC Document Number ED 016 946 (May), and in William A. Stewart (1968), 'Continuity and change in American Negro dialects', *The Florida FL Reporter* (Spring):3 ff. Though the controversy is of extreme interest to researchers in Negro Nonstandard English, it does not directly relate to the findings or argument of this paper.

3. Variously attested. See Uriel Weinreich, William Labov, and Melvin I. Herzog (1968) 'Empirical foundations for a theory of language change', in *Directions for Historical Linguistics*, ed. by W. P. Lehmann and Yakov Malkiel, 152, n. 41. Austin, University of Texas Press.

4. Ruth I. Golden (1964), 'Changing dialects by using tapes', in *Social Dialects and Language Learning*, ed. by Roger W. Shuy, 63, Champaign, University of Illinois Press. For a disclaimer, see Raven I. McDavid, Jr. (1967), 'A checklist of significant features for discriminating social dialects', in *Dimensions of Dialect*, ed. by Eldonna L. Evertts, 9, n. 3. Champaign, University of Illinois Press.

5. E. Bagby Atwood (1953), *A Survey of Verb Forms in the Eastern United States*, 30. Ann Arbor, University of Michigan Press.

6. Beryl Loftman Bailey (1968), 'Some aspects of the impact of linguistics on language teaching', *Elementary English* 45 (May):576.

7. A perhaps more vivid example of such 'cross-code' ambiguity was related to me by Professor Rudolph C. Troike of the University of Texas at Austin. A lady from Houston, named Kaiser, having arrived at a hotel in Boston to claim her reservation, said her name to the clerk, who carefully wrote 'Carser'.

8. It is certainly not the intent here to downgrade the importance of functional interference. See William Labov and Paul Cohen (1967), 'Some suggestions for teaching Standard English to speakers of Non-Standard dialects', ERIC Document Number ED 016 948 (July), for a discussion of the distinction between 'structural' and 'functional' interference.

9. The fieldwork and analysis were one phase of a project to reevaluate English instructional material and curricula in the wake of integration in five independent school districts of East Texas: Atlanta, Clarksville, Marshall, Nacogdoches, and Tyler. The project was sponsored by the school districts under grants from ESEA and NDEA, and by the Texas Education Agency. All the interviews were conducted between August and December, 1967

   The 253 informants, of whom 170 were Negro, were selected to include a wide range of ages, and of ethnic and educational backgrounds. Because grammatical as well as phonological data were of interest to the project, the interviews were in general topical and did not follow a standardized worksheet. With modifications, the interviews followed techniques suggested in Roger W. Shuy, Walter A. Wolfram, and William K. Riley (1967), *Linguistic Correlates of Social Stratification in Detroit Speech,* East Lansing, Mich., Michigan State University Press, and in William Labov (1966), *The Social Stratification of English in New York City*. Washington, D.C., Center for Applied Linguistics.

10. I do not wish to suggest that all Negro informants used particular deviant grammatical structures with the same frequency in all cases. The data have in some measure been selected to reflect what I consider to be 'basilect' structures. See William A. Stewart (1964), 'Urban Negro speech: sociolinguistic factors affecting English teaching', in *Social Dialects and Language Learning,* ed, by Roger W. Shuy, 10–18, Champaign, University of Illinois Press, for a discussion of basilect reconstruction to account for

structural interference in the learning of standard English. Further, this discovery technique is not entirely incompatible with the position of Labov, *The Social Stratification*.

11. The age of the informant, city of domicile, and my informant number follow the responses cited, in that order.

12. On the phonemic level, the mere notion of a disambiguating marker was rather thoroughly discredited by the neogrammarians, who showed that what their opponents had maintained were exceptions to sound laws on the basis of their importance to the maintenance of semantic distinctions could be accounted for on the basis of other perfectly regular phenomena. See Leonard Bloomfield (1933), *Language,* 346 ff. (New York, Holt), for a discussion. This controversy and its outcome certainly still have relevance for modern generative theory, but it is not clear that the notion of disambiguation is without validity on the syntactic level, even though our present grammatical model seems unable to handle it. To account for the phenomenon on the basis of stylistic variation certainly seems to beg the question.

13. See Note 11 above.

PART FIVE

Pidgin English

Introduction

The immense importance of the sea in early American life, documented by Chase in Part One, virtually guarantees that varieties important at sea, on islands, and in coastal areas would have a great influence on early American English. A very great deal of data on the use of pidgin English both at sea and in the continental colonies can be gathered by consulting the writings of sailors, missionaries, travelers, and other observers in many categories. According to the Leechman–Hall article of 1955 (reprinted here) the earliest American attestations are the very first ever recorded.

It would be virtually impossible to do more than hint at the vast amount of data available from uncounted numbers of writers on the use of pidgin English at sea. Many examples are given by Dillard (1972, especially ch. IV; 1975a, 1976a). Many others are given in articles by Ian F. Hancock (1969, 1972, 1976), and especially in his 1971 dissertation. Historians like Foster Rhea Dulles furnish many other examples, the numbers growing as new works are consulted. Dulles (1946), for example, quotes a very early (probably immediately after 1784, although Dulles does not so state) observer named Shaw on the conversation of one Chinese merchant: 'You are not Englishmen? . . . But you speak English word, and when you first come, I no can tell difference; but now I understand you very well. When I speak Englishman his price, he say "So much — take it — let alone." I tell him, "No, my friend, I give you so much." . . . Truly, Massa Typan, I see very well you no hap Englishman. All China-man very much love your country.' And Shaw feels 'obligated' to add the same speaker's conclusion: 'All men come first time China very good gentlemen, all same you. I think two three time more you come Canton, you make all same Englishman too.'

It is not now fashionable, in the extremely political context of present-day pidgin–creole studies, to comment on such matters as the very widespread use of phrases like *all same* (*alle samee* in some texts). See, however, Note 11 in the article by Leechman and Hall on American Indian Pidgin English (this volume: 422 and fn. 11) for an overt statement and for recognition of the relationship to *all one*.

These characteristic phrasal compounds, so firmly established in the pidgin that substitution of one word will not disguise the relationship, is one of the striking factors that has influenced the 'diffusionists', who see rather maritime transmission than bilingual interference or spontaneous outcropping of 'universals'. A universalist, Bickerton (1977) ridicules the West African Pidgin English (as well as the religiosity) of the *Religious Intelligencer* excerpts printed in Dillard (1975b) while praising P. Grade's article in the same collection (although not completely without reservation). However, both the *Religious Intelligencer* (Dillard 1975b:103) and Grade have phrasal compounds like *too much* 'very much' (where no notion of excess is present, the phrase acting merely as an intensifier) and *God palaver* 'religion'. The Chinese Pidgin English *Joss Pidgin* (the second word often spelled *Pigeon*) is one of the many compounds in which CPE substitutes *Pidgin* for *Palaver*. (In this case, following Whinnom [1965], I would insist that *palaver*, being from Portuguese and being attested in West African Pidgin English before 1710, is the original form and that *pidgin* is the 'relexification'. But *Joss*, ultimately from Portuguese *Deos*, has an equal claim to be 'original', with *God* as the lexical replacement.)

    The students of pidgin/creole diffusion have, in recent years, been unfair targets for the followers of Chomsky who would find in language, and perhaps especially in pidgin, a direct model of the structure of the mind. Such objectors have often put the diffusionists in the same box with the verbal behaviorists, although the association is not a fair one. The study of signaling systems, although obviously not all such systems are of the complexity of language, becomes a part of the study of places like the sea and the frontier, where face-to-face verbal communication may at times be difficult. The sea (with its semaphore) and the frontier (with its sign language) had marginal language systems analogous in some way to one position in the argument over 'simplification' in pidgins. To study such 'marginal' situations is not, however, to subscribe to the proposition that any language, including a pidgin, is such a signaling system.

    Outside the imagination of a few linguists, the only statements of this type which have been made, have actually come from very traditional students like dialect geographers. Cassidy (1971:212–213) actually speculates that,

> ... there would initially be a good deal of gesture accompanying speech; this would be reduced, though probably never eliminated, as the pidgin took shape. Gestures would accompany the first exclamations: shouts to attract attention (arm waving), more restrained greetings (salutes, beckonings to approach, signs to stop, parting signs). Exclamations or interjections expressing surprise, fear, amusement, warning, anger might be accompanied by gestures — which can only be guessed at.

One would say that such guessing had gone too far already, especially when there are studies of some well-developed sign systems.

Within this context, the sign language of the Plains Indians occupies something like the position of 'deaf and dumb sign language' in general linguistic studies, the obvious difference being that physical impairment had nothing whatsoever to do with the Indians' sign language. Taken over by such groups as the cowboys, who often learned only a little of it, sign language did, have some of the characteristics of signaling behavior. It is noteworthy, however, that, contrary to Cassidy's speculation, this use of the Plains Indian sign language developed rather late than early in the contact situation.

Many of the early writers (Stefánsson [1909], for example) on the relationship between a 'ships' jargon' and a 'shore jargon' have pointed up the larger vocabulary of the latter:

It has probably more than twice as extensive a vocabulary as the ships' variety and is so different from it that some white men who know the ships' jargon have employed as interpreters Loucheux Indians under the impression that the Indians spoke real Eskimo.

In fact, the distinction here seems very like what MacCarthy and Varnier, in *L'Algérien* for May 11, 1852, called *petit Sabir* and *grand Sabir*. Schuchardt (1909), who cited these authors, found the distinction of no value; but it does help to explain many things. For one thing, the ships' jargon reflects most of the concerns of the diffusionists (De Granda 1976), whereas the shore jargon is usually studied by those who find a preponderance of influence from the native language(s) of the area. Also, despite the protests of many linguists (Chumbow 1973) against any notion of 'simplification', there are, in all probability, such reductions *in the ships' jargon only*. Naro (1978) apparently means about the same thing by the term *reconnaissance language*.

In the pretelevision age, American Indian Pidgin English, analogous to ships' jargon in the same way that the plains were analogous to the sea, was familiar to Americans from many fictional sources,[1] including *The Lone Ranger*, which featured the hero's Indian sidekick Tonto. It is widely assumed that anything from such sources must involve fakery, but Tonto was played by Jay Silverheels, a real enough Indian with a reputation for interest in his people's culture and even for militancy. We all know that American movies and bad novels have given distorted pictures of some realities, but can we assume that anything is a distortion *because* it has appeared in the movies? Literary fashions change, and the 'realism' of the past generation is held up to scorn by the present, but perspective supposedly tells us that the cycles of fashion are not the straight lines of progress, and that something of what passed for realism in the past may be as reliable as what is passing for the same at present.

Mary Rita Miller, whose 1967 article is reprinted in this volume, was surely aware of all these considerations, although Reinecke et al. (1975:539) deal with her in harsh terms because she 'draws no distinction between writers who may have heard Indians speaking pidgin and those who attributed pidgin to their fictional characters'. On the general subject of dialect in fiction, see Stewart (1972). Reinecke et al. represent, however, a considerable advance over writers like Marckwardt (1958) and Laird (1975), who simply ignore American Indian Pidgin English while giving a fair amount of attention to the American Indians.

Although it is not clear how Reinecke et al. would have regarded it insofar as authenticity is concerned, the (nonfictional) literature of Western travel is full of attestations of various kinds of pidgin, including AIPE. In fact, the Reinecke et al. remark (1975:538) that even the titles recorded by Leechman and Hall, Miller, and Dillard (1972) 'are probably a small proportion of the pertinent ones' can be substantiated with great ease. Two excellent examples from the travel literature are A. D. Richardson's *Beyond the Mississippi* (1865) and James F. Rusling's *Across America* (1875). The latter, especially, abounds in AIPE attestations like 'Me been down to Indian Wells. 'Tother fellow got him knife and dollar. Good! Dieganos much friend to Gen-e-ral. Heap!'

These authors' transcriptional practices in fact, do as much to disguise the pidgin nature of the Indians' speech as to advance it as a fictional claim. For example, *got him*, a fairly clear use of the transitivizer used also in West African and Melanesian Pidgin English, would be *gotam*, or perhaps *gotum*, to a writer more aware of the pidgin tradition.

According to the very extensive attestations in Warburton (1966), the Yurok Indians of Northern California speak a pidgin English characterized by derivational patterns like, '*Cos every time he's goan hefy my knees*' (where *hefy* [verb] means 'make heavy') and by both -*et* and the more general AIPE -*um* transitivizer: '*You tellet him, Taisy you my sweetie cos I lofet you like hell*' (Warburton 1966:123). '*I tolem "Was you want?"*' (1966:151); and '*Me ketchem napoei* [salmon] *big fat one*' (1966:137). As always, there is considerable influence from the native language, especially in vocabulary like *napoei* (above), but such influence does not preclude a diffused influence from pidgin English further to the east.

In New England, AIPE was spoken, unless we are to assume that the many attestations are faked, from the early seventeenth century. A few more attestations, and a rehash of many already cited, are provided by Goddard (1976, 1978). In his 1978 article Goddard objects to the diffusionist claim in Dillard (1972:ch. IV) that AIPE represented the learning of a multilingual contact solution by American Indians from West Africans (WAPE). It is quite true that the earliest attestations of AIPE predate those of WAPE, and that it therefore cannot be proved that the former represented diffusion from the latter.[2]

It is still noteworthy, however, that the earliest representations of AIPE come from coastal or even maritime contexts. In, for example, William Bradford's *Of Plimouth Plantation* (1622), there is a description of an Indian named Samoset who, on about the 16th of March, 1621, 'came boldly among them and spoke to them in broken English, which they could well understand but marveled at it'. Samoset told of another Indian named Squanto (perhaps more accurately Tisquantum) who had been carried away in 1614 by 'one Hunt, a mr. of a ship, who thought to sell them for slaves in Spain'. Tisquantum had somehow gotten to England rather than to Spain, and had learned better English than Samoset could speak. This report, among the very earliest of anyone's use of what could well have been AIPE, certainly connects the Indians' knowledge of English to the sea and to the slave trade, if it does not give any support to the notion that AIPE derived in any sense from WAPE.

Another report earlier than the presumptive period of WAPE influence could be argued from William Wood's *New Englands Prospect* (1634), where Indians who rowed out toward an English ship and were fired upon exclaimed 'What much hoggery?', called the ship 'so big walk', and expressed the fear that it would 'bimeby kill'. *Bimeby* is familiar from worldwide pidgin English as a future marker, and was thus probably transmitted nautically. *Big* as used here seems to be a derivational device common to AIPE and WAPE (Dillard 1976a:ch. I). *Hoggery* seems quite another matter. Goddard (1977) derives it by 'phonological interference' from English *angry*, citing another attestation, John Underhill's *Newes from America* (1638). When Underhill would not respond from his ships in the mouth of the Thames River in Connecticut, the Indians cried: '*What English man, what cheere, what cheere, are you hoggery, will you cram us.*' As Goddard points out, the gloss by Underhill is: 'Are you angry, will you kill us, and do you come to fight [?]' The gloss is hardly a literal one, however, and Goddard himself points out that the derivation of *hoggery* from *angry* is an anomaly in the phonology of English-Indian borrowing practices.

If Goddard's researches have cast light on *hoggery*, however, they have not done much for *meddle*, as in the following excerpt from Benjamin Tompson's *New-Englands Crisis* of 1676, comprising King Philip's supposed speech to his people, inciting them to attack the English: '*Me meddle Squaw me hang'd, our fathers kept what squaws they would whither [sic] they wakt or slept'* (Hall 1924). This use of *meddle* as a transitive verb with a female object (perhaps with sex opposite to that of the subject, and perhaps even meaning 'copulate with', although there are not enough data to permit that conclusion with any certainty) is paralleled in a number of sources where WAPE, according to Creolist theory at least, is historically involved. R. C. Dallas's *History of the Maroons* (1803) quotes one of the Jamaicans who resisted British domination: *'Massa parson say, no mus tief, no mus meddle with somebody wife; must set down softly.* These are rather clearly the Ten Commandments, a Maroon Jamaican Creole version of 'Thou Shalt Not Steal, Thou Shalt Not Commit Adultery', etc. Plantation novelists for the continental United States have, further, sporadically recorded this sexual use of *meddle*. (William A. Stewart [personal communication] suggests a derivation from *middle*, and cites blues lyrics like: 'My father was no jockey, but he sure taught me how to ride. First in the middle, and then you sway from side to side.')

The use in Black English has, almost predictably, been explained away as a euphemism by observers like Culbertson (1972:148, wherein there is a discussion of alternation between *meddle* and *meddle with*) and euphemism is not an impossible part of the process where this *meddle* is concerned. The widespread use, on the other hand, seems to indicate that the full semantic shift took place somewhere in the pidgin English tradition; and, if Goddard's attestation is a credible one, it may have come to AIPE as well as to WAPE.

In spite of dogged avoidance of the issue by writers in various fields (e.g. Chase on *triangular voyage* and *middle passage*, this volume: 121), the slave trade was closely linked to the sea. Slave use of virtually unmodified pidgin English was distinctly coastal and insular in the early period, that being where the slaves were concentrated. The Maritime Provinces of Canada (Paddock 1966) display many of the characteristics of the language of the nautical trade, including slavery.

Whether the direct transmission of AIPE was from WAPE or not, it is not a tenable hypothesis that pidgin English (or French, Portuguese) 'arose' exclusively on the West African coast. In spite of the temptation to appeal to those Black identity groups who have accepted the Black English formulation in terms of pride in 'our own language', the evidence does not fully support such a conclusion. In Portuguese, there is the case of Papia Kristang (Hancock forthcoming), much like Papiamentu and other 'African' Portuguese-based creoles but completely lacking African speakers and any reasonable history of contact with West African languages in the formative stage. For further discussion, see Birmingham's article (this volume).

There are, in the English-based contact tradition, varieties like those of Pitcairn Island and Tristan da Cunha that clearly belong to the pidgin-creole tradition without having any African component in their populations and without any substantial language contact with Africans. According to Booy (1958), the permeation of the Tristan da Cunha lexicon by nautical terms is as great as Chase asserts for the English of the eastern United States in the eighteenth century.

The maritime, coastal, and insular associations of pidgin English, as well as its utility in multilingual situations have long been recognized. Baker (1943:13) points out how:

It [pidgin English] spread to almost every corner of the Pacific [by the close of the eighteenth century]. It was as much used by the original white inhabitants of Australia and New Zealand as it was in other parts of the South Seas. Today it is spoken by millions of people. . . . The country's native languages (. . . about twenty in number) are almost closed books to one another. In the midst of such confusion, the jargon of Pidgin English, which the riffraff and scum of the seven seas had spread across the Pacific . . . may have served as a lingua franca.

There is, in fact, no doubt that pidgin English did serve as such a lingua franca in many parts of the world, including those parts of West Africa where the slave trade was in progress and parts of continental North America where American Indians and Africans, both from extremely multilingual language areas and forced into a new kind of language contact, had the same need for a new 'jargon'. The 'riffraff and scum' who spread the jargon in the first place — or who gave the first impetus to the diffusion of a contact variety — very probably included slave traders. They also included people once thought of virtually as national heroes but now being reevaluated by history, like Commodore Perry. Accounts like that of Hawks (1856:159) include pidgin English, not so labelled of course:

Gentlemen, Doo Choo man very small, American man not very small. I have read of America in books of Washington — very good man, very good. Doo Choo man give American all provision he wants. American no can have house on shore.

History may have labeled these diffusers as scum and riffraff — or at least as exploiters — but it should be remembered that many of them were prosperous and respected (even idolized) members of their own communities in the eighteenth and nineteenth centuries. Furthermore, it was their part in the enslavement of Africans and of Indians like Samoset and Tisquantum which merited them the scorn of later generations, not the spread of pidgin English. In fact, pidgin might later become, for populations like that of New Caledonia, a buffer against a new linguistic imperialism: 'Pidgin English was so well established in the South Seas that the Germans could make no impression on it' (Baker 1943:12).

In Africa, too, the maritime pidgins were especially important in providing a lingua franca for such multilingual activities as the slave trade. (See, especially, Hancock [1976].) In the earliest attestations we have, nautical words were adapted for figurative — or shoreside — uses. W. F. W. Owen's *Narrative of Voyages to Explore the Shores of Africa, Arabia, and Madagascar* quotes a Cape Lopez African: ' "Very fine biggy house and ab got two deck", meaning that it had a ground and first floor' (Owen 1833, vol. II:177). There are some striking correspondences to American maritime uses by Africans. A Liberian informant supplies: 'She come day, go day, God send Sunday', interpreted as, 'She comes once in a while' without, apparently, ever having heard of Colcord (1945) who records, 'Come day, go day, God send Sunday', which she says was 'applied alongshore to people who work in a listless and uninterested manner, the implication being that they are clock watchers'.

The pidgin English that had flourished in the China Sea and in the Pacific in general perhaps since the seventeenth century or even earlier came to Hawaii only in the late nineteenth century (Carr 1972:3–7). The reason is obvious: The bilingual contact situation was well served by *hapa haole*, the foreign-accented Hawaiian, and only when great numbers of speakers of other languages came in did the situation obtain in which a pidgin really flourishes. Reinecke (1969) gives an account which stresses rather the on-the-spot 'creation' of pidgin in a contact situation, with emphasis on the exploitation of a Polynesian or Oriental population by Europeans. The records clearly indicate that some Hawaiians (like Henry Obookiah, who died in Connecticut in the pursuit of the evangelical activities to which he devoted the last part of his short life) learned pidgin in the maritime trade before the variety became well established in the 'Sandwich Islands'. Obookiah had sailed on a whaling vessel before Christian missionary zeal claimed him for its own, and texts like Melville's *Moby Dick* show a pidgin-like contact variety on the whaling ships.

Today, when Honolulu dwarfs any other Hawaiian city and when Oahu and Hawaii are the islands on which research projects look into the relationship between pidgin English (by now a creole or partly decreolized dialect) and education, it is easy to forget that Lahaina, on the island of Maui, was at least as important as Honolulu insofar as whaling was concerned. It may be almost forgotten, also, but the whaling industry played a bigger role than perhaps anything else in the Americanization of the islands and in the spread of the English language there. As Dulles (1933:244) puts it: 'Despite . . . the continuing feud between whalers and missionaries, it was these two elements that drew the islands steadily closer to the United States'.

Today, tourists dominate Lahaina even more than Honolulu or Hilo, and the average visitor's contact with 'pidgin' is limited to humorous decals like

PLEASE NO
STRAIGHTEN OUT
DA MESS
ON MY DESK
You goin' jam up my system!

'Local color' is supplied in columns for the Honolulu *Advertiser* which otherwise might have been written in Duluth, with lines like: 'Would you believe "Da Kine Famous Amos" with macadamia nuts?' (August 16, 1977, A–3, describing a new cookie), and 'You like one tour?' (August 15, 1977, A–6, account of a youthful tourist guide). The graffiti scrawled on the windows of half-abandoned buildings, seemingly not occupied since whaling days, include

I LIKE FOC [sic] TOURISTS

And, more respectably, the nine-member Faith Apostolic Church of Lahaina features a huge sign announcing

JESUS COMING SOON

The church may even represent a kind of survival of the days when missionaries with their moral zeal made Lahaina a competitor and alternative to the fleshpots of Honolulu.

Today, it is as easy to forget how whaling dominated the economic life of the mid-to-late nineteenth century in the United States as it is to forget the dominant maritime trade of the preceding period, slaving. It is easy to forget the importance of either today, but the records of the past preserve the reports of the importance of both slavery and whale-fishing.[3]

The vocabulary of the whalers, influential among whom where the Hawaiians ('Kanakas') spread very far. According to the influential survey by Reinecke (1969, citing Stefánsson [1909] in this regard), certain 'Hawaiian words' were thus carried to the Arctic by whalers. In Stefánsson's actual list, however, are *kau kau* (which Stefánsson compares to 'our chow chow') and *mikaninny* 'small, little, a child' which Stefánsson compares to (ultimately Portuguese) *pickaninny*, with a well-deserved question as to whether it is 'Kanaka'. Stefánsson had good reason, however, to suspect the presence of 'Kanakas'. According to

Loftis (1973:101), the name itself penetrated to the gold mining area of California:

With the leveling of rank, some of the forty-niners found it convenient to drop their old names and past histories and assume a new identity. 'French Pete', 'Kanaka Joe', 'Boston', and 'Kentuck' of Bret Harte's *The Luck of Roaring Camp* were part of the same tradition.

Literary treatments of the whalers of the nineteenth century, and of their language, are especially well known. Everybody knows that Queequeg and Tashtego of Melville's Moby Dick spoke a pidgin-like English, and that the little black cabin boy Pip spoke a dialect closely resembling other literary renditions of Black English during the period. What should be well known but never seems to be written about is that not only *Moby Dick* but *Typee, Omoo,* and *Mardi* (1963a, 1963b, 1963c) are written about whaling ships and their crews. *Typee,* it is true, only starts from a whaling ship; the central character jumps ship in the South Pacific and lives among cannibals — who turn out to be no more bloodthirsty than the money grubbers who launched the ship.

One of the more well-traveled Typees in this first book by Melville is an obvious speaker of pidgin English: '*Ah, me taboo, — me go Nukuheva, — me go Tior, — me go Typee, — me go everywhere, — nobody harm me, — me taboo* (1963:187). Melville's first-person narrator is curious to find out how Mamoo acquired his grasp of a kind of English, but finds the other reluctant to explain:

Curious to know how he had acquired his knowledge of English, I questioned him on the subject. At first, for some reason or other, he evaded the enquiry, but afterwards told me that, when a boy, he had been carried to sea by a captain of a trading vessell with whom he had staid three years . . . (1963: 187–188).

In other words, like Henry Obookiah who receives extensive attention in Reinecke (1969), Mamoo had learned his pidgin English in the maritime trade. And, ultimately, Samoset and Tisquantum of Bradford's *Of Plimouth Plantation* learned their 'broken' English in the same maritime tradition.

Some indication of the importance of Chinese Pidgin English in that maritime lingua franca tradition has been given above. There are many other sources, like Leland (1900). For the continental United States, especially the West, the same observers, like Rusling and Richardson, who provide the most accessible examples of AIPE also have material on Chinese Pidgin English:

If you call on a lady, and inquire of her Chinese servant, 'missee have got?' he will reply, if she be up and about 'Missee have got topside': or, if she be still asleep, 'Missee have got, wakee sleepee'. Not wishing to disturb her, you hand him your card and go away with, 'Maskee, maskee; no makee bobbery' (Rusling 1875:340).

For *maskee* and *bobbery* in a maritime context, see the sources cited in Dillard (1975a:38–39, 40–41). Notice also that Rusling assumes 'you' know pidgin English to speak to the Chinese servant.

Earlier writers like L. W. Jenkins, whose *Bryant Parrot Tilden of Salem at a Chinese Dinner Party* (Canton, 1819), is quoted in Miller (1969), pointed out how Chinese 'hong' merchants could communicate with Americans in pidgin English in the early nineteenth century. A financial well-wishing was: 'I now chin chin the sky and wish you may catch too much profit.' (For *chin chin* 'speak', see Granville [1962]. Carr [1972] points out how *catch* 'get' is characteristic not only of Chinese Pidgin English but also of Melanesian and Hawaiian Pidgin English.) A theological discussion could be concluded with: 'Ayay! My flinde, now no more occasion for make talke dat Josh pidgin [religious subject]. Tluly now my can see you long me tinke [think] all the same.' Miller points out what anyone who takes the trouble to examine nineteenth-century American periodicals can easily see for himself: The newspapers and magazines were full of Chinese Pidgin English. Called *China John, John Chinaman*, or collectively 'The Celestials', the Chinese brought their pidgin English, which the history of the variety in China suggests must have been known to many of them before they arrived in North America, to the attention of the general public in the United States in the nineteenth century.

Without mentioning pidgin English, Kung (1962:231) identifies *kow-tow, chow* (also *chow chow*, in use as far from California as rural East Texas), *chop-chop, joss* (from Portuguese), *fantan, mah-jongg, tong, joss house, chopstick, chop suey, chow mein, flop, yok-a-mi*, and *tong war* (the last three are quoted from Mencken, without apparent disapproval). The presence of a Portuguese term (*joss*, from *deos*) and several compounds with English words makes it seem probable that Chinese Pidgin English was at least one of the media for transmitting the words to American English.

This list of words shows no very great influence of Chinese Pidgin English on American English. There remains to be evaluated, however, the influence of Chinese and of pidgin English in general on casual styles of American speech, especially small-boy talk and baby talk (i.e. what adults use in talking to children — not language acquisition forms).

It is probable, for example, that the slangy American expressions 'You bet' and 'You betcha' either originated in or were propagated by pidgin English. Accounts in books like W. Henry Barneby's *Life and Labour in the Far, Far West* (1884:416–417) report:

Chinese and Mexican workmen are much employed here; we saw six of the former engaged in filling a cart, on our arrival at the villa. The following notice was put up outside a saloon on the Southern Pacific Railway, at a station house called Lang, which we passed this morning: — Eating House. Good, you bet.

Elsewhere, Barneby expresses a characteristic Western underevaluation of CPE:

It is a mystery how they [little settlements of frugal Chinese] get there [i.e. the mines of the Rocky Mountains] nobody wants them, nobody took them there, nobody showed them the way, and yet there they are, often barely able to speak more than a word or two of 'pigeon English' (1884:416–417).

Of course, Barneby underestimated the Chinese even more than he did their pidgin English.[4]

As Dressler's 1927 collection *California Chinese Chatter* shows, they were often busily involved in all kinds of financial and commercial affairs. The telegrams that they wrote are interesting combinations of pidgin and 'telegraphic' English. The supposed similarity of the two has led some to offer the latter as an explanation of the former, but specifically pidgin forms come through in these telegrams. It should be noted how often the 'pleonastic' pronoun (noun classifier) occurs in a medium, the telegraph, where saving words means saving money.[5] Notice also *what for* (p. 458) when *why* would have been a briefer as well as more standard form. To that degree, at least, these communications help to illustrate how pidgin English is an institutionalized language variety, not just something that 'springs up' in response to the passing needs of interlocutors.

This pronominal repetition of the subject is merely one more of the many factors that have led pidginists to point to common features present in widely dispersed pidgins. For that reason, they reject the age-old analysis 'the lexicon of English and the grammar of Chinese' — or any other language being considered at the time. For that reason also, they are wary of attempts to find special evidence of human brain structure through the analysis of pidgins or creoles.

The means of pidgin transmission was fairly obvious: the sea. The multilingual communication needs of sailors spread pidgin English, perhaps only in its 'ships' jargon' form, around the globe. The similarity of certain land areas to the sea, detailed in Part Two, seems reason enough not to be surprised that pidgin English spread across, for example, the Great Plains of North America.

Once localized on land, pidgin English may have always undergone some of the changes and 'enlargement' that Stefánsson (1909) associates with 'shore jargon'. In perhaps all cases, the native languages of the people in the area were the overwhelmingly most important factor in the 'enrichment' of the pidgin. Current work on AIPE, especially, (Leap 1973, 1974, 1975) stresses those contributions from the native languages. This is all to the good, but the diffusionist impulse of the 'ships' jargon' — perhaps spoken mainly by Indians being 'removed' to the west in the case of AIPE and involving little or no nautical contact except in the very beginning stage — should not be underestimated. That such transmission took place seems to be a fact that no longer be ignored in historical treatments.

NOTES

1. Evidence like that presented by D. G. Brinton (1887), has, however, been overlooked. Brinton showed that the numerals did not resemble those of the Lenape languages at all but did have a close resemblance to the numerals (one to ten) of Mandingo. A very similar set of numbers was reported by Joseph B. Cobb, who said he learned them from a slave who had been born in Africa, in *Mississippi Scenes* (1851, quoted in Turner [1949:308]). The resemblances are obviously close:

	Brinton's 'Nanticoke'	Brinton's Mandingo	Cobb
one	killi	kilin	kelleh
two	Filli	fula	fullah
three	Sapo	saba	subah
etc.			

Brinton reports having found these supposedly Nanticoke words in some eighteenth-century texts. The learning of African language forms by Indians in that area, at least, is no surprise, given the well-known close relations between Indians and West African slaves in the northeastern states in the eighteenth century (Greene 1942).

2. For example, the Natchitoches, Louisiana, telephone directory has, in a telephone company message in the yellow pages, an Indian 'chief' who says, 'Me wanna gettum buffalo'. (The cowboy in the same cartoon-advertisement gives the Indian dialing instructions to get Buffalo, New York.)

3. It is equally easy to forget that, in the earliest days of 'whale-fishing', colonial Whites learned some of the skills of the business from Indians, who had long practiced off-shore whaling.

4. There are innumerable works like Alexander McLeod's *Pigtails and Gold Dust* (1948) that quote Chinese speakers of what is obviously pidgin English. About half of the works identify the variety as pidgin, usually with the spelling *pigeon*. McLeod presents, for example, the picture of a Chinese servant leaving his job and providing the employer with

a substitute: 'My fliend heap good boy; he stay you; I catch-um place San Francisco' (1948:107). Elsewhere he presents a lengthy song by a Chinese laundry worker: 'Workee, workee, All same workee, . . .' (McLeod:116). This author is also one of many who represents communication between members of different minority groups, in this case a Digger Indian to a Chinese miner: 'Give Ingian man four dollars — you give white man four dollars — you give Ingan [sic] man four dollars.'

There is no denying that many of the printed examples of Chinese Pidgin English may be repeated from hearsay rather than from direct observation. Further, the transcribers were not linguists and often not even talented laymen. Still, many of the linguistic forms presented are matched in the reports of more reliable writers (Leland 1900). There are some recent surveys of Chinese Pidgin English, like Meredith (1929), but the latter unfortunately hides her light behind a not-very-unusual translation of Longfellow's *Excelsior* into Chinese Pidgin English.

McLeod, like most other authors on the Chinese in American life, has considerable material on the presence of Chinese prostitutes on the West Coast. (See the telegrams about 'women' in the excerpts from *California Chinese Chatter*.) Predictably, a Chinese-American writer like Kung (1962) would deemphasize such material or leave it out entirely.

5. For the 'pleonastic' pronouns in Black English, see Smith's article (this volume) or Tyson (1976).

DOUGLAS LEECHMAN and ROBERT A. HALL, JR.

American Indian Pidgin English:
Attestations and Grammatical Peculiarities

We are all familiar with the stereotyped broken English which writers of
Western stories, comic strips, and similar literature put into the mouths of
Indians: 'me heap big chief', 'you like um fire water', and so forth. This
type of language, however far removed it may be from the usage of most
present-day Indians, represents the continuation of an earlier tradition of
actual speech, in which a pidginized variety of English served in the
contacts between Indians and Whites, from the seventeenth century
onward. For this contact language, we may use the term *American Indian
Pidgin English* (AIPE), thus indicating its relationship to other kinds of
pidgin English.[1] That AIPE has been a true pidgin (i.e. used by both
groups in the contact situation), and not merely broken English used by
Indians alone, is well attested; here, as in other instances, the Whites
(especially traders) were the ones who taught the pidginized language to
the aborigines, and even spread words from one native language to
speakers of another:

When the white trader invaded the solitudes of the Indians, he took with him, or
soon picked up, a small stock of words which, by his constant use among the tribes,
have become, as it were, common property; thus 'squaw,' the Narragansett name
for woman, the Algonquin 'papoose' for child, 'chuck' food, and many other
words, have become universal among all the North American Indians east of the
Rocky Mountains, when speaking to a white man, or Indian not of their tribe.[2]

We have attestations of Whites using a pidginized variety of English in
speaking with Indians down to the present century, as in text 38, below.

The present article is an effort to present and analyze such material as
has been found bearing on AIPE, with the aim both of casting light on the
linguistic acculturation of the Indian and of aiding the historical study of
pidgin English as a whole.[3] Not much data is available, since many
writers[4] make their Indians speak normal English, no matter what their
actual speech may have been like.[5] However, Leechman has gathered a

This article first appeared in *American Speech* (1955):163–171. It is reprinted here by
permission of the authors and of *American Speech*.

number of reasonably trustworthy attestations of AIPE from various sources; we reproduce here the relevant passages. The two authors have discussed the material together, and Hall has prepared an analysis of its linguistic aspects.

The attestations are here presented in their original orthography, in chronological order. Each passage is preceded by its date, and is followed by an indication of its source.

1. 1641: 'They say, *Englishman* much foole, — Lazie *squaes!*' Thomas Lechford (1833), *Plaine Dealing; or, Newes from New England*, 103. Massachusetts Historical Society Collections 23. Cambridge, Mass.

2. Ca. 1673: 'Here is a specimen warrant: "You, you big constable, quick you catch um Jeremiah Offscow, strong you hold um, safe you bring um afore me, Waban, Justice Peace." — "Tie um all up, — and whip um plaintiff, and whip um 'fendant, and whip um witness."' Francis F. Drake (1927), *Indian History for Young Folks*, New York. Originally published 1884.) 93–94.

3. 1675: 'About the 15th August (1675), Captain Mosely with sixty Men, met with a Company, judged about three hundred Indians, in a plain Place where few trees were, and on both Sides Preparations were making for a Battle; all being ready on both sides to fight, Captain Mosely plucked off his Periwig, and put it into his Breeches, because it should not hinder him in fighting. As soon as the Indians saw that, they fell a Howling and Yelling most hideously, and said, *Umh, umh me no stawmerre* [understand] *fight Engismon, Engismon got two Hed, Engismon got two Hed; if me cut off un Hed, he got noder, a put on beder as dis*; with such like words in broken English, and away they all fled and could not be overtaken, nor seen any more afterwards.' Charles H. Lincoln, editor (1913), *Narratives of the Indian Wars 1675–1699*, 39. New York.

4. 1675: 'They [the Indians] will say three sleeps me walk, or two or three sleeps me do such a thing.' John Josselyn (1883), *Account of Two Voyages* (1674), 302. Massachusetts Historical Society Collections 23, Cambridge, Mass.

5. 1675–1699: '. . . an Indian, a Friend of his . . . with his Knife made a Hole in his Breast to his Heart, and sucked out his Heart-Blood: Being asked his Reason therefore, his Answer, *Umh, umh, nu, Me stronger as I was before, me be so strong as me and he too, he be ver strong Man fore he die.*' Lincoln, op. cit., p. 41.

6. 1675–1699: '. . . amongst which dead, was one who had Life in him, and was found by a Friend Indian, he took him up and said: *Umh, umh poo Ingismon, mee save yow Life, mee take yow to Captain Mosee* (Mosely).' Ibid., p. 43.

7. 1675–1699: 'The Indian answered: "Nay, mee own, English Fashion is all one Fool: you kill mee, mee kill you! No, better ly somewhere, and Shoot a man, and hee no see! That the best Soldier!"' Ibid., p. 238, quoting Cotton Mather in *Decennium Luctuosum*.

8. 1720: 'You be de white man, you have soul; when we die we fling in water, big fish come carry us to an oder place, den we live dare and die agen, and fish bring us back to an oder place.' Speech by Indian Will in William Rufus Chetwood (1720), *The Voyages of Captain Richard Falconer*. London.

9. 1756: 'Solomon [a Caughnawaga Mohawk] ended by saying "You don't know Catawba, velly bad Indian; Catawba all one devil."' Drake, op. cit., p. 196, quoting from *Col. James Smith's Captivity* (1756).

10. Ca. 1770: An anecdote of an aged Indian who had spent much time among the white people of Pennsylvania and New Jersey: 'One day, about the year 1770, he observed

that the Indians had a much easier way of getting a wife than the whites, and were much more certain of getting a good one — "for", said he, in his broken English, "white man court — court, may be one whole year! — may be two year before he marry! Well! — may be he then get *very good* wife — but may be not! — may be very cross! — Well now, suppose cross, scold as soon as get awake in the morning, scold all day, scold until sleep, — all one; he must keep *him*. [Footnote: The pronouns in the Indian language have no gender.] White people have law forbidding throwing away wife, be he ever so cross! — must keep *him* always. Well! how does Indian do? — Indian, when he sees industrious squaw, which he like, he go to him, place his two forefingers close aside each other, make two look like one, look squaw in the face — see *him* smile — which is all one *he* say *yes*! so he take *him* home — no danger *he* cross! throw *him* away and take another! Squaw love to eat meat! No husband, no meat! Squaw do everything to please husband, he do same to please squaw; live happy." ' Rev. Peter Jones (1861), *History of the Ojebway Indians*, 80. London.

11. [1790: Quotation from *The Basket Maker*, a play by John O'Keefe:]

    WATTLE — Pray my good people, didn't he owe you a few blows on the back?

    OTCHEGROS — dat put me in de mind, he did give me once a tump in de cheek, I pay you.

    SOKOKI — He did with tamahawk once take my ear.

    WATTLE —What!

    THIRD INDIAN — If Kikapous liv'd he was dis day to fight me wid hatchet — here (*offers hatchet*).

    WATTLE — O Help! Murder!

    F. Bissell (1925) *The American Indian in English Literature of the Eighteenth Century*, 147. Yale Studies in English, 68. New Haven, Yale University Press.

12. 1794: 'The letters *f. v. ph*, and *r*, are wanting in their alphabet. They therefore omit them entirely in foreign words, or pronounce them differently, for example, *Pilipp* for *Philip, Petelus* for *Petrus, Pliscilla* for *Priscilla*.' George Henry Loskie (1794), *History of the Mission of the United Brethren among the Indians in North America*, 19. London.

13. 1804–1806: 'Everything that is incomprehensible to the Indians they call big medicine.' Quoted from Lewis, by Elijah Harry Criswell (1940), *Lewis and Clark: Linguistic Pioneers*, lviii. University of Missouri Studies, Vol. 15, No. 2. Columbia, Mo., University of Missouri Press.

14. 1823: 'He replied in broken English "Indian no call this an aspen tree quake asp." "What then?" asked the inquisitive hostess. "Woman tongue. Woman tongue," answered the sagacious warrior, "never still, never still, always go." ' John Dunn Hunter (1823), *Memoirs of a Captivity among the Indians of North America*, 376. London.

15. 1823: 'Man, brave man, no cheat Indian. Indian no cheat white man.' Ibid., p. 399.

16. 1823: ' . . . the Indian replied in broken English: "Why didn't [*sic*] give fine things to him? He got no beaver, to give for fine things. White man mouth full honey, talk sweet, say many good things. This please foolish Indians. He then cheat him. He no fool Shomacassa." ' Ibid., p. 397.

17. 1823: ' . . . she indignantly replied in broken English, "White man want poison poor Indian. Whiskey bring my people to want. Whiskey kill poor Peggy. Peggy, poor daddy and mammy have no one to help 'em when Peggy dead." ' Ibid., p. 395.

18. 1826: 'An Indian woman proposed to a white man as follows: "You silly. You weak. You baby-hands. No catch horse. No kill buffalo. No good, but for sit still — read book. Never mind. Me like. Me make rich. Me make big man. Me your squaw." ' Mary Meek Atkeson (1921), 'Study of the local literature of the upper Ohio Valley with especial reference to the early pioneer and Indian tales', Ohio State University Bulletin 26(3):39 [*Contributions in English*, No. 2] quoting Timothy Flint in *Francis Berriam* (1826), I, 57.

19. 1836: 'I demanded my ducks [previously promised], he looked gloomy, and replied with characteristic brevity, "No duck — Chippewa [personal name] gone up lake with canoe — no canoe — duck by-and-by." ' Catherine Parr Traill (1929), *The Backwoods of Canada*, 175. Toronto. (Originally published 1836.)

20. 1836: 'When I asked him his name, he replied "Indian name Maquin, but English name 'Mister Walker,' very good man"; this was the person he was called after.' Ibid., p. 176.

21. 1837: Robert Montgomery Bird in his *Nick of the Woods* makes an Indian say *Quakel* for *Quaker*, a very literal following of the idea that Indians pronounce *r* as *l*. Albert Keiser (1933), *The Indian in American Literature*, 150. New York.

22. 1843: 'Strike! Nick kill cap'n — major kill Nick.' James Fenimore Cooper, *Wyandotte*, quoted by Keiser, op. cit., p. 112.

23. 1845: [An Indian, Susquesus, warns a Negro not to flog another Indian, Musquerusque, because the Huron chief] 'got tender back; never forget rope.' James Fenimore Cooper, *Satanstoe*, quoted by Keiser, op. cit., p. 113.

24. Ca. 1851: 'He [an intoxicated Indian] came staggering towards his wigwam, singing out to all whom he met, "Me goes to Methodist; me nod drink little more; me am Methodist." ' George Conway (1851), *Recollections of a Forest Life*, 42. London.

25. Ca. 1857: 'Pale-faces come, take our land, and drive us away. Pale-faces give us red-water, which make our heart feel bad and burn us up. Ugh! Den dey bring us good book, to tell 'bout Great Spirit, and make us good.' Tonowaha speaking in Preuss's *Fashions and Follies of Washington Life* (1857), quoted by Perley Isaac Reed (1918), *Realistic Presentation of American Characters in Native American Plays prior to 1870*, 114. Columbus, Ohio.

26. 1861: ' "Me very great chief, me got dree wives, all broders," meaning they were sisters.' Jones, op. cit., p. 81.

27. 1864: Thoreau says definitely from his own observation that a Penobscot [?] Indian traveling with him 'generally added the syllable *um* to his words when he could, as padlum, etc.'; e.g. 'Sometimes I lookum side-hill'; 'Sometimes I lookum locks [rocks].' Henry David Thoreau (1884–1894), *The Maine Woods*, 230 and passim. Boston, Riverside Press. (Originally published 1864.) Cf. also 'That make hard paddlum thro'; hold 'em canoe. So say old timers.' Ibid., p. 228.

28. 1864: 'Me been sick. Oh, me unwell now. You make bargain, then me go.' Ibid., p. 105.

29. 1871: 'His name was Ottawa, and he was a war chief of the Ogalalla band of the Sioux nation. He struck himself on his breast, saying "Good Indian, me", and pointing to those around him, he continued, "Heap good Indian, hunt buffalo and deer." ' Fanny Kelly (1871), *Narratives of My Captivity among the Sioux Indians*, 22. Hartford, Conn.

30. 1871: 'Me understand English; my boy make two chairs next week; pay ten shillings for 'em, eh?' Alexander Begg (1871), *Dot It Down: a Story of Life in the North-West*, 147. Toronto.

31. 1871: 'Injun very hungry — something to eat, eh?' Ibid., p. 148.

32. 1871: 'Thank ye! Chairs next week; good-bye, Injun glad; good young squaw.' Ibid.

33. 1871: 'Lying tongue; bad Sioux did that; I will have blood for it; travel-travel — will kill bad Sioux for that.' Ibid., p. 149.

34. 1892: [Old Jake has just seen an Indian climbing up the face of a cliff towards a cave; the rope breaks and the Indian is dashed on the rocks below. Old Jake runs to his assistance and pulls him out of the water in which he is lying. The Indian:] ' . . . were just able to say "Wild Cat paleface's friend. Cache up thur. Paleface can keep all." His head fell over, limber-like, and he slipped from my hands as dead as a last year's straddle-bug.' Achilles Daunt (1892), *In the Land of the Moose, the Bear, and the Beaver*, 69. London.

35. 1938: 'Sure take um home.' Edna Ferber (1938), *Cimarron*, 312. Garden City, N.Y., Doubleday, other examples of *-um*, passim.
36. 1946: ' "S'pose you in brush," he began tentatively. "You no got nothin', no gun, no bow'n arrow. — You savvy bow'n arrow?" . . . "You walk in brush, no make noise, pretty soon you see rabbit. . . . You throw 'em bone. Make big noise. Rabbit, he hear that. He scared. He know big bird make noise like that when he catch rabbit; maybe eagle, maybe big owl. He too scared, he stay, no move for long time. You go slow, go easy, catch 'em rabbit. He no run away. . . . You savvy?" ' Douglas Leechman (1946), Balaam and the Old Times', *Queen's Quarterly* 53:447–458, 449–451.
37. 1946: ' "Cold last night," he greeted me one morning. "Pretty soon winter. Pretty soon trees go yellow. Some little leaves go red. All the hillsides strong yellow and red. Very fancy. Awh, good!" ' Ibid., p. 455.
38. 1946: ' "Plane come", I announced, rather needlessly.
"I hear."
"I go now."
"Too bad", said Balaam. "Old friend now. First day you see me, you say 'like meet old friend'." ' Ibid., p. 457.

Our attested material consists largely of quotations adapted at least in part to Standard English, with occasional pidginized forms, phrases, or sentences left in their original form. We are therefore not in a position to give a complete outline of the linguistic structure of AIPE, and can only enumerate its peculiarities in terms of the respects in which our material differs from Standard English.

The phonology of AIPE is characterized chiefly by reduction of the phonemic inventory, through certain substitutions and the loss of certain phonemes, together with other scattered phenomena. The substitutions involve chiefly the replacement of a fricative by a stop: /ð/ > /d/ in *broder*, *dare* 'there', *dat, de, den, dey, dis, oder* 'other', *wid* (in the texts 8, 11, 25, 26 above); /θ/>/t/ in *tump* 'thump' (11); /θ/>/d/ in *dree* 'three' (26); /f/ > p/ in *Pilipp* (12); and /v/ > what was presumably /b/ (mentioned in 12, without any example). The retroflex or flap /r/ is replaced by /l/ in *locks* 'rocks', *Petelus* 'Petrus', *Pliscilla, Quakel, velly* (9, 12, 21, 27); and /t/ is voiced to /d/ in *beder* 'better' (3).

Loss of a vowel is found in *ver* < *very* (5). Among the consonants, /l/ is lost in clusters in *Engismon, Ingismon*, and *Mosee* 'Mosely' (3, 6); final /-r/ is lost in *poo* 'poor' (6). The initial syllable /di-/ disappears in *'fendant* 'defendant' (2). Other phenomena of phonological change include the assimilation of /t/ to /d/ before a following /d/ in *nod drink* 'not drink' (24), and the insertion of a vowel into the consonant cluster /tl/ (</tr/, see above) in *Petelus* 'Petrus' (12).[6]

In the morphology, we find a noun used uninflected, in its singular form, in *two Hed* (3). Among the pronouns, the use of the single form *me* as both subject and object is very widespread (3, 4, 5, 6, 7, 18, 24, 26, 28,

29, 30), so much so that one wonders whether the use of *I* as subject (e.g. 5, 33) is an Anglicism.[7] In the third person singular, *he* is used as a feminine (10); and we find the reduced form *a* (3).

Verb structure is characterized especially by very widespread loss of inflectional features, i.e. by the exclusive use of the simple form of the verb (3, 5, 8, 10, 15, 16, 17, 18, 19, 22, 23, 30, 35, 36, 38). This phenomenon manifests itself in the use of the simple form where Standard English has differentiated forms in the first sg. or third sg. present, or in the past: e.g. *me be* (5); *big fish come carry us* (8); *he go* (10); *Nick kill Cap'n* (22); etc. The form *been* occurs (28) as the past of *be*;[8] is *was* (5) an Anglicism? The suffix /-əm/, spelled *'em, um* (either suffixed to the verb or separate in orthography) and sometimes *'im* or *him*, occurs widely as a transitive suffix (2, 10, 14, 16, 17, 18, 27, 35, 36);[9] in one instance it forms a verbal noun: *paddlum* 'paddling' (27).[10]

The only other peculiarity on the level of inflection is the use of *all one* in the meaning 'like, as, the same as' (7, 9, 10); from the attestations it is not clear whether we are to phonemicize this as /'ɔl 'wʌn/ or /'ɔl wʌn/.[11] In word formation, the only item of note is the compound-type noun plus noun, in *baby-hands* 'having hands like a baby' (18).

Passing to the level of syntax, we find certain peculiarities in the structure of phrases. In noun phrases the absence of both definite and indefinite articles is especially widespread (8, 10, 13, 18, 25, 31, 32, 33, 34, 36, 37, 38): e.g. *we fling in water, big fish come* (8); *white man court* (10); etc., etc. A noun or pronoun attribute, with the meaning of 'possessor', occurs preceding a noun head whose meaning is 'thing possessed', in simple juxtaposition,[12] as in *yow life* (6); *white man mouth* (16); *Peggy poor mammy and daddy* (17). In one instance, a noun attribute is found following a noun head: *Justice Peace* 'Justice of the Peace' (2).

Two types of adjective phrase call for special attention. In one, an adjective head is followed by a noun modifier, with partitive meaning: *full honey* 'full of honey' (16). With a comparative, the term of comparison is introduced by *as* 'than': *beder as dis* (3); *stronger as I was before* (5).

Among verbal phrases, there are five types worthy of note. The verb is repeated, with meaning of 'continued action',[13] in *court-court* (10) and *travel-travel* (33). A verb is followed directly by another verb acting as complement in *strawmerre fight* (3) and *want poison* 'wants to poison' (7). In *talk sweet* (16), an adjective attribute with adverbial meaning follows the verb it modifies; but in *quick you catch um . . . strong you hold um, safe you bring um* (2), this type of attribute precedes the verb and its subject. An adverb of time precedes its verb in several instances (10, 11, 14, 16): e.g. *he then cheat him*.

In the structure of predicates, the center is often a noun or adjective, giving the predicate the meaning of 'equation', rather than of 'action' as in Standard English (1, 7, 10, 14, 15, 18, 23, 26, 28, 29, 31, 32, 34, 36, 37): e.g. *Englishman much foole* (1); *that the best soldier* (7); *he cross* (10); etc., etc. In two instances, the center of the predicate is an adverb or a phrase introduced by a preposition, and the meaning of the predicate is 'location': *cache up thur* (34); *you in brush* (36).[14]

Predicates are rendered negative by the use of *no* preceding the center of the predicate (7, 15, 16, 18, 36): e.g. *he no run away* (36). In 24, the negativizer is *not* (> *nod*), preceding the center of the predicate: *nod drink.*

The subject is zero ('omitted') in a number of instances (10, 14, 15, 18, 19, 23, 29, 30, 31, 32, 33, 36, 37, 38): e.g. *suppose cross* 'if he is cross' (10); *never forget rope* (23); etc., etc. In one place, a third sg. verb is used with a first sg. subject: *me goes* (24).

The order of elements in a clause is occasionally different from that of Standard English. The predicate precedes the subject in *good Indian, me* (29), and the verbal attribute precedes subject and predicate in *quick you catch um . . . strong you hold um, safe you bring um* (2). The subject is recapitulated by a pronoun in *rabbit, he hear that* (36).[15]

A stylistic feature to be noted is the use of a third sg. noun subject instead of a first sg. pronoun: *Injun very hungry* (31); *Injun glad* (32).

Among items of vocabulary, we list here such as show marked change of meaning, or have come to be considered characteristic of American Indian use of English:

Bow 'n arrow /'bonærə/ fused to one word (as shown by spelling with *'n*), 36; cf. Melanesian Pidgin /bonæra/ 'bow'.
Broder 'sibling of same sex', 26.
Heap 'very', 29.
Medicine 'magic, something incomprehensible', 13.
Much 'very', 1.
Savvy 'know', 36.
Squaw 'woman, wife' (<Narragansett), 1, 10, 18, 32. The spelling *squaes* in 1 probably stands for /skwa·z/, with *æ* as a graphic device to indicate a long vowel.
Stawmerre 'understand', 3 — /'stɔmərə/ or /'stɔmər/.
Suppose 'if', 10, 36, cf. Melanesian Pidgin /spos/, Chinese Pidgin /səpóz/ *id.*
Tamahawk, 11.

In conclusion, we may say that, so far as can be seen from the present materials, AIPE presents basically the same characteristics of linguistic reduction and restructuring as do the other varieties of pidgin English (cf. the references given in Note 1). It is worth noting that the most frequent items in our list of grammatical peculiarities are: (1) replacement of fricatives by stops; (2) use of *me* as the only first sg. pronoun form; (3) use of a single verb form derived from the English simple form; (4) the objective suffix /-əm/; (5) loss of definite and indefinite articles; (6) the equational predicate. These features are common to American Indian, Melanesian, and Chinese Pidgin English; they are also among the earliest features attested in our documentation. Their presence and extent lend further support to Hall's suggestion[16] that pidgin English, as a whole, is of basically English origin and structure, going back to substandard English and baby talk of the seventeenth and eighteenth centuries, especially as used by sailors, traders, and slavers in dealing with supposedly ignorant, childlike savages.

The authors are of course aware that the material presented in this paper is by no means exhaustive, and will be grateful for indication of further documentation or attestations of AIPE.

NOTES

1. Including the following:
   A. Chinese Pidgin English (cf. *Journal of the American Oriental Society*, 64 [1944]:95–113).
   B. Central Atlantic Pidgin English, the source of:
      1. West African Pidgin English.
      2. Taki-Taki (cf. *Language*, 24[1948]:92–116), and the speech of the Saramacca Bush-Negroes (cf. H. Schuchardt [1914], *Die Sprache der Saramakka-Neger in Surinam*. Amsterdam).
      3. West Indies varieties of creolized English, e.g. in Jamaica, the Virgin Islands, and the Bahamas.
   C. South Seas Pidgin English, the source of:
      1. The now extinct Micronesian Pidgin English (cf. *Language*, 21[1945]:214–219).
      2. Melanesian Pidgin English (cf. R. A. Hall, Jr. [1943·, *Melanesian Pidgin English: Grammar, Texts, Vocabulary*, Baltimore, here abbreviated *MPE-GTV*; and [1955], *Hands Off Pidgin English!*, Sydney.
      3. Hawaiian 'Pidgin English' (actually a creolized variety of English at the present time).
   D. Australian Pidgin English (cf. *Language*, 19 [1943]:263–267).
2. Richard Irving Dodge (1889), *Our Wild Indians*, 47. Hartford, Conn. A similar situation existed in Australia in the early days of settlement; cf. S. J. Baker (1943), *The Australian Language*. Sydney and London. On p. 220 ff. he states: 'The mixing of aboriginal dialects — that is, the migration of terms from one district to another — through the agency of the European has probably been so great that it can now never be accurately assessed. . . . The European influence therefore had two clearcut effects: (*a*) the introduction of pidgin as a lingua franca between black and white, and (*b*) the spreading of aboriginal terms of limited original use in one district to other, and often remote, districts.' White Australians still behave in this way, e.g. in ascribing Aranta terms such as *alcheringa* 'the eternal dream-time' or *churinga* 'ceremonial objects' to

aboriginal tribes far distant from Aranta territory; most recently in A. W. Upfield (1953), *Murder Must Wait*. New York.

3. Cf. R. A. Hall, Jr. (1952), 'Pidgin English and linguistic change', *Lingua*, 3:138–146.

4. For instance, such novelists as the anonymous author of *Memoirs of an Unfortunate Young Nobleman* (London, 1743); Mrs. Frances Brooks (1931) in *The History of Emily Montague*, ed. by L. J. Burpee. Ottawa. (Originally published 1796.) Washington Irving; and James Fenimore Cooper.

5. Cf. H. N. Fairchild, *The Noble Savage*, New York. 'I have found hardly any instance in which the Noble Savage of any hue speaks broken English. To make him do so would be to dispel the illusion that surrounds him. Man Friday, though an Indian, talks like an eighteenth century literary negro. Colman's Wowski has a comical jargon for which again burlesques of negro speech are evident models' (1928:475).

6. This development is parallel to that found in consonant clusters in Melanesian and most other varieties of pidgin English: e.g. Melanesian Pidgin /ækɪs/ 'axe'; /bɔkɪs/ 'box'; strɔŋ/ [sɪtɪ'rɔŋ] 'hard'; etc.

7. The same phenomenon is found in the Melanesian Pidgin of the British Solomon Islands: the normal first sg. pronoun is /mi/, but /aj/ is found in Anglicizing set phrases such as /aj prɔmɪs/ (e.g. as used in court procedure).

8. Similar to the use of /bɪn/ as past for 'be' and also as a past-tense auxiliary in Australian Pidgin (cf. *Language*, 19 (1943):265), whence it has been introduced by speakers of Australian English into Melanesian Pidgin (cf. R. A. Hall, Jr., 'Innovations in Melanesian Pidgin' [to be published in *Oceania*], §§3.24.2, 5.24.1).

9. This suffix is used similarly in Melanesian and Australian Pidgin; cf. *MPE-GTV* §2.13; *Language*, 19 (1943):265.

10. This case is similar but not wholly parallel to the Chinese Pidgin use of /-əm/ as a passive-transitive suffix forming a verbal adjective or passive participle: e.g. /spɔiləm tli/ 'a ruined tree' (cf. *Journal of the American Oriental Society*, 64 [1944]:98).

11. For the combination of *all* plus another element in similar meaning, cf. Melanesian Pidgin /ɔlsem/ 'like, as'.

12. This type of simple juxtaposition in possessive phrases (regardless of the order of the elements) is found in many pidginized and creolized languages, e.g. Chinese Pidgin (/hi haws/ 'his house'); Taki-Taki (/tigri mamá/ 'the tiger's mother'); Haitian Creole (/kaj papa li/ 'his father's house'); etc.

13. Cf. similar phrases in Melanesian Pidgin (e.g. /go go go go/ 'keep going', *MPE-GTV* 4.40) and Taki-Taki (e.g. /dyómpo dyómpo/ 'jump and jump', /náki náki náki/ 'keep on hammering', *Language*, 24 [1948]:109).

14. These two types of predicate have parallels in Melanesian Pidgin (/dɪsfɛlə haws i-bɪgfɛlə/ 'this house is big'); Australian Pidgin (/dɪs on kəntri bə'lɔŋə mi/ 'this is my own country'); Taki-Taki (/nánsi kóni mán/ 'Anansi is a clever man'); Haitian Creole (/u gasõ/ 'you are a boy'); etc.

15. Such a construction is the source of the predicate marker /i-/ in Melanesian and Australian Pidgin (e.g. /jumi tufɛlə i/go/ 'the two of us go').

16. *Lingua*, 3 (1952):145–146.

MARY RITA MILLER

Attestations of American Indian Pidgin English in Fiction and Nonfiction

The Indian is the enigma of American letters, taciturn in contrast to the American Negro, difficult to analyze linguistically. There is undoubtedly historical evidence for his silence in fiction, but part of it is because the Indian language of the campfire was not his contact language with the White. With the Anglo-Saxon settler, trapper, or scout, he spoke a much reduced jargon sometimes based on Indian vocabulary and structure, such as the Chinook jargon, but more often based on English structure. This language, stripped of inflections and of much of its power and subtlety, became the language of communication when Indian and Englishman met, although neither spoke it elsewhere. It was a pidgin.

The Indian, already handicapped by the linguistic barrier and suspicious of the intruder, retreated or was forced westward during the colonization of the United States, and had a far different linguistic relationship with the European than did the Negro, who soon lost his African tribal language and spoke the creolized pidgin of the plantation where he worked the fields or served the Whites in their homes. There is slender but unmistakable evidence that circumstances forced the development of a pidgin between Indian and settler soon after the English arrived on the North American continent and that this miniature language has continued to exist down to the present.[1] For whatever reason, the English and the Indian in English-speaking territory did not generally develop the rapport necessary for closer linguistic contact, although there were exceptions. Thus the pidgin remained a pidgin. On the other hand, the Indians in what is now the United States clung staunchly to their own languages, undoubtedly for group symbolism as well as for communication. However, the most important reason why the Indians did not embrace English lies in the curious facts of American history. These facts are so significant in the subsequent sociolinguistic development of the American Indian that they will be recounted briefly here. With the ever-increasing arrivals from Europe, one might have expected the Indian to have been assimi-

This article first appeared in *American Speech* (1967): 142–147. It is reprinted by permission of the author and of *American Speech*.

lated into the American scene, giving up his language and tribal customs and accepting Anglo-Saxon customs and language. Or, less optimistically, one might have expected a partial assimilation, the expansion of the pidgin English contact language into a creole, and later into nonstandard or Standard English. This process should have begun, to all appearances, no later than the decade following the Civil War, but circumstances have delayed it approximately one hundred years, and the exact outcome is in doubt. The reason for this delay in the assimilation of the American Indian, and therefore the delay in his linguistic assimilation, was the practice of the government of removing the Indians to territory farther west, a policy which resulted in their isolation from the mainstream of American life. Most Indians east of the Mississippi were compelled to vacate their lands in 1830 and were resettled in Indian country west of the Mississippi. The Cherokees, Creeks, Chikasaws, Choctaws, and Seminoles resisted this move bitterly, history tells us, but they were removed again in the 1850s to what is now Oklahoma. The confinement of Indians to reservations and the separate schools which were established for them kept them separated linguistically from English, and they found a pidgin sufficient for their limited contacts with speakers of English. The many glossaries of the Chinook jargon, the best known of the pidgins in the United States, and the travel books which recommended this language of a few hundred words, are evidence of the fact that Indians and Europeans did not learn each other's language in the Northwest. As the evidence of historical documents, eye-witness accounts, and older fiction amply testifies, the situation was the same throughout North America, the only difference being that other pidgins were based on English to a much greater extent.

Indian schools established on reservations probably did little more than maintain the status quo, linguistically speaking, where an Indian language was spoken at home and contacts with English were few and could be managed better with a lingua franca. Indian children were not admitted to public schools in most of the United States prior to 1890, and as a result their linguistically formative years were spent with other children who knew no standard dialect of English.

Now the picture is changing. The Indians, with the Navajos as the principal exception, are giving up their tribal languages in favor of a type of English which may have some of the characteristics of nonstandard English spoken by other minority groups in the United States. Therefore, it may be assumed that studies made concerning nonstandard language problems of the urban deprived may also be valuable for the American Indian in the more rural areas of the United States. Obviously the proper process is not to destroy the nonstandard language patterns, which still have value within the ethnic group, but to encourage the learning of an additional dialect of English, a standard dialect.

Attestations of American Indian Pidgin English are still few. They exist here and there in historical documents, in accounts of early travel in the American wilderness, and in reports of ocean voyages to the New World where brief inland excursions were a part of the trip. They exist also in tales of captivity by the Indians, of which there are quite a number. These long, emotion-packed, first-person accounts must have been sensational reading in their day, and for that reason many of them have survived. Some enterprising Anglo-Saxons also took troupes of Indians to Europe, where they made successful tours from city to city. They doubly capitalized on this by keeping diaries and publishing accounts of their experiences. Persons who lived peaceably with the Indians also wrote of their life in the American wilderness, and an occasional educated Indian recounted the story of his life. These were books of the past which captured the fancy of the reader in the nineteenth and early twentieth century in America. Here and there examples of pidgin English are to be found, although the searcher may inspect hundreds of pages without being rewarded with a single line of pidgin.

Fiction I consider to be an equally valid source of authentic pidgin speech because of my conviction that language structure cannot be manufactured at the whim of the author. The fact that the same pidgin characteristics are found in fiction as in nonfiction seems to prove this assumption beyond any doubt. American fiction about the Indian has suffered from a lack of realism, and many Indians were portrayed as noble savages with all the romantic mystery of Atala. Fortunately, this fashion in literature did not prevail everywhere, but even in realistic treatments of the Indian, speech was still a problem, either because the Indian was portrayed as noncommunicative or because he spoke in fluent and often courtly English. The author evidently did not wish to risk his reputation by reproducing nonstandard English on the written page. Nevertheless, examples of pidgin English do exist in fiction, and they may ultimately prove to be a richer source of attestations than nonfiction.

In general, the characteristics of American Indian Pidgin English as found in my corpus are the following. Verbs have many of the same reduction features found in other pidgins, the most consistent one being the lack of an equational verb: *That him . . . Um Sioux, Oglallas, me guess . . . Um a heap fool, holla yi hi.*[2] *Indian name Maquin, but English name Mister Walker.*[3] *I sure.*[4] *You fine? . . . Bellyache bad.*[5]

Verbs generally lack tense, person markers, auxiliaries, and modals, and have a single uninflected form: *Me lose um las' spling clossin' liver.*[6] *White man no eat, him . . . How you like him? . . . No eat dog.*[7] *What you do? . . . Day go up river, dey look for somethin' . . . One man no have cork-boat.*[8]

Been occurs as a past tense marker with or without an accompanying verb: *I been hate all palefaces . . . I been suppose all the same.*[9] *Ingin bin in white village.*[10]

Personal pronouns show divergences from Standard English usage, the most consistent form being *'um.* It is variously spelled by different writers as *'um, em, 'm,* or *-um,* and functions as a transitivizer with or without a following noun object: *Dey go camp gettum boss.*[11] *You get'm out quick.*[12] *Squaw make um bed; heap sleap.*[13] *We smoke um calumet together some time soon?*[14] *Um* also occurs as a subject, perhaps as a variant of *him: Um no hollar like um Yanktonais.*[15]

Um and *him* are also used as determiners: *He got mad at speyets* 'spirits' *an' have bayed* 'buried' *um in um cave.*[16] *I tell by way you look at him pine.*[17]

While *he, I, we,* and *they* are interspersed in the corpus among other forms which serve as subject pronouns, the following subject forms are those which relate American Indian Pidgin English to the pidgin family of languages: *No, him eat plenty labbit.*[18] *Him also great protection against bears.*[19] *Him white man, him hunt too. Him nice boy.*[20]

Complements and transitivizers are often missing where they might be expected: *I take.*[21] *Take alive.*[22]

Prepositions are lacking in some situations where they are usual, and the relationship is accomplished by juxtaposition: *I find trail three men.*[23] *I give pieces little May-Heegar.*[24] *Squaw go me, so come.*[25]

There is also some tendency to repeat the noun subject where standard English would employ a substitute, thus indicating possible uncertainty on the speaker's part as to which pronoun form to employ: *Wawatan know best place . . . Wawatan bring food . . . Wawatan not able to say.*[26] *Chuckwood heap glad see you.*[27] *Squaw make um bed; heap sleep.*[28]

Subjects are often omitted where they would be expected: *Like you. . . Burn bad.*[29] *Can't wait . . . Mebbe stop here, mebbe not.*[30] *Make nice baby come fast. Make mother strong.*[31]

The relator *longa* is reminiscent of Gullah: *You go longa me! . . . You go longa me now, heap klick.*[32] *White man go with Indians long trail west.*[33]

A prepositional use found in other marginal languages is the use of *for* to express purpose when followed by an uninflected verb form: *You look 'um tree, for make 'um lumber.*[34] *Squaw root for help squaw with baby.*[35]

A single use of *he* as a possessive occurs: *When he no find bear and deer, he hunt he friend.*[36] There is also a single example of the transposition of pronoun objects: *I bring him you.*[37]

Articles and plurals are few: *Catch um three beaver las' week . . . Boss he gone on river trail two, t'ree hour.*[38] *Bear no come where is this tooth.*[39] *Him heap 'fraid white mans.*[40] *No* rather than *not* serves in negation: *No talk. No talk any.*[41] *Him no stop.*[42] *No kill. Take alive.*[43] *No touch um.*[44]

Verb forms like the following may indicate the desire to avoid difficult consonant clusters; they are not unknown in other pidgins: *Tom lika chicka too . . . He shakee hand . . . Me drinka swipe galore.*[45]

There is repeated indication that the liquids [r] and [l] are confused: *He tlavel that way . . . Fink when he no shoot evlybody he lun look then he heap shoot um.*[46] This evidence for phonemic neutralization is supported in an article by J. Dyneley Prince, in which he states that the most interesting phonetic feature of the Delaware jargon in use between Indians and white settlers in 1684 was the interchange of [r] and [l].[47]

The fricative [ð] becomes [d]: *Dey on dat train. . . . Dey go up river, dey look for somethin'.*[48] *Wid a jolly tar.*[49]

The findings of this article further substantiate the existence of an American Indian Pidgin English, corroborating its chief characteristics and its essential relationship to all English-based pidgins. In addition, I attempt to consolidate the facts which have been responsible for the lingering of a pidgin among American Indians and to suggest the linguistic steps necessary to provide the Indian with a standard dialect of English.

NOTES

1. Douglas Leechman and Robert A. Hall, Jr. (1955), 'American Indian Pidgin English: attestations and grammatical peculiarities', *American Speech* 30:163–171.
2. Frank W. Calkins (1893), *Tales of the West*, part III, 7; I, 85. Chicago.
3. Catherine Parr Traill (1836), *The Backwoods of Canada*, 164. London.
4. Stewart Edward White (1902), *Blazed Trail*, 455. New York.
5. Walter D. Edmonds (1937), *Drums Along the Mohawk*, 65, 530. Boston.
6. Calkins, II, 70.
7. J. S. Coppinger (1955), *The Renegade*, 45. New York.
8. White, pp. 167, 194, 454.
9. R. Ray Baker (1927), *The Red Brother and Other Indian Stories*, 134. Ann Arbor.
10. Coppinger, p. 45.
11. White, p. 195.
12. Edmonds, p. 531.
13. Calkins, I, 118.
14. Baker, p. 135.
15. Calkins, I, 85.
16. Calkins, III, 10.
17. White, p. 168.
18. Calkins, II, 71.

19. Benedict and Nancy Freedman (1947), *Mrs. Mike, The Story of Katherine Mary Flannigan*, 123. New York.
20. White, pp. 171, 180.
21. Freedman, p. 183.
22. Baker, p. 73.
23. White, p. 454.
24. Freedman, p. 196.
25. Calkins, I, 115, 116.
26. Baker, pp. 67, 111.
27. Robert E. Callahan (1927), *Heart of an Indian*, 265. New York.
28. Calkins, I, 118.
29. Edmonds, pp. 67, 531.
30. Baker, pp. 67, 68.
31. Freedman, p. 152.
32. Calkins, I, 114, 116.
33. Baker, p. 73.
34. White, p. 168.
35. Freedman, p. 152.
36. Coppinger, p. 80.
37. Baker, p. 73.
38. White, pp. 325, 195.
39. Freedman, p. 123.
40. Calkins, II, 70.
41. W. D. Edmonds (1937), *In the Hands of the Senecas*, 7. Boston.
42. White, p. 199.
43. Baker, p. 73.
44. Calkins, I, 117.
45. Benjamin Bissell (1925), *The American Indian in English Literature of the Eighteenth Century* (Yale Studies in English 48. New Haven, Conn., Yale University Press), 153, quoting from *The Catawba Travellers or Kiew Neika's Return*, presented at Sadler's Wells in 1797, illustrating the writer's attempt to introduce Indian dialect.
46. Calkins, III, 7, 85.
47. J. Dyneley Prince (1912), 'An ancient New Jersey Indian jargon', *American Anthropologist* 14:508–524.
48. White, pp. 194, 199.
49. Bissell, p. 193.

RICHARD R. DAY and CHARLENE SATO

Categories of Transformations in Second Language Acquisition

Repetition tests have proven a useful method of measuring a child's level of language performance. Such measures have been used in studies of first and second language and second dialect acquisition (Baratz 1969; Day et al. 1975; Johnson 1975; Politzer et al. 1974; Swain et al. 1974).

Although usually presented as a number of correct repetitions, repetition test results may be categorized in a number of different ways. This report deals with the transformations which speakers of a creolized variety of English made in repeating sentences said to them in Standard English (SE). Reports on the repetition test used (the Standard English Repetition Test or SERT) are presented elsewhere (Day et al. 1975); the concern here is with four types of transformations and their changes across time.

The subjects in this investigation were students attending a laboratory school in Honolulu. They lived in an area in which Hawaii Creole English (HCE) is widely used. The subjects were given the SERT twice a year, fall and spring, in kindergarten, first, and second grades. The responses which the children gave were categorized as:

1. exact SE — the subject repeated the feature exactly as given by the test administrator.

2. other SE — the subject changed the feature slightly (e.g. *I'm* to *I am*) without changing code (SE) or meaning.

3. HCE transformations — the subject transformed the SE feature into HCE, but maintained the meaning (e.g. *didn't come* to *neva come*).

4. bust — the subject's repetition of a feature changed its meaning, was unintelligible or inaudible, or the subject did not respond.

This paper examines responses in category 3, HCE transformations, for 21 children who attended the school over three years. The first part of the paper examines the HCE transformations which the subjects gave on the first SERT administration, and then four categories of HCE trans-

A version of this article was presented as a paper at the Linguistic Society of America's Summer Meeting, Honolulu, Hawaii, 1977.

formations are presented. These categories are discussed and tentative explanations are offered as to why some categories are more resistant to change than others.

In order to have a better understanding of the HCE transformations, the features which the SERT tests should be presented. Table 1 shows the SERT sentences from Form B, with the features tested in each sentence in italics. Inspection of this table reveals that many of the crucial markers of SE grammar (e.g. negation, past tense, questions, etc.) are tested by the SERT. For the purposes of this paper, reference to a given feature will be made first by sentence number and then by a letter which distinguishes it from other features tested in the same sentence.

Table 1. *Standard English Repetition Test (SERT)*

Form B

1. Mary *didn't* come to school yesterday.
2. *I'm* not sure where my uncle *is*.
3. I think he*'s* with my father.
4. The boy *was beaten* by his sister.
5. Our teacher *doesn't* give us candy.
6. My brother*'s* reading a book and Rodney *is* too.
7. Teacher, *do you know* where my books *are*?
8. When the TV *isn't* on, I *can't* watch *it*.
9. Edward *doesn't* want to come with us because he*'s* eating lunch.
10. I *went and asked* Edward *if* his sister*'s* a tattletale.
11. Mommy, *can you tell* me what this *is*?
12. When my daddy*'s* not home my grandma *stays* with us.
13. My daddy *called* up his friend yesterday.
14. The candy*'s being passed* out over there by the sister.
15. We *didn't* go to the movies because my daddy *never came* home.

That our HCE-speaking subjects would transform SE features into HCE is not unexpected. Johnson (1975), for example, reported that black children made changes from SE to Black English. Labov et al. (1968)

reported the same thing when teenage Blacks were given repetition tests in SE.

Table 2 presents the results of six SERT administrations to the 21 subjects. At the beginning of their kindergarten year, approximately 28 percent of their responses were HCE transformations. We see from Table 2 that over time, on successive administrations of the SERT, the number of HCE transforms became fewer until, at the end of second grᵔde, only 12.6 percent were HCE transformations. Note that the largest single reduction in HCE transformations came at the end of kindergarten after seven months of schooling. Thus, when HCE-speaking children enter kindergarten at a modal age of five, about one-fourth of their responses to a SE repetition task are HCE transformations; after approximately eight months of school in which SE is the language of instruction, 20 percent are HCE transformations, and after three years, the number of HCE transformations on the same task has been more than halved.

Table 2. *HCE transformations of SERT items: Kindergarten through Second Grade (N=21)*

	Grade	Number	Percentage
Fall	K	170	27.9
Spring	K	122	20.0
Fall	1	116	19.0
Spring	1	117	19.2
Fall	2	92	15.1
Spring	2	77	12.6

The details on the HCE transformations which the subjects made are given in Table 3. Johnson (1975), in his report on reading and Black English, said that black children made three types of changes when reading SE material orally: substitution, omission, and insertion. However, our HCE-speaking children's transformations seem to make only two of the changes: substitution and omission. As we can see from Table 3, insertion does not occur. However, fine-grained analysis of the transformations suggests that these two categories of substitution and omission do not completely or accurately describe all the transforms shown in Table 3.

For example, omissions in our data are associated with at least two significant linguistic differences: surface structure differences and underlying structure differences. In the former, the feature is a part of the underlying structure of HCE, but is not present in the surface structure,

Table 3. *HCE transformations on Fall Kindergarten SERT* $(N=21)$

Sentence/Feature		N	% of HCE transformation	HCE transformation
1	*didn't*	5	2.9	*neva come*
2a	*'m*	12	7.1	Ø
b	*is*	4	2.4	Ø
3	*is*	11	6.5	Ø
4	*was beaten*	0	0.0	*beat, got beat*
5	*doesn't*	4	2.4	*don, no like*
6a	*'s*	12	7.1	Ø
b	*is*	11	6.5	Ø
7a	*do you know*	17	10.0	no *do*-support or flip-flop
b	*are*	1	0.05	Ø; *where are my books*
8a	*isn't*	4	2.4	Ø + *not; no stay on*
b	*can't*	6	3.5	*no can; cannot*
c	*it*	1	0.05	*em*
9a	*doesn't*	5	2.9	*don want; no like*
b	*'s*	11	6.5	Ø; *stay*
10a	*went and asked*	3	1.8	*wen (go) ask*
b	*if*	0	0.0	Ø
c	*'s*	2	1.1	Ø
d	*a*	2	1.1	*one*
11a	*can you tell*	7	4.1	no flip-flop
b	*is*	2	1.1	Ø; *what is this*
12a	*'s not*	8	4.1	Ø; *no stay*
b	*stays*	11	6.5	*stay*
13	*called*	11	6.5	*wen call; call*
14a	*'s*	9	5.3	Ø
b	*being*	0	0.0	*get;* Ø
c	*passed*	7	4.1	*pass*
15a	*didn't*	3	1.8	*neva go*
b	*never came*	4	2.4	*neva come; no come*

having been deleted or neutralized by a transformational rule. For example, it is grammatical in HCE to omit the past tense marker *wen* from sentences, although there is no reason to believe that it is not part of the underlying structure. (For a detailed account of this phenomenon, see Day [1973].)

For underlying structure differences, there are crucial differences between the two grammars, and certain of the SERT features, significant markers of SE, are not present in the grammar of HCE. For instance, the copula is an integral part of SE grammar, but HCE does not exhibit a similar syntactic construction.

In addition to the two types of omission, there are two types of substitution: lexical and word-order. A lexical change involves substituting an equivalent HCE word for a word in SE. A word-order change is self-descriptive — an HCE word order is substituted for a SE word order. A yes–no question in SE with a modal such as *can*, involves switching the subject and the modal, from *you can eat,* for example, to *can you eat.* A similar sentence in HCE, however, depends not on a subject–verb switch, but on a change in intonation. Thus, the yes–no question and the declarative statement in HCE have identical surface word order, but different intonation.

The final categories were established in the following manner. Responses which the HCE-speaking subjects gave were carefully examined, in addition to those responses which were predicted on the basis of the differences between the two grammars. University of Hawaii specialists in HCE were consulted on the viability of transformation categories. As a result, the following four categories were used in the investigation.

1. Transformational Rule Difference
   Examples:
   a. Copula: *be (am, is, are,* etc.)
   b. Interrogative
      1. *do*-support
      2. subject–verb inversion
      3. indirect question
2. Lexical Substitution
   Examples:
   a. Copula: *stay*
   b. Negatives: *don't, ain't, cannot*
   c. Pronominal: *em*
   d. Indefinite Article: *one*
3. Transformational Rule Difference and Lexical Substitution
   Examples:
   a. Negatives: *no, neva*
   b. Past Tense Marker: *wen (go)* + *verb*
4. Unmarked Surface Structure (i.e. present in underlying structure of HCE)
   Examples:
   a. Past Tense: *eat, call, chase (eaten — eat)*
   b. Present Tense: *stay (stays — stay)*
   c. Progressive Tense: *Ø (being — Ø)*
   d. Conditional: *Ø (if — Ø)*

The first category, transformational rule difference (TRD), means the change from SE to HCE is one which is based on a difference in rules in the two grammars. For example, SE has a rule of subject–verb inversion used in forming yes–no questions: declarative: 'John is eating'; interrogative: 'Is John eating?' The intonation may or may not be the same in SE. HCE is different. Yes–no questions are not formed by a subject–verb inversion rule; the intonation changes. This is categorized as a transformational rule difference between HCE and SE.

Lexical substitution, the second category, is the replacement of a SE vocabulary item by an HCE equivalent. The substitution of the HCE indefinite article *one* for the SE *a/an* is an example.

The third category combines the first two — transformational rule difference and lexical substitution. The fourth category, unmarked surface structure, captures surface structures differences between HCE and SE. In this category, we assume that there is no difference in the underlying structures; the difference is found in the surface representation. Of course, this involves a difference in rules between the two grammars, but the difference is in the surface structures, and this is distinct from the first category, TRD. For example, HCE has a past tense marker, *wen*, which comes before the simple form of the verb. It is not unusual for it to be absent, however. The difference between HEC and SE then would be a surface structure difference.

RESULTS

Table 4 presents the percentages of HCE transforms for the 21 subjects from Fall kindergarten to Spring second grade by category of transformation. The TRD type of transforms constitutes the majority; 63.5 percent of all transforms involved a TRD. The frequencies of occurrence of the remaining three were 17.6 percent unmarked surface structure; 11.8 percent TRD and lexical substitution, and 7.1 percent lexical substitution.

At the end of the second grade only 12.6 percent of all responses to the SERT are HCE transformations (see Table 2). Of these, the great majority are again TRDs (77.9 percent). Of the other three categories, only unmarked surface structure transforms occur with any frequency (18.2 percent). The other two categories occur as traces.

It is clear from Table 4 that both TRDs and unmarked surface structure transformations remain as viable categories of HCE transforms. The former drops from a total of 108 in Fall kindergarten to 60 in Spring second grade. The figures for the latter are 30 for kindergarten and 15 for second grade. For both categories respectively, about half again as many

Table 4. *Frequencies by type of HCE transformation of SERT items: Kindergarten through Second Grade* (N=21, SERT Items=29)

		TRD		LS		TRD		USS		Total
	Grade	N	%	N	%	N	%	N	%	N
Fall	K	108	63.5	12	7.1	20	11.8	30	17.6	170
Spring	K	85	69.7	6	4.9	7	5.7	24	19.7	122
Fall	1	86	74.1	2	1.7	8	6.9	20	17.2	116
Spring	1	85	72.6	5	4.3	10	8.5	17	14.5	117
Fall	2	62	67.4	5	5.4	9	9.8	16	17.4	92
Spring	2	60	77.9	1	1.3	1	2.6	14	18.2	77

instances occur at the end of second grade. Of course, by Spring second grade, the percentages of total SERT responses classified as TRDs and USSs are only 9.9 and 2.3 respectively.

The data in Table 4 involve all counted transformations. They do not show whether the changes across time involve the same items on SERT. If in Fall kindergarten a child transformed a particular SE item to HCE, what did the child do with the same item on each succeeding administration? Since there is an overall reduction in the number of transforms (see Table 2), and an increase in the amount of SE, presumably the changes should be toward SE. Inspection of Tables 5 through 8 confirms that, with relatively few exceptions, an item that was originally transformed into HCE was subsequently either repeated as SE or retained as an HCE transform. Note that there were few changes in the Bust category.

Of particular interest are those resistant transforms given as HCE transforms in Fall kindergarten and Spring second grade. There are 28 TRD and 15 USS items that were transformed both in Fall kindergarten and Spring second grade. Table 9 presents the actual SERT items represented by the 28 and 15 resistant transforms.

Table 5. *Fall 1972 TRD transformations across time: (spring 1973– spring 1975) by four SERT scoring categories*

	Spring Kindergarten	Fall First	Spring First	Fall Second	Spring Second
	N	N	N	N	N
HCE	46	41	43	33	29
Exact SE and other SE	53	51	58	72	70
Bust	9	16	7	3	9
Total	108	108	108	108	108

Table 6. *Fall 1972 lexical substitution transformation across time by four SERT scoring categories*

	Spring Kindergarten	Fall First	Spring First	Fall Second	Spring Second
	N	*N*	*N*	*N*	*N*
HCE	6	2	5	5	1
SE and other SE	4	7	3	6	8
Bust	2	3	4	1	3
Total	12	12	12	12	12

Table 7. *Fall 1972 TRD and LS transformations across time by four SERT scoring categories*

	Spring Kindergarten	Fall First	Spring First	Fall Second	Spring Second
	N	*N*	*N*	*N*	*N*
HCE	7	8	10	9	2
SE and other SE	10	9	9	9	16
Bust	3	3	1	2	2
Total	20	20	20	20	20

Table 8. *Fall 1972 unmarked surface structure transformation across time by four SERT scoring categories*

	Spring Kindergarten	Fall First	Spring First	Fall Second	Spring Second
	N	*N*	*N*	*N*	*N*
HCE	24	20	17	16	14
SE and other SE	4	8	12	13	16
Bust	2	2	1	1	0
Total	30	30	30	30	30

RESISTANT TRD TRANSFORMS

The bulk of the resistant transforms in the TRD category involves the copula. Since this partly reflects the emphasis on the copula in the SERT,

Table 9. Unmarked Surface Structure and transformational rule differences from Fall Kindergarten to Spring Second Grade

Subj.	No.	Feature	Fall '72	Spring '73	Fall '73	Spring '74	Fall '74	Spring '75
1	2a	I'm	I+0	I'm	I'm	I+0	I'm	I+0
2	2a	I'm	I+0	I+0	I'm	I+0	I'm	I+0
3	7a	do you know	you know	you know	you know	you know	you know	you know
	14a	's	0	0	0	0	0	0
	14c	Ved	pass	pass	pass	pass	pass	pass
4	2a	I'm	I+0	I+0	I+0	I+0	I+0	I+0
	6b	is ##	is	is	is	is	is	is
	13	called	wen call	call	call	call	call	call
5	13	's	0	's	is	0	is	0
	13	called	call	call	called	call	call	call
	14	's	0	0	0	0	0	0
	14c	Ved	V0	V0	V0	V0	V0	V0
6	6b	is ##	0	0	0	(bust)	0	0
	12b	stays	stay	stay	stay	stay	stay	stay
	13	called	call	called	called	called	called	call
	14a	's	0	0	0	0	0	0

Table 9. (continued)

Subj.	No.	Feature	Fall '72	Spring '73	Fall '73	Spring '74	Fall '74	Spring '75
7	2a	I'm	I+0	I+0	I+0	I+0	I+0	I+0
	12b	stays	[stay]	[stay]	[stay]	[stay]	[stay]	[stay]
	13	called	[call]	[call]	[call]	[call]	called	[call]
	14	's	0	0	0	0	0	0
	14c	Ved	[V0]	[V0]	[V0]	[V0]	[V0]	[V0]
8	9b	's	0	0	0	's	0	0
9	7a	do you know	you know	SE	SE	you know	SE	you know
	9b	's	0	0	0	's	's	0
10	7a	do you know	you know	you know	you know	you know	(bust)	you know
	9b	's	0	0	0	0	0	0
	12a	's not	0 not	0 not	(bust)	0 not	no stay	0 not
	12b	stays	[stay]	[stay]	[stay]	(bust)	[stay]	[stay]
	13	called	[call]	[call]	[call]	[call]	[call]	[call]
	14c	Ved	[V0]	(bust)	(bust)	[V0]	(bust)	[V0]
11	2a	I'm	I+0	I+0	I+0	I+0	I+0	I+0
	13	Ved	[V0]	[V0]	[V0]	Ved	[V0]	[V0]

12	14a	's	0	0	0	0	0
13	2a	I'm	I+0	I+0	I+0	I+0	I+0
	[13]	called	call	call	call	call	call
14	14a	's	0	(bust)	0	0	0
	2a	I'm	I+0	I'm	I+0	I+0	I+0
	3	's	0	0	0	's	0
	6a	's	's	(bust)	0	0	0
	7a	do you know	you know	you know	you know	SE	you know
	9b	's	0	0	0	0	0
	[13]	called	call	call	call	call	call
15	7a	do you know	you know	SE	SE	SE	you know

Note: Included in this table are only those responses which were HCE in Fall '72 and HCE in Spring '75. Notice that not all responses were HCE across all administrations. Some were SE; others, busts.

0 = zero (e.g. 0 copula)
SE = Standard English response (exact SE)
I+0 = HCE response (transformation)
0 = HCE response

you know = HCE response
call = HCE response
Ved = either *passed* or *chased* (exact SE)
V0 = HCE response
stay = SE response

it is uncertain that the finding indicates a special production problem for second-grade HCE speakers. However, it is likely that copular omission due to TRDs does not result in comprehension loss for these children.

Of the features which are sentence-final copulas, numbers 2b, 6b, 7b, and 11b, only 6b remains a HCE transform (TRD type) from kindergarten to second grade. But 6b is geographically not sentence-final, since *too* follows: *My mother's cleaning the house and Mary is too.*

Those copulas which are embedded in sentences remain transforms: 2a, 3, 6a, 8a, 9b, 12a, and 14a. Table 9 shows that 2a, 9b, and 14a have at least four HCE transforms.

RESISTANT USS TRANSFORMS

The category of unmarked surface structures transforms presents a less clear picture. Table 9 shows that three features — 12b, 13, and 14c — accounted for all examples of resistant USS transforms with three, eight, and four, respectively. Two of these, 13 and 14c, involve past tense — 13 is simple past and 14c tests the past participle in a passive construction. The feature 12b tests the marker *s* of the third person singular habitual. HCE does not have this morpheme. Since it is a redundant marker in SE, it might not be salient for the HCE speaker.

DISCUSSION

Only two of the four categories — TRD and USS — show resistance to change. However, the percentage of TRDs which change to SE on the final SERT administration is greater than that for the category of unmarked surface structures. That is, only 26.8 percent of the original TRDs remain as HCE transforms, while about 46 percent of the USSs are HCE transforms in Spring second grade.

We have no clear-cut explanation for this. Perhaps it indicates that the three categories concerned with rule differences and vocabulary differences are more likely to be changed to SE than the category involving surface structure differences. In acquiring SE, as measured by the SERT, it could be that the subjects focused their efforts on differences in rules and vocabulary. Of lesser importance or significance might be those areas of the grammars of HCE and SE which involve surface structure differences.

However, this must be qualified by the role which the data suggest that the location of the feature in the sentence plays in the HCE transformations. For example, the copula is tested in both mid-sentence position and sentence-final position, embedded in a complex sentence, and in a simple sentence. The copula in sentence-final position is more often repeated exactly than when it appears in other positions, even though the sentences may be less simple. Features 2a, 2b, and 3 illustrate this point. The sentence-final copula in 2b is repeated as exact SE more often than are the two contracted forms of the copula, 2a and 3.

Another qualification of the findings presented here is the nature of the four categories of HCE transformations. Let us examine, for example, what happens when the copula is taken out of the TRD category, and set up as a category by itself. Tables 10 and 11 illustrate this possibility. We see that approximately 82 percent of the TRDs become SE on the final SERT administration, while only about 59 percent of the original copula transformations are repeated as SE.

Table 10. *Fall 1972 TRD transformations minus copulas across time*

	Spring Kindergarten	Fall First	Spring First	Fall Second	Spring Second
HCE	10	8	9	3	5
Exact SE and other SE	17	16	17	24	23
Bust	1	4	2	1	0
Total	28	28	28	28	28

Table 11. *Fall 1972 copula transformations across time*

	Spring Kindergarten	Fall First	Spring First	Fall Second	Spring Second
HCE	36	33	34	30	24
Exact SE and other SE	36	35	41	48	47
Bust	8	12	5	2	9
Total	80	80	80	80	80

Of course there is more to the HCE transforms than a difference between the two grammars HCE and SE. There are other factors which could influence a subject's response on the SERT — amount of previous exposure to SE, age (Day et al. [1975], found that exact SE scores on the SERT increased with age), motivation, and so on. Significantly, few original transforms subsequently become busts, suggesting SERT performance is not affected by a child unsuccessfully trying to use SE and avoiding transformations. Across time the children either successfully switch to an SE repetition or continue to transform, thus the transformational phenomenon does not appear to interact with testing procedure to the disadvantage of nonstandard dialect speakers.

While HCE transforms demonstrate that a child comprehends SE, it is unclear what significance to attach to such responses. We have reported elsewhere (Day et al. 1975) that exact SE scores correlate significantly with scores on I.Q. tests, reading scores, and so on; however, we find no such correlations, positive or negative, with HCE transformation scores. Apparently whether a child tends to transform SE to HCE has no influence on an HCE-speaking child's school performance. Whatever the phenomenon reflects, there are no documented negative consequences and thus there appears to be no reason to discourage transformations.

REFERENCES

Baratz, J. (1969), 'Teaching reading in an urban Negro school system', in *Teaching Black Children to Read*, ed. by J. C. Baratz and R. W. Shuy, 92–116. Washington D.C., Center for Applied Linguistics.
Day, R. (1973), 'Tense neutralization in the Hawaiian post-creole gradatum', *New Ways of Analyzing Variation in English*, ed. by C.-J. N. Bailey and R. W. Shuy. Washington, D.C., Georgetown University Press.
Day R., S. Boggs, R. G. Tharp, G. E. Speidel, and R. Gallimore (1975), 'The Standard English Repetition Test (SERT): A measure of Standard English performance for Hawaii Creole English speaking children'. Technical Report #15. Honolulu, The Kamehameha Schools, Kamehameha Early Education Program.
Johnson, K. (1975), 'Black dialect shift in oral reading', *Journal of Reading* 18(7):535–540.
Labov, W., P. Cohen, C. Robins and J. Lewis (1968), 'A study of the nonstandard English and Negro and Puerto Rican speakers in New York City'. Cooperative Research Project No. 3288, Vol. 1. Phonological and Grammatical Analysis.
Politzer, R. L., M. R. Hoover and D. Brown (1974), 'A test of proficiency in Black standard and nonstandard speech', *TESOL Quarterly* 8 (1):27–35.
Swain, M., G. Dumas, and N. Naiman (1974), 'Alternatives to spontaneous speech: elicited translation and imitation as indicators of second language competence', *Working Papers on Bilingualism* 4:68–79.

ALBERT DRESSLER

Chinese Telegrams

Camptonville, Cal.,
March 7, 1874, 7:25 P. M.

Ah Jake

    If no delay all right will be there tomorrow.

9 Pd.   G G Clough

Downieville, Cal.,
March 10, 1874

Yuen Lung

Stockton, Cal

    Has Ah Chee started for Downieville. If not, tell him start right away.

Answer

14 Pd. $1.50   Ah Jake

Stockton, Cal.
March 10, 1874, 5:15 P. M.

Ah Jake

    Have your suit put off. My partner not come back yet. When he come I telegraph.

17 Collect $2.00   Ah Chee

Virginia, Nevada
March 12, 1874, 5:50 P. M.

Fong Sing

    Ah Hoey go Virginia four days ago for Downieville. If he no come to Downieville send to San Francisco for him.

21 Collect $1.25   Sam Sing

Reprinted from Albert Dressler (1927), California Chinese Chatter. San Francisco, privately printed.

Downieville, Cal.,
March 12, 1874

Hop Sing
Camptonville
Did Ah Hoey get in your place tonight by stage. If so tell him to come right up quick. Answer.
20 words Pd. 50c   Fong Sing

Downieville, Cal.,
March 13, 1874

Gee Lee
Elko, Nevada
Tell Mow Sing to come Downieville. I in trouble have a big lawsuit on my hands. If he will come I will send him money to pay all of his expenses. Answer quick.
34 words Pd. $3.50   Fong Ahug

Elko, Nevada
March 13, 1864, 3:40 P. M.

Tong Ah Hing
He can't come got business to attend to.
8 Pd.   Gee Lee

Stockton, Cal.,
March 14, 1874

Ah Jake
Start tomorrow you want me come up. Answer quick.
9 Collect $1.00   Ah Chee

Sacramento, Cal.,
March 16, 1874, 2:50 P. M.

Fong Sing Store
Tell Ah Gek that Chu Chee will be Marysville today and Downieville tomorrow.
13 Collect   Chu Chee

North San Juan, Cal.,
March 21, 1874, 6:50 P. M.

Fong Wo
Why don't Yu Wo Ah Ching come back. When will be he here. Answer quick.
15 Pd. 35c   Quong Tai Jan

San Francisco, Cal.,
March 25, 1874, 1:24 P. M.

Tai Yuen
    Don't sell your opium.
4 Pd. 75c   Kong Yuen Chong

San Francisco, Cal.,
March 25, 1874, 2:25 P. M.

Fong Wo & Co
    Opium too dear
3 Pd.   Yu Wo & Co

San Francisco, Cal.,
March 26, 1874, 10:10 A. M.

Quong Wo & Co
    Opium up to one hundred and sixty dollars. Send down some money.
We bought some before.
16 Collect   Quong Wo Lung

Downieville, Cal.,
March 27, 1874

Yen Mow
Nevada, Cal.
    Case all settled. Expense so much have no money to send. Get money
from some one else to go San Francisco.
20 words Pd $1.00   Quong Wo & Co

Downieville, Cal.,
March 28, 1874

Yu Wo & Co
717 Dupont St., San Francisco
    What the price of opium. Answer.
6 words Pd. 75c   Fong Wo & Co

San Francisco, Cal.,
March 28, 1874, 4:05 P. M.

Fong Wo & Co
    Now price hundred sixty dollars each hundred vials. Opium will be
higher.
12 Pd.   Yu Wo & Co

Virginia, Nevada
March 29, 1874, 11:33 A. M.
Yuk Tong
Yuk Tom you lie you jap boy gon Shanghi come or answer.
19 Pd. $1.00   Luk Chung

Downieville, Cal.,
March 29, 1874
Luk Chung
Virginia, Nevada
Yuk Tong all right. Don't understand what you mean. Answer.
10 words Collect   Yuk Tong

Virginia City, Nevada
March 30, 1874, 1:30 P. M.
Yuk Fong
Did the girl Wah How no come here last month. I think she is kidnapped. Answer if she was.
19 Pd. $1.00   Luk Chung

Downieville, Cal.,
March 30, 1874
Luk Chung
Virginia City
She has not come here yet. Have never heard any one speak of her before. If I do I will telegraph.
21 words Collect   Yuk Fong

Downieville, Cal.,
March 31, 1874
Won Lung
Stockton
Case settled. Ah Chee went this morning on stage.
9 words Pd. $1.00   Ah Jake

Downieville, Cal.,
April 24, 1874
Cune Chong
Marysville
Send one hundred and twenty dollars by telegraph to Fong Sing's Store. I send letter to you next mail. Trial on Monday. Answer.
23 Pd. $1.25   Lim Lung

Marysville, Cal.,
Fong Sing   April 24, 1874, 6:25 P. M.
  In few days will get men go up.
8 Pd. 50c   Chung

Downieville, Cal.,
Cune Chung   April 26, 1874
Marysville
  Clough is sick. Get good lawyer. Send money quick. Trial tomorrow
morning 10 o'clock. Case can't be postponed. Answer.
10 words Pd.   Fong Sing

Marysville, Cal.,
April 27, 1874
Received at Downieville 6:15 P. M.
Fong Sing
  Hire a lawyer and if he wins case me will send one hundred and twenty
dollars. If no win me send no money. The lawyer pay his own expenses.
Answer immediately.
32 Pd. $1.75   Lem Chung

Alleghany, Cal.,
June 20, 1874, 7:40 A. M.
Tung Wo & Co. Store
  Tell Lem Lun come over and cook for Miller. Bring two boxes opium.
Answer.
14 Pd.   Ah How

Oroville, Cal.,
July 12, 1874, 9:55 A. M.
Fong Sing, Tie Yuen
  Your woman she go Colusa. You want her go there.
10 Pd.   Lem Lun

Downieville, Cal.,
Kaw Chung   July 25, 1874
Wadsworth, Nevada
  Don't you let her go. I will come over tomorrow and see her. I want to
bring her to Downieville to live with me. What time does the train start.
Answer quick.
32 words Pd.   Fook Sing

Downieville, Cal.,
Wing Wo Chung   July 26, 1874
Wadsworth, Nevada

Fook Sing left today, will be in Wadsworth tomorrow. Tell her not to go
to wait till he comes. Answer quick.

21 words Pd. $1.25   Tai Yuen

Downieville, Cal.,
Kaw Chung   July 26, 1874
Wadsworth

I will start for Wadsworth today and meet her on the way. Tell her to
wait for me to come and if she wants to go I will let her. Don't care.
Answer.

33 words Pd. $1.75   Fook Sing

Downieville, Cal.,
Hing Wah   August 2, 1874
Auburn

Ask Ah Tom if my partners Yuck Sing's woman down there. If you find
where she stop answer immediately.

19 words Pd. $1.00   Ah Tri

Downieville, Cal.,
Ah Tom   August 2, 1874
Auburn

Go and ask Mow Sing and he will tell you all about it and answer quick
as you can.

19 words Pd. $1.00   Ah Tri

Auburn, Cal.,
August 2, 1874, 10:10 A. M.
Ah Tri

The woman is at Virginia. Come to Auburn and I will tell you heap lots.

15 words Pd.   Ah Tom

Auburn, Cal.,
August 2, 1874, 11:05 A. M.
Ah Tri

Woman went to Virginia town with How Ah Sing. You better come
here and talk to the company. Keep quiet. I know all about it. It is all
right.

28 Collect $1.50   Ah Tom

Nevada, Cal.,
Tie Yuen Company   August 3, 1874, 1 P. M.
Downieville
  Gum Sing and woman arrested. Here tomorrow. Send sixty dollars.
10 words Pd.   Fook Sing

Nevada, Cal.,
Tie Yuen Co   August 4, 1874, 6:45 P. M.
Downieville
  Man and woman in custody.
5 Pd.   E Barry

Downieville, Cal.,
Fook Sing   August 5, 1874
Care Wing Wo Ching
Wadsworth, Nevada
  Ah Tom write me Gan Que is at Auburn. You want catch her go right
away. Answer.
17 words Pd. $1.00   Tie Yuen

Wadsworth, Nevada
August 6, 1874, 11:10 A. M.
Tie Yuen
  I need two hundred dollars for expense. You send money to me and I
will return it to you.
19 Pd.   Fook Sing

Downieville, Cal.,
August 6, 1874
Fook Sing
Wadsworth, Nevada
  Come over here quick and I will see if I can let you have the money or
not answer.
19 words Pd. $1.00   Tie Yuen

Nevada, Cal.,
August 7, 1874, 11:40 A. M.
I Yum
  Barry, the woman and myself start for Downieville right away.
10 Collect Not charged   Fook Sing

Sierra City, Cal.,
August 7, 1874, 9 P. M.

Ah Luk

No tend to go, You Dicks, he snatch my money last night. I take him back Sierra Valley tomorrow twelve o'clock. Answer I pay.

24 Pd.   Ah Sing

Auburn, Cal.,

Ting Yeu   August 12, 1874, 12:30 P. M.
Downieville

Fook Sing's woman has gone to Marysville.

7 Pd.   Ah Tom

Downieville, Cal.,

Len Tin   August 12, 1874
Oroville

Send me letter about woman quick.

6 words Pd.   Fook Sing

Downieville, Cal.,

Sing Lung, Ah Yik   August 13, 1874
Marysville

Bring woman up right away will pay three hundred dollars. Answer.

Tie Yuen

13 words Pd. 75c   Fook Sing

Downieville, Cal.,

Sing Ling, Ah Yik   August 13, 1874
Marysville

Bring her in a buggy and I will meet you at Camptonville. Come tomorrow.

14 words Pd. 75c   Fook Sing

Downieville, Cal.,

Sing Lung, Ah Yik   August 13, 1874
Marysville

Watch woman close. I come tomorrow.

6 words Pd. 50c   Fook Sing

Downieville, Cal.,
August 13, 1874

Sing Lung, Ah Yik
Marysville
    Is man who took woman there. Answer.
7 words Pd. 50c   Fook Sing

Downieville, Cal.,
August 13, 1874

Sing Lung, Ah Yik
Marysville
    Will you bring man and woman. Answer.
7 words Pd. 50c   Fook Sing

Marysville, Cal.,
August 13, 1874, 8:15 A. M.

Fook Sing
    Will you come by buggy or stage. I want to meet you outside of town.
Answer immediately.
19 Collect $1.00   Sing Lung, Ah Yik

Marysville, Cal.,
August 13, 1874, 11:05 A. M.

Tie Yuen
    Tell Fook Sing Min Que is here. What you going to do. Answer quick.
16 Pd.   Sing Lung, Ah Yik

Marysville, Cal.,
August 13, 1874, 4:20 P. M.

Fook Sing
    She wants you come right away and get warrant with officer, friends
will help. You don't be afraid. We will get her sure.
23 Collect   Sing Lung

Marysville, Cal.,
August 13, 1874, 3 P. M.

Ah Sing Goon
    Hom Game Sing take woman he stop here now. Fook Sing come quick
to Marysville. Answer back.
17 Collect   Sing Lung, Ah Yik

                                                        Marysville, Cal.,
Fook Sing   August 13, 1874, 4:21 P. M.
Care Eing Yue
   Ask Fook Sing if he wants me to bring the woman back to his place.
Expenses will be about three hundred dollars. If he is willing to pay it
answer immediately. She might go off in a day or two.
42 Collect   Sing Lung, Ah Yik

                                                        Marysville, Cal.,
                                             August 14, 1874, 11:15 A. M.
Fook Sing
   I want to know whether you come or not and what way you come.
Answer.
15 Collect 75c   Sing Lung

                                                        Downieville, Cal.,
                                                         August 14, 1874
Sing Lung
Marysville
   Fook Sing go down stage this morning, be there tonight.
10 words Pd. 50c   Tie Yuen

                                                        Marysville, Cal.,
                                             August 15, 1874, 10:12 A. M.
Tie Yuen
   I saw the woman but have not arrested her. Send marriage certificate.
12 Pd.   Fook Sing

                                                        Downieville, Cal.,
Fook Sing   August 15, 1874
Marysville
   Will send the certificate next stage.
6 words Pd. 50c   Tie Yuen

                                                        Truckee, Cal.,
                                             August 26, 1874, 7:50 P. M.
Fong Sing
   I can't come tomorrow. Chinaman got killed, they want me to attend to
him.
14 Pd.   Ah Jake

Downieville, Cal.,
Fook Sing & E Barry   October 4, 1874
Nevada, Cal.
  Is the woman in jail or not. If she is I will send money. Answer quick.
20 words Pd. 80c   Tie Yuen

Marysville, Cal.,
October 5, 1874, 9:20 A. M.
Eing Goon
  Send fifty dollars down by telegraph today to pay expense of woman go
up to Nevada City. She name Gan Que. She come from Colusa today.
25 Collect   Sing Lung

Marysville, Cal.,
October 5, 1874, 4:20 P. M.
Eing Goon
  The woman is in jail here now. Send one hundred dollars today by
telegraph for expenses to take the woman up to Nevada. You no send
money she no go. Fook Sing he stop Nevada. You no got money, answer.
40 collect   Sing Lung

Downieville, Cal.,
Sing Lung   October 6, 1874
Marysville
  I have not got any money here for Fook Sing. You pay all the expenses
for the woman to go to Nevada and when Fook Sing comes up we will
send it all back to you.
37 words Pd. $2.00   Tie Yuen

Marysville, Cal.,
October 6, 1874, 4:20 P. M.
Tie Yuen
  Woman went up to Nevada this morning. I paid expenses one hundred
twenty dollars. You send money tomorrow.
18 Collect   Sing Lung

Downieville, Cal.,
E Barry   October 6, 1874
Nevada
  What do you think about this case. Have you got the woman or not.
Answer immediately.
16 words Pd. 80c   Tie Yuen

Nevada, Cal.,
October 6, 1874, 8:50 P. M.
Ah Tien, Ah Heing Store
Send one hundred dollars, we have woman.

E Barry
7 words Pd.   Fook Sing

Nevada, Cal.,
October 8, 1874, 10:45 A. M.
E Barry
Kem Sing with officer go Downieville today. Hide woman. Answer.
10 Pd.   Ah Wan

Downieville, Cal.,
October 8, 1874
Ah Yu Dick
Sierra City
Ah Chee send a dispatch to me saying that you snatch his money. Give
it back to him and not make any trouble. Answer.
25 words Pd. 55c   Ah Tri

Marysville, Cal.,
October 9, 1874, 8:10 A. M.
Eing Goon, Fook Sing
Last two time long pay fifty dollars, Colusa and policeman just now
chinaman want money. Send it quick by telegraph.
22 Pd.   Sing Lung

Marysville, Cal.,
October 9, 1874, 12:35 P. M.
Eing Goon, Fook Sing
Send fifty dollars here for tonight by telegraph hurry it quick. Answer.
14 Pd.   Sing Lung

Downieville, Cal.,
October 9, 1874
Sing Lung
Marysville
What for you want fifty dollars.
6 words Pd. 50c   Fook Sing

Nevada, Cal.,
October 13, 1874, 1:30 P. M.

Tie Yuen

When you coming to pay. If not in few days will send officer after you.

15 Pd.   Hong Hi Wien

Nevada, Cal.,
October 15, 1874, 6:30 P. M.

Fook Sing, Care Tie Yuen

If you don't settle immediately will bring sheriff up. Answer.

10 Pd.   Hong Hi

Downieville, Cal.,
October 15, 1874

Hong Hi
Nevada

Will send money down in two days.

7 words Pd. 40c   Fook Sing

Marysville, Cal.,
October 24, 1874, 8:15 P. M.

Sing Goon

Tell Fook Sing send money by telegraph come down Colusa policeman here now will wait till tomorrow money no come he go to Downieville to collect.

26 Collect   Sing Lung

Wadsworth, Nevada
October 26, 1874, 10:15 A. M.

Fook Sing

She will go down tonight if you want see her you will have to go to San Francisco.

17 Pd.   Kaw Chung

Jamison, Cal.,
October 28, 1874, 10:12 A. M.

Tie Yuen

My woman sick, is she well or not. Answer telegraph.

10 Pd.   Ah Jim

Ah Jim

Jamison

Downieville, Cal.,
October 28, 1874

She all right now. Go Jamison few days.

8 Collect 25c   Tie Yuen

Ah Jim

Jamison

Downieville, Cal.,
November 2, 1874

Your woman go to Sierra Valley be up tomorrow too much snow other way.

13 words Collect   Tie Yuen

Tie Yuen

Jamison, Cal.,
November 2, 1874, 4:30 P. M.

I go to Sierra Valley today did my woman start.

9 Pd. 25c   Ah Jim

Ah Jim

Jamison City

Downieville, Cal.,
November 2, 1874

Yes she started for Jamison this morning by eight o'clock on horse back she did not go by Sierra Valley.

20 words Collect   Tie Yuen

References to Introductions

Adams, Andy (1960), *The Log of a Cowboy.* Garden City, N.Y., Doubleday, Dolphin. (Originally published 1903).

Adams, Ramon F. (1961), *The Old-Time Cowhand.* New York, Macmillan.

— (1968), *Western Words: A Dictionary of the American West.* Norman, University of Oklahoma Press.

— (1971), *The Cowman Says it Salty.* Tucson, University of Arizona Press.

Allen, Harold B. and Gary Underwood, editors (1971), *Readings in American Dialectology.* New York, Appleton.

Asbury, Herbert (1933), *Sucker's Progress: An Informal History of Gambling in America.* New York, Knopf.

Bailey, Beryl L. (1965), 'A new perspective on American Negro dialectology', *American Speech* 40:171–177.

Bailey, Charles-James N. (1974), 'Review of Dillard, *Black English*', *Foundations of Language* 11:299–309.

Bailey, Richard W. and Jay L. Robinson, editors (1973), *Varieties of Present-Day English.* New York, Macmillan.

Baker, Sydney (1943), *The Australian Language.* Sydney, Angus and Robertson.

Baratz, Joan C. (1969), 'Who should do what to whom . . . and why?' in *Linguistic-Cultural Differences and American Education*, ed. by Alfred E. Aarons, Barbara Y. Gordon, and William A. Stewart, 75–77, 158–159. *Florida FL Reporter*, special issue.

— (1970), 'Should Black children learn white dialect?' ASHA 12:415–417.

Baratz, Joan C. (1971), '*Ain't* ain't no error', *Florida FL Reporter* 9:39–40, 54.

Baratz, Joan C. and Stephen S. Baratz (1969), 'Early childhood intervention; the social science base of institutional racism', *Harvard Educational Review* 40:29–50.

Barnaby, W. Henry (1884), *Life and Labour in the Far, Far West.* London and New York, Cassell.

Barrere, Albert and Charles G. Leland (1889), *A Dictionary of Slang, Cant and Jargon.* London, George Bell and Sons.

Bartlett, John Russell (1859), *Dictionary of Americanisms.* New York, Bartlett and Welford.

Bernard, J.R.L.-B. (1969), 'On the uniformity of spoken Australian English', *Orbis* 18:62–73.

Bickerton, Derek (1977), 'Review of Dillard, *Perspectives on Black English*', *Language* 53:466–469.

Birmingham, John (1976), 'Papiamentu: the long-lost Lingua Franca?' *The American Hispanist* 2:13.

Blanc, Haim (1954), *Communal dialects of Baghdad Arabic.* Harvard Middle East Monographs 10.

— (1968), 'The Israeli koine as an emergent national standard', in *Language Problems of Developing Nations*, ed. by Charles A. Ferguson and J. das Gupta, 237–251. New York.

Bloomfield, Leonard (1933), *Language*. New York, Holt.

Booy, D. M. (1958), *Rock of Exile. A Narrative of Tristan da Cunha*. London, J. M. Dent and Sons.

Bourke, John G. (1892), *On the Border with Crook*. New York.

Bradford, William (1622), *Of Plimouth Plantation*. London, John Belamie.

Brinton, D. G. (1887), 'On certain supposed Nanticoke words, shown to be of African origin', *American Antiquarian and Oriental Journal* 9:350–354.

Brooks, Cleanth (1935), *The Relation of the Alabama–Georgia Dialect to the Provincial Dialects of Great Britain*. Baton Rouge. LSU Press.

Bryan, George S. (1926), *Edison, The Man and His Work*. Garden City, N.Y., Doubleday.

Buffington, Albert F. (1968), 'The influence of the Pennsylvania German dialect on the English spoken in the Pennsylvania German area'. in *Helen Adolf Festschrift*, ed. by S. Z. Buehne, J. L. Hodge, and L. B. Pinto. New York, Ungar.

Carr, Elizabeth (1972), *Da Kine Talk, From Pidgin to Standard English in Hawaii*. Honolulu, University of Hawaii Press.

Cassidy, Frederick G. (1961), *Jamaica Talk*. London, Macmillan.

— (1971), 'Tracing the pidgin element in Jamaican Creole', in *Pidginization and Creolization of Languages*, ed. by Dell Hymes, 203–222. London, Cambridge University Press.

— (1975), 'Of matters lexicographical', *American Speech*:87–89.

Cassidy, Frederick G. and Robert B. Le Page (1968), *Dictionary of Jamaican English*. New York, Cambridge University Press.

Catalán, Diego (1958), 'Génesis de español atlántico', *Revista de Historia Canaria* 24:123–124.

Chippendale, Harry Allan (1951), *Sails and Whales*. Boston.

Chomsky, A. Noam (1959), 'Review of B. F. Skinner, *Verbal Behavior*', *Language* 35:26–58.

Chomsky, Carol (1971), *On Language Learning from 5 to 10. Acquisition of Syntax in Children*. Cambridge, Mass., M.I.T. Press.

Colcord, Joanna Carver (1938), *Songs of American Sailormen*. New York, W. W. Norton.

— (1945), *Sea Language Comes Ashore*. New York, W. W. Norton.

Courlander, Harold (1963), *Negro Folk Music*. New York, Columbia University Press.

Culbertson, Manie (1972), *May I Speak: The Diary of a Crossover Teacher*. Gretna, La., Eakin.

Dalby, David (1972), 'The African element in American English', in *Rappin' and Stylin' Out: Communication in Urban Black America*, ed. by Thomas Kochman, 170–186. Urbana, University of Illinois Press.

Dallas, R. C. (1803), *History of the Maroons*. London.

Dana, R. H. (1959), *Two Years Before the Mast*. New York, Bantam Books. (Originally published 1840.)

DeCamp, David and R. B. Le Page (1960), *Jamaican Creole*. Creole Language Studies I. London, Macmillan; New York, St. Martin.

De Granda, German (1976), 'A socio-historical approach to the problems of Portuguese Creole in West Africa', *International Journal of the Sociology of Language* 7:11–22.

DeQuille, Dan (pseud. of William Wright) (1889), *A History of the Comstock Lode and Mines*. New York. (Reprinted 1974 by Promontory Press.)

Dick, Everett N. (1954), *The Sod-House Frontier, 1854–1890*. Lincoln, Nebraska, Johnson.

Dillard, J. L. (1969), 'Standard average foreign in Puerto Rican Spanish', in *Studies in*

Language, Literature, and Culture of the Middle Ages and Later, ed. by E. Bagby Atwood and Archibald E. Hill, 97–108. Austin, University of Texas Press.

— (1971), 'The Creolist and the study of nonstandard Negro dialects in the continental United States', in *Pidginization and Creolization of Languages*, ed. by Dell Hymes, 393–408. London, Cambridge University Press.

— (1972), *Black English: Its History and Usage in the United States*. New York, Random House.

— (1973), 'On the beginnings of Black English in the New World', *Orbis* 21:523–536.

— (1975a), *All-American English: A History of the English Language in America*. New York, Random House.

— (1975b), *Perspectives on Black English*. The Hague, Mouton.

— (1976a), *American Talk, Where Our Words Came From*. New York, Random House.

— (1976b), *Black Names*. The Hague, Mouton.

— (1977), *A Lexicon of Black English*. New York, Seabury Press.

Dills, Marion May (1941), *The Telephone in a Changing World*. New York.

Dulles, Foster Rhea (1930), *The China Trade*. Boston, Houghton Mifflin.

— (1933), *Lowered Boats; A Chronicle of American Whaling*. New York, Harcourt, Brace.

— (1946), *China and America. The Story of their Relations since 1784*. Princeton, Princeton University Press.

Eskew, Harry and Elizabeth Eskew (1954), *Alexandria and the Old Red River Country*. Southwest Heritage Press.

Falconer, William (1805) *A New Universal Dictionary of the Marine*. London, William Burney.

Feinsilver, Lillian M. (1970), *A Taste of Yiddish*. New York, A. S. Barnes.

Ferguson, Charles (1959), 'Diglossia', *Word* 15:325–340.

Fickett, Joan (1970), *Aspects of Morphemics, Syntax, and Semology of an Inner City Dialect*. West Rush, N.Y., Meadowood Publications.

— (1975), '*Ain't, not,* and *don't* in Black English', in *Perspectives in Black English*, ed. by J. L. Dillard, 86–90. The Hague, Mouton.

Goddard, Ives (1977), 'Some early examples of American Indian Pidgin English from New England', *International Journal of American Linguistics* 43:37–41.

— (1978), 'A further note on pidgin English', *International Journal of American Linguistics* 44:73.

Goldin, H. E. et al. (1950), *A Dictionary of American Underworld Lingo*. New York, Twayne.

Granville, Wilfred (1962), *A Dictionary of Sailors' Slang*. London, A. Deutsch.

Greene, Lorenzo J. (1942), *The Negro in Colonial New England, 1620–1776*. Columbia Studies in History, Economics, and Public Law, 494. New York, Columbia University Press.

Grose, Francis (1785), *A Classical Dictionary of the Vulgar Tongue*. London, F. Leach.

Gumperz, John (1958), 'Dialect differences and social stratification in a North Indian village', *American Anthropologist* 60:668–692.

— (1962), 'Types of linguistic communities', *Anthropological Linguistics* 4:28–40.

Hall, Howard J., editor (1924), *Benjamin Tompson 1642–1714, First Native-Born Poet of America, His Poems*. Boston, Houghton Mifflin.

Hancock, Ian F. (1969), 'A provisional comparison of the English-based Atlantic creoles', *African Language Review* 7:7–72.

— (1971), 'A study of the sources and development of the lexicon of Sierra Leone Krio', Unpublished S.O.A.S. Ph.D. thesis, University of London.

— (1972), 'A domestic origin for the English-derived Atlantic creoles', *Florida FL Reporter* 10:9–11.

— (1976), 'Nautical sources of Krio vocabulary', *International Journal of the Sociology of Language* 7:23–36.

— (forthcoming), 'Malacca Creole Portuguese', in *Proceedings of the Conference on Creole Languages and Educational Development*, ed. by Dennis R. Craig.

— (forthcoming), 'Lexical expansion within a closed system'.

Hawks, Francis L. (1856), *Narrative of the Expedition of an American Squadron to the China Sea and Japan*. Washington, D.C., Beverley Tucker, Senate Printer.

Herskovits, Melville J. and Frances Herskovits (1936), *Suriname Folk-Lore*. Columbia University Contributions in Anthropology 27. New York, Columbia University Press.

Johnson, Guy B. (1927), 'Double meaning in the popular Negro blues', *Journal of Abnormal and Social Psychology*. 30:12–20.

Kahane, Henry, Renée Kahane, and Andreas Tietze (1958), *The Lingua Franca in the Levant*. Urbana, University of Illinois Press.

Katz, William Loren (1973), *The Black West*. Garden City, N.Y. Doubleday.

Kung, S. W. (1962), *Chinese in American Life*. Seattle, University of Washington Press.

Kurath, Hans (1933), 'The Linguistic Atlas of the United States and Canada', in *Proceedings of the Second International Conference of Phonetic Sciences*, ed. by D. B. Fry and Daniel Jones, 146–155. London, Longmans, Green.

Labov, William (1966), *The Social Stratification of English in New York City*. Washington, D.C., Center for Applied Linguistics.

— (1969), 'Contraction, deletion, and inherent variability in the English copula', *Language* 45:715–762.

— (1972), 'Negative attraction and negative concord in English grammar', *Language* 48:773–818.

Laird, Charlton (1970), *Language in America*. New York, World.

Lambert, Wallace E. and G. Richard Tucker (1969), 'White and Negro listeners' reactions to various American-English dialects', *Social Forces* 47:463–468.

Layton, C. W. T. (1955), *Dictionary of Nautical Words and Terms*. Glasgow.

Leap, William (1973), 'Language pluralism in a Southwest pueblo: some comments on Isletan English', in *Bilingualism in the Southwest*, ed. by P. Turner. Tucson, University of Arizona Press.

— (1974), 'Grammatical structure in native American English,' in *Southwest Areal Linguistics*, ed. by G. Bills. San Diego, Cal., San Diego Institute for Cultural Pluralism.

— (1975), *Prospects for American Indian English Linguistics*. San Antonio, Texas.

Leland, Charles G. (1900), *Pidgin-English Sing-Song*. London.

Leopold, Werner (1959), 'The decline of German dialects', *Word* 15:130–153.

Loflin, Marvin D. (1967), 'A note on the deep structure of nonstandard English in Washington, D.C.', *Glossa* 1:26–32.

— (1970), 'On the structure of the verb in a dialect of American Negro English', *Linguistics* 59:14–28.

Loflin, Marvin D., Nicholas Sobin, and J. L. Dillard (1973), 'Auxiliary structures and time adverbs in Black American English', *American Speech* 48:22–36.

Loftis, Ann (1973), *California, Where the Twain Did Meet*. New York, Macmillan.

McDavid, Raven I., Jr. (1966), 'Sense and nonsense about American dialects', *Publications of the Modern Language Association* 81:7–17.

— (1973a), 'Go slow in ethnic attributions: geographic mobility and dialect prejudice', in *Varieties of Present-Day English*, ed. by R. W. Bailey and J. L. Robinson, 258–270. New York, Macmillan.

— (1973b), 'Review of Feinsilver, A Taste of Yiddish', *Journal of English Linguistics* 7:107.

— (1975), 'Review of Elizabeth S. Bright, *A Word List of California and Nevada*', *American Speech* 50:110–112.

McDavid, Raven I., Jr. and Virginia Glenn McDavid (1951), 'The relationship of the speech of American Negroes to the speech of Whites', *American Speech* 26:3–17.

McLeod, Alexander (1948), *Pigtails and Golddust*. Caldwell, Idaho.

Major, Clarence (1970), *Dictionary of Afro-American Slang*. New York, International Publishing Company.

Marckwardt, Albert H. (1958), *American English*. New York, Oxford University Press.

Mathews, Mitford M., editor (1951), *Dictionary of Americanisms*. Chicago, University of Chicago Press.

Matthews, W. (1935), 'Sailors' pronunciation in the second half of the eighteenth century', *Anglia* 59:192–251.

— (1937), 'Sailors' pronunciation 1770–1782', *Anglia* 61:72–80.

Maurer, David (1939), 'Prostitutes and criminal argots', *American Journal of Sociology* 44:546–550.

Melville, Herman (1963a), *Omoo: A Narrative of Adventures in the South Seas*. New York, Russell and Russell.

— (1963b), *Mardi, and a Voyage Thither*. New York, Russell and Russell.

— (1963c), *Typee*. New York, Russell and Russell.

Mencken, H. L. (1919), *The American Language* (first edition). New York, Knopf.

— (1963), *The American Language: An Inquiry into the Development of English in the United States* (abridged fourth edition), ed. by Raven I. McDavid, Jr. New York, Knopf.

Meredith, Mamie (1929), 'Longfellow's "Excelsior" done into pidgin English', *American Speech* 5:148–151.

Merryweather, M. W. (1931), '*Hell* in American Speech', *American Speech* 6:433–435.

Miller, Stewart Creighton (1969), *The Unwelcome Immigrant: The American Image of the Chinese, 1775–1882*. Berkeley: University of California Press.

Naro, Anthony J. (1978), 'A study on the origins of pidginization', *Language* 54 (2):314–347.

Needler, Geoffrey D. (1967), 'Linguistic evidence from Alexander Hamilton's *Itinerarium*, *American Speech* 42:211–218.

Nemser, William (1971), 'Systems of foreign language learning', *International Review of Applied Linguistics in Language Teaching* 9:123.

Nida, Eugene and Harold Fehdereau (1970), 'Indigenous pidgins and koinés', *International Journal of American Linguistics* 36:146–155.

Owen, William F. W. (1833), *Narrative of Voyages to Explore the Shores of Africa, Arabia, and Madagascar*. New York.

Paddock, Harold (1966), 'The study of the speech of Carbonear, Newfoundland'. Unpublished MA thesis, Memorial University of Newfoundland.

Pfaff, Carol W. (1972), *Tense and Aspect in English*. Washington, D.C., US Office of Education.

Pyles, Kenneth (1952), *Words and Ways in American English*, New York, Random House.

Read, Allen Walker (1937), 'Bilingualism in the middle colonies, 1725–1775', *American Speech* 12:93–99.

— (1938), 'Assimilation of the speech of British immigrants in colonial America', *Journal of English and Germanic Philology* 37:70–79.

Reinecke, John (1969), *Language and Dialect in Hawaii*. Honolulu, University of Hawaii Press.

Reinecke, John, Stanley M. Tsuzaki, David DeCamp, Ian F. Hancock, and Richard E.

Wood (1975), *A Bibliography of Pidgin and Creole Languages. Oceanic Linguistics* Special Publication 14.

Richardson, A. D. (1865), *Beyond the Mississippi*. Hartford, Conn., Bliss and Co.

Rollins, Philip Ashton (1936), *The Cowboy: An Unconventional History of Civilization on the Old-time Cattle Range*. New York, Scribner.

Rosten, Leo (1968), *The Joys of Yiddish*. New York, McGraw Hill.

Rusling, James F. (1875), *Across America; or, the Great West and the Pacific Coast*. New York, Sheldon.

Schele de Vere, Maximilian (1968), *Americanisms; the English of the New World*. New York. Johnson Reprint Corporation. (Originally published 1872).

Schuchardt, Hugo (1909) 'Die Lingua Franca', *Zeitschrift für Romanische Philologie* 33:441–461.

Seaman, P. David (1972), *Modern Greek and American English in Contact*. The Hague, Mouton.

Şen, Ann L. (1973), 'Dialect variation in early American English', *Journal of English Linguistics* 12:50–62.

Silverman, Stuart (1975), 'The learning of Black English by Puerto Ricans in New York City', in *Perspectives on Black English*. ed. by J. L. Dillard, 331–357. The Hague, Mouton.

Stefánsson, V. (1909), 'The Eskimo trade jargon of Herschel Island', *American Anthropologist* 11:217–231.

Stewart, William A. (1967), 'Sociolinguistic factors in the history of American Negro dialects', *Florida FL Reporter* 5:1–7.

— (1968), 'Continuity and change in American Negro dialects', *Florida FL Reporter* 6:3–14.

— (1970), 'Sociopolitical issues in the linguistic treatment of Negro dialect', in *Report on the Twenty-First Annual Round Table Meeting on Linguistics and Language Studies*, ed. by James E. Alatis, 215–223. Washington D.C., Georgetown University Press.

— (1972), 'Acculturative processes and the language of the American Negro', in *Language in its Social Setting*, ed. by W. Gage. Washington, D.C.

Taylor, Douglas (1960), 'Language shift or changing relationship?' *International Journal of American Linguistics* 26:155–161.

— (1961), 'New languages for old in the West Indies', *Comparative Studies in Society and History* 3:277–288.

Tonkin, Elizabeth (1971), 'Some coastal pidgins of West Africa', *Social Anthropology and Language* 10:129–155.

Trudgill, P. (1974), 'Linguistic change and diffusion: description and explanation in sociolinguistic dialect geography', *Language in Society* 3:215–246.

Tsuzaki, Stanley (1971), 'Co-existent systems in language variation: the case of Hawaiian English', in *Pidginization and Creolization of Languages*, ed. by Dell Hymes. London, Cambridge University Press.

Turner, Lorenzo Dow (1949), *Africanisms in the Gullah Dialect*. Chicago, University of Chicago Press.

Tyson, Adele (1976), 'Pleonastic pronouns in Black English', *Journal of English Linguistics* 10:53–59.

Voorhoeve, Jan (1961), 'A project for the study of creole language history in Surinam', in *Proceedings of the Conference in Creole Language Studies*, ed. by Robert B. LePage. Creole Language Studies II. London, Macmillan; New York, St. Martin.

— (1973), 'Historical and linguistic evidence in favor of the relexification theory in the formation of the creoles', *Language in Society* 2:133–146.

Warburton, Austen D. (1966), *Indian lore of the North California Coast*. Santa Clara, Cal., Pacific Pueblo Press.

Wardhaugh, Ronald (1974), *Topics in Applied Linguistics*. Rowley, Mass., Newbury House.

Weinreich, Max (1953), 'Yiddishkayt and Yiddish: On the impact of religion on language in Ashkenazic Jewry', in *Readings in the Sociology of Language*, ed. by Joshua A. Fishman, 382, 413. The Hague, Mouton.

Whinnom, Keith (1965), 'The origin of the European-based pidgins and creoles', *Orbis* 14:590–627.

Wister, Fanny Kemble (1958), *Owen Wister Out West*. Chicago University of Chicago Press.

Wolfram, Walt (1974), 'The relationship of White Southern speech to vernacular Black English', *Language* 50:498–527.

Wolfram, Walt, R. W. Fasold and Marie Shields (1971), 'Overlapping influence in the English of second-generation Puerto Rican teenagers in East Harlem'. USOE Project No. 3–70–0033(508).

Wood, William (1634), *New Englands Prospect*. London, John Bellamie.

Yule, Henry and A. C. Burnell (1903), *Hobson–Jobson. A Glossary of Colloquial Anglo-Indian Words and Phrases, and of Kindred Terms, Etymological, Historical, Geographical and Discursive*. London.

Zettersten, Arne (1969), *The English of Tristan da Cunha*. Lund Studies in English 37.